www.wadsworth.com

wadsworth.com is the World Wide Web site for Wadsworth and is your direct source to dozens of online resources.

At *wadsworth.com* you can find out about supplements, demonstration software, and student resources. You can also send email to many of our authors and preview new publications and exciting new technologies.

wadsworth.com
Changing the way the world learns®

From the Wadsworth Series in Speech Communication

Public Speaking

Concepts and Skills for a Diverse Society

FOURTH EDITION

CLELLA JAFFE
GEORGE FOX UNIVERSITY

THOMSON
WADSWORTH

Australia • Canada • Mexico • Singapore • Spain
United Kingdom • United States

THOMSON

★ ™

WADSWORTH

Executive Editor: Deirdre Anderson
Development Editor: Eric Carlson
Publisher: Holly J. Allen
Technology Project Manager: Jeanette Wiseman
Assistant Editor: Amber Fawson
Editorial Assistant: Breanna Gilbert
Marketing Manager: Kimberly Russell
Marketing Assistant: Neena Chandra
Project Manager, Editorial Production: Cathy Linberg
Print/Media Buyer: Judy Inouye
Permissions Editor: Joohee Lee
Production Service: Cecile Joyner, The Cooper Company
Text Designer: Norman Baugher

Photo Researcher: Terri Wright
Copyeditor: Kay Mikel
Illustrators: John and Judy Waller, Carole Lawson
Cover Designer: Preston Thomas
Cover and CD Splashscreen Image: "Culture of the Crossroads" Mural © 1998 by Precita Eyes Muralists. Directed by Susan Kelk Cervantes. (McDonald's Building, 24th Street at Mission, SF, CA) www.Precitaeyes.org
Cover and Chapter-Opening Murals Photographer: Jonathan Fisher
Compositor: New England Typographic Service, Inc.
Printer: Transcontinental Printing/Interglobe
Credits continue on page 405.

Printed in Canada
1 2 3 4 5 6 7   06 05 04 03

For more information about our products, contact us at:
Thomson Learning Academic Resource Center
1-800-423-0563
For permission to use material from this text, contact us by:
PHONE: 1-800-730-2214
FAX: 1-800-730-2215
WEB: http://www.thomsonrights.com

Library of Congress Control Number: 2002113900

Student Edition with InfoTrac College Edition:
ISBN 0-534-60651-2
Student Edition without InfoTrac College Edition:
ISBN 0-534-60659-8
Annotated Instructor's Edition: ISBN 0-534-60652-0

Wadsworth/Thomson Learning
10 Davis Drive
Belmont, CA 94002-3098
USA

Asia
Thomson Learning
5 Shenton Way #01-01
UIC Building
Singapore 068808

Australia
Nelson Thomson Learning
102 Dodds Street
South Melbourne, Victoria 3205
Australia

Canada
Nelson Thomson Learning
1120 Birchmount Road
Toronto, Ontario M1K 5G4
Canada

Europe/Middle East/Africa
Thomson Learning
High Holborn House
50/51 Bedford Row
London WC1R 4LR
United Kingdom

Latin America
Thomson Learning
Seneca, 53
Colonia Polanco
11560 Mexico D.F.
Mexico

Spain
Paraninfo Thomson Learning
Calle/Magallanes, 25
28015 Madrid, Spain

Brief Contents

List of Speeches

Contents

C H A P T E R 1 8

Persuasive Reasoning Methods 336

A P P E N D I X A

Speaking in Small Groups 363

Preface

The civilization of the dialogue is the only civilization worth having and the only civilization in which the whole world can unite. It is, therefore, the only civilization we can hope for, because the world must unite or be blown to bits.

Robert Hutchins, 1967

It's a privilege to write this fourth edition. This edition reflects the many helpful suggestions of students and instructors who have used previous editions. Recent social changes also warrant this update. The political climate in the United States has changed. A different president now works with a different Congress in a different international climate. The events of September 11, 2001, and the subsequent confrontations with terrorism—war, and threats of war have made us even more aware of the importance of effective public speaking and listening in a diverse society and world.

This edition continues to be a culturally informed book that never loses sight of its fundamental purpose: to train students to be effective public speakers and listeners. It applies 2,500 principles of public speaking in a way that is sensitive to our rapidly changing pluralistic society. The recognition of diversity doesn't detract from building basic public speaking skills; rather, it broadens the repertoire of concepts, skills, theories, applications, and critical thinking proficiencies essential for listening and speaking in the twenty-first century.

Public Speaking and Diversity

I originally wrote this test to emphasize the intertwined relationship between public speaking and culture. Through public speaking, we express, reinforce, transmit, influence, and blend diverse cultures. In fact, the very human characteristics speakers aim to influence—beliefs, values, attitudes, and actions—are precisely the basic elements of diversity. In the classroom, cultural backgrounds influence students' perceptions of the role of public speaking, their perceptions of themselves as speakers, their perceptions of their audiences, and their perceptions of other speakers. Culture also influences topic selection, research methods and resources, and reasoning styles.

Understanding diversity is more important than ever because people from one cultural background increasingly find themselves in dialogue with people from other cultural backgrounds. As media and transportation technologies become even more sophisticated, the pace of cross-cultural interaction will only increase. We all need to tune in to the different ways in which people from diverse backgrounds speak and listen.

Technology has quickened the pace of cross-cultural interaction and has transformed the way teachers teach and students learn; thus, it is critical that any text provide materials that make learning dynamic and interactive. This edition continues the tradition set in earlier texts that combine text with computer materials and online resources that allow students with many learning styles to succeed.

In short, I believe that a book that teaches public speaking without strongly emphasizing diversity and fully integrating technology gives today's students an incomplete education. Consequently, this book continues to emphasize diversity and technology even as it covers basic public speaking and listening skills.

Features of the New Edition

I want to thank all the reviewers who took time to carefully review the text. These reviewers are listed on the inside front cover. I made a number of changes in response to their suggestions. Here are a few significant enhancements:

- Chapter 3 – increases coverage of plagiarism.
- Chapter 5 – rearranges material to make a more logical flow of ideas; demographic and psychological audience analysis now come before situational analysis.
- Chapter 6 – Figure 16.3 (3/e) moves to this chapter.
- Chapter 7 – adds new information about diversity in African speaking traditions.
- Chapter 13 – expands the ethical language section; includes the text of Martin Luther King's "I Have a Dream" speech.
- Appendix B, Speaking on Special Occasions – explains elements of a eulogy.
- Throughout the text—you'll notice updated photo and art images to better reflect today's public speaker, along with an increased number of student and professional speeches.

- Enhanced *Jaffe Connection* CD-ROM

  - Packaged FREE with every new copy of this Fourth Edition, the **Jaffe Connection CD-ROM** guides students to an interactive multimedia environment that encourages development of their public speaking skills. The CD-ROM also features seamless access to the **Jaffe Connection Web Site** for additional text-related activities.
  - With the **Speech Interactive** component of the CD-ROM, it's easy for students to see how the speeches printed in the text translate to real speaking situations. As students watch the CD-ROM's videotaped student and professional speeches, they answer analysis questions and complete evaluation checklists that give them insights into methods they can use *or avoid* in their own speeches—all the while developing important critical listening skills. After responding to the analysis questions or completing the checklists, students can email their responses to the instructor and see how their answers compare to author Clella Jaffe's evaluations.

  - **InfoTrac® College Edition**—The CD-ROM offers a direct link to this world-class online library, which is **FREE** with every new copy of this book—opening the door to complete articles (not just abstracts) from literally thousands of top journals, magazines, and other periodicals. Expanded throughout this edition, **InfoTrac College Edition** exercises and keywords throughout the book guide students to current online articles that enrich text topics—and give students easy access to a world of valuable information and research they can use in their speeches.
  - **NEW! Speech Builder Express,** accessible only through the **Jaffe Connection CD-ROM,** offers students an innovative Web-based speech outlining tool that utilizes interactive activities, a tutorial feature, and video clips to coach students from speech topic to formal outline. **Speech Builder Express** works in tandem with the "Build Your Speech" assignments in Jaffe's text, giving students the step-by-step guidance that results in effective speech preparation and delivery.
- The *Jaffe Connection Web site:* http://communication.wadsworth.com/jaffe
  - **Online resources for EVERY chapter!** At the **Jaffe Connection Web Site,** students can access Web links, quizzes, glossary terms, speech preparation and evaluation checklists, InfoTrac College Edition questions, and other interactive activities, keyed to chapter topics.
  - **"Stop and Check" skill-building and critical thinking exercises** encourage students to check their understanding. "Stop and Check" activities at the Web site are linked to corresponding "Stop and Checks" in the book.

Chapter-by-Chapter Features

Chapter Objectives. Each chapter begins with a preview of the chapter's goals, then pauses every few pages to provide an opportunity to probe these key concepts through *Stop and Check* activities and *Diversity in Practice* boxes.

Margin Definitions. Key terms are highlighted in bold throughout each chapter (when the term is first mentioned) and definitions are provided in the margins. These glossary terms are also provided on the *Jaffe Connection Web Site* as flashcard activities.

Stop and Check. These critical thinking exercises help students check their progress throughout the chapter. Many of these activities work in tandem with the activities available in the Student Workbook and in an interactive format on the *Jaffe Connection Web Site*.

Diversity in Practice. These reviewer-acclaimed box features enhance the book's emphasis on diversity by presenting brief summaries of public speaking traditions from a range of perspectives.

Build Your Speech. These skill-building exercises help students apply text concepts to actual speechmaking. Many of these activities work in tandem with Speech Builder Express outlining tool found on the *Jaffe Connection CD ROM*, or with forms and checklists found on the *Jaffe Connection Web Site*.

Key Terms. The perfect complement to the in-chapter Margin Definitions, a list of key terms at the end of each chapter helps students check their acquisition of important vocabulary. Using the page number provided, students can easily reference the term with its definition in context.

Application and Critical Thinking Exercises. These end-of-chapter questions help students understand and critically evaluate the chapter content and skills they've learned. Many of them employ *InfoTrac College Edition* searches, enhancing students' research finding skills. Instructors may use these exercises in a variety of ways: as individual assignments, as group assignments, or as topics for in-class discussion.

Chapter Summary. Each chapter concludes with a brief summary, highlighting the key topics covered in the chapter.

Sample Speeches. To provide you with exemplary models of the speech techniques taught in this text, this edition has even more sample speeches and sample outlines than the previous edition. You will find ample annotated sample speeches by both students and professionals throughout the text. Most of these are available on the *Jaffe Connection CD-ROM*.

Resources for Students and Instructors

This edition offers the most comprehensive array of supplements ever to assist in making this course as meaningful and effective as possible. The anchor of this program is the Jaffe Connection CD-ROM described earlier. This CD-ROM and many of the resources listed below have been thoroughly revised and expanded for this edition. Please contact your local Wadsworth/Thomson Learning representative for an examination copy and demonstration, or call our Academic Resource Center at 1-800-423-0563. Some ancillaries are available only to qualified adopters.

Student Resources

- *InfoTrac College Edition Student Workbook for Communication 2.0* (0-534-529993-3). This saleable workbook can also be bundled with the text. It focuses on human communication topics (small group, interpersonal, public speaking) and includes guidelines for faculty and students on maximizing this resource.

- *InfoTrac College Edition Student Activities Workbook for Public Speaking* (0-534-53101-2). Written by Nancy Rost Goulden of Kansas State University, this saleable workbook can also be bundled with the text. It focuses on public speaking and features extensive activities that utilize InfoTrac College Edition.
- *Student Workbook.* Written by Clella Jaffe, this workbook compliments and expands students' understanding and use of the main text. It features a welcome letter to the student and an introductory overview about the benefits of taking a public speaking course. It also features chapter-by-chapter activities, many of which are based on the text's Stop and Check and Build Your Speech activities, and includes scenario-based learning that facilitates both individual and group work. Chapter review self-tests with answer keys are also included. The workbook also contains speech assignment options, examples, and checklists. Speech preparation forms and checklists are formatted so they can be pulled out of the workbook and submitted.

Instructor Resources

- *Annotated Instructor's Edition, featuring the new Resource Integration Guide,* by *John Bourhis, Basic Course Coordinator, Southwest Missouri State University.* At the center of Jaffe's integrated team of resources, the Annotated Instructor's Edition features teaching strategies throughout, as well as a brand new feature: the *Resource Integration Guide.* This innovative tool for instructors includes grids that link every chapter to instructional ideas and corresponding supplement resources. **0-534-60652-0**
- *Instructor's Resource Manual with Test Bank.* Written by Clella Jaffe, this manual features course outlines and sample syllabi, as well as the following for every text chapter: transition notes to this new edition, chapter goals and an outline, suggestions correlating supplements and online resources, supplementary research notes, suggested discussion questions and specific suggestions for integrating student workbook activities, PowerPoint® slides, and videos. **0-534-60656-3**
- *ExamView® for Windows and Macintosh.* This cross-platform CD-ROM provides a fully integrated collection of test creation, delivery, and classroom management tools that feature all the test items found in the Instructor's Resource Manual. **0-534-60657-1**
- **Multimedia Manager for Public Speaking: Concepts and Skills for a Diverse Society, Fourth Edition.** An instructor CD-ROM with pre-designed chapter specific PowerPoint® presentations, containing hundreds of images, text, and all of the videos included on the Jaffe CD-ROM to invigorate lecture presentation and support teaching. The multimedia Manager also offers the ability to import information from previously created lectures or classroom activities. **0-534-60658-X**
- **Video Resources** All of the video clips and sample speeches included on the Jaffe CD-ROM or within the PowerPoint® presentations on the multimedia Manager are available on one of the volumes included in Wadsworth's video series; Student Speeches for Critique and Analysis (Volumes I–VIII) or CNN Today for Public Speaking, (Volumes I–IV). A table of contents of each video volume is included with the tape or available from Wadsworth Marketing at 877–999–2350 x875.
- **CNN® Today Videos: Public Speaking** Wonderful for launching your lectures, these videos integrate the news gathering power of CNN into every lecture, showing students the relevance of course topics to their everyday lives. Organized by topics covered in a typical public speaking course, each video is divided into short segments perfect for introducing key concepts. Many videos include the professional speeches featured on the **Jaffe Connection CD-ROM.**
  Volume I: 0-534-52212-2
  Volume II: 0-534-52213-0

Volume III: 0-534-52214-9
Volume IV: 0-534-52215-7
Volume V: 0-534-62407-3
Volume VI: 0-534-62411-1

Student Speeches for Critique and Analysis Video   You'll find a wide array of contemporary sample student speeches in this seven-volume set, including speeches of introduction, as well as impromptu, informative, and persuasive speeches.

Volume I: 0-534-56258-2
Volume II: 0-534-56262-0
Volume III: 0-534-56447-X
Volume IV: 0-534-56389-9
Volume V: 0-534-56454-2
Volume VI: 0-534-59458-1
Volume VII: 0-534-62406-5
Volume VIII: 0-534-62410-3

MyCourse 2.1 . . . *Our new online course builder! FREE!*   Whether you want only the easy-to-use tools to build your site or the content to furnish it, **MyCourse 2.1** offers you the simple solution for a custom course Web site that allows you to assign, track, and report on student progress, load your syllabus, and more. Contact your Thomson/Wadsworth representative for details. You can demo **MyCourse 2.1** at **http://mycourse.thomsonlearning.com**

Available to qualified adopters. Please consult your local sales representative for details.

Acknowledgments

Every book is in some way a co-created product in which an author relies on the insights and encouragement of others. Victoria O'Donnell (Montana State University), Sean Patrick O'Rourke (Furman University), and Anne Zach Ferguson (Oregon State University, Willamette University) initially encouraged me to undertake this project. In addition, many reviewers across the country provided insightful comments at various stages of the manuscript—some of which I incorporated into the text. Reviewers' names are listed on the inside of the front cover.

My daughter, Sara Jaffe Reamy, provided a student's perspective on manuscript drafts; my nephew, Mark Iles, contributed several pieces of art; and my husband, Jack, provided moral support throughout the hectic months of revision! The editors and designers at Wadsworth paid special attention to necessary details at each stage of manuscript revision. Beginning with Holly Allen, who saw the project most of the way through the first edition, and leading to Deirdre Anderson in the third and fourth editions, these editors were patient and supportive throughout the revision process. Special thanks go to the Project Manager, Cathy Linberg; the designer, Norman Baugher; the copyeditor, Kay Mikel; and the production service, Cecile Joyner.

You can help make the next edition even more useful. Please contact me through the Wadsworth Communication Web site at http://communication.wadsworth.com/jaffe or send your comments, suggestions, and other thoughts to:

Dr. Clella Jaffe
c/o Deirdre Anderson, deirdre.anderson@wadsworth.com
Executive Editor, Communication
Wadsworth Publishing Company
10 Davis Drive
Belmont, CA 94002

Public Speaking

Concepts and Skills for a Diverse Society

FOURTH EDITION

Introduction to Public Speaking and Culture

THIS CHAPTER WILL HELP YOU

- Explain three ways you can be empowered by studying public speaking

- Define culture in the context of public speaking

- Give reasons for studying public speaking from a cultural perspective

- Identify three ways culture affects public speaking

- Know how public speaking influences culture

- Identify elements of the transactional model of communication

"Culture of the Crossroads" Mural ©1998 by Precita Eyes Muralists. Directed by Susan Kelk Cervantes. (McDonald's Building, 24th Street at Mission, SF, CA)

Public Speaker
A person who prepares and delivers a presentation to a group that listens, generally without interrupting the flow of ideas.

HAT COMES TO MIND WHEN YOU HEAR THE words *public speaker?* Do you see a camp counselor telling scary stories to campers around a fire? What about a police officer explaining bicycle safety to a group of third-graders? A kayak instructor outlining basic procedures to a group of beginners? Each of these people is a **public speaker**—someone who prepares and delivers a presentation to a group that listens, generally without interrupting the flow of ideas. If you broaden the scope of public presentations to include introductions, toasts, announcements, reports, and briefings, you can see the possibilities for even more common types of public presentations.

Now you are enrolled in a public speaking class. A major goal of the course is to help you think your way through the process of planning, presenting, and evaluating effective speeches. You will assess your current skills, identify specific areas to improve, and then plan strategies to deal with the challenges of public speaking and listening. As you create first one speech and then another, you will improve along the way, adding competencies and refining those you already have (Jensen & Harris, 1999).

This course will prepare you to give speeches, but more often you will be an audience member who hears and evaluates public messages in a world that is increasingly diverse. Consequently, you need to evaluate critically the messages you hear each day. The skills needed for effectiveness in these two roles—as speaker and as listener—are the focus of this text.

How Can This Course Help You?

Although you probably do not think of yourself as a "public speaker," chances are you have given at least one talk—for example, an informative "Show and Tell" speech in grade school, a class report, or an announcement. You've undoubtedly listened to many public presentations, and you have some ideas about effective and ineffective speaking. These experiences provide a foundation on which you can build additional speaking and listening competencies. The study of public speaking principles can empower you in a number of ways. Let's consider some of them.

You Can Gain Confidence

If you are typical, the idea of giving a speech makes you at least somewhat anxious. For example, Anna confessed:

> Nothing scares me worse than public speaking. I would rather shoot myself in the foot or go bungee jumping than speak in front of people. I spend days with my stomach in knots, and when I finally get up to speak, I feel like I can't breathe. My hands shake and my legs feel like jelly.
>
> ANNA

Communication Apprehension (CA)
The fear or dread of negative responses you might experience because you speak out.

Public Speaking Anxiety (PSA)
Fear or dread specifically related to speaking in public.

Process Anxiety
Fear due to lack of confidence in knowing how to prepare a speech.

Performance Anxiety
Fear of forgetting or of presenting your speech poorly.

Anxiety or apprehension affects people in occupations as varied as politics (George Washington), acting (Harrison Ford and Bridget Fonda), and writing (Susan Faludi). *Apprehension* is the dread or fear of having something bad happen to you. **Communication apprehension (CA)** is the fear of negative reactions you might experience because you speak out (Richmond & McCroskey, 1995). CA is linked to learning style preference (Dwyer, 1998) and to inborn temperament traits such as shyness (Beatty, McCroskey, & Heisel, 1998).

A specific type of CA is **public speaking anxiety (PSA)** (Behnke & Sawyer, 1999). It has two dimensions: process anxiety and performance anxiety. When you feel unsure about the how-to of speechmaking—for example, you lack confidence that you can choose a topic, do research, and organize your ideas—you are experiencing **process anxiety.** When you worry about actually presenting your ideas—for instance, you think people will notice your shakiness or you fear you'll forget your speech—you are suffering from **performance anxiety.**

If you enter this class with some PSA, you are normal. A National Communication Association poll found that only 13 percent of eighteen- to twenty-four-year-olds feel confident about their public speaking skills, whereas 40 percent express some degree of PSA (Roper Starch, 1999). Because anxiety is so common, Chapter 2 presents detailed information about recognizing and dealing with it.

Fortunately, lack of confidence is not the same as incompetence. Competence is the ability to succeed or to do something well; you can be *competent* without feeling *confident*. Brian Spitzberg (1994) identified three elements in **communication competence:** motivation, knowledge, and skills (see Figure 1.1). Motivation must come from within you, but studying this text, participating in classroom activities, fulfilling assignments, and actually giving speeches will help you develop the knowledge and skills you need to perform competently.

Communication Competence
The ability to communicate appropriately and successfully.

Figure 1.1 Communication competence combines three overlapping elements: motivation to communicate, knowledge about communication, and skills in speaking and listening.

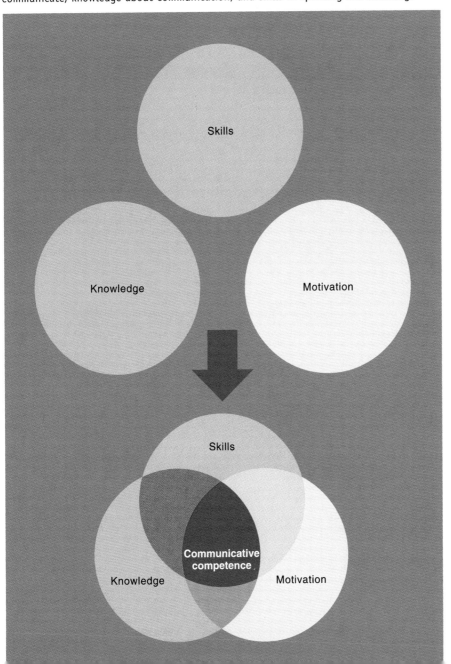

STOP AND CHECK

ASSESS YOUR CURRENT COMPETENCE

On a sheet of paper draw three overlapping circles. Label one *knowledge,* one *skills,* and one *motivation.* In each circle, write your current competencies in the public speaking context—the knowledge, skills, and motivations you already have. Then identify areas you want to improve within each category.

Web Site

You can complete this assignment online under Stop and Check Activities for Chapter 1 at the Jaffe Connection Web site http://communication.wadsworth.com/jaffe.

Many people, especially those with high levels of PSA, feel more confident as well as more competent after they complete the course (MacIntyre & MacDonald, 1998). Here are a few testimonials from former students:

Getting up in front of the class . . . built up my confidence.

MARTINA

I think it was really good that we did so many speeches because when we did it so many times, I was less nervous each time.

JENNIFER

This class is almost like a hands-on class. You learn to give speeches by giving speeches.

VICTORIA

You Can Develop Professional and Personal Skills

Ask most employers what they look for in new hires, and they will likely say, "We want employees who can listen carefully, present their ideas clearly, think critically, and exude enthusiasm." Recently, 98 percent of personnel interviewers identified both verbal and non-verbal communication skills as significant factors in hiring decisions. They overwhelmingly agreed that higher-level positions require more effective communicators and that

Competence in public speaking enables you to join in on the exchange of ideas continuously going on regarding campus, local, national, and international issues.

David Young-Wolff/PhotoEdit

communication skills are even more important in the twenty-first century (Peterson, 1997). You can develop the specific skills you need in occupations as diverse as law, nursing, management, teaching (Johnson & Roellke, 1999), and accounting (Stowers & White, 1999) in this course.

In addition to job success, the ability to present your thoughts clearly and persuasively will give you a voice in society. Rather than remaining silent, you can contribute your ideas about important issues. You can probably come up with many examples of people who use their communication skills to make a difference: students hold peace rallies and set up environmental workshops. People contribute to radio talk shows and send letters to newspaper editors. In online chat rooms, thousands of people opine about everything from sport controversies to the war on terrorism. Skillful communicators influence local, national, and even international decisions.

● Introduction ● Critiquing Guidelines ● Menu ● Assignment ● Evaluation

Wedding Toast by Mark Cavanaugh (Chapter 1)

RealOne Player   File » ⊞   _ □ ✕

(Paused) www.wadsworthmed...   0:15 / 3:19

Description
A wedding toast is not ᵃ However, Mark planned few words" at his sister usually includes someth the couple's courtship, the marriage, and extei future—often humorou speeches like this are ((spur-of-the-moment), (planned in advance, b notes with exact wordin delivery), or manuscrip and read).

Rationale
A wedding toast is a sh speech. (Several other Appendix B). These sp strengthen interperson within families, groups, Mark welcomes a broth

movie. Then, click on the Evaluation and Critique buttons above to further study the speech.

Finally, consider the value of public speaking skills in social situations. Narrating a "cousins' story" at a family reunion, telling a joke to a group of friends, and giving a wedding toast are three examples of situations where short, often impromptu speeches create strong, personal connections. Watch the toast that Mark Cavanaugh gave at his sister's wedding on the CD that accompanies this text; especially note the way his speech emphasizes the ties between family and friends.

You Can Increase Critical Thinking Skills

In ancient Greece, **rhetoric** was one of the most important subjects in the curriculum; in fact, it is one of the original seven liberal arts. This may seem surprising given the generally negative feeling people today have about the word. For instance, when asked to define *rhetoric*, Paula responded:

> Rhetoric is just talking. It's a negative word nowadays, but I don't think it always was. But presently it implies speaking just to fill up space, I think.
>
> PAULA

Rhetoric
The art of persuasive public speaking; a term often used negatively.

Phrases like "empty rhetoric" or "don't give me rhetoric; I want action!" probably influenced her thinking. However, Aristotle (trans. 1954, 1984) defined *rhetoric* as the art of using all the available means of persuasion. His text was aimed mainly at students of public speaking, but the study of rhetoric describes persuasion in many forms, including writing, advertising campaigns, rhetoric of film, and rhetoric of art.

Persuasive speaking has been important in every culture and every generation. Ancient Greeks and Romans analyzed elements of persuasion; medieval and renaissance writers added insights, and contemporary scholars develop theories and models that describe both speaking and listening. Consequently, this text covers both ancient and modern principles of rhetoric. See the Diversity in Practice box for more on the historical importance of public speaking.

One goal of a liberal arts education is the development of critical thinking skills. Critical thinkers can analyze information and sort through persuasive appeals. They can discriminate between faulty arguments and valid reasoning, follow ideas to logical conclusions, and appreciate a diversity of opinions and presentation styles. Studying rhetorical principles can help you increase your critical thinking competencies (Allen et al., 1999).

DIVERSITY IN PRACTICE

PUBLIC SPEAKING IN ANCIENT CULTURES

PUBLIC SPEAKING has its place in every society. For example, fragments of the oldest book in existence, *The Precepts of Kagemni and Ptah-hotep* (ca. 2100 B.C.), taught young Egyptians their culture's wisdom (Gray, 1946). These writings gave guidelines for both speaking and listening:

- Speak with exactness, and recognize the value of silence.
- Listeners who have "good fellowship" can be influenced by the speeches of others.
- Do not be proud of your learning.
- Keep silent in the face of a better debater; refute the false arguments of an equal, but let a weaker speaker's arguments confound themselves.
- Do not pervert the truth.
- Do not give or repeat extravagant speech that is heated by wrath.
- Avoid speech subjects about which you know nothing.
- Remember that a covetous person is not a persuasive speaker.

It was good advice then; it's good advice now!

In short, a course in public speaking offers many advantages. Your confidence will increase as you face your fears and meet the challenge of preparing and giving speeches. You can increase your speaking and listening abilities within a culture that values them. Finally, the critical thinking skills you develop along the way will help you sort through the ideas and persuasive appeals that surround you daily.

Why Take a Cultural Perspective?

The events of September 11, 2001, reminded us all that we live in a global environment where members of distinctly different cultures regularly come into contact. But not all diversity is international; in national regions and local communities you will encounter residents with diverse ethnic backgrounds, faiths, political affiliations, views about sexuality, and so on. Your community or your school may not be especially diverse, but if you understand how diversity impacts communication, you will better understand our nation and our world. That is why this text presents both the forms of public speaking most common to the United States and the speaking traditions of other cultures, in this country and abroad.

Culture
The integrated system of learned beliefs, values, behaviors, and norms that include visible (clothing, food) and underlying (core beliefs, worldview) characteristics of a society.

Co-culture
Subgroup of culture, characterized by mild or profound cultural differences, that coexists within the larger culture.

What exactly is culture? **Culture** is the integrated system of learned beliefs, values, attitudes, and behaviors that a group accepts and passes from older to newer members. Don Smith (1996), founder of Daystar University in Kenya, says it's like an onion. The outer layers represent visible elements such as clothing, art, food, and language; the deeper layers represent ideology, folk beliefs, attitudes, values, and other embedded perceptual filters that affect the way the culture's members view the world (Galvin & Cooper, 2000). In short, culture exists at a conscious as well as an unconscious level; it tends to be so pervasive that its members hardly see its effects (*Columbia Encyclopedia*, 1993; Wehrly, Kenney, & Kenny, 1999).

As members of a complex society, we share many beliefs, practices, and values. However, within each community there are subgroups, or **co-cultures,** comprised of people who are diverse in visible ways as well as in the embedded areas of belief or behavior. Think of all the co-cultural groups you can identify (for example, skinheads, Jehovah's Witnesses, bikers). Then log on to **www.yahoo.com**, click on the Society and Culture category, then click on the link to Cultures and Groups. You will find more than 12,000 groups featured. Explore a few sites that interest you. When you have done this, you will better understand why this text takes a cultural perspective.

This perspective will enable you to be a more competent communicator. Identifying audience expectations regarding the specific setting and determining what is most appropriate in it will make you a **rhetorically sensitive** person who "can adapt to diverse social situations and perform reasonably well in most of them" (Hart & Burks, 1972). Put simply, you will give each speech to an audience that has expectations regarding its length, appropriate delivery, and so on. You will be more effective if you understand and adapt to the cultural norms of your audience.

Culture Affects Public Speaking

Some cultural influences on public speaking are easy to identify. For instance, podiums for speaking are common in the United States but not in rural Australia. You will see speakers use chalkboards or white boards in U.S. classrooms and businesses but almost never at funerals. Our society also influences our speaking in less visible ways. Let's look at the core resources, technological aids, and expectations that vary from culture to culture and influence public speaking (see Figure 1.2).

Figure 1.2 Core cultural resources—beliefs, values, attitudes, and actions

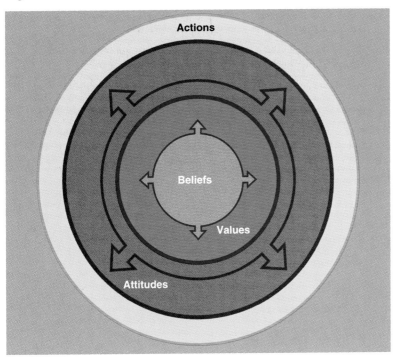

Cultures Provide Core Resources

According to communication professor W. Barnett Pearce (1989), our culture supplies us with a pool of **core cultural resources,** or "logics of meaning and action," that define our obligations as well as our taboos. These resources include a system of beliefs, attitudes, values, and behaviors that provide a foundation for every area of life including public speaking. **Beliefs** are the ideas we mentally accept as true or reject as false. **Values** are our underlying evaluations of what is important, significant, moral, or right. **Attitudes** are our predispositions to evaluate—either negatively or positively—persons, objects, symbols, and

Rhetorical Sensitivity
The ability to adapt to a variety of audiences and settings and to perform appropriately in diverse social situations.

Core Cultural Resources
Beliefs, values, attitudes, and behaviors that provide a logical basis for a culture to define what is necessary, right, doubtful, or forbidden.

Belief
Mental acceptance that something is true or false, valid or invalid.

Value
Ideal by which we judge what is important and moral.

Attitude
Predisposition to evaluate, either positively or negatively, persons, objects, symbols, and the like.

Behavior
Action considered appropriate or normal within a cultural group.

the like. Finally, **behaviors** are the actions we consider appropriate or normal. For instance, here are some foundational cultural resources for public speaking in the United States:

- A *belief* that we can change our society by speaking out and creating public policies (in contrast to cultures that consider it useless to fight fate).
- A *value* that encourages individuality (in contrast to cultural groups that emphasize conformity).
- A positive *attitude* about open forums (and negative attitudes about suppressing dissent).
- Standards for predictable speaking and listening *behaviors* that vary according to context.

These core cultural resources, and others like them, combine to create public speaking expectations. Because we value freedom and uncoerced choice, we try to respect one another's ideas. Our beliefs that individuals are intelligent and reasonable lead us to choose persuasion rather than force to influence others. In contrast, cultures with different core beliefs and values may discourage their members from expressing their ideas freely, and leaders there may use force as a means of control (Wallace, 1955).

Cultures Provide Technological Aids

Oral Cultures
Cultures with no writing and no way to record and send messages apart from face-to-face interactions.

The technology available to a culture greatly influences how its members create and exchange messages. For instance, if you lived in an **oral culture** with no writing and no technology to record and send your ideas to others, you and your audiences would have to meet face to face, and you would memorize everything you know. Oral cultures rely on poems and chants, proverbs and sayings, and stories and genealogies to summarize their values, beliefs, and history. Public performers in these cultures are like "walking libraries"; they must pass on their knowledge to someone in the next generation (Goody & Watts, 1991; Ong, 1982).

Literate Cultures
Cultures in which people record their ideas in words that can be sent across space and time; this leads to linear thinking and outlining of ideas.

The invention of writing brought about a communication revolution. People in **literate cultures** can write down their ideas and convey them to audiences separated by both distance and time. Consequently, you can read the ideas of people from other countries or from other centuries without ever seeing the communicator. In addition, you can use print resources to gather speech material, and writing out your speaking notes frees you from the limitations of memory.

Outlining is one consequence of literacy. Because letters and words follow one another in a linear fashion, speakers in print cultures tend to trace "lines" of thought and to "outline" their ideas in a linear manner. Because readers can pause and think, can analyze written claims and weigh ideas, they expect speakers as well as writers to support their claims with evidence. In this text, you'll find rules for organizing outlines and developing well-supported arguments.

In a culture with a bookstore in every mall and a newsstand in every grocery store, you can easily see the importance of literacy. However, instead of picking up a newspaper today, you probably turned on a radio or television or went online to receive information. Twentieth-century inventions have created an **electronic culture** full of media that can bring messages from around the globe into your home. You can also store and retrieve information on floppy disks, computer memory banks, and videotapes.

Electronic Culture
A culture with technology that can store information on audiotapes, videotapes, CDs, and so on. Technology shrinks the globe and enables people to communicate instantly across great distances.

The electronic revolution is changing the ways we think. The rapid-fire words and quick-cut images typical of television may be replacing the structured lines of thought typical of literacy. Cultural norms for public speaking are changing as well. Professor Kathleen Hall Jamieson (1988) argues that speeches in a media-saturated society are more conversational, personalized, dramatic, and emotional.

Few cultures have only one type of media. For instance, an oral culture that is making the transition to literacy may contain a few scribes who have mastered reading. Theirs is an *oral-literate* culture. Many people in modern oral cultures cannot read but they have radios and, perhaps, television sets. Thus, they inhabit an *oral-electronic* culture. Most people in the United States can read, but they freely use electronic devices, which results in a *print-electronic* culture. Figure 1.3 illustrates this idea (McClearey, 1997).

Figure 1.3 The three types of culture generally overlap. Can you name a culture, contemporary or historical, that is entirely oral? One that is oral–literate? How would you classify the culture of the United States? The culture in which your great-grandparents grew up?

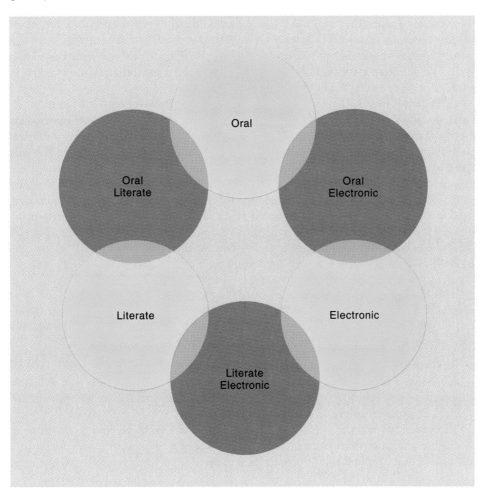

Cultures Provide Expectations About Speaking and Listening

Your cultural background influences your ideas about public speaking; your expectations, in turn, affect your comfort and often your competence when you speak in public. Cultures vary not only in the value they place on *expressiveness* and explicitness but also in the *how*, *who*, and *what* of public speaking.

Cultures Vary in Expressive and Nonexpressive Dimensions

Some cultural groups are comparatively *nonexpressive*, meaning that the members value privacy and encourage people to keep their emotions and ideas to themselves rather than expressing them. Children in **nonexpressive cultures** learn negative attitudes toward verbalization (Marsella, 1993). For example, Japanese people often associate silence with wisdom, and in some Asian cultures silence expresses power. If you think about it, it is easy to understand how people who tell their secrets might be considered less powerful than those who keep their personal opinions and knowledge private. Many Native Americans are also

Nonexpressive Cultures
Members value privacy and encourage people to keep their emotions and ideas to themselves rather than to express them publicly.

comfortable with interactions filled with silence, even between friends (Weider & Pratt, 1990). If your cultural group is comparatively nonexpressive, speaking in public may seem overwhelming (Jaasma, 1997; Kao, Nagita, & Peterson, 1997).

Expressive Cultures
Members are encouraged to give their opinions, speak their minds, and let their feelings show.

In contrast, **expressive cultures** encourage people to give their opinions, speak their mind, and let their feelings show. Many African cultures—the Anang tribe, for example—value fluency. In fact, the tribal name *Anang* means "the ability to speak wittily yet meaningfully upon any occasion" (Messenger, 1960). People of African descent who share this value are some of our country's most skilled speakers. Political leaders Colin Powell and J. C. Watts, entertainers Bill Cosby and Oprah Winfrey, and religious leaders Martin Luther King, Jr., and E. V. Hill are among them.

Differences exist within cultures and among individuals, however. One recent cross-cultural study showed that southerners are statistically more expressive than northerners even within the same country (Pennebaker, Rime, & Blankenship, 1996). Furthermore, your culture may encourage emotional expression—both verbally and nonverbally—but you may be more reserved. Interestingly, research shows that people can regulate their expressiveness to appear more or less outgoing, depending on the circumstances (DePaulo et al., 1992). For example, researchers suggest that African American speakers are encouraged to express their emotions and verbalize their ideas and opinions to create a dramatic image. However, the same speakers sometimes withhold expression to "be cool" and not let others know what they are thinking or feeling (Kochman, 1990).

Cultures Guide the "How-To" of Speaking

Communication Style
A culture's preferred ways of communicating given its core assumptions and norms.

A culture's core assumptions and norms work together to produce a preferred **communication style** (Stewart & Bennett, 1991). Elements of the communication style typically used in public presentations in the United States include the following:

- **Problem orientation.** Because of core cultural assumptions that the world is rational and ordered and that individuals can act on problems and solve them, you will hear speeches—and probably give some yourself—that attempt to resolve global, national, local, or personal issues and conflicts.
- **Directness.** In our action-oriented society, speeches tend to move in a logical way to an explicit conclusion without including a lot of side issues. This is why you often hear a "first … next … and finally" organizational pattern. Even when you tell a joke, you are expected to "get to the point."
- **Explicitness.** Speakers in public settings commonly use clear, concise, precise language instead of indirect statements and allusions. In fact, if you say "like" or "you know" a lot or give hints rather than direct instructions, you will probably be less effective in many speaking contexts.
- **Personal involvement.** In line with cultural emphases on equality and individuality, speakers typically relate to their audiences by sharing personal experiences. Look for common ground with your listeners to establish a relationship with them. If you act like a know-it-all who is superior to everyone else, you will almost surely fail.
- **Informality.** You will be more effective if you communicate conversationally. However, your public presentations should be more formal than your talks with friends.

Cultures Influence "Who" Speaks

Some cultures limit the people who may make their ideas public to adult men, for example, and sometimes just the oldest, wisest, or most knowledgeable among them (Weider & Pratt, 1990). Consequently, children, young people, nonexperts, and women may speak among themselves, but they are expected to keep silent in public arenas. If you're from such a culture, you may feel that nobody wants to hear what you have to say because you have not yet proved your wisdom or you really don't know much.

Cultures sometimes silence specific voices for a variety of reasons. For instance, the voices of the poor and oppressed, of gays and lesbians, of victims of incest and of other sufferers may be punished, ridiculed, or misunderstood (Jenefsky, 1996). Although the ideal of free speech embedded in our Bill of Rights is not always realized, it holds out the possibility for silenced individuals to speak out. Public speaking classrooms can be safe places for previously "speechless" people to find their voices.

Cultures Influence the "What" of Public Speaking

Cultures also differ in what is considered appropriate for public discussion. In some traditions, speakers give personal opinions and display their emotional involvement with their topic rather than attempt to be objective (Kochman, 1990; Sullivan, 1993; Wierzbicka, 1991). Other cultures frown on public discussions of personal feelings and viewpoints. In college classrooms, students from many traditions bring their contrasting expectations of "how to" speak well. Clearly, if they judge each other by their own culture's standards, misunderstandings and negative evaluations may result.

AP/Wide World Photos

Often the voices of women and children, minorities, or poor people are ignored or discounted. However, in May 2002, Gabriela Azurduy Arrieta from Bolivia became the first child to address the General Assembly of the United Nations. Her speech was taken seriously by U.N. members, who hear mainly from well-educated, professional adults.

In the United States, it is common to separate speakers from their words. It is possible—even likely—that you may disagree with your friends and still remain friends. Some friends, in fact, love to debate controversial topics. In contrast, Chinese and Japanese people traditionally avoid arguments, a behavior that may be traced to the Confucian idea of *hsin*, in which speakers and their words are inseparable. In these cultures, disputing someone's words publicly casts doubt on the person's honesty in general (Becker, 1988).

As you can see, factors from your background can affect how comfortable you feel in a public speaking classroom that teaches Euro-American cultural norms. What is considered competent in a classroom or in a business setting may be quite different from your cultural traditions. If so, you may have to become **bicultural,** knowing the rules for competent speaking in the dominant culture while appreciating and participating in your own ethnic speech community. In the following example, a Nigerian woman living in the United States explains how she accomplishes this:

Bicultural
Knowing and applying different rules for competent behaviors in two cultures.

> At work, . . . I raise my voice as loud as necessary to be heard in meetings. At conferences where I present papers on "Women From the Third World," I make serious arguments about the need for international intervention in countries where women are deprived of all rights. . . . Yet as easily as I switch from speaking English to Ibo [her African language], . . . I never confuse my two selves.

> Hundreds of thousands of women from the third world and other traditional societies share my experience. We straddle two cultures, cultures that are often in opposition. Mainstream America, the culture we embrace in our professional lives, dictates that we be assertive and independent—like men. Our traditional culture, dictated by religion and years of socialization, demands that we be docile and content in our roles as mothers and wives—careers or not. (Ugwu-Oju, 1993)

In summary, our cultures provide a range of appropriate communication behaviors, both verbal and nonverbal. These are the standards we often use to judge speakers as competent or incompetent. But they are not the only ways of sharing ideas publicly.

STOP AND CHECK

RECOGNIZE YOUR CULTURAL SPEAKING TRADITIONS

What public speaking traditions do you bring from your cultural heritage? How expressive were you encouraged to be? In what ways does your culture encourage or discourage you from speaking because of your ethnicity, your age, or your gender? What topics are sensitive or taboo? How might your cultural traditions affect your participation and your comfort in this course? You can answer these questions online under Stop and Check Activities for Chapter 1 at the Jaffe Connection Web site http://communication.wadsworth .com/jaffe.

To investigate this topic further, log on to InfoTrac College Edition www.infotrac-college.com and perform a PowerTrac search for the author (au) Celeste Roseberry-McKibben and read her article "'Mirror, Mirror on the Wall': Reflections of a 'Third Culture' American." Compare and contrast her list of "mainstream American" values with the information presented throughout this chapter.

Web Site

Public Speaking Influences Culture

Cultures are not static, which means that we continue to shape and mold our way of life, often through public speaking. Historically, our views of slavery and of women's roles and rights have been modified as activists insisted on reforms in speech after speech. For instance, slavery, once legal, was abolished by a constitutional amendment, and women's rights have been encoded in numerous laws. Currently, public speakers are arguing for changes in education, health care, immigration laws, and so on.

Public speakers attempt to influence society in a number of ways (Pearce, 1989):

- Some hope to *transmit* cultural beliefs, values, attitudes, and behaviors to people who do not currently hold them. For example, teachers inform students about the Bill of Rights, volunteers prepare immigrants to take the citizenship test by explaining the way our government functions, and pastors hold catechism classes to teach their church's beliefs.
- Other speakers *reinforce* or support existing cultural elements. That is, they encourage listeners to "keep on keeping on" with their current behaviors or beliefs. For instance, politicians urge people to keep voting, pastors urge their congregations to continue feeding the hungry, and teachers provide parents with tips for helping children with their homework.
- When events threaten to tear apart communities, speakers attempt to *restore* matters to a healthy state. In one city, a large, diverse group of citizens gathered to hear speakers condemn the desecration of a Jewish cemetery, and President Bush addressed the nation after terrorist attacks made us question some of our basic beliefs about safety.
- Speakers often try to *transform* their societies by bringing about social change. For instance, animal rights activists argue *for* vegetarianism and *against* wearing fur; environmental activists argue that people should use more public transportation rather than drill for more oil. Even a stable society that is relatively functional can generally be improved, and speakers appeal for causes like better health care and literacy.

In short, cultures are dynamic and changing. We speak in order to transmit cultural beliefs and behaviors, to strengthen or reaffirm what our audience already knows or does, to repair our cultures when they are in danger, and finally, to persuade audiences to change their ways of thinking or acting.

Visualizing the Communication Process: The Transactional Model of Communication

The word *communication* is so common that you may not think much about what actually happens when people communicate. The most common model is called the **transactional model,** because it depicts communication as a process in which the communicators together create mutual meanings. This model, shown in Figure 1.4, is one way to think about what is going on when you interact with others. It includes the following components, which I will define by showing how they appear in my teaching:

- As a *sender–receiver* (or source), I originate or *encode* a message—I select English words (a verbal code) to represent my ideas. As I work on my lesson plans, I keep my class in mind (receiving, in a sense, their messages from our last time together). For instance, I remember yawns from my 8 A.M. students and thankful looks from international students when I displayed key words on transparencies. I also check my email before class to see if I've received questions or comments from students that tell me what I need to define or emphasize during the class.
- My *messages* are intentional. I plan them to inform my students as well as to persuade them to value public speaking and to develop their skills. I choose language they understand, reasoning they accept, and illustrations that relate to their lives.
- I choose from a variety of *channels* to send my messages. In the classroom, the channel involves face-to-face, voice-to-ear interactions, but in a mass lecture with four hundred students in a large auditorium, I use a microphone. In addition, I also use nonverbal channels such as gestures or tone of voice, which contribute to the overall message. I can use closed-circuit television if my school has the equipment. Some professors use the Internet as a channel and offer the course online.
- *Receivers–senders*, my students in this case, hear my words and *decode* (interpret) them. Each one brings a personal background and heritage, plus individual beliefs, values, worries, and judgments, to class. Each one filters my words through personal perceptions, thoughts, and feelings, and sometimes through the influence of other listeners. Some bring laptop computers, and others take paper-and-pencil notes as they listen.

Transactional Model of Communication
Represents communication as a process in which speakers and listeners work together to create mutual meanings.

Figure 1.4 The transactional model of communication

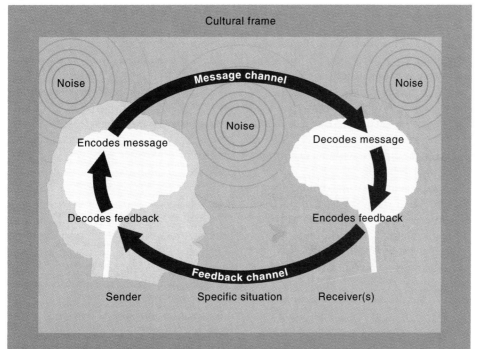

- The students send messages of their own, called *feedback*. They ask questions and discuss how to apply ideas I've presented; they nod, frown, or smile. I then decode (translate) this feedback and adapt my response: too many yawns and I ask a question or introduce a visual aid; too many frowns and I define my terminology and provide an illustration. In this transactional process of mutual sending-receiving-responding, I learn from my students and they learn from me and from one another.

- *Noise*, or static, can interfere with both message production and reception. For instance, if I have a sore throat, I may not produce enough sound to be heard. Or, in the middle of an important definition, a fire truck may go by the building (external noise). Internal noise, such as worries over being overdrawn at the bank or hunger pangs, can also disrupt the process.

- Our class takes place within a situational context that includes a five-sided classroom within a small, private university. I also speak and listen in other contexts—in faculty meetings, in discussions with my husband, in family councils, and in educational workshops. I communicate differently in each context. Students, too, choose different strategies in classroom interactions than they do in everyday conversations.

- Finally, our classroom communication exists in a larger cultural framework, in which expectations about higher education influence what is appropriate and what is not. Earlier in this chapter I discussed some ways that these cultural expectations affect our beliefs, values, attitudes, and behaviors within our technologically advanced culture.

In summary, communication is a complex, dynamic process. The transactional model attempts to depict and clarify some of the many variables that affect the way humans cooperate with one another to create meanings.

Summary

This chapter introduced the benefits you can gain when you study public speaking from a perspective of cultural diversity. This course will help you increase your competence and, perhaps, your self-confidence. It will also prepare you for participating actively in a culture that values skilled speakers and listeners. Finally, the study of rhetoric—a cornerstone of a liberal arts education—can equip you with critical thinking skills useful in everyday interactions.

By definition, culture includes both the visible and the underlying (embedded) aspects of a society, and culture influences public speaking in a number of ways. Your cultural and co-cultural traditions provide you with a set of core resources that include beliefs, values, attitudes, and behaviors that influence how you go about creating your own speeches and responding to the messages of others. In addition, this technologically advanced society provides you with a variety of resources that you can use to research your topic and present your speech. Finally, your cultural heritage provides you with expectations regarding the *how*, the *who*, and the *what* of public speaking. Of course, within each culture individual personalities and preferences also influence the ways we communicate.

Not only does culture affect public speaking but public speaking also affects culture. Speakers transmit core cultural beliefs, values, and attitudes to newcomers who must learn appropriate behaviors in specific contexts. Some speakers reinforce or support culture as it is; others repair or restore community when it is threatened. Speakers can also influence the removal or transformation of cultural elements that are outmoded or dysfunctional.

The chapter closed with a model that depicts in visual form the transactional nature of communication. This model emphasizes that both the originator of the message and the receiver must cooperate to *transact* or negotiate meaning. That is, a public speaker originates the message but remains aware of the audience and adapts to their feedback both in preparing and in speaking. Listeners participate actively by decoding the information and encoding feedback. Their communication, which can be negatively affected by both internal and external noise, takes place within a specific situation and cultural frame.

JAFFE ONLINE CONNECTION JAFFE ONLINE CONNECTION

Use your Jaffe Connection CD-ROM for quick access to the electronic study resources that accompany this text. Included on your CD-ROM are Speech Interactive and access to the Jaffe Connection Web site http://communication.wadsworth.com/jaffe, Speech Builder Express, and InfoTrac College Edition. Use the list of links, activities, and exercises included in this section as a guide to your CD-ROM and Web site resources for Chapter 1. In addition to these resources, the following Key Terms and Application and Critical Thinking Exercises are included online.

KEY TERMS

public speaker (4)
communication apprehension (CA) (4)
public speaking anxiety (PSA) (4)
process anxiety (4)
performance anxiety (4)
communication competence (5)
rhetoric (7)
culture (8)
co-culture (8)
rhetorical sensitivity (9)
core cultural resources (9)
belief (9)

attitude (9)
value (10)
behavior (10)
oral cultures (10)
literate cultures (10)
electronic culture (10)
nonexpressive cultures (11)
expressive cultures (12)
communication style (12)
bicultural (13)
transactional model of communication (15)

APPLICATION AND CRITICAL THINKING EXERCISES

1. Sometimes people do not see themselves as public speakers, because they define the word *public* too narrowly. They think of public speakers as politicians speaking at conventions but not as homemakers testifying before a local school board. Write your definition of "publics." Then, make a list of specific publics you have already addressed and those you may address someday.
2. Using InfoTrac College Edition, look up the key words "public speaking." You will get hundreds of hits. Find the article titled "Expert Offers Tips on Public Speaking" by Steve Finlay (It's in the April 1, 2002, issue of *Ward's Auto World*.) What does this article say about the importance of speaking and listening skills for automobile dealers? What tips does the author give for overcoming anxiety? How might the article apply to public speaking in an occupation that interests you?
3. To gain experience in speaking publicly, prepare an announcement (using the guidelines in Appendix B) and deliver it to your classmates. You can find upcoming campus or community events in the newspaper, on posters, or on bulletin boards around campus.
4. Interview a person working in the field you hope to enter when you graduate. What opportunities exist for public speaking within that occupation? Ask if and how public speaking is related to the higher-paying, more prestigious jobs within the field.
5. What stereotypes do you hold about the word *rhetoric?* The Internet has many sources of information on this topic. Visit http://eserver.org/rhetoric/ and follow at least two links you find there. This will help you understand the value of rhetoric. Throughout this course, listen for the word *rhetoric* as it is used on radio or television. Watch for it as you read newspapers or magazines. Each time you encounter the word, decide whether it's being used negatively, positively, or in a neutral manner. Note if any of the sources speak of rhetoric as essential in a free society.
6. Using InfoTrac College Edition, do a PowerTrac search for the text words "Sacramento: America's most integrated city." Read the article. What did you learn about cultural diversity that you did not already know?

7. Work with a group to evaluate the role of public speaking in creating and maintaining your college or university.
   - What role did public speaking have as the founders launched your institution?
   - How does your school currently use public speaking to recruit newcomers?
   - What role does ceremonial speaking, such as convocations or commencement addresses, have in maintaining the vision and the values of your institution?
   - When issues threaten to divide your campus, how do groups and individuals use public speaking to negotiate differences?
   - How is your campus preparing for the twenty-first century? How does public speaking function to move your school from the present to the future?

8. In a small group, make a list showing how public speaking is similar to everyday conversation and how it differs. Use the communication model to guide your thinking.

9. I used my classroom communication to illustrate the transactional model of communication. Select a communication event from your own life and use that to identify and explain each element of the model.

THE JAFFE CONNECTION WEB SITE

The Jaffe Connection Web site features review questions about the Web links, Stop and Check activities, and InfoTrac College Edition exercises referenced throughout the chapter. You can access this site via your CD-ROM or at http://communication.wadsworth.com/jaffe.

Web Links

1.1 Our Many Co-Cultural Groups (page 8)
1.2 The Value of Rhetoric (page 17)

Stop and Check Activities

1.1 Assess Your Current Competence (page 6)
1.2 Recognize Your Cultural Speaking Traditions (page 14)

InfoTrac College Edition Exercises

1.1 Recognize Your Cultural Speaking Traditions: Comparing Cultural Values (page 14)
1.2 Speaking and Listening Skills for Auto Dealers (page 17)
1.3 Cultural Diversity in an Integrated City (page 17)

SPEECH INTERACTIVE ON THE JAFFE CONNECTION CD-ROM

Watch the following special occasion speech by Mark Cavanaugh and answer the questions for analysis under Speech Interactive on your Jaffe Connection CD-ROM.

SAMPLE SPEECH

WEDDING TOAST
by Mark Cavanaugh   (Reprinted with permission)

Thank you all again for dealing with the heat.

I think everyone finally is relaxed and hopefully they'll enjoy the afternoon as the sun goes down.

This is the last of the big weddings at the Cavanaugh household. Baby Deirdre has grown into a beautiful woman and is now Mrs. Anderson and we are so happy about that.

We do things a little bit backwards here at the Cavanaugh household. Usually you plant something in memory of a big event, we seem to cut things down.

I was talking to Pete Wensberg who grew up right across the way our whole childhood and he goes;

"What ever happened to that big pine tree?"

and I said; "Well that came down for Susan's wedding."

"Well what ever happened to that little minnow pond? That little pond you had over in the corner?"

I said "Well we filled it in for Clare's wedding." and he said;

"Well hey, at least you got rid of that poison ivy!" and I said,

"Well, that's for Deirdre's wedding."

So, Deirdre, I know it doesn't sound glamorous but I know the landscape crew enjoys the fact that they don't have to deal with it.

I really want to thank Deirdre for allowing Leo and me to walk you down today. It was very special.

We know Dad was with us the whole way, his spirit and so was Shirley's.

The one thing that I'll always remember and is very special for Dave and Deirdre, is that both Shirley and Leo got to know the individual that their son and daughter was going to marry.

That is something that they'll take with them forever because I think both of them cherished the fact that they were truly in love and it is something I know Dave and Deirdre will be able to look back on with a lot of pride.

My favorite memory will be literally intercepting Dave's call to Dad. Those of you that were at the rehearsal dinner last night heard Mom's phone call from Dave when she was down waiting with Clare for the premature birth of Henry, and I was back here with Dad—babysitting Dad—making sure things were going OK at the homestead.

Well the phone call came in. It was like 10:00 at night and we had just gotten off the phone with Mom—kind of did a check to see how Clare was doing—and I'm thinking "Who's calling at 10 o'clock at night?" So I get the phone.

"Ah, yes, is Mr. Cavanaugh there?" and I said,

"Yeah, he's in the bathroom brushing his teeth right now. Can I ask who's calling?"

"Ah Mark, It's Dave."

"Oh Dave, hey. How are you doing?"

"Oh, ah, I didn't know you'd be home."

"Yeah, well. Let me get him." I say, "Dad, it's Dave."

Dad says "Hey, this could be the call! You know they're going hiking this weekend. They are going away for the weekend to Colorado."

So I sat bed side with Dad and I'm thinking "Oh my God, it's like the draft pick!"

So the one thing I'm always going to remember is Dad's huge smile. You know his eyes welling up and him saying "Oh, I'd be honored for you to have my daughter's hand in marriage."

And it was awesome. Leo couldn't be happier. So it was like a father and son bonding thing.

I walked back to my room at the end of the house and thought "Ah, this is great" and was kind of choked up and all of a sudden I hear Leo lying in bed saying, "Now get *your* act together."

Giving Your First Speech: Developing Confidence

THIS CHAPTER WILL HELP YOU

- Develop your speechmaking skills

- Explain the five canons of rhetoric:

  invention, disposition, style,

  memory, and delivery

- Understand physiological and

  psychological anxiety

- Develop strategies to deal with

  nervousness

- Learn skills for effective rehearsal

- Deliver your first speech

Detail from "Family Life and Spirit of Mankind"
Mural ©1977 by Susan Kelk Cervantes and Judith
Knepher Jamerson. (Leonard R. Flynn School,
East Wall, Army Street at Harrison, SF, CA)

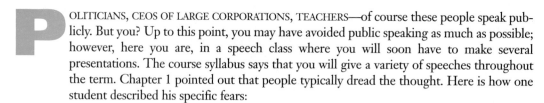

POLITICIANS, CEOS OF LARGE CORPORATIONS, TEACHERS—of course these people speak publicly. But you? Up to this point, you may have avoided public speaking as much as possible; however, here you are, in a speech class where you will soon have to make several presentations. The course syllabus says that you will give a variety of speeches throughout the term. Chapter 1 pointed out that people typically dread the thought. Here is how one student described his specific fears:

> Public speaking has always been hard for me, mainly because I'm shy and very self-conscious. I'm afraid of making a mistake and looking stupid in front of others. I also have the problem of not being able to bring across the message I want because I always stumble in speeches.
>
> CALEB

Public speaking anxiety (PSA) is common—in fact, one study reported that 20 percent of students in public speaking courses have severe PSA (Robinson, 1997). The same study showed that learning the how-to of public speaking helps demystify the speechmaking process and provides students with the skills they need to create good speeches. In addition, learning specific strategies for dealing with nervousness related to speech delivery increases students' overall competence. Assess your PSA by taking the test in the Stop and Check box.

STOP AND CHECK

ASSESS YOUR PUBLIC SPEAKING ANXIETY

Take this test to self-assess your anxiety regarding public speaking. In the blank beside the statement, write the number of the response that best reflects your feelings.

- (0) Strongly disagree
- (1) Disagree
- (2) Agree
- (3) Strongly agree

____ 1. I begin to get nervous the moment the speech is assigned.
____ 2. I feel panicky because I don't know how to create a speech.
____ 3. I usually feel nervous the day before I have to speak.
____ 4. The night before the speech I can't sleep well.
____ 5. I'm afraid people will think I'm dumb or boring or weird in some way.
____ 6. On the morning of the speech, I am really tense.
____ 7. I find it difficult to think positively about giving a speech.
____ 8. I think my physical reactions are greater than those that other people experience.
____ 9. During my speech I actually think I'll faint.
____ 10. I continue to worry even after the speech is over.

ADD YOUR SCORES.

_____ Total score

0–5   You are virtually fearless.
6–15   Your level of anxiety is quite normal.
16–25   Your level of anxiety may give you problems.
26–30   Consider making an appointment with your professor. Go back and look at the areas that bother you most, then develop specific strategies from the chapter to help you with your unique stresses.

Web Site

This test is also available online under Stop and Check Activities for Chapter 2 at the Jaffe Connection Web site. Or take an interactive version of the Personal Report of Public Speaking Anxiety (PRPSA) on the Web site. Click on "Book Companion Web Site" from the Web site http://communication.wadsworth.com/jaffe. Then click on "PRPSA Survey" under "Course Resources" on the left navigation bar.

Whether your anxiety is minimal or great, the goal of this chapter is to help you decrease your process anxiety as well as your performance anxiety. First, let's look at the skills you need to create a speech, then we will turn to commonly suggested strategies for reducing anxiety.

Develop Speechmaking Skills: Overcome Process Anxiety

"Good morning, class, according to the syllabus, your first speech is coming up next week. Today, I'll describe the assignment ..." Students commonly begin to experience tension when they first hear these words (Behnke & Sawyer, 1999). What causes their anxiety? For many, it's fear of the unknown—they don't know what to say or how to say it (Bippus & Daly, 1999). To an extent, you can lessen your dread by studying speech principles, observing others speak, and actually speaking yourself. As speechmaking becomes more familiar, you will feel less panicky.

Think of it this way: When you are learning any new skill, you follow the guidelines fairly closely at first. Only after you have mastered the basics and feel more confident do you begin to take liberties. Remember when you first learned to drive a car? You concentrated on every move; later, the process of shifting, steering, and braking became automatic. Public speaking is similar. Early on, your instructor may ask you to follow the guidelines closely. Once you are more experienced, you will feel freer to be creative in your preparation.

This section describes rhetorical traditions that draw from a 2,500-year history. In classical Greek and Roman academies, educators closely studied the "how-to" of speechmaking. They divided the entire process into five major categories: (1) creating the speech, (2) organizing speech materials, (3) choosing effective language, (4) learning the major ideas, and (5) delivering the speech. In each category they identified a *canon* (a set of principles, standards, norms, or guidelines) that students need to master to become effective orators. They called these five categories, and the principles within them, the five **canons of rhetoric** (Cicero, 1981).

Canons of Rhetoric
Principles, standards, norms, or guidelines for creating and delivering a speech.

A student who has process anxiety worries about creating the speech itself; one who has performance anxiety worries about actually delivering the speech.

Michael Newman/PhotoEdit

Create Your Speech: The Canon of Invention

Canon of Invention
Principles for designing a
speech that meets a need a
specific audience has.

The **canon of invention** provides guidelines relating to the content of a speech. Just as an inventor designs a product that solves a particular problem, you will design a speech that meets a need for a specific audience in a specific situation. The principles of invention help you analyze your audience, select an appropriate topic and purpose, gather evidence, and develop reasonable and logical arguments and explanations. Obviously, the content of your speech is vital; that is why this text devotes nine chapters to the norms found in the canon of invention.

Consider Your Audience

Begin the process of invention by thinking of your classroom as a *mini-culture* (see the Diversity in Practice box for more on this). Look around and note factors that might influence your speaking choices. What can you tell about your classmates' backgrounds and interests? At first you will probably notice obvious categories such as age or gender, but look for details like wedding rings, books from other courses, religious jewelry, or clothing choices. Strike up conversations before or after class as a way to become acquainted. Ask people their majors or where they're from. All these strategies will help you think of your audience as a group and as individuals within the group.

In addition, consider the situation in which you will speak. Inspect the room itself. Is it well lighted and well ventilated? Will your speech compete with external noise? Consider the time of day your class is held. Will your classmates be sleepy or hungry? Being mindful of details such as these will help you move to the next task—choosing your subject and purpose.

DIVERSITY IN PRACTICE
YOUR CLASSROOM CULTURE

WE GENERALLY think of cultures as large national entities or as smaller co-cultural groups within them. However, various groups—even groups as small as your class— develop distinct ways of doing things; consequently, each becomes a *mini-culture* with its own set of beliefs, values, and norms or rituals (Staley & Staley, 2000). If this seems confusing, think of the differences between a speech class and a physics class. Or contrast two history classrooms. In one, the professor lectures every period; in the other, a professor uses discussions and small groups to present course concepts.

Similarly, one speech class may develop a warm, open, supportive climate. Class members believe that each student can succeed; they value each person's feelings; and they create rituals—such as learning each other's names and greeting one another as the class gathers. In contrast, another class might develop a closed, hostile, or competitive culture wherein its members feel defensive and unsuccessful; these students reveal their values when they ignore one another and sleep or study during speeches.

Instructors generally state their core beliefs, values, and behavioral norms during the first class session. They typically emphasize their belief that public speaking is important, and they affirm values of openness, honesty, and diversity. They also state their expectations about respectful listening and speaking behaviors. Students also contribute to classroom culture. Consequently, what you and your classmates believe about one another, what you value, and how you act combine to create the culture that develops in your classroom.

Examine Luis Proenza's speech to a diverse audience using InfoTrac College Edition to locate his speech, "The Melting Pot: Finding Solutions to Cultural Differences." It was published in *Vital Speeches* of March 1, 2002, p. 361. Proenza, President of the University of Akron, gave this speech at his university's commencement exercises. Analyze how he stayed audience centered. What, if anything, could he have done to be more audience centered?

Choose a Topic

"Oh, no! What will I talk about? Why am I doing this?" These may be some of your biggest questions, and later chapters will provide you with detailed guidelines covering these concerns. However, your first assignment is probably an introduction—either of yourself or of a classmate; consequently, topic choice is partly done for you. But finding an interesting focus remains challenging. When introducing a classmate, set up an interview and discover one or more novel or unusual details about the person's background, experiences, or interests. Focus your speech around these details. A self-introduction may create more anxiety. You must reveal something about yourself within a fairly short time period, and you must decide what personal information you are willing to share. Whatever your speech assignment, consider these guidelines:

- **Be sure you understand what is expected.** It is embarrassing to prepare a speech carefully, only to discover—on speech day—that you've misunderstood the assignment. Generally your instructor provides specific guidelines that explain the time expectation and the general requirements for the speech. Study them carefully and ask questions if something is unclear. Also, study the examples at the end of the chapter and in Appendix C, and watch the videos on the CD that comes packaged with this text. They will help you understand how other students successfully completed similar assignments.
- **Choose to reveal something unusual.** Avoid boring your audience with something everyone has experienced; search for a novel and unique focus. Students have told about unusual jobs (working as a pyrotechnician, the person who sets off fireworks displays), vacations (a trip to New Zealand), and volunteerism (taking a therapy pet into nursing care facilities).
- **Select a significant topic.** Your topic should be important enough to discuss. Have you had life-changing experiences? Have you learned important lessons that others could also learn? Consider working your personal adventures or insights into a speech. Mona's speech, reprinted at the end of the chapter, described her decision to return to school after a divorce. Jessica related her family's experiences when her brother was born with Down syndrome. It's located in Chapter 15. Jason's self-introduction, outlined in Appendix C, described a dangerous hiking adventure. All of these speeches are on the CD that accompanies this text.
- **Consider your listeners' sensibilities.** Your purpose is not to shock your audience by revealing things that are too personal or embarrassing. Think twice before you reveal personal information about sensitive subjects such as sex, money, and religion. And here is another chance to be culturally sensitive; in your preparation, try to think from the diverse perspectives of audience members.
- **Try out your ideas on people you trust.** Discuss your audience and your assignment with them. If you have two or three ideas, ask your friends to give their opinions about each one.

If you have been thinking of your audience all along, you will have a good sense of what are and are not appropriate subjects for your speech.

Identify Your Purpose

When you have selected your topic, identify your reason for speaking by considering your audience once again. What response do you want from them? Answering this question will provide you with your general purpose. Your early speeches will probably focus on one of the following three goals:

- Do you want them to learn something? If so, your general purpose is to *inform*.
- Do you want them to respond by believing or doing something? Are you trying to reinforce their beliefs or behaviors? Then your general purpose is to *persuade*.
- Do you want them simply to laugh and enjoy themselves? If so, your purpose is to *entertain*.

As you might imagine, these purposes often overlap. In your introductory speech, your major goal will be to inform the class about either yourself or another classmate, but you will also want to be at least somewhat entertaining.

Gather Speech Materials

Because you are not an expert on many of the topics you choose, you must consult outside resources to fill in gaps in your knowledge. Commonly, you will find supporting materials in oral, print, and electronic sources (see Chapter 7). A speech of introduction is somewhat different in that it relies less on outside research and more on personal experiences or on an interview with the subject; however, you may also consult library resources to improve the speech. For example, Brigit knew about New Zealand from her visit to the country, but outside research provided her with additional information about its history.

In your speeches, highlight interesting and unusual events or experiences such as volunteer work in a nursing home with a therapy pet. Gather information from print and electronic resources, interviews, and personal experiences.

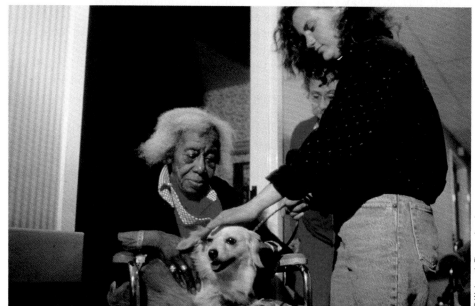

© Wadsworth–Thomson Learning

When interviewing, schedule your meeting for an uninterrupted time in a quiet place. After class, over email, or by telephone, arrange the details regarding place and time you will meet—then be on time. Bring a list of questions and tape record your conversation (with permission only) or take notes as you talk. Be sure you understand your interviewee by asking questions such as "Did I hear you correctly when you said you took your dog into convalescent homes?" or "I'm not sure I know how therapy pets are screened for safety. Could you clue me in?" Summarize at the end so you don't leave with misconceptions.

For additional information, consult print sources. For example, books or magazines can provide you with more facts about topics like therapy pets. You might even look up background information on a topic when you are introducing yourself. For instance, Michael described his personal experiences as a pyrotechnician, and he added information about fireworks that he'd found in library research.

If you have an encyclopedia on CD-ROM, look there for information. Videos or television are other resources for speech materials. If you have access to the Internet, you can explore various Web sites to locate interesting or significant background information. A word of caution, however: Internet sources can provide both excellent and poor or even fraudulent data; Chapter 7 provides guidelines for thinking critically about information you find online. Also, take advantage of InfoTrac College Edition materials. You received a password to the InfoTrac College Edition database when you purchased a new copy of this textbook. Use it to access hundreds of magazines, newspapers, journals, encyclopedias, and other features that have been screened for legitimacy.

Organize Your Ideas: The Canon of Disposition or Arrangement

After you have gathered information, you must arrange the ideas so that they will make sense to your audience. Principles of speech organization make up the **canon of disposition** or **arrangement.** Of course, there are many ways to organize a speech, and cultures vary in their "patterns" or organizational styles. Before organizing your speech, consider your listeners' culture, which influences their expectations.

Canon of Disposition or Arrangement
Guidelines for organizing a speech.

Most speeches in the Western speaking tradition have three major parts: the introduction, the body, and the conclusion. To be an effective speaker, you first orient your audience toward the subject in an introduction. This leads to the body of the speech, the part that generally takes up most of your speaking time, where you explain and develop your major ideas. After your major points, leave your listeners with a memorable conclusion. Taken as a whole, the outline looks like this:

> I. Introduction
> II. Body
> III. Conclusion

I. INTRODUCE YOUR TOPIC

Your first speech may vary slightly from this pattern, but in general an introduction has these four major functions that date back to the first-century Roman educator Quintilian (trans. 1920–1922):

- Orient the audience by drawing their attention to your subject.
- Motivate them to listen by relating the topic to their concerns.
- Demonstrate that you are a credible speaker on the subject by linking yourself with the topic.
- Preview the major point of the speech by stating the central idea.

II. DEVELOP THE BODY OF YOUR SPEECH

In the body of your speech, present and develop your major ideas, using sufficient evidence for clarification and support. There are many ways to organize speeches: topical, problem–solution, cause–effect, and so on. Using these patterns results in a linear arrangement, as shown by this outline of a cause–effect speech:

A. Causes
   1. First cause
      a. Support
      b. Support
   2. Second cause
      a. Support
      b. Support

B. Effects
   1. First effect
      a. Support
      b. Support
   2. Second effect
      a. Support
      b. Support

Although linear patterns are common, your cultural background, your learning style, or your personality traits may lead you to visualize your speeches as moving in wavelike patterns or in spiraling forms. Chapter 9 illustrates both traditional and alternative organizational forms. You'll find an additional pattern for narrative speeches in Chapter 15.

III. CONCLUDE MEMORABLY

To be most effective as a speaker, don't stop abruptly; instead, provide a sense of closure that ties your ideas together and leaves your audience with something to take away with them. Conclusions often have these elements:

- A transition to the conclusion
- A summary of the major ideas
- A reference to the introduction
- A final memorable statement

Connect Your Ideas

Your major work is done, and it's time for weaving your ideas together so that your speech flows smoothly from point to point. The words and phrases that link your ideas with one another are called **connectives**. Simple connectives include words such as *first, next,* and *finally.* More complex sentences, such as "After the initial shock of my accident, I began the painful rehabilitation process," summarize where you have been and where you are going in your speech. Put simply, connectives help your listeners keep their place in the speech by linking the various points to one another and to the speech as a whole.

Once you have your materials and the general framework or organizational pattern, you can begin to select precise wording and then learn your speech well enough to deliver it to an audience. The principles for these aspects of speechmaking are found in the final three canons of rhetoric: style, memory, and delivery.

Choose Suitable Language: The Canon of Style

When asked, "What do you think it means when someone says, "I like your style?"" several students responded:

> . . . you would most likely mean that you like the way I carry myself or the way I act.
>
> MATT

> It would probably mean that you like something about my personality or the way I handle things and people.
>
> JOSH

According to *The American Heritage Dictionary of the English Language, 4th Edition* (accessed online at **www.bartleby.com**), they're right. Style can mean a person's individuality as expressed in his or her actions and tastes. However, in rhetoric, **style** means language; the **canon of style** contains the principles for using language effectively in both speaking and writing. (That's why you consult style manuals in your writing classes.)

Put the finishing touches on your ideas by polishing the words you use, always with an ear tuned to your listeners. Here are a few general guidelines for effective use of language in public speaking:

- Choose appropriate vocabulary and grammar for both the occasion and the audience. This means adapting your vocabulary to audience characteristics such as occupation, age, or educational level.
- Omit language that may offend your listeners. Eliminate swear words as well as language that demeans people on the basis of their sex, race, or age.
- Choose words that listeners understand. Either define technical terms or eliminate them and choose more familiar language.
- Use fewer slang expressions. The language used in public speeches is generally more formal than the language used in everyday conversation.

More detailed information on the canon of style is provided in Chapter 13.

Learn and Present Your Speech: The Canons of Memory and Delivery

Because they lacked TelePrompTers and the like, Roman educators taught young orators elaborate techniques for learning their speeches by heart. In fact, the **canon of memory** is often called the lost canon because so few people in this culture rely on memory alone, and because **memorized delivery** is highly risky. Forgetting even a few simple words can lead to public embarrassment—something you definitely want to avoid! Also, in your first speech stay away from **manuscript delivery,** in which you prepare your entire speech beforehand, down to the exact words, then read it to your audience. As you might imagine,

Connectives
Words and phrases that you use to tie your ideas together.

Style
In rhetoric, style means language.

Canon of Style
Principles for choosing effective language.

Canon of Memory
Guidelines to help you remember your ideas.
Memorized Delivery
Learning the speech by heart, then reciting it.
Manuscript Delivery
Reading a speech.

reading your speech means you will lose important eye contact with listeners. Also avoid **impromptu delivery,** in which you stand up and speak with little preparation beforehand. Instead, make it your goal to use **extemporaneous delivery,** in which you determine in advance the organizational outline and the major ideas. Before you speak, put key ideas on note cards. Write single words, phrases, and statistics to jog your memory as you deliver your speech. Then, during the speech itself, choose your words as you go. Chapter 14 elaborates on these four delivery methods, and Chapter 11 gives you additional ideas to help you remember your speech.

Principles found in the **canon of delivery** also provide guidelines on nonverbal behaviors, such as gestures and eye contact that strengthen your performance. More details on delivery are covered in Chapter 14. Briefly, you will be more skillful if you remember the following:

- Make eye contact with your listeners.
- Have pleasant facial expressions.
- Avoid a monotone voice.
- Smile at appropriate times.
- Be conversational.
- Stay within the time limits.

Focus throughout not on giving something *to* your audience but on creating something *with* them.

You will be more competent in creating your speech if you follow the guidelines found in the five canons of rhetoric. To summarize, begin by analyzing your audience, selecting a topic and purpose, and gathering materials (invention). Then organize or arrange your ideas into meaningful patterns (disposition), choose appropriate language (style), and learn your major points (memory), so that you can present them effectively (delivery). Now you are prepared for the rehearsal that will help you perform your speech well.

For additional material on the canons of rhetoric, check the Internet Web site sponsored by Brigham Young University at `http://humanities.byu.edu/rhetoric/canons.htm`. This URL and all the Web sites referenced in this text are maintained for you on the Jaffe Connection Web site.

Impromptu Delivery
Speaking with little advanced preparation.

Extemporaneous Delivery
Preparing a speech carefully in advance but choosing the exact wording during the speech itself.

Canon of Delivery
Rules or standards for presenting your speech.

STOP AND CHECK
USE THE CANONS TO ASSESS SAMPLE SPEECHES

Listen to the speeches of introduction on the CD that comes with the text. Evaluate each one according to how well it meets the guidelines given in the chapter. Does the speaker understand the assignment? Is the speech novel and significant enough to maintain interest? Is the speaker sensitive to the intended audience? Does the speech seem well organized? Is the language interesting? How well rehearsed does it seem to be? What advice, if any, would you give each speaker to improve the speech? These questions are available online under Stop and Check Activities for Chapter 2 at the Jaffe Connection Web site.

Web Site

Develop Rehearsal Skills: Overcome Performance Anxiety

Nervousness manifests itself in two forms: physiological and psychological. **Physiological anxiety** is your bodily response to the feared event itself. **Psychological anxiety** manifests itself in worry, dread, and feelings of inadequacy that may start when your speech is assigned and peak about the time you open your mouth to speak. This student describes both types:

Physiological Anxiety
Bodily responses to a perceived threat (increased heart rate, adrenaline rush).

Psychological Anxiety
Mental stress about a perceived threat.

I was anxious about my speech from the first moment I knew about it. I became most worried the night before and the day of the speech. I worry about how I present my speech, and I'm not very confident in my abilities. Once I stand in front of the class, I become rigid and my stomach is in knots. I generally turn red (shades) and talk differently (due to nerves).

EILEEN

This section discusses a number of specific skills you can use in combination to overcome both kinds of nervousness (Sawyer & Behnke, 1999).

Develop Strategies to Deal with Physiological Responses

Fight-or-Flight Mechanism
Physiological mechanism your body automatically activates when threatened to enable you to fight or to flee.

You know from experience how your body responds to dangerous situations. A process called the **fight-or-flight mechanism** takes over, and your body energizes you either to fight the threat or to run away from the danger. Unfortunately, your body doesn't distinguish between physically threatening situations, where you actually need the extra physical energy to make your escape, and psychologically threatening experiences, where your increased heart rate, butterflies, and adrenaline rush only add to your stress. In speech situations, your physiological anxiety is typically highest when you face your audience and begin your introduction (Behnke & Sawyer, 2001). As you progress, you will probably begin to feel more relaxed, becoming even more at ease during the conclusion (see Figure 2.1). If you are like most people, your stress will be minimal during the question-and-

Figure 2.1   Knowing that anxiety is greater in certain periods can help you control your nervousness by planning strategies that enable you to get through these periods.

SOURCE: FROM BROWNELL & KATULA (1984). REPRINTED BY PERMISSION OF THE EASTERN COMMUNICATION ASSOCIATION.

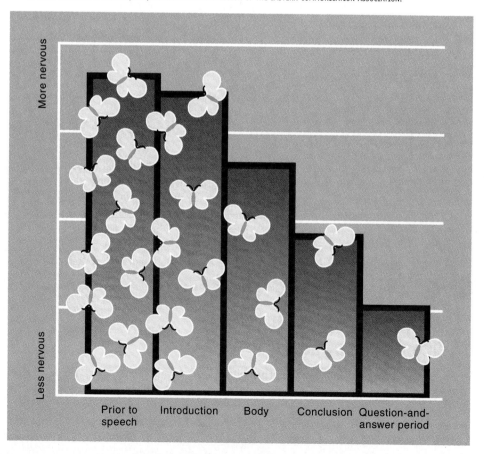

answer period immediately following the speech, although some physiological symptoms may linger. Here's how one student described the process:

> As I sit in class my anxiety level increases by the minute. Right before and as I walk to the front of the room, I use all my power to hide how nervous I am. I take a deep breath and start talking. During the beginning of my speech, anxiety is the worst. My nervous habits show through most in the beginning. As I continue my speech, it gets easier and I become more comfortable. By the conclusion, I'm usually cool, calm, and collected!
>
> EMILY

To counteract physical tension, engage in some form of physical exercise before class—lift weights, walk, or run your tension away. Listen to soothing music. Don't skip breakfast or lunch, and limit sugar and caffeine if these substances make you feel wired. When you get to the classroom, focus on relaxing your major muscle groups and breathe slowly and deeply just before you speak.

These additional tactics may ease your anxiety:

- Plan a compelling introduction to help carry you through the anxiety peak at the beginning of the speech. When you arrive in the classroom, silently repeat the goal of the speech, the main ideas, and your introduction so you will start well.
- Use visual aids when appropriate, especially at the start of your speech. These ease tension because they give the audience something to look at besides you.
- Deliver your introduction from notes rather than reading it or reciting a memorized text. If you read a prepared text, you risk failing to engage your audience. A memorized introduction is hazardous because this is such a high-anxiety point in your speech.

Develop Strategies to Deal with Psychological Anxiety

Although you know better, you may still hear an internal voice say, "I don't know what I'm doing. I'll forget halfway through. I probably won't get my ideas across. They'll see my knees shake." Self-talk is called **internal monologue (I-M)** (Howell, 1990). Negative self-talk adds to your discomfort, but it's not fatal. Researchers have identified two areas of vulnerability: your level of confidence (I've never done this before; I'm embarrassed about my looks; I'll flunk) and your expectations regarding the audience's reactions (they'll make fun of me; they don't want to hear what I have to say; they won't pay attention; they'd rather be somewhere else) (Bippus & Daly, 1999; MacIntyre & MacDonald, 1998). This type of anxiety generally peaks just before you speak (Behnke & Sawyer, 2001).

Internal Monologue (I-M)
Self-talk.

Control Your Internal Monologue

You can learn to control I-M by a process called **cognitive modification** in which you identify negative thoughts and replace them with positive ones (Robinson, 1997). Think positively in three areas: about the message, about the audience, and about yourself:

Cognitive Modification
Identifying negative thoughts and replacing them with positive ones.

- To think positively about the message, select a topic that interests you and is beneficial to your audience. Give yourself enough time for research and organization. Be sure of your pronunciation; check the dictionary to make sure you know how to say unfamiliar words.
- To promote positive thoughts about the audience, remember that other students are probably just as nervous when they speak, and they are not experts in your subject. Assume that they want you to succeed, and focus on the purpose of your speech. (If your first language is not English, think of how your audience would feel if they had to give a speech in *your* native language.)
- Maintain a positive self-image by focusing on the things you do well. Remind yourself that your worth as a person is unrelated to your skill as a novice public speaker and that competence develops with experience.

Todd Eckelman

Before your speech, find a quiet place to rehearse. Learn your main ideas and practice giving the speech differently each time instead of trying to memorize it word for word.

Visualization
Rehearsing by using your imagination to envision your speech from start to finish.

Use Visualization

Another helpful strategy, one that many athletes use before performances, is called **visualization**. Visualization is a form of positive self-talk or mental strategizing in which you see yourself successfully performing a complex task. Professors Joel Ayres, Theodore Hopf, and their associates have guided many students in using visualization techniques to ease their PSA. They found that students who use these techniques during their preparation are less apprehensive and report fewer negative thoughts during their speeches (Ayres & Hopf, 1989; Ayres, Hopf, & Ayres, 1994).

Ayres and Hopf suggest the following:

1. Find a quiet place and picture all the details from the beginning to the end of your speech.
2. Seat yourself mentally in the audience and pretend you are watching yourself give the speech.
3. Imagine your speaking self as a competent, well-prepared performer who stands confidently, stresses important words, pauses effectively, and makes appropriate gestures.
4. Think about the audience responding positively with nods, smiles, and interest.
5. Continue to visualize yourself finishing your speech, gathering your notes, making final eye contact with the audience, and leaving the podium or other speaking space.
6. Finally, imagine yourself back in the audience, delighted to be through!

Two key elements accompany successful visualization: You must create vivid images, and you must control the images you generate (Ayres, Hopf, & Edwards, 1999).

Rehearse

After your speech is fully planned and outlined and you have taken steps to deal with your nerves, find a quiet place where you can deliver your speech out loud, using your note cards. Recruit friends, family, roommates—anyone who can act as an audience, provide feedback, troubleshoot problems, and give you practice speaking in front of a group. Plan to rehearse several times, each time selecting slightly different wording. Focus on looking away from your notes and communicating in a conversational manner. Practice may not make perfect, but the more prepared you are, the better you will feel about your presentation.

BUILD YOUR SPEECH
YOUR FIRST SPEECH

Using the five canons of rhetoric, prepare a speech in which you introduce yourself or your classmate. As you prepare this speech, consider the following questions:

1. Do I understand the assignment?
2. Is my topic somewhat unusual? If not, do I have a unique or novel approach?
3. Is the topic significant enough to discuss?
4. How will I adapt this speech to this audience?
5. Which friends can I ask to listen to my ideas?

You can build your speech for this initial and all subsequent assignments using Speech Builder Express, your online speech outlining tool accessible via your Jaffe Connection CD-ROM. Speech Builder Express uses interactive activities and video clips to coach you from speech topic to formal outline. Once you log in, you can create and save up to five speech outlines and, if requested, email them to your instructor.

Summary

It is not enough simply to get up in front of an audience and talk; good speaking requires thought and preparation. The Greeks and Romans identified a set of principles or standards—a canon—for each of five areas of speechmaking: invention, disposition, style, memory, and delivery. Use guidelines from the canon of invention to consider your audience's characteristics and interests and take into account their responses to the time of day and temperature in your classroom. After that, select a unique, significant, and appropriate topic. Decide whether your major purpose is to inform, persuade, or entertain, then gather materials that will provide the information you need to present your topic adequately. Consult oral, print, or electronic resources as you do your research.

Organize your ideas into a culturally meaningful pattern using norms from the canon of disposition to create an introduction, body, and conclusion. Choose appropriate wording (canon of style) and learn your major ideas (canon of memory) so that you can extemporaneously deliver your speech (canon of delivery).

Finally, deal with your nerves by rehearsing wisely. Know when to expect the highest levels of anxiety and plan accordingly. Plan specific activities to counteract the physical tension brought on by the fight-or-flight mechanism. Then work to control your internal monologue by cognitive restructuring, substituting positive thoughts for negative ones. Visualize yourself performing your speech successfully from beginning to end. Use vivid images and control your imaginary scenario so that you succeed in giving your speech.

Doing these steps thoughtfully and thoroughly enables you to walk into your classroom with confidence on speech day. Thus, you will be able to deliver your speech more competently.

JAFFE ONLINE CONNECTION   JAFFE ONLINE CONNECTION

Use your CD-ROM and the Jaffe Connection Web site http://communication.wadsworth.com/jaffe to review the following concepts, answer the review questions, and complete the suggested activities.

KEY TERMS

canons of rhetoric (23)
canon of invention (24)
canon of disposition or arrangement (27)
connectives (28)
style (28)
canon of style (28)
canon of memory (28)
memorized delivery (28)
manuscript delivery (28)

impromptu delivery (29)
extemporaneous delivery (29)
canon of delivery (29)
psychological anxiety (29)
physiological anxiety (29)
fight-or-flight mechanism (30)
internal monologue (I-M) (31)
cognitive modification (31)
visualization (32)

APPLICATION AND CRITICAL THINKING EXERCISES

1. Consider the role of preparation and rehearsal in increasing your speaking competence. What effect does last-minute preparation have on competence? What effect does it have on anxiety? Knowing this, how do you plan to prepare for your next speech?
2. Rank from 1 to 5 (easiest to hardest), the five canons of rhetoric in order of difficulty for you personally.
____ Invention: audience analysis, topic selection, purpose, research
____ Disposition: organization or arrangement and connection of ideas

____ Style: choice of appropriate language
____ Memory: remembering what you want to say
____ Delivery: actually presenting your speech

Which is easiest? Why? Which is hardest? Why? Identify specific strategies you can use to work on the areas that challenge you most.

3. Log on to www.whitehouse.gov and explore the site. How might links found on this site help you apply principles of invention such as topic selection and research?

4. Use InfoTrac College Edition to search for the term "public speaking anxiety" (PSA). Note the number of hits you get. Sometimes researchers do not use terminology commonly used by the public. In a new search, look up the familiar term "stage fright." How many hits do you get? Look for the article titled "So Long, Stage Fright" in the June 2000 issue of *Success* magazine. Compare the advice given by Dilip R. Abayasekara, a non-native speaker of English, with the advice for overcoming anxiety presented in this chapter.

5. At the top of a sheet of paper write the name of an occupation that interests you. Then, down the left side of the page, list the five canons of rhetoric, leaving several spaces between each one. Beside each canon, identify ways that the skills developed within the canon will be useful in the job you named. For example, how will identifying a purpose or doing research help a nurse or an engineer? How will organizing ideas help a teacher or computer programmer?

6. Work with a group to analyze your classroom audience using the suggestions on page 24. In light of material from Chapter 1, and from your experiences, discuss some adaptations you might make to be successful with this group. For instance, how might the group influence your choice of topics? How might you adapt to diversity? How might the classroom itself, the time of day of the class, and other outside factors affect your speaking?

7. Within your classroom, you will generally use extemporaneous delivery; however, the other modes of delivery are sometimes more culturally appropriate. With a group, write down the four modes: memorized, manuscript, impromptu, and extemporaneous. Beside each, identify specific instances in which that mode would probably be the most effective. For instance: impromptu delivery—most wedding toasts; manuscript delivery—graduation speeches. After you have identified several specific examples, discuss with your group some guidelines that you think speakers should follow for each type of delivery.

THE JAFFE CONNECTION WEB SITE

The Jaffe Connection Web site features review questions about the Web links, Stop and Check activities, and InfoTrac College Edition exercises referenced throughout the chapter. You can access this site via your CD-ROM or at http://communication.wadsworth.com/jaffe.

Web Links

2.1 The Canon of Style (page 28)
2.2 Canons of Rhetoric (page 29)
2.3 Applying Principles of Invention (page 34)

Stop and Check Activities

2.1 Assess Your Public Speaking Anxiety (page 22)
2.2 Use the Canons to Assess Sample Speeches (page 29)

InfoTrac College Edition Exercises

2.1 Reliable Research Sources (page 26)
2.2 Your Classroom Culture: Analyzing a Speech for a Diverse Audience (page 24)
2.3 Overcoming Public Speaking Anxiety (PSA) (page 34)

Build Your Speech Featuring Speech Builder Express

2.1   Your First Speech (page 32)

SPEECH INTERACTIVE ON THE JAFFE CONNECTION CD-ROM

Watch the following Speech of Self-Introduction by Mona Bradsher and answer the questions for analysis under Speech Interactive on your Jaffe Connection CD-ROM. In addition to Mona's speech, Speech Interactive features Jason Kelleghan and Jessica Howard's introductory and narrative speeches referred to on page 25.

Student Speech with Commentary

SELF-INTRODUCTION
by Mona Bradsher

My name is Mona Bradsher. I'm a junior, although I'm older than most juniors at our school. In my speech, I want to introduce you to a very persuasive six-year-old. Through her, you'll learn why I have come back to finish my college degree after a ten-year break from school.

When I was eighteen, I started college like many of you. But, unlike most of you, I dropped out when I was twenty—in the middle of my sophomore year. I left school because I wanted to get married to a man named Jason. I'd met him the summer before, and we had fallen in love. Jason and I did get married and we had a daughter, Sasha.

In my case, the fairy tales were wrong: Jason and I didn't live happily ever after. We divorced just before our fifth wedding anniversary. So there I was—a twenty-five-year-old single mom with a child to raise. My income was pretty low, because I didn't have enough education to get a job that paid well. It was hard to get by on what I could make and the small amount of child support that Jason paid each month. We didn't go out for dinners or movies, but we did eat healthy meals at home. We didn't have money for a nice car, so we used the bus system. When Sasha was sick, I'd have to work extra hours to pay the doctor's bill and the cost of prescriptions. So it was tough, and I worried that as my daughter got older I wouldn't be able to support her on what I made. I felt really trapped.

Last year Sasha started school. One day she came home and told me her teacher had taught them about the importance of education. Sasha's teacher had put up a chart showing the difference between what high school graduates and college graduates make. Her teacher also talked about how education helps every person fulfill his or her individual potential and lead a fuller life. The teacher told all the children that education was the most important gift they could give themselves. So Sasha said to me, "Mommy, now that I'm going to school, why don't you go too?"

At first I told Sasha that mommy had to work to pay for our apartment and food, but Sasha would have none of that. She insisted that I should go to school. I don't know how many of you have tried to argue with a very insistent six-year-old, but take my word for it: You can't win! Because my daughter was so persistent, I checked around and found out there is an educational loan program specifically for older students who want to return to school and complete their education. I qualified, and I'll keep getting the loan as long as I maintain a B average. So far, my average is above that because Sasha and I have a deal: We study together for three hours every night.

And that's why I'm here now. That's why I've come back to finish my degree after a ten-year break. I'm here because my daughter reminded me of the importance of education. If I can learn an important lesson from a six-year old, then I can learn other important lessons from the teachers at our university.

Mona's self-introduction is a personal experience narrative that explains why she is an "older than average" student in a class comprised mainly of younger students.

She summarizes her marriage and divorce quite briefly, but she piles up details when she describes her life as a poor, single working mother. Notice how she uses vivid images to get her listeners emotionally involved in her story.

Mona is tapping into strong cultural values—the value of education, of perseverance, and of hard work.

She doesn't really tell students "Don't get married too young; stay in school." But her narrative persuasively argues that the choice she made brought difficulties she could have avoided if she had stayed in school. (Chapter 15 provides more details on the functions of narratives.)

Ethics and Diversity

THIS CHAPTER WILL HELP YOU

■ Define ethics

■ Describe three responses to diversity

■ Identify characteristics of dialogical speaking and listening

■ Distinguish between monological speaking and dialogical speaking

■ Explain three guidelines for speaking in a democracy

■ Discuss ethical responsibilities of listeners

■ Give examples of two kinds of unethical research

Detail from "Family Life and Spirit of Mankind" Mural ©1977 by Susan Kelk Cervantes and Judith Knepher Jamerson. (Leonard R. Flynn School, East Wall, Army Street at Harrison, SF, CA)

AYED YASIN WAS SELECTED AS ONE OF THREE STUDENTS to speak at Harvard University's 2002 commencement exercises. Yasin, a former president of the Harvard Islamic Society, chose as his speech title "Of Faith and Citizenship: My American *Jihad*." Reaction was swift. The controversy centered around the word *jihad*, which the *Boston Globe* called "one of the most controversial words in any language" (Healy, 2002). Concerned students argued that Yasin should be free to speak his mind, but he should not be given a university-sanctioned platform to condone violence; at least one person sent Yasin a death threat. University president Larry Summers urged seniors to remain calm, "Especially in a university setting, it is important for people to keep open minds, listen carefully to one another, and react to the totality of what each speaker has to say." But David Adelman, a graduating senior, argued, "Using such a contentious issue is unnecessary at this time" ("Outrage at Harvard," 2002).

Both Zayed Yasin and his critics faced an **ethical dilemma.** What obligation did the critics have to make sure his rights to free speech were upheld? What was the most ethical way to listen to his ideas? To respond to them? In light of September 11, 2001, and of Palestinian suicide bombings in Israel, what obligation did Yasin have to other students, including members of Hillel, Harvard's Jewish students' group, with whom he'd previously clashed? Would his speech have been more appropriate if it were not delivered at a commencement ceremony?

As the situation played out, Zayed dropped the word *jihad* from the title, most of the students listened politely when he delivered the speech, a few protested, and a few gave him a standing ovation ("Speech on *Jihad*," 2002).

The situations you face may not be so dramatic, but you make ethical communication choices each day. When you stand up for what you believe to be true, when you respectfully invite someone who has a different perspective to speak, when you check facts so that you don't pass on faulty information, or when you resist the temptation to plagiarize a speech, you are making a positive ethical choice.

Professor Vernon Jensen (1997) defines **ethics** this way:

> . . . [your] moral responsibility to choose, intentionally and voluntarily, oughtness [what you should do] in values like rightness, goodness, truthfulness, justice, and virtue, which may, in a communicative transaction, significantly affect [yourself] and others. (p. 4)

Put another way, when you communicate ethically, you make a conscious decision to speak and listen in ways that you, in light of your cultural ideals, consider right, fair, honest, and helpful—to others as well as to yourself. This is not always easy, especially in a pluralistic culture.

In our complex society and diverse world, you probably know both individuals and groups who believe and behave in ways almost opposite to you. These differences seem irreconcilable, leading to tension between you and those with whom you otherwise have much in common (Pearce, 1989). Fortunately, the U.S. Constitution protects the free expression of a wide range of ideas, even those that others find offensive or disgusting; however, you are not free to say just anything. You can't legally yell FIRE! in a crowded theater, for example; nor can you intentionally slander another person's reputation by spreading information you know to be false. Consequently, you must balance tensions between your rights and your responsibilities to others. Jensen suggests you concentrate on both, and he coins the term **"rightsabilities"** to emphasize this double focus.

But how is this done? How do we determine right and wrong in public speaking? Should you leave some things unsaid? When? Who decides? On what basis? This chapter presents some of the principles that have emerged as people have grappled with these ethically challenging questions. First we will examine common responses to diversity, and then discuss guidelines for ethical speaking, listening, and researching in a complex culture.

Ethical Dilemma
Ethical question or problem that arises when a communicator must balance important but competing beliefs and values.

Ethics
Making a conscious decision to communicate in ways that you, in light of your cultural ideals, consider right, fair, honest, and helpful to yourself and others.

"Rightsabilities"
Phrase coined by Professor Vernon Jensen to highlight the tension that exists between our right to free speech and our responsibility for our speeches.

Responses to Diversity

To illustrate the range of differences between individuals and national groups, Porter and Samovar (1994) created a maximum–minimum scale (see Figure 3.1). The end marked "minimum" shows comparatively small differences: for instance, environmentalists and developers share educational, monetary, and legal systems (they may even sit side by side in church and shop at the same supermarket), but they disagree about the balance between environmental and business interests. At the "maximum" end of the range are national groups that have divergent languages, histories, religious traditions, forms of government, and core philosophies. Diversity, even at the minimum end of the scale, is often divisive and can lead to hearings, open disputes, or marches; differences at the maximum end may result in boycotts, sanctions, or wars. Three common responses to diversity are resistance, assimilation, and accommodation.

Resisting Diversity

Resisting groups or individuals defend their own beliefs and traditions against change; in extreme situations, they attack people who differ from them (Berger, 1969). The intensity of their attacks ranges from physical assaults, terrorist bombings, or war to active persecution and intolerance and to milder challenges that ignore, discount, or ridicule divergent ideas. Here are some examples:

Resisting
Response to diversity in which you refuse to change, defend your own positions, or attack others.

Figure 3.1 The minimum–maximum scale of sociocultural differences

SOURCE: SAMOVAR & PORTER, 1994

- Michael Lerner, an American rabbi who criticizes Israel and sympathizes with Palestine, has received emails that say "You subhuman leftist animal. You should be exterminated." To protect himself, police suggested he install an alarm in his house (Byrne, 2002, p. 23).
- A conservative student newspaper at the University of California, Berkeley printed a negative story about a Chicano group that advocates a revolt against white people. Some conservatives were harassed and a few received death threats. Someone broke into their offices and took 3,000 copies of their newspaper (Sorokin, 2002).

It is easy to label hate crimes or death threats as unethical, but what about taunting or simply ignoring people who differ from you?

Resistance can be positive. Resisting groups often speak out against perceived social injustices. For instance, the decade of the 1960s was characterized by civil rights, antiwar, and student protest movements. Today, resistance is expressed as activists rally on behalf of the environment, third world debt relief,

AP/Wide World Photos

We watched in stunned horror as avowed enemies of the United States used civilian airplanes as weapons to take down the World Trade Center and hit the Pentagon on September 11, 2001. This is an extreme example of resistance to diversity.

Assimilating
Response to diversity in which you surrender some or most of your ways and adopt cultural patterns of another group.

Accommodating
Response to diversity in which you listen and evaluate the views of others; both sides adapt, modify, and bargain to reach mutual agreements.

Multivocal Society
Society that actively seeks expression of a variety of voices or viewpoints.

Voice
Ideas, opinions, and wishes of a person or group that are expressed openly and formally.

animal rights, and so on. Activists often justify their methods by reasoning that the ends they seek warrant the means they use. To learn more about resistance groups, use the Internet search engine www.alltheweb.com to search for the exact phrase "protest movement," and read an article about a local or global resistance movement.

Assimilating Diversity

Instead of defending one's own ways and attacking others, people who are **assimilating** reject or surrender their background beliefs and practices to embrace those of another group (Berger, 1969). For example, a woman whose parents are both public school administrators decides to home school her own children. A Jew becomes a Buddhist. An immigrant learns English and never again speaks her first language. Individuals and co-cultural groups often assimilate in one area or another, but they rarely change entirely. In the United States where choice is a dominant value, people are free to change their ideas and lifestyles; however, ethical implications arise when individuals passively allow themselves to be coerced or manipulated into changing without critically examining good reasons for the change.

To understand assimilation in greater depth, log on to InfoTrac College Edition and use PowerTrac to search for the article titled "Vietnamese-Americans Fight War of Identity, Assimilation." In this personal narrative, Phat X. Chiem describes his family's efforts to be "Vietnamese" as well as "American."

Accommodating Diversity

People who show a willingness to hear and evaluate diverse views are **accommodating** to diversity. This means they are open-minded and willing to rethink their ideas—perhaps to surrender some, to modify others, and to keep still others relatively intact. Accommodation is important in a **multivocal society,** one that actively encourages a variety of voices. In this sense, **"voices"** means ideas, opinions, and wishes of a person or group that are expressed openly and formally (Gates, 1992).

In their book *Transcultural Leadership*, Simons and his colleagues (1993) describe individuals who acknowledge real differences between groups but learn enough about other cultures to communicate effectively while remaining rooted in the values and language of their own traditions. They actively look for shared cultural checkpoints, and they cooperate with different people and groups to adapt and create new forms that transcend a single tradition or worldview. Gates (1992), who is chair of Harvard University's W. E. B. DuBois Institute, summarizes the ideals of a multivocal society. In it, co-cultural groups recognize that they hold divided opinions, yet individuals and groups work together to forge a civic culture that accommodates both differences and commonalities. The meeting described in Diversity in Practice: The Homosexuals and the Baptists illustrates one attempt between two groups to confront some of their differences in face-to-face conversations.

In summary, your decisions to resist new ideas or to embrace them with relatively few questions, to block voices from being heard or to create space for a multivocal society have ethical implications for both speaking and listening in a pluralistic society. Let's now turn to specific resources offered within our culture for people who want to be ethical speakers, listeners, and researchers.

THE HOMOSEXUALS AND THE BAPTISTS

IN OCTOBER 1999, Jerry Falwell, a Baptist pastor and founder of the Moral Majority, invited 200 gay men and lesbians to meet with 200 members of his Thomas Road Baptist Church. He wanted to bring church members face to face with homosexual people for a discussion of ways to tone down antigay rhetoric in light of the rise in hate crimes against gays and lesbians (Cloud, 1999).

The Reverend Mel White, Falwell's long-time friend and ghostwriter of Falwell's biography, had come out of the closet and now heads an interfaith movement to end religious policies directed against gays. Over the years, White has repeatedly asked Falwell to avoid antigay rhetoric that might incite violence against homosexual people. Falwell himself realized the impact of hate after several shootings occurred in which gunmen expressed anti-Christian sentiments, and he set up the October gathering between the two divergent groups.

Jerry Falwell predicted "For the first time in history, we will have talked without fighting" and Mel White mused, "How do two people who see each other as a threat talk to each other in nonhate language?" (Rossellini, 1999). The answer is unclear, but the question highlights the difficulties inherent in communicating ethically when people disagree on fundamental issues.

To investigate the topic of inflammatory rhetoric directed toward a group, go to the Internet at www.google.com. Search for the exact phrase "gay bashing" or "Japan bashing" or "evangelical bashing," and read an article written from the perspective of a person whose co-cultural group is being bashed.

STOP AND CHECK
YOUR RESPONSES TO DIVERSITY

Examine your own responses to diversity. In what areas do you resist diverse ways of believing and behaving? When, if ever, do you march or openly protest differences? What perspectives, if any, do you ignore or put down? In what areas, if any, have you changed your beliefs or behaviors and assimilated diverse perspectives into your personal life?

You can complete this assignment online under Stop and Check Activities for Chapter 3 at the Jaffe Connection Web site.

Web Site

Speaking Ethically

The emphasis on ethical speaking goes back thousands of years. The Latin motto *vir bonum, dicendi peritus* (the good person, skilled in speaking) inspired generations of Roman orators. Educators in Rome urged their students to combine good character with knowledge about the world and skill in speaking. These instructors knew the power of words and the ethical implications of persuasive public speaking. Simply put, speakers can urge their listeners to behave abominably, or they can inspire them to better their world.

Vir Bonum, Dicendi Peritus
"The good person, skilled in speaking."

Your concern with ethics should begin as soon as you receive your speech assignment. What responsibilities do you have to your audience? To your topic? To yourself? A number of speech scholars have set forth guidelines you can use to speak ethically. They fall into two major areas: dialogical principles and democratic principles.

Use Dialogical Principles

Think back to how you first learned to communicate. Chances are you spent a lot of time listening and then practicing words and phrases with parents and older relatives. According to the **dialogical theory** of communication, these first conversations formed the

Dialogical Theory
Theory that conversation is the foundation for all communication; speakers and listeners work together actively to co-create meaning.

foundational pattern for all your other communication, even public speaking (Schwandt & Soraya, 1992). Although public speaking is different from conversations in many ways, you and your listeners can at least take a dialogical, rather than a monological, attitude toward each other.

Dialogical Speakers
Speakers who value traits such as authenticity and openness and who consequently show respect for their audience.

Communication ethics scholars explain that **dialogical speakers** value authenticity, honesty, inclusiveness, and openness. They try to take listeners' perspectives and responses seriously. In contrast, **monological speakers** impose their agendas, hide their motives, and discount the needs of the audience. Avoiding monologue and thinking dialogically is one way to incorporate ethics into your communication (Arnett & Arneson, 1999; Johannesen, 1996).

Monological Speakers
Speakers who impose their own agenda regardless of the needs of their audience.

Avoid Unethical Monologue

By definition, monological speakers engage in one-sided communication; that is, they talk—the audience listens. This does not mean that monological communication is always unethical. In fact, we sometimes willingly seek out political or religious speakers who arouse our emotions and urge us to behave and believe as they do.

Ethical issues arise when monological speakers believe their goals and their agendas are important enough to *impose* on others. They treat their listeners as objects to command or manipulate rather than as equals with whom they have a relationship. This type of monologue goes against our cultural values of equality and uncoerced choice. Johannesen (1996) explains that monological speakers often try to dazzle and impress audiences with their prestige or authority in an attempt to mold others in their own image.

Some act as if they were puppeteers, pulling just the right strings to evoke the desired responses in their listeners. One example of monological speaking took place in Seattle where a financial planner convinced a group of Chinese immigrants with limited English to risk their savings on investments that he knew were shaky. He cynically played on his listeners' desire for financial security to satisfy his own desire for profit.

Seeds of Peace is one organization that believes in the value of dialogue. It brings together teenagers from Palestine and Israel to communicate in face-to-face interactions.

Courtesy Seeds of Peace, www.seedsofpeace.org

The key to unethical monologue is that the speakers show varying degrees of "self-centeredness, deception, pretense, . . . domination, exploitation, and manipulation" (Johannesen, 1996, p. 68). To succeed, however, these speakers need cooperative audiences who let themselves be swayed by words or by an impassioned delivery. The historical example of Hitler shows the devastating results that can occur when a speaker treats his audience as automatons that can be organized and energized for evil purposes. It is noteworthy that Hitler was opposed by many Germans who were willing to die rather than follow his rhetoric.

Choose Ethical Dialogue

If you log onto InfoTrac College Edition and search for the key word "dialogue," you will get more than 5,000 hits. The articles describe dialogue between diverse groups on local, national, and international levels. Dialogue is so important that the United Nations designated the year 2001 as the Year of Dialogue among Civilizations. Secretary General Kofi Annan (2001) explained:

> The United Nations itself was created in the belief that dialogue can triumph over discord, that diversity is a universal virtue, and that peoples of the world are far more united by their common fate than they are divided by their separate identities.

In *The Magic of Dialogue,* Yankelovich (1999) describes several instances in which dialogue helped change history for the better. At the international level, Mikhail Gorbachev, former head of the Soviet Union, said that the turning point in the Cold War was a conversation in which he and President Reagan respectfully discussed their values and aspirations for their respective countries. Dialogue also helps people at local and regional levels. A project called San Diego Dialogue, sponsored by the University of California at San Diego (UCSD), regularly brings together businesspeople and community leaders from Mexico and San Diego to deal with once-intractable border and regional problems. (You can learn more about this project at their Web site www.sandiegodialogue.org.)

Dialogue is a mind-set about communication more than a set of rules about communication; it corresponds closely to cultural values on freedom of choice, honesty, and openness (Jensen, 1997). Dialogue requires three conditions: equality, empathy, and examination (Yankelovich, 1999):

- *Equality* means that you and your listeners respect one another and consider each other's opinions to be important and worthy of consideration.
- *Empathy* means you all try to understand the others' perspectives. You show compassion and a willingness to identify emotionally with one another.
- *Examination* means that you are willing to scrutinize your own and others' assumptions with an open mind. You avoid a know-it-all attitude.

In meaningful conversations, communicators pay attention, consider one another's ideas, and contribute their own ideas. Similarly, in dialogical public speaking you want your listeners to be mentally involved and responsive, reflecting the communication model in Chapter 1. Geissner uses the term ***respons*-ibility** to describe this speaker–listener involvement (McGuire & Slembek, 1987). Ideally, dialogical listeners work with you—and everyone gains as a result.

A commitment to dialogue doesn't mean you must give up your personal biases or strong beliefs; in fact, you may *never* agree with some people, and you may try to persuade them to adopt your viewpoint. But you won't manipulate or trick them; you'll be honest and seek the common ground that benefits everyone. The Baptists and the gays featured in the Diversity in Practice box on page 41 still disagreed on many issues after their meeting, but their dialogue contributed to honest discussion, not just stereotyping and name-calling.

In short, a commitment to dialogical principles involves authenticity, honesty, and openness. You take seriously your audience's perspectives and responses. An example of a

*Respons-**ibility**
Speakers and listeners respond to one another and come to mutual understandings.

dialogical financial planner is one who sees her audience's concerns and goals, then guides them toward investments that meet their needs as well as hers. In most cases, a dialogical attitude is more ethical than a monological approach.

Practice Democratic Principles

Dialogical principles focus on your relationship with your audience; democratic guidelines focus more on the ethical issues you face when you create the speech itself (Johannesen, 1996; Wallace, 1955). Events in the twentieth century often highlighted the tension between free speech and responsible expression within a democracy. McCarthyism in the 1950s, anti-war and black power protests in the 1960s, disputes over music lyrics in the 1980s, a Ku Klux Klan march in New York City in 1999—all these happenings brought the freedom versus responsibility issue to the fore. In response, a committee of the National Communication Association (NCA) developed a credo that summarized ethical principles that hundreds of speech professors signed on to. The latest version of this credo is reprinted in the Diversity in Practice box.

DIVERSITY IN PRACTICE
NCA CREDO FOR ETHICAL COMMUNICATION

QUESTIONS OF right and wrong arise whenever people communicate. Ethical communication is fundamental to responsible thinking, decision making, and the development of relationships and communities within and across contexts, cultures, channels, and media. Moreover, ethical communication enhances human worth and dignity by fostering truthfulness, fairness, responsibility, personal integrity, and respect for self and others. We believe that unethical communication threatens the quality of all communication and consequently the well-being of individuals and the society in which we live. Therefore we, the members of the National Communication Association, endorse and are committed to practicing the following principles of ethical communication:

- We advocate truthfulness, accuracy, honesty, and reason as essential to the integrity of communication.
- We endorse freedom of expression, diversity of perspective, and tolerance of dissent to achieve the informed and responsible decision making fundamental to a civil society.
- We strive to understand and respect other communicators before evaluating and responding to their messages.
- We promote access to communication resources and opportunities as necessary to fulfill human potential and contribute to the well-being of families, communities, and society.
- We promote communication climates of caring and mutual understanding that respect the unique needs and characteristics of individual communicators.
- We condemn communication that degrades individuals and humanity through distortion, intimidation, coercion, and violence, and through the expression of intolerance and hatred.
- We are committed to the courageous expression of personal convictions in pursuit of fairness and justice.
- We advocate sharing information, opinions, and feelings when facing significant choices while also respecting privacy and confidentiality.
- We accept responsibility for the short- and long-term consequences for our own communication and expect the same of others.

SOURCE: Endorsed by the National Communication Association, November 1999. Reprinted by permission of the National Communication Association.

Develop a Habit of Research

During your speech, you are your listeners' primary source of information. Consequently, you owe it to them to know what you're talking about, and you need to do your homework before you speak. Let's say you're discussing a complicated issue such as immigration reform, don't settle for just a surface understanding; instead, do research in a number of sources and seek out diverse perspectives. Search out the positions taken by the major political parties. How do typical border states respond? Look for perspectives of immigrants. Identify the social class issues that apply. Give your audience the breadth of information they need to form reasoned and wise conclusions.

Be Honest and Fair

Honest speaking means you present your information as truthfully as you can. Don't exaggerate a problem and make it seem greater than it actually is. Don't distort or twist information. Statistics can be particularly misleading, so find out as much as you can about numbers you present. For instance, you might find statistics showing that wine, used in moderation, can be healthy, but the statistics come from studies funded by the wine industry. Does this mean they are inaccurate? Not necessarily, but probe further and see if impartial sources produce similar statistics.

Be fair and balanced. Give your subject an evenhanded treatment rather than presenting only the arguments that support your position. You can hear examples of unbalanced presentations whenever you listen to talk radio. There, biased hosts and their carefully screened callers "discuss" issues and problems. In political ads, you'll also find slanted, emotional appeals aimed at scaring people. In addition, the Internet contains thousands of advocacy Web sites that exist to provide a one-sided view of a specific topic. For example, you can present a more balanced view of gun control issues if you consult both www.handguncontrol.com and www.nra.org (the National Rifle Association Web site).

Practice Civility

Talk-show host Jerry Springer's guests yell verbal insults and attack one another; talking heads on all-news channels interrupt and shout at each other; politicians use negative ads against their opponents. The common lack of civility in public discourse led one commentator to coin the term *drive-by debating* to describe this phenomenon (Hackney, as quoted in Bartanen & Frank, 1999, p. 38).

Civility is a social virtue that involves self-control or moderation; it contrasts with pride, insolence, and arrogance. Civil speakers and listeners are more than simply polite. They choose persuasion, consultation, advising, bargaining, compromising, and coalition building. Civility is related to two concepts presented earlier: accommodation and dialogical public speaking. Both require people to understand, to appreciate opposing perspectives, and to accept the outcome when their own position does not prevail. Cultures across space and time, from the ancient Greeks to modern Asian cultures, have promoted civility as an ethical principle (Barrett, 1991; Bartanen & Frank, 1999).

An example of civility came after Election 2000. After five weeks of counting and court decisions, George W. Bush was declared President of the United States by a single Electoral College vote. That night, both men gave speeches that were models of civility. Gore first conceded, then Bush accepted the results:

> while I strongly disagree with the court's decision, I accept it. . . . I know that many of my supporters are disappointed. I am too. But our disappointment must be overcome by our love of country. . . . While we yet hold and do not yield our opposing beliefs, there is a higher duty than the one we owe to political party. This is America and we put country before party. We will stand together behind our new president. (Gore, 2000)

Civility
Self-control or moderation, in contrast to pride or arrogance; civil speakers persuade, consult, and compromise rather than coerce and manipulate.

Although Election 2000 was hotly contested, Vice-President Al Gore conceded the presidency, and George W. Bush accepted it in courteous speeches.

Republicans want the best for our nation, and so do Democrats. Our votes may differ, but not our hopes. I know America wants reconciliation and unity. I know Americans want progress.... Together, guided by a spirit of common sense, common courtesy and common goals, we can unite and inspire the American citizens. (Bush, 2000)

 You can watch these speeches on the CD that comes with this text.

This is by no means a complete list of democratic principles. However, use these to think about ethical speaking in a pluralistic culture. Since diversity is pervasive, you must decide how you can best respect (and live comfortably with) this diversity (Jensen, 1997).

 To learn more about ethical speaking in a democracy, use the PowerTrac feature on InfoTrac College Edition and search for the article titled "National Tragedy Should Breed Political Civility." Note the author's four suggestions for civil public discourse.

Listening Ethically

The dialogical attitude applies to listening as well as speaking. Certainly you cannot listen to everyone; you simply don't have the time. But listening respectfully to people empowers them. Although you may not agree with a speaker's ideas, allowing that person to speak recognizes the individual as a significant person whose ideas and thoughts are important enough to hear. Think about how positive you feel when someone who disagrees with you still takes time to ask what you believe and how you came to your conclusions. Sincere questions, those that are not meant as personal, sneering attacks, show that listeners are really trying to understand your viewpoint.

In contrast, there are many ways to silence speakers. Let's say two people are conversing; one person says, "I don't want to hear this" and walks away, leaving the other person frustrated! The same thing can happen in public speaking settings. Someone leaves in the middle of a speech, or two or more members of the audience, often seated near the back, whisper and laugh throughout. These people are doing two things: (1) indicating disrespect for the speaker and the ideas being presented, and (2) being disrespectful of fellow listeners who wish to hear the speech. **Hecklers** are also silencers when they shout down a speaker in an attempt to keep others from hearing the speech. Choosing not to listen when you could do so implies that the speaker's ideas are not significant or worth your time.

Hecklers
People who taunt, insult, ridicule, or shout down another person.

However, when you hear a speaker who is obviously passing on false information, what do you do? Do you confront the speaker in front of others? Do you plan a speech to counter the ideas and present more accurate information? Do you ask questions that enable other listeners to detect the misinformation? Do you write a letter to the editor? These are all possible responses. Think about your ethical responsibilities as a listener, and ask yourself these questions:

In a society in which issues are decided by informed people, do I expose myself to a number of arguments, or do I listen only to the side with which I already agree? In short, do I listen with an open mind?

Do I fulfill my ethical responsibilities to other listeners by not distracting them?

Do I fulfill my responsibilities to speakers by letting them know they are being heard?

Do I encourage speakers to meet ethical standards? This may mean that I ask for further information about their sources or that I point out relevant information they omit. (Holzman, 1970; Jensen, 1997)

Researching Ethically

Thomas's speech started dramatically:

> How would you react if I told you that inside this box there was a snake? Would you frantically jump up on top of your desk? Would you panic and let out a shrill scream? Would you run hysterically from the room? If you answered yes to one or more of these questions, chances are you have a phobia of snakes.

STOP AND CHECK

HECKLING

University audiences are sometimes rowdy. Here are some examples: In the 1980s both Jeane Kirkpatrick and George Bush were heckled at the University of Minnesota when they were members of the Reagan administration. At the University of California, Berkeley, Jeane Kirkpatrick was heckled so loudly that she left the stage without finishing her speech rather than trying to talk over or around the hecklers (Nordlinger, 2001).

A recent incident at the midyear graduation ceremony at California State University at Sacramento received a 2002 Jefferson Muzzles Award from the Thomas Jefferson Center for the Protection of Free Speech. (The center gives these awards annually to draw attention to violations of free speech principles and to foster appreciation for First Amendment rights. You can access this site at http://www.tjcenter.org/muzzles.html.)

Janis Besler Heaphy, publisher of the *Sacramento Bee,* was invited to address about 17,000 students and guests at the ceremony. She included the following in her speech:

> . . . the world changed on September 11th. . . . The terrorist attacks awakened a sense of patriotism long dormant in this country. We have been reminded of our greatness and how lucky we are to be Americans. But that blessing comes with responsibilities. . . .

Heaphy continued by cautioning against the government's expanded surveillance powers, the FBI's use of racial profiling, and the proposed military tribunal to try accused terrorists.

As she began questioning government actions relating to terrorism, many in the audience became restless. Some booed and stomped their feet; others heckled her. Their jeers were so loud that the university president stood and asked the audience to hear Heaphy out. She continued speaking, but soon some in the audience broke into a "chant clap." The president again called for calm, but Heaphy decided to return to her seat without finishing the speech.

Later, newspaper editorials and letters to the editor ranged from those who were sent into "deep depression about the state of mind of educated people who should know better" (Haiman, 2001) to those who argued that newspapers tend to defend "a liberal's right to free speech" but are less concerned about hearing out conservative ideas (Dutton, 2001).

(continued)

QUESTIONS

- What do you think were the listeners' motivations for their behaviors?
- What ethical responsibilities do audience members have toward Ms. Heaphy? Toward the other listeners? Toward their own political positions? Which should assume the most importance in this setting? Explain your choice.
- Do you agree with the writer of the letter who said that heckling or booing a liberal speaker tends to draw more media response than when a conservative speaker is shouted down? Why or why not?
- Is there ever a place for heckling? If so, when or where might it be appropriate? If not, why not?

You can answer these questions online under Stop and Check Activities for Chapter 3 at the Jaffe Connection Web site. You can read the text of Ms. Heaphy's address and the university president's response at http://www.csus.edu/news/121701commencements.htm.

Students listened intently, but the professor frowned. This opening scenario sounded too familiar, and a quick check of department speech files turned up an identical outline submitted in a previous term. Obviously Tom's speech was plagiarized, which is a specific ethical breach. During the same term, Junko made up a statistic, which is an act of fabrication. To avoid these ethical mistakes, it is important that you understand just what plagiarism and fabrication are.

Avoid Plagiarism

Plagiarism
Presenting the words or ideas of others as if they were your own.

Plagiarism means that you present the ideas and words of others as if they were your own, without giving credit to the originators. According to plagiarism.org (2002), this type of cheating is increasingly common in the age of the Internet; in fact, this site states that as many as 30 percent of all students plagiarize on every written assignment they complete. Purdue University's Online Writing Lab (2002) recognizes that even well-intentioned students may be confused about the many rules they must adhere to. You can find out more about this at http://owl.english.purdue.edu. Here's that site's definition of plagiarism:

> . . . the unacknowledged use of somebody else's words or ideas. While other cultures may not insist so heavily on documenting sources, American institutions do.

The Online Writing Lab distinguishes deliberate plagiarism from possibly accidental plagiarism. Students deliberately plagiarize when they borrow, buy, or steal another student's speech or written outline and present it as if it were their own work. Tom's speech on phobias, mentioned previously, was deliberately copied.

Presenting the words and ideas of others without giving credit to the source, either in the speech itself or in the outline, may be intentional or done out of ignorance, as in the following case. Jeremy spoke on cryonics, the process of deep-freezing a live creature and later thawing it to return it to life. He vividly described a dog that was frozen and revived using this process. As he spoke, his instructor kept thinking "I've heard this before," and she suspected that Jeremy was giving a "frat file" speech. After class, her files turned up a cryonics outline from a previous term. The two outlines were markedly different although both contained the identical frozen dog passage. She concluded that Jeremy was clearly not giving a frat file speech but that he had used a source the first speaker used—and neither gave credit to the original. Intentional or not, plagiarism is comparable to stealing. (Generally, you are responsible for acquainting yourself with plagiarism rules, so you have no basis for pleading ignorance of them.)

According to Purdue University's Online Writing lab, you should give credit when you use

- Somebody else's words or ideas—whether you found them in library resources, the Internet, films or television shows, recordings, advertisements, letters from friends, and so on.
- Information from interviews, conversations, or email.
- Someone else's unique phrases.
- Diagrams, illustrations, charts, photographs, and figures.

You do not need to document

- Personal experiences, observations, conclusions, or insights.
- Common knowledge, such as folklore or traditions within your cultural group.
- Generally accepted facts—the kind of information you find in five or more sources or information you think your audience already knows or could easily find in reference material.
- Results of experiments you personally conduct.

Within your speech, name your source if you use someone else's materials. For example, when you use a direct quotation, introduce it as such. When you paraphrase someone else's ideas, cite the originator. When you present a diagram or chart on a PowerPoint slide or on an overhead transparency, be sure to write the source somewhere on the slide. Here are some specific ways students have provided source information as they spoke:

- Faith Smith, President of the Native American Educational Services College in Chicago, argues that using Native American symbols in sports is derogatory, stereotypical, and often blatantly racist.
- According to an article in the *Wall Street Journal*, women in state and local governments hold only 31 percent of the top administrative jobs.
- According to a record producer in the cartoon strip *Doonesbury*, "Drummers are extinct."

Chapter 11 describes ways to document sources on your outline. Be sure to list your references at the end using a standard format such as MLA (Modern Language Association) or APA (American Psychological Association). These style manuals are available on the Internet or in the reference section of the library; they will show you how to cite just about any source—from a book to a personal letter; from a CD to an Internet Web page.

Plagiarizers risk severe penalties if discovered. Look in your college or university's handbook, and you will find plagiarism rules and the consequences for breaking them. Typically, plagiarizers receive an "F" for the assignment. More serious breeches may result in temporary suspension, permanent expulsion, and/or a notation on one's permanent record, which can seriously affect a student's life!

Avoid Fabrication

Besides using the words and ideas of others, some speakers **fabricate,** or make up, information or guess at numbers and then present them as factual. They cite references they haven't consulted. In addition, they pass along rumors or unsubstantiated information. For instance, rumor mills report the alleged facelifts of famous entertainers, allegations the stars contend are fabrications. It would be easy to research the topic of plastic surgery, discover one of these rumors, and then use it as an example; however, doing this perpetuates a falsehood.

The best way to avoid fabrication is to use a number of sources and to be alert for conflicting information. Thoroughly check any discrepancies before you present information as factual.

Fabricate
Make up information or repeat a rumor without sufficiently checking its accuracy.

STOP AND CHECK

WOULD YOU USE QUESTIONABLE STATISTICS?

Kilolo is researching the topic of breast cancer. She finds several sources that say women have a one in eight chance of developing the disease. However, as she does more extensive research, Kilolo discovers a *New York Times* article that calls this figure "faulty." If a woman lives to be 110, then, yes, the cumulative probability that she will develop this type of cancer is one in eight, but even 80-year-old women are not at that high level of risk. The chances are closer to one in one thousand for women under 50. A spokesperson for the American Cancer Society admits that the one in eight figure is more metaphor than fact, but she believes it's used for good ends—it increases awareness of the disease and makes women concerned enough to seek early detection. Some physicians, in contrast, point to an "epidemic of fear" created by the inflated numbers (Blakeslee, 1992).

QUESTIONS

- Should Kilolo use the one in eight figure because she's seen it in five or six sources? Why or why not?
- What do you think of the American Cancer Society's decision to continue using the figure when they know it is inaccurate? Is this ethical?

Web Site You can answer these questions online and submit them to your instructor under Stop and Check Activities for Chapter 3 at the Jaffe Connection Web site.

Summary

People in pluralistic cultures have belief, value, attitudinal, and behavioral differences that range from superficial to fundamental. You can respond to diversity in a number of ways. If you choose to defy or resist, you will bolster your positions and (perhaps) attack or ignore diversity. If you choose to assimilate, you will surrender some aspect of your own cultural tradition and adopt a new way. Finally, when you accommodate diversity, you accept differences and work with others to create a society in which all can live together.

Our culture provides both dialogical and democratic resources that you can use to speak and listen ethically. Choose a dialogical rather than an unethical monological relationship with your listeners. That is, rather than imposing your thoughts and ideas on others, respect your listeners as equals, have empathy with their perspectives, and examine both your own and your listeners' assumptions in an honest, open manner. Democratic principles remind you to develop a habit of research, to present your materials honestly and fairly, and to respond to diversity with civility.

Listening also calls for ethically responsible actions. Allowing people to speak empowers them, giving them a voice and allowing others to hear their ideas. However, when speakers present incorrect or misleading information, you are faced with ethical decisions in which you need to balance your rights and responsibilities against the rights and responsibilities of the speaker and other listeners. Vernon Jensen coined the term *rightsabilities* to highlight the tension you feel.

As you present your materials, be sure to cite your references and check a variety of sources to avoid the ethical problems of plagiarism or fabrication. Plagiarism occurs when you present the ideas or words of another person as your own without giving credit to the original source. Fabrication occurs when you make up material or present something as factual when it is not.

JAFFE ONLINE CONNECTION JAFFE ONLINE CONNECTION

Use your CD-ROM and the Jaffe Connection Web site http://communication.wadsworth.com/jaffe to review the following concepts, answer the review questions, and complete the suggested activities.

KEY TERMS

ethical dilemma (38)
ethics (38)
"rightsabilities" (38)
resisting (39)
assimilating (40)
accommodating (40)
multivocal society (40)
voices (40)
vir bonum, dicendi peritus (41)

dialogical theory (41)
dialogical speaker (42)
monological speaker (42)
respons-ibility (43)
civility (45)
heckle (46)
plagiarism (48)
fabrication (48)

APPLICATION AND CRITICAL THINKING EXERCISES

1. Draw a minimum–maximum scale that represents diversity on your campus. Identify differences at the minimum end of the range. Work your way up the scale and identify increasingly greater areas of diversity that may be seen as conflicts. When and how do campus speakers address this diversity?

2. With a small group of your classmates, discuss the following: Use the scale you made in Exercise 1 to decide what diversity issues on your campus provide opportunities for people with different beliefs, values, or behaviors to encounter one another. Which of the three ways of dealing with differences—resistance, assimilation, or accommodation—do members of your student body most commonly use? Assess the ethics of their responses.

3. With a small group in your classroom, discuss ways that people who hold diverse perspectives on a controversial topic might engage in dialogue. (For example, pro-choice advocates meeting with pro-life activists; born-again Christians talking with committed Muslims; animal rights activists meeting with research scientists; the leaders of Iraq meeting with the leaders of the United States.)

4. With a small group of your classmates, discuss speakers who demonstrate opposite characteristics of one of the elements depicted in the Latin phrase *vir bonum, dicendi peritus:*

   • *A person lacking in character who is a skilled speaker.* Make a list of people skilled in speaking but who are not "good" persons. (Hitler tops most people's list.) What problems do these skilled orators bring about in the world?

   • *A person of excellent character who is unskilled in speaking.* Identify situations, real or hypothetical, in which good people want to do something that will better their world but lack the skills needed to present their ideas to others who could join their efforts.

5. Log on to the Internet and go to www.un.org, the home page of the United Nations. Follow the links to Kofi Annan's speech given at Seton Hall University's School of Diplomacy and International Relations in February 2001. Read the speech, then identify concepts that are even more important after the events of September 11, 2001, the

war on terrorism, the rise in Palestinian-Israeli conflict, and the Indian-Pakistani conflict that have taken place since that speech.

6. Use your own values and beliefs as well as the guidelines described in this chapter to write an ethical code that states the principles by which you want to speak and listen.

7. Evaluate yourself as a responsible listener. How do you avoid silencing speakers? Use the questions in the section on Listening Ethically on page 47 to guide your self-evaluation.

8. Using InfoTrac College Edition, do a PowerTrac search for the title "Junk Journalism." Read this article about media coverage of the missing Washington, D.C., intern, Chandra Levy. Identify the rumors, unsubstantiated information, and fabrications that were published. To see the effect of this coverage, use PowerTrac to search for the article titled "California Voters Just Say No to Gary Condit."

THE JAFFE CONNECTION WEB SITE

The Jaffe Connection Web site features review questions about the Web links, Stop and Check activities, and InfoTrac College Edition exercises referenced throughout the chapter. You can access this site via your CD-ROM or at http://communication.wadsworth.com/jaffe.

Web Links

3.1 Protest Movements Promote Change (page 40)
3.2 Inflammatory Rhetoric Toward a Group (page 41)
3.3 Dialogue Brings Leaders of Border Communities Together (page 43)
3.4 Getting a Balanced View of Gun Control Issues (page 45)
3.5 Heckling and Principles of Free Speech (pages 47–48)
3.6 Plagiarism Rules in the Internet Age (page 48)
3.7 Kofi Annan's Speech on International Relations (page 52)

Stop and Check Activities

3.1 Your Responses to Diversity (page 41)
3.2 Heckling (pages 47–48)
3.3 Would You Use Questionable Statistics? (page 50)

InfoTrac College Edition Exercises

3.1 Cultural Assimilation of a Vietnamese American (page 40)
3.2 Choose Ethical Dialogue (page 43)
3.3 Four Suggestions for Civil Public Discourse (page 46)
3.4 How Media Coverage Fabrication Affects Others in Missing Intern Story (page 52)

SPEECH INTERACTIVE ON THE JAFFE CONNECTION CD-ROM

Using your Jaffe Connection CD-ROM, watch the clips of Al Gore's concession speech and George W. Bush's acceptance speech under Speech Interactive, and then answer the questions for analysis.

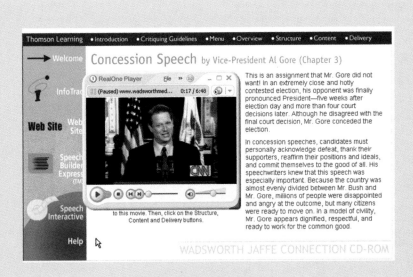

Effective Listening

THIS CHAPTER WILL HELP YOU

- Appreciate the importance of listening skills
- Name two linguistic barriers to listening
- Describe cultural factors that hinder listening
- Explain how personal barriers affect your listening
- Draw and explain four specific thought patterns that are common during listening
- Use cultural schema to improve your listening
- Discuss diverse cultural listening styles
- Identify strategies to improve your comprehensive listening
- Improve your critical listening skills
- Practice dialogical listening through nonverbal feedback
- Give appropriate verbal feedback

"Learning Wall" Mural ©1989 by Keith Sklar. (SFSUD Headquarters, Franklin and Hayes Streets, SF, CA)

THINK ABOUT ALL YOUR COMMUNICATION ACTIVITIES DURING a typical week. Then rank the following activities—reading, writing, listening, and speaking—in order according to the amount of waking time you normally spend doing each one:

_____ reading _____ writing _____ listening _____ speaking

If you ranked listening first, you're like the average person, who spends about 50 percent of the time listening and less than 18 percent each reading, writing, and speaking. An ancient proverb, attributed to Zeno of Citium, endorses this bias toward listening: "We have been given two ears and but a single mouth in order that we may hear more and talk less."

If we listen so much, we should be pretty good at it. Right? Unfortunately, we often fail to give this vital skill as much attention as we give other communication skills. Compare the number of reading, writing, and speaking courses to the number of *listening* courses your college or university offers. Schools offer many writing, literature, and speech courses, but no listening to comprehend or critical listening course. Instead, instructors incorporate listening in other courses.

Because listening is so vital, this chapter begins by stressing its importance. Then we will look at areas of listening you may need to improve. Finally, you will learn some strategies to help you become a more effective listener.

Listening Skills Are Valuable

As the introduction pointed out, listening is the communication skill we use most and study least. However, good listening can be one of your most valuable assets. In fact, if you use the search engine www.alltheweb.com and search for the exact phrase "listening skills," you will get more than a quarter of a million hits! Obviously, many people in this culture believe strongly that listening is important. However, they are typically overconfident about their abilities, thinking that they remember 75 to 80 percent of what they hear, when, in fact, average listeners recall only about 25 percent (Roach & Wyatt, 1995).

Listening skills are valuable in a number of ways:

- *We listen most.* Listening is the most commonly used job skill; employers mention understanding and following instructions (skills linked to comprehensive listening) as the next most common (Maes, Weldy, & Icenogle, 1997). Think of how much time you spend listening for information and directions in college; your skill determines your success in your courses. Because you listen so much, you will be more productive if you do it well.
- *Good listening skills are good job skills.* The most successful people are generally effective listeners. Barbers, doctors, journalists—even politicians—understand the need to listen; in fact, during campaigns politicians often go on "listening tours."
- *Listening and being heard empowers people and aids personal relationships.* Bentley (1998) begins an article on listening this way: "Most people would agree that having someone listen to you makes you feel better—mentally and physically. In fact, according to Ralph G. Nichols, who is regarded as the father of listening, 'The most basic of all human needs is to understand and to be understood. . . . The best way to understand people is to listen to them.' Thus, being listened to is one of our most basic needs" (p. 56). Use InfoTrac College Edition, to search for Bentley's article "Listening Better: A Guide to Improving What May Be the Ultimate Staff Skill." What specific suggestions does he offer to improve your listening skills?

These are only a few of the reasons listening is important; you can probably think of additional ways good listening habits make life easier. Pause now for a moment and ask yourself how your listening helps or hinders your comprehension of course work. What personal relationships benefit or suffer as a result of your listening behaviors? How is listening vital in a job you currently hold or plan to have someday? Keep these questions in mind as you study the remainder of the chapter.

Barriers to Listening

The Chinese character for listening (Figure 4.1) combines the symbols for ears, eyes, and heart, thus reinforcing the idea that good listeners are wholly involved in the listening process. Most of us don't start our days thinking "I'm going to be a terrible listener today." We intend to listen well; however, we face linguistic, cultural, and personal barriers. Understanding these barriers and devising strategies to deal with them will help you listen more effectively.

Linguistic Barriers

Diversity shows up in language variations within the United States. Walk down the streets of New York City, and you'll hear Spanish, French, Russian, accented English, Farsi—more than one hundred languages are spoken in that city alone. Compare the slang that teenagers invent and the phrases their grandparents use, the terminology that skateboarders use and the legalese that only lawyers understand. Clearly the potential for linguistic misunderstandings is great.

Language Differences

A shared language is vital for understanding. If you don't know a speaker's language, you'll need an interpreter or you won't be able to decode the message. Even then, because languages and the ideas they embody are so different, you probably won't understand everything the speaker is saying. (See Chapter 13 for more on how language differences can affect comprehension.)

Accents or dialects can also hinder your ability to distinguish the words you hear. Regional accents, ethnic dialects, accents influenced by a first language—all these require you to pay special attention to discriminate between words. Nonstandard syllable stress and pronunciation differences can create problems. For instance, in one class an international student gave a speech on *beerd* watching. His instructor was puzzled as to who watched beards until he realized the speaker's pronunciation of the vowel sound in *bird* was confusing. A French speaker pronounced the word *atmosphere* as "at-MOS-feer." An African pronounced *alarm* as "AL-arm." Their audiences had to concentrate carefully to understand each word.

Figure 4.1 The Chinese character that translates as "listening" emphasizes its holistic nature by combining the symbols for ears, eyes, and heart.

Vocabulary Differences

Misunderstandings can also occur if you don't share the speaker's vocabulary. This may happen for a variety of reasons. For example, the speaker may use highly technical jargon common to a particular field of study. One scholar at a convention read the following sentence:

> Urging a dialogue between neurology and culturalology, Turner suggests that the rhythmic activity of ritual, aided by sonic, visual, photic, and other kinds of "driving" may lead to specific neuronal activity that leads to social cohesion and feelings beyond verbalization. (Delroy, 1992)

The other scholars in the audience may have understood her, but you'd be lost, right?

Ears · Eyes · Heart · **Listening**

Jacques Chenet/Woodfin Camp & Associates

Nelson Mandela speaks English with British and South African syllable stress and pronunciation patterns; you may have to listen closely to understand his message.

Cultural Allusions
References to historical, literary, and religious sources that are familiar in a specific culture.

Additionally, some speakers have large vocabularies due to their study of Latin or Greek, two languages that provide the roots for almost 80 percent of English words. Many people learn new words through wide reading of literature or through self-help books such as *Thirty Days to a More Powerful Vocabulary.* When you don't share a speaker's vocabulary, you will have difficulty understanding the speech. For instance, in her speech to the 1992 Democratic National Convention, Barbara Jordan, former representative from Texas, said this:

> We must frankly acknowledge our complicity in the creation of the unconscionable budget deficits, acknowledge our complicity and recognize, painful though it may be, that in order to seriously address the budget deficits, we must address the question of entitlements, also. . . . [T]he baby boomers and their progeny are entitled to a secure future.

Because she was speaking to a relatively well-educated audience, most attendees could figure out what she was talking about, but some listeners, both those in the convention hall and those watching on television, would have a hard time defining such words as *complicity, unconscionable,* and *progeny.*

Cultural Barriers

You may also fail to understand a speaker's **cultural allusions,** or references to specific historical, literary, and religious sources. You can probably think of things that are familiar in your culture or co-culture that might confuse someone from a different group. Here are a few examples:

- A person who grew up in the Big Band era doesn't know who Ricky Martin or Eminem are.
- A Christian doesn't understand a Muslim speaker's reference to *zakat.*
- A student taking philosophy understands Kant's Categorical Imperative, but many of his classmates don't.
- A Kenyan student refers to Jomo Kenyatta, whom he assumes his audience recognizes as founding president of Kenya, but many of his American classmates have never heard of Kenyatta.

In our pluralistic society and multicultural world, each group draws from different historical events, cultural heroes, literary or oral traditions, and religious resources. In a pluralistic setting, you may be unfamiliar with these culture-specific references. It is up to the speakers to be sensitive to differences and explain allusions or choose areas of common knowledge.

Personal Barriers

Personal distractions can obstruct your listening. For example, William identified some of his listening problems:

> Sometimes I become aggressive; sometimes I get defensive when I feel attacked. I have attention deficit disorder; at times I am easily distracted by others around me. I let my feelings for people get in the way.
>
> WILLIAM

William's response is fairly typical. A number of personal factors can hinder your listening. *Physical factors* (hearing loss, sleep deprivation, hunger pangs, the flu) can affect your ability or your desire to focus on a speech.

Psychological factors can also keep you from listening closely: You just had an argument with a friend; you have a huge test coming up in your next class; your bank account is overdrawn; a relative is going in for medical tests. The mental worry that accompanies psychological stressors can take your energy away from listening.

Stereotypes and prejudices can also hinder listening. You **stereotype** when you put people into a category, then assume that they will fit the characteristics of the category. If you are **prejudiced,** or biased, you listen to the speaker with pre-formed judgments, which may be either negative or positive. To illustrate, a student once remarked: "He wore white socks! I can't take a guy seriously if he wears white socks with a suit!" Students who support abortion rights listen approvingly to a speaker from Planned Parenthood but block out one representing Right to Life, and vice versa.

Paying attention is another major factor in listening effectiveness. Here Gail discusses some of her thought patterns as she struggles to focus on the speech:

> I'm easily distracted. . . . It's easy for me to either focus on one particular thing that has been said, and then sort of drift off, exploring it further in my own mind, or—and this applies more specifically to someone whose speaking style or subject does not impress me—float off on unrelated topics ("I wonder where she gets her hair cut?"). Also, depending on the subject, I can get easily bored.
>
> GAIL

Often, listening is hard work. For one reason, you can think far more rapidly (about 500 words per minute) than the fastest speaker can talk (about 300 words per minute). Most speakers average about 150 words per minute, leaving you with 350 words per minute of a **speech–thought differential,** also called **"leftover thinking space"** (Lundsteen, 1993). These four specific thought patterns, illustrated in Figure 4.2, are common during listening:

- *Taking small departures from the communication line.* These small departures can hinder your comprehension, but they can also help you follow the message if, during them, you produce your own examples, relate the material to your personal experiences, answer the speaker's rhetorical questions, and otherwise interact with his ideas.
- *Going off on a tangent.* When this happens, you depart from the speaker's line of thinking and seize on one of her ideas, taking it in your own direction. You stop listening; one idea leads to another, and before you know it, you're in a daydream, several subjects removed from the topic at hand.
- *Engaging in a private argument.* Here, you begin to challenge and argue internally before you've heard the speaker out. Your thinking runs a parallel course to the speaker's ideas. You close your mind, stop trying to understand the speaker's reasoning, and carry on a running argument as you listen. In contrast, effective critical listeners identify arguments that don't make sense, but they withhold their final judgment of the overall argument until they have heard the entire speech.
- *Taking large departures from the communication line.* In this pattern your attention wanders off into unrelated areas; you bring it back and focus on the speech for a while; then, off it goes again, and you find yourself thinking about a totally unrelated topic. This cycle repeats indefinitely (Lundsteen, 1993).

As you can see, listening can be difficult when linguistic, cultural, and personal factors get in the way. Assess your listening skills by completing the test in the Stop and Check box. In the remainder of the chapter, you will discover some strategies you can use to become a better listener.

Stereotype
Place someone in a category, then assume the person fits the characteristics of the category.

Prejudiced
Having pre-formed biases or judgments, whether negative or positive.

Speech–Thought Differential
The difference between the rate you think (about 500 words per minute) and the rate you speak (about 150 words per minute).

Leftover Thinking Space
Another term for the difference between your thinking rate and your speaking rate.

Figure 4.2 These four thought patterns are typical during listening. The first can be productive, but the rest characterize poor listening.

SOURCE: WOLVIN, ANDREW D., & CAROLYN GWYNN COAKLEY, 1993, *PERSPECTIVES ON LISTENING*, ABLEX PUB. CO., NORWOOD NJ, P. 115.

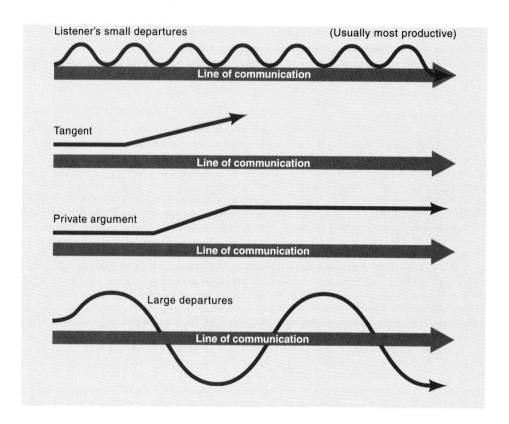

STOP AND CHECK
LISTENING SKILLS SELF-ASSESSMENT

Evaluate your listening by taking this test. Then create a personal plan you can use to become a more effective listener. How often do you engage in these listening behaviors? First, write the letter that most accurately indicates your behavior; then tabulate your listening score using the key that follows the questions.

A = almost always
B = usually
C = sometimes
D = rarely
E = almost never

How often do you

_____ 1. Get lost in a speech because your vocabulary is small?

_____ 2. Turn off a speaker who proposes a position different from one you hold?

_____ 3. Feel anger, defensiveness, fear, or other emotions when you disagree with the speaker?

_____ 4. Get distracted by external factors, such as noises outside the room?

_____ 5. Get distracted by internal preoccupations, such as personal worries or stresses?

_____ 6. Carry on a running argument with a speaker instead of hearing her or him out?

_____ 7. Go off on a tangent?

_____ 8. Have a short attention span and lose your place in a long speech?

_____ 9. Stereotype a speaker and let that affect how you listen?

_____ 10. Give up trying to understand a speaker's accent and tune the speaker out?

KEY

For every A give yourself 2 points.
For every B give yourself 4 points.
For every C give yourself 6 points.
For every D give yourself 8 points.
For every E give yourself 10 points.

Total score _____

More than 90	Your listening skills are exceptional.
Between 76 and 90	You are above average.
Between 60 and 75	Your skills are about average.
Below 60	You are probably not as effective as you could be.

If you scored below 80, develop a listening plan that identifies specific strategies you can use to improve your listening. The rest of this chapter will provide you with some of these key strategies.

This self-assessment test is also available online under Stop and Check Activities for Chapter 4 at the Jaffe Connection Web site.   **Web Site**

Strategies to Improve Listening

Being mindful of your thought patterns during the listening process will help you develop strategies for understanding and retaining material more effectively. A combination of resources from within your culture, along with nonverbal and note-taking skills, will help you become a better listener.

Use Cultural Schemas

A set of cultural expectations, called listening schemas, can help you organize and understand messages (Figure 4.3). **Schemas** are the mental plans, blueprints, or models that you use, first to perceive information, then to interpret, store, and recall a speech (Edwards & McDonald, 1993). Think of how you listen to a story. If you're typical, you have a mental model of what a good story is like. You then use this model to interpret a specific story—whether to take it seriously, how to draw lessons from it, what parts are worth remembering, and so on.

Schemas
Mental plans or models that guide your perception, interpretation, storage, and recollection of a speech.

You formulate your schemas through listening to many and varying speeches. For instance, because you've heard many announcements, you have a pretty good mental picture of what they are like—they follow a somewhat predictable pattern. Similarly, you learn what to expect from a demonstration speech, an entertaining story, a news report, a funeral eulogy, or an award presentation because you've heard a number of speeches in each category.

The Diversity in Practice box on Cultural Listening Styles identifies some listening expectations that are common in other cultural and co-cultural groups.

Figure 4.3 Our minds contain a number of schemas or models that help us listen and respond to specific types of speeches.

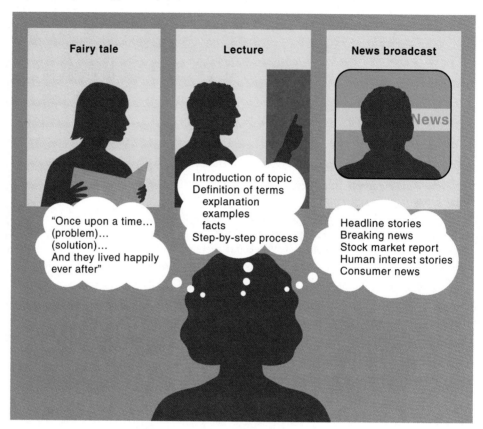

DIVERSITY IN PRACTICE
CULTURAL LISTENING STYLES

THE WAYS LISTENERS approach public speeches reflect differences in worldviews and behaviors among cultural groups. Knowing some cultural variations will make you more mindful of listening diversity. Here are a few examples:

- A Javanese listening schema: On the island of Java, listeners repeat phrases they like to a neighbor. This results in a buzz of voices throughout the speech, signaling the speaker that the audience is receiving it well (Tannen, 1989).
- An Asian listening tradition: In cultures that emphasize unity, listeners expect speakers to develop oneness with them rather than present divisive ideas. Both speakers and audiences share the responsibility for making communication successful (Sitkaram & Cogdell, 1976).
- Another Asian tradition: Audiences listen in silence, feeling that noise breaks the concentration required to attend to a speech. Applause can signal suspicion, similar to booing by an audience in the United States; some listeners do not even applaud at the end of the speech so that the speaker will remain modest (Sitkaram & Cogdell, 1976).
- An African American schema: In some contexts, the entire audience participates in a "call and response" pattern, which reflects African traditions. The speaker's statements (calls) are punctuated by the listeners' reactions to them (response), with the result that the audience is, in a real sense, talking back to the speaker. Because no sharp line distinguishes speakers and listeners, both cooperate to create the message (Daniel & Smitherman, 1990; Smith, 1970).

- U.S. student preferences: In a recent cross-cultural study of student listening prefer-ences, American students reported liking messages that are short and to the point. They tend to prefer speakers with whom they can identify (women more so than men) (Kiewitz et al., 1997).
- German student preferences: German students prefer precise, error-free messages; disorganized presentations frustrate and annoy them. They are much less concerned about identifying personally with the speaker (Kiewitz et al., 1997).
- Israeli student preferences: Israeli students prefer complex and challenging informa-tion that they can think over and evaluate before they form judgments and opin-ions. The length of the message is relatively unimportant (Kiewitz et al., 1997).

You can read the entire study of cross-cultural student listening preferences on InfoTrac College Edition; use PowerTrac to search for the author Kiewitz and find the article titled "Cultural Differences in Listening Style Preferences: A Comparison of Young Adults in Germany, Israel, and the United States."

Know Your Listening Purpose

Just as you have speaking goals, you also have listening goals. You turn on the radio for entertainment; but, when a commercial comes on, you tune out—or you evaluate the claims critically, deciding whether the product interests you. You listen to a lecture to understand-ing a subject better, then you lunch with friends and hear them vent about a test. For each type of listening, you shift your strategies to meet your listening goals more effectively. Here, we focus on listening to comprehend and listening to evaluate messages.

Improve Your Comprehension

Think of all the times you listen for information: Your boss gives directions for your next project; a friend directs you to the financial aid office; a radio reporter tells you where an accident blocks traffic. And, according to the student handbook of the University of Minnesota, Duluth (2002), an average student spends fourteen hours each week in class lis-tening. Listening to learn, or **comprehensive listening,** is a vital skill in many areas of life.

Several strategies can help you better comprehend material. For example, jot down the vocabulary words; look up unfamiliar words and concepts. To develop skills for identifying major ideas and important supporting materials, study Chapter 8 (supporting information) and Chapters 9 through 11 (organization) in this text. Here are some specific tips for over-coming those departures from listening that were presented in Figure 4.2.

Comprehensive Listening
Listening to learn, under-stand, or get information.

- *Prepare in advance.* Prepare for lectures and labs by reading the related material in the text or by looking up background information. Study the list of major textual concepts usually found at the chapter opening; skim the chapter and notice headings and bold-faced terminology; read the summary. Look at the pictures and diagrams before you go to class. Or look for supplementary information on the Internet.
- *Use attention directing strategies.* To overcome departures and tangents from the speech, both large and small, take notes. Direct your attention to specific areas of the message; for example, listen for and write down the main ideas, focus on practical "things I can use," or listen for examples that will help you remember concepts.
- *Enhance the meaning.* Use small departures productively by asking yourself questions that link the material to your personal experiences and ideas. For example: "Who do I know who is like that?" "Isn't that what happened to my grandmother?" "How on earth does that work?" "What is the next step going to be?" "Does this match what I learned in another class?" Elaborate on the ideas mentally by creating images in your mind or by referring to what you already know or have experienced.
- *Look for organizational patterns.* Use organizational skills from the canon of disposition to help you remember material. For instance, identify the main points and watch for

Effective note-taking is one way you can improve your comprehensive listening skills.

signals such as "first," "next," or "finally" that will help you understand a series of steps. Be alert for words like "therefore" or "in contrast" that connect one idea to another (Lundsteen, 1993).

● *Use strategies that complement your personal learning style.* For instance, if you learn best by hearing, get permission to tape the lecture or speech and replay it at a later time. If you learn best by creating linear outlines, use a laptop computer or notebook and outline the main points and important supporting information. If you are more graphically oriented, make a mind map and draw connections between ideas. Draw useful illustrations in the margins of your notes. (I personally include the lecturer's examples in my notes, because I learn and remember abstract ideas best when I tie them to real-life situations.)

● *Don't ignore the speaker's manner.* A confident, intense involvement with the subject adds a dimension that says "This is important, pay attention" or "I care about this topic and so should you." In contrast, a tentative, apologetic, or apathetic manner may lead you to conclude "This is not very important material" or "This speaker doesn't seem very sure of this material, how can I be?"

In summary, comprehensive listening requires skill in understanding words and ideas, in identifying major ideas and supporting materials, in connecting new material with old, and in recalling information. This type of listening corresponds with the general speech purpose to inform. We now turn to critical listening skills that you'll employ when you hear a persuasive speaker.

Improve Your Critical Listening Skills

Persuasive speakers surround you and urge you to buy, to sign petitions, to donate, to accept a religious belief, or to use a particular product. You need to develop critical listening skills to sort out competing claims for your allegiance, your beliefs, your money, and your time. A critical approach means that you ponder and weigh the merits of various appeals rather than accepting them without reflection. **Critical listening** skills build on comprehensive listening skills but add questions such as these:

Critical Listening
Listening that requires you to reflect and weigh the merits of persuasive messages before you accept them.

● What is this speaker's goal?
● Does this message make sense?
● Where does this information come from?
● What are the benefits of adopting the speaker's ideas?
● What problems, if any, go along with this position?
● Am I being swayed by my emotions?
● Should I trust this speaker?

In short, critical listening is one way to live out the cultural saying "Don't believe everything you hear." Sharpening these skills will guide you as you sift through all the persuasive appeals each day brings. Chapters 8 and 18 provide tests you can use to evaluate evidence and reasoning.

In a diverse culture, as noted earlier, you are sometimes tempted to seek out speakers who affirm your ideas. They bolster your beliefs and actions, especially if the dominant society challenges them. The following examples may clarify this listening purpose:

● People who give money to support needy children attend a banquet where they hear narratives describing how their gift literally saved lives. These stories convince them to continue their donations.

- Members of synagogues, churches, mosques, and temples gather weekly to reaffirm their beliefs about God.
- Every year on the anniversary of the Supreme Court decision *Roe v. Wade*, supporters on both sides of the abortion issue attend rallies to hear speakers who reaffirm their position.
- Members of neo-Nazi groups organize gatherings in which speakers passionately argue for the merits of white supremacy.

If you find one of these settings comfortable, you may find yourself reacting enthusiastically by clapping, nodding, or verbally encouraging the speaker. Because you are involved with the topic, you may accept questionable arguments or emotional appeals that support your cause. However, you need to test these messages as you would any other persuasive speech. Think how different history would be had Hitler's listeners evaluated his messages critically (Ridge, 1993; Wolvin & Coakley, 1993).

STOP AND CHECK

DEVELOP STRATEGIES TO LISTEN MORE EFFECTIVELY

Return to the Listening Skills Self-Assessment you completed on pages 60–61 and note each question you answered with an "A" or a "B." Using materials from the section on Strategies to Improve Listening, develop strategies that will help you overcome the listening barrier implied in each question. You'll find a Listening Skills Development Plan under Stop and Check Activities for Chapter 4 at the Jaffe Connection Web site. You can use this form to record your strategies. To investigate this topic further, log on to InfoTrac College Edition and perform a PowerTrac search for the author Arleen Richman. Read her article "Listen Up!" What additional tips does she give for effective listening?

Web Site

Practice Dialogical Listening

Remember the diagram of communication from Chapter 1? As you listen to a public speech, you provide feedback, often nonverbal but sometimes verbal. This section will examine both nonverbal and verbal interactions. As you read, remember that cultural expectations influence appropriate feedback behaviors.

Give Appropriate Nonverbal Feedback

Your posture, your movements, even the distance you sit from the speaker can help you send feedback more effectively.

Posture

Your posture communicates involvement and helps you focus your attention. Face the speaker squarely. Even if you are sitting in the corner of the room, you can turn toward the speaker more directly. Lean forward slightly. When you are thoroughly engrossed in a speech, this posture—being "on the edge of your seat"—is natural. Let your body assume a relaxed, open position.

Distance

Think about the difference in your attentiveness if you sit in the far corner of the back row where people walk by an open door, or if you sit front-and-center where you have fewer outside distractions. Which seat contributes more to your learning? One study, illustrated in Figure 4.4, found that instructors interact more regularly with students who are sitting in the first two or three rows, toward the center (Hybels & Weaver, 1992). It makes sense that the more you interact with the speaker, the more you will understand and remember.

Figure 4.4 In the formal seating arrangement depicted in this classroom diagram, the "action zone" is shaded red. Students who sit in this zone interact more with the instructor. Those in the area shaded yellow interact less frequently, and those in the unshaded area have the fewest number of interactions.

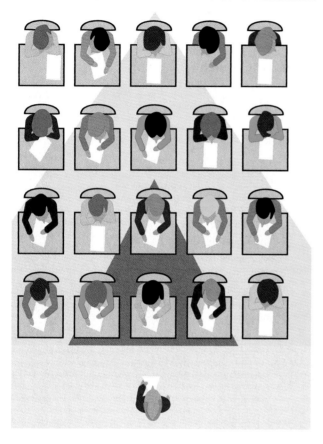

Movements

Avoid disruptive behaviors such as fidgeting, shuffling papers, or drumming your fingers on the desk. Instead, support the speaker by making eye contact, which also helps focus your attention. Smiling at an amusing anecdote, nodding in support of a major point, or applauding when appropriate also increase your involvement and help the speaker.

A speaker who looks out at attentive listeners may actually become more interesting. One campus legend relates how a boring professor began the semester by standing only at the lectern and reading from his notes. His students decided to act *as if* he were a fascinating lecturer. Whenever he moved away from his notes, ever so slightly, they all leaned forward a bit, made eye contact, and used supportive motions. According to the story, the professor was eventually walking back and forth across the front of the room, lecturing animatedly!

Give Appropriate Verbal Feedback

"What's her source of information?" "Where can I write for further facts?" "Hmmm ... that happened to my friend!" "How is he defining that particular word?" Questions and comments such as these arise as you listen. When you know that a question-and-answer period will follow a speech, jot down your questions and comments. Of course, there are many different types of questions; here are a few common categories (Goodman & Esterly, 1990).

Loaded Questions

Loaded Questions
Questions containing implications intended to put the speaker on the defensive.

You can put a speaker on the defensive by the implicit assumptions your question contains. These are **loaded questions.** Let's say a reporter asks the president "When are you going to start keeping your promises about Medicare reform?" The question is loaded because it implies (1) that the president made the promise, and (2) that he is failing to keep it. In addition, the word *when* is not really asking for a time. That is, the expected answer is not "Well, I thought I'd start that on the morning of June 16, just before lunch."

Closed Questions

Closed Questions
Requests for brief, specific answers.

Closed questions ask for brief, specific answers. Use them when you seek precise information or want to verify your understanding. The question "Are you a member of the NRA?" asks for a yes or no response. "When did Billy the Kid die?" asks for a specific date. "What Web site do you use most?" asks for a specific Internet address. "Who wrote the *Chronicles of Narnia*?" requires a specific name.

Open Questions

Open Questions
Requests for more lengthy responses.

Open questions invite longer answers. For instance, "What do you think are the best ways to help children deal with the death of a classmate?" allows the speaker to select from a number of possible responses. Other examples include "What suggestions do you have for dealing with unwanted email?" or "How will your spending habits change now that you've destroyed your credit cards?"

Clarification Questions

When you are confused, ask for more information. Here are some examples of **clarification questions:** "Could you explain the difference between the Russian Old Believers and the Molokan Russians?" "What did you mean when you said we might never have been born without gays in the military?"

Clarification Questions
Requests to clear up confusing ideas.

Requests for Elaboration

If you want a speaker to further expand on her ideas, **request for elaboration:** "You told us that some of the Founding Fathers grew hemp. Could you elaborate on that?" "Can you provide more information about the cost and availability of the eye chip?" "Could you give more details on theories about the causes of school shootings?"

Requests for Elaboration
Questions asking for more information.

Comments

Instead of asking questions, you can **comment** by providing information from your own experience or research. For instance, after a speech on bulimia, one person provided statistics she had heard on a television show. Another briefly shared a story about her bulimic sister's treatment. If you know some data in the speech is incorrect (for example, let's say the speaker gives outdated statistics), you can provide updated information. Your questions and comments are part of the co-creation of meaning that involves both a speaker and a participating audience. (Not all cultures participate equally in this co-creation of meaning process, as the Diversity in Practice box titled Saving Face explains.)

Comment
Information from personal experience or research

DIVERSITY IN PRACTICE
SAVING FACE

QUESTION-AND-ANSWER periods are rare in some cultural groups. For instance, in the context of traditional Chinese or Japanese public speaking, listeners are supposed to understand the speaker. Asking a question is an admission that they're not intelligent enough to unravel the speaker's shades of meaning. In addition, questions reflect on the speaker's ability to communicate effectively; that is, if listeners are confused and have questions, the speaker failed to communicate. Finally, to preserve the speaker's "face," it is considered inappropriate to question a speaker's information—and thus, his or her character—in front of others (Becker, 1991; Sueda, 1995).

In summary, listening is not easy. Speakers can be boring, subjects are often complex and difficult, your emotions may get involved, and your daily stresses can influence how well you listen. Being aware of your thought processes during listening and actively working to focus your attention on the speech will help you become a better listener. Then, consider yourself a co-creator of meaning who actively interacts with the speaker, both nonverbally and verbally, to create mutual meanings.

Summary

Listening is the communication activity that we do most and study least. Listening is important in your personal and occupational life. However, listeners often face a number of cultural as well as personal barriers that impede effective listening. Linguistic barriers, misunderstanding vocabulary words, or the use of cultural allusions all make comprehension difficult. In addition, personal and psychological factors, such as physical tiredness, stresses and worries, stereotypes and prejudices, and wandering attention patterns, can hinder listening.

Fortunately, you can devise strategies to listen more effectively. Use cultural schemas or mental blueprints to guide the perception, interpretation, storage, and recollection of what you hear. Know your listening purpose and identify strategies to help you comprehend information or critically evaluate persuasive messages.

Finally, practice dialogical listening by contributing appropriate nonverbal and verbal feedback during the speech. Nonverbal actions communicate that you are interested in the speech; they also help you pay attention. Useful nonverbal elements include a posture that communicates involvement, a distance that helps focus your attention, and movements that support rather than disrupt the speech. When you have an opportunity to interact verbally with a speaker, ask questions or provide comments that elaborate on the topic. However, be aware that after-speech questions and comments are inappropriate in some cultures.

JAFFE ONLINE CONNECTION   JAFFE ONLINE CONNECTION

Use your CD-ROM and the Jaffe Connection Web site http://communication.wadsworth.com/jaffe to review the following concepts, answer the review questions, and complete the suggested activities.

KEY TERMS

cultural allusions (58)

stereotype (59)

prejudiced (59)

speech–thought differential (59)

leftover thinking space (59)

schemas (61)

comprehensive listening (63)

critical listening (64)

loaded questions (66)

closed questions (66)

open questions (66)

clarification questions (67)

request for elaboration (67)

comment (67)

APPLICATION AND CRITICAL THINKING EXERCISES

1. Think about the Chinese symbol that stands for listening (see Figure 4.1). In what way do you use your ears, eyes, and heart when you listen to your classmates? Your professors? A speaker whose ideas support your own opinions? A speaker with whom you totally disagree?

2. Using the diagrams in Figure 4.2 as models, draw a diagram that depicts your listening pattern during the last lecture you heard. Next, draw a diagram that depicts your listening pattern during the last conversation you had with your best friend. Draw a third diagram that shows your listening pattern during your last major conversation with a family member. Compare the three. What conclusions can you draw about your listening patterns in various contexts?

3. Listen to a speaker who takes a position that differs dramatically from your views; you may find such a speaker on radio or television (for example, a person whose lifestyle differs from yours, one who disagrees about politics, someone whose views on a social issue such as capital punishment diverge from yours, or a person with different religious beliefs). As you listen, jot down your thoughts and your feelings, then evaluate your listening effectiveness.

4. Practice the nonverbal skills of active listening in one of your courses. That is, use posture, space, and movement to help focus your attention on the lecture. Afterward, evaluate whether your nonverbal behaviors helped you pay attention and recall the class material.

5. In the next group of classroom speeches, select one speech that you will follow by verbally interacting with the speaker. During the speech, jot down several questions you plan to ask.

6. Log on to InfoTrac College Edition and do a PowerTrac search for the title "Shut Up Already! A Surefire Way to Learn the Value of Listening." It tells about college student Brett Banfe, who challenged himself to be silent for a year. Read the article to find out what he learned, then design an experiment using silence that could help you and your classmates improve your listening skills.

7. Go to www.usu.edu/arc/idea_sheets/, a Utah State University site that provides many student aids. Link to "active listening skills" in the communications resources, or study the ideas in "listening skills for lectures" in the study skills resources. Use the suggestions you find there to help you create your Listening Skills Development Plan under Activities for Chapter 4 at the Jaffe Connection Web site.

THE JAFFE CONNECTION WEB SITE

The Jaffe Connection Web site features review questions about the Web links, Stop and Check activities, and InfoTrac College Edition exercises referenced throughout this chapter. You can access this site via your CD-ROM or at http://communication.wadsworth.com/jaffe.

Web Links

4.1 Listening Skills (page 56)
4.2 How to Develop Listening Skills (page 69)

Stop and Check Activities

4.1 Listening Skills Self-Assessment (pages 60–61)
4.2 Develop Strategies to Listen More Effectively (page 65)

InfoTrac College Edition Exercises

4.1 Listening Skills on the Job (page 56)
4.2 Cross-Cultural Student Listening Preferences (page 63)
4.3 Listen Up! (page 65)
4.4 What Silence Teaches About Listening (page 69)

SPEECH INTERACTIVE ON THE JAFFE CONNECTION CD-ROM

Watch the persuasive speech "Embryo Adoption" by Paul Southwick on the Jaffe Connection CD-ROM and answer the questions for analysis under Speech Interactive for Chapter 4. (The speech text is in Appendix C.)

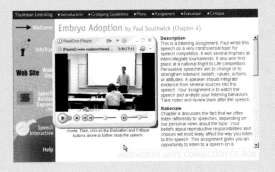

Audience Analysis

THIS CHAPTER WILL HELP YOU

■ Describe various audience motivations

■ Tell how demographic audience analysis helps you adapt your speech to the audience

■ Develop a questionnaire to assess your listeners' psychological profile

■ Explain how the situation affects your audience

■ Analyze your audience's perception of your credibility

"Educate to Liberate" Mural ©1988 by Miranda Bergman, Jane Norling, Maria Ramos, Vicky Hamlin, Arch Williams. (Hayes Street and Masonic, SF, CA)

EVERY YEAR, COLLEGES AND UNIVERSITIES RECOGNIZE AND HONOR outstanding instructors. The University of Washington, for example, commended the following professors and listed some characteristics that set them apart:

- Senior lecturer, James Green (anthropology) says, "I try to tailor my presentations to what I think is on the minds of people 18 to 20 years old . . . you make yourself sensitive to what people are saying and how they're responding to you."
- Professor Priti Ramamurthy (women's studies) says, "I try to get [students] to see how the headlines are connected to their own lives."
- David Domke (communication) has the ability "to connect with students one-to-one, even though they sit among hundreds of others in the classroom" (Luce, 2002, pp. 33–34).

Audience Analysis
Identifying audience characteristics to communicate more effectively.

Listening Speaker
Dialogical speaker who hears audience interests and concerns before, during, and after a speech.

All these teachers understand the importance of sensitivity to students at every step of lecture preparation. They use the skills of **audience analysis** to think carefully about a specific class and find resources to communicate most effectively with those students. They take a dialogical perspective and become **listening speakers** (Holzman, 1970), who hear audience interests and concerns before, during, and after their presentations. Because your relationship with your audience is complex, this chapter examines your perception of your audience and the situation as well as their perception of you.

Analyze Who Is Listening

A good speech is one that's prepared for a particular group at a particular time; even politicians, salespersons, or university recruiters, who present the same material repeatedly, adapt their material to each audience and each setting. This section explores ways you can think about a specific audience and a specific speaking situation.

Consider Audience Motivations

Why do audiences gather? What attracts them? What holds them? Answering these questions provides clues about your audience's motivations and helps you prepare each speech

Passive listeners comprise most speech classes; their goal is to earn course credit—listening to you is required. With passive audiences, carefully choose relevant topics and present interesting information about them.

Dick Blume/The Image Works

more effectively. Audiences assemble for several reasons. Many years ago, H. L. Hollingsworth (1935) identified the following six types of audiences:

1. **Pedestrian audiences** randomly and temporarily come together because something grabs their attention—perhaps a salesman's flashy demonstration of a food processor, the impassioned voice of an activist in an outdoor forum, or the humorous stories of a sidewalk entertainer. Your challenge with these audiences? To attract listeners and keep their interest long enough to present your message.

2. **Passive audiences** listen to speeches to accomplish other goals. For instance, some teachers attend a job-related workshop, not because they're fascinated by the topic but because their principal insists they attend. Most speech classes consist of passive listeners who attend class, not just to hear speeches but to receive academic credit. Some take the course reluctantly! To be effective, select an interesting topic and help your audience understand its relevance to their lives.

3. **Selected audiences** voluntarily and intentionally gather to hear about a topic (for example, windsurfing) or to hear a particular speaker (perhaps a famous author). A **homogeneous audience** is comprised of members who share an attitude—whether positive or negative. Speaking to an audience with a positive attitude can be fun, but you must develop your ideas clearly so that listeners understand and accept them. Facing a negative or **hostile audience** presents an entirely different set of challenges. (Chapter 17 discusses how to deal with this type of audience.)

4. **Concerted audiences** voluntarily listen because they more-or-less agree that the subject is important, but they don't know what they can do about it. They need you to motivate them and give them specific directions. Students sometimes organize rallies around national or campus events. For instance, in the weeks after September 11, 2001, people gravitated to public places where leaders comforted them and described specific things they could do to help victims and to prevent future acts of terrorism.

5. **Organized audiences** already know about the topic and are motivated and committed to act, but they need specific, "how-to" instructions. Students at my university participate in overseas service trips to Romania. They meet before their trip and learn how to get their passports, what type of clothing to pack, how to say a few basic Romanian phrases, and what cultural differences they can expect.

6. **Absent audiences** are separated from the speaker; they listen through radio, telephone conferencing, television, videotapes, or videoconferences—live or days (even years!) later. Advances in technology make this type of audience more and more common. When you speak to absent audiences, remember they can easily change channels or tune you out. Focus on being interesting and relevant, and use conversational delivery as if you were speaking to one listener at a time.

The same audience member may vary in motivation from meeting to meeting. Let's follow a student through several sessions that precede a trip she takes to Romania. She first hears about a service trip during an announcement in her social work class (passive); she shows up at an informational meeting (selected) to learn more about Romania. Next, she gets additional information about various service possibilities in that country (concerted). After she is accepted for a specific trip, she attends meetings to get specific details for the trip (organized). She may even check out a videotape about Romania from the university's library (absent).

As you might imagine, an audience is not always homogeneous. For instance, a mostly passive audience such as your classroom may have several students who select both the topic and the instructor; a mostly organized audience may include passive listeners who are just tagging along with friends. Regardless, you'll be more effective if you consider the fundamental motivation of your audiences and plan speeches that are sensitive to their interests and needs.

Pedestrian Audiences
Random, temporary, and accidental audiences that did not intend to hear a speech.

Passive Audiences
Groups who listen to accomplish other goals.

Selected Audiences
Groups that choose to listen to a selected subject or speaker.

Homogeneous Audiences
Listeners who are similar in attitude.

Hostile Audiences
Listeners who are negative toward the topic or the speaker.

Concerted Audiences
Listeners who are positive toward a topic but don't act; they need motivation and a plan.

Organized Audiences
Motivated listeners who need specific instructions.

Absent Audiences
Intentional listeners separated in distance and time who are reached through various media.

Analyze Audience Demographics

One of the most common ways to consider your audience is through **demographic audience analysis,** in which you analyze listeners according to the groups or populations they represent. In some situations, demographic factors help you tailor your remarks specifically. However, if you are not careful, you may classify your listeners into categories and then stereotype them. Remember that each person belongs to many groups, and membership in a specific group is more **salient** (it matters, or is significant) in some situations than in others (Collier, 1994). Rothenberg (1998) summarizes the complexity of demographic analysis:

> When we engage in [demographic analysis], we should never lose sight of the fact that (1) any particular woman or man has an ethnic background, class location, age, sexual orientation, religious orientation, gender, and so forth, and (2) all these characteristics are inseparable from the person and from each other. . . . It is also true that . . . we may have to make generalizations about the experience of different groups of people, even as we affirm that each individual is unique. (p. 2)

In short, because no one is simply a "lawyer" or a "Latina" or a "senior citizen," analyze your listeners' identification with various groups *in light of your specific speaking situation.* These categories are common in demographic analysis: ethnicity, race, religion, gender, marital status, age, group affiliation, occupation and socioeconomic status, and region. Let's look at each of them in more detail.

Ethnicity

Ethnicity refers to a group's common heritage and cultural traditions usually having national and religious origins (Collier, 1994; O'Neil, 1999). For example, the Russian Old Believers who live in the Willamette Valley of Oregon are a distinct ethnic group, distinguished from their European American and Mexican American neighbors by language, clothing, cultural heroes, and religious traditions (Jaffe, 1995). The urban areas of the United States are especially diverse. For example, members of more than 150 ethnic groups (speaking 114 languages) reside in Queens, New York. Ethnicity is a complex concept, in part because many people have ancestors from more than one group.

Ethnic identity assumes more or less salience depending on the context. A person of Norwegian descent in a fairly homogeneous audience—such as a Scandinavian festival—is consciously aware of her ethnicity. However, the same person in your speech class probably considers her educational and occupational goals to be more important than her Norwegian roots.

Race

Ethnicity is often linked to **race,** but the two are not identical. Racial categories are generally based on physical characteristics such as skin color or facial features; however, races are not clearly distinct, and characteristics that supposedly identify one race are also found in other populations. For example, populations in Africa, India, Australia, New Guinea, and the Southwest Pacific all have dark-brown skin, but they're unrelated (O'Neil, 1999). Moreover, millions of Americans come from mixed racial backgrounds that blur the lines between groups (Marmor, 1996). President Clinton (2000) addressed racial issues in his State of the Union Address. He cited scientists such as Alan Templeton, an evolutionary and population biologist at Washington University, who argue that there is no genetic basis for distinct racial categories; we are "99.9 percent the same." However, race is a "social category," and unfortunately such categories are often associated with stereotypes. If you assume that a person or group will have specific abilities, skills, or behaviors associated with these stereotypes, you are being **racist.** You can read a first-person account showing the complexity of racial and ethnic classifications at http://mapage.noos.fr/dardelf/Race.html. Identify the various labels the author has been tagged with. What conclusions has she drawn?

Religion

It is an old saying that it is better to avoid both religion and politics in social conversation. This reflects the deep feelings many people have on these topics. Of course it is permissible to speak publicly on religion, but it is necessary *in every speech* to be sensitive to the possible range and intensity of religious beliefs within your audience. I've heard students, totally oblivious to their Jewish classmates, say "when we all go home to celebrate Christmas." Some listeners identify themselves as members of a particular faith yet see their religion as peripheral to their identity. For others, religion is a central factor in their everyday lives. Religious traditions are often linked to ethnicity, and disparagement or dismissal of a group's sacred texts, heroes, or rituals often evokes intense emotional reactions—even among people who hold them loosely.

Sex and Gender

Don't confuse sexual differences—being biologically male or female—with gender differences, which are cultural. **Gender** is a cluster of traits culturally labeled as masculine, feminine, or androgynous (containing both masculine and feminine characteristics). To illustrate, women often change an infant's diapers, and some cultural groups consider this a feminine task; however, nothing in a man's biological makeup prevents him from cleaning up a baby. Thus, diaper changing can be an androgynous act. In our rapidly changing society, we continually examine and negotiate gender-associated characteristics, changing our notions of "proper" behaviors for men and for women. If you assume a man or a woman will think or act in a certain way because of his or her sex, you are being **sexist.**

An audience member's identity as male or female is salient at events like a Million Man March or a Promise Keepers rally and a "Women in Science" conference or a mother-daughter banquet. However, all-male or all-female audiences can be drawn to a speech by their members' political affiliation, educational level, or another factor. For example, engineers at a workshop on disaster preparedness may all be women, but their interest in safety is what motivates them to attend, not their biological sex.

Gender
Clusters of traits culturally labeled as masculine, feminine, or androgynous.

Sexist
Assuming someone will act or think a certain way because of gender.

Marital Status/Sexual Expression

Take into account the interests and perspectives of both the married people and the singles in your audience. In addition, consider your listeners' sexual orientation and their sexual activity. Don't assume they're all heterosexual—or that they're all sexually active. One student speaker made unwarranted assumptions on a campus with an active Greek system. He advised his listeners to attend a fraternity party, scope out interesting women, persuade one to drink heavily, then invite her to an upstairs bedroom to "look at the goldfish." Some listeners laughed, but others were offended by his assumptions about women, fraternities, drinking, and heterosexuality. Married students were amused at his immaturity but bored with his speech.

Age

Not surprisingly, age influences an audience's motivations and concerns. Globally, cultures distinguish between generational groups, and market researchers in the United States identify and then target age cohorts because different generations were brought up differently, experienced different events, and pursue different social missions (Morton, 1998). Here are some common labels for, and descriptions of, these generations:

- *Mature Americans* are in two categories. Those who were born before 1924 have adapted to enormous cultural changes. As young people, these seniors lived through the Great Depression and World War II, listened to the radio but not television, and drove Model Ts instead of SUVs. Mature Americans born between 1925 and 1945 tend to be adventurous and determined to remain youthful. Their teachers read the Bible, prayed in school, and fretted about students who chewed gum!

- *Baby boomers*, 77 million of them, were born between the end of World War II and the early 1960s. Older boomers remember the assassinations of President Kennedy and Martin Luther King, Jr. Boomers tend to be individualistic, driven, and "me"-centered. Some avoided the draft, experimented with drugs, and organized protests. Boomers grew up with television, but they took along typewriters, not computers, when they went off to college.

- *Generation Xers*, the first latchkey generation, are a racially and culturally diverse group whose 44.5 million members were born between 1963 and 1978 (or 1981). They came of age in a media-dominated society with access to network television and cable, CD-ROMs, VCRs, and videogames (O'Donovan, 1997). Socially, they grew up with high divorce rates, legalized abortion, a huge national deficit, and a series of political scandals. Some researchers describe them as fun loving and routine hating, reactive and angry. Younger Gen Xers have used personal computers since they were six years old, so their outlook on life and their view of technology is vastly different from that of seniors (Halstead, 1999).

- *The millennium generation*, born after 1978 (or 1981, according to some sources), inherited many social and environmental problems; consequently, they tend to be more civic-minded (and less angry) than Gen Xers. The millennium generation was born into the "twitch speed" era of MTV and personal computers, in which technology makes everything seem to move faster (Prensky, 1998). One student speaker referred to eighteen- to twenty-four-year-olds as the "I-generation," or Internet generation.

Although people in each group have individual differences, members of a generational cohort tend to be moved by appeals and allusions that another generation might not understand. For example, when Elizabeth Dole was running for president she addressed a group of young, female students at Harvard Law School, her alma mater. In her speech she described her 1950s struggle to convince her mother that she should go to Harvard Law and have a career. Her listeners couldn't relate to her story. Most of them grew up in achievement-oriented families within a society that now encourages women to plan for a professional life. Figure 5.1 illustrates the complicated nature of demographic analysis.

Group Affiliation

People form groups to share interests, experiences, or hobbies. Veterans of Foreign Wars, Wheelchair Athletes, Alcoholics Anonymous, and members of fraternities or sororities are examples. Often these groups invite guest speakers to meetings. Because group identity is highly salient in these situations, you should draw on common experiences and shared beliefs and values. For instance, if you're with the Young Democrats, find heroes within that party that you can praise, even if your political loyalties lie elsewhere.

Occupation/Socioeconomic Status

Differences in educational level, income, occupational choice, and social class status can all be salient in particular situations. Knowing your classmates' job experiences and their academic majors can help you adapt more specifically to unique elements within your classroom. In addition, consider that seniors and sophomores may differ in their perspectives. In the world of work, computer engineers or physicians may differ in sex, ethnicity, religion, and sexual orientation, but similar interests and experiences give them commonalities you can draw upon. Furthermore, comfortably middle-class individuals may have little in common with those who struggle to make ends meet when the topic is stock market investing; however, a topic such as cheating is relevant across economic lines.

Regions

You know that Japanese or Nigerian audiences require different speaking strategies, but what if you move from one state or region to another? Although people in the United States share much in common, people in various regions tend to have somewhat different charac-

FIGURE 5.1 These silhouettes represent a single audience member who is influenced by many demographic factors that are interwoven with individual traits and personality characteristics. In one situation, the listener's age is the more salient factor; in another, her region and group affiliation matter more.

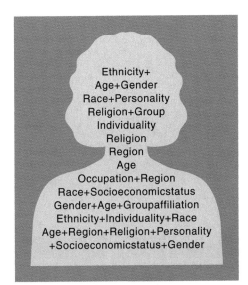
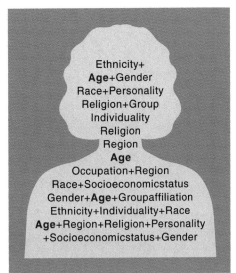
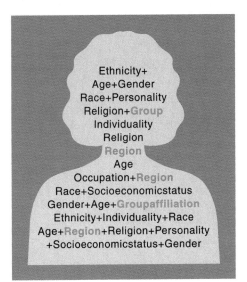

teristics due to climate, history, language, economic base, politics, and so on. These differences influence their interests and perspectives (Andersen et al., 1987).

You can see this principle in practice if you follow a presidential candidate around the country. He discusses hurricane damage with Florida residents, but not with Oregonians. His emphasis in Silicon Valley differs from that in the ranchlands of the West. Issues important in Vermont (with 97.6 percent whites) and in Hawaii (29 percent white, non-Latino) will vary. He recognizes that an inhabitant of New York City may have more in common with a San Franciscan than she does with a person from upstate New York. The rural New Yorker may be more similar to an Iowan than to her Manhattan cousin ("America 2000: A Map of the Mix," 2001).

In summary, demographic audience analysis is a way of considering your listeners in terms of categories, based on such elements as ethnicity, gender, age, group affiliation, and regional identity. Instead of stereotyping listeners, try to use the more inclusive model depicted in Figure 5.1. Know that demographic categories can guide you as you select materials and organize your speech, but in each individual, these elements function together rather than separately.

STOP AND CHECK

ANALYZING YOUR AUDIENCE

Web Site

Use the Audience Motivations and Demographics form shown here to analyze your classroom audience. For your own speech assignment, you can access this form on the Jaffe Connection Web site.

THOMSON WADSWORTH

Home | Press Room | Contact Us | Find Your Rep | BookShop | Services | Disciplines

5. Audience Analysis

Book Info
Companion Sites
Discipline Home

Wadsworth : Companion Website

INSTRUCTOR RESOURCES   NEED A PASSWORD?

CHAPTER RESOURCES
Chapter 5
Activity
Infotrac Exercises
Preparation Form
Tutorial Quiz

COURSE RESOURCES
About the Author(s)
Communication Links
Documentation
Glossary
Handbook
Infotrac Exercises
PRCA-24 Survey
PRPSA Survey
Research
Sample Chapters
Student Center
Visual Overview Demo
Careers
Communication Links
Events

ANCILLARIES
Book Supplements

[Back]

Preparation Form:
Evaluate Your Audience (Audience Motivations and Demographics)

Name:		Date:	

In general, this audience:		True	False
Is passive.			
Is selective.			
Is organized.			
Is absent.			
Is hostile to the subject of the speech.			
Is neutral to the subject of the speech.			
Is supportive of the subject of the speech.			
Is interested in the speech subject.			

Ethnically:		True	False
The audience members are similar.			

To further investigate the topic of demographic audience analysis, log on to InfoTrac College Edition and perform a PowerTrac search for the journal *Marketing to Women*. Select three articles (most are very short) and tell how you might prepare to speak to the group of women presented in each article. (Articles include topics such as radio listening habits and groups such as cheerleaders, book club members, and Gen X mothers.)

Analyze the Audience's Psychological Profile

Natalie really wanted to speak about a vegetarian diet, but she didn't want to repeat information everyone knew. So prior to speaking, she made a **psychological profile** of her classmates by creating a questionnaire that she asked audience members to fill out prior to making her speech. She wanted to know what her listeners already knew, how they felt, what they considered important, and how they actually ate. In other words, she assessed their psychological approach to her topic. To determine your audience members' psychological profile, think about their beliefs, values, and attitudes regarding your subject.

Psychological Profile
Assessment of an audience's beliefs, values, and attitudes.

Beliefs

A **belief** is a mental acceptance that something is true or false, correct or incorrect, valid or invalid (Rokeach, 1972). Our beliefs may be based on study or investigation or on conviction without much factual information or knowledge. And we may have misconceptions. When Natalie evaluated her listeners' beliefs, she used open questions such as these that allowed for a variety of responses:

Belief
Mental acceptance that something is true or false, correct or incorrect, valid or invalid.

- What do you think are the benefits and drawbacks of a vegetarian diet?
- If you don't eat meat, why not?
- If you eat meat, what might convince you to stop?
- What are some categories that vegetarians fall into?

She added some closed questions such as these:

Is a vegetarian diet healthy?
_____ yes
_____ no
_____ I'm not sure

She discovered that a few classmates avoided eating meat, but they didn't really understand how to combine proteins. Most couldn't identify three kinds of vegetarians, and half thought that a vegetarian diet was too difficult to follow during college. However, three persons were confirmed vegans who ate no animal products and who regularly downloaded information about vegetarianism from the Internet. In short, three people had a fairly deep understanding of a vegetarian diet, but most had little information and many misconceptions.

Because they must create an audience out of people who are not intending to listen to a speech, speakers sometimes use unusual means to attract attention to their topic.

Jack Jaffe

Attitudes

Our tendencies to like or dislike, to have positive or negative feelings, are called **attitudes.** Attitudes have an emotional component that involves feelings and values, a mental component that involves beliefs, and a behavioral component that influences actions. For instance, Americans tend to *feel* positively toward work because they *believe* it's linked to success, which they *value*, so they *act* by setting personal goals and striving to accomplish them.

Researchers use **scaled questions** to measure attitudes along a range or continuum from highly positive to highly negative. Attitudes can also be neutral, meaning that listeners

Attitudes
Preferences, likes and dislikes, that involve beliefs, feelings, and behaviors.

Scaled Questions
Questions asking for responses along a continuum; used to assess attitudes.

probably haven't thought enough about the subject to form an opinion. Here are typical scaled questions that Natalie might use to assess audience attitudes:

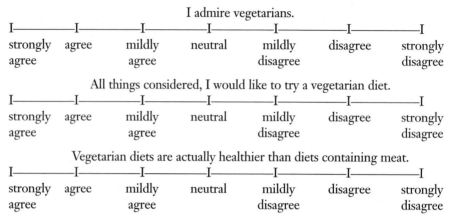

I admire vegetarians.

I————————I————————I————————I————————I————————I————————I
strongly   agree   mildly   neutral   mildly   disagree   strongly
agree   agree   disagree   disagree

All things considered, I would like to try a vegetarian diet.

I————————I————————I————————I————————I————————I————————I
strongly   agree   mildly   neutral   mildly   disagree   strongly
agree   agree   disagree   disagree

Vegetarian diets are actually healthier than diets containing meat.

I————————I————————I————————I————————I————————I————————I
strongly   agree   mildly   neutral   mildly   disagree   strongly
agree   agree   disagree   disagree

Notice that the first statement identifies feelings, the second looks at a predisposition to act, and the third assesses beliefs. All three—feelings, behaviors, and beliefs—work together to create attitudes. It is easier to speak when the audience shares your attitude toward your topic, whether it's negative or positive. However, your task becomes more complex when audience attitudes are diverse. Natalie, a vegetarian, knew that she'd have three sympathetic listeners, but most were mildly or moderately negative toward vegetarianism. Two were downright hostile; one of them lived on a beef cattle ranch and the other's grandfather was a butcher. Knowing the range of attitudes within the audience helped her plan a good speech.

Values

Values
Ideals by which we judge what is important and, consequently, how we should behave.

Values are the standards we use to judge what is good or bad, beautiful or ugly, kind or cruel, appropriate or inappropriate. U.S. cultural values include choice, individualism, fair play, progress, freedom, equality, and the like. Almost every topic you choose touches on your values because you at least consider the subject important enough to discuss. However, you directly address value questions when you use words such as right or wrong, moral or immoral, important or insignificant. As with attitudes, it's helpful to think of value judgments as existing across a range. The **Ethical Quality Scale (EQS)** provides a way to visualize gradations of opinion regarding ethical questions (Jensen, 1997). Although this scale deals with ethical or moral judgments, you could easily adapt it for judgments related to beauty, fairness, and other value issues.

Ethical Quality Scale (EQS)
A graphical representation of gradations of opinion regarding issues of value.

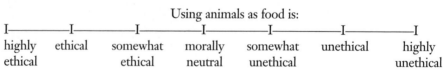

Using animals as food is:

I————————I————————I————————I————————I————————I————————I
highly   ethical   somewhat   morally   somewhat   unethical   highly
ethical   ethical   neutral   unethical   unethical

Natalie found that some classmates judged vegetarianism as highly ethical, whereas others felt it was morally neutral. Even the beefeaters didn't care what Natalie ate as long as she didn't try to push her diet on them. Because values are our assumptions about what is good, we often respond with strong emotions when they are challenged. Natalie is passionate about vegetarianism, but the rancher's daughter may become equally passionate if Natalie implies that the beef industry is immoral.

Although we have discussed beliefs, actions, attitudes, and values as separate entities, the truth is that they're intertwined, and they affect your audience's interest in your topic. Take a listener who doesn't know much about writing a résumé but has a positive attitude because a good résumé will help him be successful, which he values. Contrast him to a woman who knows she needs to wear seatbelts, who values safety, and who buckles up automatically. Her interest in a seatbelt speech is probably minimal.

STOP AND CHECK

CONSTRUCT A QUESTIONNAIRE

This Combination Questionnaire combines closed questions, open questions, and scaled questions on the topic of road rage. Using your topic, construct a questionnaire that you can use to analyze your classmates' psychological profile. A questionnaire form is available for your own speech assignments on the Jaffe Connection Web site.

Web Site

A Combination Questionnaire

Name (optional) _____

Age _____   Sex _____   Major _____

Have you experienced road rage?   _____ yes   _____ no   _____ not sure

Have you been the object of road rage?   _____ yes   _____ no   _____ not sure

Place an X on the point of the scale that best indicates your response to the sentence.
Use the following codes:

SA	=	strongly agree
A	=	agree
MA	=	mildly agree
N	=	no opinion
MD	=	mildly disagree
D	=	disagree
SD	=	strongly disagree

Sometimes I get so angry at other drivers, that I feel
I could do something that might endanger their safety.

```
|---------|---------|---------|---------|---------|---------|
SA        A        MA        N        MD        D        SD
```

Angry drivers in other cars pose threats to my safety.

```
|---------|---------|---------|---------|---------|---------|
SA        A        MA        N        MD        D        SD
```

Road rage is a serious national problem.

```
|---------|---------|---------|---------|---------|---------|
SA        A        MA        N        MD        D        SD
```

How would you define road rage?

What effect do you think it has on its victims?

What is the best way to deal with this phenomenon?

What kinds of road rage, if any, are worse than others?

To learn more about this topic, log on to the Internet and go to the Web page "Questionnaire Design" at the site http://www/quickmba.com/marketing/research/qdesign. Pay particular attention to the advice on content, wording, and sequencing questions.

Assess the Situation

You have considered your listeners' motivations, and you have thought about demographic categories. Now think about the specific situation in which your speech takes place. Many aspects of the situation can affect your audience. Time and the environment are two basic considerations.

Take into account the effect of the situation on your listeners. Distractions they encounter in an informal outdoor situation like this are different from distractions in a cold, noisy indoor classroom.

© Wadsworth–Thomson Learning

Consider the Time

Two aspects of time affect public speaking. First, consider what time of day your class is held and the effect that may have on your audience. Think of those 8:00 A.M. listeners who stumble into the room brushing sleep from their eyes. Does anyone come to class after working a night shift? What about classes just before lunch, when people are hungry? Or those just after lunch, when they're sleepy? What differences might there be between day classes and evening classes? Evaluate these questions, and adapt your talk appropriately. For instance, you might be more animated when listeners are sleepy, or you might shorten your speech when it's very late.

Also, consider the *cultural* time system. In the United States, time is commonly seen as a line that is cut into segments, each lasting a specific duration, with distinct activities assigned to each (Jaffe, 1995). Take this class, for example. You chose this particular class partly because it fills a time slot you had available. The clock tells you when class starts and when it is over. In this setting, the date and length of your speech are important. (You may be graded down if you don't appear on the assigned date, or give a speech of the assigned length.) Your listeners expect you to work within this time pattern.

In contrast, listeners from a culture or co-culture with a more relaxed sense of time often focus less on starting precisely on time and fitting their remarks into a rigid time frame, as the following example illustrates. An American professor went to Brazil to teach psychology in a 10:00 A.M.-to-noon class (Burgoon, Butler, & Woodall, 1989). Of course, he carried his cultural expectations with him, and he began speaking close to 10 o'clock. However, students arrived as late as 11 o'clock without signs of concern or apology. At 12:15 P.M., everyone was still in the classroom, asking questions. Finally, at 12:30 P.M., the professor ended the class and left. The students, however, seemed willing to stay even longer.

Consider the Environment

Once I taught in a small college theater that was painted black. Floors, ceiling, chairs—everything was black. We met there twice before I called the schedule desk and requested a different room. The black theater is only one of many instances where the room itself can work against you. Windowless spaces, those too small or too large, rooms located by a noisy stairwell—all may affect your audience, whether or not they recognize it.

Other environmental considerations include the room's temperature (too hot, too cold), the weather outside (sunny and beautiful, stormy and icy), noise (an air conditioner, heater), and other items that might affect your listeners' comfort or draw their attention. You'll be a better speaker if you consider these aspects of your situation and adapt accordingly.

In summary, you form perceptions of your listeners by analyzing the demographic categories and groups to which they belong, their psychological profile, and the specific situation in which you will speak. The professors who earn teaching honors adapt to demographic, psychological, and situational factors as they teach. For more information on situational analysis, go to InfoTrac College Edition and do a PowerTrac search for the title "One Speaker's Pet Peeves." What similarities and differences do you find when analyzing a classroom versus a business situation?

To complete a situational analysis of your audience, use the questionnaire included under Stop and Check Activities for Chapter 5 at the Jaffe Connection Web site.

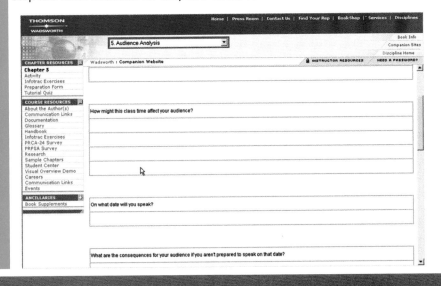

Web Site

Consider Your Audience's Perception of You

While you are forming impressions of your listeners, they are busily forming perceptions of your **credibility**—impressions about your character, your intentions, and your abilities. They begin their evaluation of you before your speech, modify it while you speak, and carry away a lasting impression after you are through (McCroskey, 1993).

Credibility
Listeners' impressions of your character, intentions, and abilities that make you more or less believable.

Be Aware of Prior Credibility

Let's say a former president comes to your campus to speak on foreign policy. You go to the speech assuming that he will know about the subject. Or, one of your classmates is on the fencing team, so when she arrives on her speech day with fencing equipment in hand, you

Rudy Giuliani brings prior credibility to his speeches because of his performance as mayor of New York City during its greatest crisis. However, within each speech, he must again demonstrate that he is competent and trustworthy.

AP/Wide World Photos

Prior or Extrinsic Credibility
Credibility speakers bring to the speech because of their experience and reputation.

expect her to have an insider's perspective on the topic. This type of credibility, the reputation or expertise of speakers that makes them believable even before they say a word, is called **prior** or **extrinsic credibility.** Practically speaking, you probably won't have prior credibility within your classroom, because most students lack the credentials or reputation that make their classmates see them as experts. Therefore, you'll need to establish some link between the topic and yourself in your introduction. Chapter 10 describes how to do this, and the Diversity in Practice box here provides some cross-cultural information on this topic.

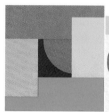

DIVERSITY IN PRACTICE
PRIOR CREDIBILITY IN OTHER CULTURES

CULTURES VARY IN THEIR EVALUATIONS of prior credibility. Age and gender loom large in some Native American cultures. When the occasion calls for "saying a few words," younger males and women in these cultures will seek out older males to speak for them. Weider and Pratt (1990) relate the story of a young woman who spoke for herself and her husband on a public occasion. Her elders scolded her for not knowing how to act!

In Kenya, credibility is linked to wealth, social status, education, age, and ethnicity. Interestingly, wealth can come in the form of wives, children, cattle, or money, but wealth in itself is not the only criterion. The more credible speakers are those who have used their wealth to help others. In addition, especially in rural areas, unmarried men or a man with few children or no sons is not considered authoritative. Furthermore, in a country with forty distinct groups, ethnicity is also important. Members of certain groups have higher credibility within the country as a whole (Miller, 2002).

Your age as a speaker will probably affect your audience, either positively or negatively. Because U.S. culture celebrates youth and actively looks for fresh ideas, young people often receive as much or more attention than older speakers. In contrast, listeners in a culture that respects the wisdom and experience that come only with age may pay less attention when you are young and more attention when you are older. Consider this potential difference whenever you adapt to a culturally diverse audience.

Demonstrate Credibility in Your Speech

Demonstrated or Intrinsic Credibility
Obvious knowledge the speaker shows during the speech.

Regardless of your reputation, you must demonstrate credibility as you speak. Not surprisingly, this is called **demonstrated** or **intrinsic credibility.** Think of the student on the fencing team. If she couldn't name pieces of equipment or describe a fencing match, you would decide she was no expert. What will your audience look for as they decide whether you are credible? They will want evidence that you are knowledgeable about the subject. Consequently, it is important to do careful research and cite your sources. Define unfamiliar terminology, give examples, tell your personal experiences with the subject, and otherwise show your thorough understanding of the subject. Finally, be prepared to answer questions afterward.

Your listeners will also expect you to be calm and poised. Think of it this way: If you're agitated during a classroom presentation, your audience may wonder why you can't control yourself. In contrast, if you are poised, they will perceive you more favorably.

Take Terminal Credibility into Account

Terminal Credibility
Final impression listeners have of a speaker.

Relief! Your speech is over and you're through. But wait. Your listeners continue to evaluate you. The overall impression you leave, your **terminal credibility,** is a balance between the reputation you brought to your speech and the expertise you demonstrated as you spoke.

Terminal credibility is not permanently fixed. If your listeners eventually discover that some of your information was incorrect, they will lose confidence in you. For example, suppose one of your classmates praises the pharmaceutical product Ritalin that is used to treat attention deficit disorder (ADD). In a previous speech, she mentioned that her little brother had ADD, so she had some prior credibility for this speech. In the speech itself, she provides facts and figures that describe the prescription drug: what it is, what it does, what doctors say about it. You're impressed. A month later, a physician suggests that your cousin take Ritalin, and you do further research on the drug. You learn that your classmate's speech was clearly one-sided; she presented only the positive side of the medication. Your final impression of her credibility plummets.

Summary

You and your audiences are involved in an interactive process in which you form impressions of one another. You assess your listeners' motivations as well as demographic characteristics such as age, ethnicity, race, religion, gender, marital status, group affiliation, occupation and socioeconomic status, and region; however, you also realize that these characteristics are only salient at specific times and in specific circumstances.

Analyze also your audience's psychological profile as it relates to your topic. What do they already know or believe? How do they feel about your subject? What attitudes and underlying values influence their interest? Developing a questionnaire with various types of questions will help you identify their responses to specific aspects of your subject.

Finally, situational characteristics also affect your audience. The time of day, the length of your speech, and the noise level or temperature in the room influence their interest and attention. Do what you can to minimize environmental distractions.

Your listeners are actively evaluating you. Before your speech, they assess your reputation. During your speech, they form impressions of your credibility and your overall trustworthiness based on cultural criteria such as sound evidence, source citation, overall knowledge, and composure. After you've finished, your listeners may continue to assess your credibility, either positively or negatively.

This is one of the most important chapters in this text. As award-winning teachers know, sensitivity to a specific audience is not an option. It is essential to good speechmaking.

JAFFE ONLINE CONNECTION   JAFFE ONLINE CONNECTION

Use your CD-ROM and the Jaffe Connection Web site http://communication.wadsworth.com/jaffe to review the following concepts, answer the review questions, and complete the suggested activities.

KEY TERMS

audience analysis (72)
listening speaker (72)
pedestrian audiences (73)
passive audiences (73)
selected audiences (73)
homogeneous audiences (73)
hostile audiences (73)
concerted audiences (73)

organized audiences (73)
absent audiences (73)
demographic audience analysis (74)
salient (74)
ethnicity (74)
race (74)
racist (74)
gender (75)

sexist (75)

psychological profile (79)

beliefs (79)

attitudes (79)

scaled questions (79)

values (80)

Ethical Quality Scale (EQS) (80)

credibility (83)

prior or extrinsic credibility (84)

demonstrated or intrinsic credibility (84)

terminal credibility (84)

APPLICATION AND CRITICAL THINKING EXERCISES

1. Identify times when you have been a member of each type of audience: pedestrian, passive, voluntary, concerted, organized, and absent.

2. What occupation(s) most interest you? Think of opportunities you might have to address each type of audience listed in Exercise 1 within your chosen occupational field. Which type of audience is most common in that occupation? Which is least common?

3. Choose one of these topics, and talk with a small group of your classmates about the different ways you would develop a speech for each of the following audiences:
Topic: Your school's administrators are discussing a policy that will abolish all competitive sports on campus.

Audiences

- Your classmates
- A group of prospective students
- Alumni who are consistent donors to the school
- Basketball team members

Topic: The United States should double its foreign aid budget.

Audiences

- Senior citizens
- A high school government class
- The local chapter of the League of Women Voters

4. Log on to InfoTrac College Edition and do a PowerTrac search for the article "Marquee Speaker Adds Prestige to Engagement." Working with a small group of classmates, use information from this article to identify a speaker you'd like to invite for an imaginary event on your campus. For example, you might plan a leadership conference for high school students, an alcohol abuse workshop for dormitory residents, or a sports recognition banquet for athletes and their parents. What local, regional, or nationally known figure would make a good speaker for your event?

5. Using InfoTrac College Edition, do a PowerTrac search for the article "Teens Tuning Into Booze-branded 'Alcopop' Ads." Who was polled? What questions were asked? What audience interests and attitudes did pollsters find that you would need to consider if you were planning a speech on the topic of 'alcopop' ads targeted to new youthful customers?

6. Try to see yourself as your classmates see you. At this point in the term, what credibility do you bring to each speech? How can you demonstrate credibility in your next speech? How do you think your audience sees you after you're finished?

7. In 1981 *Washington Post* reporter Joel Garreau wrote *The Nine Nations of North America.* You can find a summary of his ideas online at
http://www.harpercollege.edu/~mhealy/g101ilec/namer/nac/nacnine/na9intro/nacninfr.htm.
Follow the link to your region and see if you agree with his description of the area in which you live. Then link to another region. How might a speaker from your region adapt to an audience in this other region?

THE JAFFE CONNECTION WEB SITE

The Jaffe Connection Web site features review questions about the Web links and InfoTrac College Edition exercises referenced throughout this chapter. You can access this site via your CD-ROM or at http://communication.wadsworth.com/jaffe.

Web Links

5.1   Ethnic and Racial Identity (page 74)
5.2   Construct a Questionnaire: Questionnaire Design (page 81)
5.3   Nine Nations of North America (page 86)

Stop and Check Activities

5.1   Analyzing Your Audience (page 78)
5.2   Construct a Questionnaire (page 81)
5.3   Do a Situational Analysis (page 83)

InfoTrac College Edition Exercises

5.1   Analyzing Your Audience: Marketing to Women (page 78)
5.2   Situational Analysis (page 82)
5.3   Prestigious Speakers (page 86)
5.4   Teen Poll About "Alcopop" (page 86)

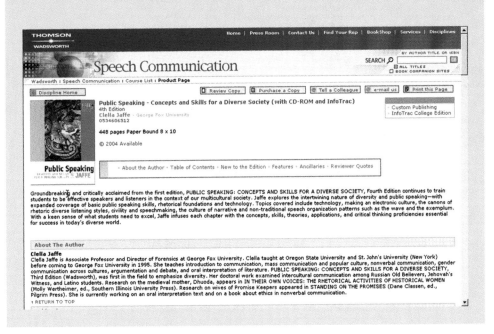

Selecting Your Topic and Purpose

THIS CHAPTER WILL HELP YOU

- Choose your speech topic
- Narrow your topic to fit the situation
- Identify both a general purpose and a specific purpose for your speech
- Write a central idea that states the main concept of your speech

Detail from "Family Life and Spirit of Mankind"
Mural ©1977 by Susan Kelk Cervantes and Judith
Knepher Jamerson. (Leonard R. Flynn School,
East Wall, Army Street at Harrison, SF, CA)

THERE ARE LITERALLY MILLIONS of topics in the world; in fact, there are so many possible subjects that selecting just one that's appropriate for a classroom speech may feel daunting. The subject can't be too broad or too complex (after all, most speeches are limited to ten minutes at the most); it should be interesting—to you as well as your audience; it should be relevant; it should be novel . . . there are numerous factors to consider.

Is there a surefire method you can use to select a topic that fits you, your audience, and the occasion? Probably not, but here are techniques that students have used:

> The way I usually come up with topics is by looking around and noting what things I see that I think are interesting. I evaluate whether or not they would make good speech topics. Also, I will take things that puzzle me or torque me off.
>
> AMY

> When I choose a topic, I analyze the parameters first: time limit, any given topic area, audience . . . then I think of something I'm interested in. If nothing comes to mind, I file the assignment in my thoughts—and often something during the day sparks an interest.
>
> JOY

> I spend a lot of time on the Internet, so I naturally go online and browse for topics. A site such as www.yahoo.com provides links to newspapers and magazines that include international and national topics, business and entertainment news. I always find several topics that interest me.
>
> TERRENCE

Regardless of method, eventually you will come up with a number of possible subjects. The key—as Amy, Joy, and Terrence point out—is to find something you are comfortable with, something that is significant enough to discuss publicly. This chapter will give you guidelines for choosing your topic, narrowing it to a manageable size, and then selecting your purpose and focus.

Choose Your Topic

Choosing a topic is generally up to you because most instructors don't assign specific subjects. You can avoid being overwhelmed at the open-endedness of your assignment by examining five areas: the significance or need to discuss possible topics, your personal interests and experiences, other courses you're taking, current events, and international and cultural subjects.

Assess Your Audience's Need to Know

Topics are everywhere. What did you eat for lunch? Who is your favorite recording artist or group? What is the traffic like in your town? Everyday topics such as these often result in interesting speeches (Christensen, 1998). However, look for a significant topic—one that needs to be discussed to bring about change, increase your audience's understanding, or highlight important cultural values and beliefs (Bitzer, 1999; Vatz, 1999). Evaluate possible topics from your audience's perspective (see Figure 6.1). What do they already know about the subject? What more do they need to know? Does it affect their finances? Their future? Their health? Will it appeal to their curiosity?

One key to keeping audience interest is to provide novelty, presenting something unfamiliar or presenting a familiar topic in a different way (McKeon, 1998). One student violated this principle and showed her audience how to make a peanut butter and jelly sandwich. (Take two slices of bread; put peanut butter on one slice and jam on the other; put them together.) She wasted her classmates' time; they'd known this recipe since kindergarten. Is her topic completely out of line? Not necessarily. Another student researched the

FIGURE 6.1 Topics range from personal to global in scope. Whatever topic you choose, always evaluate it from your listeners' perspective. They are usually interested in personal topics or in things that are relevant to their daily concerns. Take care to develop your subject in a novel way that connects to their interests.

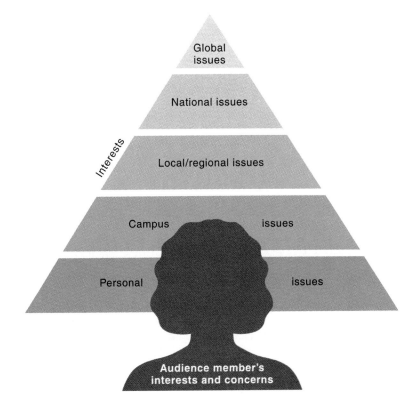

nutrients in peanuts, talked about their fat content, explained the history of peanut butter, and discussed vegetarian recipes that use peanuts. Many of his facts were novel and potentially valuable to those who were on a tight food budget.

In short, choosing a topic that meets your audience's need to know and presenting your subject in a novel way are two fundamental principles in speechmaking. When audience members already know a lot about your subject, you'll be more successful if you dig for supplementary information or select another topic that will not waste their time. (Chapter 16 discusses this in more detail.)

Consider Your Personal Interests

Generally, good public speakers are curious, and your natural curiosity can generate possible topics (Murray, 1998). What do you know and care about? What would you like to explore further? What is your major? Your occupational goals? What pets do you own? What interesting topics have you seen on television? What irritates you? What changes would you like to see in society? Here are ways some students used personal interests to create speeches:

- Paula spent a summer in Israel; she spoke about Israeli–Arab conflicts.
- Maria read a magazine article saying that lottery winners weren't always happy. You can read her speech outline on this topic at the end of Chapter 9.
- Lorinda took an art class and became fascinated with Mark Rothko's painting. She explained his life and his work.

In addition, search through your unique life experiences for subjects. You are who you are because of what you know and what you've experienced (Christensen, 1998). Draw from knowledge arising from your family background, jobs, hobbies, or recreational interests.

- Students who fought forest fires as a summer job have spoken about containment of fires.
- Josh is a drummer; he chose a particular type of drum (the African *dundun* drum) for his topic. (His outline is included in Appendix C.)
- Fadi works with the homeless; he believes they are not receiving enough attention, so he advocated increased funding for low-cost housing.

Speaking on topics that fascinate or concern you has obvious advantages. When you are truly interested in your subject, you are more enthusiastic about it. This enthusiasm often helps you concentrate on your topic rather than your insecurity as a speaker. In addition, if you appear to be bored by your topic, why should your audience be interested?

Look for Topics from Other Courses

Another good source for speech topics can come out of your major (or other) course work. For example, if you're taking anthropology, look at the table of contents in your textbook for potential topics such as marriage customs, kinship patterns, or gender differences among cultures. Giving a speech on an interesting topic from another class has the added advantage of helping you learn material for that course.

Don't hesitate to use research you have done for a paper in another course if the subject is an appropriate speech topic. To illustrate, as part of a nursing course, Jack wrote a paper on Cherokee beliefs and practices. He used some of the same material in his classroom speech on Native American medicine. Remember, however, if you adapt a paper, you must tailor the information to your particular classroom audience.

Investigate Current Events

Newspapers, newsmagazines, and television shows are good sources of appropriate topics. Skim headlines or surf Internet news sites, jotting down current issues that interest you. Major newsmagazines (*Time* and *Newsweek*, for example) are also available on InfoTrac College Edition (do a PowerTrac search for the magazine name). Also, don't overlook television program guides as a source of subjects. This list came from just one day's television schedule:

Navy SEALs	mummies	Portuguese pickled fish
Palm Beach	dog shows	solar explosions
NASCAR racing	DEA agents	male ballet dancers
driving lessons	vaudeville	1930s Paris
bullies	brainwashing	armored car robberies

Topics from current events usually address a need in society. The fact that they are important enough to discuss in the print or broadcast media means that they are significant to many people. And, because they are publicly covered, you should be able to find information easily.

Consider International and Cultural Topics

You may find it easier to think of personal (how to write a résumé) or national (terrorism) topics because these are close to our lives and they regularly appear in the news. However, don't overlook international subjects, especially if you have traveled abroad or if you were born outside the United States. Explore your own cultural heritage and experiences. For instance, someone of French ancestry could examine French attitudes toward Euro-Disney, located just outside Paris. Someone who works at McDonald's might look at varying management styles in the Japanese or British franchises. A student from India might speak about Bollywood (the Indian equivalent to Hollywood headquartered in Mumbai, formerly called Bombay). You can also peruse newspapers, magazines, and television broadcasts that regularly report on trade, global investments, or international crime, all topics of increasing importance in the twenty-first century.

Check the Internet for cultural topics. For example, you can find excellent resources on race and ethnicity at www.georgetown.edu/crossroads/asw/. Georgetown University manages this Web page, which provides links to sites for Native Americans and Americans of African, Asian, and Latino origin. A category designated "other" links you to additional information on immigration, Italian American resources, and cultural institutes for specific groups.

A word of caution: If you choose an international or cultural topic, be sure to make connections to your listeners' here-and-now concerns. For example, suppose your subject is land mines, which seems pretty far removed from your campus world. Think of ways your classmates could identify with the topic. Would they empathize with the plight of innocent villagers who lose limbs when they step on a mine? Do any listeners have friends or relatives in the military who might encounter these weapons? What about their tax dollars that finance specialists who detonate the mines? Could you tie the topic into fundamental values, such as the desire for a world at peace or for freedom and justice for all? Your challenge is to find these connections and help your audience see the relevance of your topic to their lives.

This icon depicting Holy Anna of Novgorod is located in a chapel in Eskelstuna, Sweden. A speaker from a Swedish or an Orthodox Christian background could explain the history or function of icons. An art major could describe the artistic features of icons.

Narrow Your Topic

Once you've selected a broad topic, you must narrow it sufficiently so that you can discuss it in a short classroom speech. As an example, let's consider the general topic of animals. Obviously, you can't discuss "Animals from A to Z" in seven minutes; however, you can focus on a single species, on a controversy like wearing fur, or on dangerous pets. Consider using a mind map as a way to let your ideas flow. Figure 6.2 illustrates how to start with a broad subject and narrow it to a series of more realistic classroom topics. Use your creativity to approach the topic from a personal, national, or even international level.

Careful work early in the term will produce several subjects you can use throughout the term. Let's say Figure 6.2 is Katherine's mind map.

- Her first presentation, a self-introductory narrative, relates an experience she had when she volunteered to take her dog as a therapy animal into a nursing home.
- Next, she gives an informative speech describing how to adopt a retired greyhound.
- Later, she reports on the use of hormones in beef production.
- Finally, she argues that environmental laws that protect the spotted owl have gone too far.

Three sample speeches or outlines on animal topics are included in this text: (1) "Terrestrial Pulmonate Gastropods" at the end of Chapter 12 and on the CD that accompanies the text; (2) "The Benefits of Hunting" at the end of Chapter 18; and (3) "Dolphin Communication" in Appendix C. As you can see, "animals" is a broad general topic that provides a wealth of material for specific speeches.

Figure 6.2 A mind map of topics related to animals.

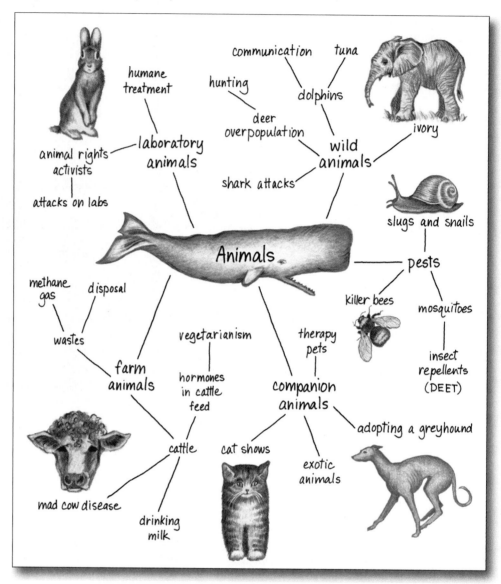

Choose Your Purpose and Focus

You don't just "accidentally" give a public speech; instead, you speak to accomplish specific goals or purposes (Scofield, 1999). Before each speech, clarify what you want to achieve by identifying your general purpose and tentatively formulating a specific purpose for that particular speech. (You will continue to refine your specific purpose as you work on your speech.) Writing out a summarizing statement helps both you and your listeners understand the central idea that you'll develop.

Identify Your General Purpose

Almost 2,000 years ago, St. Augustine (416/1958), who was a rhetoric teacher long before he was a saint, identified three purposes for speaking publicly: to teach, to please, and to move. In the eighteenth century, George Campbell (1776/1963) identified four purposes:

STOP AND CHECK

IDENTIFY SEVERAL USABLE TOPICS

Make a list of ten to fifteen major topic areas that interest you, then narrow your list to two or three. Make a mind map for each topic on your narrowed list.

If you select these general areas early, you can be alert throughout the term for information to use in your speeches. Let's say you are looking for material on eating disorders; you can scan weekly TV schedules for shows that feature the topic. You can also set up interviews with professionals as well as people who have experienced eating disorders. Because you have the topic clearly in mind, you have plenty of time to gather up-to-date materials to create a good speech.

If you begin early enough, you can create a file for each speech, photocopying or clipping articles from newspapers or magazines, taking notes on lectures, or videotaping related television programs. At speech time, you will have many resources available for a good presentation, including a number of audiovisual aids that a last-minute scramble might not produce.

to enlighten the understanding, to please the imagination, to move the passions, and to influence the will. In this century, Alan Monroe (1962) said we attempt to inform, entertain, stimulate through emotion, or convince through reasoning. Today, most speech instructors identify three **general purposes:**

- *To inform,* in which your intention is to explain, teach, describe, or provide a basis for your audience to have a greater understanding of your topic. Within the broad subject of animals, for example, you might inform your audience about killer bees, methane gas produced by farm animals, or deformities in frogs caused by environmental pollution.
- *To persuade,* in which you intend to convince or motivate your audience in some way. You might gather evidence to convince your listeners that deer hunting is beneficial to the environment or to persuade them to donate money to their local humane society.
- *To entertain,* in which you help your audience release tension through laughter by taking a humorous look at your subject. For instance, speeches on pet psychiatrists or pet wardrobes can be funny.

General Purposes
A speaker's general purpose could be to inform, to persuade, or to entertain.

These purposes often overlap. Take the case of a university recruiter. She attempts to persuade her listeners to attend the school she represents, both by informing them about the university and by entertaining them with humorous accounts of campus life. In addition, she knows that a variety of listeners calls for a blend of purposes: She entertains the alumni (and encourages donations), informs the parents or spouses about financial aid, and persuades prospective students to fill out application forms.

Classroom instructors usually assign the general purpose for your classroom speeches. For instance, if you are assigned to give an informative speech, focus your research on discovering and presenting factual material that will increase your audience's knowledge or understanding of your topic. If your assignment is to persuade, select convincing and motivating materials that will influence your listeners to believe and act in the ways you desire. (Chapter 17 details ways you can narrow your persuasive speech purposes.) If you're asked to be entertaining, choose a ridiculous event or situation and use strategies such as exaggeration and word plays to highlight humorous aspects of the topic. Although you may not be asked to give an entertaining speech in the classroom, maintaining interest rather than boring your audience will help you accomplish your other speech purposes. Figure 6.3 shows how to come up with a variety of speech purposes for a broad topic such as animals.

Figure 6.3 How to generate a number of topics about animals for different purposes.

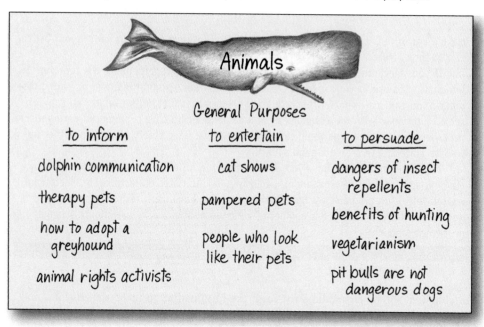

STOP AND CHECK

NARROW YOUR PURPOSE

Make a diagram similar to the one in Figure 6.3, using one of the subject-area mind maps you made for the Stop and Check exercise on page 95.

Identify Your Specific Purpose

Specific Purpose
The cognitive, affective, or behavioral responses a speaker desires.

Cognitive Effects
Influences on beliefs, understandings, and other mental processes.

Affective Effects
Influences on listeners' feelings.

Behavioral Effects
Influences on audience actions.

Jen chooses DEET, a chemical commonly used in insect repellents, for her topic. Next, she must decide exactly what she wants to accomplish with her listeners, so she begins to focus on a **specific purpose,** the response she wants from her audience. She can focus on one of three areas: thinking, feeling, or doing.

- If her intention is to guide her listeners' thoughts, she aims for **cognitive effects** that will inform their understanding or convince them to believe her claims.
- If she hopes to influence their feelings, she'll target **affective** or emotional **effects.**
- Finally, **behavioral effects** are the actions she wants audience members to perform as a result of her speech.

In short, Jen must clarify what she wants her listeners to know, feel, or do and write her goals in a specific purpose statement. She keeps the desired response in mind by using the words "my audience" within this statement, and she uses an infinitive phrase. Here are some specific purpose statements she might formulate, depending on her general speech purpose:

- To inform my audience about the chemical makeup of DEET and the way our bodies process this chemical. (Cognitive effect: The audience will know more about a common product.)
- To persuade my audience to believe that DEET is a health hazard when it is misused. (Cognitive effect: The audience will be convinced of the link between misuse of the chemical and health problems.)

- To persuade my audience to fear the misuse of DEET. (Affective effect: The audience will have an emotional response and develop a negative attitude toward misuse of these insect repellents.)
- To persuade my audience to use DEET properly and only when necessary. (Behavioral effect: The audience will be motivated to do something as a result of this speech.)

Although many instructors ask their students to begin the specific purpose with the phrase "to inform my audience," some professors prefer that their students write the specific purpose as a statement of the outcome they want to produce in their listeners—one that specifies the desired audience response:

- As a result of my speech, my audience will *know* the chemical makeup of DEET and understand how our bodies process it.
- As a result of my speech, my audience will *believe* that misusing insect repellents with DEET is potentially dangerous.
- As a result of my speech, my audience will *have a negative attitude* about misuse of DEET.
- As a result of my speech, my audience will use insect repellents that contain DEET properly and with caution.

At this stage of preparation, Jen has this much of her speech formulated:

Topic:	The dangers of DEET
General purpose:	To persuade
Specific purpose:	To persuade my audience to use insect repellents that contain DEET properly.

By formulating her general and specific purpose early, Jen can focus additional research more effectively. She will search out facts, descriptions, and explanations for most speech purposes, but especially if her goal is to inform. If she wants to prove links between DEET and health problems, Jen will need scholarly studies and opinions from experts. In addition, examples and comparisons will help her motivate her listeners to care or to act.

After you've selected both your general and specific purposes, you are ready to begin formulating one statement that captures the major idea of your speech. This is known as the central idea.

Write Your Central Idea

The **central idea** is your summary statement of the main ideas of your speech. It's as if someone were to say "Tell me in one sentence what you're going to speak about. No details,

Central Idea
A single-sentence summary of the main idea of the speech.

Within a broad topic such as animals, you can find many suitable subtopics for classroom speeches. Insect repellents, dolphin communication, and adopting greyhounds that have finished their racing careers are three examples.

© Pictor International/Pictor International, Ltd./PictureQuest

just the bottom line. A complete sentence, not a question." The single-sentence digest or abstract you come up with is your central idea; it is also called the core idea, subject sentence, residual message or, for English essays, the thesis statement. This sentence states what you want your audience to remember after your speech is over. The following guidelines will help you formulate your central idea more effectively:

Write a single declarative sentence

> that makes a statement about the subject matter and

> > summarizes the content of the speech

> > > in a reasonable, simple manner

> > > > that is precise enough to guide you and your audience. (Engnell, 1999)

Notice, for example, the contrast between these correctly and incorrectly written central ideas:

Correct: DEET, a chemical compound that is found in insect repellents, is dangerous when it is misused, but carefully following directions can prevent serious health problems.

Incorrect: Why should you use insect repellent with caution? (This is a question, not a declarative sentence.)

Incorrect: We must first define what DEET is. Then we will find out why Americans have overlooked DEET's damaging effects. Finally, we will look at ways you can protect yourself when using DEET-based insect repellents. (The rule is one sentence, not three.)

Incorrect: Why you should be careful about using DEET-based insect repellents. (This is a fragment rather than a complete sentence.)

Begin to formulate your central idea as soon as you've selected your topic and decided on your general and specific purposes. Then allow yourself plenty of time to explore and develop your thesis—the approach, the slant, the point of view you'll develop, the general direction you'll take (Griffin, 1998). The process of invention takes time and energy; new ideas will emerge and others will seem less important, so don't be afraid to revise your direction as you do additional research, preparation, and organization. As this student explains:

> I tend to have running dialogues in my head, sometimes even out loud. While I talk to myself, I work out particulars. I answer questions I've posed to myself ("Well, really, Gail, if you argue that, where will you go? It's too huge!" or "Now does that really make sense?"). My answers often lead me to modify my central idea as I continue my preparation.
>
> GAIL

Here are some additional examples from student speeches that show the relationship between topic, general purpose, specific purpose, and central idea.

Topic:	Dolphin communication
General purpose:	To inform
Specific purpose:	To inform my audience about studies in the area of dolphin–dolphin and human–dolphin communication.
Central idea:	Dolphins are intelligent creatures who communicate with other dolphins and with human researchers.

(A complete outline of this speech is included in Appendix C.)

Topic:	Medical misinformation on the Internet
General purpose:	To persuade
Specific purpose:	To persuade my audience that medical misinformation on the Internet is a problem that can be solved if we take three corrective steps.

Central idea: Medical misinformation is rampant on the Internet, but a code of conduct for Web sites, government regulations, and personal action can protect consumers.

(This speech outline appears at the end of Chapter 7.)

Topic: Sleep deprivation
General purpose: To persuade
Specific purpose: To persuade my audience that sleep deprivation is a national problem that can be solved through personal and societal effort.
Central idea: Sleep deprivation, which has several causes, affects millions of Americans every day; society can help, but most of the solutions are personal.

(An outline of this speech appears in Appendix C.)

DIVERSITY IN PRACTICE
DOES REQUIRING ONE SPEECH ON "COMMUNICATION AND CULTURE" INCREASE STUDENTS' EMPATHY?

LORI CARRELL (1997) reported the results of research done in a medium-sized Midwestern university. The goal of the study was to determine if student *empathy,* or the ability to take diverse perspectives, increased when diversity issues became part of the course. Underlying the research was the assumption that competent communicators are those who can view issues from multiple perspectives. Four groups participated in the study: a control group had no special treatment; another group took an entire course in intercultural communication; another discussed concepts related to diversity at several points during the term; finally, another group had a one-shot assignment to give a public speech on a "communication and diversity" topic.

The results indicated that students who studied intercultural communication for a whole term significantly increased in empathy. Those who discussed diversity issues often throughout the semester also increased in empathy. However, students who gave only one diversity speech had no significant gains in empathy.

What does this mean to you? How might an increase in empathy make you a more competent communicator? What connections can you see between the ability to take a variety of perspectives and the diversity concepts presented in this text and in your classroom? How might your topic choices make you more sensitive to issues of diversity?

In the speech itself, usually in your introduction, state or paraphrase your central idea. This prepares your audience for what you are going to talk about and guides them as they listen. See how these students incorporated their central idea in the introduction of their speeches to inform their audiences directly of their purpose for speaking:

- Today, I will explain the concept of dolphin intelligence, dolphin-to-dolphin communication, and dolphin communication with humans.
- Today we will explore the dangers associated with medical misinformation on the Internet. First, as consumers we would be wise to know where incorrect medical information has been found. Second, we'll see why there is so much misinformation on the net. And, finally, we will all learn what we must do to avoid being misled when using medical information gained online.
- We must first wake up to some of the alarming effects of sleep debts, then we can open our eyes to better understand their causes, and finally cozy up to some solutions at both the personal and the societal levels.

Here are two additional central idea statements. The CD that comes with this text shows how both speakers actually worded their statements when they delivered their speeches.

- Prescription drug advertisements are often deceptive, and this has negative effects on consumers, but you can take steps to protect yourself. (Damien Beasley)

Cultural amnesia, which results from a lack of knowledge and overall ignorance, is widespread; this can have negative effects on our freedoms and democratic values but we can work nationally and individually to solve this problem. (Amy Zavala)

In summary, topic and purpose selection are obviously important aspects of speech-making; however, this process can be frustrating. You can focus your preparation more effectively if you select a subject that interests you, narrow it to a manageable subtopic, formulate general and specific speech purposes, then summarize your main concepts in a central idea or thesis statement that you want your audience to remember after your speech.

BUILD YOUR SPEECH
GENERAL PURPOSE, SPECIFIC PURPOSE, AND CENTRAL IDEA

Choose three topics from this list (or select three topics that you can talk about without doing much research). Write out the general purpose, a specific purpose statement, and the central idea for an impromptu speech about each topic.
- Online shopping
- Stress relievers for college students
- Simple breakfasts
- Free things to do in our community
- Going to the movies
- Exercising regularly
- Study tips

Access Speech Builder Express to record a general purpose, specific purpose, and central idea for your own speech assignments.

Summary

As you begin the process of choosing a speech topic, look for one dealing with something your audience needs to know. Then, examine your personal experiences, other course work, current events, and international stories for subjects that will contribute to your listeners' knowledge. Be sure to find a topic that interests you! By doing careful work early in the term, you can produce a list, or a series of files, on topics that will interest both you and your listeners.

After selecting your topic, focus on your intention or major purpose for the speech. Then, write the specific purpose that names the response you want from your listeners. The central idea comes next. This single sentence summarizes the major content of your speech in a way that guides both you and your listeners. Begin to formulate your central idea early in the speech, but be willing to revise it as you proceed in your research.

JAFFE ONLINE CONNECTION **JAFFE ONLINE CONNECTION**

Use your CD-ROM and the Jaffe Connection Web site http://communication.wadsworth.com/jaffe to review the following concepts, answer the review questions, and complete the suggested activities.

KEY TERMS

general purpose (95)	affective effects (96)
specific purpose (96)	behavioral effects (96)
cognitive effects (96)	central idea (97)

APPLICATION AND CRITICAL THINKING EXERCISES

1. Design a mind map on the general topic of education after high school.
2. Work with a small group of your classmates to create a mind map based on a very general international topic such as Japan, world trade, ethnic wars, or the United Nations. Use a blank transparency or a large piece of paper to record your ideas; then display your mind map for the entire class.
3. Use InfoTrac College Edition to look up information about humor in speeches. Do a PowerTrac search for author Brian Wiersema, and read his article on the use of humor in business speeches. What benefits does he say humor has in the business context? How might you incorporate humor in your speeches?

4. Discuss in a small group ways you could add the element of novelty to the following common topics: seatbelts, tea, television, weddings.
5. The Web site www.schoolelection.com/persuasive/speechtopics.htm lists 850 subjects that high school students identified as the best informative and persuasive topics they'd heard. Skim through these lists and identify five topics in each list that would be appropriate for college or university students, and five that are clearly high school level subjects.
6. For additional information on St. Augustine, one of the great figures of rhetoric, go to www.lcc.gatech.edu/gallery/rhetoric/figures/Augustine.html and read the section "Augustine on Rhetoric." This advice was given seventeen centuries ago. Which principles still apply?

THE JAFFE CONNECTION WEB SITE

The Jaffe Connection Web site features review questions about the Web links, Stop and Check activities, and InfoTrac College Edition exercises referenced throughout the chapter. You can access this site via your CD-ROM or at http://communication.wadsworth.com/jaffe.

Web Links

6.1 Browsing for Topics (page 90)
6.2 Race and Ethnicity (page 93)
6.3 Topics Listed by High School Students (page 101)
6.4 St. Augustine on Rhetoric (page 101)

Stop and Check Activities

6.1 Identify Several Usable Topics (page 95)
6.2 Narrow Your Purpose (page 96)

InfoTrac College Edition Exercises

6.1 Newsmagazines (page 92)
6.2 Using Humor in Speeches (page 101)

Build Your Speech Featuring Speech Builder Express

6.1 General Purpose, Specific Purpose, and Central Idea (page 100)

SPEECH INTERACTIVE ON THE JAFFE CONNECTION CD-ROM

Using your Jaffe Connection CD-ROM, watch and listen to Damien Beasley and Amy Zavala deliver their central ideas (pages 99 and 100 of this chapter). Watch and listen to any of the other informative or persuasive speeches included under Speech Interactive. Can you identify the speaker's central idea?

Researching Your Speech in an Electronic Culture

THIS CHAPTER WILL HELP YOU

■ Plan your research

■ Distinguish between primary and secondary sources

■ Gather oral, print, and electronically stored resources effectively

■ Include ethnic and international sources in your research

■ Use the Internet critically

■ Record your information in a way that is suited to your learning style

"Time After Time" Mural ©1995 by Betsie Miller-Kusz.
(Collingwood Street near 19th Street, SF, CA)

MBER'S TOPIC WAS HEPATITIS C; Krista chose the Electoral College; Kaliope decided to speak about television violence. However, none of these students was an "expert" on her topic. They all faced the challenge you face—once you have selected and narrowed your topic, you must gather information to support your ideas.

Gathering effective supporting materials is part of the canon the Romans called "invention." It combines several skills that contribute to your developing competence in speechmaking. As you select materials for use in your speech, you must:

- Know how to find the data you need to support your ideas
- Formulate a research plan
- Critically evaluate sources and choose the best materials available
- Record your findings in a systematic way

This chapter presents information on the research process, with the goal of helping you accomplish these four major tasks effectively.

Gather Materials for Your Speech

To gain a variety of perspectives about your subject, instructors usually ask you to consult from three to seven sources, including both primary and secondary materials. You should be able to find oral, print, and electronic data easily; however, selecting the *best* information requires you to use your critical thinking skills throughout. This section will discuss effective ways to plan, conduct, and evaluate your research.

Plan Your Research

Reference Librarian
Library specialist whose job is to help you find research information.

Laurie Lieggi, a **reference librarian** at George Fox University, says students often wait until the last minute, thinking they can pop into the library once, spend a couple of hours in attack mode, get speech materials that are easy to find, and leave—choosing to be satisfied with whatever they can find immediately (personal interview, July 20, 1999). Many go to the Internet first, and, because it's convenient, want to use it exclusively. Lieggi likened this type of research to eating at fast food restaurants. Fast food alone fails to provide the nutrients, variety, and quality of meals you carefully prepare at home.

Consult a reference librarian if you need help during any stage of your research.

You will use your research time more wisely if you sit down and plan a search strategy, even before you head to the library. The following tips will help you:

- *Budget enough time.* Good research is time consuming, and if you think you'll get wonderful, usable information in one short session, you will be disappointed. Consequently, on your calendar, set aside more than one block of time for research.
- *Get to know your library.* Because each library is different, visit or tour the one you will use the most. Also, consult the how-to pamphlets and brochures your campus librarians have prepared to explain specific features available in your library.
- *Include a librarian in your research plan.* Librarians are paid to assist you; be sure to consult them when you need help. Laurie said, "I'm a reference librarian because I want to be available to students. That's what I enjoy. Every question is a puzzle, and I get to help a student solve a puzzle." Besides, who knows your campus library better than the people who work there daily? In larger academic libraries, **subject librarians** have a library degree plus an advanced degree in another discipline.
- *Let your topic guide your research.* This chapter suggests a number of research sources, but you may not need them all in a single speech. Instead, identify the best sources for your particular subject. For instance, if you're speaking about a current event, include a nightly network or cable news program in your plan. For a speech on pet overpopulation, consider an interview with the head of your local humane society. For a speech about whitewater rafting, helpful resources might include personal experiences, books, articles in sports magazines, and Internet Web sites.
- *Identify key terms to use when you search computerized catalogs, databases, or the Internet.* Think creatively, consult a librarian, or find the Library of Congress Subject Headings in the reference section of the library. For example, Marcus searched for "disabled" and "housing" with little success until his librarian suggested he use the word "handicapped." Then he found all the information he needed (which shows that headings are not always current in usage). Subject terms can be highly specific. For example, to find material on the Civil War, type in "United States—History—1861–1865—battles." If you start with the more general term (civil war), you'll end up with sources about civil wars in ancient Greece, nineteenth-century Bolivia, and today's Congo. Many online databases have browse, thesaurus, or index features that can help you identify specific key terms.
- *Identify experts in the field (if known).* You'll save some research time if you know the names of recognized experts on your topic. Search for these names in the library's resources under "authors," or try to work an interview with a campus expert into your plan.
- *Make critical evaluation a part of your plan from the outset.* So many resources are available nowadays that you might feel you're drowning in data—some highly credible, some very questionable. Find out as much as you can about every source you use, whether book, article, Web site, or personal interview. Then compare sources. Some will be OK, some pretty good, and some excellent. Choose the best.
- *Keep a running list of all your sources as you search.* This way, you can easily assemble your final bibliography and return to a source if necessary. If you are using the Internet, create a directory for your bookmarks if your computer has that feature.
- *Plan to use a variety of sources.* Remember the fast food analogy? You wouldn't eat only Big Macs, so don't expect to use only the Internet or newspapers or encyclopedias or any other credible source. Strive to find diverse perspectives so you can approach the topic from a number of viewpoints.

This is not an exhaustive planning list, but using these tips will help you focus your search more effectively. The rest of the chapter will guide you in carrying out your overall plan.

Subject Librarian
Librarians who are specialists in a particular subject such as law or medicine; they may have an advanced degree in the subject.

STOP AND CHECK
BEGIN YOUR RESEARCH PLAN

THOMSON	Home | Press Room | Contact Us | Find Your Rep | BookShop | Services | Disciplines
WADSWORTH	

7. Researching Your Speech in an Electronic ...

Book Info
Companion Sites
Discipline Home

CHAPTER RESOURCES   Wadsworth : Companion Website   🔒 INSTRUCTOR RESOURCES   NEED A PASSWORD?

Chapter 7
Activity
Hot Content
Infotrac Exercises
Preparation Form
Tutorial Quiz

[Back]

COURSE RESOURCES
About the Author(s)
Communication Links
Documentation
Glossary
Handbook
Infotrac Exercises
PRCA-24 Survey
PRPSA Survey
Research
Sample Chapters
Student Center
Visual Overview Demo
Careers
Communication Links
Events

ANCILLARIES
Book Supplements

Preparation Form:
    Your Research Plan

Name: _____ Date: _____

                            My Research Plan

A. General topic: _____

B. Narrowed topic: _____

C. General purpose: _____

D. Specific purpose: _____

E. Tentative central idea: _____

F. Budgeted time: (day) _____ (time) from _____ to _____ (place) _____
                      (day) _____ (time) from _____ to _____ (place) _____
                      (day) _____ (time) from _____ to _____ (place) _____

Web Site

Before you even go into the library, use the research plan illustrated here, filling in sections A to G, to begin creating your research plan. Then read the rest of this chapter to identify and evaluate the best type of material for your specific topic. Additional Stop and Check activities in this chapter will help you refine your research strategies.

    The research plan is available online under Stop and Check Activities for Chapter 7 on the Jaffe Connection Web site.

Distinguish Between Primary and Secondary Sources

Primary sources are created by individuals and groups who are directly involved in events at the time they take place. You'll find primary sources in several categories. **Original documents,** such as letters, interviews, news footage, and minutes of meetings, were written or created by insiders who were personally involved in events. **Creative works** include books, paintings, poems, and dance performances. **Relics** or **artifacts** are cultural objects such as jewelry, tools, buildings, clothing, and other created items.

    Secondary sources are a step away from the actual persons or events under study, produced by nonparticipants who summarize and interpret the original reports. Although they may have been created when the events occurred, they can also appear months, decades, even centuries later. Examples include history books, critical reviews of artistic performances, and scholarly articles.

    As you do research, distinguish between primary and secondary sources. Although both are useful, you can appreciate the difference between a participant's account and an outsider's summary or interpretation of the same event. You can use personal experiences as well as three basic means to gather both primary and secondary materials:

- Collect information from oral interviews with both primary and secondary sources.
- Discover speech materials in print.
- Find data through media channels.

Primary Sources
Information from people actually involved in the event.
Original Documents
Letters, news footage, minutes of a meeting, and other evidence recorded by a primary source.
Creative Works
Poems, dances, paintings, writings, and other aesthetic creations.
Relics or Artifacts
Culturally significant creations such as buildings, jewelry, or tools.
Secondary Sources
Information provided by nonparticipants who summarize and interpret events or people.

You can conduct a face-to-face interview, or you can tune into televised interviews conducted with experts as well as laypeople.

Draw from Your Personal Experiences

You have probably chosen your topic because it relates in some way to your own interests and experiences. Don't overlook your personal experiences; instead, examine your connection with the topic for usable information. For demonstration or how-to speeches, your personal expertise may make you more believable. Students have also worked their experiences into speeches on immigration, Ritalin, bee keeping, cartooning, arranged marriages, and so on.

Consider Oral Sources

When you get information in direct, face-to-face interactions, you are consulting **oral sources,** whether in a one-on-one interview or a one-to-many lecture. To record this information, use written notes, audiotapes, or videotapes.

Oral Sources
Direct face-to-face informants.

Interview a Knowledgeable Person

Well-planned interviews can help you clarify confusing ideas by questioning people who know your subject firsthand. **Experts** are people whose study, experience, or occupation makes them knowledgeable. For example, to update this chapter, I interviewed a reference librarian; my students have interviewed chiropractors, police officers, construction workers, and other professionals. You can also interview a **layperson** or **peer**—someone who has gained insights and formulated opinions through ordinary living. I could have interviewed students who have learned to use library research tools effectively. Their insights, though not scholarly, often contain practical wisdom.

Expert
Person whose knowledge is based on research, experience, or occupation.

Laypeople or Peers
Ordinary people whose knowledge comes from normal, everyday experience.

Most potential interviewees have full schedules, and they're doing you a favor when they agree to be interviewed, so consider these factors:

- *Give your interviewee an idea of your speech topic and the kind of information you need.* This is especially important if you are interviewing non-native English speakers. To think through and prepare their answers, these interviewees may want you to submit written questions before you meet.
- *Be conscious of the time.* When you make the appointment, estimate the length of time it will take, then respect those limits! Although different cultural groups have different norms regarding punctuality, arrive on time. If anyone is late, let it be your interviewee. If you absolutely can't keep your appointment, give the person as much notice as possible.

● *Prepare in advance.* Write out your questions so you will remember everything you want to ask. (Written questions also keep the interview focused.)

● *Take careful notes.* Make sure you've understood correctly by reading your notes back to the interviewee, who can then make corrections or additions. Ask questions such as "Is this what you mean?" or "Did I understand you correctly when you said . . . ?"

● *Aim to understand your topic from your interviewee's perspective.* If you interview people whose ideas and actions clash with yours, practice civility. Listen politely, and try to understand how they came to believe or behave the way they do.

● *If you want to tape the interview, ask for permission* in advance, and place the recorder in full view.

When you cannot meet in person, consider a telephone interview, following the same guidelines regarding questions, advance preparation, and punctuality. Technology stretches our concepts of interviewing. Email, for instance, allows you to contact a source directly in a question-and-answer format similar to an interview. In fact, thousands of experts permit Web sites such as **www.askanexpert.com** to list their email addresses because they want to share their knowledge in hundreds of areas (Rodrigues & Rodrigues, 2000). In addition, you can regularly see or hear interviews on cable stations, on news programs, and over radio. Some shows even allow you to call or fax your questions to the expert.

Attend Lectures and Oral Performances

Don't overlook lectures or oral performances such as poetry readings as sources. The key is to take careful notes or use a tape recorder—with advanced permission, of course. (Some well-known lecturers are syndicated and their contracts prevent you from recording them; fortunately, they often sell tapes of their most popular lectures.) Again, through electronic means such as television or videotapes you can "attend" lectures or performances; camera close-ups may even give you the feeling of having a front-row seat.

To investigate this topic further, log on to InfoTrac College Edition and perform a PowerTrac search for the article "Top-Notch Interviews." Read the author's ten tips and identify specific things you might incorporate in your interviews.

STOP AND CHECK

REVISIT YOUR RESEARCH PLAN

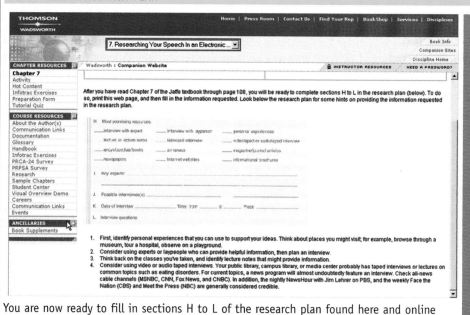

Web Site

You are now ready to fill in sections H to L of the research plan found here and online under Stop and Check Activities for Chapter 7 on the Jaffe Connection Web site.

1. First, identify personal experiences that you can use to support your ideas. Think about places you might visit; for example, a museum, a hospital, a playground.
2. Consider using experts or laypeople for helpful information; plan an interview.
3. Think back on the classes you've taken, and identify lecture notes that might provide information.
4. Consider using video- or audiotaped interviews. Your public library, campus library, or media center probably has taped interviews or lectures on common topics such as eating disorders. For current topics, a news program will almost undoubtedly feature an interview. Check all-news cable channels (MSNBC, CNN, Fox News, and CNBC). In addition, the nightly *NewsHour with Jim Lehrer* on PBS, and the weekly *Face the Nation* (CBS) and *Meet the Press* (NBC) are generally considered credible.

Use the Library

Libraries contain a variety of materials including printed matter, pictures, maps, videotapes, and audio recordings. These materials have academic credibility because of the number of screenings they undergo before they are acquired. Book publishers employ editors and reviewers to validate each manuscript. Magazine and newspaper editors screen articles and hire fact checkers to correct errors. However, library materials still require critical evaluation. You'd expect to find opinions on editorial pages and in syndicated columns, but you must also watch for unsupported statements wherever they may be. Also, specific publications have a bias, which is sometimes stated forthrightly: the *New Republic* proclaims its liberal bias, and the *National Review* proudly labels itself conservative. Other publications and books have an unstated bias that you must discern. For example, newspapers and book publishers tend to emphasize certain subjects or perspectives more than others. This is one reason your instructor asks you to consult several sources.

Almost all college libraries have converted to online computerized programs to help you locate information quickly and easily (American Library Association, 1999). If you have not done so already, spend some time becoming familiar with your own library's cataloging system. The research principles discussed next are similar for libraries with card catalogs and those with computerized systems.

DIVERSITY IN PRACTICE
RESEARCH IN KENYA

DIFFERENT CULTURAL GROUPS have different traditions regarding research. For instance, Kenyan students described typical speech preparation in their culture:

- "Audiences in the African context do not expect researched and memorized speeches, but speeches compiled spontaneously and using the speaker's wisdom."
- "Public speaking in Africa is not . . . something that someone will spend a week researching."
- "In the African context there are less rules to follow, or at least the emphasis is not as much as it is in the West." (Miller, 2002, p. 174)

Kenyan students, however, noted that research and preparation is becoming more common in their country.

Even within the United States, the type of research described in this chapter is not required for every speech. (Examples include the narrative speeches described in Chapter 15 and the special occasion speeches described in Appendix B.)

Books

Each library book is cataloged in several ways, by subject, author, title, and key words. For example, Sally McClain's book about the Navajo Code Talkers is found under the author, McClain, Sally; under the title, *Navajo Weapon: The Navajo Code Talkers;* and under the subject, Native Americans, Navajo. Key words include *Navajo* and *Code Talkers* and *encryption.*

Look carefully at the copyright date that appears in the front of the book and in the catalog information. For topics such as bicycle helmets or breast cancer treatments, up-to-date materials are essential. However, some subjects—*honesty,* for example—draw from philosophical, religious, and cultural traditions that go back thousands of years, and books written in 1910 may still be credible.

The Reference Section

What was the murder rate in New York City in 2000? Who were the signers of the Declaration of Independence? When was the Taj Mahal built? To help you find specific information quickly, your library contains hundreds of reference works including encyclopedias, dictionaries, and sources for statistics.

General Encyclopedias
Collect and summarize information on a wide array of topics.

Encyclopedias   **General encyclopedias,** such as the *Encyclopedia Americana* and *Collier's Encyclopedia,* collect and summarize information on thousands of topics. They provide a helpful overview of your topic early in your research. The *Encyclopedia Britannica* is especially useful for international topics. An encyclopedia's index can often guide you to several related subjects, and the bibliography at the end of each article suggests other sources of information. Many encyclopedias are available online, some for a fee; however, many libraries pay the fees so that you can find information without charge.

Specialized Encyclopedias
Summarize information in specific subject areas.

In addition to general encyclopedias, the reference section includes **specialized encyclopedias** that provide information on specific subject areas. If you want to know about a particular bird, look in the *Encyclopedia of Birds.* Psychological depression? There is a whole encyclopedia on that topic alone. How about the *Encyclopedia of Computer Software,* or one on architecture? These are all available. Use your judgment in evaluating the publication date. The encyclopedia about computer software is rapidly outdated, whereas the one about birds remains useful for many years.

Encyclopedias are also available on CDs or loaded onto personal computers. Microsoft *Encarta* and *Compton's Multimedia Encyclopedia* are but two examples. These electronic encyclopedias contain sound clips, speeches, movie segments, and thousands of visuals.

Dictionary
Provides definitions and other information about words or terms.

Dictionaries   The most familiar type of **dictionary** provides definitions, historical sources, synonyms, and antonyms for words. However, you can find specialized dictionaries in the reference section, including ones devoted only to pianists, to psychotherapy, or to American slang. If your computer's software program has a built-in dictionary, simply type in a word and the definition and pronunciation will appear on your monitor.

Sources for Statistics   Consult the *Statistical Abstracts of the United States* (a government document) for U.S. statistics on a variety of topics including population, health, education, crime, government finance, employment, elections, the environment, and defense. This book shows historical trends as well as current statistics. In addition, almanacs such as the *World Almanac* provide statistical information.

Online Reference Materials   You can access thousands of reference materials online. Here are a few suggestions:

- Use the "references" category at www.yahoo.com to link to encyclopedias, dictionaries, books of quotations, and statistical sources.
- You can get to Webster's Dictionary's Web site by typing in /www.m-w.com/dictionary or try www.bartleby.com for the American Heritage Dictionary.

- You might want to bookmark www.refdesk.com, an amazing site that provides links to hundreds of additional reference materials. (My students often thank me for introducing them to this site.)
- If you're looking for statistics, try the site that advertises itself as the "gateway to over 100 United States Federal agencies," www.fedstats.gov.
- For information on national or global populations, access the U.S. Census Bureau's site at www.census.gov. This user-friendly, reliable site records each new birth automatically; consequently, population figures change regularly (Hawkes, 1999).

© Wadsworth–Thomson Learning

Periodicals

Periodicals are issued once during a period of time—weekly, monthly, quarterly, or annually. They range from popular or general interest magazines like *Time, Sports Illustrated*, and *MacLean's* (Canada) to more specialized periodicals such as *Hiker's World* or *Vital Speeches of the Day*. Popular magazines are easy to understand and have contemporary examples, up-to-date statistics, illustrations, and quotations from both experts and laypeople.

In addition, libraries also house **trade** and **professional journals,** such as the *Quarterly Journal of Speech*, which contain topics of interest to specific occupations and the research findings of scholars writing in academic areas. Some of these articles may be too technical for classroom speeches; others, however, provide excellent materials.

You'll find current issues on file and older issues archived, often on microfiche or microfilm. These two storage devices require that you use specialized machines, usually having a print capability so that you can copy articles you need. Currently, most major magazines and many scholarly journals are on the Internet, and you can easily download and print a hard copy of articles that you need. InfoTrac College Edition contains hundreds of magazines and journals (Figure 7.1).

> Library books, magazines, and newspapers have a measure of academic respectability because of the selection process they undergo before they appear on the shelves.

Periodicals
Magazines or journals issued at regular intervals.

Trade or Professional Journals
Journals that pertain to specific occupations or areas of academic research.

Congressional Digest: The Pro and Con Monthly

Look at this periodical if you are researching a controversial topic. The *Congressional Digest* is an independent storehouse of information that represents multiple viewpoints. Each issue examines a single topic (affirmative action, farm policy, environmental protection) being discussed in Congress. For instance, a recent issue covers bankruptcy reform and examines the interests of both debtors and creditors. You will find a timeline of bankruptcy legislation and recent congressional actions. A glossary of terms, an overview of the issue, the current bankruptcy code, and directions to helpful Internet sites precede a presentation of pro and con arguments made by members of Congress.

An annual index presents titles (for example, *Drunk Driving: Setting National Standards*) and subjects (health care, statehood proposals, foreign relations) from 1921 to the present. More helpful are the detailed tables of contents for topics covered from 1981 to the present. When you need to understand both sides of an issue, save valuable time and check this source early.

Newspapers

Newspapers generally cover current events in greater depth than radio or television news broadcasts. You'll find reports on current issues and events, along with opinion pieces by editors, syndicated columnists, and readers who submit letters to the editor. Many newspapers also print humorous articles, obituaries, human interest pieces, and critical evaluations of movies, plays, books, art exhibits, and musical performances.

FIGURE 7.1 InfoTrac College Edition has thousands of articles, updated continually. Use the password that accompanied a new copy of this text to access this database.

SOURCE: InfoTrac College Edition © Gale Group.

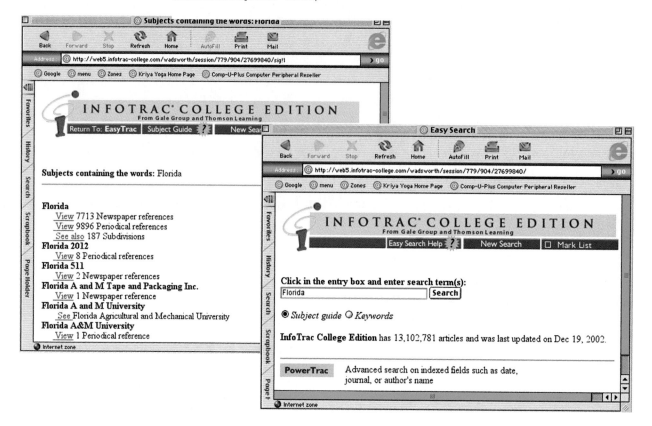

Daily, weekly, and monthly newspapers range in size from metropolitan papers with international circulation to small student papers. Some are specifically targeted toward various cultural and ethnic groups (see the Diversity in Practice box for more on this). A few are dubbed the "elite media" because they are known for high-quality, detailed reporting, and papers with smaller circulation often use their stories. Three major newspapers in this category are the *New York Times*, the *Washington Post*, and the *Los Angeles Times*. Most school libraries carry at least one of these elite papers, and all are available over the Internet. If you don't regularly read such a paper, you might want to compare one day's edition with the same day's local newspaper.

The *New York Times* is an excellent source of primary documents because it reprints a number of them in part or in whole. Consequently, if you want to read the text of the president's inaugural address, you can find it in its entirety in the *Times*. You will also find excerpts of testimony given at Senate hearings, presidential remarks made at press conferences, and majority and dissenting opinions on significant Supreme Court decisions.

Indexes

An easy way to locate articles from scholarly journals, popular magazines, and newspapers is to use indexes. Look in reference books or in computerized databases that index journals; the *ERIC* index for the field of education is one example. The *Readers' Guide to Periodical Literature* is invaluable for locating articles in popular magazines from 1900 to the present; its editors list each article in alphabetical order by subject, author, and title. Also indexed

DIVERSITY IN PRACTICE

INTERNATIONAL AND ETHNIC PRESSES

Netscape: Newspapers US and Worldwide - refdesk.com

Location: http://www.refdesk.com/paper.html   What's Related

refdesk.com

NEWSPAPERS - USA AND WORLDWIDE
Wed, Dec 18, 2002
DISCLAIMER

United States Newspapers by State

National	Idaho	Missouri	Pennsylvania
Alabama	Illinois	Montana	Rhode Island
Alaska	Indiana	Nebraska	South Carolina
Arizona	Iowa	Nevada	South Dakota
Arkansas	Kansas	New Hampshire	Tennessee
California	Kentucky	New Jersey	Texas
Colorado	Louisiana	New Mexico	Utah
Connecticut	Maine	New York	Virginia
Dist. of Columbia	Maryland	North Carolina	Vermont
Delaware	Massachusetts	North Dakota	Washington
Florida	Michigan	Ohio	West Virginia
Georgia	Minnesota	Oklahoma	Wisconsin
Hawaii	Mississippi	Oregon	Wyoming

U.S. News Archives
Searchable Newspaper Archives

WORLD NEWSPAPERS

AFRICA
Algeria | Benin | Egypt | Ethiopia | Ghana | Guinea | Ivory Coast | Kenya | Liberia | Madagascar | Mauritius | Morocco | Namibia | Nigeria | Reunion Island |
Seychelles | Senegal | South Africa | Swaziland | Tanzania | Tunisia | Uganda | Zambia | Zimbabwe |

ASIA
Bangladesh | Bhutan | Brunei | Cambodia | China | India | Indonesia | Japan | Kazakhstan | Laos | Macau | Malaysia | Maldives | Mongolia | Nepal | North Korea |
Pakistan | Philippines | Saudi Arabia | Singapore | South Korea | Sri Lanka | Taiwan | Thailand | Uzbekistan | Vietnam |

CARIBBEAN
Antigua and Barbuda | Bahamas | Barbados | Bermuda | British Virgin Islands | Cuba | Dominican Republic | Grenada | Haiti | Jamaica | Netherlands Antilles |
Puerto Rico | Trinidad and Tobago | Virgin Islands |

CENTRAL AMERICA
Belize | Costa Rica | El Salvador | Guatemala | Honduras | Nicaragua | Panama |

EUROPE
Albania | Andorra | Austria | Belarus | Belgium | Bosnia-Herzegovina | Bulgaria | Croatia | Cyprus | Czech Republic | Denmark | Estonia | Finland | France |
Georgia | Germany | Gibraltar | Greece | Hungary | Iceland | Ireland | Italy | Latvia | Liechtenstein | Lithuania | Luxembourg | Macedonia | Malta | Moldova | Netherlands |
Norway | Poland | Portugal | Romania | Russia | Scotland | Slovakia | Slovenia | Spain | Sweden | Switzerland | Turkey | Ukraine | United Kingdom | Yugoslavia |

MANY LIBRARIES carry newspapers from around the world. Consulting one or more of these papers allows you to gain different perspectives, to hear voices other than those you will find in local or national sources. Many of these papers are also on the Internet. Check out the *World Press Review,* a monthly magazine that prints excerpts of translated materials from international papers; its editors identify the bias of the source, whether conservative, liberal, or moderate.

Also search out materials representing diverse perspectives within the United States. Organized labor, African Americans, gays and lesbians, Catholics, and Muslims, to name a few, all publish periodicals that reflect their interests and perspectives. If your library doesn't subscribe to periodicals you need, look for them online. The Internet search engine www.yahoo.com provides links to more than 8,000 newspapers and magazines, including alternative, regional, and international periodicals. Or go to InfoTrac College Edition's log on page and click on the list of journal names this resource provides; you'll find a wide variety of diverse perspectives there.

are broad topics with a number of subheadings, as this sample entry found under *Medicinal Plants* demonstrates:

Botany, Medical

   Weeds for wellness [medicinal weeds used by the Mayans] C. Hardman, il *Américas* v 54 no3 p4-5 My/Je 2002.

Each entry gives the title, author's name, magazine, volume, and page number. The il indicates that the story is illustrated.

To use a computerized index, type in key words. You should get a number of hits; many will have an *abstract* (brief summary) that helps you decide which are worth looking up. For example, while researching his speech on the Promise Keepers (men who join together publicly to pledge that they will be faithful husbands and fathers), Diego typed in both "Promise Keepers" and "Men's Movement." He skimmed abstracts from more than twenty articles, marked those that seemed suitable, printed the references he'd marked, then went directly to the magazines and journals to read the articles.

Major newspapers also provide tools to help you locate specific articles. For instance, the *New York Times Index* provides the date, page, and column location of almost every news article that has appeared in its pages since 1851. Each annual index lists articles alphabetically under one of four types of headings: subject, geographic name, organization, and personal name. Since 1962, the foreword has summarized each year's important events. The index itself is a source of information for brief answers to questions such as "Is the teenage birthrate rising or falling?" or "How many rhinoceroses are left in the wild?"

Use Mass Media Resources

Turn on your radio, catch the news on television, or watch a program such as *60 Minutes* for speech materials. In fact, if your topic is current and is certain to be discussed on the day's news, plan to take notes, tape the portion of the program in which the topic is discussed, or purchase a videotape or transcript of the broadcast. That way, you can play back the tape or read the transcript carefully to check the accuracy of your information.

As you watch or listen, distinguish between primary and secondary sources, between factual news reporting and editorial opinion. For example, *The NewsHour with Jim Lehrer*, on public broadcasting stations, usually begins with factual information about a subject. Then Lehrer assembles experts who discuss the subject for as long as fifteen minutes. This part of the broadcast consists of opinions and interpretations as well as eyewitness accounts. Some guests, such as a representative of the Jordanian government, are primary sources. Others, such as a U.S. professor of Middle Eastern studies, are secondary sources.

In addition, check your library's holdings of films, videotapes, and audiotapes, or contact one of the many organizations that circulate recordings and tapes of lectures. For example, medical organizations provide tapes on such topics as ethical treatment of patients with highly contagious diseases. Action groups of all kinds offer audio- and videotaped information about the issues that concern them. Other resources are as close as your local video store.

Use Internet Resources

Internet
A system that links computers around the world; likened to a web or superhighway.

In the United States we are saturated with information, opinions, and persuasive appeals, and the **Internet** has multiplied the amount of available information by geometric proportions. In fact, there is so much information online that you could literally spend the rest of your life in front of your computer, skimming a screen full of data every ten seconds, and you would never run out of material. Rather than become overwhelmed by all the available data or accepting it at face value, you should understand how to do research online. First, let's focus on benefits and cautions relating to Internet research, and then we will examine how to evaluate the materials you find.

What Is the Internet?

Within the last decade, millions of people gained access to this vast communication system that links computers globally. Originally designed for military and scientific purposes, today's Internet is somewhat like a spider web (the "World Wide Web"), a road system (the "Information Superhighway"), or a huge mall with numerous entrances, information centers, levels, concourses, and specialized areas (Harnack & Kleppinger, 1998). Wonderful as this tool is, finding credible information on the Internet is different from finding reliable resources in a physical library. Enormous advantages—and several disadvantages—result from the fact that the Internet is:

1. *Democratic.* Anyone who can gain access to the Internet has a chance of being heard. Personal or private email, as well as public books, newspapers, and academic journals, are online. The information on many sites has not been checked for accuracy. Furthermore, no one organizes Internet documents or makes sure you will find a genuine match between your key words and the documents you find.

2. *Global.* You can access documents from your town or from around the world that are helpful—but potentially overwhelming.

3. *Up-to-the-minute.* Facts, such as weather information and breaking news, are as close as your computer terminal. In fact, the Internet is especially good for current topics related to popular culture, computer science, or government documents.

4. *Interactive.* You can send email messages and join chat groups. If you like, you can play chess at any time of day or night with someone on the other side of the globe.

5. *Free.* Although you may have to pay for access to the Internet, most of the materials there are free. Furthermore, many, even most, public libraries as well as campus libraries and computer centers have terminals that anyone can use without cost (Hacker, 1998).

You've probably surfed the net before, but you may not have used it for serious academic research. Think of it as a cyberspace library, but enter this library cautiously. The net has highly screened, reputable material alongside and sometimes linked to unregulated sites. For instance, a university sponsored and maintained site, such as the *Medieval Sourcebook* of Fordham University, may be just a few clicks of your mouse away from a medieval reenactment Web site created and maintained by a person who relies more on fantasy than fact. Another illustration: You can access the *Denver Post* online and find a serious, well-researched report about a political candidate. On the same site, you can link to a forum in which anyone can state an opinion about the same candidate, factually based or not, in complete anonymity.

You may find interesting, even accurate information on the medieval reenactment site or in the forum, but you'll be more credible if you present data that your listeners recognize as coming from quality institutions and organizations. For more information about the Internet, see the following Web sites:

- Walt Howe, When did the Internet start? A brief capsule history: `www.delphi.com/navnet/faq/history.html`
- Internet Update at `www.itworks.be/I_Update/current.html`

Researching Online

Taking the on-ramp to the electronic superhighway puts you into a system that links millions of electronic sites. However, your computer must follow a set of rules to access that information. First, you'll need a **browser**—a software program such as Netscape Navigator or Microsoft Internet Explorer that helps you find and display information on your computer screen. Most Internet materials are stored on Web pages written in a computer code or language called **hypertext markup language (HTML),** with highlighted links. Click on a link, and your computer connects you to the related site.

Each site has an address called a **URL (uniform resource locator).** When you know the address of a specific site, type it accurately into the address box on your browser; even one small mistake in capitalization or punctuation will result in a dead end. The URL has a number of elements, as these examples show:

`http://www.foxnews.com`
`http://www.stemnet.nf.ca`
`http:` tells your computer the protocol or kind of link to make

Browser
A software program that helps you find and display Internet information.

Hypertext Markup Language (html)
A computer code, or browser language, used to store material on the Internet.

Uniform Resource Locator (URL)
A set of letters, numbers, and symbols that function like an address for a specific Web site.

// shows that the link will be to another computer

www. names the server where the file is located, in this case, the World Wide Web

foxnews/stemnet names the owner of the Web site

.com shows that the owner is a commercial site (**.org** is a nonprofit organization; **.edu** means an educational institution owns the site; **.gov** indicates a government site)

.nf.ca signals a foreign site; **.nf** stands for Newfoundland; **.ca** means Canada (other foreign sites include **.fr** for France, **.jp** for Japan, and **.uk** for the United Kingdom)

Subject Directory
Searches the Internet by subject categories.

Use a Subject Directory Once you're on the Internet, you'll need search tools, which fall into two general categories: subject directories and text indexes. A **subject directory** is similar to your telephone book's *Yellow Pages* where your fingers "walk" to a general category (physicians); there you look for more specific designations (dermatologists). Finally, you home in on specific information (the doctor closest to your home). Use a subject directory to locate information about broad topics such as greyhound adoption. By typing "adopt greyhound" in the search box, you'll get several hits—Web pages of satisfied owners, links to adoption agencies, even a list of available dogs in your area.

Yahoo! (**www.yahoo.com**) is a popular subject directory (Figure 7.2). Its home page provides links to categories such as education, entertainment, society and culture, reference, and health. Select a general category, then choose from successive menus until you come to Web sites that look promising. Or skip this route and simply type key words into the search box on the screen, then press SEARCH. Yahoo then provides a list of hits with links to other search tools. Check also the Argus Clearinghouse (**www.clearinghouse.net**), which monitors many subject guides or "webliographies." In addition, the Internet Public Library (**www.ipl.org**) and the Library of Congress home page (**http://lcweb.loc.gov**) provide excellent links to search tools with information on all Internet sources.

Finding the correct search term can be challenging, but you can turn to the librarians at **www.ipl.org** for assistance. They'll use their organizing skills to help you find interesting, useful information. Internet Public Library reference librarians at **www.ipl.org/ref** will even answer specific questions by email.

Figure 7.2 Yahoo.com is just one of many popular subject directories.

SOURCE: Copyright © 2003 Yahoo! Inc. All Rights Reserved, http://www.yahoo.com

Figure 7.3 alltheweb.com, a powerful text index, allows you to search for exact phrases.

SOURCE: Copyright © 2003 Fast Search & Transfer ASA.

Use a Text Index For other types of searches, a **text index** is a better choice, especially if your topic is obscure or limited, because text indexes allow you to search for exact phrases. Type in a key word, a series of words, or an entire line from a specific work. Here you'll need to use your skills for identifying and finding key terms. If your term is too broad, you may end up with over 100,000 hits. Not very helpful!

A powerful text index, www.alltheweb.com was introduced in the fall of 1999 (Figure 7.3). In a matter of seconds, this index will search more than a billion sites on the Internet. Other text indexes include AltaVista at http://altavista.com, Google at www.google.com, Metacrawler at www.metacrawler.com, and Dogpile at www.dogpile.com. Let's say your topic is bankruptcy reform; go to Dogpile and type in "bankruptcy reform" and press FETCH. You'll get many hits; some will be duplicates. Each hit comes with a short annotation so that you can make quick judgments about the source and usefulness of the site.

How to Evaluate Internet Resources

Powerful search tools will probably overwhelm you with information. How on earth can you sort through 315,442 hits on the subject of "lottery winners"? You'll probably be tempted to take the easiest material to access and get on with your life; however, this strategy may not be best, so exercise critical judgment about the sources and content they contain (Internet Source Validation Project, 1999).

Source Even before you click onto a document, begin evaluating its source by looking at its URL. A document with a .gov or .edu notation is sponsored and maintained by an institution with a reputation to uphold; .com sites are commercial, and .org Web pages are sponsored by organizations with varying reputations (Figure 7.4). When you enter the Web page, look for the name and email address of the person who created or maintains the site; this gives an additional basis for assessing source credibility. Try to determine the author's occupation, educational background, and expertise. Can you contact him or her? Would knowledgeable people consider the source to be accurate, expert, and reliable?

Content First, look for a site rating. Teams of outsiders often evaluate sites to see if they provide complete, current, and thorough coverage of a topic. These evaluators also look at the way materials are organized to see whether or not the site is user friendly. A rating,

Text Index
Search engine that looks up specific phrases and obscure topics.

Figure 7.4 The Raven Sky Sports site is sponsored by a commercial enterprise; compare that site with the official USHGA organization site on hang gliding.

SOURCES: Courtesy Raven Sky Sports, www.hanggliding.com. Courtesy United States Hang Gliding Association, Inc., www.ushga.com.

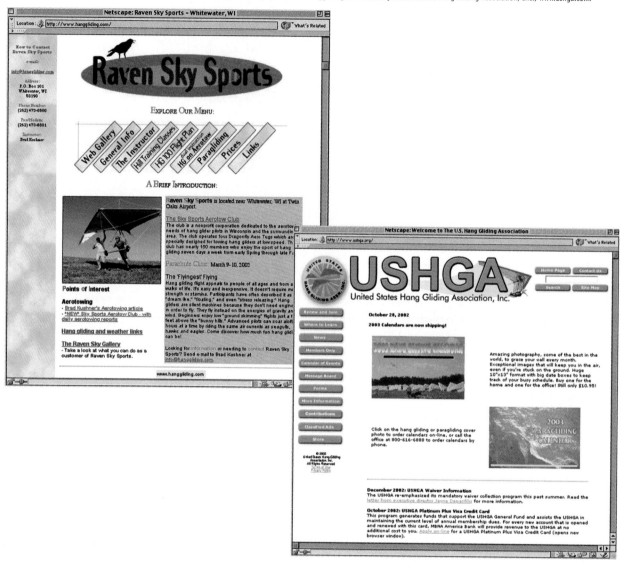

although helpful, does not guarantee that the document contains accurate or high-quality materials, so do your own site rating based on these tips:

1. *Determine the intent or purpose of the site.* Is the page designed to provide information, to entertain, or to sway opinion? What audience does it appear to address?
2. *Look for a bias.* Does the material emphasize one perspective over another, or is it relatively objective? Is it free of gender or ethnic stereotyping? Does the creator or sponsor have a personal or commercial goal? Does the source have an established position on the topic?
3. *Check timeliness.* Is the information (especially statistical data) up to date? Is the site maintained regularly?
4. *Assess accuracy.* How is the material similar to what you've found in other sources? Would reputable sources accept the ideas as plausible and accurate? Look for links. Do these sites appear to be reputable as well? Does the document list its sources? Its methodology?

5. *Finally, consider organization.* If you have your choice between two sites that appear to be equal in accuracy and quality of information, choose the one that is easier to use (Hawkes, 1999).

For example, a search using www.google.com for the topic "medical misinformation" turned up these documents, among others:

⬤ *CNN Food and Health News: Medical misinformation on the information superhighway.*
CNN is well-known for its reporting on medical news, but the article is dated August 30, 1995. Millions of Web pages have been added to the Internet since then; however, the report may contain some principles for evaluating Internet information that are generally valid.

⬤ *Charlatans, Leeches, and Old Wives: Medical Misinformation, by Susan Detweiler, the Detweiler Group. Searcher, 9(3), March 2001.*
The home site for this journal is *Information Today, Inc.*, the magazine for users and producers of electronic information services. It provides a great deal of information, including phone numbers, addresses, and email addresses of the group as well as the author.

⬤ *Second Opinions by Barry Groves, Ph.D.* (Has .uk—United Kingdom—in the URL).
A link, "about Barry Groves," provides information that helps you decide if he's credible or not. He was trained as an electronics engineer and served in the Royal Air Force. He became interested in food and diets, and earned a Ph.D. in nutritional science. He has written in some credible journals.

⬤ *Urban Legends and Folklore* (www.about.com).
This site provides many amusing examples that could be useful in adding colorful examples to a speech on the topic.

In short, you must use your critical thinking abilities whenever you log onto the Internet. More detail about critical analysis is found in Quianna Clay's outline at the end of the chapter; it deals with medical misinformation on the Internet.

STOP AND CHECK
CRITICAL THINKING AND THE INTERNET

Although the Internet is wonderful, use its information with care. Mixed in with verifiable facts and research data, texts of nineteenth-century British novels, and pictures of Roman architecture, you'll find commercials and rumors and opinions that you cannot verify because many Internet contributors are anonymous and not accountable.

1. Use the guidelines provided in the text to assess the reliability of the following sites. That is, evaluate the source and the content (the purpose, bias, timeliness, accuracy, and organization) of information you find on an organizational site for hang gliding, available at www.ushga.org, and on a specific commercial site such as www.hanggliding.com.

2. Then go to www.whitehouse.gov and read the biographical information you find there about the President of the United States. Assess the content. What is the purpose, the bias, the timeliness, and the accuracy of this biographical information? Use a subject directory such as www.yahoo.com and search for the president by name. Follow at least one link there and, using the same tests for site content, compare the biographical information you find there with the information the White House presents.

3. Of the sites you reviewed in activities 1 and 2, which materials are more apt to be verifiable? Which features more expert contributions? Which materials were probably

(continued)

Web Site

not screened or edited? What are the strengths and limitations of each type of material? That is, when would you be likely to use each source effectively?

Sometimes you will find hoax sites that look legitimate, but are really prank Web pages that mimic and poke fun at the real thing. For example, typing **.net** instead of **.gov** in the White House Internet address leads you to a prank site set up to look official. Go to **www.whitehouse.net** and see for yourself.

You can access these links and answer these questions online under Stop and Check Activities for Chapter 7 on the Jaffe Connection Web site.

Record Your Information

Obviously you won't remember everything you discover during your search, so you need a strategy for recording your findings. Then, when you sit down to organize your speech, you will have the necessary information at your fingertips and you can easily classify your ideas into themes and patterns. There are three common methods of recording research information: photocopies or printouts of material, mind maps, and note cards. Choose the one that matches your individual learning style. Then use a standard bibliographic format to list your sources at the end of your outline.

Photocopy or Print Your Materials

One advantage of photocopying your materials is that you have the entire resource in front of you. Use copy machines available in most libraries to copy articles from books, newspapers, and periodicals for one-time use. Or download and print material from the Internet. Be sure you write the source (in standard bibliographic form) directly onto your photocopies or downloaded materials. Then, using highlighters, identify major ideas and salient information.

To see how this works, consider the speech topic "medical misinformation on the Internet." The prospective speaker photocopies pages from books and newspapers; she also clips articles from her own subscription newspapers and magazines. She makes sure to copy the entire reference at the top of each page. Then, using one color for major points and a second color for examples and quotations, she highlights the material relevant to her subject. When she finally organizes and outlines her ideas, she simply spreads out her photocopied and highlighted articles and weaves the materials together into a coherent speech.

Whenever you copy materials, you are using the intellectual property of another person who has a right to profit from its use. Fortunately, the **Fair Use provision** in the federal Copyright Act allows you to print and use materials for nonprofit educational purposes; therefore, photocopying materials for one-time speech research is within your legal rights as a student (Kirshenberg, 1998).

Fair Use Provision
The provision in the federal Copyright Act that allows free use of materials for educational and research purposes.

Create a Mind Map

If your learning style is more holistic, consider making a mind map. Chapter 6 showed how to use a mind map to generate speech topics, but you can use a similar process to record and sort topical information. One advantage of this method is that you can classify and subdivide your materials as you gather them.

Here's how a topical mind map works. First, identify the subject of your speech in the center of the page, using a diagram or drawing. Then, draw a line to attach each subtopic to this center. Show further subdivisions by drawing radiating lines under your subtopics. If you have a lot of material, you may have to make a separate page for each major point. See Figure 7.5 for a mind map about medical misinformation. Be sure to list your sources. If there's room, write your references directly onto your mind map; however, if your space is limited, make source cards or list your references on a separate piece of paper.

Figure 7.5 A sample mind map to record information.

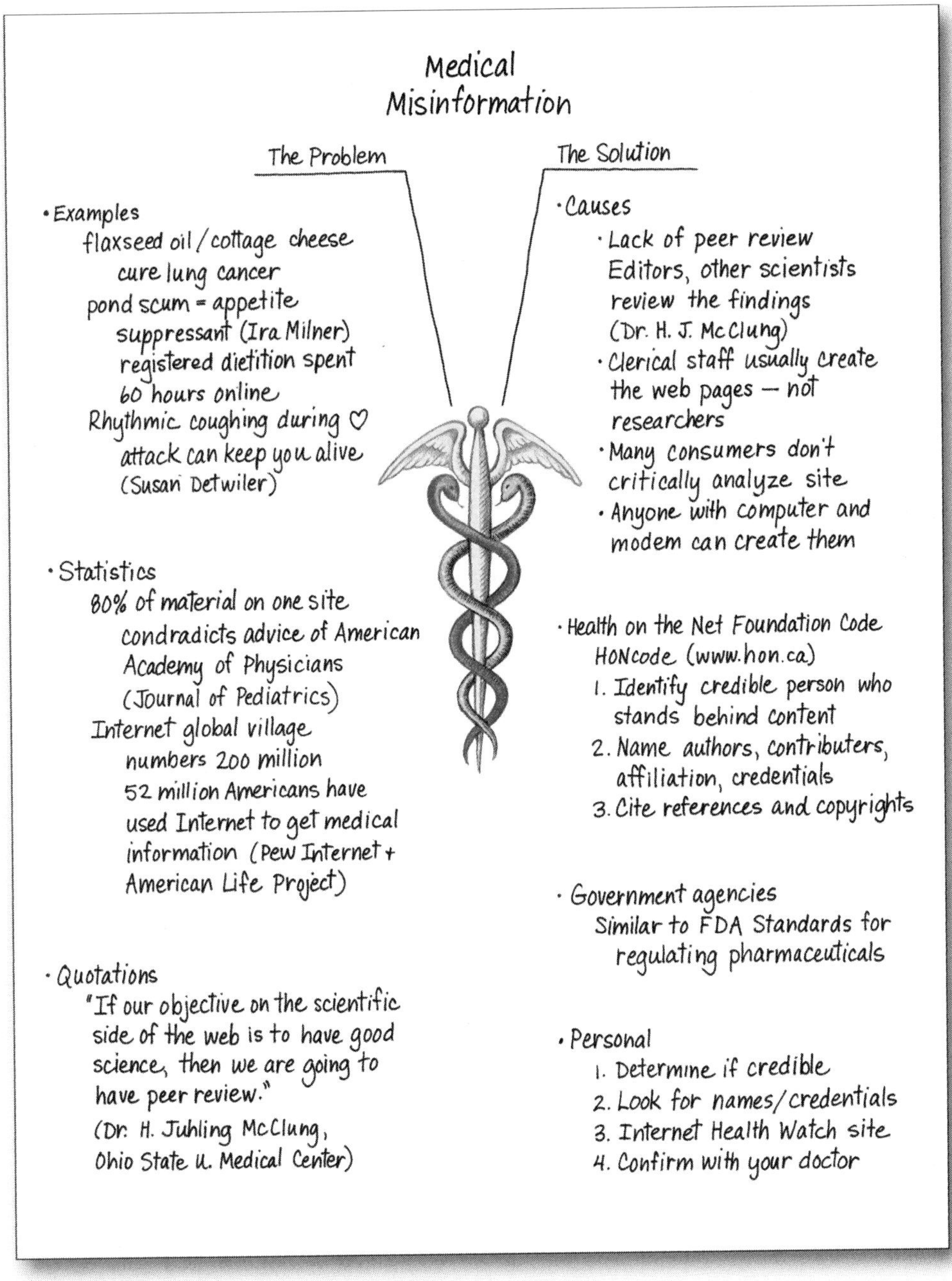

Write Note Cards

A more structured approach is to use 3 × 5 or 4 × 6 cards. This method has many advantages: The cards are small enough to handle easily, you can cite your sources directly on each card, and you can easily classify your information. Sort your material into major categories by using two basic kinds of note cards: source cards and information cards.

Source Cards

Begin by making a separate card for each source, using a standard bibliographic format. **Source cards** include the author, date, title, place of publication (for books), or newspaper or magazine title, followed by the page number or URL where you found the information. You can **annotate** your bibliography, meaning that you write a brief description of the information you found in the book or article. Make source cards for materials gathered from interviews and films as well. See Figure 7.6 for an example.

Source Cards
Cards used to record bibliographic information.
Annotate
To summarize a book or article's contents on a source card.

Figure 7.6 Source cards contain bibliographic information. Annotated cards also include a brief summary of the material found in the source.

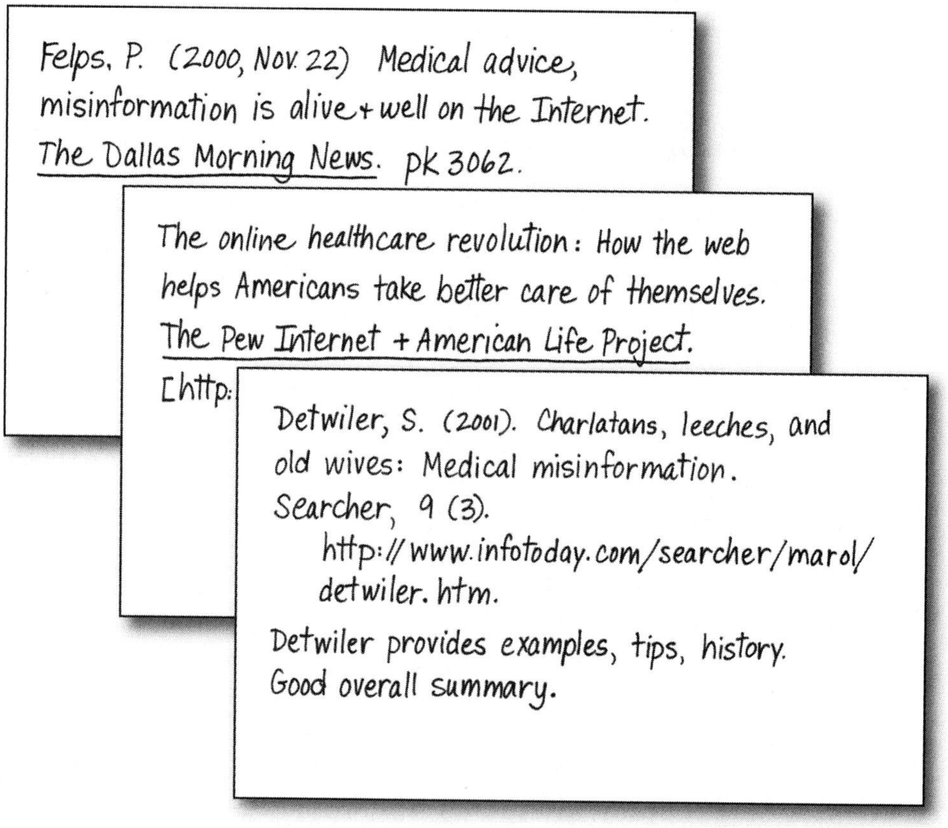

Felps, P. (2000, Nov. 22) Medical advice, misinformation is alive + well on the Internet. The Dallas Morning News. pk 3062.

The online healthcare revolution: How the web helps Americans take better care of themselves. The Pew Internet + American Life Project. [http:

Detwiler, S. (2001). Charlatans, leeches, and old wives: Medical misinformation. Searcher, 9 (3). http://www.infotoday.com/searcher/marol/detwiler.htm.

Detwiler provides examples, tips, history. Good overall summary.

Information Cards

Next, write down important data, creating a separate **information card** for each different idea, statistic, quotation, example, and so on. On the top of each card, write a heading that classifies the information into a category that may later become a main point. Also, label the card with an abbreviated source citation so that when you use the material in the speech, you can cite its source. Figure 7.7 shows examples of information cards.

The advantage of this method is that you can separate your cards into piles, then move them around, placing your major point at the top and arranging your supporting information below. You can easily change the order of both your points and your relevant supporting materials before writing the outline.

Information Card
Card for recording and categorizing important data.

Use a Standard Format to Cite Your Sources

To avoid plagiarism, give credit to the sources you use by creating a bibliography at the end of your outline. List all your sources in alphabetic order using a standard bibliographic format found in the style or publication manual your instructor recommends. The reference section of your library has many popular style manuals, including ones from the American Psychological Association (APA) and the Modern Language Association (MLA). To find specific sites online, go to www.alltheweb.com and search for the exact term "APA Style

Figure 7.7 Use a different information card for each source, and classify each card according to the major idea the information supports. Include an abbreviated source citation on each card.

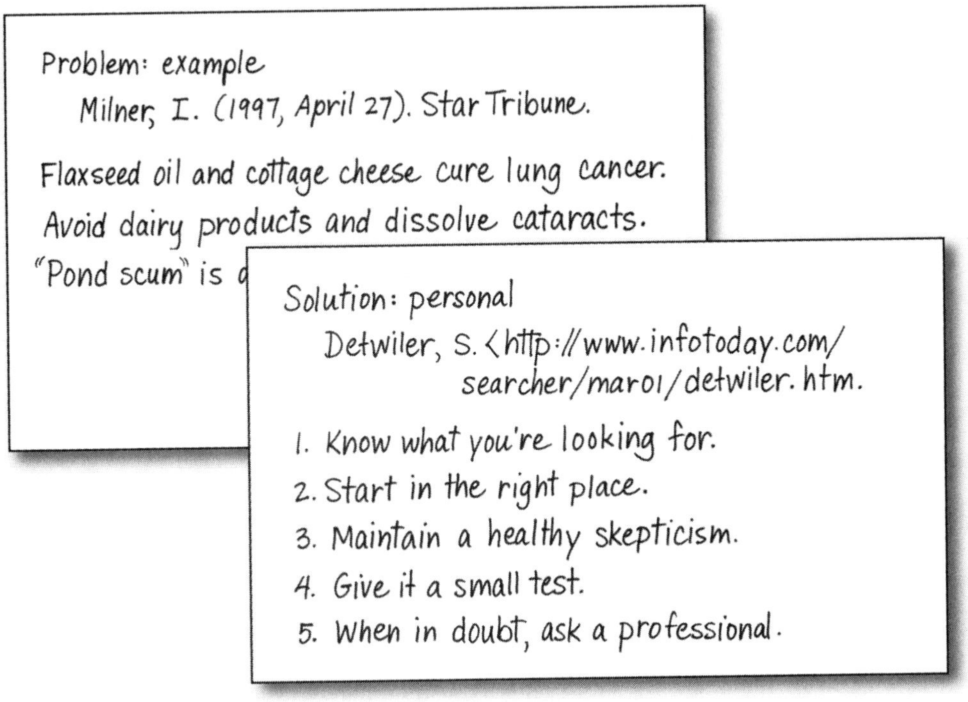

Problem: *example*
   Milner, I. (1997, April 27). Star Tribune.

Flaxseed oil and cottage cheese cure lung cancer.
Avoid dairy products and dissolve cataracts.
"Pond scum" is a

Solution: *personal*
   Detwiler, S. < http://www.infotoday.com/
                 searcher/mar01/detwiler.htm.

1. Know what you're looking for.
2. Start in the right place.
3. Maintain a healthy skepticism.
4. Give it a small test.
5. When in doubt, ask a professional.

Manual," or "MLA Style Manual." You will get hundreds of hits with links to further information about bibliographic citations, often furnished by professors and librarians. Good examples of APA source citations can be found at http://puffin.creighton.edu/psy/TLB/writadv.html.

In summary, an important part of the research process is recording information so that it is readily available when you put your speech together. If you approach the research task holistically, you may download or photocopy your materials and use highlights to identify important information. Or, you may make mind maps, using images as well as words to record the results of your research. If you like a structured, linear method, note cards may be your best choice. The important thing is that you find a way to remember your ideas. Then use a standard bibliographic format to list your sources alphabetically.

STOP AND CHECK
COMPLETE YOUR RESEARCH PLAN

Return a final time to your research plan, and complete sections O and P here or online under Stop and Check Activities for Chapter 7 on the Jaffe Connection Web site. Make any other alterations that seem justified in light of what you have learned in this chapter.

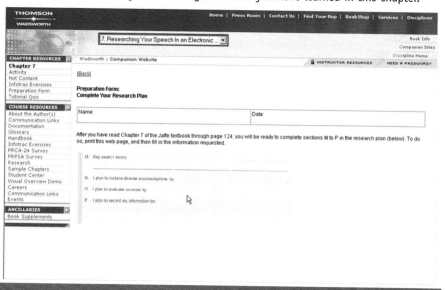

Web Site

Summary

Part of your competence in speechmaking is your ability to gather information. You'll be more effective if you set aside plenty of time to explore your topic using a research plan that is appropriate for the subject. Look for both primary and secondary sources of material: primary sources are original documents and other firsthand information; secondary sources interpret, explain, and evaluate the subject.

You can find both primary and secondary materials in face-to-face interactions and in print sources such as books, periodicals, and newspapers, published in traditional library forms as well as online. Consider also the wide variety of visual and audiotaped materials available to you. Throughout your research, search out diverse perspectives including international, ethnic, and alternative viewpoints.

Through the Internet, you can access literally millions of documents from local, national, and global sources—some highly credible, others useless. Use a subject directory to look up general topics. If you can't find information on specific or unusual topics or if you're looking for specific phrases, go to a text index. Sift through the materials you find by evaluating each source as well as the purpose, bias, timeliness, accuracy, and organization of each site's content. Constantly record your findings, using a method that meets your learning style preferences, whether photocopying, making a mind map, or using source and information cards. On the bibliography that accompanies your outline, cite your sources using a standard form that you can find in a style or publication manual.

JAFFE ONLINE CONNECTION JAFFE ONLINE CONNECTION

Use your CD-ROM and the Jaffe Connection Web site http://communication.wadsworth.com/jaffe to review the following concepts, answer the review questions, and complete the suggested activities.

KEY TERMS

reference librarian (104)
subject librarian (105)
primary sources (106)
original documents (106)
creative works (106)
relics or artifacts (106)
secondary sources (106)
oral sources (107)
expert (107)
laypeople or peers (107)
general encyclopedias (110)
specialized encyclopedias (110)
dictionary (110)

periodicals (111)
trade or professional journal (111)
Internet (114)
browser (115)
hypertext markup language (html) (115)
uniform resource locator (URL) (115)
subject directory (116)
text index (117)
Fair Use provision (120)
source cards (122)
annotate (122)
information card (123)

APPLICATION AND CRITICAL THINKING EXERCISES

1. If you have not already done so, visit your campus library. Locate and browse the reference books, the newspapers and periodicals, and the indexes and guides to them.
2. Make a file containing handouts prepared by the librarians in the library you'll use most often, and consult these during your research. (Examples: HOW TO: Locate U.S. Government Documents; HOW TO: Cite References According to the APA Manual; Periodicals Collection: A Service Guide.)
3. Make a list of library resources that provide an alternative perspective on subjects. That is, discover what subscriptions your library has to international, ethnic, and alternative newspapers and magazines. Read an article in at least one of the resources.
4. Using InfoTrac College Edition, type in key words relating to your speech topic. Select a number of articles and skim those that appear interesting.
5. Set aside an hour to explore newspapers and magazines on the Internet. A subject index such as www.yahoo.com or www.refdesk.com/newspapers provides links to many news sites. With your classmates, select an interesting, significant current event and surf around, clicking on links related to that event. Then, discuss the value as well as the drawbacks of doing research over the Internet.

6. To learn more about finding credible information on the Internet, take the tutorial provided by the University of California, Berkeley. It's available at www.lib.berkeley.edu/teachingLib/Guides/Internet/FundInfo.html#outline. Click on the link to style sheets for information about citing Internet sources. The section "Evaluating Web Pages: Why and How" also provides useful information.

7. Think about the different ways to record information. Which method—photocopies, mind maps, or note cards—would you most likely use? Which would you least likely use? When might you combine methods? Discuss your research style with a classmate.

8. Cooperate with your entire class to research a current event or an issue such as gun control. Go to the library and find and photocopy a print article, or download information from an Internet site. Or interview an expert or layperson. Make sure that some students consult mainstream sources and that others seek out diverse perspectives. Bring your information to the next class meeting and discuss and evaluate the various sources and data by determining the purpose, the source bias, the timeliness, the accuracy, and the organization of the material.

THE JAFFE CONNECTION WEB SITE

The Jaffe Connection Web site features review questions about the Web links, the Stop and Check activity, and InfoTrac College Edition exercises referenced throughout the chapter. You can access this site via your CD-ROM or at http://communication.wadsworth.com/jaffe.

Web Links

7.1   Ask an Expert (page 108)
7.2   Online Reference Materials (pages 110–111)
7.3   What Is the Internet? (page 115)
7.4   Online Library Assistance (pages 115–116)
7.5   Internet Subject Directories (page 116)
7.6   Powerful Online Text Indexes (page 117)
7.7   A Google Search for Medical Misinformation (page 119)
7.8   Bibliography Style Manuals Available Online (page 124)
7.9   University of California, Berkeley Internet Tutorial (page 126)

Stop and Check Activities

7.1   Begin Your Research Plan (page 106)
7.2   Revisit Your Research Plan (page 108)
7.3   Critical Thinking and the Internet (pages 119–120)
7.4   Complete Your Research Plan (page 124)

InfoTrac College Edition Exercises

7.1   Interviewing (page 108)
7.2   InfoTrac Journal Names List (page 113)
7.3   Speech Topic Search (page 125)

STUDENT OUTLINE WITH COMMENTARY

MEDICAL MISINFORMATION ON THE INTERNET
by Quianna Clay

General Purpose: To persuade

Specific Purpose: To persuade my audience that medical information on the Internet is often faulty but they can protect themselves by being critical consumers.

Central Idea: The Internet contains a plethora of medical misinformation that has several causes, but foundations, the government, and consumers can help.

Introduction

I. Did your know that flaxseed oil and cottage cheese can cure cancer, or that pond scum can suppress your appetite?

   A. Registered dietician Ira Milner spent sixty hours online and found a plethora of such misinformation (*Star Tribune*, 4/27/97).

   B. The *Wall Street Journal* (October 19) says the Internet is quickly becoming the most powerful, overwhelming, and potentially dangerous source of information.

II. We might laugh at these examples, but people can get deadly information online.

   A. According to the Pew Internet and American Life Project (2000), fifty-two million Americans have used the Internet to get medical information.

   B. However, sites often give bad information; 80 percent of the material on one site contradicts the advice of the American Academy of Physicians (*Journal of Pediatrics*, June 1998).

III. Today we will explore the dangerous problem of medical misinformation, we'll look at some causes, and we'll learn how to protect ourselves from being misled.

Body

I. The World Wide Web and the Internet are increasingly accessible.

   A. The Times Mirror Center for the People and Press reported that five million people used the Internet in 1994; twelve million were added in 1995, and millions more go online each year (*Consumer Health Information Source Book*).

   B. Today, more than two hundred million people are in the Internet global village (Pew Internet and American Life Project).

   C. At least 37 percent have sought medical information (National Health Council).

      1. Many turn to the Internet first.

      2. Users often trust university-based Web pages, but this is not always the case.

         a. One university page suggested that children who have diarrhea should fast and drink sports beverages.

         b. However, the American Academy of Pediatrics says these beverages are low in electrolytes, which the body loses as a result of diarrhea (*Journal of the American Medical Association*, August 1997).

II. There are many causes for the incorrect information that is available online.

   A. The main one is lack of peer review on the Internet.

      1. Print publications are judged by the credibility of the author, the publication's editorial content versus its advertising commitments, its educational values versus product promotion, and the number of scientific facts it presents.

      2. Dr. H. Juhling McClung (Ohio State University Medical Center) says, "If our object on the scientific side of the Web is to have good science, then we are going to have to have peer review."

Commentary (right margin):

Quianna gains attention with amusing examples of misinformation. She then spells out the problem and the need for consumers to be critical thinkers. Throughout she demonstrates credibility by citing respectable sources.

Here she previews the three main ideas she'll develop in the speech.

This section describes the problem.

Here, she echoes the contrast between print and Internet sources highlighted in this chapter.

Quianna emphasizes that anyone with the basic skills and equipment can create a Web page.

B. Researchers are often not involved directly in the creation of Web pages.
  1. Clerical staff who may be unfamiliar with the subject matter often create them; they may make many errors.
  2. Anyone with a computer, modem, and twenty dollars can create a Web page.
    a. The pages may be incomplete, inaccurate, or misleading (*Journal of the American Medical Association,* April 1997).
    b. Anonymous writers may have a personal agenda, no formal medical training, or a profit motive off of unsuspecting consumers.
C. Internet users also have themselves to blame.

Search engines are neutral, which requires each researcher to sift through numerous hits with care.

  1. Many people trust search engines to lead them to quality sites (*Annals of Internal Medicine,* July 1995).
  2. However, savvy users know that searches do not distinguish among sites; they just count the times a key word appears within a site, then they direct the user to the site with the most matches.
  3. Unfortunately, many Internet novices are unaware of the pitfalls awaiting them.
III. Fortunately, several steps can be taken to improve the quality of medical information on the Internet, and we can personally look for correct, reliable information.

In this solution section, Quianna points out that many people are concerned about erroneous materials available online and are creating standards and guidelines for Web site creators.

A. Some standards should be in place to ensure the safety of those who seek medical information on the Web; the Health on the Net Foundation has formulated a code of conduct (*Consumer Health Information Sourcebook,* 1998).
  1. Identify a credible person or group who stands behind the information provided.
  2. Name the authors and contributors as well as their affiliations and credentials.
  3. Cite all references and copyright information used to create the site.
B. In addition, governmental agencies need to take a more active role in regulating medical information on the Internet.
  1. They should follow the lead of the FDA, which explored new standards for pharmaceutical advertising on the net.
  2. Melissa Mancavage, public health adviser for the FDA notes, "Current regulations on prescription drugs differ between print and broadcast medium. The Internet presents additional challenges."

Quianna summarizes the guidelines for assessing Internet information found on pages 117–119.

C. We consumers must determine if a site is credible, using suggestions issued by the Department of Health and Human Services (*Consumer,* June 1996).
  1. Determine who maintains the site.
    a. Government sites like those maintained by the National Institutes of Health or the Centers for Disease Control.
    b. Private practitioners or organizations may have financial or political agendas that influence their material and their links.
  2. Look for a listing of names and credentials of people who contributed to the site; see if you can contact them with questions or inquiries for more information.
    a. Look for links to other sites; good sites don't consider themselves the only source of information.
    b. Be cautious, however; sites have no control over who links to them, and unscrupulous groups could link to more trustworthy sources in an attempt to look more credible.
  3. Log on to the "Internet Health Watch" site, which evaluates other health Web sites.
    a. Reuters Health Information Service sponsors this site, and Dr. John Renner, founder of the Consumer Health Information Research Institute in Independence, Missouri, maintains it.
    b. Renner evaluates three sites each week on their technical content, credibility, usefulness, and linkage characteristics.

    4. Most important, remember that the Internet should complement, not replace, the physician–patient relationship, and have your physician corroborate information you find on the net.

Conclusion

  I. Now, knowing where cases of inaccurate medical information have been found, knowing the causes of such misinformation, and being armed with tools that can correct the situation allows us to exercise caution.

 II. So the next time you are on the Internet and you begin to consider pond scum or cottage cheese as a cure for what ails you, keep these words in mind: *Caveat emptor*—let the buyer beware.

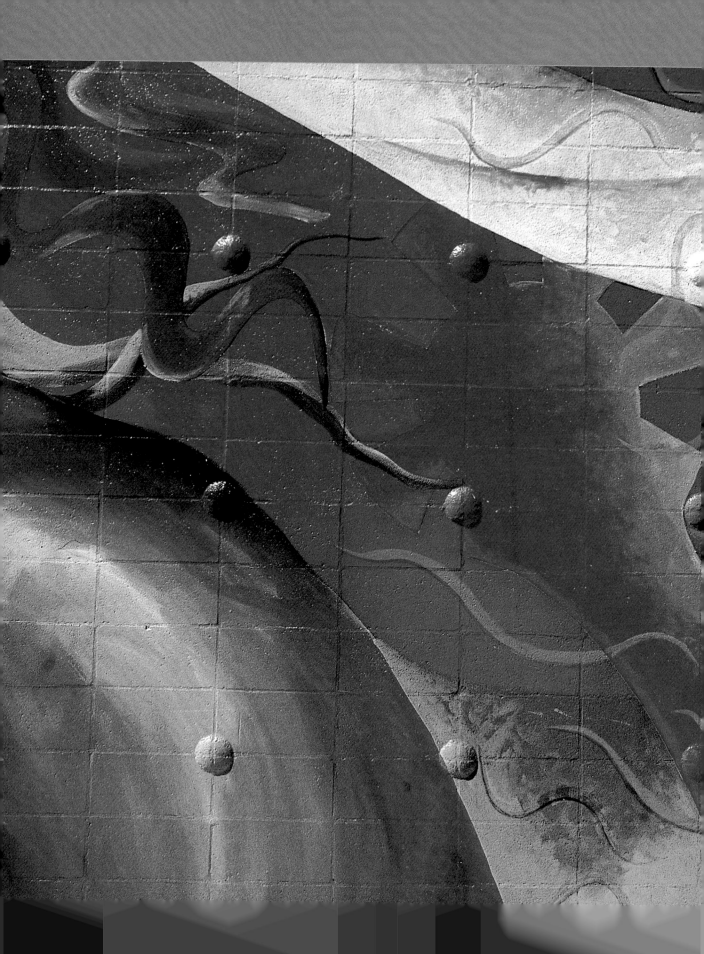

Choosing Supporting Materials

THIS CHAPTER WILL HELP YOU

■ Distinguish between fact and

opinion and know how to test

factual data

■ Use examples effectively

■ Quote authoritative sources

■ Select numerical data carefully

■ Distinguish between literal and

figurative analogies

THINK ABOUT YOUR DECISION-MAKING PROCESS. How do you choose a car, decide on a vacation site, or select a college or university? Do you read promotional brochures? Do you talk to friends or trusted advisers? Do you look for facts and opinions on the Internet? Most people make decisions only after they ask these kinds of questions: "Why should I buy that?" "Why go there?" "What is the overall cost?" They seek evidence—facts, figures, examples, and recommendations from knowledgeable people—to support their decision. So it is with other decisions we make. We want support for the behaviors and the ideas we choose. And, not surprisingly, when we hear speeches, we expect speakers to support their ideas with some kind of evidence.

Each culture has its own rules for determining what counts as acceptable evidence. In the United States, we commonly look for facts, examples, quotations, statistics, and analogies to support our ideas. Rather than accept all information at face value, we follow cultural standards for weighing evidence, accepting some as valid and rejecting other data as inadequate, irrelevant, or inaccurate. This chapter looks at the typical kinds of evidence used in public speaking. Following the presentation of each type of evidence you will find a Stop and Check section to help you think critically about the quality of the data or evidence, both when selecting materials for your own speeches and when listening to the speeches of others.

Provide Facts

Probably most of the information you discover about your subject will be factual, and in Euro-American culture people typically demand facts before accepting an idea or proposal. **Facts** are data that can be verified by observation, and **established facts** are those consistently validated by many observers as true; they include generally accepted definitions and descriptions. You judge factual information as true or false. Facts derive from a variety of sources, as these examples reveal:

Facts
Data verifiable by observation.

Established Facts
Data verified consistently by many observers.

- The origin of the word *coffee* is disputed. Some say it derives from the Arabic word *qahwah*; others say it comes from Kaffa, the province in southwest Ethiopia that is considered coffee's birthplace. [source: dictionary]
- N'Djamena is the capital city of the Republic of Chad. [source: *Information Please Almanac*]
- Fetal alcohol syndrome, a condition caused when a pregnant woman consumes substantial amounts of alcohol, is one reason for mental retardation in children. [source: empirical research studies conducted by scientists]

DIVERSITY IN PRACTICE
VISUAL EVIDENCE: CHICANO MURALS

MARGARET LEWARE (1998) argues that murals—like those in this text—make statements about ethnic pride, community activism, and cultural revitalization. (She examined Chicano/a murals in Chicago.) Study a couple of murals. Look for images such as mythical beasts, Aztlan, or a pink rose (associated with the Virgin of Guadalupe); look for portraits that resemble community members. How might these combine to define identity, reflect the people's needs, and celebrate their history? LeWare says, ". . . the murals argue that Mexican American people need not assimilate or give up their culture to survive in an urban center that is both geographically and socially distant from Mexico and from the Southwest."

This article is available on InfoTrac College Edition. It's in the journal, *Argumentation and Advocacy,* Winter 1998.

Use Definitions

You can **define,** or give the meaning of a term, in a number of ways. Looking in a dictionary provides the meaning generally accepted in common usage. For his remarks on the root causes of terrorism, Tariq Karim (2002) cited two dictionaries:

> What is terrorism? The *Chambers Twentieth Century Dictionary* (1976 edition) defines it as an "organized system of intimidation." The *Merriam-Webster Collegiate Dictionary* (current edition) defines it as "the systematic use of terror especially as a means of coercion." The word "terror" is derived from Middle English, inspired by middle French, Latin and Greek, from words which mean to frighten, to cause one to tremble or be afraid, or to flee; or to arouse a state of intense fear.

Because his source is well known, most people would agree that, yes, this is what terrorism is. However, Karim adds his personal interpretation:

> To my mind, terrorism is Terrorism (with a capital "T"). It recognizes no caste, creed, religion, race, ethnicity, or physical and political boundaries. It stalks a global theatre. Its specter will haunt us everywhere, in all societies, unless we stand up against it, unitedly, and indict its perpetrators.

Here, Karim interjects his personal **opinions** or interpretations into his definition. Stating personal opinion, either yours or someone else's, adds a subjective interpretation that is open to question. For instance, some listeners might be confused by his distinction between terrorism and Terrorism.

Define
Give the meaning of a word.

Opinions
Subjective interpretations of facts; can be questioned.

Provide Vivid Descriptions

Descriptions provide details about a subject—details of size, shape, sounds, colors, and so on. In his address to the nation following the September 11 attack, President Bush (2001) described the world's response to our horrifying experience:

> America will never forget the sounds of our national anthem playing at Buckingham Palace, on the streets of Paris and at Berlin's Brandenburg Gate. We will not forget South Korean children gathering to pray outside our embassy in Seoul, or the prayers of sympathy offered at a mosque in Cairo. We will not forget moments of silence and days of mourning in Australia and Africa and Latin America.

The details (our anthem, specific buildings, the children, naming various continents) help the audience form mental pictures of the world's response.

Describe
Create an image or impression through vivid words.

Ed Kashi/CORBIS

Arabs and Arab Americans say that inaccurate information about them is often presented as if it were true. To avoid passing along incorrect material, check a variety of sources.

The danger in using factual material is that it is easy to pass on unverified or inaccurate material. For instance, Camilla quoted from the speech, "Brother Earth, Sister Sky," which she attributed to Chief Seattle over one hundred years ago. Had she searched further, she would have discovered that the speech was actually constructed in 1972 by a screenwriter named Ted Parry for a film about ecology. (InfoTrac College Edition includes a number of articles that provide accurate information about the authorship of the speech.)

With the current explosion of available information, especially through the Internet and other electronic sources, distinguishing facts from opinions is now more important than ever.

STOP AND CHECK
THINK CRITICALLY ABOUT FACTS

Sometimes Arab Americans say that they are stereotyped and misunderstood, and that a lot of incomplete or incorrect information circulates regarding them—especially after the events of September 11. For example, many people assume that most Arab Americans are Muslims; this is true in some U.S. communities with large Arab American populations, but the fact is, overall most Arab Americans are Christians. To make sure your information is accurate, apply the following three tests:

1. *Check for accuracy or validity.* What's the truth about Arab Americans' religious affiliation? What's the percentage of Christians? Of Muslims? One source said a small proportion of Arab Americans embrace Judaism or the Druze religion. Is this true? How many?

2. *Are the facts up to date?* In the first wave of Arab immigration (1875–1920) most newcomers were Christians from Lebanon and Syria. In the second wave (1940s) more students and more Muslims immigrated; however, many Christians also came from Palestine during this decade. What are the current religious affiliations of today's immigrants?

3. *Consider the source.* One information source for journalists is the *Detroit Free Press.* It's prepared a fact sheet called "100 Questions and Answers about Arab Americans," which is available online at **www.freep.com/jobspage/arabs/arab1.html**. What credibility does a major newspaper have? What other sources might provide information?

In short, test facts by asking three questions: Is this true? Is this true now? Who says so?

Use Examples

Examples
Specific instances used to support ideas.

Have you ever listened to a speech that seemed abstract and irrelevant until the speaker used an example showing how the topic affected someone like you? Most likely, your interest increased because of the illustration. Choose short or long, real or hypothetical **examples,** or specific instances, to support your ideas because of their numerous benefits. David explains:

> The speeches that are interesting usually start with an example—often from that person's life. It shows the communicator is human. The story adds credibility . . . and leads the audience into the speech, almost like a conversation; this lets the speaker earn the audience's trust.
>
> DAVID

In addition, examples attract attention. Narrative theorists argue that we listen for examples and stories that make abstract concepts and ideas more concrete and relevant (MacIntyre, 1981). Moreover, illustrations help listeners identify emotionally with your subject. When the example rings true to their personal experience, your listeners' internal dialogue runs something like this: "Yes, I've known someone like that" or "I've seen that happen—this seems real." Finally, using examples can enhance your personal credibility. Your listeners want to know that you are involved in real-world experiences. Examples let your audience see that you understand the practical implications of your theories and ideas.

You'll find two major types of examples: real and hypothetical. Both types can be further differentiated by length. Some are very brief; others are longer and more detailed.

Use Real Examples

Real examples, those that actually happened, provide your listeners with concrete, real-life illustrations of your concepts. For instance, John's topic is culture shock. He defines the term, then begins his discussion of the first stage, the honeymoon stage. His audience listens politely, but their attention really perks up and they more clearly understand the emotions associated with this stage when he tells about Sara's experiences during her first few weeks as a nanny in Belgium. (An outline of this speech appears in Chapter 11.)

Real Examples
Actual happenings.

As you gather materials, look for experiences of people, as well as events or happenings in institutions, countries, and so on to illustrate your ideas. Because real examples actually occurred, you can provide specific names, dates, and places. For instance:

- To illustrate a speech about the downside of winning the lottery, Maria presented William, whose brother hired a hit man to kill him; Daisy, whose friend sued for half her winnings (because he had prayed that she'd win and she did); Debbie, whose sisters no longer spoke to her because she refused to pay their bills. (Maria's outline is located at the end of Chapter 9.)
- Examples showing how the culture of the United States has been enriched through the contributions of Arab Americans include Christa McAuliffe (the teacher who died in the Challenger spaceship), Doug Flutie (NFL quarterback), Donna Shalala (former Secretary of HUD), Candy Lightner (the mother who founded MADD), Ralph Nader (presidential candidate), and John Zogby (pollster).
- For his speech on the overconsumption of sugar, Hans told the story of Arnold Scott, a fifteen-year-old who weighed more than 300 pounds; his mother noticed that Arnold was losing weight rapidly and was constantly thirsty. She took him to the hospital where doctors diagnosed this obese fifteen-year-old with Type II diabetes. (Hans's outline is at the end of this chapter; excerpts from his speech can be seen on the CD that accompanies this text.)

You can also use examples from your own experience, which bolsters your credibility by linking you personally to the topic. John used personal examples from his semester in Africa to illustrate his progress through the stages of culture shock. As a result, his listeners found him to be more credible; he not only had book learning, he knew firsthand what culture shock was like.

Personal stories have great impact here as well as in other countries. In Kenya, for example, focus group participants rated them as probably the most convincing type of example. One Kenyan said, "We believe you only really know about something if you've experienced it" (as cited in Miller, 2002, p. 178). In fact, some group members thought personal narratives should be placed in a separate category of supporting material because their impact is so different from other types of narratives.

Consider Hypothetical Examples for Sensitive Topics

Sometimes you may use a **hypothetical example,** which means that the specific incident did not really occur but something like it did or could happen. This type of example contains elements of several different stories woven together to create a typical person whose

Hypothetical Example
Not a real incident or person, but true to life.

experiences relate to the topic. For instance, in a speech about teen suicide, instead of revealing details about a specific person you actually knew, you might combine elements from the lives and deaths of various teenagers to create a typical victim. If you choose a hypothetical example, tell the audience you're doing so by saying something like this: "Let's say a thirteen-year-old girl named Susan lived in a large city . . . we'll make that Los Angeles."

Indeed, because of the cultural value on privacy, hypothetical examples may be more appropriate than real ones when you're dealing with sensitive issues such as mental illness or sexual behaviors. For this reason, speakers whose work involves confiden-tiality—physicians, ministers, counselors, and teachers—often use hypothetical examples. Family counselors who present workshops on parenting, for instance, tell hypothetical stories of good and bad parenting skills without revealing incidents from the lives of specific clients, whose real predicaments are confidential.

Charles Gupton/corbisstockmarket.com

You can also create an imaginary scene that invites your listeners to personalize your topic. These scenes are especially effective at attracting attention and getting audience members to become emotionally involved. Here's one that would be a good opening illustration for a speech on problems that lottery winners face:

> Imagine that you just won the lottery. You can't sleep; you're so excited! You call everyone you know, and for a few days you bask in the joy of being an instant millionaire. Notice I said a few days. A week after you win, relatives you've never seen start asking for loans. A few days later, a friend sues for half the money, arguing that she encouraged you to buy the ticket, and without her urging, you'd still be poor. . . . The demands and the expectations pile up—so much so that you may almost wish you'd never bought that ticket!

Although hypothetical examples can work well in informative speeches, select real examples when your purpose is persuasion. Imaginary scenarios are generally less persuasive. Think of it this way: your listeners will more likely be persuaded by something that *did* happen than by something that *might* happen.

Speakers whose work involves confidentiality often describe hypothetical characters whose predicaments typify their clients' problems.

Combine Brief Examples

Examples don't have to be long. In fact, you may prefer to use a series of short illustrations; however, one brief example is easily missed or disregarded, so string together two or three—especially to gain attention in the introduction. By layering example upon example, you give audience members a number of mental images they can use to visualize your subject. Hans used three common foods as examples of grocery store items that contain surprising amounts of sugar:

- We'd expect cranberry-tangerine cocktail to be good for us, but a quick reading of the ingredient label reveals that corn syrup is the second ingredient in the juice.
- The first ingredient in one of the most popular breakfast cereals, one promoted by sports champions, is whole wheat—but sugar is next. Corn syrup and brown sugar are also on the ingredient list.
- A single can of cola contains about ten teaspoons of sugar.

Create Emotional Connections with Extended Examples

Extended examples include many details; each one gives your listeners another opportunity to identify emotionally with the subject of the story. Use them to clarify, to explain in depth, and to motivate your listeners. Look at how each detail in this illustration makes the story more poignant. The subject is the need for cheap AIDS medicines in Africa:

> Thirty-five-year-old Veronica Mngoma was diagnosed with AIDS more than a year ago, but her doctors in South Africa didn't even tell her that drugs could prolong her life. Why? She earns only $33 a week working in a furniture company, so she simply can't afford the $750 per month treatments that would make her condition a chronic disease rather than a death sentence. This mother of three is now pencil-thin and weak. She opens her sore-filled mouth to whisper, "I worry about my children." Like millions of other AIDS sufferers worldwide, Mngoma needs access to cheaper medicines. (Mabry, 1999)

Listeners can identify with one or more of the details: Ms. Mngoma's three children, her money worries, her helplessness and hopelessness. These help them connect with her plight and care about her situation. Because extended examples provide more distinct elements that engage listeners, they are generally more compelling. (Chapter 15 gives detailed information about organizing and evaluating narratives or well-developed stories that can function as the entire speech.)

Extended Examples
Longer incidents whose many details make them more compelling.

STOP AND CHECK

THINK CRITICALLY ABOUT EXAMPLES

Let's say you're reading for a speech about social anxiety and you come across the example of Grace Dailey, who experienced panic attacks so severe that she often had to leave college lectures. To help her get her degree, her professors agreed to leave the classroom door open during lectures, and they let her take tests alone (Schrof & Schultz, 1999). To evaluate the usefulness of an example such as this, ask yourself the following questions:

1. *Is this example representative or typical?* That is, do Grace's responses represent typical responses in the population of students with social anxiety? Or does her case seem extreme? This test relates to the probability of occurrence. Although the example may be possible, how *probable* is it?
2. *Do you have a sufficient number of examples?* Are enough cases presented to support the major idea adequately? How many people like Grace are attending colleges? Your listeners should be able to see that the issue you discuss is extensive, affecting a lot of people.
3. *Is the example true?* Did Grace actually leave lectures? How did such a shy woman convince her professors to work with her? Or, if it is hypothetical, does it ring true to what we know about the world and the way it operates?

Quote Culturally Acceptable Authorities

Remember this childhood challenge?

You make a statement.
Your friend responds, "Who says?"
"My teacher says!"
"Well, who's he? What does he know?"

To bolster your expertise on a topic, it helps to quote sources your listeners will see as authoritative. For instance, when Hans discussed the harms of sugar consumption, he presented the conclusions reached by research scientists and physicians.

Josh Nauman

Mentally reactivate this question-and-answer scenario as you gather speech materials. Whatever your subject, think of your audience as responding, "Who says?" Then identify the type of authority you think your audience would believe given your topic and purpose. Would you look for opinions of scholars or scientists? Wise women? Medical practitioners? Literary or scriptural texts? Quoting the words of authoritative sources will bolster your ideas if—and only if—your audience views the source as credible on the topic.

Every culture identifies sources it considers insightful enough to comment on particular topics; these can include seers, teachers, elders, academic experts, religious leaders, and written texts—authoritative sources vary among cultures and co-cultural groups. Quoting well-recognized and culturally appropriate sources can be valuable, especially if you are not known as an expert on your topic. By doing so, you demonstrate that knowledgeable, experienced people agree with your conclusions. Stating someone's exact words is a **direct quotation.** However, when the material is extensive, you're often better off summarizing the quotation in a **paraphrase.**

As Chapter 7 pointed out, two kinds of authorities can provide valuable material: experts and laypeople (peers). To show that your sources are credible, in your speech state who they are, why you believe their testimony, and why your audience should believe them.

Direct Quotation
Presenting the exact words of the source.

Paraphrase
Summarizing the source's ideas in your own words.

Quote Culturally Accepted Experts

Both education and experience are important in the United States, so look for opinions of **experts**—people considered credible because they know about a topic from study or from work-related experiences. Expert testimony comes from scholars, elected officials, and practitioners such as doctors or other professionals. Here is expert testimony, some of it taken from articles found on InfoTrac College Edition, that fits well in a speech about overconsumption of sugar:

Expert
Person considered an authority because of study or work-related experiences.

- Director of the Center for Science and the Public Interest and author of *Liquid Candy*, Michael Jacobson, says "Soda pop is junk. It has no vitamins, no minerals, no protein and no fiber" ("A Sweet Deal?," 1999).
- Helen Cook, a clinical nutritionist and master herbalist in Ajax, Ontario, Canada, believes that eating mounds of sugar is like putting cheap oil and gas into your car (Peters, 2000).

⚬ Christopher Gardner and his colleagues, research scientists at Stanford University, found that participants' triglyceride levels went up 30 percent on a convenience-food diet but went down 25 percent on a plant-food diet loaded with grains, salads, vegetables, and other whole foods with fiber (Liebman, 1998).

Because most people in the audience have probably never heard of any of these experts, it's up to the speaker to provide information that will help listeners decide whether they are credible. Giving information about the expert's institutional affiliation or explaining terms like R.D. (registered dietician) are ways to clarify the person's credentials. Notice that two of these examples paraphrase rather than directly quote the experts.

Sometimes a well-known person holds surprising opinions. That is, we commonly expect people to agree with the conventional wisdom of others who are similar to them in some way. Consider these examples:

⚬ William F. Buckley, Jr., a well-known conservative writer and journalist, supports legalization of drugs, a position not generally associated with conservatives.
⚬ Nat Hentoff, a writer and editor associated for many years with the liberal New York newspaper *The Village Voice*, takes a pro-life position, one that surprises many readers of the *Voice*.

Using unexpected testimony like this can be powerful evidence in persuasive speeches. Why? Because your listeners will reason that persons who go against their peers have thought through their opinions carefully.

Quote Credible Peers or Laypeople

U.S. cultural values include individual expression and equality among people. Therefore, the opinions of "regular people" who know about a subject because of firsthand experiences also carry weight. These **peer** or **lay sources** may not know scientific facts and related theories, but they can tell you how it feels to be involved as a participant. What do laypeople report about sugar consumption? In an article about vending machines in schools, several nonexperts spoke out ("A Sweet Deal?," 1999):

Peer or Lay Sources
People considered credible because of firsthand experiences with a topic.

⚬ Thirteen-year-old Bridget Hickson drinks one twenty-ounce bottle of soda before her 8:00 A.M. classes. At lunch, she guzzles two more bottles. "I like the way it tickles my throat," she reports. The soda costs her about $2.70 per day and puts about fifty teaspoons of sugar into her body.
⚬ Tyler Bilek, whose middle school is deciding whether or not to install vending machines, favors them, "Kids bring soda in from home anyway. At least it would benefit the school if they bought it here."
⚬ Jordan Ellis, in contrast, disagrees, "We don't need any more sugar being pumped into our bodies, especially not at school."

Put simply, the thirteen-year-old who guzzles soda and the middle school students, one who favors and the other who opposes installation of vending machines, all add participants' perspectives that a speaker can use to good advantage in developing a speech.

Quote Sayings, Proverbs, and Words of Wisdom

Every culture provides a store of sayings, proverbs, phrases, and words of wisdom that encapsulates ideas, beliefs, and values considered important. Cultural words of wisdom come from literature and oral traditions, from well-known and anonymous sources, from philosophical and political treatises. Here are a few examples:

⚬ This, above all, to thine own self be true. (literature)
⚬ It takes a village to raise a child. (African proverb)

- You shall know the truth, and the truth shall set you free. (religious text)
- Ask not what your country can do for you; ask what you can do for your country. (political speech)
- The greatest good for the greatest number [of people]. (philosopher)

Sayings do not always originate from well-known sources. You can also quote authoritative figures in your own life, as long as your audience respects the source. This speech excerpt illustrates how this works:

> My parents—and especially my father—taught me to draw an invisible line. He said to me, "Farah, you decide how you want other people to treat you, and if somebody crosses that line and it's unacceptable to you, just walk away from it. Don't let people treat you the way that they feel you should be treated. Have people treat you the way *you* feel you should be treated."
>
> That was good advice then. It is good advice now. (Walters, 1992)

Walters expects her audience to accept her father as a credible source of wisdom because this culture respects (although we sometimes reject!) the advice of friends and families.

Religious writings also provide rich sources of material when the audience accepts the text as valid. The evangelist Billy Graham, for example, commonly uses the phrase "The Bible says . . ." when he intends to invoke the ultimate authority. If his audience includes people of religious affiliation other than Christian, it is conceivable that they will discount Graham's source at least to some degree.

To find sayings, proverbs, and wise words you can use in your speeches, log on to the Internet and go to a search engine such as Yahoo! (www.yahoo.com), which links to a "Reference" category that includes many sources for quotations. Follow the links that interest you. (The Diversity in Practice box provides additional details about the importance of proverbs in some African cultures.)

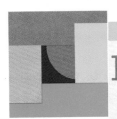

DIVERSITY IN PRACTICE
PROVERBS IN A WEST AFRICAN CULTURE

IN AN ARTICLE ENTITLED "Your Mother Is Still Your Mother" (Tembo, 1999), the author describes the importance of proverb usage among the Igbo people of Nigeria, West Africa, where proverbs both contain and transmit cultural wisdom. Chinua Achebe, a famous African author, calls them the Igbo's "horse of conversation." Adults who are considered wise conversationalists invariably use proverbs effectively, and every full and functioning adult in the village community learned to use proverbs properly during childhood. Each competent user understands each proverb's meaning and discerns the situations in which a specific proverb fits.

Use the information given and the skills you've developed through your usage of InfoTrac College Edition to find and read this entire article.

STOP AND CHECK
THINK CRITICALLY ABOUT QUOTING AUTHORITIES

Look back at the quotations of experts and laypeople relating to sugar. Ask yourself these questions about each source cited.

1. *What is the person's expertise?* Michael Jacobson's? Christopher Gardner's? Helen Cook's? Is it relevant to the subject under discussion?
2. *Is the person recognized as an expert by others?* How could you determine his or her reputation?

3. *Is the peer or layperson stating an opinion commonly held by others like him or her?* In other words, is it a typical or representative view? Do Tyler and Jordan typify middle school students? Do most middle school students drink as much soda as Bridget? Or is she an extreme example?

4. Because you don't have the entire article, you cannot assess the context for the person's words. However, whenever possible, *ask if the words are taken out of context.* That is, do they fairly represent the speaker's intended meaning? Words can be distorted so that the quoted person appears to hold a position not actually held.

To investigate this topic further, log on to InfoTrac College Edition and search for the exact words "taken out of context." Read one of the articles and identify the effect this has on the person quoted incorrectly.

Use Statistics Carefully

In our society, people tend to like numbers. We begin measuring and counting in preschool. We study the results of opinion polls and statistical research. Many consider numbers and measurements to be credible and trustworthy—hard facts. Consequently, effective use of numerical support may increase your credibility, causing you to appear more competent and knowledgeable. Commonly, numerical information enables us to understand the extent of an issue or problem or to predict the probability of some future happening.

In short, numerical data can be useful; however, it has unique drawbacks. In general, statistics are short on emotional appeal because they don't involve listeners' feelings, and too many in a speech may bore your audience. Furthermore, numerical information can be misleading. If you present obviously biased information, your listeners may distrust you. Consequently, take extra care to use enumeration and statistics both accurately and sparingly.

Enumeration
A count.

Presenting numerical information creatively can help your audience understand it better. William Dakin, a tax counsel for Mobil Corporation, could have simply said that the company's tax return was thousands of pages long; however, he made his point more dramatically by showing the stacked pages.

Provide a Count

Enumeration means counting. Providing a count helps your audience understand the extent of a problem or issue: how many people are injured in accidents annually, are diagnosed with a disease, have adopted a child over two years old, and so on. Two major tips will help you use enumeration more effectively.

1. *Round your numbers up or down.* There are two good reasons for doing this. First, listeners find it hard to remember exact numbers. For instance, instead of saying "When I searched on the Internet for information about Arab Christians, I got 4,569 hits," it is better to say "more than 4,500 hits," or "close to 5,000 hits." In addition, numbers related to current topics are likely to change rapidly. As you know, the number of Web sites on any given topic is constantly being revised.

2. *Make numbers come alive by comparing them to something already in your listeners' experience.* Let's take pro wrestling, for example. The sport attracts 35 million cable viewers each week, but

David Schull/New York Times

just how many people is that? A quick Internet search for statistics shows that it is approximately the population of Canada and Norway combined. Giving your audience something concrete, such as the population of two familiar countries, helps them to better understand the concept of 35 million.

Here's how First Lady Laura Bush (2001) explained the number of people killed in the September 11 terrorism act:

> If we remember a person a day, a child born on September 11 will be entering college before we are finished remembering all those who were killed.

Regina Lewis also used specific details to explain how much information is available on an Internet search engine's database:

> Within two seconds, the search engine Google provides you with enough information that, if it were printed out, would create a stack of paper 140 miles high. ("How to Become a Good Googler," 2002)

Both Mrs. Bush and Ms. Lewis give their listeners specific, meaningful details that clarify the numbers they are presenting.

Choose Statistics with a Critical Eye

The statistics most commonly used in speeches include means, medians, modes, percentages, and ratios (see Figure 8.1).

Figure 8.1 This pictograph shows lottery winnings of twenty-five participants. The mean or average was $5,700; the median or midpoint was $3,000. However, most people won $2,000—the mode. When a few extreme instances lead to unrealistic conclusions, the median or the mode is often more useful than the mean.

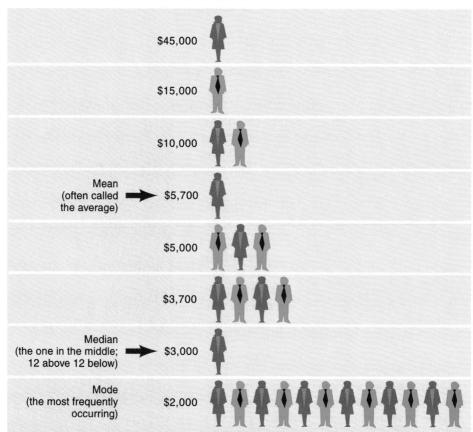

	$45,000
	$15,000
	$10,000
Mean (often called the average) ➡	$5,700
	$5,000
	$3,700
Median (the one in the middle; 12 above 12 below) ➡	$3,000
Mode (the most frequently occurring)	$2,000

Mean

The **mean** is the *average* of a group of numbers. To calculate the mean, add up all the specific measurements and divide by the total number of units measured. Here are some examples:

- A speech on women's issues might compare the mean ages at which women get married in the United States, in Spain, and in Zambia.
- A speech on credit debt could report the average number of credit cards per household (14.27), the average outstanding balance on those cards per household ($7,034), and the average late fee charge in 2002 ($28.79) compared to 1995 ($12.64) (Lim, 2002).
- A student leader might compare the mean tuition figures of other similar universities to a proposed tuition increase at her own school to argue against rising tuition costs.

The mean is skewed when extreme figures at either end of the range would make the comparison less useful. Just average the annual incomes of nine people who work for minimum wage and one billionaire to understand the limitations of the mean.

Mean
Average of a group of numbers.

Median

The **median** is the middle number in a set of numbers that have been arranged into a ranked order: half the numbers are above it and half below it. In the example of the billionaire and the minimum wage earners, the median is a way to give your listeners a more realistic picture.

Median
Middle number in a set of numbers arranged in a ranked order.

Mode

The **mode** is the number that appears most commonly. For example, on some college campuses, a few first-year students are sixteen, more are seventeen, some are in their twenties, thirties, or forties, but most are eighteen—the modal number. A few nurses in one hospital earn $25 an hour; a few earn only $14, but the modal rate for nurses' pay is $18 per hour.

Mode
Most frequently occurring number.

Percentages

Use **percentages** to show the relationship of a part to the whole, which is represented by the number 100. Public speakers commonly use percentages, as in the following example (which is illustrated in Figure 8.2):

Percentages
Figures that show the relationship of the part to the whole, which is represented by the number 100.

Figure 8.2 Seventy-nine percent of legal immigrants to the United States go to one of seven states.

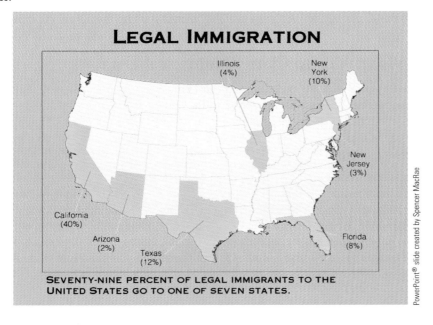

During the forty years from 1880 to 1920, at least 12 million immigrants fleeing poverty and persecution in European countries flocked to the United States. Since 1965, when the immigration laws were changed, at least that many more have entered the United States—both legally and illegally. Of legal immigrants, 79% go to one of seven states, as the map shows.

Rate of Increase or Decrease
A percentage that uses an earlier baseline figure to compare growth or decline.

Often you'll find the percentage stated as a **rate of increase** or **decrease,** which compares growth or decline during a period of time to a baseline figure from an earlier period. Treat these rates with caution, for unless you know the baseline number the rate of increase or decrease is relatively meaningless. Case in point: If a company employs two people in the year 2002 and adds an additional employee in 2003, the rate of increase is 50 percent. However, if a company employs 100 people in 2002 and adds an additional employee in 2003, the number of new employees is the same, but the rate of increase in the larger organization is only 1 percent. The reverse is also true. The two-person company that loses one employee decreases by half, or 50 percent; the large company hardly notices a loss of one. As you can see, when baseline numbers are initially very low, the rate of increase is potentially astounding!

Here are some crime rates that are typical of statistics you will come across in your research (National Center for Victims of Crime, 2000). Each is followed by a short analysis question:

- Males experience violent crime at rates 28 percent greater than females; however, females are raped and sexually assaulted at 7.5 times the rate of males. *(Why do you think the authors reported the figure relating to males as a percentage but the number relating to females as a multiple? What is 7.5, stated as a percentage?)*
- The U.S. rate of children and teens killed by gunfire is 12 times higher than in the twenty-five other industrialized countries combined. *(Any deaths are lamentable, but we cannot determine the magnitude of the problem from this information. What if the other countries only have 10 such deaths? What if they have 20,000?)*

Ratios

Ratio
A numerical relationship shown by numbers such as 1 in 10.

Often we present relationships between numbers as a **ratio,** rather than as a percentage; consequently, you'll commonly find 10 percent and 1 in 10 used interchangeably. Twenty-five percent, similarly, is stated as 1 out of 4. Ratios are especially helpful when the percentage is very small; for example, .000001 percent equals 1 case in 100,000. As a result, you'll be more effective if you say, "18 out of 100,000 teens died of gunshot injuries in 1989, up from the 12 per 100,000 recorded in 1979," than if you give the figures as percentages.

Use Visual Aids to Clarify Numerical Data

Because numerical data are sometimes difficult to understand, present them in visual form whenever you can. William Dakin, shown in the photograph on page 141, used stacks of paper to illustrate his point. The pictograph of Figure 8.1 and the map of Figure 8.2 are both visual aids. Figure 8.3 shows the value of a table to help your audience visualize complex numbers. Imagine trying to understand a speaker who simply says this:

Child care workers are underpaid. Men who graduate from college average more than $51,804 annually; women graduates average $33,615. Men who have some college earn an average of $33,161 compared to women in the same category who average $22,445. Even men with a high school diploma average $27,665, and women who have graduated from high school earn on the average $19,309. Compare all these salaries to the average of $15,488 that the highest paid child care workers earn.

Figure 8.3 A table effectively depicts complex numerical data in a way that listeners can easily grasp.

Comparative Salaries of Child Care Workers		
	Average for all men	Average for all women
College graduates	$51,804	$33,615
Some college	$33,161	$22,445
High school diploma	$27,865	$19,309
Highest paid child care worker	$15,488	

Is your head spinning? Do you remember any of this data? Now, imagine that the speaker either gives you a handout or projects a transparency with Figure 8.3 on it. How are your responses different? In what ways does the visual enable you to grasp the material better?

You can see that different types of data call for different types of visual aids. Because visual aids are vital in American culture, this text devotes Chapter 12 to the topic of creating and displaying visual materials.

STOP AND CHECK

CRITICALLY ANALYZE NUMERICAL DATA

Because numbers are easy to manipulate, evaluate them carefully with these questions before you use them.

1. *What is the source of the numbers?* Does the source have an interest such as a possibility of financial gain that would make high or low numbers more desirable?
2. *Are the numbers up to date?* Using a count or a percentage that is old is generally not applicable to current conditions.
3. Before you use startling rates of increase, *look at the baseline figures of the percentages.* Note any other relevant factors that might affect this rate.

For further information about testing your numbers, log on to InfoTrac College Edition and do a subject search for "statistics." Click on the "subdivisions," then link to the articles in the "analysis" subdivision. Read one that interests you, noting the guidelines for statistical interpretation.

Find Compelling Comparisons

We often learn new information or understand new ideas better if we can compare and contrast the new to something familiar. A **comparison** or **analogy** points out similarities between things: "The hail felt like a rain of golf balls" or "Her family is a circus and she's the clown." Put simply, we understand the unfamiliar better by finding points of comparison to something that's already in our experience. Comparisons can be literal or figurative.

Comparison or Analogy
Stating similarities between two things.

Use Literal Analogies

Literal Analogies
Comparisons between two actual things that are alike in important ways.

When you compare things that are similar in important ways, you are using **literal analogies.** For example, a Pakistani speaker, Liaquat Ali Khan (2002), explained to the U.S. Senate how his country was founded:

> Pakistan was founded so that millions of Muslims should be enabled to live according to their opinions and to worship God in freedom. . . . Like some of the earlier founders of your great country, these Muslims, though not Pilgrims, nevertheless embarked upon an undertaking, which, in aim and achievement, represented the triumph of an idea. That idea was the idea of liberty, which has had its ardent followers in all climates and all countries. When our time came, its call summoned us, too, and we could not hold back.

By showing the similarities of his country's founding to that of the United States, by linking both countries in their shared values, Khan's listeners could understand why Muslims broke away from India's Hindu population to create Pakistan. You can access the complete article on InfoTrac College Edition to learn more about Khan's views.

Here's another example. In a classroom speech on the pros and cons of fetal-cell transplantation, Chris Patti showed how proponents on both sides of this controversial issue literally compare the dead fetus to other dead bodies:

> Supporters of transplantation believe that the fetus is essentially a cadaver. They reason that adult cadavers are used in research with the consent of their families. So why shouldn't fetal cadavers be used to develop more effective methods of treating debilitating diseases? John Robertson, a law professor at the University of Texas, says that the dead fetus is essentially an organ donor and that its usable organs should be used to treat horrible diseases.
>
> . . . Critics of fetal tissue research and transplantation believe that the fetus is essentially a victim. They ask, "Should we do harm so that good may come?" Their answer is no. Arthur Caplan, Director of the Center for Biomedical Ethics at the University of Minnesota, argues against using a victim to save the lives of others. "Society will not tolerate killing one life for another," he asserts.
>
> CHRIS

Contrasts
Stating differences between two things.

Sometimes you will find that pointing out *differences*, or showing **contrasts** between a new concept and a more familiar one, is effective. For example, when Betty explained the Japanese educational system, she described its differences from schooling in the United States as well as its similarities. Andres explained lacrosse by contrasting it with the more familiar games of baseball and football.

Create Vivid Figurative Analogies

Figurative Analogies
Stated similarities between two otherwise dissimilar things; requires an imaginative connection.

When you highlight similarities between otherwise *dissimilar* things, you're using **figurative analogies.** These analogies require your listeners to apply their imagination and integrate likenesses between two otherwise different things or ideas. In a convocation speech at Queens College in North Carolina, a music professor compared personalities to various melodies:

> . . . each of us has a unique melody. . . . Some of you are quiet, soft, and lyrical. Others are rhythmic and energetic. Some are majestic and somber. Yet others may be whimsical and funny. Still others are cool and mellow. And truthfully, some of you are like the new styles of music, you are just way out there. Regardless, your melody is your own sound, your own style, your essence, your identity. (McClain, 2001)

Fouling out, having a game plan, scoring a slam dunk—all these are figurative analogies comparing life to a sporting event. Can you identify other common examples?

George Tarbay, NIU Media Services

In short, figurative analogies connect familiar images with those less known. Many of the students in the audience could identify characteristics of musical genres—ballads, soft rock, jazz, heavy metal—that resemble different people.

STOP AND CHECK
THINK CRITICALLY ABOUT ANALOGIES

Evaluate your use of comparisons and contrasts. To test literal analogies, make sure the two items are alike in essential details. For instance, you could mislead your audience by comparing the work of a police officer in Houston, Texas, to another in Sioux Falls, South Dakota. Although they're alike in many ways, they are not fundamentally the same. Comparing the Houston officer to one in Los Angeles or Miami is more appropriate because all three operate in urban settings with diverse populations. Sioux Falls officers, on the other hand, have more in common with police officers in smaller cities in Michigan and Nebraska.

To test figurative analogies, be sure the comparison is clear and makes sense. Can your listeners make the necessary connection of ideas?

To learn more about both literal and figurative analogies, log on to InfoTrac College Edition and do a subject search for "analogies."

Summary

It is vital to support your ideas with evidence that listeners can understand so that they see reasons for your major ideas. Select facts, including definitions and descriptions, that you can verify in a number of sources. In addition, select facts that are up to date. Further, during your research, distinguish factual material from opinions and take care not to pass on distorted or incorrect information.

Most listeners respond to examples, and using specific incidents as supporting material functions to make abstract concepts more concrete and relevant. In addition, illustrations help listeners identify emotionally with your topic by means of real or hypothetical, brief or extended, examples. To be effective, examples should be representative, sufficient in number, and plausible.

The use of quotations can enhance your credibility if you are not considered an expert on a topic. Directly quote or paraphrase the opinions of experts and lay or peer sources. In addition, quote cultural proverbs, written texts, and even words of wisdom from relatively unknown sources that your audience will accept as credible.

In a society that tends to be impressed by quantification, the judicious use of enumeration and statistics may increase your audience's acceptance of your ideas. However, be sure that your numerical support is understandable, up to date, and used in ways that do not create misleading impressions. Visual aids are often helpful in clarifying complex numerical data.

Finally, comparisons or analogies are an additional means of support. Literal analogies compare or contrast two actual things; figurative analogies compare two things that are generally considered different but share one specific likeness. Both types add vividness to your speeches.

As you interweave facts, examples, numbers, testimony, and analogies, you give your listeners more reasons to accept the conclusions you present.

JAFFE ONLINE CONNECTION   **JAFFE ONLINE CONNECTION**

Use your CD-ROM and the Jaffe Connection Web site http://communication.wadsworth.com/jaffe to review the following concepts, answer the review questions, and complete the suggested activities.

KEY TERMS

facts (132)
established facts (132)
define (133)
opinions (133)
describe (133)
examples (134)
real examples (135)
hypothetical examples (135)
extended examples (137)
direct quotation (138)
paraphrase (138)
expert (138)

peer or lay sources (139)
enumeration (141)
mean (143)
median (143)
mode (143)
percentages (143)
rate of increase or decrease (144)
ratio (144)
comparison or analogy (145)
literal analogies (146)
contrasts (146)
figurative analogies (146)

APPLICATION AND CRITICAL THINKING EXERCISES

1. Bring to class a current edition of a newsmagazine or newspaper. With your classmates, choose an issue from the week's news. Collect and display information by divid-

ing the chalkboard into sections, one for each kind of evidence: facts, examples, quotations, numerical data, and analogies. Contribute information from your magazine or paper, cooperating with your classmates to fill the board. Evaluate the evidence using the tests presented in this chapter.

2. Log on to InfoTrac College Edition and do a PowerTrac search for the article "The Immortal Ten." Come to class prepared to discuss the origin of one of the common sayings presented.

3. Do a PowerTrac search for the journal *Vital Speeches* on InfoTrac College Edition. Read Solomon Trujillós's speech titled "The Hispanic Destiny: Corporate Responsibility" and identify the kinds of supporting materials he uses. Evaluate the effectiveness of the strategies in gaining and keeping your attention. Where does your attention perk up? Where do you find yourself losing interest? How do you think the actual audience responded to the speech?

4. Go to the online edition of *U.S. News & World Report* at www.usnews.com/usnews/home.htm. Read the cover story and find examples of a fact, expert and peer testimony, a statistic, and an analogy.

5. With a small group of your classmates, evaluate the effectiveness of the following pieces of evidence taken from student speeches. What kind (or kinds) of evidence does each excerpt represent? Is the evidence specific or vague? Does the speaker cite the source of the evidence adequately? Does it meet the tests for the type of evidence it represents?

- A recent study showed that at least three out of four black children who were placed in white homes are happy and have been successfully incorporated into their families and communities.

- According to the *Natural History of Whales and Dolphins*, dolphins communicate through a system of whistles, clicks, rattles, and squeaks. These clicking sounds are not only used for navigation in the deep waters but they may also be used to convey messages. Pulsed squeaks can indicate distress, while buzzing clicks may indicate aggression.

- As far as deaths [from killer bees] are concerned, Mexican officials report that only sixteen people have died in the last three years as a result of their stings. That number is similar to the number who die of shark bite. As one Texan put it, "The killer bee will be no more a threat to us than the rattlesnake."

- According to New Jersey Congressman Frank Guarini, "American families play amusement ride roulette every time they go on an outing to an amusement park."

- As reported by the *World Press Review Magazine,* the Japanese use of disposable chopsticks has resulted in the destruction of half of the hardwood forests in the Philippines and one-third of the forests in Indonesia. This trend will likely continue as long as the Japanese use twelve billion pairs of throwaway chopsticks a year, which is enough wood to build 12,000 average-sized family homes.

- In 1988, fetal brain cells were implanted deep into the brain of a fifty-two-year-old Parkinson's victim. Traditional treatments all failed this person. Now, he reports that his voice is much stronger, his mind is sharper and not confused, and he can walk without cane or crutches.

THE JAFFE CONNECTION WEB SITE

The Jaffe Connection Web site features review questions about the Web links, Stop and Check activities, and InfoTrac College Edition exercises referenced throughout the chapter. You can access this site via your CD-ROM or at http://communication.wadsworth.com/jaffe.

Web Links

8.1 Arab American Fact Sheet (page 134)
8.2 Finding Quotations Online (page 140)
8.3 *U.S. News & World Report* Online (page 149)

Stop and Check Activities

8.1 Think Critically About Facts (page 134)
8.2 Think Critically About Examples (page 137)
8.3 Think Critically About Quoting Authorities (pages 140–141)
8.4 Critically Analyze Numerical Data (page 145)
8.5 Think Critically About Analogies (page 147)

InfoTrac College Edition Exercises

8.1 Visual Evidence: Chicano Murals in Chicago (page 132)
8.2 Distinguishing Fact from Fiction Online (page 134)
8.3 Expert Opinions (page 138)
8.4 Nigerian Wisdom Transmitted Through Proverbs (page 140)
8.5 Using Facts Out of Context (page 141)
8.6 Guidelines for Statistical Interpretation (page 145)
8.7 A Pakistani's View of the Founding of Pakistan (page 146)
8.8 Think Critically About Analogies: Understanding Literal and Figurative Analogies (page 147)
8.9 Common Maxims (page 149)
8.10 Identifying Supporting Materials (page 149)

SPEECH INTERACTIVE ON THE JAFFE CONNECTION CD-ROM

Read the following outline by Hans Erian and watch excerpts from his persuasive speech under Speech Interactive on your Jaffe Connection CD-ROM. In addition to Hans's speech, Speech Interactive features Paul Southwick's persuasive speech, "Embryo Adoption," which uses a metaphor throughout. The transcript of Paul's speech is found in Appendix C.

STUDENT OUTLINE WITH COMMENTARY

OVER-CONSUMPTION OF SUGAR
by Hans Erian

General Purpose: To persuade

Specific Purpose: To persuade my audience that overconsumption of sugar is contributing to obesity and related diseases, but something can be done about it.

Central Idea: Too much sugar can lead to obesity and Type II diabetes, but national awareness, plus personal commitment to good health, can help.

Introduction

I. Fifteen-year-old Arnold Scott weighed three hundred pounds; he developed symptoms that led to a diagnosis of Type II diabetes.

  A. Type II diabetes, usually associated with adults, is increasing among children and leaving them vulnerable to blindness, heart and kidney disease, and stroke at ages as young as thirty (*Newsday*, 7/20/99).

  B. Dr. Barbara Lindner of the National Institute of Diabetes, Digestive Diseases, and Kidney Diseases linked the rise in diabetes to a rise in obesity, and obesity is on the rise because of sugar.

    1. The *Nationwide News* of August 21, 2001 reported that, of the ten most-bought foods bought at the supermarket, most are sugar-filled junk foods (*New York Times*, 2/16/02).

    2. A Georgetown University study showed that 25 percent of adult calories come from sugar; for kids, it's closer to 50 percent.

II. The average person in this room consumes about 125–150 pounds of sugar per year.

  A. *Consumer Reports on Health* of August 2001 says that increases in blood sugar levels lead to increases in disease and death.

  B. Americans are consuming too much unhealthy sugar without realizing it.

III. Today we will explore two major causes of sugar overconsumption, then we'll examine negative effects, and finally we'll look at ways to nationally and personally deal with the problem.

Body

I. The two main reasons for increased consumption of sugar are ignorance and increased consumption of soda pop.

  A. The FDA and the sugar association have been fighting a linguistics tug-of-war since about 1970 over the definition of sugar.

    1. Fructose is the good sugar, the kind found naturally in fruit.

    2. Bad sugar, the kind in most foods, comes under names like sucrose, dextrose, and high fructose corn syrup, which may be confusing because of the word "fructose" in it.

    3. Common items in local stores can lead to confusion.

      a. Here's a cranberry-tangerine juice drink that we'd expect to be healthy, but the second ingredient is high fructose corn syrup.

      b. Wheaties ingredients include whole wheat, sugar—and also corn sugar and brown sugar, other bad sugars; can this be the breakfast of champions?

  B. The second reason is the increased consumption of soda.

    1. Coca Cola contains sucrose and has about ten teaspoons of sugar per pint.

Commentary (right margin):

Hans prepared this speech when he was on his college speech team. He begins with an extended example full of details that he developed when he delivered his speech.

These are startling facts.

Here he quotes an expert who links the problem to sugar consumption.

Additional statistics help establish the extent of the problem.

The average college student's consumption is sobering and piques interest.

He previews his major points.

He distinguishes between two types of sugar.

Showing common foods shows how easy it is to be deceived about products.

He'd be wise to double check his numbers, but most of us can imagine how many cases of soda that adds up to!

2. The consumption of soda increased by 43 percent to eighty-five gallons per year since 1987; that's 555 cans annually for every American (*San Jose Mercury News*, 1/17/99).

TRANSITION: Now that we've seen the increased use of sugar because of ignorance and soda pop, we will see the negative effects this is having on our health.

II. This amount of sugar is having a negative impact on our health.

The *New York Times* is a credible source, but I'd like to hear him also cite the study that this information is based on.

   A. There is convincing new evidence between weight gain in children and the consumption of soda pop (*New York Times*, 9/9/01).

     1. Obesity is directly linked to soda pop consumption regardless of the amount of food you eat or lack of exercise.
     2. Perhaps this is because the body has trouble adapting to intense concentrations of sugar taken in liquid form.

   B. Obesity is linked to many diseases, including high blood pressure, high cholesterol, and heart disease as well as cancer and diabetes.

These statistics support his claim of a link between cancer and obesity.

     1. Obesity is now considered the Number Two killer in the United States because it causes cancer.

       a. Obese people are 70 percent more likely to get pancreatic cancer, which has a 95 percent mortality rate (*New York Times*, 10/9/01).
       b. The U.S. Department of Health links it to post-menopausal breast cancer and colon cancer.

     2. Obesity is linked to diabetes.

       a. Since 1991, adult obesity increased by 60 percent, and the percentage of overweight kids has doubled (*Hartford Courant*, 9/9/01).
       b. Children and adolescents are developing Type II diabetes, a disease associated with people over forty-five years of age.

Dr. Bernstein is an "expert" who uses nature metaphors—tidal wave and avalanche.

       c. Dr. Gerald Bernstein predicts that, if left unchecked, there will be five hundred million diabetics worldwide in twenty-five years, leading to a tidal wave of suffering and an avalanche of health care bills.

TRANSITION: Now that we see that Americans are consuming too much sugar and it's destroying our health, we need to decrease our sugar intake.

The solution is two-pronged: national and personal.

III. We can do something on a national and a personal level.

   A. On a national level we need to increase our awareness and decrease soda pop consumption.

In a society in which consumers are bringing lawsuits against fast food businesses, Brownwell's recommendation regarding ads is timely.

     1. Kelly Brownwell, director of Yale University's Eating and Weight Disorders, recommends regulation of ads aimed at children to provide equal time for nutritional and pro-exercise messages.
     2. She also suggested changing the price of foods to make healthier foods less expensive than sugar-laden ones.

This recommendation is also workable. A few months after Hans gave this speech, the Los Angeles School Board voted to take these machines out of their schools.

     3. Schools could disable the school vending machines during class time, stripping them of sweets, or putting a new tax on them, which may discourage students from buying sweets (*New York Times*, 2/16/01).
     4. We might also impose a tax on soft drinks in general.

TRANSITION: These are just a few ways to provide incentives for people to get healthy and eat less sugar.

B. We would like to have someone else help us get healthy, but what is really needed is a personal commitment to health.

1. Start off slow and follow Dr. Robert Owen's advice; he wrote *Optimum Wellness*, and he suggests you have dessert a few times a week or a can of pop a couple of times a week.
2. In fact, the World Health Organization suggested that up to 10 percent of calories can come from sugar, but try to stick to healthy sugars.
3. In addition, be a label reader.

Conclusion

I. Now that we have looked at the misconceptions regarding sugar and what they lead to, you can decrease your sugar intake.
II. This will prevent more people from ending up like Arnold Scott who takes insulin injections just to stay alive.

Realistic solutions are practical enough for people to put into practice. Moderation, as his expert suggests here, is very doable.

He concludes by returning to his sad opening story.

Organizing Your Speech

THIS CHAPTER WILL HELP YOU

■ Organize your main points

■ Identify and use a number of linear patterns, including chronological, spatial, causal, problem–solution, pro–con, and topical

■ Identify and use more holistic, alternative patterns when they are appropriate, including the wave, the spiral, and the star

"Desaparecidos Pero no Olvidados" Mural ©1999 by Carlos Madriz, Josh Short, and Mabel Negrette. (Balmy Alley, Balmy and 24th Street, SF, CA)

y now, you have chosen and carefully focused your topic. Even so, your research probably produced so much information that you feel overwhelmed. How do you sort through it all to make an understandable speech—one that hangs together with a number of main points that have some sort of logical connection? Good speakers find ways to organize their thoughts and present their ideas in patterns that audiences can follow and remember. Otherwise, they frustrate their listeners, as Heidi and Gail point out:

> If an audience is confused or overwhelmed with disarrayed information, not only is the speech difficult to understand but the whole underlying credibility of the rhetor is diminished.
>
> Heidi

> Organization is everything. . . . I consider it being kind to your audience as well as yourself.
>
> Gail

Guidelines for organization fall into what the Romans called the *canon of disposition.* This chapter begins with general tips for identifying and organizing main points, moves on to explain some linear organizational patterns, and concludes with holistic, alternative methods of arranging the body of your speech.

Organize Your Main Points

Although the body is the middle part of your speech, it is the part that you plan first. As you collected information, you probably identified a number of subcategories such as causes or proposed solutions, or a chronological time line in which events occurred. Identifying these patterns can help you determine major points and focus supporting materials under each one. At the outset, consider the following general tips for organizing main points.

Limit the Number of Points

Cognitive psychologists say we learn better when we portion blocks of information into three to seven major units (which explains why your telephone number is divided into three and four digit segments). Consequently, your listeners will remember your speech better if you develop a limited number of main ideas: most instructors recommend three to five points.

At this point in your preparation, return to the central idea you developed in Chapter 6. If you clearly identified the direction of your speech, you can now begin to flesh it out. For instance, Maria wants to convince her classmates that the lottery winners are often unhappy, and people who want to be wealthy are better off spending their money elsewhere. So she initially sets out this central idea:

> The lottery is a form of gambling that often leads to unhappiness.

During the research process, Maria's material clusters into three major points: (1) the lottery itself—its history, profitability; (2) the problems winners encounter; and (3) alternatives to buying lottery tickets. So she revises her central idea to read like this:

> The lottery, a form of gambling, raises money for good causes; however, winning often creates enormous problems for the winners, and they would be better off spending their money elsewhere.

Her major points are now easy to identify:

   I. Lotteries are a form of gambling that raise money for good causes.
  II. Lottery winners often have enormous problems as a result of winning.
 III. Most people would be happier if they found an alternative to playing the lottery.

Support Each Point with Evidence

Chapter 8 described numerous ways to support the major ideas of a speech, among them facts, examples, quotations, numerical information, and analogies. At this stage, Maria sits down with her articles about lottery winners and arranges specific pieces of data under each main point. Here's an example of her first major point:

I. Lotteries are a form of gambling that raise money for good causes.
   A. *Webster's Dictionary* identifies the lottery as a popular form of gambling.
      1. Winners pay to participate, generally by purchasing tickets at a uniform price.
      2. Winners are determined by chance.
   B. Lotteries generate revenues for good causes.
      1. The earliest lottery, organized in London in 1680, raised money for a municipal water supply.
      2. A French lottery helped pay for the Statue of Liberty.
      3. Lotteries helped support the Jamestown Colony and the American Revolution.
      4. They provided funds for Harvard, Princeton, and Dartmouth.
      5. Current lotteries in New Hampshire and Oregon, among other states, provide educational funding.

Order Your Points Effectively

For some topics, the ordering of points flows logically. Obviously, starting with an explanation of lotteries in general, moving to the problems that winners encounter, and suggesting alternatives is more logically satisfying to Maria's audience than if she were to suggest alternatives, discuss the problems, then explain what lotteries are. For other speeches, the natural flow is less obvious. A topic such as recreational opportunities available in a particular region might have the following organization:

I. Bungee jumping
II. Hang gliding
III. Hot air ballooning
IV. Windsurfing

No logical reason dictates that bungee jumping must come first and windsurfing last. In fact, the speaker might start with windsurfing which happens on a river, then move to the airborne sports. Or he might move from the least expensive to the most costly, depending on the audience. If these sports are centered in specific places, he might move from the nearest to the most distant options.

With these principles in mind, you can now choose from a number of organizational patterns that will best work for your speech.

Traditional Patterns

From listening to speakers throughout the years, you have developed some schema for organizational patterns. Some patterns work especially well for presenting facts and information; others are better for persuasive messages (see Chapter 17). This section presents six traditional patterns that can help you organize a wide variety of topics: chronological, spatial, causal, problem–solution, pro–con, and topical.

Chronological Organization

In a **chronological pattern,** the sequencing—what comes first and what follows—must occur in a given order. Because this pattern develops an idea as it transpires over a period

Chronological Pattern
A pattern that presents points in time or sequential order.

A chronological pattern is useful for topics that describe ordered sequences. One example is the life cycle of a butterfly.

Edward R. Degginger/Bruce Coleman, Inc./PictureQuest

of time, consider using a chronological pattern for biographical speeches, those that recount historical events, and those that explain processes, stages, or cycles.

It stands to reason that a biographical speech is often developed chronologically because an individual's life unfolds across a period of years. Here is a sketch of the main points of a speech about a person's life, organized chronologically:

James Nahkai, Jr., was a Navajo Code talker.
I. His early life on the Navajo Reservation
II. His experiences as a Code Talker in the U.S. Marine Corps
III. His later participation in the Navajo Tribal Council

Chronological organizational patterns also function effectively when you describe historical events:

The Civil War cost more lives than any other war.
I. Events preceding the war
II. The war years
III. Reconstruction of the South

Process Speech
A speech that describes a sequence of steps or stages that follow one another in a fairly predictable pattern.

Process speeches generally feature a chronological pattern. In such a speech, several steps or stages follow one another in fairly predictable sequences. You can describe natural as well as social processes. This skeleton outline shows the chronological organization of a natural process.

A baby's first year
I. The newborn
II. Development during the first three months
III. Three- to six-month-old babies
IV. Six- to nine-month-old infants
V. Nine-month to year-old babies

Many social, psychological, or personal processes also occur in patterned sequences or cycles. Norma summarized Professor Steve Duck's "theory of relational dissolution" in this brief outline:

Four phases are typical when a relationship dissolves.
I. Intrapsychic—one or both partners ponder what to do about the relationship.
II. Dyadic—they talk to one another about breaking up.

III. Social phase—other people are told about their breakup.

IV. Grave-dressing phase—they rationalize the breakup.

The key to chronological speeches is that events *must* occur in a sequence and follow a clear "first, next, finally" pattern. In a disease, for instance, symptoms follow rather than precede infection with a virus. Occasionally, however, speakers vary the pattern by beginning with the final point before showing the events that led up to it. For instance, the speaker could first describe a divorced person rationalizing the divorce ("grave-dressing" phase), then flashback and provide details about the first three phases.

Spatial Organization

You can also organize the points of your speech spatially by place or location. The **spatial pattern** is less common, but it is good for speeches about places or about objects that are made up of several parts. For example, a guide showing a group how to use the campus library probably will provide a map and describe what is located on each floor. Beginning with the ground floor, she works her way up to higher floors. If you were to describe the effects of alcohol on the human body, you might move from the brain downward to the heart and other organs. The order in which you present your points doesn't matter with some topics, as this speech outline (which is divided geographically) demonstrates:

Spatial Pattern
Presents points by place or location.

Major global earthquake areas
  I. Eastern European fault lines
 II. The Pacific "Ring of Fire"
III. The Rift Valley in Africa

Objects that you describe from top to bottom, bottom to top, or side to side lend themselves well to spatial organization. For example, a brick pathway in a garden is constructed in four layers: gravel, heavy-duty weed barrier fabric, sand, and bricks. Consequently, people who make their living by explaining gardening techniques use a spatial pattern. Similarly, exercise instructors often begin with head and neck exercises and work down the body spatially.

Causal Organization

Because they have learned Euro-American thought patterns, people in the U.S. culture tend to look for causes that underlie events. For this reason, you might choose a **cause–effect pattern** to discuss problems by examining the reasons underlying the problem (the causes) and the implications they have for individuals or for society at large (the effects). There are two basic causal organizational patterns: cause-to-effect and effect-to-cause. Here is a cause-to-effect outline for a speech on amusement park tragedies:

Cause–Effect Pattern
Presents reasons (causes) and implications (effects) of a topic.

Amusement park tragedies injure thousands of people annually.
  I. Causes
     A. Equipment failure
     B. Operator failure
     C. Rider behavior
 II. Effects
     A. Personal risks
     B. Needless tragedies

For some topics, you might decide it is more effective to look first at a problem's effects on an individual or group before you explore its causes. This is an effects-to-cause organization pattern.

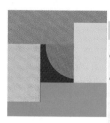

SOME AFRICAN ORGANIZATIONAL PATTERNS

IN MANY AREAS OF THE WORLD, speakers choose patterns markedly different from those presented in this text. Two such examples come from Africa.

MADAGASCAR

Elders in the Merina tribe use a four-part organizational pattern when they speak (Bloch, 1975):

1. First is a period of excuses in which the speaker expresses his humility and reluctance to speak. He uses standard phrases such as "I am a child, a younger brother." He sometimes relates well-known stories and proverbs.
2. He follows this by thanking the authorities for letting him speak at all. He uses a formula that thanks God, the president of the republic, government ministers, the village headman, major elders, and finally the people in the audience.
3. In the third section, he uses proverbs, illustrations, and short poems as he makes his proposal.
4. He closes by thanking and blessing his listeners.

KENYA

The body of the speech is not necessarily linear. In fact, a circular pattern, somewhat like a bicycle wheel, is more typical. The hub or center of the wheel is the single main point that ties the entire speech together. The speaker then wanders out repeatedly from the central point, telling stories and providing other supporting materials and stories that tie back to the main idea. To an outsider, the speech might seem boring or illogical, but Kenyan listeners are able to follow the logic that ties the points together (Miller, 2002).

People in the United States consume too much sugar.
   I. Effects include obesity—even in young children
      A. Linked to cancer
      B. Linked to heart disease
      C. Linked to Type II diabetes in children
  II. Causes of overconsumption of sugar
      A. Lack of awareness about the presence of sugar in common foods
      B. Consumption of carbonated drinks

Problem–Solution Organization

Problem–Solution Pattern
Describes a problem and a possible solution(s) to it.

In line with their core beliefs that life presents a series of problems to be solved, people in the United States often approach global and national issues, as well as personal problems, as challenges to understand and solve through knowledge and effort. (Some cultures, in contrast, believe it is futile to fight fate.) Thus, a **problem–solution pattern** is common. Not surprisingly, if you choose this pattern, you first look at the problem—sometimes examining its causes and effects—then propose solutions. Here is an outline for an informative speech on elder abuse that uses this pattern:

The high cost of prescription drugs is affecting the health of many elderly persons.
   I. Prescription drugs are increasingly costly.
      A. Causes of the problem
      B. Effects of the problem

II. Several solutions have been proposed.
  A. Governmental solutions
  B. Personal solutions

Some speakers choose to present problem–solution approaches to personal as well as national or global topics. This outline shows the major points in a speech about a personal issue:

Hair loss affects millions of people.
  I. Women as well as men experience hair loss.
    A. Causes of the problem
    B. Effects of the problem
  II. There are several solutions on the market.
    A. Medications
    B. Hairpieces
    C. Bonding techniques
    D. Transplants

When the purpose of your speech is informative, introduce your listeners to a variety of solutions. In persuasive speeches, however, it is most effective to propose several solutions, then focus on the one solution you believe should be implemented. Chapter 17 returns to the problem–solution pattern and explains additional organizational plans commonly used for persuasive speeches.

Pro–Con Organization

In the United States, speakers and audiences commonly explore arguments both for and against controversial issues. If you give a speech that summarizes both sides of an issue, you may find the **pro–con arrangement** useful. Classify all the arguments in favor of the issue under the pro label, then list the arguments against it under the con label. Here is an example of a pro–con organization:

Pro–Con Arrangement
Presents arguments in favor of and arguments against an issue.

The Hawaiian sovereignty movement has both proponents and opponents.
  I. Arguments in favor of an independent nation of Hawaii
    A. The 1989 annexation was illegal because the Senate never approved it.
    B. Promises made in the 1920s to return lands to Native Hawaiians have not yet been kept.
    C. The 1959 statehood vote is meaningless because independence was not a ballot option.
    D. In 1993, President Clinton apologized for the illegal overthrow of 1898.
  II. Arguments against an independent nation of Hawaii
    A. Most residents of Hawaii are not Hawaiian natives.
    B. Changing the current legal, economic, political, and military systems would be difficult.
    C. Other less drastic, solutions would solve the problems.

This organizational pattern works best in informative speeches, when your purpose is to enlighten people on the nature of an issue. By presenting both sides, your listeners can weigh the evidence and evaluate the arguments for themselves. When your purpose is persuasive (you are advocating acceptance of one set of arguments rather than another), you generally will choose a different pattern. Chapter 17 examines persuasive techniques.

Topical Organization

If your material doesn't really fit into any of these organizational patterns, arrange your points topically, which is the most widely used pattern. A topical arrangement classifies the major points into topics or subdivisions, each of which is part of the whole. Although every

AP/Wide World Photos

The major points of a speech on sovereignty for the Hawaiian Islands can be organized in a number of ways, including pro–con, topical, chronological, and spatial.

Topical Arrangement
A pattern that divides a subject into subtopics, each of which is part of the whole.

point contributes to an overall understanding of the subject, the points themselves can be ordered in various ways. For instance, Jen used the following **topical arrangement** for her classroom speech on animal communication:

Animals communicate for four purposes:
 I. Aggression
 II. Appeasement
 III. Courtship
 IV. Identification

Perhaps she did so accidentally, but Jen arranged her points in alphabetical order. She could have changed the order in several ways. For example, making identification the first point then discussing appeasement, courtship, and aggression proceeds from calm, more social animal behaviors to more intense, antisocial behaviors.

Choosing the Best Traditional Pattern

Because you can develop the same topic in a number of ways, choose the organizational pattern that works best given your purposes and your supporting materials. For instance, in addition to the pro–con outline about Hawaiian sovereignty just presented, other patterns could be used to effectively organize an informative speech on the subject. Here are three examples:

Chronological: The Hawaiian Sovereignty movement gained supporters during the 1990s.
 I. In the early 1990s, a few people supported Hawaiian sovereignty.
 II. In November 1993, President Clinton apologized for the U.S. treatment of Hawaii.
 III. In 1994, the Ohana Council members, led by "Bumpy" Kanahele, declared Hawaiian independence.
 IV. In August 1998, Native Hawaiians and supporters held an Aloha March in Washington, DC.
 V. In 1999, a sovereignty convention was held.

Spatial: Four Hawaiian regions are so different that each one would experience sovereignty uniquely.
 I. Ceded lands include 1.5 million acres of crown lands.
 II. Two hundred thousand acres were promised to homesteaders in the 1920s.
 III. Some islands have been purchased and developed by individuals such as Bill Gates.
 IV. Some islands have been developed for tourism and other industries.

Topical: Supporters of sovereignty fall into three general categories.
 I. Independence, with international recognition as a sovereign nation
 II. Nation-within-a-nation status, similar to Native American tribes in the United States
 III. Status quo, but with reparations and full control of Hawaiian trust assets granted to Native Hawaiians

BUILD YOUR SPEECH
DEVELOPING YOUR MAIN POINTS

Write your topic here:

_____

Begin the process of organizing your material into main points. Study the evidence you found in your research, then check ✔ all that apply.

- ❏ The topic unfolds in *stages*.
- ❏ The topic unfolds in *steps*.
- ❏ *Ordered dates* are important to this topic.
- ❏ There is a *before, during, and after* pattern.
- ❏ The topic takes place in *distinct locations or places*.
- ❏ Several *causes* are mentioned.
- ❏ Several *effects* are present.
- ❏ The topic describes a *problem*.
- ❏ There is a *solution or solutions* to a problem.
- ❏ There are *pro arguments* for a particular position.
- ❏ There are *con arguments* against a particular position.
- ❏ There are several *topical points* that don't really fit into one of these patterns.

Write your tentative central idea here

_____
_____
_____

In light of the boxes you checked and your tentative central idea, select the organizational pattern that would work best with your speech. _____

_____

Revise your central idea, if necessary _____

_____
_____
_____

Identify three to five main points and write them here:

_____
_____
_____
_____
_____

You can access Speech Builder Express at the Jaffe Connection Web site for help developing main points for your speech assignments.

Alternative Patterns

In addition to the traditional patterns usually taught in public speaking classes, researchers are looking at other organizational patterns commonly used by women and ethnic speakers. For example, Cheryl Jorgensen-Earp (1993) examined a number of alternative patterns that women have used historically. She argues that many speakers are uncomfortable with the standard organizational patterns due to cultural backgrounds or personal inclinations.

Figure 9.1 The wave pattern.

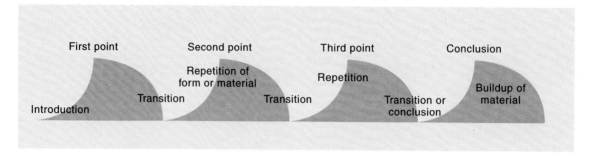

Organic Pattern
Alternative pattern that provides a clear speech structure in a less linear form.

As alternatives, she proposes several less direct and more **organic patterns** that provide a clear structure for a speech but have a less linear form. Jorgensen-Earp uses diagrams or pictures to describe these patterns, comparing them to a wave, a spiral, and a star (Zediker, 1993).

The Wave Pattern

This pattern, illustrated in Figure 9.1, consists of repetitions and variations of themes and ideas. Major points come at the crests of the waves. You follow each crest with a variety of examples leading up to another crest, then repeat the theme or make another major point. Use one of two types of conclusions: either wind down and lead the audience gradually from your topic, or make a transition, then rebuild, so that your final statement is a dramatic peak. African Americans, as well as women, often use the **wave pattern** in speeches (Jorgensen-Earp, 1993).

Wave Pattern
A repetitive pattern that presents variations of themes and ideas with major points presented at the crest.

Perhaps the most famous wave pattern speech is Martin Luther King, Jr.'s "I Have a Dream." King used this memorable line as the crest of a wave that he followed with examples of what he saw in his dream; then he repeated the line. He concluded with a dramatic peak that emerged from the final wave in the speech—repetition and variation on the phrase "Let freedom ring." (Dr. King's entire speech is reprinted at the end of Chapter 13.)

An excerpt from Sojourner Truth's "Ain't I a Woman?" speech illustrates this pattern:

> That man over there says that women need to be helped into carriages, and lifted over ditches, and to have the best place everywhere. Nobody ever helps me into carriages, or over mud-puddles, or gives me any best place!
>
> And ain't I a woman?
>
> Look at me! Look at my arm! I have ploughed and planted, and gathered into barns, and no man could head me!
>
> And ain't I a woman?
>
> I could work as much and eat as much as a man—when I could get it—and bear the lash as well!
>
> And ain't I a woman?
>
> I have borne thirteen children, and seen them most all sold off to slavery, and when I cried out with my mother's grief, none but Jesus heard me!
>
> And ain't I a woman?

As you can see, this can be a very powerful technique to stir the emotions of listeners. One student used the following outline to introduce a classmate.

Who is this man?
    A. Example of his accomplishments
    B. Example of personal characteristics

Who is this man?
    A. Additional information about his accomplishments
    B. Another example of personal characteristics

Who is this man? . . . He's . . . [our classmate]!

In short, between the major points of your speech, use a barrage of specific and general examples that illustrate and support your main ideas. Employ repetition and variation throughout. Although the examples in this section repeated a phrase, this is not a requirement. You can use the repetitive style by stating main points that are similar in intensity but differently phrased.

The Spiral Pattern

Shanna was asked to talk to high school students about selecting a college. She decided to create a hypothetical student, Todd, and have him appear in three scenarios, each one costing more money and taking him further from home. She visualized a **spiral pattern,** illustrated in Figure 9.2, as she framed her speech. First, she described his choices and experiences at a local community college. Next, she sent Todd out of town but kept him at a public institution within the state. Finally, she placed Todd at a private university across the continent from his hometown. Because each major scenario was more difficult or more dramatic than the preceding one, her speech depicted Todd moving from smaller to larger adjustments. Figure 9.3 illustrates how she might write out her points in spiral form.

The spiral pattern is often useful for speeches on controversial topics that build in dramatic intensity. Men who suffer partner abuse is one example. A series of narratives might revolve around a hypothetical character named Dan who lives with an abusive partner. In the first scenario, Dan is abused verbally. In the second, he receives a black eye and a broken nose. In the final scenario, his partner rams him with her car and he is hospitalized with life-threatening injuries. Each scene builds in tension, with the most controversial scenario reserved for the final spiral.

Spiral Pattern
A repetitive pattern with a series of points that increase in drama or intensity.

Figure 9.2 The spiral pattern.

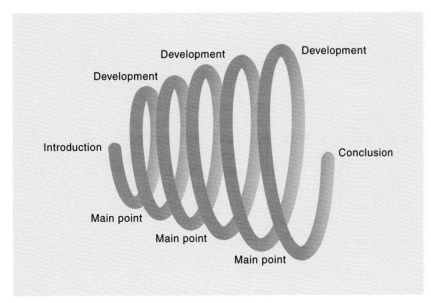

Figure 9.3 The spiral pattern helps Shanna organize her points to show Todd's progress through increasingly dramatic situations.

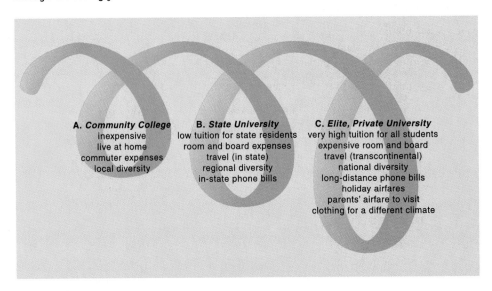

A. Community College
inexpensive
live at home
commuter expenses
local diversity

B. State University
low tuition for state residents
room and board expenses
travel (in state)
regional diversity
in-state phone bills

C. Elite, Private University
very high tuition for all students
expensive room and board
travel (transcontinental)
national diversity
long-distance phone bills
holiday airfares
parents' airfare to visit
clothing for a different climate

Star Pattern
Presents relatively equally weighted speech points within a thematic circle that binds them together; order of points may vary.

The Star Pattern

Each point in a **star pattern** speech, illustrated in Figure 9.4, is more or less equally weighted within a theme that ties the whole together. You might use this variation on the topical pattern if you were to present the same basic speech to a number of audiences. By visualizing your major points as a star, you have the flexibility of choosing where to start and what to emphasize, depending on what's relevant for a specific audience. To illustrate, you might begin with a point your audience understands or agrees with, then progressively move to points that challenge their understanding and agreement. For inattentive audiences, begin with your most dramatic point. For hostile audiences, begin with your most conciliatory point. This pattern has the advantage of allowing you to make audience adaptations quickly and still have your speech work effectively.

There are two ways to develop the points of the speech. One way is to state the point, support or develop it, then provide a transition to the next point. Alternatively, you could develop each point fully and then state it. Base your decisions on the type of audience and the nature of your various points.

The final element in the pattern is a thematic circle that binds all your points together. By the close of the speech, your listeners should feel that the circle is completed and the theme is fulfilled. For instance, Jan presents seminars on investment management using the general theme of financial security, with points on retirement plans, medical insurance, growth investments, and global funds. With some audiences, she begins with retirement plans and ends with global investments; with others, she begins with growth and global funds and ends with medical insurance and retirement plans.

The star pattern is common during election years. Candidates share the underlying theme "Vote for me!" Furthermore, they stake out their position on a number of different issues. However, instead of giving the same "stump speech" to every group, they order the issues and target specific points to specific audiences. For soccer moms a candidate might begin with education and end with crime issues; for elders, the same candidate might begin

Figure 9.4 The star pattern.

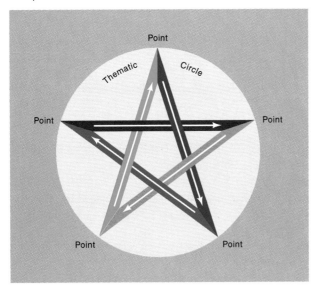

by discussing Social Security and end by presenting educational policies. Figure 9.5 provides an example. Think of these repetition patterns as a form that is common in songs. Each verse provides a different development of the song's theme, while the lyrics are repeated exactly unchanged in the chorus. Keep in mind throughout your preparation that these patterns require as much organizational planning as the other more linear formats.

Figure 9.5 This college recruiter visualizes her speeches as points of a star enclosed in the overall theme "Apply to this college." The order of her points depends on her specific audience—sometimes she starts with the sports program, sometimes with campus life, sometimes with the academic reputation of the college.

STOP AND CHECK

DEVELOP YOUR SPEECH USING AN ALTERNATIVE PATTERN

Write your topic here:

_____

For a wave pattern:
Identify each wave that you will develop with supporting evidence. Write the repetitive phrase at the crest of the wave, then below it, identify the supporting material you will use. Use Figure 9.6.

For a spiral pattern:
Identify the loops of your spiral speech. Then identify the supporting material you will use to develop each loop. Use Figure 9.7.

For a star pattern:
Identify your major points and write one on each point of the star. (You do not have to have five points.) In the circle that connects the points, write out the central theme of your speech. Use Figure 9.8.

You can access Speech Builder Express on the Jaffe Connection Web site for help in outlining your speech assignments.

Figure 9.6 Identify each wave that you will develop with supporting evidence. Write the repetitive phrase at the crest of the wave. Below the crest, identify the supporting material you will use.

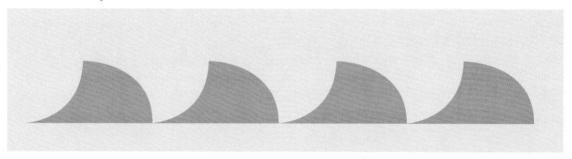

Figure 9.7 Identify the loops of your spiral speech. Then identify the supporting material you will use to develop each loop.

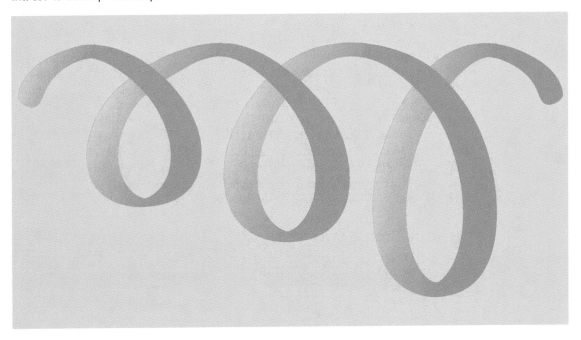

Figure 9.8 Identify your major points and write one on each point of the star. (You do not have to have five points.) In the circle that connects the points, write out the central theme of your speech.

Summary

After you gather information for your speech, you must organize it into a pattern. Begin with the body of the speech, and choose from among several linear patterns to organize your major points. Common organizational frameworks include chronological, spatial, causal, pro–con, problem–solution, and topical patterns. These patterns are appropriate for several types of speeches; causal and pro–con are especially good for informative purposes. However, the six patterns discussed here are not the only ways to organize materials; Chapter 17 presents several additional methods typically used in persuasive speeches.

Furthermore, nonlinear patterns are typical in diverse settings, as the examples from Madagascar and Kenya and the alternative patterns show. Women and ethnic speakers, for example, commonly select holistic or organic patterns such as the repetitive wave or the spiral. Speakers who want flexible points within a major theme pattern may represent their ideas in the form of a star. Regardless of the pattern, traditional or alternative, you must carefully identify your main points and then develop them with supporting materials.

JAFFE ONLINE CONNECTION   JAFFE ONLINE CONNECTION

Use your CD-ROM and the Jaffe Connection Web site http://communication.wadsworth.com/jaffe to review the following concepts, answer the review questions, and complete the suggested activities.

KEY TERMS

chronological pattern (157)
process speech (158)
spatial pattern (159)
cause–effect pattern (159)
problem–solution pattern (160)
pro–con arrangement (161)

topical arrangement (162)
organic pattern (164)
wave pattern (164)
spiral pattern (165)
star pattern (166)

APPLICATION AND CRITICAL THINKING EXERCISES

1. Outline one of the speeches available on your CD-ROM. (Don't use one of the Speeches of Introduction; they usually have a slightly different organizational pattern.) Is the organizational pattern easy to discern? What suggestions, if any, could you give the speaker about arranging the points of the speech?

2. With a small group of your classmates, take a topic such as abortion, divorce, alcohol on campus, or immigration and organize major points in as many of the following patterns as you can: topical, chronological, spatial, cause–effect, pro–con, problem-solution, spiral pattern.

3. Use InfoTrac College Edition to do a PowerTrac search for the journal *Vital Speeches*. Read several speeches and identify each speaker's main points and his or her organizational pattern.

4. Read or listen to a recording of a speech by an African American speaker such as Vernon Jordan, Malcolm X, or Martin Luther King Jr. (The speeches of Malcolm X can be found in his autobiography.) What basic organizational pattern does the speaker use? Can you find examples of the wave pattern within the speech?

5. Use the exact phrase option on www.alltheweb.com to search for "I have a dream" or "Ain't I a woman?" How many hits do you get? Both of these speeches have inspired groups as well as individuals, showing the power of rhetoric to influence a culture. Follow one of the links to find out more about King's or Sojourner Truth's vision.

6. Take the theme of creativity or the theme of perseverance. Then work with two or three classmates and discuss how you might create a speech organized around the wave, the spiral, or the star pattern. *Hint:* Think of three famous people who persevered . . . each one in a more dramatic way. Or use examples from your school's sports teams, your personal lives, lives of entertainers, and so on.

THE JAFFE CONNECTION WEB SITE

The Jaffe Connection Web site features review questions about the Web links and the InfoTrac College Edition exercises referenced throughout the chapter. You can access this site via your CD-ROM or at http://communication.wadsworth.com/Jaffe.

Web Links

9.1   "I Have a Dream" and "Ain't I a Woman?" Speeches (page 171)

Stop and Check Activities

9.1   Develop Your Speech Using an Alternative Pattern (pages 168–169)

InfoTrac College Edition Exercises

9.1   Identify Main Points in a Speech in *Vital Speeches* (page 170)

Build Your Speech Featuring Speech Builder Express

9.1   Developing Your Main Points (page 163)

SPEECH INTERACTIVE ON THE JAFFE CONNECTION CD-ROM

Watch any of the speeches listed on Speech Interactive on your Jaffe Connection CD-ROM to determine the organizational patterns used.

STUDENT OUTLINE WITH COMMENTARY

YOU HAVE MY DEEPEST SYMPATHY: YOU JUST WON THE LOTTERY
by Maria DiMaggio

General Purpose:	To persuade
Specific Purpose:	To persuade my audience that winning the lottery is not as great as it's perceived to be and that they should invest their money in alternative ways.
Central Idea:	The lottery, a form of gambling, raises money for good causes; however, winning often creates enormous problems for the winners, and they would be better off spending their money elsewhere.

Introduction

 I. You have my deepest sympathy; you just won the lottery.

 II. Most of us would be shocked if someone said we'd won $20 million, then offered us condolences; however, hundreds of lotto winners have discovered the downside of winning big.

This is a problem-solution organizational pattern.

III. I used to think I'd be the happiest person in Brooklyn if I could just win a million dollars, but my research about lottery winners convinced me to spend my money elsewhere—and I hope you'll follow my example.

IV. Today, I'll explain what the lottery is, then describe various problems that winners face, and point out alternatives if you really want to spend money foolishly.

Body

I. Lotteries are a form of gambling that raise money for good causes.
   A. *Webster's Dictionary* identifies the lottery as a popular form of gambling.
      1. Winners pay to participate, generally by purchasing tickets at a uniform price.
      2. Winners are determined by chance.
   B. Lotteries generate revenues for good causes.
      1. The earliest lottery, organized in London in 1680, raised money for a municipal water supply.
      2. A French lottery helped pay for the Statue of Liberty.
      3. Lotteries helped support the Jamestown Colony and the American Revolutionary War.
      4. They provided funds for Harvard, Princeton, and Dartmouth.
      5. Current lotteries in New Hampshire and Oregon, among other states, provide educational funding.

II. Unexpected problems arise for lotto winners.
   A. Their dreams of instant riches are not fulfilled.
      1. Money is given out over twenty to twenty-five years.
      2. A lotto "millionaire" gets about $50,000 annually—before taxes, delinquent taxes, past-due child support, and student loans are taken out.
      3. Winners who run short on cash cannot draw from their winnings.
      4. They cannot use their winnings as collateral to get a loan.
      5. They cannot liquidate their future winnings.
   B. Many suffer personal loss and rejection.
      1. William Post won $16.2 million but watched his brother go to jail, convicted of hiring a hit man to kill William.
      2. Debbie won $6.85 million but lost contact with her sisters, who stopped speaking to her when she declined to pay their debts.
      3. Bernice took a day off work to claim her $1 million; her job was given to someone else.
      4. Daisy won $2.8 million but went through a painful lawsuit.
         a. Her son's friend sued for half the winnings because she asked the friend to pray that she'd win.
         b. He prayed, she won, so he thought he was entitled to some of her money.
         c. The court ruled against him, saying he couldn't prove his prayers caused her to win.
   C. Lotto winnings don't necessarily bring happiness.
      1. A study of people with the best of luck and those with the worst of luck supported this conclusion.
      2. Accident victims weren't as unhappy as expected; however, lottery winners were more unhappy and took less pleasure in life than expected.
   D. Heaven help the heirs if a lotto-winning relative dies and leaves them a fortune.
      1. They must immediately pay estate taxes on the unpaid total, with monthly penalties added after nine months.
      2. Taxes on a $20 million lotto inheritance are more than $5 million.

The problem section comes in two main points; first she gives some background information.

In this point, Maria describes problems for the winners and their heirs.

III. If you have extra money, you could spend it in far more profitable ways.
   A. Invest in the stock market.
   B. Donate your extra money to a charitable organization and claim a tax deduction.
   C. Indulge yourself: buy cable, eat lobster once in a while, buy season tickets to a sporting or a cultural event, get an exotic pet.
   D. If you like to think your lotto money supports education, you can donate to my college fund!

Conclusion
   I. I hope I've convinced you that playing the lotto is not all it's advertised to be.
   II. I've explained what the lottery is, the problems it can cause, and some alternative ways to get rid of money.
   III. So the next time you see a new lotto multimillionaire, consider sending your sympathies rather than your congratulations.

This is the solution section of the speech.

Beginning and Ending Your Speech

THIS CHAPTER WILL HELP YOU

■ Develop an introduction for your speech that gains attention, motivates the audience to listen, establishes your credibility, and previews the speech

■ Develop a conclusion that signals the end, summarizes, provides psychological closure, and ends with impact

■ Link the parts of the speech to one another through skillful use of connectives such as signposts and transitions, internal previews, and internal summaries

"The Chant of the Earth, The Voice of the Land" Mural ©1991 by Betsie Miller-Kusz. (Market Street and 19th Street, SF, CA)

MAGINE THAT YOU'RE LISTENING TO THESE TWO INTRODUCTIONS:

Would you watch an execution? Today, I'll enlighten you with some information about television coverage of live executions.

On May 16th, [2001], three hundred people solemnly [filed] into a Midwest auditorium to participate in a unique American experience: the telecast of a live execution. In order to watch Timothy McVeigh die, he must have tried to kill you or murdered a member of your family on April 19, 1995. . . . No one will really know the tangle of competing motives in that remote viewing room. After all, we see death on TV every day—in the news, in the coverage of auto races and in virtually all television dramas. Why would anyone expend so much time, effort, and anguish simply to watch another human die on television? (Statham, 2001)

Stop for a moment and think of the impression each speaker created at the outset. How do you feel about being "enlightened"? Which introduction gains your attention? Arouses your curiosity? Which speaker seems more prepared? More credible?

This chapter will help you lead your listeners skillfully into your subject and, at the end, conclude in a way that summarizes your thoughts and leaves a memorable impression. You will also learn how to connect your ideas to one another and to the speech as a whole.

Plan Your Introduction

After you have planned the body of your speech, then work on your introduction. As Chapter 2 pointed out, the Roman educator Quintilian (1920–1922) identified four purposes for an introduction:

1. To draw the listeners' attention to the topic
2. To motivate the audience to listen
3. To establish yourself as knowledgeable about the topic
4. To preview the major ideas of the speech

In addition, remember to include the essential definitions or background information that listeners need in order to understand your subject. By including these elements in your introduction, you'll answer four basic listener questions up front: What's this all about? Why should I listen? Why should I listen to you? What will you be covering? Figure 10.1 depicts the function of the introduction as a way to answer these listener questions. We will look at each question in this section.

Gain Attention

Gaining attention is the first step in the listening process, so you must immediately answer your listeners' question, "What's this speech about?" Introduce your topic in a creative way. Some speakers—students as well as professionals—simply announce their subject like this: "Today, my speech is about polar bears." Although this does introduce the topic, it's not very creative; good speakers often choose more effective techniques. Here are a few strategies for introductions that will be discussed in this section.

- Ask a question.
- Provide a vivid description.
- Begin with a quotation.
- Use an audio or visual aid.
- Tell a joke or funny story.
- Refer to a current event.
- Begin with an example.
- Start with startling numbers.

Figure 10.1 The introduction functions to answer these four questions that your listeners have.

Ask a Question

Choose either a rhetorical or a participatory question. **Rhetorical questions** are the kind listeners answer in their mind; **participatory questions,** in contrast, call for an overt response, such as a show of hands or a verbal answer. Quianna Clay's speech (outlined in Chapter 7) began with two rhetorical questions:

> Did you know that flaxseed oil and cottage cheese can now cure lung cancer? Or, that avoiding dairy products will dissolve cataracts? Well, neither did registered dietician Ira Milner, until he spent 60 hours online and found a plethora of such medical misinformation.

Her listeners respond internally to these rhetorical questions; many know someone with lung cancer or with cataracts, and they are aware of typical medical procedures for these conditions. Most listeners can conjure up a mental picture of a scoop of cottage cheese or a glass of milk. The incongruity of these "cures" intrigues the audience and draws them into the topic.

In contrast, sometimes you want a visible response from your listeners. If so, you must make it clear that you want them to respond physically. For instance, ask for a show of hands or call on a member of the audience to answer a question you pose. A professional speaker (Davidson, 2001) asked his audience to take out a pen or pencil and write down the age to which they expected to live, then he asked these questions:

> By a show of hands please, how many put in at least age 70? Just about everyone in the room. How many put in at least age 80? How many put at least age 90? Still a healthy number, isn't there? And how many put at least age 100? How about 105? . . . The people who raised their hands for 90 or 100 are likely to be accurate . . . but the paradox of living to 100 or 105 is that it's wasted if each day flies by quickly.

For a question to capture the audience's attention, it must be sufficiently intriguing. Here are three examples of ineffective questions that came from actual speeches. The first is too broad; the second too specific; the third too unusual for most people to relate to.

Rhetorical Questions Questions that listeners answer in their minds.
Participatory Questions Questions that listeners answer overtly.

How many of you have ever purchased an album, cassette, or compact disk?

Have you ever had your finger almost sliced off and left hanging by a small piece of skin?

Have you ever visited a harem?

Both types of questions, rhetorical and participatory, help establish dialogue between speakers and listeners because they invite audience response, whether mental or physical.

Provide a Vivid Description

Draw your audience's attention to your subject by describing a scene in such vivid language that your listeners are compelled to visualize it mentally. The scene can be either real or imaginary. Here is Danae's opening for her classroom speech on arachnophobia (fear of spiders):

Imagine yourself just hanging out one morning, minding your own business, when a large, monstrous body, fifty times your size, casually approaches you then, suddenly, lets out a blood curdling scream, hurls a giant bowl your way, and takes off running. Sound familiar? It would if you were the little spider that had the misfortune of getting just a little too close to Little Miss Muffet of nursery rhyme fame. I venture to say that we all have had to deal with spiders at some time in our lives. They seem to be everywhere, especially at this time of year. What causes this Muffet-type reaction? It just may be arachnophobia—the irrational fear of spiders. (Wirth, 1999)

Begin with a Quotation

You can often gain listener attention with a quotation or a familiar cultural proverb. These quotations or adages can be *about* a subject or, in the case of a biographical speech, by the subject. Choose a saying that encapsulates your overall theme and cite its source. For example, Professor Thomas Martin (2001) began one address with the following quotation from the *Hobbit*:

Yesterday morning I rose at 3 A.M. to drive 200 miles to Omaha, Nebraska, in order to fly to Hartford, Connecticut. When the alarm went off at 3, I was immediately reminded of Bilbo Baggins's response to Gandalf who had asked him to leave his hobbit hole and venture forth with him into the world.

Gandalf: "I am looking for someone to share in an adventure that I am arranging, and it's very difficult to find anyone."

Bilbo: "I should think so in these parts! We are plain, quiet folk and have no use for adventure. Nasty, disturbing uncomfortable things! Make you late for dinner! I can't think what anybody sees in them."

I, like Bilbo, wanted to stay in my hobbit hole. . . . Gandalf, as you might remember, did not allow Bilbo to stay home.

Another example comes from Leslie's speech about Disneyland. She opened with a quotation by Walt Disney:

In the center of the Magic Kingdom stands a statue of Walt Disney and Mickey Mouse holding hands. It is named "Partners," and under it Mr. Disney states why he wanted to first open Disneyland, "We believe in our idea: a family park where parents and children could have fun together."

Quotations can also come from song lyrics, poems, or scriptural texts. Or they may originate in family sayings or in memorable words spoken by someone such as a high school soccer coach. For instance, for a speech on perseverance, one such opening might be "My grandmother used to say, 'It's a great life if you don't weaken.'" The Internet can help you

Josh Nauman

Draw listeners' attention to your topic at the outset of your speech. One effective attention-gaining strategy is to use a visual aid like this Navajo rug.

locate thousands of quotations. Use a search engine such as www.yahoo.com and follow the quotation link, located under references, or go directly to sources like www.quoteland.com or www.bartleby.com.

Use an Audio or Visual Aid

You can use posters, charts, tape recordings, and other visual and audio materials successfully in drawing attention to your topic. If you like humor, consider using an overhead projector or in-focus machine to display a relevant cartoon that you've transferred to a transparency or scanned onto a computer disk. Here are some examples: Tom displayed a large poster of an automobile at the outset of his speech explaining how to buy a car overseas. Mary began with seven seconds of taped sounds made by humpback whales. Jennifer, whose topic was Peter Ilich Tchaikovsky, played a short clip from *The Nutcracker Suite*.

Tell a Joke or Funny Story

Professional speakers often begin by telling a joke that creates an informal, humorous atmosphere at the outset of the speech. If you are good at telling jokes and funny stories, you might try this strategy; however, you can also embarrass yourself by beginning with a joke that flops! To avoid this, test your joke in advance on some friends and let them decide if it's really funny. Make sure your joke relates to the topic of your speech. Otherwise, although you will gain attention, you won't draw it to your subject. Here is a riddle that could be used to begin a speech on learning a second language:

> You know the word for a person who knows three languages? It's trilingual.
>   What's the word for a person who knows two languages? Right, it's bilingual.
> What do you call a person who knows only one language?
>   The correct answer is, "an American!"

Although most of the students in the rest of the world gain a measure of proficiency in English as well as in their own languages, most students who graduate from high schools in the United States know only English.

Refer to a Current Event

To identify with your listeners and establish common ground, you can begin with well-known current happenings—airplane crashes, campus controversies, well-publicized trials, elections, and the like. For example, after the terrorist attacks of September 11, 2001, thousands of speakers made reference to that incident. Here's how one speaker mentioned two current issues in his October 2001 speech (Novelli, 2001):

> Here we are: Six weeks after the terrorists attacks in New York and Washington; fighting an unconventional war against terrorism unlike any we have ever seen; but also, right in the middle of the major league playoffs to see who will get to the World Series. Life speeds on.

 This speech or another that begins with a reference to a current event is available through InfoTrac College Edition. Do a PowerTrac search for the journal *Vital Speeches* and see how others have used current events in their speech openings.

Begin with an Example

As Chapter 8 pointed out, examples provide your listeners with the opportunity to become emotionally involved with your topic. Everyone likes a good story, and when we hear of real people involved in real situations, we generally become more attentive. One speaker (Farmer, 1999) used this extended example in his introduction to a speech about the Internet.

> You may have heard the stunning story of the Russian sailor who had to practice telemedicine—on himself. This sailor was participating in a race in South Africa. He was alone in his boat when he became injured, with a major infection on his elbow. In true Internet style, he communicated his symptoms through satellite email to an emergency room doctor in Boston. The Boston doctor became very alarmed, concerned that the sailor was in imminent danger. So he guided the sailor—via satellite email—through surgery that the sailor performed on himself. He drained his abscess, stopped his bleeding, managed to survive all of this and then, for good measure, he won the race.

Here's another example from a speech describing the process of getting a marriage annulled:

> After twenty-three years of marriage, four children, a year of separation, and fifteen years of divorce, a man tells his ex-wife that he has decided to get an annulment in the Catholic Church.

Start with Startling Numbers

Numbers and statistics can be dry; however, they can also capture and hold your listeners' attention if they are shocking enough or if they are put into an understandable context, as this example illustrates:

> According to the Centers for Disease Control, 72 percent of young adults eat too much fat, and fewer than one in five follow recommended dietary guidelines. That means that, in this classroom with twenty-five students enrolled, we might predict that eighteen people indulge in too many hamburgers and milkshakes and that twenty people routinely ignore their physicians' nutritional recommendations. I confess, I'm talking about myself here.

Although this is not an exhaustive list of successful openings for speeches, it provides you with examples of openings commonly used by public speakers in a variety of settings.

DIVERSITY IN PRACTICE
CONSIDERING ORGANIZATIONAL CULTURE

CHAPTER 1 pointed out that culture includes both the visible, stated aspects of a group's way of life as well as the more embedded beliefs and assumptions that guide group members. The concept of **organizational culture** extends this definition to recognize that organizations and institutions also have histories, traditions, hierarchies, rituals, folklore, and so on that make them function as small cultures within the larger society. Insiders know the group's way of life; newcomers must learn it. For example, Microsoft differs from IBM; St. John's University (Catholic sponsored) is unlike George Fox University (Quaker sponsored) in many ways.

Whenever you speak within an organization, learn as much as you can about its culture before you create your speech—even expectations for introductions can differ in specific settings. For example, a business leader from the community recently gave the commencement address at my university. She did not start with a statistic, a visual aid, or any other attention strategy mentioned in this chapter; instead, she first referred to the occasion, congratulated the graduates, and expressed respect for the university—acknowledging both the organization and the cultural event (graduation) before introducing the topic of her speech. It would have seemed abrupt and strange to the graduates and their families on this special occasion if she had launched into her speech immediately.

To see how speakers adapt their introductions to specific organizations, go to your library and look at several issues of the journal *Vital Speeches of the Day* or log on to InfoTrac College Edition and do a PowerTrac search for the journal *Vital Speeches*. Select three or four talks given by a guest speaker at a ritual event. Read the introductions to see if and how the speaker recognizes elements of the organization's culture in his or her opening remarks.

Organizational Culture
The way of life of a specific organization that includes its history, traditions, heroes, folklore, vocabulary, rituals, and ways of doing things.

The purpose of an introduction is not simply to gain attention; it must draw attention *to your topic.* One student ignored this rule and slapped the podium loudly; when listeners jumped to attention, he said, "Now that I have your attention, I am going to talk about animal overpopulation." His introduction failed because, even though it attracted attention, it was not relevant to his subject.

Give Your Audience a Reason to Listen

Once you have your listeners' attention, it is important to answer their question, "Why should I listen to this speech?" You may think your topic is important and interesting, but your listeners may see it as boring or irrelevant. Jill faced this challenge when she came from Hawaii to study at Oregon State University; there she gave a speech on Hawaiian sovereignty. Most OSU students had never heard of the controversy about returning Hawaii to Hawaiian rule, and the issue was remote from their everyday lives. Jill met this challenge by relating to her Oregon audience as follows:

> Although you may not be aware of the issue of Hawaiian sovereignty, you may someday vote on whether or not to allow Hawaiians to again be a sovereign nation instead of a state.

You can frame your topic within a larger issue; for instance, computer viruses are a crime issue, and elder abuse is part of a nationwide problem of violence against the helpless. A speech on polar bears does not directly relate to listeners in most classrooms; however, treatment of polar bears is connected to larger issues such as animal rights and animal overpopulation. Here's one way to relate this topic to an urban audience.

At this point, you may be curious about polar bears, but you may not think much about them. After all, the only polar bears in New York are in the zoo. However, the problem with polar bears in Canada is similar to problems here on Long Island with a deer population that is getting out of control. What do we do with animals that live close to humans?

One of the important characteristics of humans is their ability to learn new things. And at times, you give speeches to increase your audience's knowledge or to satisfy their curiosity. For instance, few people in the classroom will ever have their marriage annulled, but 58,000 annulments are granted annually to U.S. Catholics—and 24.5 percent of the population claims affiliation with the Catholic Church. Here's how Maureen related her topic, "The Annulment Process," to her audience:

> Since at least two people in this classroom are Catholic, this subject should be of interest to you. For those of you who are not Catholic, I hope this information will help you better understand one aspect of the Catholic religion.

Many issues that don't seem to directly impact your listeners may actually affect their pocketbooks, whether or not they know it. National issues that rely on tax dollars for support are in this category—issues such as public radio and television, weapon development, and Medicare. Chapter 18 provides more details about some of the needs, wants, emotions, and values that motivate people to listen to speeches.

Establish Your Credibility

After you have the audience's attention and have given them a reason to listen to your topic, give them a reason to listen to you by linking yourself to your topic. Typically, you do this by briefly sharing your subject-related experiences, interests, and research findings. Mention your major, courses you have taken, television shows that first interested you, and so on. Maureen linked herself to her topic of annulment through her personal experiences.

> The annulment process is of particular interest to me since I am a divorced Catholic who is engaged to be married to a Catholic man.

Audiences recognize Chuck Colson's credibility when he speaks on prison reform. After the Watergate scandal, this Nixon aide served time in prison, then began a prison-reform organization. Your listeners, however, won't know your qualifications, so you'll have to explain your link to your topic.

AP/Wide World Photos

Here are some additional ways students have linked themselves to their topics:

I became interested in the topic of polar bears when I saw a video about them.

I read an article about Charlotte Beers, a woman who broke through "the glass ceiling" to become the first woman to hold a top position in a multibillion-dollar advertising agency. I realized that this is the barrier I have personally encountered in a variety of managerial positions I have held at various firms, and I decided to examine "the glass ceiling" by doing additional research.

During the past three summers, I worked for a plumbing contractor, which piqued my interest in contaminated drinking water. I later read articles on the topic in *Time Magazine* and *Consumer Reports*.

I became interested in the topic of antioxidants because of my childhood. I always begged for Coco-Puffs, but I got oatmeal and bananas instead. So I developed my health consciousness from my mother who fed me fruits and vegetables and other good foods.

Establishing your credibility is optional if another person introduces you and connects you with the topic or if your expertise is well established. However, even professionals who speak on topics outside their area would do well to link themselves with the topic. Let's say an engineer is speaking at a school board meeting about adoption of a districtwide sex education program. Her experiences as a parent are more salient in this context than her engineering expertise.

Preview Your Ideas

You may have heard the old saying, "Tell them what you're going to say; say it; then tell them what you said." The **preview** serves the first of these functions. It is the short statement you make as the transition between the introduction and the body of your speech in which you state some form of your central idea. Heidi explains the importance of a preview for listeners.

> It obviously helps to have an idea of where the speaker is headed. The preview provides a brief synopsis of what key points will be expanded upon. The speech then should continue in the order first declared.
>
> HEIDI

Preview
The transition from the introduction to the speech body; some form of the central idea.

Here are three student previews that alert each audience to the speaker's organizational pattern. Previews like these aid listeners who are taking notes or outlining the talk.

DIVERSITY IN PRACTICE
A NAVAJO (DINÉ) SPEECH INTRODUCTION

NOT EVERY cultural group begins a speech by first gaining attention, next relating to audience interests, then establishing their credibility. Speakers at Diné Community College (formerly Navajo Community College) first answer the listeners' question, "Who are you and what's your clan affiliation?" Students thus begin their classroom speeches by telling their names (who they are) and identifying their clan affiliation (knowing this helps listeners understand the roots of their life). Until this personal, identifying information is shared, neither the speakers nor their listeners can feel at home (Braithwaite, 1997).

Before we can drift off for a good night's sleep, we must first wake up to some of the alarming effects of sleep debt, then we can open our eyes to better understand their causes, and finally we'll cozy up to some solutions at both the personal and the societal levels.

Today, I'll retell the story of the boy who cried "wolf" with a few character changes. The boy who cries "wolf" is the American government, and the wolf we are to fear, I'll call industrial hemp.

Today, I will discuss the annulment process, provide statistics surrounding this issue, and detail some of the emotional and spiritual considerations related to it.

In short, a good introduction draws attention to your topic, relates the subject to your listeners, links you to the subject, and previews your major ideas.

STOP AND CHECK

CREATE AN INTERESTING INTRODUCTION

Web Site

Select one or two of the following central ideas. Then work with a classmate to create an introduction that answers the four questions your listeners ask regarding any subject. You can also write these introductions online and email them to your classmates. Look for this activity under Stop and Check Activities for Chapter 10 on the Jaffe Connection Web site.

- Arachnophobia, the irrational fear of spiders, has three major causes and two basic treatments.
- The five stages typical of the grief process are denial, anger, bargaining, depression, and acceptance.
- Elder abuse is an increasing problem in our society, but several solutions have been proposed.
- Many women, as well as men, experience hair loss, and they look to medications, hairpieces, bonding techniques, and transplants to solve the problem.
- You can save money at the supermarket on produce, meat, cereal, and bakery items.
- Thousands of students default on federal student loans every year, leaving taxpayers with their school tabs.

The listener's questions are:

1. What's this about? (Identify several strategies to gain attention to the topics you choose. Which do you think are more effective?)
2. Why should I listen? (How could you relate the topics to audience interests or experiences?)
3. Why should I listen to you? (How might a speaker establish credibility on each subject?)
4. What will you be covering? (How would you preview the main ideas of each topic you choose?)

To learn more about different ways to begin a speech, log on to the Internet and go to www.gallaudet.edu/~engwweb/writing/introconslu.html. There you'll find one topic (deaf education) with several different opening options. Alternatively, you could review the introductions of the speakers featured on the CD that comes with this text. Evaluate how well each introduction fulfills the criteria described here.

Conclude with Impact

Your conclusion leaves your audience with a final impression of both you and your topic. This is the time to provide closure through a summary and a satisfying or challenging closing statement without adding new information. Appearing disorganized at the end can negate the positive impressions your audience held during the speech. Like the introduction, the conclusion has several important functions: to signal the end, to summarize the main points, to provide psychological closure often by a reference to the introduction, and to end with an impact.

Signal the Ending

Just as your preview provides a transition to the speech body, your signal makes the audience aware that you're concluding. Both beginning speakers and professionals use common phrases such as "In conclusion" or "Finally." However, these transitions are more creative:

> We now know that when we feel the need to escape from our world and enter into the zones of biting insects, dousing ourselves too liberally with DEET for protection carries some risks.

> Today we've taken a look at our National Debt. Our national sleep debt, that is.

Don't overlook nonverbal actions as a way to signal to your conclusion. For instance, pause and shift your posture or take a step away from the podium. You may also slow down a bit and speak more softly. Combining both verbal and nonverbal transitions generally works well.

Review Your Main Ideas

Briefly summarizing or recapping your main points fulfills the "Tell them what you said" axiom, as the following reviews or summaries illustrate:

> We've explored ways that sleep deprivation affects us in three areas: in our personal lives, in our relationships, and in our workplaces.

> I hope that I have increased your knowledge about oxidation and convinced you that antioxidants are one way to prevent heart disease, arteriosclerosis, strokes, chronic illnesses, and even cancer.

Many speakers combine their transition statement with their summary as this example shows:

> Now that we have looked at the shark as it really is [transition phrase] maybe you now realize that its reputation is really inaccurate and that humans present a greater threat to the shark than sharks present to humans [restatement of the central idea].

Provide Psychological Closure

Looping back to something from your introduction—which one writing professor calls an "echo"—provides your audience with a sense of psychological closure. Here's the professor's explanation:

> The echo is the inside joke of writing [or, in our case, speaking]. By repeating or suggesting a previous detail—a description, word, question, quote, topic or whatever— you make a point with that which is already familiar to your [audience]. It's a way of putting your arm around the [audience member] and sharing a bit of information that only the two of you can appreciate.

Read this short article for yourself by logging on to the Internet and searching www.alltheweb.com for the exact phrase "Echo in introductions and conclusions." Look in your introduction for something that you could finalize here at the end. For instance, if you began with an example, complete it in the conclusion. Or, refer to startling statistics or to quotations you presented in the opening. Here are some examples:

> The inhabitants of Churchill, Manitoba, aren't wrong to fear the polar bears who wander into their towns, but carrying rifles may not be the best way to protect themselves against this already endangered species.

> Five thousand needless deaths can be eliminated each year if people understand the dangers of DEET and protect themselves against its harmful effects.

> For those eighteen of us in this classroom who eat too much fat and the twenty of us who regularly ignore our doctor's nutritional advice, there's hope.

End Memorably

Finally, plan to leave a positive and memorable impression. During the few minutes you speak, audience members are focusing their attention on your subject. When you finish, however, each listener will return to his or her thoughts, moving away from the mental images you co-created throughout the speech. So end with impact by choosing some of the same types of material you used to gain attention in the beginning:

- End with humor.
- Ask a thought-provoking question.
- Use a quotation.
- Issue a challenge.
- Tie the subject to a larger cultural theme or value.

Using humor and using quotations are two memorable ways to end a speech. Quoting a well-known humorist such as Mark Twain is one way to combine the two.

© Bettmann/CORBIS

Look at some of the speeches and outlines provided in the text and notice the different and creative ways that students memorably end their speeches. Here are a few effective endings:

> The woman whose twenty-three-year marriage ended in annulment is more common than you might think. Although she considered an annulment inconceivable, she did not contest her ex-husband's request for one. She realized that the annulment did not erase the existence of her marriage, but it allowed her ex to have good standing within the Catholic Church.

> So, next time you are on the Internet and you begin to consider pond scum or cottage cheese as a cure for what ails you, you may want to keep these words in mind: *Caveat emptor*—let the buyer beware.

Eventually, when you are working in the "real world," be aware of the glass ceiling and try to help those around you. Working together, we will crack the glass and dismantle the ceiling.

In summary, a good conclusion provides a transition to your conclusion, summarizes your major points, gains psychological closure, and finishes with a thought-provoking closing statement.

STOP AND CHECK
EVALUATING INTRODUCTIONS AND CONCLUSIONS

Here you'll find an introduction and conclusion for two different speeches. Read through each set, then answer the questions that follow it. You can complete this activity online under Stop and Check Activities for Chapter 10 at the Jaffe Connection Web site.

Introduction: Six of the ten leading causes of death among Americans are diet related: heart disease, cancer, stroke, and diabetes mellitus, as stated by the *Vegetarian Times* magazine. Everyone here would like to live a healthy life, right? Today, I will explain the advantages of being a vegetarian to your health and to the environment.

Conclusion: Because I have this information, I have reduced my consumption of meat lately, and I ask you to do the same thing. Being a vegetarian is not that bad; you're improving your health and, at the same time, saving the environment. Don't forget, once you're old and suffering from a heart ailment or cancer, it will be too late. Take precautions now.

- Does this introduction make you want to hear this speech? Why or why not?
- How does he gain attention?
- How does he relate to the audience? Is this effective?
- Do you think he is a credible speaker on the topic?
- Could you write a brief outline of his major points from his preview?
- Is his conclusion as effective as his introduction? Why or why not?

Introduction: What is the easiest way to raise $125,000 for research for Multiple Sclerosis? That's right. Swim 1,550 miles down the Mississippi River like Nick Irons did. Nick, a twenty-five-year-old, swam the murky waters of the Mississippi to raise money to research a disease his father has. Many people would think this was a crazy thing to do, because they don't know about the disease. Only one in ten George Fox students surveyed had the slightest idea of what MS was. My dad has had MS for eight years, and I really didn't know a lot about the disease until I researched it and found out a lot more than I expected. Since most people are unclear about MS, I will first define the disease, describe some of its effects, and tell you what is known about the cause, the cure, and the medications that are currently used.

Conclusion: In conclusion, little is known about the causes and cures of MS. It is a disease that attacks the central nervous system, impairing many senses. Next time you question why a person swam over 1,500 miles down a dirty river, make sure you know why and have a clear understanding of the cause. A lot is being done to find a cure for this debilitating disease. It will be found.

- What would you say is the most effective part of her introduction?
- What's the most effective element of her conclusion?
- Which is better: her introduction or her conclusion? Why? What improvements, if any, would you suggest she make?

(continued)

Web Site

To investigate this topic further, log on to the Internet and go to www.dc.peachnet.edu/~drobinso/students/concl.html. There you'll find a number of introductions and conclusions taken from student essays. Each one is followed by evaluative comments from other students in the class. Although this exercise was created for a writing class, you'll find insightful critiques that will help you evaluate your speech introductions and conclusions.

Review the conclusions of the persuasive, informative, and narrative speeches featured on Jaffe Speech Interactive. Do the speakers signal the ending of the speech, review their main ideas, provide psychological closure, and end memorably?

Connect Your Ideas

Connectives
Words, phrases, and sentences used to lead from idea to idea and tie the parts of the speech together smoothly.

After you plan the speech body and formulate the introduction and conclusion, you'll add the final touches to polish your speech. These are **connectives**—the words, phrases, and sentences that lead from one idea to another and tie the various parts of the speech together smoothly. They function as tendons or ligaments that hold your speech together and help your listeners keep their place as you talk. The most common types of connectives are signposts, transitions, internal previews, and internal summaries.

Signposts and Transitions

Signposts
Simple connectives like first, next, and finally that help listeners keep their place in the speech.

Signposts are similar to signs along a highway—those markers that help drivers know how far they've come and how far they must go. In much the same way, speech signposts help your listeners orient themselves to their place in your speech. Words such as *first*, *next*, and *finally* introduce new points and let your listeners sense the flow of your ideas. Other phrases that help your speech flow include *most importantly*, *in fact*, and *for example*. Here are some examples:

- *First*, sleep deprivation affects your life in general.
- *The final step* occurs when the case is submitted to the judge for a decision.
- *On the other hand*, the computer does have a lot of things going for it.
- *In addition*, brain wave patterns can be measured and analyzed.

Transitions
Summaries of where you've been and where you're going in your speech.

Transitions summarize where you have been and where you are going in the speech. You can use them both between points and within a single point. Here are some simple transitions *between* major points:

> We have looked at what oxidation is [where you've been]; now let's examine what antioxidants are and what they can do to help prevent oxidation in the arteries [where you're going].

> The problem, as you can see, is a complex one because both the people and the polar bears need protection [a summary of the last point]; however, two solutions have been proposed [a preview of the next main idea].

> Although the glass ceiling is widespread [where you've been], it is not shatterproof [where you're going].

Transitions can also lead from subpoint to subpoint *within* a major point. For example, Tamara's major point, "There are several causes of amusement park tragedies," has three subpoints: equipment failure, operator failure, and rider behavior. After she describes the first two causes, she transitions to the final one by saying this:

While both equipment and operator failure cause accidents [first and second sub-point], a number of tragedies are additionally caused by rider behavior [third sub-point].

Here's another example. Jenny's speech about Golden Seal Root (GSR) has this as one of its major points: People use GSR both internally and externally. She first describes the internal uses, then transitions to the second use by saying this:

Not only do people use Golden Seal Root internally [first use], they also apply the herb externally [lead-in to second use].

Internal Previews and Internal Summaries

Internal previews occur within the body of your speech and briefly summarize the sub-points you will develop under a major point. For instance, Tamara might say this:

Experts agree that there are three main causes of amusement park tragedies: equipment failure, operator failure, and rider behavior.

This internal preview helps her audience see the framework she'll use as she develops her major idea related to causes of accidents.

If you summarize subpoints after you've made them but before you move to another major point, you're using an **internal summary.** Thus, Tamara could have summarized her section on causes before moving on to the effects of amusement park accidents in this way:

In short, we have seen that equipment failure, operator failure, and rider behavior combine to create thousands of tragedies annually.

After she finished discussing the uses of Golden Seal Root, Jenny could have summarized her entire point by saying:

In summary, people use GSR both internally and externally.

Connectives, then, are words, phrases, and complete sentences you'll use to connect your ideas to one another and to your speech as a whole. They serve to introduce your points, to preview and summarize material within a point, and to help your listeners keep their place in your speech.

Internal Previews
Brief in-speech summaries that foretell the subpoints you'll develop under a major point.

Internal Summary
Restatements of the ideas within a subpoint.

Summary

After you've organized the body of your speech, plan an introduction that will take your listeners from their various internal mental worlds and move them into the world of your speech. Do this by gaining their attention, relating your topic to their concerns, establishing your credibility on the subject, and previewing your main points. Finally, plan a conclusion that provides a transition from the body, summarizes your major points, gives a sense of closure by referring back to the introduction, and leaves your listeners with a challenge or memorable saying. Throughout your speech, use connectives to weave your points and subpoints into a coherent whole.

JAFFE ONLINE CONNECTION   **JAFFE ONLINE CONNECTION**

Use your CD-ROM and the Jaffe Connection Web site http://communication.wadsworth.com/jaffe to review the following concepts, answer the review questions, and complete the suggested activities.

KEY TERMS

rhetorical questions (177)
participatory questions (177)
organizational culture (181)
preview (183)
connectives (188)

signposts (188)
transitions (188)
internal previews (189)
internal summary (189)

APPLICATION AND CRITICAL THINKING EXERCISES

1. Before your next speech, trade outlines with others in your class. Use the guidelines in this chapter to evaluate your classmates' introductions, conclusions, and connectives—advising them on what they do well and what you think they could improve. When you get your outline and suggestions back, make adjustments that would improve these sections of your speech.

2. Outline a speech given by one of your classmates. Evaluate the effectiveness of the introduction and conclusion. What suggestions, if any, would you give the speaker to improve the beginning or the ending?

3. Review the section on credibility in Chapter 5—what your audience thinks of you. How and why does a good introduction and conclusion affect the audience's perception of you? How and why does a poor start or finish influence their perception?

4. Log on to InfoTrac College Edition and do a PowerTrac Search for the journal *Vital Speeches*. Find three different speeches with interesting titles, for example, "Lawyers: Law Is a Jealous Mistress" (July 1, 2002), "The Lasting Legacy of George Washington" (April 15, 2002), and "The Secret of Gun Violence in America" (August 1, 2001). Read each one and evaluate the effectiveness of the introduction by using criteria developed in this chapter.

5. Read the conclusions of the same speeches you studied in the previous exercise. Evaluate the conclusion using the criteria in the text. Does the speaker provide a transition? Review the major points? Provide psychological closure? End memorably? What changes, if any, would you make that would improve the conclusion?

6. To see an example of an effective introduction, log on to InfoTrac College Edition and use your PowerTrac skills to search for a speech by John Ramsay titled, "At home with books: Reading is fundamental." It's in *Vital Speeches* for March 15, 1999, vol. 65, no. 11.4. Why do you think this introduction is so effective?

7. Log on to the Internet and use the search engine www.alltheweb.com to search for the exact phrase "introductions and conclusions." You should find many sites that were created by both writing and speech instructors. Go to one of the sites for writers and compare and contrast the guidelines for writers with those for speakers that you find in this text. What are the similarities? The differences? How do you account for these differences?

THE JAFFE CONNECTION WEB SITE

The Jaffe Connection Web site features review questions about the Web links, Stop and Check activities, and InfoTrac College Edition exercises referenced throughout the chapter. You can access this site via your CD-ROM or at http://communication.wadsworth.com/jaffe.

Web Links

10.1 Finding and Using Quotations (page 179)
10.2 Deaf Education Speech: Different Openings (page 184)
10.3 Evaluations of Introductions and Conclusions (page 188)

Stop and Check Activities

10.1 Create an Interesting Introduction (page 184)
10.2 Evaluating Introductions and Conclusions (page 187)

InfoTrac College Edition Exercises

10.1 Using Current Events in Speech Introductions (page 180)
10.2 Considering Organizational Culture: Adapting Speech Introductions (page 181)
10.3 Use Chapter Criteria to Evaluate Speech Introductions (page 190)
10.4 Evaluate an Effective Introduction (page 190)

SPEECH INTERACTIVE ON THE JAFFE CONNECTION CD-ROM

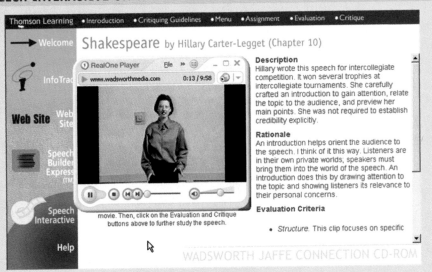

Watch the speech introduction clip from Hillary Carter-Liggett's informative speech titled "Shakespeare" and answer the questions for analysis under Speech Interactive on your Jaffe Connection CD-ROM. Then examine the following outline carefully.

STUDENT OUTLINE
WITH COMMENTARY

PETER ILICH TCHAIKOVSKY
by Jennifer Gingerich

General Purpose:	To inform
Specific Purpose:	To inform my audience about some of Peter Tchaikovsky's background and musical accomplishments.
Central Idea:	Tchaikovsky was a great Russian composer who was, and is still, given much credit as a musician.

Introduction
  I. Some of you may recognize this music [*The Nutcracker Suite*].
      A. If you do, go ahead and raise your hands as soon as you recognize it. [Play the recording.]
      B. [See how many recognize the music, and give an appropriate response.]
      C. You may have recognized the music as *The Nutcracker,* but do you know the composer—Peter Ilich Tchaikovsky, who was born in 1840?
  II. I first became interested in Tchaikovsky when I was a little girl.
      A. I heard the Portland Symphony perform the *1812 Overture* with live cannons.

In her introduction, Jennifer relates to her audience after she establishes her credibility. What do you think of the effectiveness of this? How well does her overall introduction fulfill the functions of a successful opening?

B. I grew up listening to works by Tchaikovsky, such as *The Nutcracker Suite* and his *1812 Overture.*

C. I even played some of his music on my violin in orchestra class.

D. The more I heard Tchaikovsky's music, the more I liked it, and he soon became my favorite composer.

III. Tchaikovsky even has distant connections to Goshen College!

A. All of us have heard his music.

B. Even more importantly, Tchaikovsky visited the United States a little over 107 years ago and performed in a place where some Goshen students will soon perform.

IV. Today I will share some things I've learned about Tchaikovsky including his background, his lasting works, and his concert that opened Carnegie Hall.

Body

I. First of all, Tchaikovsky was destined to be a musician.

A. Peter had many musical talents as a young boy.

1. He made up tunes and plunked them out on the piano.

2. His mother taught him to play waltzes.

3. Not only did he play tunes, he also tapped out rhythms.

B. Although he showed talent, his destiny was not obvious to everyone, because at age 10 his father sent him to law school.

1. Law was a stable and profitable career.

2. In contrast, musicians led hard lives during that time.

C. Tchaikovsky left law school at age nineteen because his passion for music was too strong.

1. In her 1942 biography, *Stormy Victory,* Claire Purdy quotes Tchaikovsky as saying, "My musical talent—you cannot deny it—is my only one."

2. Because music was both his talent and passion, Tchaikovsky decided to focus solely on developing his musical gifts.

II. Composing full time was a wise career choice, for Peter Ilich Tchaikovsky began to write outstanding compositions that gained him lasting national and international adoration.

A. Tchaikovsky was well loved in Russia for his talent.

B. *The Nutcracker* is performed every Christmas to this day.

C. In their 1940 book, *Living Biographies of Great Composers,* authors Henry and Dana Lee Thomas state that Tchaikovsky's music "translates him into an entirely different world . . . in which he can . . . become an . . . instrument in the hands of a higher power."

III. Lastly, Tchaikovsky's talents were such that he was invited to conduct his works at the opening of Carnegie Hall.

A. The *New York Times* article, "Music Notes," written on February 22, 1891, announced that Tchaikovsky was to open Carnegie Hall; the author added, "This Russian is one of the strongest composers of our time, and his appearance here will be a musical event of much importance."

B. According to the 1979 book *The Music Makers,* edited by Victor Stevenson, Tchaikovsky toured America, creating a musical sensation.

Conclusion

I. In conclusion, Tchaikovsky was a great composer who was destined to be a musician and who wrote great works that gained him lasting recognition.

Underline all the connectives you can find in the body of this outline. (Remember that an outline is not the same as a speech text. It's only the framework or skeleton that she'll elaborate on.) Jennifer builds connectives in her outlines so that her points hold together and her speech flows from point to point.

With all the information storage technology available today, Jennifer can actually locate and read newspaper articles that are more than 100 years old.

II.   Tchaikovsky came to this country to open the great music hall that our own Goshen College Chamber Choir will be performing in on March 28.

III. I hope that I have helped you today to see the influence this wonderful composer has had on my life and the lives of many around the world.

References

Purdy, C. L. (1942). *Stormy victory: The story of Tchaikovsky.* New York: Julian Messner, Inc.

Stegmeister, E. (1973). *The new music lovers handbook.* New York: Harvey House, Inc.

Stevenson, V. (Ed.). (1979). *The music makers.* New York: Harry N. Abrams.

Thomas, H., & Thomas, D. L. (1940). *Living biographies of great composers.* Garden City, NY: Halcyon House.

Musical notes. (1891, February 22). *The New York Times,* 13.

Identify the ways this conclusion signals the end and reviews the main points. How effectively does she create psychological closure? What other ending choices could she have made? For example, what if she turned on *The Nutcracker Suite* when she said "In conclusion," and ended the speech with the music playing softly?

Putting It All Together: Outlining Your Speech

THIS CHAPTER WILL HELP YOU

- Outline the contents of your speech in a linear form
- Prepare note cards or a speaking outline
- Record your ideas in a more organic pattern

"Family Life and Spirit of Mankind" Mural ©1977 by Susan Kelk Cervantes and Judith Knepher Jamerson. (Leonard R. Flynn School, East Wall, Army Street at Harrison, SF, CA)

LTHOUGH STUDENTS SOMETIMES PROTEST, "Why should I write an outline? I'm preparing a speech, not writing an essay," instructors have good reasons for requiring speech outlines. An outline is to a speech as a skeleton is to the body; it's like steel girders to a skyscraper. A good outline highlights your speech's framework and displays your ideas and their relationships to one another. Many students eventually recognize that the discipline of outlining teaches them valuable skills. For example, in the semester after she took a public speaking course, Michelle thanked me for teaching outlining skills:

> The organizational skills I learned in communication class have been valuable tools in several areas. Not only did learning how to outline allow me to develop clear, focused speeches, but it also helps in organizing and focusing papers and presentations in all my other classes.
>
> MICHELLE

You've already done most of the work for creating an outline. That is, you've researched your topic (Chapter 7), selected supporting materials (Chapter 8), and identified ways to organize the body, introduction, and conclusion of your speech (Chapters 9 and 10). You've already seen the value of clearly identified points, each one supported by carefully chosen data. In fact, you may have already made a **rough draft outline** of your main points and supporting materials. This chapter will help you tie together all your efforts from preceding chapters and complete a formal outline that will function as the framework or skeleton for your thoughts.

Outlines differ from a **script** or **text,** which includes every word you say. And both differ from the **speaking notes** you take with you to the podium. Compare and contrast the script at the end of Chapter 2 with the outline at the end of Chapter 9 and the speaker's notes presented later in this chapter.

Experienced speakers know that there's no single way to outline a speech correctly; the more speeches you give, the more you'll find a way that works best for you considering your individual learning style. This chapter presents tips for making conventional outlines, followed by a description of how to prepare speaking notes. It concludes with ideas for more holistic methods of pulling together a speech that take into account diversity in individual thinking styles.

Rough Draft Outline
A preliminary outline that's not yet formatted formally.

Scripts or Texts
The actual text of the speech; includes every word you say.

Speaking Notes
The key words and phrases you take with you to the platform when you speak.

How to Prepare a Content Outline

Content Outline
A formal record of your major ideas and their relationship to one another in your speech.

Most instructors require a **content outline,** a record of the speech's major ideas or materials and their relationship to one another. Although instructions vary in specific details, several general guidelines can help you prepare content outlines.

Begin with a Heading

Give your speech a title, then include the general purpose, the specific purpose, the finalized central idea, and the organizational pattern that you've developed using principles found in Chapters 6 through 9. The heading is a nutshell look at what you plan to accomplish. Here is the heading John used for his speech about culture shock.

Topic:	The Five Stages of Culture Shock
General Purpose:	To inform
Specific Purpose:	To inform my audience of the stages of culture shock and to demonstrate these with real-life examples.
Central Idea:	Culture shock is a psychological process that typically progresses through five stages: honeymoon, disintegration, reintegration, autonomy, and interdependence.
Organizational Pattern:	Chronological

Use a Standard Format

Before the advent of computers and word processing programs, students had to use their typewriters' tab feature to line up points and subpoints. Fortunately, most computer software programs now have a number of formatting features or style tools that automatically put in some of the features discussed in this section. Learning to use them will save you time and effort as you create content outlines.

Alternate Numbers and Letters

Show the relationship of the parts of your speech to one another by alternating numbers and letters in a consistent pattern. For example, identify your major points using one of the patterns described in Chapter 9. Then designate each major point with a Roman numeral. Under each main point, identify first-level supporting points and give each one a capital letter head (A., B., C., . . .). Second-level supporting points get Arabic numerals (1., 2., 3., . . .), and third-level points are designated with lowercase letters (a., b., c., . . .) The following system is typical:

I. Major point
  A. First-level supporting point
    1. Second-level supporting point
    2. Second-level supporting point
      a. Third-level supporting point
      b. Third-level supporting point
  B. First-level supporting point
II. Major point
  A. First-level supporting point
  B. First-level supporting point

Computerized word processing programs that autoformat outlines can save you time and energy when you actually sit down to write your speech outline.

© Peter Chapman Photography

Coordinate Points

Use the principle of **coordination;** this means that your major points all have basically the same value or weight. All your second-level points are similar in value, and so on. In the following outline, the problem and the solution are major points. First-level points—causes and effects—are coordinated approximately equally. Each first-level point is further supported by coordinated second-level points.

Coordination
Points are arranged into various levels; the points on a specific level have basically the same value or weight.

I. Problem
  A. Causes
    1. First Cause
    2. Second Cause
  B. Effects
    1. First Effect
    2. Second Effect
    3. Third Effect
II. Solution
  A. The plan
  B. Cost
  C. Benefits

Indent

Indentation is yet another way to help you see the interrelationship of your materials. For example, the A and B headings line up visually as do the second- and third-level supporting

Indentation
Formatting by spacing inward various levels of points.

points. Consequently, the formatting itself helps you "see" your main ideas and the points under them.

Write Your Points in Sentence Form

Complete sentences allow you to see the content included in each point. For example, John's introduction to his speech on culture shock *could* use only phrases, like this:

I. *Craik* in Ireland
II. Travelers abroad
III. My Kenyan experiences
IV. Five stages

It's obvious that someone reading his outline would not know what each point actually covers. His phrases might function adequately as a speaking outline; however, both John and his professor will have a better idea of his speech content if he uses the following full-sentence outline for the major points in his introduction.

I. You're in Ireland when a man offers you some craik (pronounced "crack"); should you be surprised or offended?
II. Whenever you enter another culture, you can expect to go through culture shock.
III. I experienced this process when I spent the summer in Kenya.
IV. People typically experience five stages of adjustment to a new culture: honeymoon, disintegration, reintegration, autonomy, and interdependence.

Parallel Points
Making the points similar in type.

Another key is to construct **parallel points.** That is, don't write out some points as declarative sentences and others as questions. Avoid mixing phrases and complete sentences, and don't put two sentences in a single point—all of which this student did when she originally outlined her major points:

I. What is Multiple Sclerosis (MS)? [a complete sentence in question form]
II. The Big Mystery! [a sentence fragment or phrase]
III. Who? [a single word in question form]
IV. Effects . . . Symptoms of MS. [an incomplete sentence]
V. There are three prominent medications being used right now to treat MS. These are talked about in the magazine *Inside MS.* [two declarative sentences]

Here's how her rewritten points should look:

I. Multiple Sclerosis (MS) is a disease of the central nervous system.
II. The causes remain a mystery.
III. Its victims tend to share age, gender, and regional characteristics.
IV. The condition affects eyesight and bodily coordination.
V. Most physicians prescribe one of three major medications.

Use the Principle of Subordination

Subordination
Placement of supporting points under major points.

The word **subordination** comes from two Latin root words: *sub,* or under, and *ordinare,* or place in order. This means that all first-level points support and are placed under major points; all second-level points support first-level points and are put under them, and so on. Return to the previous example and think critically about the speaker's points. Are all her first-level points equal? Or do some seem more logically to follow others? What would happen if she used a problem–solution pattern for first-level points, then subordinated the other material to the second level of support? Her outline would now look like this:

I. Multiple Sclerosis (MS) is a disease of the central nervous system. [problem]
    A. Its causes remain a mystery. [causes of the problem]

B. Its victims tend to share age, gender, and regional characteristics. [affected persons]

C. It affects eyesight and bodily coordination. [effects of the problem]

II. Most physicians prescribe one of three major medications. [solution]

Coordinating her major points into a problem–solution pattern is a much more effective way to organize this speech. And subordinating three points—the causes, the victims, and the effects of MS—under the problem section of this speech creates a more logical flow of ideas.

In summary, a good content outline begins with a heading and uses a standard format that includes coordinated points arranged by alternating letters and numbers and by indenting material in a way that shows the relationship of ideas to one another. It's written in complete sentences that are parallel in construction, and contains supporting materials arranged underneath the major ideas.

John Streicher's outline, with commentary, pulls all of these elements together, providing you with a good model outline and an explanation of how John organized and outlined his speech. His professor asks for a list of references at the end of each speech, as well as an outline of both the introduction and conclusion. (Some instructors ask their students to write out the beginning and ending and outline only the body of the speech.) Here is John's complete content outline.

STUDENT OUTLINE WITH COMMENTARY

THE FIVE STAGES OF CULTURE SHOCK
by John Streicher

Topic:	The Five Stages of Culture Shock
General Purpose:	To inform
Specific Purpose:	To inform my audience of the stages of the psychological phenomenon known as culture shock and to demonstrate these stages with real-life examples.
Central Idea:	Culture shock is a very real psychological process that typically progresses through five stages: honeymoon, disintegration, reintegration, autonomy, and interdependence.
Organizational Pattern:	Chronological

Introduction

I. You're in Ireland when a man offers you some *craik* (pronounced "crack"); you're surprised and offended, but should you be?

II. Whenever you enter another culture, you can expect to go through culture shock.

A. In *The Five Stages of Culture Shock,* Paul Peterson defines culture shock as "an internalized construct or perspective developed in reaction or response to a new or unfamiliar situation."

B. Culture shock typically involves several stages of adjustment.

III. I experienced this process when I spent the summer in Kenya.

A. Customs were so different that I often felt I was missing what was going on.

B. However, working my way through several stages taught me valuable coping strategies that make me more sensitive to newcomers to our culture.

IV. Today, I will identify and describe five stages people typically experience when they enter a new culture: the honeymoon, disintegration, reintegration, autonomy, and interdependence stages.

By writing out his heading, John made sure the focus of his speech is clear and that his outline accomplishes his stated purposes.

Specifically identify your introduction, your body, and your conclusion. This introduction gains attention, relates to the audience, establishes credibility, and previews the major points. Each element is assigned a separate Roman numeral.

Point IV, the preview, functions as the transition between the introduction and the speech body. It tells the audience to listen for chronologically organized information about the stages of culture shock.

John labels the body of his speech. He uses the principle of coordination; each point identifies a single stage. In his first major point, he sets up a pattern he'll modify and use to develop each point. He defines the stage, explains typical responses, provides examples, and ends with helpful tips for navigating the stage.

Subpoints B and C are first-level points that are made up of both second- and third-level supporting materials.

Again, John first defines and explains the stage, then ends with survival tips.

His first-, second-, and third-level supporting points are subordinated by means of indentation and alternating numbers and letters.

Notice that all his points are phrased as declarative sentences and that he includes only one sentence per point.

Frustration climaxes the third point, so here is a good place to write out a transition statement rather than use a signpost. John separates his transition from the lettering and numbering system.

Body

I. The Honeymoon stage is first; it represents your initial contact with the culture.
    A. Your previous cultural identity isolates you from belonging in that culture.
        1. You'll be surrounded by strange sights, sounds, and smells.
        2. You will not understand what others expect of you.
    B. But you typically feel like a tourist—excited, adventuresome, even confident.
        1. People in the host culture may be kind and helpful.
        2. You may be oblivious to your errors.
            a. Students in a Venezuelan airport made unintentional errors.
            b. A woman on a bus in the Bahamas showed a naïve attitude.
    C. You can take steps during this stage to help you through the later stages.
        1. Begin a journal that records both your positive and negative experiences.
        2. Act like a tourist and find things you enjoy doing.
            a. Look for cultural offerings in the area.
            b. Find areas of natural beauty that you can retreat to, both now and later.
        3. Plan a vacation for six months down the road.
        4. Build a support system.
            a. Make contacts with people in the area.
            b. Keep in touch with family and friends at home by letter, email, and phone.

II. In about two to eight weeks, you enter the Disintegration stage–wherein the novelty has worn off, and unexpected things begin to happen.
    A. You're no longer a spectator; you must solve practical problems.
    B. Typically, you'll experience confusion (Help! What do I do now?), failure (I'm inadequate), and self-blame (It's all my fault).
    C. You can take steps to help yourself through this stage.
        1. Take care of yourself physically.
        2. Continue to learn the language and the nonverbal communication system.
            a. When she was a nanny in Belgium, Sara spoke French with the children's family, but she also took a French course at a nearby university.
            b. Look for cues to nonverbal expectations.
            c. Record your insights in your journal.

III. Two to three months later the Reintegration stage lets you shed your self-blame and interact within the culture.
    A. You may reject the "overwhelmed feeling" and stand up for yourself.
    B. However, you may feel anger and rejection toward the host culture.
        1. An anthropologist in Africa opposed perceived injustice in the legal system.
        2. Some exchange stereotypes about their hosts with others like themselves.
        3. Some go home.
            a. Five to 30 percent of people on overseas assignments return early.
            b. Companies lose up to $400,000 per returnee.
    C. Plan ways to get through this stage positively.
        1. Go on the vacation you planned during the Honeymoon stage.
        2. Avoid talking negatively about your hosts with your own group.
        3. Record your frustrations in your journal.
    (Transition: You've adjusted to the Honeymoon, Disintegration, and Reintegration stages from here, you either regress or you move toward greater understanding in the Autonomy and Interdependence stages.)

IV. After three to six months, you'll find balance at the Autonomy stage.
    A. You can relax and understand, rather than criticize, the host culture.
    B. You'll negotiate effectively in the setting that's foreign to you.
    C. Some tips will help you through this stage.
        1. Don't overestimate your abilities and commit a blunder.
        2. Do some serious shopping, because you're less likely to be "taken."

V. Finally, after about nine months, you come to the final stage—Interdependence.
  A. Consider yourself bicultural or multicultural.
    1. You aren't controlled or dominated by cultural differences.
    2. You can demonstrate trust and sensitivity.
    3. This stage is best demonstrated by an American in Kenya.
  B. You begin to assume responsibilities and privileges in your new culture.

A signpost leads to his last point.

Conclusion
  I. I hope this helps you understand the process of integrating into a new culture.
  II. People typically experience five adjustment stages: Honeymoon, Disintegration, Reintegration, Autonomy, and Interdependence.
  III. Even if you don't go abroad, you can better understand immigrants.
  IV. And go ahead, have some *craik*—the Irish slang word for a good time!

By setting apart the conclusion, he makes sure that he's crafted a memorable ending that summarizes the speech and is both purposeful and brief.

Bibliography
  Coping with culture shock. (1999, March 23, last updated). Carnegie Mellon Office of International Education. Available online at: www.oie.studentaffairs.cmu.edu/students/guidebook.98/cultshock.htm.
  Culture shock. (1999, December 2, last modified). Comox Valley International College—School of English Language. Available online at: www.cvic.bc.ca/c_shock.htm.
  Culture shock: Survival manual. (1999). Technical University of Budapest International Education Center. Available online at: www.khmk.bme.hu/surv/studo1.ssi.
  Drake, W. (1997). Managing culture shock: 25 slides with notes. Available online at: www.culturebank.com/sepiv/realshock/.
  Furnham, A., & Bochner, S. (1986). *Culture shock*. New York: Methuen.
  Jordan, P. (1992). *Re-entry*. Seattle: Youth with a Mission.
  Loss, M. (1983). *Culture shock*. Winona Lake, IN: Light and Life Press.
  Pederson, P. (1995). *The five stages of culture shock*. Westport, CT: Greenwood.
  Storti, C. (1990). *The art of crossing cultures*. Yarmouth, ME: Intercultural Press.

This bibliography is formatted in the American Psychological Association (APA) style. Ask your instructor which format he or she prefers, but always include a list of the references you consulted during your speech preparation.

BUILD YOUR SPEECH
EVALUATE YOUR CONTENT OUTLINE

Use Speech Builder Express to prepare your content outline. When you have finished your outline, evaluate it using the Evaluate Your Content Outline checklist under Preparation Forms for Chapter 11 at the Jaffe Connection Web site http://communication.wadsworth.com/jaffe.

Web Site

How to Create Your Speaking Outline

Although content outlines help you organize your ideas and visualize your points in relationship to one another, they differ from your **speaking outline**—the outline you take with you to the podium. Content outlines are written in full sentences, but speaking outlines use full sentences in two places only: transition statements and direct quotations. Instead, they are **key word outlines,** using just enough important phrases or words to jog your memory as you speak. This section describes two major formats for key word outlines: note cards and speaking outlines.

Speaking Outline
The outline you take with you to the platform.

Key Word Outline
An outline using important words and phrases that will jog the speaker's memory.

Use Note Cards

Write your key words out on note cards—either 3 × 5- or 4 × 6- inch cards are most common. Using note cards in delivery offers several advantages. For one thing, they are smaller, less noticeable, and easier to handle than a standard sheet of paper. They are sturdy enough not to waver if your hand trembles. And if you deliver your speech without a podium, you can hold your cards in one hand and still use the other to gesture. Here are some tips for creating note cards:

- Use purchased cards, or make your own.
- Write legibly; print or type key words in capital letters; double or triple space your lines.
- Number your cards so that you can put them in place quickly if they get out of order.
- Write on only one side of each card because turning note cards over can be distracting.
- Delete nonessential words—use only key words and short phrases.
- Use no more than five or six lines per card, and space your lines so that you can find your place instantly. For longer speeches, don't crowd additional information onto your cards; instead, use more cards.
- Highlight important ideas and circle or underline words you want to emphasize during delivery.
- Put words such as *pause* or *slow down* on your cards to serve as delivery reminders.

Avoid this speaker's mistake, and keep your speaking notes largely invisible. Don't wave them around or tap the cards on the podium. Move from card to card or page to page unobtrusively; however, let your audience see you refer to your notes when you're giving direct quotations or complicated statistics.

Figure 11.1 Your note cards are highly individualized. That is, you make a personalized set of key term cards that will jog *your* memory.

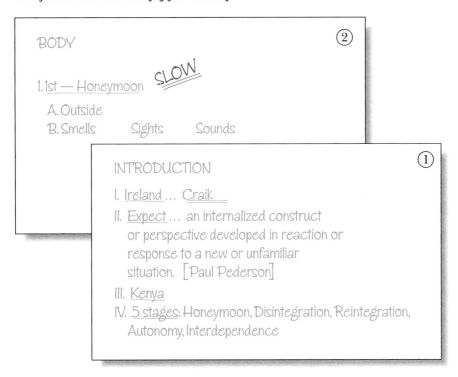

- Practice in front of a mirror using your note cards. Revise them if they are not as helpful as you would like.
- When you actually give your speech, use your cards unobtrusively. Never wave them around. However, when you read a direct quotation or give complicated statistics, hold up a card and look at it frequently to show your audience that you are being as accurate as possible ("Preparing the Delivery Outline," 1999).

Figure 11.1 shows two of the note cards for John's speech on culture shock.

Create a Speaking Outline

Another strategy is to create a speaking outline by typing out key terms on a standard-size sheet of paper. Many of the tips for creating note cards apply to key term outlines, but there are some minor differences as the following tips point out:

- Use plenty of space to distinguish between the various sections of your speech.
- Use highlighter pens to distinguish the sections easily. For example, underline signposts and transition statements in orange, and use a different colored highlighter for the introduction, the body, and the conclusion.
- Use different font sizes and formatting features to break up visual monotony and direct your eyes to specific places as you go along. For example, in Figure 11.2 the preview alternates lowercase and capitalized words.
- If you have several sheets of notes, spread them across the lectern in such a way that you can still see the side edges of the lower pages. Then when you move from one page to another, slip the top sheet off in an unobtrusive motion and tuck it at the bottom of the pile.

Figure 11.2 Speaking outlines contain key words to remind you of your ideas and advice words to remind you of your delivery.

Introduction
   I. Ireland—**craik** ("crack")—offensive?   **RELAX !!**
  II. <u>expect</u> C.S.
     A. Paul Peterson *The Five Stages of Culture Shock*
       "an internalized construct or perspective
       developed in reaction or response
       to a new or unfamiliar situation."
     B. A progression.
 III. my **Kenyan** experiences.   **DON'T RUSH !!!**
     A. felt missing out.
     B. learned coping strategies.
     C. apply to newcomers here
 IV. <u>FIVE</u> stages:
     • honeymoon,
     • **DISINTEGRATION**
     • reintegration,
     • **AUTONOMY**
     • interdependence.

Body
   I. **First = Honeymoon**
     A. Don't belong
       1. sights, sounds, smells.
     B. excited   adventuresome confident   <u>**like a tourist.**</u>
       1. helpful **hosts**
       2. **oblivious** to errors   **S - L - O - W !!**
         a. <u>**students**</u>   **Venezuelan**   **airport.**
         b. <u>**woman**</u>   **bus**   **Bahamas**

● If a lectern is unavailable, place your pages in a dark-colored notebook or folder that you hold with one hand while gesturing with the other. (Angle your notebook so that the audience doesn't see your pages.)

Figure 11.2 shows the first page of a speaking outline for the culture shock speech.

In short, speaking from brief notes, rather than reading from an outline or trying to memorize your speeches, allows you to remember your major ideas and supporting materials. Moreover, you can maintain eye contact with the audience, secure in the knowledge that if you lose your train of thought you can easily glance at these notes to regain your place.

BUILD YOUR SPEECH
EVALUATE YOUR SPEAKING OUTLINE

Using Speech Builder Express, click on the Completing the Speech Outline option to preview your content outline. Using this complete outline, you can easily prepare your speaking outline or note cards. You can then evaluate your speaking outline using the Evaluate Your Speaking Outline checklist included under Preparation Forms for Chapter 11 at the Jaffe Connection Web site http://communication.wadsworth.com/jaffe.

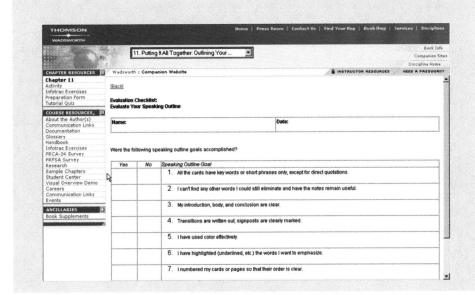

Web Site

How to Work with an Alternative Pattern

The Diversity in Practice box titled Individual Cognitive Style (p. 208) discusses thinking styles and their influence on outlining. If your cognitive style leans toward more global or imagistic thinking, you may choose one of the alternative patterns, such as the wave, spiral, or star described in Chapter 9. Consequently, your depiction of your speech's content will be less conventional, but you can still design an appropriate representation of your ideas and their relationship to one another by using the tips provided here (Jorgensen-Earp, n.d.):

- First, decide on the pattern you will use to organize your materials; you may find it useful to sketch the diagram.
- Then write out your main points.
- With your pattern in mind, indicate what you will use for developmental material, subordinating this material under the point it supports.
- Indicate how you plan to begin and end your speech; then write out key transition statements.
- Use standard indentation and numbering only if it's helpful.

Figure 11.3 provides an example of John's culture shock speech that's now formatted into a spiral pattern.

Figure 11.3 This figure depicts the contents of the culture shock speech as visualized in a spiral form.

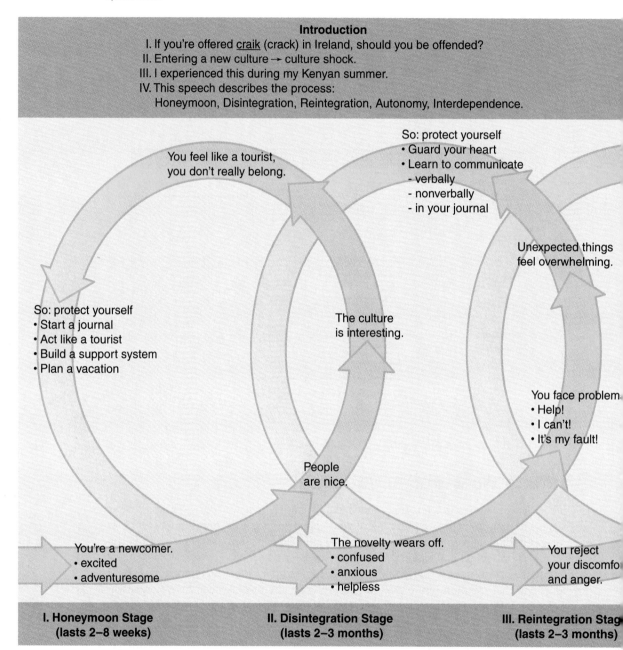

Introduction
I. If you're offered <u>craik</u> (crack) in Ireland, should you be offended?
II. Entering a new culture → culture shock.
III. I experienced this during my Kenyan summer.
IV. This speech describes the process:
  Honeymoon, Disintegration, Reintegration, Autonomy, Interdependence.

You feel like a tourist, you don't really belong.

So: protect yourself
• Guard your heart
• Learn to communicate
  - verbally
  - nonverbally
  - in your journal

Unexpected things feel overwhelming.

So: protect yourself
• Start a journal
• Act like a tourist
• Build a support system
• Plan a vacation

The culture is interesting.

You face problem
• Help!
• I can't!
• It's my fault!

People are nice.

You're a newcomer.
• excited
• adventuresome

The novelty wears off.
• confused
• anxious
• helpless

You reject your discomfo and anger.

I. Honeymoon Stage
(lasts 2–8 weeks)

II. Disintegration Stage
(lasts 2–3 months)

III. Reintegration Stag
(lasts 2–3 months)

Summary

As part of the speechmaking process, it's important to understand and show the ways that your points and subpoints relate to one another. For this reason, you'll probably be asked to outline your ideas in a linear form, using alternating letters and numbers and careful indentation. Coordinate your main points and subordinate supporting materials under them. Write your content outline in complete sentences, and include a list of references at the end.

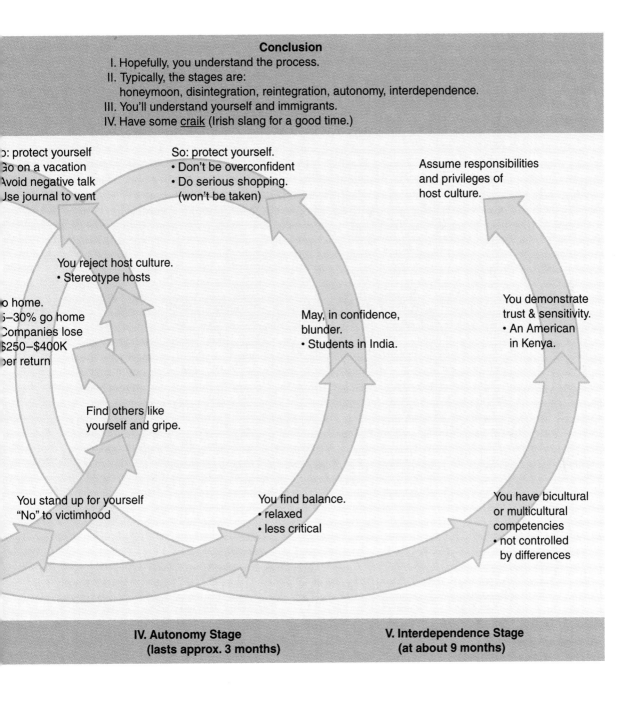

Conclusion
I. Hopefully, you understand the process.
II. Typically, the stages are:
　　honeymoon, disintegration, reintegration, autonomy, interdependence.
III. You'll understand yourself and immigrants.
IV. Have some <u>craik</u> (Irish slang for a good time.)

o: protect yourself
Go on a vacation
Avoid negative talk
Use journal to vent

So: protect yourself.
• Don't be overconfident
• Do serious shopping.
　(won't be taken)

Assume responsibilities
and privileges of
host culture.

You reject host culture.
• Stereotype hosts

o home.
5–30% go home
Companies lose
$250–$400K
per return

May, in confidence,
blunder.
• Students in India.

You demonstrate
trust & sensitivity.
• An American
　in Kenya.

Find others like
yourself and gripe.

You stand up for yourself
"No" to victimhood

You find balance.
• relaxed
• less critical

You have bicultural
or multicultural
competencies
• not controlled
　by differences

IV. Autonomy Stage
(lasts approx. 3 months)

V. Interdependence Stage
(at about 9 months)

However, content outlines do not go with you to the podium. Instead, take a speaking outline that consists only of key words; this will enable you to remember your main points but prevent you from reading your speech verbatim.

A linear outline is not the only way to record your ideas; in fact, one way to recognize diversity is to admit that people with various learning styles may actually benefit from using an alternative way of recording the speech content. Experiment to find what works best for you. If you choose to use an alternative pattern, you may find it helpful to record your ideas as a simple diagram, then arrange your major ideas and supporting materials on it.

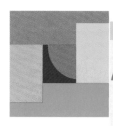

INDIVIDUAL COGNITIVE STYLE

Cognitive Style
Comprised of the modes you
typically use to think, perceive, remember, and solve
problems; it's influenced by
your culture but unique to
you.

ANY DISCUSSION OF DIVERSITY is incomplete without a mention of individuality, and in a chapter on outlining, it's important to note that each person's **cognitive style** (sometimes called thinking style or learning style) is unique. Consequently, every classroom contains "a diverse population of learners" ("Thinking and Learning Skills," 1999). Your cognitive style is comprised of the modes you typically use to think, perceive, remember, and solve problems. Our cultures influence our styles to an extent, but your particular way of processing information is unique to you (Irvine & York, 1995).

In 1981, the cognitive scientist Roger Sperry won the Nobel Peace Prize for his research in brain hemispheric dominance. His studies revealed that the right brain processes information more globally, intuitively, and artistically; in contrast, left-brain processes are more linear, analytic, logical, and computational. Most people use both hemispheres of their brains, but one side or another tends to be dominant (Giller, n.d.; Riding & Cheema, 1991). This text is obviously not intended to describe the finer points of cognitive science research. However, the diversity of cognitive styles and the fact that they reflect both a personal and a cultural orientation does fit the emphasis of this text.

What does this mean in a chapter on outlining? Well, the traditional form of outlining presented here and in most other public speaking texts involves a more leftbrain way to frame a speech—a way that may or may not match your preferred cognitive style. Consequently, although you are required to produce a linear outline, your personal style may be more holistic—and when you organize speeches in contexts outside the classroom, you may want to know alternative, more organic ways of showing your points. The last section of this chapter describes some alternative ways of showing your speech ideas.

To learn more about this topic, log on to the Internet and do an InfoTrac College Edition PowerTrac search, or go to a subject directory (such as www.google.com) and search for "thinking styles," "right-brain/left-brain," "learning styles," or other related terms. If you're interested in identifying your personal style, look for an online learning styles test on the site www.namss.org.uk/lstyles.htm.

JAFFE ONLINE CONNECTION   JAFFE ONLINE CONNECTION

Use your CD-ROM and the Jaffe Connection Web site http://communication.wadsworth.com/jaffe to review the following concepts, answer the review questions, and complete the suggested activities.

KEY TERMS

rough draft outline (196)   parallel points (198)
scripts or texts (196)   subordination (198)
speaking notes (196)   speaking outline (202)
content outline (196)   key word outline (202)
coordination (197)   cognitive style (208)
indentation (197)

APPLICATION AND CRITICAL THINKING EXERCISES

1. Outline an in-class speech given by one of your classmates. After the speech, give the outline to the speaker and ask him or her to check its contents for completeness and faithfulness to the speech.
2. Using the same outline, ask another student to evaluate your formatting—use of indentation, alternating numbers and letters, complete sentences, and the like.
3. Before you give your next speech, work from your content outline and prepare a speaking outline. Let one of your classmates evaluate both outlines and make revisions that would improve either one or both.
4. Use InfoTrac College Edition and do a PowerTrac search for the speech "Closing the Digital Divide" in the journal *Vital Speeches*. Create speaking note cards or a speech outline for the speech. Bring your note cards or outline to class for discussion.
5. Visit Purdue University's Online Writing lab at http://owl.english.purdue.edu. Search for the topic "outline" and read the material you find at the link "Developing an Outline."
6. Many speech instructors have created Web sites that provide information about content outlines and speaking outlines. Two of the better sites are www.hawaii.edu/mauispeech/html/outline_a_speech.html and www.smsu.edu/com/com115/outlines.htm. What additional tips did you find at these sites?
7. Using Ron St. John's site at Maui Community College (see Exercise 6), find the sample student outline "How to Buy a Baseball Bat" and critique it.

THE JAFFE CONNECTION WEB SITE

The Jaffe Connection Web site features review questions about the Web links and InfoTrac College Edition exercises referenced throughout the chapter. You can access this site via your CD-ROM or at http://communication.wadsworth.com/jaffe.

Web Links

11.1 Individual Cognitive Styles (page 208)
11.2 Tips for Outlining a Speech (page 209)
11.3 Evaluating Sample Speech Outlines (page 209)

InfoTrac College Edition Exercises

11.1 Information on Individual Cognitive Styles (page 208)
11.2 Create Note Cards from a Speech (page 209)

Build Your Speech Featuring Speech Builder Express

11.1 Evaluate Your Content Outline (page 201)
11.2 Evaluate Your Speaking Outline (page 205)

Visual Aids: From Chalkboard to Computer

THIS CHAPTER WILL HELP YOU

- Explain the value of visual aids in your public speeches
- Determine the advantages and disadvantages of using various presentation technologies, including overhead projectors, classroom boards, poster boards and flip charts, handouts, slides, and data projectors
- Choose helpful visual aids for each speech, including objects, models, people, lists, charts, graphs, photographs, drawings and maps, and audio and video resources
- Explain the principles of computer-generated visuals
- Give guidelines for using visual aids
- Create your personal visual presentation plan

"Immigrant Pride Day Community Mural" Mural ©1998 by Precita Eyes Muralists. (Mission District, SF, CA)

SOME VISUAL AIDS are legendary—as horror stories:

> One student killed, skinned, and cleaned a live fish in front of her stunned classmates. Another thought it would be creative and dramatic to open his speech on terrorism with a role-played scenario. Just as he got up to speak, he'd arranged for a couple of friends dressed in fatigues and carrying fake automatic weapons to burst into the classroom and order everyone to hit the floor. He didn't anticipate his classmates' reactions: some screamed, others cried. One began hyperventilating and had to go to the emergency room. (She had immigrated from a country in which terrorist incidents were common.) Someone called 9-1-1. As you might imagine, class ended immediately.

Other visuals are memorable for positive reasons:

> One speaker gave an inspirational message on shedding bad habits and replacing them with positive behaviors. He began his speech in ragged, dirty clothing, but as he talked, he removed one item after another and replaced each with a clean, new garment.

In this era of advanced technology, you'll almost certainly use visual aids when you make public presentations. Clearly, visual aids can be memorable—either positively or negatively—and you'll be a more competent speaker if you know how to create and display visual support in a positive way. The purpose of this chapter is to prepare you to use visual aids that will enhance your message and create positive impressions about you.

Visual Aids Transcend Culture

Despite a proliferation of media in this century, the use of visual aids is not new. In oral cultures, speakers use objects as well as words to clarify their ideas and help their listeners better understand abstract concepts. For instance, in the sixth century B.C., the Jewish prophet Jeremiah used a ruined linen belt as an object lesson to symbolize the decay that would come to the kingdom of Judah as a result of disobeying God (Jer. 13). In addition to clarifying ideas, people learn and remember better when they use more than one sense to take in information, and in an image-saturated culture they expect visual support. Think of your own listening experiences. Don't you learn more and remember more from speakers who use posters, charts, models, maps, objects, and graphs than from those who don't even use the chalkboard?

No, visuals are not new, but the number and kinds available are different from those used even ten years ago. And the future promises even greater technological diversity. For example, **multimedia presentations** involving text, audio, still images, and video are now commonplace. Visual support also enhances communication in pluralistic settings.

Multimedia Presentations
Combinations of text, music, still images, animation, and video.

DIVERSITY IN PRACTICE
IF YOUR FIRST LANGUAGE IS NOT ENGLISH

NONNATIVE SPEAKERS of English worry that their English will not be understood or that they will make mistakes when they address their American classmates. Visuals offer nonnative speakers the following advantages:

- By putting key words on your visual, even if you have accented English, your listeners can see as well as hear your words. This enables them to understand you more clearly.
- When you provide something for your audience to see, their focus—at least part of the time—is on your visual rather than on you. This may lessen your anxiety.
- Using visuals helps you remember your speech. Words on a list or pictures in a flow chart, for instance, remind you of your main points.

Reynolds (1996) emphasizes their value as a tool in international marketing. And visuals can help presenters who must speak in a second language, as the Diversity in Practice box on page 215 explains.

Choosing the Right Type of Presentation Technology

You can probably list a number of ways to display visuals—in fact huge corporations exist for the sole purpose of providing machines and materials for creating and displaying visual aids. To prove this, log on to the Internet, go to www.alltheweb.com, and search for the exact phrase "visual aids." (You should get more than 240,000 hits!) The 3M Company, for example, makes transparencies, plastic envelopes to store them, frames to hold them, machines to project them, and so on. This section covers a number of common ways to display visual aids—each with advantages as well as disadvantages.

Overhead Projectors

Overhead projectors are everywhere—they're in classrooms, businesses, and other organizations throughout the United States and across the globe. In fact, they're the most widely used means of display in businesses today (Muhovic, 2000). They allow you to enlarge and display an image on a wall or a screen so that everyone can see it, even in a large auditorium. Using an overhead projector has many other advantages. Transparencies are simple and inexpensive to make; the film is available in most campus bookstores, print shops, or office supply stores—and it comes in colors. You can easily store and transport transparencies. You can also overlap them by simply placing one on top of another.

Draw freehand directly onto the transparency or trace a cartoon, map, or other drawing from any printed copy. For a more professional look, use a copier to transfer a printed image to the plastic transparency. Or insert a transparency into your printer and print onto it directly from your computer. I personally like to write directly on a blank transparency, using it in place of a chalkboard and eliminating the need to turn my back to the audience.

Skillful use of an overhead projector adds to your audience's perception of your competence. However, poor skills can have the opposite effect. For best results, here are a number of things to remember:

- Before you begin speaking, turn the machine on and adjust the focus of your transparency. Then turn the machine off until you're ready to use your visual.
- If you are using a list of words on a transparency, consider cutting the transparency into strips and displaying each strip as you discuss the point it makes (Becker & Keller-McNulty, 1996).
- If you want to draw your listeners' attention to some part of your visual, point to your transparency instead of the screen. To avoid showing that you're trembling, use a pointed object, placing it where you want your listeners to focus; then move your hand away from the projector.

Classroom Boards

Classroom boards are part of the standard equipment in most educational settings. Boards have several advantages. They're almost always available in the classroom. They're great for explaining unfolding processes such as working out a math problem. They also encourage informality, which is appropriate in some public speaking settings. Finally, they are useful in settings that include speaker–audience interactions, such as brainstorming sessions (anonymous reviewer, 1994).

Unfortunately, boards have three major drawbacks:

- You can't prepare your visual beforehand. Having an unprepared visual creates additional anxiety for speakers who like to have everything, down to the visuals, ready and rehearsed in advance.
- Most people don't write well on boards. Their visuals, consequently, look unprofessional.
- When you write on the board, your back is turned to your audience, and you're talking to the board. This is probably the major drawback of boards in general.

Boards continue to evolve. Some have a copier machine button at their base. Push it, and the attached machine transfers what you wrote on the board onto an $8\frac{1}{2} \times 11$-inch piece of paper suitable for making into handouts. Furthermore, technicians can set up electronically linked magnetic boards in several sites for use during a teleconference session. With this technology, what you draw or write in Seattle appears simultaneously on boards in Hong Kong, Sao Paulo, and Cairo (Martel, 1984).

Poster Boards and Flip Charts

For convenience and economy, use large sheets of poster board to display your visuals. It's readily available in a variety of weights and colors at campus bookstores or art supply stores. You'll also need an easel of some sort to support your posters. If you watch Congress on C-SPAN, you can see major public figures using poster board to display charts and graphs. Speakers who deliver the same speech over and over—financial planners, for example—regularly use professionally prepared posters. Posters are effective with relatively small audiences, but at greater distances they're difficult to see. These tips will enable you to make more professional-looking posters.

- Use rulers or yardsticks to ensure straight lines and avoid a "loving-hands-at-home" look.
- Use more than one color to attract and hold audience interest.
- If you plan to use the poster repeatedly, stick-on letters will make it look more professional.
- Protect your poster from becoming bent or soiled by covering it with plastic to transport it. If you use the same posters repeatedly, carry them in a portfolio.

Flip Charts
Tablets you prepare in advance or create on the spot; turn to a new page or tear off and display pages as you finish them.

Flip charts are tablets, lined or unlined, that are commonly used in businesses and organizations but are less frequently seen in classrooms. The paper in them varies from tablet thickness to stiffer weights. Larger flip charts work well in conference rooms; smaller ones are used for presentations to only a few listeners.

Flip charts can be useful, especially if you repeat the same speech to various, fairly small audiences. You can even use small tabletop flip charts for presentations to individuals or small groups of people when other means of display are unavailable.

Jose Pelaez/corbisstockmarket.com

Flip charts can function like a classroom board, especially in brainstorming-type situations where you engage in a great deal of interaction with your audience. For example, ask listeners at the beginning of your presentation to contribute ideas that you will later incorporate into your talk. Tear off the series of lists you and your listeners create, and pin or tape them to the wall. If you use a flip chart in this way, you must overcome the same disadvantages you faced with a classroom board. When you turn to write on the chart, your back is turned toward the audience. In addition, they may not be neat or professional looking.

Flip charts are also good for "building" a diagram in front of the audience. Prepare the entire visual lightly in pencil. Then, during your presentation, trace over the lines for a professional-looking drawing that appears to be done on the spot. You can be sure that all the words are spelled correctly beforehand, and you can use the chart as a giant prompt card.

If you make the same presentation repeatedly for different audiences, prepare a series of lists, charts, or drawings in advance on heavier weight tablets. Then use the flip chart much as you would use a series of posters, exposing each new visual as you discuss it. The separate visuals will stay in order. In addition, because the cover is very stiff, the tablet can stand alone on any table. This makes it a useful way to display your visuals when no other equipment, such as an overhead projector, is available (anonymous reviewer, 1994).

DIVERSITY IN PRACTICE

TRAVELING AND TALKING

TODAY, THOUSANDS of professionals create visual aids for use abroad. Many engineers, marketers, physicians, and computer specialists who today cross oceans to speak never thought, when they took their beginning speech courses, that they'd eventually speak internationally. Someday you may join their numbers.

In an issue of *Electronic Design Magazine,* columnist Bob Pease (1998) tells of trips to South America and Asia where he presented material he'd given numerous times in the United States. Stateside, he had displayed more than 400 transparencies (weighing over five pounds) of technical drawings and explanations. Before he left, he toyed with the idea of creating special transparencies with subtitles translated into Portuguese and Spanish. Good idea? Well, adding 400 transparencies per language would add ten pounds of bulky weight to his briefcase. Besides, he'd need help creating the subtitles. In the end, Pease ran out of time and used his English-language visuals.

Jeff Radel (1999), from the University of Kansas Medical Center, emphasizes that the United States is not the center of the universe; the size of slides available here is not globally uniform. As a result, slots in slide projectors and carousels differ in size, and the number of slots varies to accommodate thicker or thinner slides. Consequently, speakers who plan to use slides overseas should make sure that standard U.S.-sized equipment is available there.

Seymour (1996) also addresses equipment problems. Before leaving the United States, speakers should check the voltage used in the other country's outlets and make sure their power-line cords can fit into foreign adapters. True, a wide prong that won't fit can be ground off with sandpaper or emery boards, but it's easier to check adapters and purchase appropriate equipment before departure. In short, presenters who depend on visual aids should carry a variety of backup equipment when they go on the road.

These articles, and others that deal with speaking internationally, are available on InfoTrac College Edition.

Handouts

You can provide each listener with a brochure, pamphlet, photocopy, or other handout. These valuable visuals free listeners from having to take extensive notes, and they let audience members leave with material they can study later ("Five Keys," 1997). In addition a handout can provide supplementary information you don't have time to cover in your speech. They are less common in the classroom than in business settings, but students have used them effectively. One spoke on a health-related topic; he passed out professionally made brochures from his campus health services; another passed out an information sheet describing an origami project. In other settings, companies provide sales representatives with brochures and other handouts for potential customers. Members of committees, such as a university board of trustees, often receive an entire book of supplementary reports and visuals.

When you use handouts, your primary challenge is to let your handout supplement your message, not replace it. To use these visuals more effectively, do the following:

- Distribute them, face down, before you begin speaking; then, at the point you discuss the material on them, ask your listeners to turn them over.
- Mark the points you want to emphasize with a letter or number so you can easily direct your audience to specific places on your handout. Let's say you distribute a map of an entire state, but you want to talk about three areas. Mark the first with an "A," the second with a "B," and the third with a "C." Then, as you discuss each point, draw your listeners' attention to it.
- Put identical material onto a transparency and project it as you speak—highlight on the transparency information you want them to find on their handout.

For a summary of characteristics found on effective handouts, log on to the Internet and go to this site sponsored by Kinko's Copy Service: www.amcity.com/buffalo/stories/1997/10/13/smallb3.html.

Slides

Slides, like overhead transparencies, can be projected onto a screen where fairly large audiences can see them. You can make slides from photographs; in addition, with a number of computer programs, you can make slides directly from your personal computer. One drawback: slides are less visible in well-lit rooms, and you may find yourself speaking in the dark when you use them.

Common slide projectors have a carousel-type tray in which you place your slides in order. Each time you want to project a different slide, press a button on your hand-held control. To enhance your professionalism, put a black slide between sections of content so that you can pause to talk with your audience while avoiding a blast of white light or leaving a picture or diagram up so long that it's distracting or boring (anonymous reviewer, 1994).

Data Projectors

Data projectors connect directly to a computer and project what's on the monitor onto a screen. This technology allows you to prepare all your visuals using a presentation program such as Microsoft's PowerPoint. After you create your program of slides, put the entire series on a disk. Then on the day of your presentation, simply slip your disk into the computer and press any key to bring up the images you've created. To change a slide, click the

STOP AND CHECK
BEGIN YOUR VISUAL PRESENTATION PLAN

D. Most promising types of visuals (check those that apply, and write specifics in the blank):

_____ object (what, how used?) _____

_____ model (what, how used?) _____

_____ person (who, how used?) _____

_____ list (specifically?) _____

_____ table (of what?) _____

_____ chart type _____ that shows _____

_____ graph(s) type _____ depicting _____

_____ photograph(s) of _____

_____ drawings of _____

_____ maps of _____

_____ audio support of _____

_____ videotape of _____

Assess the equipment that is available for your classroom speech by filling in sections A–C on the audiovisual aid plan shown here. Try to visualize yourself using various kinds of visual display technology during your speech. My Visual Aid Plan is available online under Stop and Check Activities for Chapter 12 on the Jaffe Connection Web site.

Web Site

mouse. Fit in a plain slide wherever you plan to discuss material that you don't plan to support visually. The student speech at the end of the chapter illustrates this technique. It's available on the CD that accompanies this text.

This technology may or may not be readily available in your classroom, but workplaces of the future will certainly have highly developed data projectors to display computer-generated visual support. Keeping current with state-of-the-art display equipment is a real plus in the workplace.

Choosing the Right Type of Visual Aids

Prepare your speech first, then decide where a visual would enhance your message and select the type that would work best given your material (Muhovic, 2000). A variety of visual aids can all function to make your ideas more understandable, although one type is often better than another. The key is to choose the *best* visual, not the one that's easiest to make. This section will discuss a variety of visuals:

- Three-dimensional objects, models, and people
- Lists, charts, and graphs
- Photographs, drawings, and maps
- Audio- and videotaped resources

Objects

Imagine a basketball coach trying to convey the finer points of dribbling without using a basketball. Or think of an origami instructor explaining how to fold a crane without providing origami paper so audience members can do the project as well as hear about it. These scenes are hard to visualize because we need to see as well as hear a verbal description of some subjects. For this reason, actual three-dimensional objects are useful, especially in speeches that demonstrate a process.

Your topic determines whether or not an object would be a realistic visual aid. For example, what object could you use for a speech about the Bermuda Triangle? Black holes? Welfare reform? It's nearly impossible to think of something appropriate. However, with a little creative thinking, you can sometimes come up with ideas for communicating your point through touch, smell, or taste. Here are some examples:

- Sky used beekeeping equipment for a speech on honey production.
- Shelly gave each listener a tuft of unprocessed wool and a piece of yarn to touch as she discussed yarn making.
- Melissa provided small samples of freshly ground coffee to smell for her talk on coffee roasting procedures.
- Juan had his classmates chew sticks of gum during his talk about the origins and evolution of gum.

Models are good choices for visuals when an actual object is too large or too small or otherwise too difficult to bring into the classroom.

Jeff Greenberg/PhotoEdit

However, objects are not always appropriate. For instance, it's illegal to bring in firearms, and it's unwise to use live animals that may be difficult to manage, as Denis found out. His nervous wolf dog detracted from his speech because wary listeners focused on the size of the animal's teeth, not Denis's words! Some objects are impractical. Marko couldn't think of a way to bring his motorcycle into the classroom. (Fortunately, his class was willing to walk to a nearby parking lot where he spoke from the seat of his bike.) In short, objects must be legal, accessible, and practical.

Objects can be invaluable or they can be detractions. Follow these guidelines for the effective use of objects with your speech:

- Be sure the object is large enough for everyone to see, or provide each listener with an individual object.
- Don't pass your objects around. If you do, some members of the audience will focus their attention on the visual rather than on your speech, and by the time everyone actually gets the object you may have completed the speech.

Models

When you can't bring actual objects into the classroom, use a **model** or realistic facsimile instead. Scaled-down models depict larger objects, such as buildings, dinosaurs, or cars. In contrast, enlarged models show larger versions of very small objects such as atoms, ants, or eyeballs. Teachers often use models such as skeletons, brains, or hearts when they cannot bring the real objects into their classrooms. Sometimes you can make your own model, or you can borrow one from a professional to display during your speech.

One student's topic was his summer job as a pyrotechnician, or fireworks display technician. Because federal regulations (and common sense) prevented him from bringing explosives into the classroom, he made a model of the spherical explosive device, complete with a fuse. He also brought the actual cylinder into which he dropped lit explosives while on the job. Finally, he wore the actual jumpsuit and displayed the safety helmet that he wore.

Model
A facsimile of an object that you can't easily bring to the speech.

People

Use friends, volunteers from the audience, even yourself to demonstrate a concept. For example, to point out the problems inherent in judging people by their looks, Nancy introduced her friend to the class. Then, during the course of the speech, she used makeup, hair gel, and black clothing to transform her friend from a "preppy" into a "Goth" in just a few moments. Also, consider ways to use the audience as a whole—you might ask fellow students to stand and participate in an exercise of some sort. Don't overlook yourself as a visual aid. Consuelo, a first aid instructor, used her wrists and neck to show the location of major arteries.

In short, an object, a model, or a person is almost indispensable in certain types of speeches—especially demonstration speeches. However, when it's unrealistic to use them, turn to the many other types of visuals available to you.

Lists

Lists are **text-based visuals,** meaning that they rely on written words more than on visual images. Lists might incorporate clip art in a minor way, but their value depends on the words and numerical information they display. That is, without clip art, the message would still come through; without the words or numbers, it would not.

Lists are popular for speeches organized chronologically because you can easily make a list out of anything that's done in stages or that occurs in steps. For example, a list of the kinds of animal communication, as shown in Figure 12.1a, would help listeners better

Text-based Visuals
Carry meaning in the written words rather than visual images.

Figure 12.1 Common visuals include (a) a list, (b) a flowchart, and (c) an organization chart.

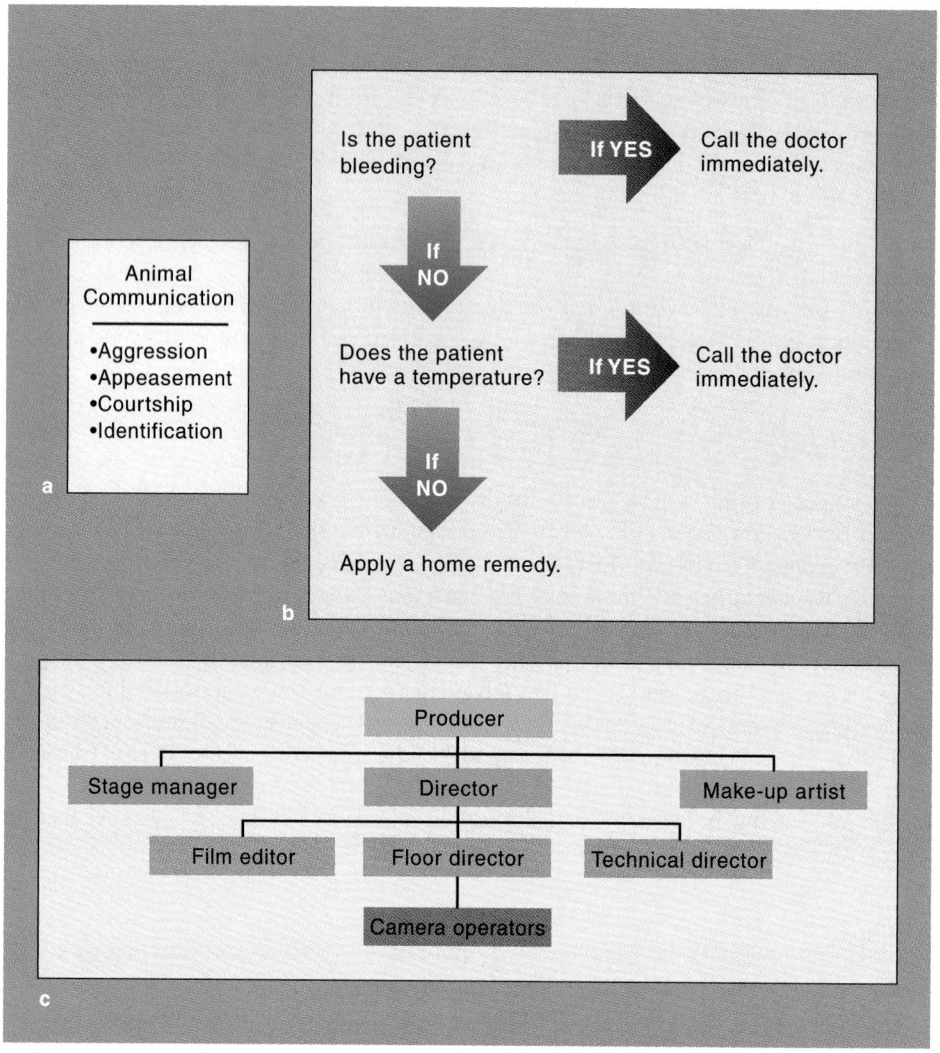

organize and remember the major types. Lists can also summarize in words or phrases the key points of more detailed material used in topically arranged speeches. You'll use lists more effectively if you remember the following guidelines:

- Don't put too much information on your visual. For instance, if your list is too detailed, your listeners may simply read it, discover the same information as in your speech, then stop listening.
- Follow the six-by-six rule: Use no more than six lines, no more than six words per line (Davidson & Kline, 1999).
- Use words and phrases rather than long sentences or whole paragraphs.
- Avoid the impulse to write out your main points, then read them to your audience (Becker & Keller-McNulty, 1996).

Charts

Flowcharts
Show the order or directional flow in which processes occur.

The two basic types of charts are flowcharts and organizational charts. **Flowcharts** show the order in which processes occur. You can often recognize them by the use of arrows indicating directional movement. Flowcharts can include drawings (pictorial flowcharts), or they may simply be a series of labeled shapes and arrows. Figure 12.1b illustrates a portion of a flowchart.

Organizational charts show hierarchies and relationships. A family tree, for example, is an organizational chart showing the relationships among family members. The chart in Figure 12.1c shows the relationship among various individuals involved in television production.

Organizational Charts
Show hierarchies and relationships.

Photographs

Although photographs provide an actual view of an object, a person, or a scene, the saying "A picture is worth a thousand words" is not necessarily true. Photographs are of little use if your audience can't see them. Consequently, any photo you show to the entire class should be poster size at least. This ensures that each listener can see the details of the picture.

However, because enlargements are sometimes difficult to acquire and because prints themselves are generally too small to be seen in even the smallest classrooms, you must figure out how best to show photographs you've deemed to be essential. Here are three effective ways to display pictures:

- Tricia found four pictures of Harry Truman at various stages of his life. She cut and taped them onto one piece of paper; then she made a photocopied handout for each classmate.
- Alene transferred a black-and-white photograph of a newborn baby to a transparency; then she used an overhead projector to project it onto a plain wall in the classroom. Throughout her speech on fetal development, the image of the baby framed her presentation.
- Bunnasakh brought six carefully selected slides to introduce her classmates to her country, Thailand.

Despite some successes, it's easy to use photographs ineffectively, and you should avoid two common mistakes:

- Don't pass photographs around. As with objects, the person closest to the speaker sees all the pictures and hears their explanation, but the person at the back of the room sees the photographs long after they were described.
- Don't show pictures from a book. For instance, John walked back and forth across the front of the room, showing several photographs in a book that didn't fully open. Some students had to squint to see the pictures, and holding the book put John in an awkward posture. Also, he had to spend time flipping from page to page. This was obviously an ineffective way to present his pictures.

Graphs

Have you ever felt bombarded with statistic after statistic? Speeches full of numerical data are often boring, difficult to follow, and impossible to remember unless you use graphs to represent the numbers in diagram form. Graphs are a type of **image-based visuals** that communicate via a figure or other image. Depicting your material in one of four types of graphs allows your listeners to see how your numbers relate to one another.

Image-based Visuals
Carry meaning in visual images; written words are secondary.

Line Graphs
Display in a linear form one or more variables that fluctuate over a time period.

1. **Line graphs** depict information in linear form; they are best for showing a variable that fluctuates over a period of time, such as the changes in college enrollment over two decades. Moreover, they are good for showing the relationship of two or more variables—for instance, comparing the number of male and female students during the same period. (Figure 12.2a shows fluctuation in funding of three projects over a six-year period.)

Figure 12.2 Major types of graphs: (a) a line graph, (b) a bar graph, (c) a pie graph, and (d) a pictograph.

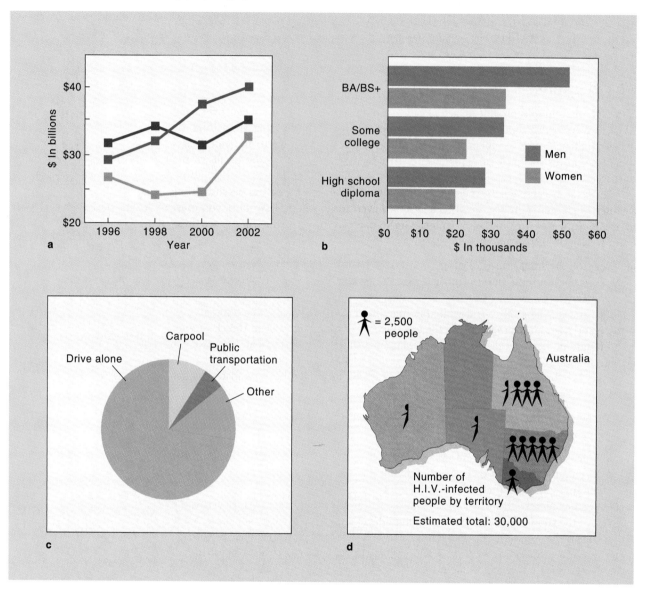

Bar Graphs
Compare data from several groups by using bands of various lengths.

Pie Graphs
Circles divided into portions that represent parts of the whole or divisions of a population.

Picture Graphs or Pictographs
Present data in pictures, each representing a certain number of individual cases.

2. **Bar graphs** are useful for comparing data from several groups. For instance, numerical information comparing the salaries of men and women with differing educational levels is displayed on the bar graph in Figure 12.2b.

3. **Pie graphs** are circular graphs that are especially good for showing divisions of a population or parts of the whole. The pie graph in Figure 12.2c depicts the way typical Americans get to work; you could use it in a speech about carpooling or public transportation.

4. **Picture graphs** or **pictographs,** the least common of the four types, are especially effective for data that relate to objects or people. Each picture represents a certain number of individual cases, as Figure 12.2d demonstrates.

Drawings and Maps

Drawings can be invaluable, either alone or added to lists or other visuals as decorative or supplementary support. If you can't even draw stick figures, you can at least trace or photocopy a commercial drawing onto a transparency or a handout. Or let your computer come to your rescue. Most computer graphics packages have extensive clip art files of prepared drawings that you can easily add to your visuals. This partial list gives you some ideas of how to use drawings.

- Substitute drawings for illegal firearms, nervous wolf dogs, inaccessible motorcycles, buildings that are too large, or insects that are too small to bring into your classroom.
- Insert a cartoon when it perfectly illustrates your point and adds humor to your talk.
- Add a **diagram**—a line drawing or graphic design that serves to explain, rather than realistically depict, an object or a process—to illustrate the acid rain cycle or the circulatory system.

Diagram
Drawing or design that serves to explain, rather than realistically depict, an object or process.

Maps are drawings that visually represent spaces. We map the heavens as well as the earth; we map weather; and we even talk about mind maps—maps of information. Choose from the following kinds of maps:

- **Political maps** show the borders between nations and states, but such maps are easily outdated in a rapidly changing world. For instance, any world map dated before 1990 is obsolete; since then, a number of countries, including the Soviet Union and Yugoslavia, have been dismantled, and new political boundaries have been drawn.
- **Geographic maps**—those showing mountains, deserts, lowlands, and other natural features—do not go out of date.
- Blueprints and floor plans of buildings, maps of routes between two points, city maps, campus maps—the list goes on. Figure 12.3 depicts a map of a Native American kiva.

Political Maps
Show current borders for states and nations; rapidly outdated in fast-changing world.

Geographic Maps
Show mountains, deserts, and other natural features—not outdated.

Figure 12.3 A floor plan of a building is a type of map. This Native American kiva is one example.

SOURCE: MARK ILES

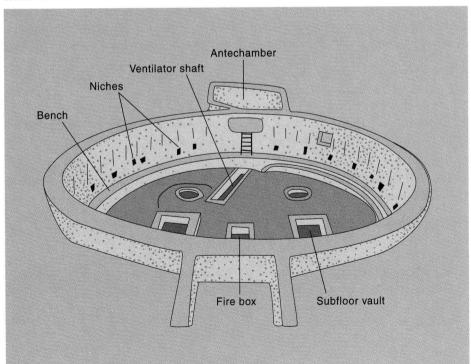

If you want to draw your listeners' attention to specific features on the map, mark the spot with a letter or number. Then, during your speech, ask listeners to focus on that specific feature.

In short, we use a variety of visuals to illuminate ideas, clarify concepts, help audiences organize and remember material, and present abstract concepts more concretely. Three-dimensional objects, and text- or image-based visuals can be indispensable in a visually oriented society. However, in some cases, recordings of sounds or images are even more effective support.

Audio and Video Resources

Think of the difference between hearing a speech about *dundun* drums and actually hearing the drums. Or think of the greater understanding you get when you can see and hear a film clip showing the sights and sounds of a rodeo compared to a poster showing a list of its major events. Although audio and visual support require extra preparation and planning, they can help you convey certain types of information.

Audio Resources

Audio support is particularly important with music-related topics. Portable electronic keyboards, guitars, ethnic musical instruments, and so on can add to your speech—as can tapes or CDs. All these enable your audience to hear the sounds you are explaining, ranging from reggae music to the music of a particular composer (as demonstrated in the speech about *dundun* drums, outlined in Appendix C).

Although it's less commonly done, you can effectively use sounds other than music. In her speech on whales, for instance, Mary Beth played a tape of a whale song and asked her listeners to identify the source of the sound. Use your creativity to think of other ways to incorporate short sound clips—sounds from nature, traffic noises, conversations—to enhance your presentation.

Video Resources

College recruiters visit high schools, bringing along videos of their institutions, complete with background music and interviews with administration, faculty, and students. In many cases, the images themselves provide most of the message. The recruiter simply introduces the video, then fields questions afterward.

In the classroom, your goal with videotapes is to supplement, not replace, your ideas using some of the massive amounts of visual resources available to you—including clips from television shows, feature films, advertisements, and home movies. By carefully selecting short segments to illustrate your points, you can clarify your ideas dramatically and memorably, as these examples demonstrate.

- Lisa made the *Guinness Book of Records* for being part of the largest tap dancing group ever assembled at one time for a performance. As she explained ways to get listed in the famous record book, Lisa used a fifteen-second video clip that her mother had recorded.
- Mary Beth's whale speech ended with a ten-second clip taken from a television program, showing a number of whales playfully leaping in and out of the water.
- Andrew discussed the differences between men's and women's gestures. To illustrate, he brought a fifteen-second commercial showing a male and female interacting. As he introduced his topic, he played the tape. Then, as he discussed each point, he again played the tape—this time with the sound turned off—pausing the tape at various places to illustrate the point he was making.

All these students were successful because they preplanned carefully. They selected short clips that illustrated, rather than substituted for, their words; they cued up their tapes in advance; and they planned carefully exactly when they'd start and stop the tape.

Enabling listeners to see or hear about your topic is important in many public speaking settings today. Indeed, it's almost necessary in some presentations, such as demonstrations. Skillful construction and use of visuals will distinguish good speakers from adequate ones, and as you learn to work with visuals, your competence will increase.

STOP AND CHECK

CONTINUE YOUR VISUAL PRESENTATION PLAN

Return to your Audiovisual Aid Plan shown on page 217 and available online under Stop and Check Activities for Chapter 12. Review your speech outline or think of the material in your speech and decide which ideas need to be supplemented by which types of visual or audio aids. Then fill in section D. On a separate sheet of paper, make a preliminary sketch of the material you plan to use on each visual.

For additional advice on choosing the best type of visual or sketching out your material, visit the online tutorial series sponsored by the University of Kansas Medical Center, located at www.kumc.edu/SAH/OTEd/jradel/effective.html.

Use Computer Technology to Create Visuals

So much technology is available to create and display visuals that you may be tempted to overuse visual support and forget that oral delivery is still the key to a good presentation. Put simply, 400 visuals, fabulous though they may be, taken by themselves won't replace one well-prepared and polished speaker who explains her ideas clearly. In fact, an article in the *New York Times* suggested that overused bulleted points, bar graphs, flowcharts, and the like have taken the life out of public speaking and made some talks seem like old-fashioned grade school filmstrips (Zuckerman, 1999). Perhaps he was overreacting, but his point was good: a flashy "presentation" cannot substitute for good ideas. Keep in mind that the technological tools and design principles described in this section are helpful only insofar as they help listeners understand your ideas.

Take Advantage of Technological Tools

Computers enable you to produce high-quality, professional visuals quickly and easily. The simplest way to create visuals on your computer is to use a word processing program and type in the information that you will eventually transfer to a handout or a transparency. Although word processors are simple to use, you don't have to create boring documents. By adjusting fonts, letter sizes, line spacing, and formatting, you can create visually appealing lists, tables, and charts. You can also add bullets, borders, and clip art to make your visuals even more attractive.

Let a **graphics program** do the hard work of converting your statistical data into graphs. Among the better-known graphics programs are Harvard Graphics, StatView, Delta Graph, Freelance Graphics, and Adobe Illustrator. You don't have to be a genius or a computer whiz to use these packages successfully, as their user's manuals are quite friendly.

Graphics Programs
Computer programs that convert statistical data into graphs.

Presentation Programs
Computer software to create a package of lists, tables, graphs, and clip art.

Scanner
Machine that converts a photograph or image from print to electronic data that can be stored on a disk.

Presentation programs are software packages written to help you create a series of lists, tables, graphs, and so on, then transfer them to slides, transparencies, or a computer disk for use with a data display machine. If you don't personally have a presentation program, visit your school's computer lab and search for Microsoft PowerPoint, Adobe Persuasion, or a similar program.

Experiment with backgrounds, fonts, and colors. You can easily create graphs and charts, and you can either illustrate your visuals with clip art from more than 200 drawings and diagrams or use a **scanner,** which lets you copy and store in electronic form photographs or other images from books, magazines, or other print sources. You can then add these images to your slides. Presentation programs also allow you to import or download images from the Internet, to add video clips or animation, or to use music and create a multimedia presentation. The speech at the end of the chapter shows how one student used a series of PowerPoint slides to support her ideas. You can view it on the CD that accompanies your text.

Design Your Visuals for Impact

If you work with a presentation program, you'll have access to so many design features that you may be tempted to overdo things and create a series of slides that impress, but fail to enlighten your audience. For example, with PowerPoint you can create transitions between slides as well as build on individual slides. This means you could program every slide to **transition** onto the screen differently—one wipes from the left, another appears from the top down, another dissolves, a fourth appears in a checkerboard pattern. You could similarly program individual slides to **build,** which means that lines of text come onto a slide only when you press the mouse or touch a computer key. You could easily end up with slides that contain lines of text flying in from the left, the right, the top, the corner, flashing on and off, one letter appearing at a time with clicking sound effects, and so on—creating a mishmash of movement that doesn't communicate your *ideas* at all.

Experiment with a presentation program for fun, but in the end you are better off following rules for simple, well-designed visuals. This section describes a number of design principles that will help you make pleasing, but effective, visuals.

Transition
The way each slide in a series appears on the screen.
Build
Lines of text appear on individual slides when you touch a computer key or press the mouse.

Choose a Readable Font

Whether you make your visuals by hand or rely on a computer, make readability your primary concern. One key is to choose a **font**—a complete set of letters and numbers of a given design—that helps, rather than hinders, your audience's ability to read it. Here are some tips for readability that you can see illustrated in Figure 12.4.

1. Choose title or sentence case, and avoid all capital letters.
   - USING ALL CAPITAL LETTERS IS MORE DIFFICULT TO READ— BESIDES YOU'RE NOT SHOUTING AT YOUR LISTENERS, SO WHY CAPITALIZE?
   - Title Case (Capitalizing the First Letter of Important Words) is Easier to Read.
   - Sentence case (capitalizing only what you'd capitalize in a sentence) is also readable.
2. Use a **serif font** (with cross lines at the top and bottom of letters) rather than a **sans serif font** (with no cross lines) when you use a computer to create your visuals.
   - A serif font is easier to read because the serifs lead your eyes from one letter to another ("Readability," n.d.).
   - Sans serif fonts are less readable; use them for titles.
3. Avoid cutesy but hard-to-read display fonts, even if your computer program offers a plethora of choices, some very artistic and interesting. If you are handwriting your visual, write legibly in plain lowercase letters.

Font
A complete set of letters and numbers of a given design.

Serif Font
A font with cross lines at the top and bottom of letters.
Sans Serif Font
A simple font with no cross lines on each letter.

Figure 12.4 Both serif and sans serif fonts are useful on classroom visuals. Avoid fancy display fonts that don't pass the readability test.

Serif fonts such as these are easier to read; using boldface makes them even more visible.

Palatino	**Palatino (bold)**
Times New Roman	**Times New Roman (bold)**
Bookman	**Bookman (bold)**

Sans serif fonts are useful for titles and headings.

Helvetica	**Helvetica (bold)**
Optima	**Optima (bold)**
Avant Garde	**Avant Garde (bold)**

Tempting as they may be, you're wise to avoid fancy display fonts that are difficult to read.

Zapf Chancery	***Zapf Chancery (bold)***
COPPERPLATE	**COPPERPLATE (BOLD)**
𝔚ittenberger 𝔉raktur	**𝔚ittenberger 𝔉raktur (bold)**

- A font such as Wittenberger Frattur, besides being less readable, can draw attention to itself.
- Fonts like Copperplate can be difficult to read.
- Cursive fonts like Zapf Chancery are generally less readable.

4. Remain consistent from visual to visual. That is, if you use Helvetica for your title on the first visual, use it on every visual. Do likewise for the subtitle and text fonts.

For more information about fonts in general, log on to the Internet and go to www.google.com. Do a search for all the words "readability of serif fonts" or "font size."

Use Size and Space Wisely

One key to well-designed visuals is font size, which is measured in **points.** A good general rule is to use a 30–36 point font size for titles on computer visuals and overhead transparencies. Use 24 point for the next level of information and 18 point for the third level.

Points
The unit of measurement for font size.

Use other formatting features to make your slides visually appealing. For example, you might center the title, underline the subtitle, and bullet the points to help your audience see the relationship of your ideas to one another better. Also, pay attention to the overall balance of the slide—spread the information across the visual rather than bunching the text into the upper left quadrant.

Don't try to cram too much information on each visual; instead, limit yourself to one idea per visual, and leave plenty of white space so that your listeners' eyes can find their place easily. The *maximum* amount of material recommended is six lines, no more than 40 or 45 characters per line. While you're still planning out your visuals, write in your material, then go back and edit out every unnecessary word or figure. In other words: simplify, simplify, simplify.

Color and Emphasis

Use color to add interest and emphasis. According to the 3M Company, color has the following four advantages:

1. It attracts attention and holds audience interest.
2. It increases learning, retention, and recall of informative messages.
3. It adds persuasiveness to messages.
4. It motivates audiences to participate.

Select colors for your text words and images that contrast with the background color. For white or ivory-colored posters and clear transparencies, choose high-contrasting black or dark blue, not yellows or oranges. Red can be a good emphasis color when used sparingly, but Muhovic (2000) warns that red is a "culturally loaded" color—in the United States it symbolizes anger ("seeing red") or danger (being "in the red"). For computer-generated slides, experiment until you find a color combination you like. Try yellow lettering, followed by white then lime green, on a dark blue background. Notice the difference when you try red or green on the same dark blue. To avoid a cluttered look, limit yourself to three colors for your entire series of slides.

Color is one way to emphasize ideas. For example, use brightly colored bullets to draw attention to a list. Or vary the color of a word or phrase you want to stand out. You can also underline or use italics or boldface fonts to highlight and accent something specific.

In summary, focus on principles of good design—on readability, on sizing and spacing your words and figures, and on choosing color combinations that will make your words readable and provide emphasis where you want it. These principles will keep you mindful of the fact that your aids are just that: aids. They aren't your message, and they aren't a display of personal artistic or computer skills.

STOP AND CHECK

COMPLETE YOUR VISUAL PRESENTATION PLAN

Return to your Audiovisual Aid Plan first shown on page 217 and available online under Stop and Check Activities for Chapter 12. Make any revisions you'd like; next, sketch out each visual—paying attention to the size and spacing of your words and images. Select appropriate colors and decide which words or phrases you want to emphasize. Then go to work on your text- or image-based visuals. If you plan to use audio or video support, make arrangements now for the equipment you'll need. And have fun!

Web Site

General Guidelines for Using Visual Aids

Although each type of visual aid has specific techniques for successful use, you can build your skills in preparing and presenting visual aids by applying these general guidelines.

- Whatever type of visual you choose, be sure it can be seen in the room where you will speak.
- Don't create a visual for its own sake. For example, a presenter who says, "Today, I'll talk about 'character,'" and the word "CHARACTER" appears on a slide is not clarifying a complex point or strengthening a bond with the audience. She's created what professional presenter Joan Detz (1998) calls a "dreaded" word slide that doesn't really add to a message. In short speeches (six to ten minutes), Muhovic (2000) suggests you use no more than three visuals selected because they show the speech structure, support your concepts, or show relationships between ideas.
- Display visuals only when you discuss them; then cover them.
- Talk to your audience, not to your visual.
- Rehearse using your visuals. If you don't have access to a projector or easel during your practices, use a table as a "projector." Or visualize yourself using your posters or transparencies—where you'll stand in relation to them, how you'll point out specific features on them, what you'll do with them when they're not in use.
- Don't violate your audience's norms or expectations to the point where you shock, offend, revolt, or anger listeners. One student showed pornographic photographs to illustrate her speech about pornography. When you shock or violate expectations so severely, you may never regain attention, and your credibility—especially in the area of good sense—suffers as a result.
- Whenever machines are involved, have a Plan B in case the technology fails. Imagine what will happen if the slide projector jams, the light on the overhead projector burns out, or the videotape machine eats your tape. An alternate plan, usually in the form of a handout, saves your speech. Demonstrating your composure in case of equipment failure is another way to enhance your credibility (anonymous reviewer, 1994).

Summary

As a speaker in a visually oriented culture, it is to your advantage to use visual support effectively. Visuals illustrate your ideas, keep your audience focused on your speech, and make abstract ideas more concrete. Although visuals are not new, the amount and kind of support available now is unprecedented.

To display your visuals, choose a means that suits your topic and the room in which you will speak. Overhead projectors, chalk or white boards, poster boards, flip charts, handouts, slides, and computer projectors are additional ways to present your visual aids. All have advantages and disadvantages, and you should take care to have a Plan B in case your equipment fails. These are all ways to display your visuals, but they are not the visuals themselves.

Choose from several types of visuals. Objects, persons, or models comprise three-dimensional visuals. In addition, you can sometimes incorporate touch, smell, and taste into your presentation. Choose text-based lists, or image-based charts, graphs, photographs, drawings, or maps. Finally, select audio or video clips when they would best clarify your ideas.

Emerging technologies, led by advances in computer engineering, are guiding us into a century in which you will have access to even more sophisticated presentational equipment. High-tech boards that can be connected globally are but one example. Even now, you can use word processing programs, graphics packages, and presentation programs to create professional-appearing visuals.

Throughout, remember that visual support should enhance rather than replace your speech. For this reason, use principles of design including readability, size and spacing, and color to your advantage. Furthermore, display visuals only when you are discussing them, and talk to the audience, not to the visuals. Carefully edit your tapes and videos, and make sure they are visible and audible for everyone.

In conclusion, don't overlook the importance of competent use of visual materials as a way to enhance your credibility. Keep in mind that professional-looking resources create more positive impressions than those that appear to be scribbled out just minutes before your presentation. Further, the disastrous case of equipment failure may actually increase your credibility, if your listeners see you handle the stressful situation with composure. Finally, demonstrate your good sense by selecting and presenting only visual support that does not violate your listeners' expectations.

JAFFE ONLINE CONNECTION • JAFFE ONLINE CONNECTION

Use your CD-ROM and the Jaffe Connection Web site to review the following concepts, answer the review questions, and complete the suggested activities.

KEY TERMS

multimedia presentations (212)
flip charts (214)
model (219)
text-based visuals (219)
flowcharts (220)
organizational charts (221)
image-based visuals (221)
line graphs (221)
bar graphs (222)
pie graphs (222)
picture graphs or pictographs (222)
diagram (223)

political maps (223)
geographic maps (223)
graphics programs (225)
presentation programs (226)
scanner (226)
transition (226)
build (226)
font (226)
serif font (226)
sans serif font (226)
points (227)

APPLICATION AND CRITICAL THINKING EXERCISES

1. Observe public speakers—for instance, professors in other courses—who regularly use visuals. What kind(s) of visual displays are most common? Which do you see used least? Evaluate the speakers' use of the visuals; that is, do they use them well, or should they read this chapter? Explain.
2. Which technology for displaying visuals will you probably use for your classroom speeches? Which would you not consider? In your future employment, what equipment do you think you'll use the most? The least? Why?
3. Think about speeches you've heard during the last week. What kinds of visuals, if any, did the speakers use? When would visuals have made it easier for you to listen to and understand the material?
4. Discuss with a small group of your classmates how you would best display a drawing in (1) a large auditorium, (2) a classroom, (3) a speech given outdoors, and (4) a presentation in someone's living room. (Several means may be appropriate.)
5. What kind of visual might work most appropriately for a speech on each of these topics:
   • The circulatory system
   • The physical effects of smoking on the lungs

- The fabled "silk" trading route
- Ozone depletion
- Changes in mortgage interest rates over two decades

6. Make a visual using a word processing program on your computer. Experiment with fonts. Use your software's print preview function to look at the overall balance of the visual; adjust line spacing and font size as necessary.

7. Use InfoTrac College Edition and do a PowerTrac search using the text words "using visual aids" or the key words "visual aids." Look for an article about visual aids in an international or multicultural situation. Read it and summarize the information it presents about adapting visuals to foreign or heterogeneous audiences. Or read and summarize an article that gives advice on using visual aids successfully.

8. Browse the Internet using your favorite search engine, and find and read material on several sites about visual aids. Analyze the credibility of each site. (That is, does the URL contain an .edu or a .com? Why might that make a difference? Who wrote the materials? When? What links can you find? With this information, assess the overall usefulness of each site.) Take notes as you work and bring them to class so you can discuss your findings with a small group of your classmates.

THE JAFFE CONNECTION WEB SITE

The Jaffe Connection Web site features review questions about the Web links and the InfoTrac College Edition exercises referenced throughout the chapter. You can access this site via your CD-ROM or at http://communication.wadsworth.com/jaffe.

Web Links

12.1 Visual Aids Search (page 213)
12.2 Characteristics of Effective Handouts (page 216)
12.3 Kansas University Medical Center Visual Aids Tutorial (page 225)
12.4 Readability of Fonts (page 227)

Stop and Check Activities

12.1 Begin Your Visual Presentation Plan (page 217)
12.2 Continue Your Visual Presentation Plan (page 225)
12.3 Complete Your Visual Presentation Plan (page 228)

InfoTrac College Edition Exercises

12.1 Traveling and Talking: Using Visual Aids Internationally (page 215)
12.2 Adapting Visual Aids to a Multicultural Audience (page 231)

SPEECH INTERACTIVE ON THE JAFFE CONNECTION CD-ROM

Watch the informative speech *Terrestrial Pulmonate Gastropods* by Shaura Neil, and answer the questions for analysis under Speech Interactive on your Jaffe Connection CD-ROM.

STUDENT SPEECH WITH VISUAL AIDS
WITH COMMENTARY

TERRESTRIAL PULMONATE GASTROPODS
by Shaura Neil

In a flash, I am surrounded by a huge terrestrial pulmonate gastropod. The creature lunges at me; in a mad scramble for survival, I try to fight off the beast. All of a sudden . . . salt begins to fall from the sky. The ionic compound saves my life as the beast begins to wither

In this speech, Shaura uses PowerPoint-generated slides, a three-dimensional object, and her hands (to illustrate the slug's movements). Her computer is hooked up to an LCD display, which is on standby before she begins. She reactivates it and bring up each slide by clicking the mouse.

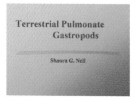

Shaura has inserted a blank slide after each visual. She displays the blank until the place in her speech that requires the next visual.

She uses hand motions to mimic the latching on motion of a masticating slug.

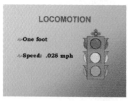

up and die in front of me. I awaken from my dream and stare at the poster on my wall. I have just had a nightmare involving one of my favorite animals—the slug. In my nightmare salt saves me from a giant slug, but, in reality, it is salt that is the slug's worst nightmare.

If you live in Oregon, you've seen them, these snails-with-no-shells; and, like other Oregonians, you may have been tempted to send the little creatures to slug heaven by salting their slimy backs.

Because I have encountered slews of slugs, I decided to do some research on them—including ways to get rid of them.

Display first slide.

Today, I'll share some interesting facts about slugs and explain their contribution to the environment. Then, I'll describe their major predators and discuss inhumane and humane ways to rid your yard of these creatures.

Slugs are intriguing creatures. They have an average life span of one to six years and grow to be approximately one and a half to ten inches long. Slugs have amazing eating patterns; they spend most of their active hours devouring food and can masticate several times their own body weight in one day. What do they eat? Well . . .

Display "Food Fit for a Slug" slide.

Slugs will consume a wide variety of food, including lichens, green plants, worms, centipedes, certain insects, animal feces, AND . . . even other slugs.

Display a blank slide.

To feed, a slug first extends its mouth over its desired substance, and then the slug uses its jaw to latch onto the food with its tongue. A slug's tongue contains over 27,000 sharp, backward-pointing teeth. Because a slug has teeth upon its tongue, it is nearly impossible for it to bite its own tongue.

Display "Locomotion" slide; she formats it so that it builds line by line as she discusses the material on it.

For locomotion, the slug crawls on its belly, or, to use a more scientific term,

Click to add the line "One foot."

its "foot." A slug's foot enables it to move because of a series of rippling muscles along the bottom of the foot that propel the slug along. The muscles move in a wavelike motion. Having only one foot can present a variety of problems for the slug.

Click to add the line "Speed: .025 mph."

Slugs can attain a maximum speed of .025 miles per hour. That's only $2\frac{1}{2}$ hundredths of a mile . . . which figures out to 44 yards an hour—less than $\frac{1}{2}$ a football field in distance. And that's just the speediest slugs! Also, it can create quite an embarrassment when one slug trips another slug.

Click to add the line "Slug Slime."

A second crucial aspect of a slug's locomotion involves its "slug slime." This slime is vital because it simultaneously increases traction and "greases the skids" of the slug's path. The slime is used not only for movement, but for moisture control, mating, and self-defense. How is it protective? When a slug feels threatened it secretes large amounts of the slime, generating a thick, protective coat. A slug's slime also absorbs water. This amazing feature explains why it is impossible to rinse slug slime from your skin after you have finished handling the beast.

Display next blank slide.

The slug's mating ritual is quite unique. A slug's courtship can last for hours and involves ritualized bouts of lunging, nipping, and side-swiping. Slugs are hermaphroditic, meaning that they contain both male and female reproductive organs. Perhaps unfortunately for the slug, slugs require another slug to mate with in order to receive a proper blend of genetic coding. However, the blend cannot be too drastic; a slug can only mate with other slugs of the same species. For example, a banana slug will only mate with another banana slug. This prevents the ghastly occurrence of slug mutts.

Slugs are not only fascinating creatures, they also contribute to the environment.

Display "Slugs and the Environment" slide.

Slugs disperse seeds and spores through their waste elimination, break down decaying plant matter, and help to reduce the population of dozens of other small pests, such as spiders and beetles. The absence of slugs would no doubt hurt the ecosystem.

Display the "Slug Killers" slide.

Despite their contributions to the environment, slugs have many predators.

Small mammals, snakes, amphibians, some species of birds, carnivorous beetles, and other slugs all seek to devour the slug. Slugs have very few defense mechanisms against predators of species other than their own. Slugs are colored to blend in with their surroundings and they can secrete their slime, as mentioned above. However, against other slugs, slugs have an amazing strategy. It is common for two slugs to engage in a life or death struggle. In this struggle the two slugs lock tongues. At the commencement of the battle the victor flips his opponent on its back, leaving it to fry in the sun. Do not become caught in the midst of a battle between two slugs.

There remains one predator of slugs that has not been mentioned—the human. I am now going to bring out a visual aid. Those of you with weak stomachs please, look away.

Bring forth from a paper bag a container of salt.

Every year, hundreds of innocent slugs are brutally slaughtered through the use of salt by humans. The simple use of NaCl induces an unnecessary and excruciatingly painful death for the slug. Salt creates an ionic imbalance in the slug, impelling it to crawl out of its own slime and rapidly dehydrate. Because slugs have numerous nerve endings all over their body, salt causes undue pain as they die.

Insert a blank slide.

There are alternatives to salt. Slug poison is less painful to the slug and can be found at a local hardware store. However, poison creates problems of its own. Poison can be fatal to children and to small pets if consumed. Consequently, parents, pet owners, and city dwellers are wisely cautioned not to use slug poison.

Used coffee grinds placed at the base of plants in a garden are very effective in deterring slugs. The aroma and texture of the grinds is unpleasant to slugs and they will avoid that territory. The only downfall of this method is that grinds must be replaced every day because, once they lose their aroma, they are useless.

Alcohol can also be an effective slug repellent. Slugs are attracted to beer, so if you set a bowl of beer near a garden, the slugs will gravitate to it and drink alcohol in the beer, which is fatal. Once again, the drawback to this method is that the beer must be replaced daily. There is also the consideration of having to look at dead slugs . . . and dispose of them. Furthermore, family members may no longer want to eat out of a bowl that once held dead slugs. Still, beer is a more humane option than salt.

After learning all of these marvelous facts about slugs, it is my hope to prevent the further use of salt in eliminating them. I plead with you all to end this atrocity. As a slug-lover and an ambassador of peace for slugs everywhere I urge everyone to please, skip the salt.

Her transition summarizes one point and introduces the next. She displays the next slide, which has a point-by-point build programmed in.

VIDA 生命 LIFE VITA

©1977 GRETCHEN ROSENBLATT

Choosing Effective Language

THIS CHAPTER WILL HELP YOU

- Explain how words are linked to culture and meaning
- Distinguish between the denotative and connotative meanings of words
- Define dialects and jargon, and explain when they are appropriate in public speaking
- Tell how the ability to name or label groups and issues is linked to power
- Give examples of epithets, euphemisms, and ageist and sexist language
- List six guidelines for effective language in public speaking
- Understand how alliteration, rhyme, repetition, personification, hyperbole, metaphor, and simile can make a speech more interesting
- Give guidelines for listening and speaking in linguistically diverse contexts

"Life" Mural ©1997 by Gretchen Rosenblatt. (16th Street and Market, SF, CA)

ANGUAGE NOT ONLY conveys your ideas. Your word choices also provide clues about your region of origin, age, educational level, income level, sex, ethnicity, and occupation. Here are a few examples:

Regional distinctions: Oregonians might purchase a can of *pop*; New Yorkers would call it *soda*. Oregonians wonder what a *frappe* is, but they understand *milkshake* immediately.

Male–female distinctions: Women might call a blouse *plum* or *mauve* or *lilac*. Men might call it *purple*.

Occupational distinctions: Communication professors say things like, ". . . the exclusions that characterize the historical practice of the bourgeois public sphere are constitutive of the concept itself . . ." (Asen, 1999). Stockbrokers, barbers, and dentists don't talk like this.

In the study of rhetoric, language falls within the canon of style, which is the focus of this chapter. First, it looks at some aspects of language and examines how our vocabularies both reveal and express cultural assumptions. Next, it provides tips for effective language choices in U.S. classrooms. Finally, it discusses ways of speaking in linguistically diverse settings.

Language Reflects Culture

Languages
Verbal codes consisting of symbols a speech community uses to communicate.
Symbols
Signs that represent or stand for objects and concepts.

Languages are verbal codes made up of a system of symbols that a community of language speakers uses to share their ideas. **Symbols** are signs that represent or stand for objects and concepts the community shares. However, for these signs to be meaningful, the persons who use them must understand them similarly. To illustrate, we sometimes use symbols in the form of simple drawings to convey ideas such as those depicted in Figure 13.1.

If you're familiar with these symbols, you know them as (a) recycle, (b) no smoking, (c) a curve in the road, and (d) New Mexico. Some, like the highway sign, are well known—all drivers learn its meaning to pass their licensing exam. Less familiar is the *zia*, or sun symbol, which represents my home state of New Mexico. Obviously, if you're unfamiliar with a sign, you won't be able to decipher its meaning.

Words
Verbal symbols that stand for or represent ideas

Although we can represent some ideas by pictograms or drawings, we can't draw pictures to communicate every concept. So each society has developed a language system made up of **words**—verbal symbols that stand for or represent cultural ideas. Each member of the culture learns the language in order to communicate and interact within the group.

Words and Meaning

In *New Words and a Changing American Culture*, Raymond Gozzi (1990) explains that words are the names we give to our "cultural memories." They serve as "markers of cultural attention" or shared experiences that we consider significant enough to name. Put another way, one or more people in a culture notice a phenomenon, formulate an idea about it, and label it—they encode their idea into a word. The process looks something like this.

Long ago humans:
1. Noticed a phenomenon—some creatures can fly.
2. Formed a concept—all these creatures have two legs, two wings, a beak, and feathers.
3. Created a label—for this category of flying animals, the label *bird* (English), *oiseau* (French), *pájaro* or *ave* (Spanish).

According to this theory, our vocabulary names what our society identifies as significant, and our labels carve out our interpretations of our world, forming the social realities in which we live, think, and act. An example might help. Think of the words you know for different kinds of snow. There's *snow*, of course, maybe *blizzard*, *downy flakes*, and *sleet*, but

Figure 13.1 Four signs or symbols: (a) recycle, (b) no smoking, (c) a curve in the road, and (d) New Mexico.

can you think of more words to represent snow? This task would be easier if you were an Eskimo, for Eskimos have named many different kinds of snow. Does that mean they perceive varieties of snow that you do not? Maybe. It almost certainly means that knowing subtle differences between kinds of snow is significant in that culture.

It's easy to see how humans create words for objects such as birds, snow, buildings, or chairs. However, words also label less tangible experiences, actions, feelings, and ideas. To understand this better, think of the meanings (if any) you attach to the word *Watergate*. Before Richard Nixon's presidency, a small number of people associated the word with an apartment complex in Washington, D.C. However, after the famous break-in and subsequent presidential resignation—along with the movie (*All the President's Men*), books, interviews, and articles that surrounded those events—the word *Watergate* came to symbolize scandal. Even today, reporters coin terms like *Trooper-gate*, *Whitewater-gate*, and *Enron-gate* when political scandals arise.

DIVERSITY IN PRACTICE
DIALECTS

A **DIALECT** IS A VARIANT FORM OF A LANGUAGE. There are many English dialects: One is British English (BritSpeak); others include American English, Black English (ebonics or African American Vernacular English, AAVE), international English, and a variety of other regional and ethnic group variations ("Dialects Doing Well," 1998). The dialect most common in institutions such as education, business, and broadcasting is **Standard English.** It is the language of print—and the version of English widely used in U.S. public speeches.

You may speak a dialect other than Standard English. Although your dialect functions well in many settings, you may choose to be bi-dialectical, meaning that you use one version of English around family and friends and another in public contexts. This is called **code switching.** Pauline Jefferson, for instance, uses Standard English when she transacts business with customers in her bank and when she makes public presentations for her coworkers. However, when she speaks before a small female audience in her local church, she switches codes, alternating between Standard English and AAVE.

For more information about this topic, log on to the Internet and use a search engine like www.alltheweb.com to search for the exact term *code switching* or go to www.slanguage.com for a look at English slang terms that vary by city. Also, the site http://www.americandialect.org, sponsored by the American Dialect Association, offers scholarly and less-academic links to information on dialects such as ebonics, the Ocracoke Brogue, and American Sign Language.

Dialect
A variant form of a language.

Standard English
The English dialect most commonly used in public speaking and in U.S. institutions.

Code Switching
Changing from one language code to another.

Our languages change to reflect cultural transformations. Among the more than 10,000 words added to English in the last few decades are *gridlock*, *serial killer*, *microchip*, *junk food*, and the *mall*. Sportscaster Chick Hearn added the terms *slam dunk* and *air ball*. When your grandparents were growing up, there were no malls or junk food, no gridlock or slam dunks. They either didn't exist or they weren't important enough to name (Gozzi, 1990). English also adopts words from other languages, including *coffee* from the Arabians, *ambiance* from the French, and *kamikazi* from the Japanese. And meanings change over time. If you read a Shakespearean play, you'll be struck by the differences between the English of Shakespeare's time and the English of today.

Denotative Meaning

Denotative Meaning
What a word names or identifies.

Words denote or "point" to an object or abstract idea; thus, the denotative meaning is what the word names or identifies. The following list might clarify this further. You'll find several categories followed by examples of words that denote or stand for objects or ideas within each:

Real objects: rocks, buildings, necklaces, tea
Imaginary things: unicorns, Martians, elves, Superman
Qualities of objects: softness, generosity, width, height
Feelings: anger, envy, peace, love
States of being: happiness, depression, contentment, gratitude
Abstractions: justice, quarks, conscience, success
Actions: exercising, singing, eating, studying

When you look up words in the dictionary, you find their denotative meanings; for instance, the label *police officer* denotes "a member of a police force" ("Merriam-Webster Online," 2002).

Ambiguous
Word that identifies more than one object or idea; its meaning depends on the context.

Some words stand for more than one idea; their meaning is **ambiguous** in that their context determines how we interpret them. For instance, the word *pot* has at least five meanings:

- A rounded container used chiefly for domestic purposes
- A sum of money, as in the total amount of bets at stake at one time (the jackpot)
- An enclosed frame of wire, wood, or wicker used to catch fish or lobsters
- Slang for marijuana
- Ruin, as in "her business went to pot" ("Merriam-Webster Online," 2002)

You know that when you cook in a pot, you're thinking of the first meaning. But when you discuss legalization of pot, you're not talking about laws regulating cooking containers or billiard shots! The context determines the meaning.

As you plan language for your speech, make sure to use the correct word in the correct context to denote your intended meaning. Use a dictionary or thesaurus if you need to. Increasing your vocabulary and discriminating among shades of meaning between words is a good idea, for the greater your vocabulary, the more power you will have to communicate your thoughts precisely.

Connotative Meaning

Connotative Meaning
Emotional overtones, related feelings, and associations that cluster around a term.

Although words denote objects and concepts, they also carry emotional overtones or **connotative meanings.** That is, words not only stand for ideas but also represent feelings and associations related to the concepts. To illustrate, *police officer* has different connotations for different individuals depending on their experiences. Some people like police officers because of relatives or friends who are officers; others have had negative experiences with officers that left them with a generalized fear or mistrust of people in this profession. Each person's reactions form the connotative meanings of *police officer* for that individual.

Language can be emotionally charged—either positively or negatively—and we commonly substitute a more neutral word for one with negative connotations. To discuss this further, we now turn to epithets and euphemisms.

Epithets

Epithets are words or phrases that describe some quality of a person or group (often with negative connotations). For example, one political party calls the other *extremists* because opinion polls show that voters respond negatively to the term. Within hours, the attacked party counters with the term *big government spenders,* another negative term. Words like *nerd*, *pig* (for police officers), *queer*, and *nigger* are negative epithets that function to frame perceptions about the group. For example, calling anti-abortion advocates *anti-choice* creates a negative image, whereas the group's self-chosen title, *pro-life*, has positive connotations.

Members of labeled groups often try to lessen the negative power of the epithet by accepting and using the term themselves. Police officers take the letters of the word *pig* and reinterpret them to form the slogan *P*ride, *I*ntegrity, *G*uts. Similarly, some homosexuals take the epithet *queer* and transform it for use in slogans such as "We're queer and we're here" or in labels such as Queer Nation. One who did so explained, "We have to take the power out of these words" (Ray & Badle, 1993).

Euphemisms

Euphemisms, in contrast, are words or phrases that substitute an agreeable or inoffensive term for a more direct one that might offend, embarrass, or suggest something unpleasant. We regularly use euphemisms for things we hesitate to speak of, such as bodily functions (*go to the powder room*), religion (*the Man Upstairs*), and death (*passed away*). Euphemisms also mask unpleasant situations, like corporate layoffs. It sounds better for a company to *downsize* than to *fire* or *lay off* workers.

Public speakers often use euphemisms for controversial actions, ideas, and policies. For example, government officials call new taxes *revenue enhancement* or *investments in America* to soften the reality of planned tax increases. Similarly, military officers use the term *collateral damage* rather than *bombing of civilians* to describe the unpleasant results of a military action. Learn more about this subject by logging onto the Internet and using a search engine such as **www.dogpile.com** to search for the word *euphemisms*.

Watch for connotative language in your research. For example, a military leader calls an opponent a *warlord* rather than an *influential leader*. Politicians label their opponents *obstructionists* who *attack* and *destroy* legislation, whereas they, of course, *stand up for the rights of ordinary people*. By carefully choosing their words, these speakers hope to create perceptions that produce the spin or interpretation they want.

Jargon

Jargon is a specialized, technical vocabulary and style that serves special groups (doctors, lawyers), interests (feminism, knitting), and activities (football, gardening). For example, football has specialized meanings for *drive* and *down*

Epithets
Words or phrases with powerful negative connotations, used to describe some quality of a person or group.

Euphemism
Word or phrase that substitutes inoffensive term for potentially offensive, embarrassing, or unpleasant things.

Jargon
A specialized, technical vocabulary that serves the interests and activities of a particular group.

Use of jargon—a set of technical words associated with a topic—is appropriate in contexts where everyone knows the terms. However, undefined jargon in a speech to a lay audience is generally more confusing than enlightening.

and *safety*. When everyone in your audience knows the meaning of the jargon, it's appropriate to use it. However, if you're communicating with nonspecialists, you'll need to define and clarify technical terms to avoid excluding listeners. By translating jargon, you demonstrate your rhetorical sensitivity.

In summary, languages are systems of symbols—words that denote or stand for ideas and evoke feelings or connotative meanings that differ from person to person. Carefully choose your words, making sure that you use the correct word in context. Pay attention to connotative meanings—either positive or negative—that listeners might attach to your words. You can demonstrate that you are rhetorically sensitive by adapting your dialect and your jargon to your audience and the occasion. As you do this, you are taking into account the cultural implications of your terminology.

STOP AND CHECK

THINK CRITICALLY ABOUT DENOTATIVE AND CONNOTATIVE WORDS

Test your understanding of meanings with these exercises:

1. Whenever they launch a new product, marketers carefully select terminology that will have positive connotations for consumers. Look up two or three advertisements in your favorite magazines, then list some of the words you find in each ad. What is the denotative meaning of each word on your list? Now jot down some of your personal connotations for each term. Evaluate the overall marketability of the term itself.

2. Work with your classmates to make a list of the car models owned by class members (Mustang, Explorer, Sport, and so on). Within a small group identify the denotative meaning of each word. Then discuss the connotative associations you think the manufacturers hope will sell the car.

For additional information, log on to the Internet and go to http://www.wuacc.edu/services/zzcwwctr/connotation.txt, a Web site from Washburn University that has exercises that test how connotations differ among various individuals. For an additional exercise about denotative and connotative words, go to Stop and Check Activities for Chapter 13 at the Jaffe Connection Web site.

Web Site

Use Language Ethically: Inclusive Language

Language choices have ethical implications because words and phrases can include or exclude, affirm or dismiss individuals or entire groups (Johannesen, 1996). The University of Tasmania's publication, *Just Talk: Guide to Inclusive Language*, declares:

> Discriminatory language is that which creates or reinforces a hierarchy of difference between people. It is therefore both a symptom of and a contributor to, the unequal social status of women, people with disabilities and people from various ethnic and social backgrounds. (Currey & Mumford, 2002)

In the last few decades, there has been an emphasis on using nondiscriminatory language. Emory University's (2001) Statement on **Inclusive Language** recommends, "A recognition of the full humanity of all peoples should prompt an attempt to speak and think in ways which include all human beings and degrade none." Using inclusive language can increase your credibility. For example, Seiter, Larsen, and Skinner (1998) found that speak-

Inclusive Language
Ethical terminology that affirms and includes, rather than excludes, persons or groups of people.

ers who put down persons with disabilities or focus on the disability rather than on the individual lose credibility, likability, and persuasiveness. Here are several guidelines for sensitive use of language.

Avoid Language That Privileges One Group over Another

Sexist language subtly influences the way we view the sexes by giving priority to males, their activities, and their interests. **Ageist language** portrays older people in ways that privilege youthfulness and demean or devalue age. (To illustrate, phrases like *feel younger* or *look ten years younger* subtly reinforce the notion that youth is better than age.) **Racist language,** similarly, privileges one racial or ethnic group and degrades or devalues others. Nonsensitive language also highlights physical conditions, ignores sexual orientation, and so on.

Nonparallel language—language that does not treat women and men the same—is a specific linguistic form that reinforces differences and privileges males. It's nonparallel to designate a female by adding a suffix to a male term, as in *actor-actress*, and *steward-stewardess*. It's also nonparallel to mark job titles, as in a *male nurse* or a *female judge*. (Would you ever say a *female nurse* or a *male judge?*) Differing terms of address are also nonparallel; a woman may be called *Mrs. Alberto Sanchez*, but you won't hear *Mr. Jane Andrews*. Similarly, couples may be perceived as *man and wife* but not as *woman and husband*.

Joel Simon

Avoid Stereotyping

Try to recognize and avoid stereotypes. For instance, common misconceptions are that older people are closed minded, less capable mentally, unhealthy, physically unattractive, lonely, and poor. This shows up in language that perpetuates these stereotypes: *set in her ways, losing his marbles, ready for a nursing home*, and *well-preserved* (to describe an attractive elderly person) (Freimuth & Jamieson, 1979).

Stereotypes of gay men as effeminate, athletes as stupid, Native Americans as alcoholics, welfare recipients as single women of color, Democrats as pro-choice (about 40 percent claim to be pro-life), and Chinese Americans as Buddhists (most are Christian) are just a few examples.

Avoid Creating Invisibility

Language can make people and groups invisible. Take, for example, the use of the "generic he." People who are now your grandparents' age learned to use *he* to designate a person of either sex, as this illustration from a 1938 speech text shows.

> When one has settled upon a subject and has some notion of what *he* wishes to do with it, *his* immediate concern is with the materials, the stuff out of which *his* speech is to be woven. *He* must have ideas and data with which to hold attention and to make and impress *his* point [italics added]. (Winans, 1938)

Such language implies that only males speak in public.

The use of the suffix *man* creates similar problems. Replace words like *chairman, mailman, caveman*, and *policeman* with the inclusive labels *chair, mail carrier, cave dweller*, and

In cultures where elderly citizens are highly respected, ageist language is not the issue that it is in the United States, where youth is valued. Here, ageist language can demean older people by subtly influencing listeners to perceive them negatively.

Sexist Language
Negatively influences the way listeners see men or women.
Ageist Language
Negatively influences the way listeners see older people.
Racist Language
Language that privileges one racial group over another
Nonparallel Language
Does not treat the two sexes equally.

police officer. Other examples: Language that assumes relationships are all heterosexual or that *Americans* equals *U.S. inhabitants*. (Canadians, Brazilians, and Guatemalans are also *Americans*.)

Avoid Demeaning Epithets or Slurs

As previously discussed, when epithets frame negative perceptions of a group, avoid using them. Think about negative labels commonly applied to elderly people: *old duffer*, *little old lady* (in tennis shoes), *granny*, *gramps* or *pop*, *old biddy*, *old hag*, and *dirty old man*. These all create mental images that demean seniors. Other examples of slurs include *woman driver*, *sissy*, *dumb jock*, *dumb blonde*, *welfare queen*, *fag*, or *dyke*.

Avoid Dismissive Language

Language can be applied to people in ways that discount the importance of their ideas, as these examples show: elderly people are *too old*, *senile*, *no longer in the thick of things*, *over the hill*. Phrases like *just a secretary*, *white trash*, and *typical female* are often used as disdainful put-downs.

Avoid Undue Emphasis on Differences

Don't mention differences unless they matter in the context of the speech. For instance, instead of saying "the *Latina* nurse" or "my *African American* physics professor," simply say "the nurse" or "my physics professor." Also, don't mention someone's competency as if it were unusual for that group: Instead of "an *intelligent* welfare recipient," simply say "a welfare recipient." Don't describe the disabled as helpless people to be pitied and aided. Also, don't suggest that they are more heroic, courageous, patient, or special than others, and never use the word *normal* to contrast them with others (Currey & Mumford, 2002).

In short, terminology is not neutral. The words you select have the power to influence your listeners' perceptions, not only regarding issues but also regarding individuals and groups. The fact that some language choices demean or put down groups or individuals raises ethical questions and colors your listeners' views about you. Making sure that your word choices are inclusive is one way to show respect for diversity, and doing so will likely enhance your personal credibility.

STOP AND CHECK

AVOIDING DISCRIMINATORY LANGUAGE

With a small group of your classmates, select a group that has been put down or demeaned by language use. This may include women, specific ethnic groups, religious groups, or groups with alternative lifestyles.

1. Make a list of some terms that outsiders have used to label members of the group.
2. Then list some labels the group places on itself.
3. Assess the connotative meanings associated with the words on each list.

With a few classmates, talk about ways you can select language sensitively with respect to the specific group you've chosen.

To investigate this topic further, log on to the Internet and use a search engine such as www.google.com or www.alltheweb.com to search for an exact term such as *sexist language*, *ageism*, or *racism*.

Use Language Effectively

Several principles in the canon of style will help you use language more effectively in your speeches. Choose language that is accurate, appropriate, concise, clear, concrete, and interesting.

Be Accurate

Be accurate in your word choices. One form of inaccuracy is to use similar sounding, but incorrect, words called **malaprops**—named after the fictional Mrs. Malaprop in Richard Sheridan's comedy *The Rivals*. She consistently used the wrong word, to the great amusement of her audience. Children are noted for their use of malaprops or cute sayings. For example, a little boy who was discussing eating habits with his mother asked, "If you're a *vegetarian*, why don't you fix our cat?" He obviously confused the word with *veterinarian*.

Malaprops
Using one word instead of another that sounds similar but has a different meaning; often humorous.

Malapropism is cute for children, but embarrassing for adults. One cabinet official, speaking before a group of physicians, stated that alcohol could lead to *psoriasis* [sir EYE uh sis] of the liver. Soon, she realized that her listeners were chuckling. When she recognized her mistake, she laughed too, and quickly acknowledged that, of course, she meant *cirrhosis* [sir OH sis] of the liver. She obviously knew the difference between psoriasis (a skin disease) and cirrhosis.

It's a wise policy not to use a dictionary word without knowing the context in which it's commonly used. For example, a Japanese student described a car wreck that, in her words, "*distorted* the car door." Her Japanese–English dictionary came up with *distort* to convey the idea that the car was *bent*, *caved in*, or *dented*. Although the word does mean *crooked*, *deformed*, or *contorted*, no native speaker of English would use *distorted* in the context of a dented fender. (For additional examples of Japanese speakers whose dictionaries misled them, log on to InfoTrac College Edition and read the article titled "Say What You Mean / Donotation and Connotation."

Finally, use standard grammar in contexts that call for Standard English. Nonstandard forms such as *me and him* (instead of *he and I*) or *they was* (instead of *they were*) can create negative impressions in a job interview or other public presentation. The key is to adapt your grammar to fit the occasion. (To check grammatical forms, use the grammar-checking feature on your word processor, or go to `http://www.bartleby.com/index.html`, a site sponsored by Columbia University.)

Be Appropriate

Match your language to the topic, the audience, the situation, and yourself as an individual. Generally, your language in public settings is more formal, containing less slang than you'd use in everyday life; however, your audience and the situation should be the final influence over your linguistic choices. For example, you would use different words and different levels of formality to speak to homeless people gathered in a park than you would to address members of an alumni association at a formal banquet, even with the same topic. Similarly, language used in a lecture differs from language used in a eulogy.

Using a dialect is appropriate for some speakers, but not for others. An African American, for instance, might use African American Vernacular English (ebonics) when it's expected and appropriate; however, a Euro-American or an Asian American who used ebonics, even in the same setting, would probably be out of line.

Be Concise

Because directness is valued in the United States, we commonly eliminate unnecessary words, called **verbiage.** Here's an example from a caller on a radio talk show: "What they

Verbiage
Nonessential words.

did is they took the issue and distorted it, and how they did it is they did it by . . ." He would have been more concise had he said, "They distorted the issue by . . ."

Students often clutter their speeches with too many words. This example from a student speech on the value of learning a second language shows both how he actually gave the speech and how he could have given it:

As he gave it:

I became interested in this topic *upon the constant hounding of my father urging me* to take a foreign language, preferably Japanese, *the reason being is because* my major is business, and the Japanese are dominating the international business scene.

As he might have given it:

I became interested in this topic because my father constantly hounded me to take a foreign language—preferably Japanese. He reasoned that my major is business, and the Japanese are dominating the international business scene.

Although brevity or conciseness is valued in the United States, many other cultures value flowery words and language; what we may consider verbiage, other groups may regard as good verbal skills as Diversity in Practice: Understanding Aristide explains.

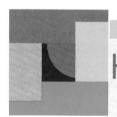

DIVERSITY IN PRACTICE
UNDERSTANDING ARISTIDE

Haitian President Jean-Bertrand Aristide's speaking style often confuses American congressional leaders and administration officials. According to *U.S. News & World Report*, Aristide "speaks a cultural tongue Americans don't understand" (Zimmermann & Goode, 1994, p. 32). He is a master of competitive oratory, a type of speechmaking that features indirect language, laced with proverbs and metaphors, and he commonly uses a stylistic device called "throwing pwent" which is intentionally indirect and ambiguous. Contrast this with the public speaking tradition explained in this chapter, which emphasizes clarity, concrete wording, and elimination of vague terminology, and you can see the potential for misunderstandings on both sides.

 To read this article, log on to InfoTrac College Edition and do a PowerTrac search for the phrase *throwing pwent*.

Be Clear

The purpose of public speaking is to clarify ideas rather than make them hard to understand. One of the best ways to be clear is to avoid jargon, but because many topics involve technical terms, you may have to look up jargon words to translate them into understandable English. Jesse failed to do this in his discussion of how AIDS is transmitted:

We've all been taught that AIDS is perinatal and that it is transmitted through sexual contact.

Following the speech, someone asked what *perinatal* meant. Jesse didn't know; the word came from an article he'd read, and he had not looked it up. (*Perinatal* actually means "associated with the birth process, the period immediately before, during, or just after the time of birth.") If he'd taken the time to look up the word, Jesse could have said instead,

We've been taught that AIDS is transmitted from mother to child perinatally—that is, during the birth process—and that it is transmitted through sexual activity.

This version would have been more effective, for the brief definition clarifies the word's meaning.

Wadsworth–Thomson Learning

Create vivid images by using concrete words. Saying that someone is a *bagpiper* is more specific than calling him a *musician*; but musician is more specific than the term *entertainer*.

Be Concrete

Another important aspect of style, one that can help your listeners form precise understandings, is to choose **concrete words**—those that are specific rather than abstract, particular rather than general. Think of words as ranging along a scale of abstraction such as this:

abstract/general	animal
	vertebrate
	mammal
	dog
concrete/particular	greyhound

Concrete Words
Specific, rather than general or abstract terms.

If you say, "She owns a greyhound," your ideas are much more concrete than if you say, "She has a mammal." But "She has a mammal" is more concrete than "She owns an animal." The more distinct and specific the words you choose, the more vivid your images and the more precise your meanings.

Here is an excerpt from a speech on electronic drums that is exceptional for its use of concrete language (Pettit, 1990):

> Picture your stereotypical rock drummer: shaggy, smells, looks, and sometimes acts like a lower primate, body type—lean and wiry, definitely the fast-twitch kind of muscles, and they aren't in the head. And it always seems that they're the first in the band to OD. On the Muppets TV show, the drummer's name was "Animal," and they kept him chained to his set of drums.

As you can see, concrete images help you picture the sights, movements—even the smells—of drummers. This is an example of language that appeals to listeners' senses.

Vague words have indefinite boundaries and, consequently, are imprecise in defining a concept. For example, what is a *hill*? When does it become a *mountain*? Who is *old*? A child thinks a nineteen-year-old is old, but a nineteen-year-old thinks old is being forty-five. What is *large*? *Small*? Compared to what? A *giant* pizza is not on the same scale as a giant building. You can lessen your use of vague words by choosing specific details to define or illustrate what you mean. Let's say you're speaking of a *small* inheritance. Give a dollar figure that shows what you consider *small*. One listener may think $2,000 is *small* whereas another has $20,000 in mind.

Vague Words
Imprecise terms that have indefinite boundaries.

STOP AND CHECK

CHOOSING MORE ACCURATE WORDING

The purpose of this exercise is to raise your awareness of vague words that we typically use in place of more precise ones. For example, *get* is a common verb that can often be replaced with a more concrete term. In the blank that follows each sentence, replace the *get* or its past tense *got* with more precise wording.

Can you *get* the telephone, please? _____

What did you *get* for your birthday? _____

Why did you *get* angry about that? _____

I'm *getting* ready to outline my speech. _____

He *got* a thousand dollars just for giving one speech! _____

It *got* cold last night. _____

He *gets* nervous just before he speaks. _____

After I studied the calculus problem for over an hour, I finally *got* it!

_____

You can *get* information 24 hours a day on the Internet. _____

After he *gets* here, we can leave. _____

You can complete this activity online under Stop and Check Activities for Chapter 13 at the Jaffe Connection Web site.

Web Site

Be Interesting

A major reason for speaking is to help your listeners see, feel, and remember the information you present. Colorful, vivid language helps keep listener attention and interest. You can make the language of your speech more memorable by using alliteration, rhyming, repetition, personification, hyperbole, metaphors, and similes.

Alliteration

Alliteration
Words with recurring initial sounds

Alliteration is the use of words that have the same recurring initial sounds. For instance, the keynote speaker at a conference used the alliterative phrase "*Ch*oose *ch*ange or *ch*ase it" to organize her presentation. Another speaker referred to the writer, Harriet Beecher Stowe, as "very *p*roper, *p*rimly dressed, and *p*recisely spoken" (Carnahan, 1999). In her speech about seat belts, Natalie used alliteration: "Don't let *f*ate *f*orecast your *f*uture. Buckle up."

One way to help listeners remember the main ideas in a topical message is to alliterate the main points. A speech coach used this alliterative pattern.

Good team members have:

Commitment.
Communication.
Competitiveness.

Rhyming

Rhymes
Words that end in the same sound.

As you know, **rhymes** are words that end in the same sounds. You can rhyme single words, phrases, or lines. For an example of a speech that is rhymed throughout, listen to a recording made by a rap artist. Although it is possible to rhyme an entire speech, you will probably use rhymes in more limited ways. In his speech about electronic drums, Bob rhymed three words within one sentence:

So I want to examine this new world of the push-button beat and pose the question to you: "What or who would you rather have in your band, a *mean* and *clean* drum *machine* or a stereotypical rock drummer?"

You can also use rhymes effectively for wording the main points of your speeches. Here are two examples:

We are faced with two choices:
> Retreat
> Compete

Workplaces typically have three generations of employees (Peters, 1999):
> Boomers
> Bloomers
> Zoomers

As you might imagine, this stylistic device often enables listeners to remember major points more easily.

Repetition

Technically, there are two ways to use **repetition.** One is to repeat the same word or phrase at the beginning of clauses or sentences. For example, Ronald Reagan's (1986) tribute to the Challenger crew of seven astronauts who lost their lives when their spacecraft exploded included these repetitive clauses: "We will cherish each of their stories, *stories of* triumph and bravery, *stories of* true American heroes." Another type of repetition restates the same phrase at the end of a phrase or a sentence. Lincoln's famous phrase, "government of *the people*, by *the people*, for *the people*" is an example. This speech excerpt, which shows two repeated phrases, comes from a talk by a Native American speaker (Archambault, 1992):

> This idea is not original with me. It was taught to us by a great leader of the Lakota people—my people—Chief Sitting Bull. *He taught us* that Indian children could succeed in modern society and yet retain the values of their culture, *values such as* respect for the earth, for wildlife, for rivers and streams, for plants and trees; and *values such as* caring for each other and for family and community. *He taught us* that we must leave behind more hope than we found.

Repetition
Saying the same word or phrase at the beginning or at the end of clauses or sentences.

Personification

Personification means giving human characteristics to nonhuman entities. These entities include animals, countries, natural objects and processes, and social processes. Native American Chief Seattle (1853/1971) used personification in an 1853 speech before the Governor of the Washington Territory:

> Yonder sky that has wept tears of compassion upon my people for centuries untold, and which to us appears changeless and eternal, may change.

Personification
Giving human characteristics to nonhuman entities.

Hyperbole

Hyperbole (hype) is the use of exaggeration for effect. For example, politicians say things such as, "If we don't do something about health care, there will be *no more* jobs" or "If we don't do something about AIDS, there will be *no more* people." They use these exaggerations to indicate that the problems are serious and deserve government attention.

Although hyperbole can be effective, excessive hype can lessen the speaker's credibility. Some exaggerations border on the ridiculous, and people feel the speaker is overreacting or lying. Moreover, instead of focusing on the policy the discussion often changes focus to the hyperbole itself. *No* jobs? Really? *No* more people? At all? In the classroom, Zack's use of hyperbole similarly created a negative impression:

> Imagine a world where you have *no* trees, *total* pollution, and a landfill in *every* neighborhood. This is where we are heading because of our abuse of the land and lack of concern for ways to replenish the earth and her resources. There is a way

Hyperbole
Using exaggeration for effect.

where each person . . . could help, maybe even solve the problem. It's called recycling.

ZACK

His point that recycling will contribute to the preservation of natural resources is a good one. However, saying *no* trees, *total* pollution, and *every* neighborhood overstates the case; furthermore, although recycling may help, it will not *solve the problem* of environmental pollution in and of itself. Thus, Zack's exaggerations might lead listeners to question his reasoning in general, and because this hype was in his introduction, to discount his ideas from the very beginning.

Metaphor

Metaphors
Implied comparison in which one thing is spoken of as being something else.

The use of metaphor is discussed extensively in other places throughout this text (see Chapters 8 and 18). To review, **metaphors** are implied comparisons in which one thing is spoken of as being something else; the words *like* and *as* are not used. To Professor Michael Osborn (1997), speech students are builders who frame and craft their speeches, or they are weavers who intertwine verbal and nonverbal elements into a successful performance, or they're climbers who scramble over barriers or obstacles such as speech anxiety on their way to a successful speech. In a speech given at Kansas State University on the anniversary of women's suffrage, newscaster Bernard Shaw (1993) used a metaphor comparing democracy to food preparation.

> Democracy is not a smooth sauce. . . . Democracy is the lone dish in constant need of seasoning, stirring, tasting. Democracy is never . . . never done.

Mixed Metaphor
Combining metaphors from two or more sources, starting with one comparison and ending with another.

Similes
Short comparisons that use the word *like* or *as* to compare two items that are alike in one essential detail.

One danger in using metaphors is the possibility of beginning with one comparison and ending with another. This is called a **mixed metaphor.** To illustrate, a panelist on a television news broadcast said the following about deploying U.S. troops:

> We must solve the root problem, or the line will be drawn in the sand, and we'll be back in the soup again.

As you can see, he combined three images: *root* compares the problem to a plant; the *line drawn in the sand*, an uncrossable boundary; and *soup*, a food. By going in three directions with his comparison, this speaker left his listeners with no clear image.

Simile

Archetypal symbols—sunrise and sunset, sickness and health, parent and child—are widely used as metaphors by people all over the globe.

Similes are similar to metaphors in that they compare two items that are unlike in most ways but alike in one essential detail. However, they differ from metaphors in that they explicitly state the connection, and they contain the word *like* or *as*. Jesus often used similes in his teachings, as this example demonstrates:

> The kingdom of heaven is *like* a grain of mustard seed, which a man took, and sowed in his field. Which indeed is the least of all seeds: but when it is grown, it is the greatest among herbs, and becomes a tree, so that the birds of the air come and lodge in the branches thereof. (Matthew 13:31–32)

Similarly, Chief Seattle (1853/1971) used vivid similes, as this excerpt from his speech indicates:

> [The white] people are many. They are *like* the grass that covers vast prairies. My people are few. They resemble the scattering trees of a storm-swept plain. . . . There was a time when our people covered the land *as* the waves of a wind-ruffled sea cover its

Kyle Krause/Index Stock Imagery/PictureQuest

shell paved floor, but that time long since passed away with the greatness of tribes that are now but a mournful memory.

When you read through speeches, you will see some metaphors and similes emerge and reemerge. Some arise from our experiences of being human. For instance, all human groups experience day and night, sickness and health, seasonal changes, and family relationships. Osborn (1967, 1977) calls these **archetypal symbols,** because all humankind understands them. Other comparisons relate to cultural modes of transportation (the ship of state) and sports (the game of life), and as the culture changes, new metaphors linked to electronic technology are emerging (experiencing static, feeling wired).

Archetypal Symbols
Recurring metaphors and similes that arise from shared human and natural experiences.

Language and Pluralistic Audiences

In classrooms across the country, students with the following linguistic diversity commonly sit side by side:

- Some are monolingual (speak one language only).
- Others are bidialectical (speak two English dialects).
- A few are multidialectical (speak three or more English dialects).
- Some are bilingual (speak two languages).
- A few are multilingual (speak three or more languages).

Communicating in a linguistically diverse setting can be complicated and frustrating. However, you can plan ways to adapt to multilingual situations that will be beneficial to everyone involved.

Adapt to Multilingual Situations

When you speak to a linguistically diverse audience, don't assume you'll be instantly understood. Take a hypothetical student, Ryan, whose only language is Standard English. His classmates include people who speak Spanish and English, Japanese and English, ebonics and Standard English, and Mandarin Chinese and English. Because he wants to speak effectively, he adapts his speech by using a few simple strategies:

- Before preparing his outline, he tries to "hear" the terminology and jargon related to his topic in the way a non-native speaker of English might hear it.
- When possible, he chooses simple words that most people would understand; however, he does not talk "down" to his audience.
- He identifies words that might be confusing and uses them on visual aids, which he displays as he talks.
- He defines difficult words and jargon terms as he goes along.
- He builds in redundancy or repetition by saying the same idea in a number of different ways.

Put simply, being mindful of linguistic diversity allows Ryan to strategically select language that communicates effectively with listeners from various linguistic backgrounds.

When you're an audience member who's listening to a nonfluent speaker, you must put forth more-than-normal effort to make the experience satisfying, both to the speaker and to yourself. Remember that the major goal of any speech is communication of ideas, not perfection of language skills. As you listen, concentrate on the ideas rather than on each specific word. This may require a special kind of patience as well as the ability to take the perspective of the communicator. **Perspective taking** means that you put yourself in the other person's shoes. That is, you try to imagine what it would be like to give a speech in a foreign language to a group of native speakers of that language. Also, keep in mind that nonfluency is linked to inexperience in your language, not to lack of intelligence or lack of

Perspective Taking
Putting yourself in another person's shoes.

education (Lustig & Koester, 1993; Simons, Vazquez, & Harris, 1993). These additional tips can help you listen more effectively:

- Approach the speech with a positive attitude, expecting to understand.
- Listen all the way through. Make special efforts to keep your mind from wandering in the middle of the speech. It may help to take notes.
- Practice *respons*-ibility in co-creating meaning. Plan to give appropriate nonverbal feedback to demonstrate your interest, patience, and support for the speaker.
- Control your negative emotional responses. Let's face it, it is difficult to deal with linguistic barriers, and people often get frustrated or bored when there are language differences.
- Don't laugh, even if the speakers do, at their language skills. Often they laugh nervously to relieve tension (Thiederman, 1991a, 1991b).

Adapt to an Interpreter

Although using an interpreter may seem remote now, you may eventually have to communicate through someone who translates your words into another language, including sign language. If you have occasion to use an interpreter, here are a few things to remember.

On your CD-ROM, watch Kelly Bilinski and Uriel Plascencia team up. He speaks in Spanish; she interprets.

Josh Nauman

- Keep your language simple. Do not use overly technical or uncommon words.
- In advance of the speech, provide your interpreter with an outline of your speech so that he or she may check the meaning of any unfamiliar words. The interpreter may also use it during your speech as a guide to what you will say next.
- When your interpreter translates into another language, speak in short units. Don't try entire paragraphs; rather, speak one or two sentences, then allow the interpreter to speak.
- Consider looking at the interpreter as he or she speaks. This will indicate that you are ready for the translation; it also signals the audience to look at the interpreter rather than at you.
- Because it takes two to three times longer to speak through an interpreter who translates into another language, shorten your speech accordingly.

Remember that using interpreters is not easy, but without them, you could not communicate your ideas effectively. Consequently, work on maintaining a positive attitude throughout the speaking event. (Appendix C provides an example of a classroom speech, delivered in Spanish and interpreted into English by a fellow student. It's available on the CD-ROM that accompanies this text.)

Summary

Language is a tool that humans use to communicate with one another and build complex societies. We use words to name our cultural memories—meaning that we label those things we notice and need to know in order to survive; in short, we name the events, people, and things we find important. Languages are dynamic, with words being added, borrowed, and discontinued in response to social changes.

Words denote or stand for objects, actions, and ideas; jargon, a technical vocabulary common to members of an occupation, can confuse outsiders who don't know its meaning. More important, words have connotative meanings that consist of the feelings and associations that the word implies. Epithets generally carry negative connotations, whereas euphemisms put negative things more positively. In recent years, people have become concerned about the power of words—especially those used in discriminatory ways—and have worked to eliminate sexist, ageist, racist, and other noninclusive language from acceptable vocabulary.

Your speaking effectiveness will depend largely on how well you can put your ideas into words. Thus, there are several guidelines for using language effectively in public speaking. First, be accurate in both your vocabulary and grammar. Further, use language that is appropriate to the audience and occasion, and to you. Eliminate extra words and phrases that make your speech less concise. Define jargon in an effort to be clear, and select concrete words that will enable your listeners to form more precise meanings. In addition, choose interesting words, and consider using alliteration, rhyme, repetition, personification, hyperbole, metaphors, and similes that draw from shared cultural references.

Finally, it is probable that you will be in a public speaking situation where you either speak in a second language—necessitating the use of an interpreter—or listen to a speaker who has the accent of another language. In these situations, it is most important to communicate ideas rather than have linguistic precision. If you listen to a speaker from another linguistic background, take the responsibility of listening with an open mind in a supportive manner.

JAFFE ONLINE CONNECTION · JAFFE ONLINE CONNECTION

Use your CD-ROM and the Jaffe Connection Web site http://communication.wadsworth.com/jaffe to review the following concepts, answer the review questions, and complete the suggested activities.

KEY TERMS

languages (236)
symbols (236)
words (236)
dialect (237)
Standard English (237)
code switching (237)
denotative meaning (238)
ambiguous (238)
connotative meaning (238)
epithets (239)
euphemisms (239)
jargon (239)
inclusive language (240)
sexist language (241)
ageist language (241)
racist language (241)

nonparallel language (241)
malaprops (243)
verbiage (243)
concrete words (245)
vague words (245)
alliteration (246)
rhymes (246)
repetition (247)
personification (247)
hyperbole (247)
metaphors (248)
mixed metaphor (248)
similes (248)
archetypal symbols (249)
perspective taking (249)

APPLICATION AND CRITICAL THINKING EXERCISES

1. One Internet Web page, titled "Incredible Facts" (accessed at http://bg-info.com/humor_-_facts.html), claims that the English word with the most dictionary meanings is *set*. Use a dictionary to look up this word and see if you agree or if you can prove that this is wrong. If you use a print edition instead of an online dictionary, thumb through the book and look for other ambiguous words with more than ten meanings.

2. Use a Web search engine such as www.google.com or www.dogpile.com and look up the word *ebonics*. Download and print off at least two articles and bring them to class with you. In a small group discuss one of the following questions; afterward, share your group's conclusions with the entire class:

- Identify some ways that ebonics differs from Standard English.
- What controversies swirl around ebonics? Why do you think the dialect is controversial?
- What do linguists say about the dialect?
- What are the arguments in favor of instruction in ebonics?
- What are the arguments against instruction in ebonics?

3. Interview a member of a specific occupation, and make a list of jargon terms associated with the job (for example, carpenters, waiters, foresters, pharmacists, truckers, bankers). Discuss your list with a classmate. How many terms do you know? Which terms are unfamiliar? If you were listening to a speaker from that occupation, how might the speaker translate the jargon so that you would better understand?

4. Log on to InfoTrac College Edition and do a PowerTrac search for the article "Straight Talk" in the June 10, 2002, issue of *Network Computing*. It contains two letters to the editor explaining how and why to clarify jargon. Come to class prepared to give two reasons to minimize jargon and describe two tips that tell you how to do so.

5. Find a speech by a Native American or a speaker from another culture. W. C. Vanderwerth's book, *Indian Oratory* (University of Oklahoma Press, 1971), is a good place to look for historical Native American oratory, or search InfoTrac College Edition using PowerTrac for the journal *Vital Speeches*, which provides contemporary speeches. Locate the metaphors and similes in a speech. Note the differences, if any, between the metaphors of that culture and your own.

6. When (if ever) might you use an interpreter in the future? When might you listen to a speech delivered with the assistance of an interpreter? (Consider speeches you might watch on television.) When (if ever) might you give a speech in a second language? When might you listen to a speaker who is presenting a speech in a second language?

7. If you know a second language, prepare a short speech in your own language, then work with an interpreter who presents your speech in English as you give it in your language. For example, Maria prepared her speech in Italian and had an Italian-speaking classmate interpret when she gave it to the class—some of whom spoke Italian, some of whom didn't. Paula prepared her speech in Romanian and brought her cousin to class to translate because all her classmates were monolingual.

THE JAFFE CONNECTION WEB SITE

The Jaffe Connection Web site features review questions about the Web sites, Stop and Check activities, and InfoTrac College Edition exercises referenced throughout the chapter. You can access this site via your CD-ROM or at http://communication.wadsworth.com/jaffe.

Web Links

13.1 English Slang and Dialect Differences (page 237)
13.2 Euphemisms Soften Controversial Ideas (page 239)
13.3 Test Connotations for Different Individuals (page 240)
13.4 Monitor Your Language Sensitivity (page 242)
13.5 Checking Your Grammar (page 243)
13.6 Be Aware of Multiple Meanings of Some Words (page 251)
13.7 What Is Ebonics? (page 251)

Stop and Check Activities

13.1 Think Critically About Denotative and Connotative Words (page 240)
13.2 Avoiding Discriminatory Language (page 242)
13.3 Choose More Accurate Wording (page 246)

InfoTrac College Edition Exercises

13.1 Japanese English Language Bloopers (page 243)
13.2 Throwing *Pwent* (page 244)
13.3 The Use and Misuse of Jargon (page 252)
13.4 Metaphors and Similes from Other Cultures (page 252)

SPEECH INTERACTIVE ON THE JAFFE CONNECTION CD-ROM

Read Martin Luther King, Jr.'s speech, "I Have a Dream," and focus especially on his skillful use of metaphors and repetition. What other instances of vivid language do you find? After you have studied the speech, watch a portion of it under Speech Interactive on your Jaffe Connection CD-ROM.

PROFESSIONAL SPEECH
WITH COMMENTARY

I HAVE A DREAM
by Martin Luther King, Jr.

This speech was delivered on the steps of the Lincoln Memorial on August 28, 1963. The occasion was a March on Washington for Jobs and Freedom; the audience numbered about 250,000 people. It was televised and reprinted in newspapers. The Seattle Times, April 4, 1993, calls it "the most famous public address of 20th Century America."

1. Five score years ago, a great American, in whose symbolic shadow we stand signed the Emancipation Proclamation. This momentous decree came as a great beacon light of hope to millions of Negro slaves who had been seared in the flames of withering injustice. It came as a joyous daybreak to end the long night of captivity.

   [1] King opens with images of light and darkness.

2. But one hundred years later, we must face the tragic fact that the Negro is still not free. One hundred years later, the life of the Negro is still sadly crippled by the manacles of segregation and the chains of discrimination. One hundred years later, the Negro lives on a lonely island of poverty in the midst of a vast ocean of material prosperity. One hundred years later, the Negro is still languishing in the corners of American society and finds himself an exile in his own land. So we have come here today to dramatize an appalling condition.

   [2] Here is his first series of repetitions: "one hundred years later . . ."

3. In a sense we have come to our nation's capital to cash a check. When the architects of our republic wrote the magnificent words of the Constitution and the Declaration of Independence, they were signing a promissory note to which every American was to fall heir. This note was a promise that all men would be guaranteed the inalienable rights of life, liberty, and the pursuit of happiness.

[4] Analyze how he uses the bank of justice metaphor.

4. It is obvious today that America has defaulted on this promissory note insofar as her citizens of color are concerned. Instead of honoring this sacred obligation, America has given the Negro people a bad check, which has come back marked "insufficient funds." But we refuse to believe that the bank of justice is bankrupt. We refuse to believe that there are insufficient funds in the great vaults of opportunity of this nation. So we have come to cash this check—a check that will give us upon demand the riches of freedom and the security of justice. We have also come to this hallowed spot to remind America of the fierce urgency of now. This is no time to engage in the luxury of cooling off or to take the tranquilizing drug of gradualism. Now is the time to rise from the dark and desolate valley of segregation to the sunlit path of racial justice. Now is the time to open the doors of opportunity to all of God's children. Now is the time to lift our nation from the quicksands of racial injustice to the solid rock of brotherhood.

[5] Here and in paragraphs 6, 9, and 22–27 he uses archetypal metaphors— seasons, thirst, weather, mountains.

5. It would be fatal for the nation to overlook the urgency of the moment and to underestimate the determination of the Negro. This sweltering summer of the Negro's legitimate discontent will not pass until there is an invigorating autumn of freedom and equality. Nineteen sixty-three is not an end, but a beginning. Those who hope that the Negro needed to blow off steam and will now be content will have a rude awakening if the nation returns to business as usual. There will be neither rest nor tranquility in America until the Negro is granted his citizenship rights. The whirlwinds of revolt will continue to shake the foundations of our nation until the bright day of justice emerges.

6. But there is something that I must say to my people who stand on the warm threshold, which leads into the palace of justice. In the process of gaining our rightful place we must not be guilty of wrongful deeds. Let us not seek to satisfy our thirst for freedom by drinking from the cup of bitterness and hatred.

[7] Language changes over time; in 1963 the term "Negro" was common; today, it is rarely used. He refers to black and white children [¶ 17], but not to "blacks." That term came later in the 1960s. Today, we commonly hear the term "African American."

7. We must forever conduct our struggle on the high plane of dignity and discipline. We must not allow our creative protest to degenerate into physical violence. Again and again we must rise to the majestic heights of meeting physical force with soul force. The marvelous new militancy which has engulfed the Negro community must not lead us to distrust of all white people, for many of our white brothers, as evidenced by their presence here today, have come to realize that their destiny is tied up with our destiny and their freedom is inextricably bound to our freedom. We cannot walk alone.

[8] Here's another repetitive series: "we cannot be satisfied as long as . . ."

[8] "until justice rolls down . . ." is a paraphrase of the Biblical passage, Amos 5:24.

8. And as we walk, we must make the pledge that we shall march ahead. We cannot turn back. There are those who are asking the devotees of civil rights, "When will you be satisfied?" We can never be satisfied as long as our bodies, heavy with the fatigue of travel, cannot gain lodging in the motels of the highways and the hotels of the cities. We cannot be satisfied as long as the Negro's basic mobility is from a smaller ghetto to a larger one. We can never be satisfied as long as a Negro in Mississippi cannot vote and a Negro in New York believes he has nothing for which to vote. No, no, we are not satisfied, and we will not be satisfied until justice rolls down like waters and righteousness like a mighty stream.

[9] Notice the religious terminology that King, an ordained minister, uses throughout.

9. I am not unmindful that some of you have come here out of great trials and tribulations. Some of you have come fresh from narrow cells. Some of you have come from areas where your quest for freedom left you battered by the storms of persecution and staggered by the winds of police brutality. You have been the veterans of creative suffering. Continue to work with the faith that unearned suffering is redemptive.

[10] This short repetitive phrase ("Go back . . .") is almost dwarfed by the more famous phrases in the speech.

10. Go back to Mississippi, go back to Alabama, go back to Georgia, go back to Louisiana, go back to the slums and ghettos of our northern cities, knowing that somehow this situation can and will be changed. Let us not wallow in the valley of despair.

11. I say to you today, my friends, that in spite of the difficulties and frustrations of the moment, I still have a dream. It is a dream deeply rooted in the American dream.

12. I have a dream that one day this nation will rise up and live out the true meaning of its creed: "We hold these truths to be self-evident: that all men are created equal."

13. I have a dream that one day on the red hills of Georgia the sons of former slaves and the sons of former slave owners will be able to sit down together at a table of brotherhood.

14. I have a dream that one day even the state of Mississippi, a desert state, sweltering with the heat of injustice and oppression, will be transformed into an oasis of freedom and justice.

15. I have a dream that my four children will one day live in a nation where they will not be judged by the color of their skin but by the content of their character.

16. I have a dream today.

17. I have a dream that one day the state of Alabama, whose governor's lips are presently dripping with the words of interposition and nullification, will be transformed into a situation where little black boys and black girls will be able to join hands with little white boys and white girls and walk together as sisters and brothers.

18. I have a dream today.

19. I have a dream that one day every valley shall be exalted, every hill and mountain shall be made low, the rough places will be made plain, and the crooked places will be made straight, and the glory of the Lord shall be revealed, and all flesh shall see it together.

20. This is our hope. This is the faith with which I return to the South. With this faith we will be able to hew out of the mountain of despair a stone of hope. With this faith we will be able to transform the jangling discords of our nation into a beautiful symphony of brotherhood. With this faith we will be able to work together, to pray together, to struggle together, to go to jail together, to stand up for freedom together, knowing that we will be free one day.

21. This will be the day when all of God's children will be able to sing with a new meaning, "My country, 'tis of thee, sweet land of liberty, of thee I sing. Land where my fathers died, land of the pilgrim's pride, from every mountainside, let freedom ring."

22. And if America is to be a great nation this must become true. So let freedom ring from the prodigious hilltops of New Hampshire. Let freedom ring from the mighty mountains of New York. Let freedom ring from the Alleghenies of Pennsylvania!

23. Let freedom ring from the snowcapped Rockies of Colorado!

24. Let freedom ring from the curvaceous peaks of California!

25. But not only that; let freedom ring from Stone Mountain of Georgia!

26. Let freedom ring from Lookout Mountain of Tennessee!

27. Let freedom ring from every hill and every molehill of Mississippi. From every mountainside, let freedom ring.

28. When we let freedom ring, when we let it ring from every village and every hamlet, from every state and every city, we will be able to speed up that day when all of God's children, black men and white men, Jews and Gentiles, Protestants and Catholics, will be able to join hands and sing in the words of the old Negro spiritual, "Free at last! Free at last! Thank God Almighty, we are free at last!"

[11] Here is King's most famous repetitive sequence—the one that gave the speech its title. Notice that he follows it with two additional repetitions: "with this faith" and "let freedom ring."

[19] He is quoting from the Biblical book of Isaiah 40:4–5.

[21] This is a very common patriotic song.

[22–27] This repetitive series, which recognizes geographical diversity but emphasizes the unity that comes with freedom, brought roars of approval from the crowd.

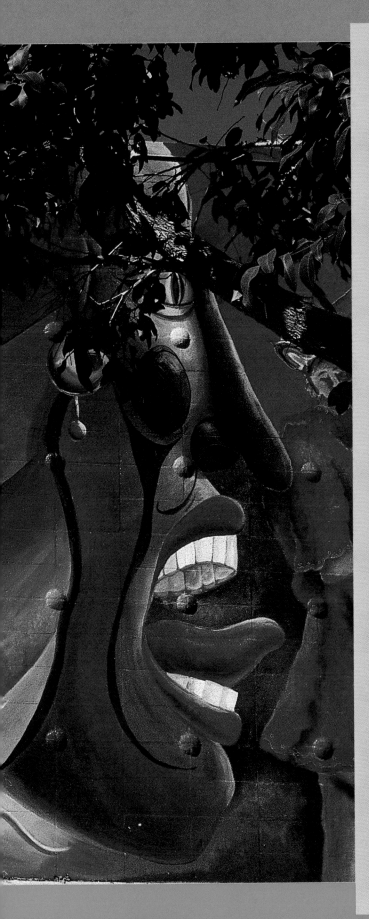

14

Delivering Your Speech

THIS CHAPTER WILL HELP YOU

■ Describe how personal appearance, clothing, and accessories can affect public speaking

■ List three functions of gestures and explain how each can be used in public speaking

■ Understand how eye contact makes a difference in your delivery

■ Describe elements of your voice that influence your message

■ List four methods of delivery

■ Discuss ways to use technology effectively in speech delivery

"Carnaval" Mural ©1995 by Joshua Sarantitis, Emmanuel Montoya, and Precita Eyes Muralists. (PG&E Yard Wall, 18th and Harrison, SF, CA)

COMPARE NEWS REPORTERS you've seen—Ann Curry, Peter Jennings, Dan Rather, Connie Chung. Each, arguably, has a similar message ("Today's happenings are . . ."). Similar words, yes, but each reporter creates a different impression based on personal appearance, manner, and vocal quality—in short, delivery.

Delivery
The verbal and nonverbal behaviors you use to perform your speech.

Delivery—the way you perform your speech—includes not only your words but also the way you present them. To deliver your speech competently, you must understand effective nonverbal communication and develop skills for using your appearance, gestures, and voice to create a positive impression. In the last three decades researchers have learned a great deal about nonverbal communication, gaining insights you can apply when you speak. The chapter discusses personal appearance, movements or mannerisms, and vocal variations that can enhance or detract from your words. It elaborates on the four major types of delivery introduced in Chapter 2 and concludes with ways to adapt your delivery when you use technology.

Maximize Your Personal Appearance

Impression Management
Self-presentation, using the metaphor of a staged drama in which we use props and personal mannerisms to create and maintain impressions of ourselves.

Erving Goffman (1959) develops the concept of **impression management** in his influential book, *The Presentation of Self in Everyday Life*. Goffman compares our self-presentation to a dramatic performance in which we attempt to create and maintain impressions of ourselves as if we were on a stage, using a combination of props and personal mannerisms to accomplish this. Your listeners form initial impressions of you based on the way you look: your physical appearance, your clothing, and your accessories.

Make the Most of Your Physical Appearance

You have several relatively permanent physical features that disclose information about you. For example, just by looking at you others can infer your sex, general age range, racial background, height, weight, and body type. Unfortunately, some audiences will stereotype you based on your personal appearance. As Chapter 5 pointed out, an audience may disregard younger speakers or pay less attention to women or minorities.

Physical features or conditions can also make you reluctant to speak publicly—less-than-perfect skin, crooked teeth, visible birthmarks, above-average or below-average weight or height, poor eyesight, a cane or wheelchair (Bippus & Daly, 1999). Because this culture saturates us with images of physically perfect bodies, any perceived difference often causes anxiety; you may feel that you're in the limelight being scrutinized. Remember, however, that people do see your features, but they generally don't focus on them throughout your entire speech. If you worry about your appearance, one of your best strategies is to have an interesting topic and a good opening statement that draws people's attention to your subject rather than to your looks.

Regardless of features, you can pay special attention to grooming, which is vital in this culture (Arthur, 1997). In fact, the proverb "Cleanliness is next to godliness" shows that neatness can be almost as significant as natural beauty. And you can enhance your presentation by smiling and gesturing appropriately. Moreover, your listeners don't only see your physical characteristics; your clothing and accessories are an important part of the total impression you create.

Choose Appropriate Clothing and Accessories

Dirk always wore black—typically a black T-shirt with the name of a rock band and a picture on the front showing a creature with fangs that dripped blood. However, on speech days he wisely chose a more conservative black polo shirt. Some authors—notably John

Molloy (1976) of *Dress for Success* fame—have made a fortune telling people that their clothing choices influence the way others perceive them. This principle applies to your classroom, where a good general rule is to select clothing that is slightly more formal than normal. For example, instead of a sweatshirt with writing on it, substitute a plain pullover sweater on speech day. Resist the temptation to wear your favorite baseball cap turned backward. Clothing that is too tight or too revealing is less appropriate than more conservative wear.

Before you speak anywhere, it's a good idea to check out clothing expectations. Let's say your job requires you to give a presentation at an unfamiliar organization. You should find out in advance if members generally wear tailored or less-formal clothing. One student was invited to speak at a staff retreat at her university, but she was embarrassed because she failed to do this:

> I was overdressed! I didn't realize it was a retreat setting, and everyone was dressed very casually.
>
> SEANA

Accessories—the objects you carry or add to your clothing—include jewelry, glasses, briefcases, notebooks, or folders. Not long ago, one of my classes reminded me that accessories do matter. Out of laziness, I'd been carting around my materials in a cardboard box. Students advised me that a leather briefcase would be more impressive! In your classroom and elsewhere, the basic rules for accessories are that they be simple, appropriate, and of the best quality you can afford.

There are ethical implications in impression management. That is, we may try to create an impression that truly reflects who we are, or we may try to deceive our audiences to one degree or another. Speakers who present verbal and nonverbal messages that they themselves believe are termed **sincere**. In contrast, speakers who make strategic choices to control nonverbal messages to create false or misleading impressions are termed **cynical**. They don't believe their own messages.

Tammy Faye Bakker-Messner gained fame as a televangelist and co-founder of a Christian TV network; however, to many, her extreme use of makeup and accessories overshadows her message of love and goodwill.

Accessories
Objects you carry or add to your clothing.

Develop Effective Mannerisms

Your manner—or the way you speak, move, and look at the audience—is an area of nonverbal communication that you can control to a significant degree. Mannerisms discussed in this section include gestures and eye contact.

Control Your Gestures

Body movements range from large motions, such as posture, walking, and gesturing, to very small movements, such as raising one eyebrow. Ekman and Friesen (1969) classified the functions of **gestures** into several categories, which nonverbal scholars commonly use. Three are especially applicable to public speaking: emblems, illustrators, and adaptors.

Sincere
Speakers presenting verbal and nonverbal messages they themselves believe.

Cynical
Speakers presenting verbal or nonverbal messages they don't believe, attempting to create a false image.

Gestures
Body movements or motions, whether large or barely noticeable.

AP/Wide World Photos

Emblems

Emblems
Gestures that stand for words or ideas; a head nod means yes.

Emblems are gestures that stand for words or ideas. You'll occasionally use them in public speaking, as when you hold up a hand to ask for quiet. Your forefinger to your lips in a "sh-h-h-h" gesture functions in the same way. Not surprisingly, emblems vary across cultures. For instance, Ethiopians put one forefinger to their lips when silencing a child, but they use four fingers when they are communicating with adults. The sign that stands for "A-OK" in the United States refers to money in Japan (Richmond & McCroskey, 2000) and is an obscene gesture in some Latin American countries. Richard Nixon discovered this when he exited a plane in Latin America and responded to a reporter's question, "How was the trip?" by signaling "A-OK!"

Illustrators

Illustrators
Gestures that add emphasis to or illustrate verbal messages.

Illustrators are gestures that illustrate or add emphasis to your words, and you'll likely use them during your speeches. Illustrators function in a variety of ways:

- To accent words and phrases. For example, "We should *all* vote" [extend your hands and arms outward].
- To show spatial relationships. For example, "It's about *this* [extend your hands to show the distance] wide."
- To point to objects. For instance, "Look at this [point to the area on the map] part of the ocean."

Make sure that your illustrators are purposeful. It's easy to wave your arms about randomly or to repeat a meaningless gesture that listeners may find distracting. Watch two or three speeches on the Jaffe Connection CD; turn the sound down and focus on how the speakers use their hands and arms to make effective points—or simply to make meaningless movements.

Adaptors

Adaptors
Gestures that betray stress or fear.

If you use too many **adaptors**, a third kind of gesture, you may alert your audience to your nervousness, because adaptors can betray stress or fear. There are three kinds of adaptors:

- **Self-adaptors** are those in which you touch yourself. Fidgeting with your hair, licking your lips, scratching your face, and rubbing your hands together during your speech are a few examples.
- **Object adaptors** involve touching things. Here you play with your keys or jingle change in your pocket, pull at necklaces or earrings, twist a ring, or tap your pencil or note cards.
- **Alter-adaptors** are gestures you use in relationship to the audience. For instance, if you fold your arms across your chest during intense questioning, you may be subconsciously protecting yourself against the perceived psychological threat of the questioner.

Because adaptors indicate anxiety or other stresses, especially when they appear to be nervous mannerisms, strive to eliminate them.

Self-adaptors
Touching yourself (like scratching) when you're stressed.

Object Adaptors
Nervously touching or playing with items like pens or jewelry.

Alter-adaptors
Gestures, like folding your arms protectively, that betray nervousness about the audience.

Make Eye Contact

> I find it hard to listen to speakers who look down, not giving full attention to the audience.
>
> LARISA

In the United States, where direct eye contact communicates honesty and trustworthiness, it's important to look at the audience. The phrase "Look me in the eye and say that" is partly premised on the cultural notion that people won't lie if they're looking at you. **Eye contact** also communicates friendliness. In interpersonal relationships, for instance, one person who purposefully avoids the other's gaze is signaling a lack of interest in developing a relationship.

You may need to practice making direct eye contact. Tempting as it is to look at your notes, the desktops in the front row, the back wall, or out the window, all these gazes communicate that you're uncomfortable. Avoid this impression by looking around the room in at least three general directions: at the listeners directly in front of you, those to the left, and those to the right. Because of your peripheral vision, you can generally keep most listeners within your vision as you change the direction of your gaze.

Finally, look at various people within the room—not just at one or two. And resist the urge to make more eye contact with audience members you perceive as more powerful. For example, you may want to look more at your instructor than at your classmates, at men more than at women, but try to avoid these behaviors. As part of a job application process, one would-be professor addressed the faculty members; unfortunately, he made noticeably more eye contact with the male than with the female professors—largely ignoring the female department chair. Needless to say, he wasn't hired!

Eye Contact
Looking audiences in the eye; communicates friendliness in the United States.

What is effective about this speaker's nonverbal appearance? (Evaluate his clothing, grooming, eye contact, and gestures.) What impression would you get if he gave his whole speech using the body position shown on the left? On the right?

Wadsworth–Thomson Learning
Wadsworth–Thomson Learning

What is typical in the United States is not universal. For instance, Japanese communicators use less direct eye contact. It's not unusual to see downcast or closed eyes at a meeting or a conference; within Japanese culture this demonstrates attentiveness and agreement rather than rejection, disinterest, or disagreement. Additionally, Nigerians as well as Puerto Ricans consider it disrespectful to make prolonged eye contact with superiors (Richmond & McCroskey, 2000).

 For additional information on gestures and eye contact, log on to InfoTrac College Edition and search for the key words *eye contact, nonverbal gestures,* or *body language.*

Vary Your Vocal Behaviors

When friends call on the phone, you recognize their voices instantly because of distinctive vocal features. And even without seeing someone—as when you listen to the radio—you can identify speakers as young or old, male or female, Southerners or New Yorkers, native or non-native speakers of English. Moreover, you can often detect moods such as boredom, hostility, or enthusiasm. Understanding two important aspects of vocal behaviors will help you become a better public speaker: pronunciation and vocal variation.

Pronounce Your Words Clearly

Pronunciation, the way you actually say words, has several components including articulation and stress or accenting. Your pronunciation can reveal your regional origin, ethnicity, or social status.

Articulation and Stress

Articulation
The way you enunciate or say specific sounds.

Stress
Accenting syllables or words.

Articulation is the way you say individual sounds such as *this* or *dis, bird* or *beerd.* Some speakers reverse sounds—saying *aks* instead of *ask.* **Stress** is the way you accent syllables or whole words—*poe-LEESE* (police) or *POE-leese,* for example. Some people alter both articulation and stress, for instance, comparable (*COM-purr-uh-bul*) becomes *come-PARE-uh-bul*; potpourri (*poe-per-EE*) becomes *pot-PORE-ee.* When you're in doubt about a pronunciation, consult a dictionary. You'll find that some words, such as *status,* have two acceptable pronunciations—*STAY-tus* and *STATT-us.* When the dictionary provides two variations, the first is considered preferable (*PREFF-er-uh-bul*).

Regional Origin

You've probably noticed regional variations in pronunciation and articulation. The following list illustrates just a few:

- There are differences in the *extent* to which sounds are held. Southern speakers typically draw out their sounds, resulting in the "southern drawl."
- Many Bostonians add an *r* at the end of a word such as *tuba.* Listen to a speaker from Massachusetts, and you'll hear *tuber.*
- Speakers from different regions often articulate sounds differently. Go to Brooklyn and you'll hear *oi* instead of *er* (*thoity* means *thirty*).

Ethnicity

Ethnicity is another factor that may affect pronunciation. Dialects such as an Appalachian dialect or African American Vernacular English have distinctive articulation and stress patterns. Furthermore, non-native speakers of English use accents that reflect articulation and stress patterns from their first language. In a multilingual world and in pluralistic classrooms, there are bound to be accents, and as travel and immigration continue to shrink the world, you'll hear even more in the future. Unfortunately, we tend to judge one another on the basis of regional and ethnic dialects and accents; however, the letter in Diversity in

IMMIGRANTS, DON'T BE IN SUCH A HURRY TO SHED YOUR ACCENTS

THIS LETTER to the editor appeared in the *New York Times*, March 21, 1993.

To the Editor:

You report that immigrants in New York City are turning to speech classes to reduce the sting of discrimination against them based on accent. . . . I'd like to tell all my fellow immigrants taking accent-reduction classes: As long as you speak fluent and comprehensible English, don't waste your money on artificially removing your accent.

I am fortunate enough to be one of the linguistically gifted. I even acquired an American accent before I left China for the United States five years ago. From the day I set foot on this continent till now, the praise of my English has never ceased. What most people single out is that I have no, or very little accent. However, I know I do have an accent. . . . I intend to keep it because it belongs to me. I want to speak and write grammatically flawless English, but I have no desire to equip myself with a perfect American accent. . . .

America is probably the largest place for accents in English because the entire nation is composed of immigrants from different areas of the world. This country is built on accents. Accent is one of the most conspicuous symbols of what makes America the free and prosperous land its own people are proud of and other people long to live in.

I work in an urban institution where accents are an integral part of my job: students, faculty and staff come from ethnically diverse backgrounds. Hearing accents confirms for me every day that the college is fulfilling its goal to offer education to a multicultural population.

I wonder what accent my fellow immigrants should obtain after getting rid of their own: a New York accent? a Boston accent? Brooklyn? Texas? California? Or go after President Clinton's accent?

Fellow immigrants, don't worry about the way you speak until Peter Jennings eliminates his Canadian accent.

YanHong Krompacky

Practice: Immigrants, Don't Be in Such a Hurry to Shed Your Accents, presents a good argument for acceptance of a variety of accents.

Social Status

Differences in pronunciation often indicate social status. This is the premise for the classic movie *My Fair Lady*. Eliza Doolittle *says* the same words as Professor Higgins, but her pronunciation marks her as an uneducated member of the lower class. The professor takes her on as a project. By changing her pronunciation—and other nonverbal variables, such as dress and grooming—she eventually passes as a Hungarian princess.

Use Vocal Variation

Around 330 B.C., Aristotle understood the importance of vocal characteristics in creating an impression on listeners. We continue to discuss these three important components of voice identified in his text *Rhetoric:* volume, pitch, rate—and the variations in each.

> It is not enough to know what we ought to say; we must also say it as we ought. . . . It is, essentially, a matter of the right management of the voice to express the various emotions—of speaking loudly, softly, or between the two; of high, low, or intermediate pitch; of the various rhythms that suit various subjects. These are the three

things—volume of sound, modulation of pitch, and rhythm—that a speaker bears in mind (Aristotle, trans. Roberts, 1984).

Vocal Variations
Changes in volume, rate, and pitch that combine to create impressions of the speaker.

What kinds of impressions do **vocal variations** create? For one thing, listeners like speakers with pleasing vocal variations. One student summarized delivery skills that leave positive impressions on him:

> An audience stays in tune when the speaker's voice changes, adding life to the message. An animated speaker is also more interesting than a "block" of ice. The speaker must be interested in what he/she is saying in order to be convincing.
>
> DAVID

In addition, several studies (Burgoon et al., 1989; Ray, 1986) conclude that audiences typically associate vocal characteristics with personality traits. For instance, here are just a few common associations:

Loud and fast speakers: self-sufficient, resourceful, dynamic
Loud and slow speakers: aggressive, competitive, confident
Soft and fast speakers: enthusiastic, adventuresome, confident, composed
Soft and slow speakers: competitive, enthusiastic, benevolent

Is there a relationship between your voice and your credibility? Various studies indicate that audiences make a number of associations about your trustworthiness based on your voice. Speak faster and you may be considered more intelligent, objective, and knowledgeable. If you're a male, you may be seen as dominant, dynamic, and sociable. Speak with a moderate rate and you may give the impression of composure, honesty, people orientation, and compassion (Burgoon et al., 1989).

Make vocal variations work for you. For example, use a slower rate when you're giving key points and speed up for background material (Davidson & Kline, 1999). Change your vocal inflections if your audience appears to be losing interest; that is, add pitch variation and slightly increased volume and rate to communicate enthusiasm (Hypes et al., 1999).

Meanings can vary depending on your tone of voice, rising or falling inflection, or stressed words. For instance, a movie character is accused of shooting a clerk in a convenience store. When the sheriff asks, "Why did you shoot the clerk?" the suspect responds,

Whoopi Goldberg uses her distinctive vocal features along with variation in rate, volume, and pauses to create a style that's uniquely her own.

AP/Wide World Photos

"I *shot* the clerk?" (pause) "*I* shot the clerk?" At the trial, the sheriff testifies that the accused confessed twice, clearly saying, "I shot the clerk." The sheriff says the statement as if it were factual, whereas the suspect's rising voice inflection and stressed words indicate that he's asking a question—drastically changing the meaning of the literal words. For additional tips on vocal variation, log on to the Internet site provided by the Birmingham, Alabama, Toastmasters at **www.angelfire.com/tn/bektoastmasters/Toastmasters5.html**. Practice some of the suggested exercises you find there.

Pause for Effect

Finally, consider your use of pauses. Pauses can be effective, or they can be embarrassing—to both you and your listeners. Effective pauses are intentional; that is, you purposely pause between major ideas, or you give your audience a few seconds to contemplate a difficult concept. Judith Humphrey (1998) urges speakers to slow down and use lots of pauses as this quotation illustrates.

> [C]onsider this: when does the audience think? Not while you're speaking, because they can't think about an idea until it's delivered. They think during the pauses. But if there are no pauses, they won't think. They won't be moved. They won't act upon what you say. The degree to which you want to involve the audience is reflected in the length of your pauses. (p. 472)

To learn more about pauses, you can read this article for yourself on InfoTrac College Edition. Look for the title "Executive Eloquence"; step 7 describes effective delivery.

Pauses can also function as punctuation marks. For example, at the end of the body of the speech, you might pause slightly, move one step backward, then say, "In conclusion . . ." Your pause functions as a comma that signals a separation in your thoughts.

In contrast, ineffective pauses or hesitations can disrupt your fluency and signal that you've lost your train of thought. **Unfilled pauses** are silent; **filled** or **vocalized pauses** are your *uh* or *um*, *like* and *you know* sounds. Beginning public speakers, as well as many professionals, use vocalized pauses. However, too many *ums* can be distracting, so work to keep them to a minimum.

Unfilled Pauses
Silent pauses.

Filled (Vocalized) Pauses
Saying *um* or *uh* or other sounds during a pause.

Put It All Together

Chapter 1 defined communicative competence as the ability to communicate in a personally effective and socially appropriate manner (Spitzberg, 1994). The key is to find what delivery works best for you in a given situation. For instance, consider these two presentation styles: confident and conversational. A **confident style** incorporates vocal variety, fluency, good use of gestures, and eye contact to create an impression of dynamism as well as credibility. If you're naturally outgoing, this style may best fit your personality. However, in some situations—funerals, for example—you'd choose a more **conversational style,** one that's calmer, slower, softer, and less intense, but still maintains good eye contact and gestures (Branham & Pearce, 1996). Listeners associate this style with trustworthiness, honesty, sociability, likableness, and professionalism, and it may actually fit you better if your personality is more laid-back. But someone who generally speaks more conversationally can adapt for occasions—a rally, for instance—where excitement runs high and people expect a more enthusiastic delivery. Both styles are persuasive.

Don't worry if you are not yet a dynamic, confident speaker. Instead, work on creating your personal delivery style—using your appearance, mannerisms, and vocal variations to your advantage. Then, choose a mode of delivery that fits the specific context.

Confident Style
A way of speaking characterized by effective vocal variety, fluency, gestures, and eye contact.

Conversational Style
Speaking that's comparatively calmer, slower, and less intense, but maintains good eye contact and gestures.

Select the Appropriate Type of Delivery

Tim forgot that his classroom speech was due until his name was called, so he just stood up and "winged" a talk. Quianna memorized her speech (see the outline at the end of Chapter 7) because, as a member of the University of Alaska's speech team, she presented this speech more than twenty-five times in competition. The attorney general read her commencement address at the Ivy League school, and excerpts of it were reprinted in the *New York Times*. Juan Gonzalez prepared his closing arguments carefully, but when he actually faced the jury, he delivered his final appeal using only his legal pad with a few scrawled notes. These speakers illustrate the four major types of delivery, introduced briefly in Chapter 2: impromptu, memorized, manuscript, and extemporaneous. (The CD that accompanies this text has examples of each type of delivery.)

STOP AND CHECK

THINK CRITICALLY ABOUT DELIVERY

Political candidates often illustrate the link between delivery and effective speaking (Brookhiser, 1999; Shipman, 2000). For example, Ronald Reagan was called the "Great Communicator," and Bill Clinton's speaking skills are legendary. In contrast, many politicians want to be president, but some are termed "charismatically challenged." One man's voice was described as "somewhere between that of a dentist's drill and the hum of a refrigerator . . ." (Simon, 1999, p. 16). Another's delivery was called wooden, earnest, solemn, uptight; in fact, he tended to discount delivery and focus instead on speech content. Enter the consultants. Some handlers spun their candidate's style as *authentic*. In contrast, other consultants sat beside their candidate, watching and rewatching videotaped speeches, analyzing his volume, his rate, his gestures, his facial expressions. They coached him to loosen up . . . leave the podium, spread his arms, smile, wear cowboy boots, trade in his blue suit for warmer brown more casual clothing. The candidate finally admitted what good public speakers know—no matter how wonderful his ideas, his message would go largely unheard if the audience slept through his delivery.

Within small groups in your classroom discuss the following questions:

1. What qualities are important in a president? How does presidential image matter? What do you think of the consultants' decision to capitalize on his unremarkable delivery by calling it "authentic"? Do you think a candidate should undergo a makeover or should he "be himself," regardless?
2. On MTV's campaign coverage, young people were asked their impression of one candidate. A person responded, "Uh, uh, old." What difference does it make if a president looks old?
3. President William Taft (1909–1914) weighed around 300 pounds. Could he be elected today? Why or why not? Is this good or bad?
4. Why have no women yet been elected to the presidency? When do you predict that the United States will elect its first female president?
5. Could Abraham Lincoln—with his looks and awkward mannerisms—be elected in this television-dominated society? Why or why not?
6. How do you judge your classmates' abilities based on the way they present themselves?

Web Site   You can answer these questions online and, if requested, email your response to your instructor.

Impromptu Delivery

Use **impromptu delivery** when you must think on your feet. This mode requires the least amount of preparation and rehearsal, because impromptu speeches are given on the spur of the moment, meaning that you don't prepare them in advance. However, in a sense, your entire life—your knowledge and experience—prepares you for these speeches. Let's say you attend a wedding reception, and you're asked to tell a funny story spontaneously about the bride and groom. You won't have time to spend weeks in preparation. Instead, you'll think quickly and draw from your experience with the couple to find material for your speech.

Most people shudder at the thought of speaking without preparation and rehearsal, especially if their performance will be rewarded or punished in some way—such as by a grade or a job evaluation. However, a few students give an impromptu speech when the professor has assigned one that's to be carefully prepared. Bad strategy!

Impromptu Delivery
Delivering the speech as you create it.

Memorized Delivery

Memorized delivery used to be common. Roman orators, for example, planned their speeches carefully, then memorized them word for word. As a result, they could give the same oration repeatedly. In many oral cultures, tribal orators memorize the stories and legends of the tribe, a tradition that ensures that the exact stories continue throughout succeeding generations.

College students who successfully memorize speeches are those, such as Quianna Clay and Paul Southwick, who repeat each speech dozens of times in intercollegiate speech tournaments. However, you'll rarely hear memorized speeches in the classrooms or in offices, boardrooms, churches, and clubs of contemporary cultures. Consequently, it's not advisable to rely on this method. Regardless of this advice, some students think memorizing will help them overcome their fears. One international student confided:

> I think if I memorize the entire speech including the pauses, gestures, posture, etc., I will feel more comfortable delivering the speech and I will be less nervous.
>
> Lambros

However, the opposite often happens. Standing in front of their audiences, beginning speakers often forget what they've memorized. Some pause (ineffectively), look toward the ceiling, repeat the last phrase in a whisper, repeat it aloud, then look hopelessly at the instructor. When this happens, they end up embarrassed. Recently, I met an elderly lady who vividly remembered her college speech class. She said she was scared to death to give

Memorized Delivery
Delivering a speech you've learned word for word.

her speech on the topic of spanking, so she decided to memorize it. Unfortunately, memory failed her, and her resulting embarrassment has stayed with her for more than fifty years!

Another drawback is that memorized speeches are generally not delivered conversationally. Put simply, they don't sound natural. Rather than engaging in a dialogue with the audience, the speaker appears to be concentrating on recalling the exact words of the speech.

Manuscript Delivery

Manuscript Delivery
Reading a speech.

When you write your speech out and read it, you're using **manuscript delivery.** In general, reading your speech is not recommended. In fact, Hypes et al. (1999) call this "the most inactive method of presenting," one that enables a speaker to impart a lot of information—most of which the audience soon forgets. Active speaker–listener interactions, in contrast, keep the participants' attention longer, involve them mentally, and make the speech more enjoyable.

Despite the disadvantages, on some occasions—especially formal ones such as commencement addresses—manuscript delivery is acceptable, even necessary. Further, you may use a manuscript if you speak on radio or television when exact timing is essential. (Barbara Bush's speech, located in Appendix C and available on the CD that came with this text, is an example of effective manuscript delivery.)

For competent manuscript delivery, type your entire script in capital letters, using triple spacing. Then, go over your speech, using a highlighter or underlining the words you wish to accent. Make slashes where you plan to pause. Finally, practice the speech until you can read it in a natural manner, with as much eye contact as possible. Conversational delivery is essential, because most people don't like to be read to, especially if you never pause or look up.

Although manuscript delivery is sometimes appropriate, you generally won't speak in such formal settings nor will you appear on radio or television. And manuscript delivery is inappropriate for most classroom speeches. The final type of delivery—extemporaneous—is generally the preferred mode, and this is the method you'll most commonly use.

Extemporaneous Delivery

Extemporaneous Delivery
Preparing and rehearsing a speech carefully in advance, but choosing the exact wording as you deliver the speech.

In contrast to impromptu speeches, you prepare extemporaneous speeches carefully in advance but don't plan every single word. Instead, outline your major ideas, and use note cards with cue words during your delivery. To illustrate how a professional speaker prepares for **extemporaneous delivery,** consider the case of Ted Robinson, a Honolulu clergyman:

Robinson works all year long on his forty talks. Every summer he takes a one-month study leave, during which he spends about two weeks collecting ideas and setting up forty separate file folders for forty different topics. Throughout the year, he adds ideas to his files. On a weekly basis, he prepares in the following way:

- On Wednesday he pulls up the folder with the topic of the week, looks at the ideas he has collected, then spends his time narrowing his purpose.
- On Thursday he organizes a tentative outline, admitting, "Often, the hardest part is to start. Sometimes it takes another day to jell."
- On Friday he enters his empty church, goes to the pulpit and preaches the sermon—twice. As he does, he rewrites, crosses out, changes, and omits ideas on his tentative outline.
- On Saturday he follows the same procedure—two more times in an empty building. Finally, at 9:00 that evening, he sits down with a 5 × 8 card and jots down a key word outline, which he then memorizes.
- On Sunday he reviews his outline and heads off to deliver his talk. (Krauss, 1993)

Let Robinson act as a model. Begin the process of researching and organizing your speech well in advance. Give yourself plenty of time to let your ideas jell. Write out your outline, and put the main ideas on note cards (see Chapter 11). Then, practice, practice, practice—aloud, to your friends, as you drive. On the day of the speech, review your outline and your notes and go to class with the confidence that comes from thorough preparation.

Of the four types of delivery, three—impromptu, manuscript, and extemporaneous—are used with some regularity in the United States. Each has its strengths and weaknesses. In general, extemporaneous delivery is most commonly used in public presentations, and it is the one you will use in most of your classroom speeches.

Use Technology Competently

Technology provides many delivery aids that can amplify your voice and record your words in audio or video form. Because microphones are so common and because instructors as well as employers often videotape speeches, knowing basic principles for delivering your speech, using technological aids, is important. Increasing numbers of nonprofessionals—politicians, doctors, educators, social activists, and the like—are mastering these valuable skills. And to prepare you for speaking in an electronic culture, this chapter closes with tips for using technology.

Using Microphones

Microphones enable people with ordinary voices to project their words over greater distances. Because you'll probably use microphones (mikes) at some point, let's review several types of mikes as well as guidelines for using them effectively.

The types of mikes available fall into two basic categories: fixed and portable. Each type has advantages and disadvantages. **Fixed microphones** are attached to a podium or a stand. Although they project your voice adequately and allow you to use both hands, they limit your movements, forcing you to stay within the pickup range of the mike. Generally, these mikes have a short, flexible "neck" that you can adjust upward or downward or from side to side a few inches. **Portable microphones** include handheld versions (corded or cordless) and small clip mikes that attach to your clothing. **Lavaliere mikes** are portable mikes that fasten around your neck by a thin cord. These all give you considerably more freedom to move around the room. However, handheld mikes limit you slightly because you have only one hand free to gesture with or to handle notes.

No matter which microphone you use, there are several guidelines to follow. Test the mike before you speak, and ask the sound technician to make necessary adjustments at that time. Remember that each mike has its own **pickup range**—the distance you can hold it from your mouth, pick up the sound, and transmit it effectively. This is especially important to consider with a fixed mike. If you find the microphone is not projecting your voice well, move it toward you; don't bend toward it, assuming an unnatural posture. Speak in a conversational voice. Too much volume may distort your words, so step away from the mike if you intend to raise your voice. Finally, be careful not to touch or jar the microphone or mike stand, which can create intrusive and grating sounds.

Adapting for Videotaped Speeches

The simplest kind of video recording requires only one camera operator, using a portable handheld or fixed camera with a single camera angle. More sophisticated presentations require a variety of professionals including producers, stage managers, lighting directors, makeup artists, directors, and editors who work together to create a polished product.

Fixed Microphone
Mike attached to a podium or stand.

Portable Microphone
Handheld or clip mike that can be carried.

Lavaliere Mike
A portable mike worn like a necklace.

Pickup Range
The greatest distance at which a mike can be held and still pick up sound and transmit it effectively.

Don't do what this speaker is doing—leaning into the microphone to talk. Instead, work with a sound technician beforehand; he or she will adjust the mike's pickup range for your natural stance.

AP/Wide World Photos

Regardless of the level of sophistication, cameras call for slight adjustments in appearance and movement. For example, the choices you make about your personal appearance can add to or subtract from an overall positive impression:

- Both men and women commonly use makeup to minimize shine and to conceal or camouflage blemishes. The key is to look natural rather than made up.
- Wardrobe consultants suggest that some clothing looks better on film (Ross, 1989). For instance, blue or gray tones photograph better than solid black or white, and off-white or pastel shirts or blouses appear better than stark white. Shiny, highly reflective fabrics may cause glare, and busy patterns and very small plaids or stripes often appear distorted on film.
- Accessories matter. When choosing jewelry, remember that "less is more"—in both amount and flashiness. Ties should be simple, in conservative colors.

As you might imagine, the choices you make in makeup, clothing, and accessories can strengthen your overall presentation or become the focus of your listeners' attention. Furthermore, because the camera is a close-up medium, you should adapt your gestures and eye contact, at least slightly, when your speech is videotaped. Here are a few guidelines:

- Because the camera can zero in on your face by using extreme close-up (ECU) shots, every blink, every small eyebrow movement will show. With this in mind, be aware of your facial expressions, and control those that do not contribute to your verbal message.
- Control your body movements. In general, sweeping gestures, walking, scratching, touching your hair, nervous mannerisms, and other nonessential motions detract.
- Work to be graceful and fluid in the movements you do use. Relax so that you appear comfortable.
- If you're working with several cameras, look at the one with the red light on.

A good strategy is to study videotaped speeches of both effective and ineffective speakers. Mute the sound, then closely inspect the speaker's gestures and eye contact to find elements that contribute to an overall positive or negative impression.

Using a TelePrompTer

TelePrompTer
Screen, located beneath the camera lens, on which the words of the speech scroll up during a filmed speech.

If you ever speak on television, you may use a **TelePrompTer,** a handy machine that eliminates your worries about forgetting your speech. TelePrompTer screens, located just beneath the camera lens, project your script line by line, enabling you to read it while looking directly at the camera (somewhat like reading the credit lines that unroll on your television screen at the end of a program). During a rehearsal session, work with a technician who controls the speed of the lines so that the text unrolls at your speaking rate. The technician can circle key words or underline phrases that you want to emphasize. Because this is a special form of manuscript delivery, practice reading so that your delivery sounds conversational, as if you were simply talking to your audience.

Summary

By increasing your knowledge of nonverbal communication, you can make choices that will create positive impressions as you deliver your speech. The notion that good speakers manage nonverbal aspects of delivery, affecting listeners' impressions, is at least as old as Aristotle—and he surely didn't invent the idea. Modern scholars continue to explore specific aspects of appearance, mannerisms, and vocal variations that create positive or negative impressions in audiences.

You can make strategic choices in the way you dress, in your grooming, and in the accessories you use to communicate your competence. Your mannerisms—gestures, eye contact, and vocal variation—are also important in creating impressions of dynamism, honesty, and other characteristics of credibility. As you learn to use nonverbal communication effectively, your competence in public speaking increases correspondingly.

Of the four major types of delivery, memorization is common in oral cultures and in competitive speech tournaments, but it is less frequently used elsewhere. You may speak spontaneously in the impromptu style, or you may read from a manuscript. More commonly, you'll join the ranks of extemporaneous speakers—preparing in advance but choosing your exact wording as you actually speak.

You may use technology to present your speech. The most common technological aid is the microphone; consequently, it is important to know various types of mikes and how to use them effectively. Speeches that are videotaped call for careful clothing, accessories, and makeup choices as well as control of body movements. Finally, TelePrompTers help you read a script as you're being filmed.

As with all attempts to influence others, the attempt to manage impressions has ethical implications. Speakers who believe in both the verbal and nonverbal messages they are sending are said to be sincere, but those who try to create false or misleading impressions are termed cynical.

JAFFE ONLINE CONNECTION   JAFFE ONLINE CONNECTION

Use your CD-ROM and the Jaffe Connection Web site http://communication.wadsworth.com/jaffe to review the following concepts, answer the review questions, and complete the suggested activities.

KEY TERMS

delivery (258)

impression management (258)

accessories (259)

sincere (259)

cynical (259)

gestures (259)

emblems (260)

illustrators (260)

adaptors (260)

self-adaptors (260)

object adaptors (261)

alter-adaptors (261)

eye contact (261)

articulation (262)

stress (262)
vocal variations (264)
unfilled pauses (265)
filled (vocalized) pauses (265)
confident style (265)
conversational style (265)
impromptu delivery (267)
memorized delivery (267)

manuscript delivery (268)
extemporaneous delivery (268)
fixed microphones (269)
portable microphones (269)
lavaliere mikes (269)
pickup range (269)
TelePrompTer (270)

APPLICATION AND CRITICAL THINKING EXERCISES

1. The combination of environment, appearance, and mannerisms forms a "front." Whether intentional or unwitting, the front influences the way observers define and interpret the situation. With this in mind, why do some people appear to be something they're not? Why do some speakers appear to be competent or trustworthy, and you later discover they aren't? Have you ever tried to put on a front (anonymous reviewer, 1993)? If so, when? Why? What are the ethical implications of fronts?

2. Write a script for an ad selling one of these products:
   • Used car dealership
   • Perfume
   • Vacation to South America
   • Brand of cola
   Bring your script to class and exchange it with a classmate. Demonstrate the type of vocal variation you would use if you were delivering this ad.

3. If possible, videotape one of your speeches, then watch yourself on video. Specifically pay attention to your gestures, noting your use of emblems, illustrators, or adaptors. Plan specific strategies to improve your gestures, eliminating those that create negative impressions and strengthening those that produce favorable impressions.

   Watch the tape again. This time, evaluate your eye contact. Throughout your speech, notice the way you use your voice. Check for appropriate rate and volume; be alert for pauses, and count the number of "ums" you use, if any. Discuss with a partner from class how you can improve these nonverbal aspects of delivery.

   If you can't videotape a speech, create a worksheet that identifies the elements of delivery mentioned in the chapter. Give it to a classmate just before your speech, and have him or her specifically note nonverbal aspects of your delivery; afterwards, discuss with that person strategies you can use to improve problem areas.

4. With a small group of your classmates, make a set of guidelines for delivery that's appropriate to your classroom's unique culture. For example, would you change the advice about clothing or accessories presented in this chapter? What might you add that's not covered here? (Prepare for this discussion by having some in the group use InfoTrac College Edition to do a PowerTrac search for the subject *public speaking* and others to do a search for *gestures*. Read a couple of articles that discuss speech delivery and list the tips you find there.)

5. Some colleges and universities offer public speaking courses online. With a group of your classmates, discuss the pros and cons of this practice. How might it work? What would be the drawbacks? Would you take such a course? Why or why not? (Prepare for this discussion by logging on to www.alltheweb.com, and searching for all the words *public speaking course online*.)

THE JAFFE CONNECTION WEB SITE

The Jaffe Connection Web site features review questions about the Web links, Stop and Check activities, and InfoTrac College Edition exercises referenced throughout the chapter. You can access this site via your CD-ROM or at http://communication.wadsworth.com/jaffe.

Web Links

14.1 Vocal Variation (page 265)
14.2 Online Public Speaking Courses (page 272)

Stop and Check Activities

14.1 Managing Impressions (page 260)
14.2 Think Critically About Delivery (page 266)

InfoTrac College Edition Exercises

14.1 Using Nonverbal Gestures, Eye Contact, and Body Language (page 262)
14.2 Using Pauses Effectively (page 265)
14.3 Speech Delivery (page 272)

SPEECH INTERACTIVE ON THE JAFFE CONNECTION CD-ROM

Watch examples of memorized, extemporaneous, manuscript, and impromptu speeches under Speech Interactive on the Jaffe Connection CD-ROM. Speech Interactive also features Barbara Bush's commencement speech at Wellesley College and Paul Southwick's speech "Embryo Adoption" discussed in this chapter.

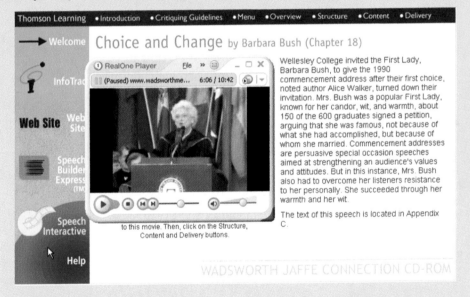

Telling Narratives

THIS CHAPTER WILL HELP YOU

- Explain how narratives function to explain, to persuade, and to entertain
- Apply three tests for narrative reasoning
- List elements of narratives
- Give guidelines for using language effectively in narratives
- Identify the five parts of an exemplum

Detail from "Culture of the Crossroads" Mural ©1998 by Precita Eyes Muralists. Directed by Susan Kelk Cervantes. (McDonald's Building, 24th Street at Mission, SF, CA)

LACE YOURSELF IN JONESBOROUGH, TENNESSEE, on a warm fall day. You're in a tent with hundreds of people listening to a man dressed in overalls narrate the story of his boyhood in Mississippi with a thick southern accent. From the "Tall Tales Tent" down the street and the "Family Tales Tent" next to yours, you occasionally hear bursts of laughter and applause. You are just one of some 8,000 visitors who annually trek to the storytelling festival in this, Tennessee's oldest town. If you can't visit Jonesborough, check your local listings for a closer festival hosted by one of 225-plus storytelling organizations nationally (Watson, 1997). Or turn on public radio and listen to Garrison Keillor's stories of Lake Wobegon on his weekly program, *Prairie Home Companion*.

Storytelling is universal; it has existed in every culture during every era. As a result, we live in a "story-shaped world" (Wicker, 1975). We tell stories about real people and real events, and we make up narratives of imaginary worlds peopled with imaginary characters. Lawyers frame their prosecution or defense arguments as narratives, and politicians present their political visions in story form. Coaches, teachers, members of the clergy, and comedians all routinely tell stories. The scholar Roland Barthes states the importance of narrative in this way:

> The narratives of the world are numberless. . . . Narrative is present in every age, in every place, in every society; it begins with the very history of [humankind] and there nowhere is nor has been a people without narrative. All classes, all human groups, have their narratives, enjoyment of which is very often shared by [others] with different, even opposing, cultural backgrounds. . . . Narrative is international, transhistorical, transcultural: it is simply there, like life itself. (as quoted in Polkinghorne, 1988, p. 14)

Ordinary citizens as well as international leaders use narrative reasoning; it is especially common among women and speakers from ethnic groups such as African Americans and Native Americans (Cortese, 1990). In fact, stories are so much a part of every culture that Walter Fisher (1984a, 1999) calls us **homo narrans,** the storytelling animal. This chapter begins with a discussion of narrative functions, followed by tests for narrative reasoning or merit. The last half of the chapter discusses important components of narratives and concludes with a useful organizational pattern, the exemplum.

Homo Narrans
A Latin phrase that identifies humans as storytelling animals.

Narrative Functions

Storytelling
An oral art form we use to preserve and transmit commonly held ideas, images, motives, and emotions.

Storytelling is "an oral art form for preserving and transmitting ideas, images, motives and emotions with which everyone can identify" (Cassady, 1994, p. 12). Stories tell about the past, highlight human emotions and drives, and illuminate cultural ideals. Tales from a variety of groups illustrate facets of the cultures, identify common themes, and show cultural differences, leading audiences to self-awareness and cross-cultural understandings at the same time (Anokye, 1994). Here we look at three functions of stories: to inform, to persuade, and to entertain.

Informative Narratives

What's it like to go to that college? What happens to the money I donate to a charity? What took place during the *Titanic*'s last hours? Answers to questions such as these often come in the form of narratives. Before you entered college, did you talk to students who explained campus life by telling stories about classes, professors, registration, and social events? From hearing both positive and negative tales, you began to anticipate the good as well as the bad of college life. Hearing about a single mother whose child got medicine because of your charitable donation leaves you satisfied that your gift was used wisely. And the fate of the *Titanic*—whether presented in oral, written, or filmed versions—still fascinates millions of

Storytelling is universally used to pass on important cultural ideas. Here, Kitbidin Atamkulov is recounting the epic tale of Manas, the Kirghiz hero, to his entranced listeners—both young and old.

Franz Lanting/Minden Pictures

people globally. The scholar Didier Coste (1989) says that our narratives present our culture's understandings of natural, social, and ultimate things.

Explaining Natural Phenomena

We use stories to explain natural phenomena. Why are cats and dogs enemies? The Kaluli tribe from Papua New Guinea explains this in a myth. Where do babies come from? Parents dust off the "birds and the bees" story for a new generation. How did the world come into being? Scientists across international borders weave together facts and ideas into narrative accounts such as the big bang theory. When combined with evolutionary narratives, these accounts can profoundly affect our perceptions of the world (Spangler & Thompson, 1992). Of course, many cultural groups modify or reject outright these scientific stories; instead, they offer explanations (often irreconcilable) of their own. Did the defendant kill the victim? Prosecutors and defense lawyers offer competing explanations that jury members and onlookers must weigh and compare, finally accepting the murder story that makes the most sense to them.

Explaining Society and Institutions

Stories also explain how cultural institutions or structures came into being. Think of your history texts: They're peopled with characters who faced dramatic choices, overcame hardships, invented useful as well as harmful machines, and made mistakes. These stories explain the founding of our country, its wars, blameworthy scenes of slavery as well as praiseworthy scenes of the Constitutional Convention. (Naturally, history books from other countries have different explanations of some of the same events.) Frequently, historical facts are obscured by myths, and a variety of scholars offer alternative explanations. For example, "Afrocentric" historians and feminist "her-storians" tell different narratives from those told by "malestream" scholars. Log on to InfoTrac College Edition and look for an article called "Stone Camels and Clear Springs." This drama, which features audience participation and feedback as it retells the history of the Salar people, can be found in the journal *Asian Folklore Studies* (1990).

Organizations and groups as well as cultures have unique stories that explain their history and traditions. Your college has a story, as does your family. Couples relate the saga of their relationship in story form (Sternberg, 1998). An InfoTrac College Edition search for the key word *storytelling* yielded hits that described narratives in courtrooms, social work settings, business boardrooms, churches, health care facilities, and ceramics studios. One hit led to a speech by a communication professional whose job involves "corporate story-telling"; put simply, he helps men and women tell their organizations' stories in clear and compelling ways (Gresh, 1998).

Explaining Ultimate Things

Another genre of philosophical and religious stories attempts to explain ultimate realities—to answer such questions as "Who are we?" "What is our purpose on earth?" "What happens after death?" "How should I live a moral life?" These stories explain the rituals that give meaning to religious adherents, rituals that are usually based in historical events. Jewish people, for instance, narrate the story of the Maccabees as they light Hanukkah candles. Muslims tell of the Prophet's flight to Medina during the fast of Ramadan. Christians remember the death and resurrection of Jesus as they celebrate Easter. In short, religious beliefs and practices are grounded in stories that followers have preserved over generations, stories that give ultimate meaning to the lives of adherents. (The Diversity in Practice feature explores narrative traditions in Native American cultures.) Listening to stories is one way we learn about processes and concepts, a way we answer our own questions and tell others about nature, society, and ultimate things.

DIVERSITY IN PRACTICE
NATIVE AMERICAN NARRATIVE TRADITIONS

SEVERAL NATIVE groups of North America differentiate among stories in the following ways (Bierhorst, 1985):

Eskimos distinguish between *old* stories and *young* stories.
Winnebago natives tell both *waikan* (sacred) or *worak* (narrated) tales.
Pawnees differentiate between *false* stories, which are fiction, nonfiction, or a mixture of both, and *true* stories, which are the old, sacred tales.
Tlingit natives tell *tlagu* stories (of the long ago) and *ch'kalnik* tales (it really happened).

You can see from these labels that cultural groups distinguish between different kinds of stories. Some ancient stories, called **myths**, communicate the group's answers to the ultimate questions of life; they differ from stories that aim to entertain or serve less significant functions. For this reason, R. C. Rowland (1990) calls them the most powerful narratives—they are the stories people use to define the good society and to solve problems that are not subject to rational solutions.

For examples of Native American stories, log on to the Internet and search for the exact phrase *Native American tales*. Read two tales that interest you personally from two different tribes. How are they alike? How are they different?

Myths
Powerful ancient stories told to communicate a culture's answer to ultimate questions about life's purpose and meaning.

Persuasive Narratives

Does a low carbohydrate diet help people lose weight?

> Yes. My mother's been on one for three months and she's lost 35 pounds; let me tell you about her lifelong struggle to control her weight . . .

How should children treat other people's belongings?

> Once upon a time, a little girl named Goldilocks went to the home of three bears . . .

Do UFOs exist?

Well, one day the most interesting thing happened to me! It was like this . . .

Persuasive stories motivate listeners to choose some behaviors and avoid others, to act and to keep on acting—to volunteer their time on a regular basis, for instance. Stories (about UFOs, for example) also convince people that something is or is not true. Finally, narratives present hopeful visions of the future that audiences will want to aspire to and bleak scenarios they'll want to avoid.

Motivational Narratives

You have undoubtedly heard stories that provide models or examples of successful people (who behave in certain ways or adhere to social norms and values) or people who fail (who suffer the consequences of socially unacceptable actions). Either way, these **exemplary narratives** persuade people within a culture to choose some actions and avoid others. These examples illustrate the exemplary function.

Exemplary Narratives
Stories that provide examples or models of culturally appropriate or inappropriate ways to live.

- Clara "Mother" Hale opened Hale House in Harlem to care for drug babies and babies with AIDS. Her story models what ordinary people can do when they decide to fight injustice.
- Dave Roever is badly scarred as a result of his Vietnam injuries. His personal testimonial about facing adversity provides a positive model for others in difficult circumstances.
- The fictional character Pinocchio serves to caution children not to lie.
- A personal story about a spending spree and your resulting credit problems motivates your listeners to use their credit cards wisely.

Exemplary narratives told publicly are powerful partly because they flesh out culturally admired traits that can be quite abstract. For instance, what is courage? Go hear Dave Dravecky tell his life story. In the prime of his baseball career, this athlete lost his pitching arm and shoulder to cancer. Or listen to one of the Navajo code talkers tell about his experiences in the Marine Corps during World War II. The lessons these men learned through their experiences are models for others who face life challenges of their own.

Stories model actions such as hard work by people like Yolanda Tavera, who grew up as a migrant child following the crops but now coordinates migrant education for an entire school district. Motivational speakers describe entrepreneurs such as Bill Gates, who dropped out of Harvard and founded the Microsoft Corporation. Although the characters change, the plot is similar in every case: the people begin with little except vision and perseverance and end up successful in their fields. Others would be wise to follow their example.

Not all stories model how we should live; some provide a cautionary message, showing us how *not* to behave. These narratives are also powerful because of their emotional content. A police officer tells horror stories about teenagers whose careless driving killed carloads of innocent people. Her hope is that the emotional impact of the stories will influence beginning drivers to take care behind the wheel. Health professionals tell frightening tales of people who practiced unsafe sex, with dire consequences. The purpose of each story is to influence people to avoid specific behaviors.

Speakers also use stories to influence listeners' beliefs, actions, or attitudes. In fact, narrative reasoning is so effective that Aristotle classified it as a type of **deliberative speaking,** the kind of speaking that gives people information and motivates them to make wise decisions regarding future courses of action. Persuasive stories function in two ways. They provide a rationale *for* a particular course of action, a proof of its *necessity*. At other times, they provide good arguments *against* a particular course of action.

Deliberative Speaking
A form of speaking that gives people the information and motivation they need to make wise decisions regarding future courses of action.

The late James Nahkai Jr. was one of many Navajo code talkers who narrated their true-life adventures in World War II. These heroic Navajo Marines created an unbreakable code based on their native language and helped win the war in the Pacific. A 2002 movie, *Wind Talkers*, tells a fictionalized (and sometimes inaccurate) version of their story.

Photo © Kenji Kawano

Some stories are unpleasant to hear, for their telling exposes a societal wrong that needs to be righted. Speakers often use emotionally involving narratives to motivate others to intervene, to make a difference, to improve the lives of the needy. Here is a persuasive narrative told by the founder of a volunteer network that cooks and delivers more than 1,200 meals daily to needy people.

> I hugged the heavy bag of donated groceries and began to climb the five long flights of stairs to Richard's studio apartment. I remember feeling a strong sense of satisfaction knowing that I was bringing help to a dying man who was all alone. That satisfied glow disappeared the instant I saw him.
>
> Richard lay propped up in a bed, his swollen features all distorted by AIDS-related disease. He hadn't eaten in two days, so when I approached his bedside he eagerly grabbed the grocery bag. I watched him reach again and again in the bag to find something, anything, that he could eat . . . now. Bread mix, oatmeal, canned beans, a box of macaroni and cheese—there was nothing ready to eat and no way he could get out of bed to cook. He finally gave up.
>
> Then he looked up at me still clutching the empty bag, the useless assortment of ingredients strewn across the bed and floor. For a moment we just stared at one another. Then I made a promise I wasn't sure how I would keep. But I promised to bring him meals for as long as he needed, and I vowed that no one else in the same situation would ever have to face the unthinkable combination of AIDS and starvation. That was nearly seven years and 300,000 meals ago. (Ganga Stone, n.d.)

Ms. Stone tells this personal narrative with persuasive intentions. If she can effectively persuade listeners to identify with both Richard and herself, a woman determined to change a negative situation, they may begin to look for personal ways to relieve the suffering of people like Richard. If they become concerned enough, they may tell the story to others, inviting more and more people to attack such problems.

Not only do persuasive stories change individuals, they also contribute to changes in policies on wider levels. On the campus level, for example, stories about a series of muggings have convinced administrators to establish policies that correct the problem. On the national level, widely circulated tales about oil spills led to tighter regulations for oil tankers. International tales of terrorist groups' activities led the United States to seek out and destroy terrorist cells in many parts of the world.

Visionary Narratives

Narratives do more than recount the past or the present. Science fiction, for instance, paints bleak scenarios of out-of-control technology or, conversely, depicts a bright future if machines are harnessed and controlled. Stories about the future can give hope, as shown when a physician comforts parents with an "after surgery this child will walk again" narrative. On a more mundane level, investors have poured millions of dollars into stocks based not on past earnings but on visions of future wealth.

Inspiring narratives also suggest ideals that go beyond your listeners' current beliefs and experiences, confronting them with possibilities and visions, expanding their understandings of themselves and their lives (Kirkwood, 1992). Through the **rhetoric of possibility,** you show what might be, and you move others to envision a future that they then make real. A famous example is Dr. Martin Luther King Jr.'s 1963 call to be a nation in which all are judged "not by the color of their skin, but by the content of their character." His vision inspires us to this day, but it's still not a reality, and we must continue to work together to make that vision come true. To see how vital the vision remains, log on to the Internet and search for the exact phrase *I Have a Dream*. Follow links to a couple of sites from the more than 20,000 hits you will get.

Rhetoric of Possibility
Points out what can be, not what is.

Persuasive stories can influence a few people or millions. They act as examples of both wise and unwise behaviors; they provide a rationale *for* or *against* a policy, and they present a vision of what might be.

Entertaining Narratives

Let's face it: not all stories are full of profound meanings. Sometimes we tell them just to relax and have a good time. For example, storyteller Jackie Torrence (1998) calls some stories "Jump Tales," for they end with a "BOO!" and we tell them because we love the shivers they give. Children's stories, urban legends, and television sitcoms are examples of narratives that feature unusual or quirky characters in unusual or quirky situations. Humorous stories also come in the form of extended jokes or in exaggerated situations carried to the extreme (Cassady, 1994).

Entertaining stories are told in gatherings large and small. Friends tell friends the funny things they saw or did during the day. Parents and grandparents tell silly stories to bored kids during road trips; campers entertain one another as the campfire dies down. You've probably told your share of entertaining stories to at least a few people. Log on to the Internet and search for *silly stories* or *jokes*, for *scary stories, urban legends,* or *campfire tales*. The number of hits you get in each category should give you some idea of the popularity of entertaining stories. (www.alltheweb.com turned up more than one million hits for *jokes!*)

The great rhetoric scholar Kenneth Burke (1983) summarizes the variety of narratives we use as "the imaginative, the visionary, the sublime, the ridiculous, the eschatological (as with . . . Purgatory . . . [or] the Transmigration of Souls), the satirical, every detail of every single science or speculation, even every bit of gossip . . ." (p. 859). We are indeed storytelling animals.

STOP AND CHECK

YOUR NARRATIVE PURPOSES

Of all the stories you've recounted within the last twenty-four-hour period, estimate the percentage you told for the following purposes:

_____ to inform
_____ to persuade
_____ to entertain

Do you think these percentages will change when you're out of college and working full time in your chosen career? If so, what kind(s) of stories will you probably tell more? What kind(s) will you tell less frequently? Discuss with a small group of your classmates how you will probably use narratives to do the following in your career area:

• Explain natural things
• Explain organizational or social realities
• Explain ultimate things
• Motivate people to believe or act in specific ways
• Present a vision of the future
• Entertain an audience

Evaluating Narrative Reasoning

Stories aren't equally valuable, and we need to test them to see if they are sensible and worthy of being told. Some are true and honest; others are false, mistaken, or downright lies (Burke, 1983). But how do we judge them? And if we're faced with competing narratives, how do we weigh and decide which is best? To answer these questions, narrative theorists offer three major tests of narrative logic (Fisher, 1999).

Narrative Coherence
Deciding if a narrative is understandable or sensible.

1. Does the story have **narrative coherence**? That is, is it understandable? Does it hang together in a logical way? Do the events within the story itself follow one another in a predictable sequence? Do the characters act and interact in ways that are probable, given their personalities and cultural backgrounds? Or do some things seem out of character or out of order?

Narrative Fidelity
Testing if the narrative faithfully represents how the world works.

2. Is the story a true or faithful representative of what you know about the world and the way it works? Fisher (1984a, 1984b) terms this **narrative fidelity.** In other words, does the story make sense within the larger cultural framework? If it is a myth, folktale, or hypothetical story, does it contain important truths that demonstrate appropriate ways to live?

Narrative Merit
Testing whether or not a narrative is worth telling.

3. Does the **narrative** have **merit**? Does it deserve to be told? Is the message important or worthwhile? Does it draw conclusions or motivate people to behave in positive ways that result in ethical outcomes for individuals and for society as a whole? Put simply, it's important to evaluate the desirability of passing on the narrative.

We weigh priorities when we choose whether or not to repeat a story; one that creates problems for the individuals involved and their families can provide a good example for other people. For instance, members of the press discussed the appropriateness of reporting that two California high school girls, who were kidnapped, but rescued when police surrounded and killed their attacker, had been raped. (A police officer eventually confirmed the crime.) The girls themselves chose to describe their ordeal to *People Magazine*, hoping that their story would help take the stigma out of rape (Crary, 2002). Gossip about a political candidate's marriage or the suicide attempts of a public figure's child also pose questions of narrative merit. If details of a person's private life are merely entertaining, many people refuse to relate them; however, if the story reveals a person's character or tendency to behave negatively, it might be appropriate to tell.

Good stories aren't necessarily true—fiction has its place—but stories that are blatantly false and result in harm to others are wrong to tell. History provides many examples of leaders who spread lies, with disastrous consequences. Here's one: In the Middle Ages, people circulated narratives about Jews poisoning the water supply of villages, stories that resulted in the murder of many Jewish people and produced irreversible negative consequences on individuals and on society as a whole.

Animals are sometimes the characters in stories—especially in children's tales where they inform, entertain, or persuade children to act in culturally appropriate ways.

Guidelines for Narratives

Because you have been hearing and telling stories all your life, the elements of the narrative schema are probably quite familiar. This section covers five important elements of a good story: the purpose, characters, sequence, plot, and language.

Identify Your Purpose

If you give a narrative speech or tell a narrative as part of a larger speech, consider your purpose carefully. What function do you want the narrative to fulfill? Is its major purpose to inform, persuade, or entertain? Will it present a vision of possibilities that your audience has not yet considered? Remember that even when a story is mainly told for entertainment purposes, it generally conveys a lesson or point.

Develop the Characters

It almost goes without saying that stories contain characters. Many narratives involve fictional characters such as animals or natural objects that are personified or given human traits—for instance, talking trees. Moreover, obviously imaginary characters such as dragons, talking train engines, genies in bottles, and other fanciful characters are widely used to convey important cultural values. Aesop's fables, for instance, have featured animals to communicate western cultural wisdom for more than 2,000 years. Coyote stories, similarly, communicate the wisdom of various Native American groups.

Depending on your purpose, stories about actual people who act—meaning they move, speak, form relationships, and interact with others—are often more effective. These characters are motivated by their distinctive personality traits, ethnic and religious background, educational experiences, and social background, and these factors influence their choices.

Develop the Plot

Characters in a good story face some sort of challenge that tests their assumptions, values, or actions. The way they respond to the challenges and the resulting changes in their lives form the **plot** or action of the narrative. During this period of change, natural processes,

Plot
The story's action.

such as growing up, occur. The characters also meet physical, psychological, and economic challenges. They have accidents; they begin and end relationships; they lose their possessions in a tragic fire, and so on. How they deal with these challenges provides the point of the story.

Select Vivid Language

Narrative speaking requires careful attention to language. Vivid word choices and details bring the story to life and enable your listeners to feel as if they are there. Detailed descriptions in stories do more than simply convey information. They help create the scene and provide a sense of authenticity by providing specific names, places, and times that meet your listeners' psychological preference to set events in space and time (Tannen, 1989). Consider these features of style as you plan the language of your narratives: use of details, constructed dialogue, and listing.

Provide Detailed Descriptions

Details are important in several places. At the beginning, when you orient the audience to the plot of the story, include enough descriptive material so your audience will have a sense of the context. When you come to the key action, provide important details your audience can use to clearly understand the changes taking place within the characters. Finally, use a cluster of details in the climax of the story to drive home your main point.

Tony goes from school to school, telling stories in both English and Spanish. He also advises children to tell their own stories vividly by providing three details about the characters, the setting, the problem, and the solution.

The opening details function to set the story in a time and a place. For this reason, mythical stories often begin with the formulaic phrase, "Once upon a time in a faraway land." Listeners who have heard fairy tales immediately pull up their mental "fairy tale schema" and listen to the story through that filter. Setting a truelife narrative in a specific place and time functions to draw listeners into the world of the story. A college student who started her narrative, "When I was a junior in high school, I was enrolled in a very small private school in the mountain country of Montana," immediately activated her listeners' "personal experiences" schema. Regardless of the actuality of the tale, details about the setting help listeners place themselves psychologically in the story's space.

A word of caution: take care to include just the right amount of detail. Certain details are vital, but others are irrelevant for a variety of reasons. First, there may be *too many details*. Just ask a child to tell you about a movie he saw, and you will probably get bogged down in details, maybe even missing the point of the story entirely, because young storytellers don't always separate *relevant* details from *interesting* ones. In addition, details can be inappropriate if they reveal more than listeners want to know. For instance, narrators can disclose intimate or horrifying information that causes listeners to focus on the details and miss the point. For these reasons, evaluate details carefully in light of your specific audience, then edit out irrelevant or inappropriate material. Watch the CNN clip "Bilingual Storyteller" on the CD provided with this text, and notice the way Tony uses details to make his stories more vivid.

Construct Dialogue

Created or **constructed dialogue** between major characters adds realism to a story. By adding vocal variety that conveys the personalities and the emotions of the characters during your delivery, you further increase not only your involvement but your listener's involvement as well. For example, compare these two ways to report actions:

> He told me to move my car, but I didn't, because I was only going to park for a moment. The next thing I knew, he threatened me.

Constructed Dialogue
Created conversation between characters that adds realism to a story.

Contrast the different effect it would have on your audience if you create a dialogue, then use different "voices," volume, and rate for each character, like this:

> He rolled down his car window and yelled, "Hey, kid, move your pile of junk!"
>
> I turned down my radio and explained through my open window, "I'll just be here a minute. I'm waiting for my mother."
>
> He jerked open his car door, stomped over to my car, leaned into my window and said slowly through clenched teeth, "I said, (pause) 'Move . . . your . . . pile . . . of . . . junk, *kid!*'"

As you can see, creating a scene with vivid, memorable dialogue is far more likely to involve your listeners in your dilemma, causing them to place themselves in the scene with you. By increasing listeners' emotional involvement in the story, you keep their attention and have greater potential for communicating the point of your speech.

Create Lists

Lists increase rapport with an audience because they introduce specific areas of commonality with the speaker. For instance, saying "I packed my bags and checked twice to see if I had forgotten anything" gets across the message, but specific details that are familiar to fellow travelers enliven it, as this example illustrates:

> As I packed for Europe, I was afraid I would forget something vital. I looked through my bag for the seventh time. Toothpaste? Check. Toothbrush? Check. Toilet paper? (I'd been told to bring my own.) Check. Deodorant? Yep. Yet something seemed to be missing—as I was to discover in an isolated village in Germany.

Again, the details involve listeners actively as they create mental images for each item in the list. As you can see, the language of narrative does make a difference. Because narrative is one way of appealing to emotions, it is vital that your audience is involved in the story, and word choices that increase audience involvement make your story more powerful and memorable.

STOP AND CHECK
ANALYZING A FOLKTALE

Log on to the Internet, using a search engine like www.alltheweb.com and search for the term *folklore*. Download a folktale from another culture. Compare the way it's constructed with the guidelines presented here. What is the purpose of the story? Are the characters real or imaginary? What details provide clues to their personality and motivations? What is the plot of the story? How does the storyteller incorporate vivid language, use of details, dialogue, and lists? How is the story similar to one that's typical of narratives from your culture? Is it different? If so, how?

You can complete this analysis online under Stop and Check Activities for Chapter 15 at the Jaffe Connection Web site. Bring your analysis to class and prepare to discuss your conclusions with a small group of your classmates.

The Exemplum Pattern

Exemplum
An organizational pattern in which a narrative is used to illustrate a quotation.

A common narrative pattern, used by speech teachers for hundreds of years, is the **exemplum** (McNally, 1969). It has five elements. When you use this schema, include all five elements; without them, the narrative is just another narrative. The five parts of the exemplum follow one another in this pattern:

1. State a quotation or proverb.
2. Identify and explain the author or source of the proverb or the quotation.
3. Rephrase the proverb in your own words.
4. Tell a story that illustrates the quotation or proverb.
5. Apply the quotation or proverb to the audience.

Select your narrative from personal experiences, from historical events, or from episodes in the life of someone else. Choose one that represents, illustrates, or explains something important to you, perhaps a turning point in your life. Identify a lesson or point to your story, then find a quotation that supports this point. You can use a commonly quoted saying, such as "silence is golden," or you can go to sources of quotations (listed topically and by author) that are found in the reference section of the library or online. As Chapter 7 pointed out, a subject index such as www.yahoo.com links you to many such sources including *Bartlett's Familiar Quotations*, *Classic Quotations*, and *Words of Women*.

In his classroom exemplum, Paul Lee used his personal experience of immigrating to the United States to reinforce the importance of all citizens working to create a better society. Here is a summary of his major points.

1. *Quotation*: "Ask not what your country can do for you; ask rather what you can do for your country."
2. *Source*: President John Kennedy, the thirty-fifth President of the United States, said this in his Inaugural Address.
3. *Paraphrase*: In other words, instead of taking for granted the things our country has to offer, we should actively seek opportunities to improve our country.
4. *Personal narrative*: Immigrating to the United States from Hong Kong posed many challenges and hardships as the family learned a new language and customs. Eventually, family members proudly took the oath of citizenship—with all the rights and privileges that it brought—before a presiding judge who welcomed the new citizens with Kennedy's challenging words.
5. *Application*: Everyone—both native born and immigrants—should reflect on the privilege of being in the United States; each listener should think of some way to make the country better for all.

In summary, an exemplum builds around a quotation that you develop by telling a narrative. This pattern is useful when your speech goal is to reinforce cultural values. The CD that comes with your text provides examples of two narrative speeches: Jessica Howard's exemplum and Gail Grobey's persuasive narrative, both of which are reprinted at the end of this chapter.

Summary

In every society narrative is present as a form of reasoning or sense making. Narratives both reflect and shape cultural beliefs and values, and hearing narratives from other cultures highlights both commonalities and differences between groups. Narratives in all cultures function in three ways: to inform, to persuade, and to entertain. Explanatory narratives provide answers for why and how things are the way they are. Exemplary narratives are stories with a moral or point that listeners should—or should not—imitate. Other persuasive narratives provide reasons to do or *not* to do a particular action. In addition, narratives help us envision possibilities that we had not imagined before. Finally, some narratives are just plain fun, and we listen to them to be entertained.

Some stories are better than others, but every good story should be coherent, it should have fidelity, meaning that it represents some aspect of the real world, and it should be worthy of being told. To evaluate a story's merit, consider its effect on society, its effect on individuals, and its overall truthfulness about life.

When you tell stories, work on five elements: purpose, characters, sequence, plot, and language. Vivid language is especially important because it brings characters to life and makes the action more compelling, causing listeners to identify with more elements of the story. The exemplum is an excellent way to organize a narrative speech that is constructed around a quotation. It begins with the quotation, provides information about the source, and paraphrases the saying. An illustrative story forms most of the speech that concludes with a stated lesson or moral to the story.

JAFFE ONLINE CONNECTION JAFFE ONLINE CONNECTION

Use your CD-ROM and the Jaffe Connection Web site http://communication.wadsworth.com/jaffe to review the following concepts, answer the review questions, and complete the suggested activities.

KEY TERMS

homo narrans (276)
storytelling (276)
myths (278)
exemplary narratives (279)
deliberative speaking (279)
rhetoric of possibility (281)

narrative coherence (282)
narrative fidelity (282)
narrative merit (282)
plot (283)
constructed dialogue (285)
exemplum (286)

APPLICATION AND CRITICAL THINKING EXERCISES

1. What narratives do you use to explain the world of nature? The social world? Your family? Other groups to which you belong? The ultimate meanings in life? Do your stories ever clash with the narratives of others? If so, what do you do about these differences?

2. Share with a group of classmates a few examples of exemplary narratives you heard while you were growing up. In what ways were they intended to influence your behaviors? How successful were they?

3. In what settings have you heard inspiring life stories? Have you ever shared your personal saga of overcoming some challenge? If so, describe the occasion. Where might you give one in the future?

4. Think of stories that you have only heard orally. Who are the "legends" in your family, your sports team, your religious group, living group, or university? What lessons do their stories provide? What values or actions do they help you remember and perpetuate?

5. Many speeches are given in the form of a narrative, or an extended narrative takes up a significant part of the speech. Chief Joseph's speech in Appendix C is one example. Read through it to see how he uses a story to drive home his point.

6. The exemplum pattern is useful in a variety of settings. With a small group of your classmates, sketch out themes and suggest the types of supporting narratives that would be appropriate on each of the following occasions:
   - A sports award banquet
   - A luncheon meeting of a club such as Rotary or Kiwanis
   - A religious youth group meeting
   - A scholarship presentation ceremony
   - A Fourth of July celebration
   - A keynote address to a conference focusing on issues relevant to female physicians

7. Do a PowerTrac search on InfoTrac College Edition for the journal *Asian Folklore Studies*, and skim an article in it. Suggested titles: "Myths of the Czech Gypsies," by N. and J. Pavelcik (April 2001), or "Hunters' Lore in Nuristan," by A. Degener (June 2001). Briefly summarize the article to share with your classmates.

8. On InfoTrac College Edition, do a PowerTrac search for the key word *storytelling*. Read a couple of articles and look for tips that can help you tell stories more effectively.

9. Do a PowerTrac search for the journal *Vital Speeches*, and look for the narrative speech entitled "Storytelling: The Soul of an Enterprise" by Sean Gresh (December 1, 1998). Read the speech (the story of his life and career choices), then decide how effective you think it was with the specific audience in the particular situation.

10. Go to the National Storytelling Festival's (Jonesborough, Tennessee) home page www.storytellingfestival.net and follow the link to Featured Tellers. Read about three storytellers who represent diverse perspectives.

THE JAFFE CONNECTION WEB SITE

The Jaffe Connection Web site features review questions about the Web links, Stop and Check activities, and InfoTrac College Edition exercises referenced throughout this chapter. You can access this site via your CD-ROM or at http://communication.wadsworth.com/jaffe.

Web Links

15.1 Native American Stories (page 278)
15.2 Entertaining Stories (page 281)
15.3 Analyzing a Folktale: Locate and Compare a Folktale from a Different Culture (page 285)
15.4 Search a Subject Index for Quotation Sources (page 286)
15.5 National Storytelling Festival Featured Storytellers (page 288)

Stop and Check Activities

15.1 Your Narrative Purposes (page 282)
15.2 Analyzing a Folktale (page 285)

InfoTrac College Edition Exercises

15.1 Narratives in *Asian Folklore Studies* (pages 277, 288)
15.2 Corporate Storytelling (page 278)
15.3 Tips for Storytelling (page 288)
15.4 The Story of Sean Gresh (page 288)

SPEECH INTERACTIVE ON THE JAFFE CONNECTION CD-ROM

Watch and listen to the following exemplum by Jessica Howard and the narrative speech by Gail Grobey and answer the questions for analysis under Speech Interactive on your Jaffe Connection CD-ROM. You can also access the CNN clip "Bilingual Storyteller" under Speech Interactive for Chapter 15 on your CD-ROM.

EXPEMPLUM
by Jessica Howard

Jessica Howard's (2000) classroom exemplum built on her personal experiences as big sister to a Down syndrome child. Here are her main points.

Josh Nauman

1. **Quotation.** "When one door of happiness closes, another opens; but often we look so long at the closed door that we do not see the one which has opened for us."

2. **Source.** Helen Keller was born in 1880; nineteen months later she contracted a fever that left her blind and deaf. When she was seven, her tutor, Anne Sullivan, taught Helen to communicate through sign language, Braille, and other alternative methods of sharing ideas. Helen learned to speak and to read lips using her hands. She eventually graduated from several colleges with high honors. Throughout her life, she overcame obstacles in an extraordinary way, never letting her disabilities thwart her ambitions.

3. **Paraphrase.** Ms. Keller's life shows that when circumstances close one pleasant option, it's easy to focus on the loss and fail to see possibilities that open up in another area.

4. **Narrative.** Before I turned thirteen, my mom told us she was pregnant with her fourth child. We three girls teased her because she was thirty-eight years old, but deep down we were all excited. Unfortunately, complications arose and tests revealed that the baby was a boy who had Down syndrome.
I could tell you in my own words how I felt, but I came across a metaphor by Emily Kingsley, mother of a child with a disability, that captured my emotions.

    Kingsley says a pregnancy is like planning a trip to Italy. An excited traveler buys guidebooks and makes plans to see art and buildings and remnants from ancient Rome. She even learns handy Italian phrases. After months of eager planning the day arrives, and she packs her bags and gets on the plane. Several hours later the plane lands, not in Italy, but in Holland where she discovers she must stay! Holland is not a terrible place, but this traveler wanted to go to Italy, and it takes her a while to adjust. Pretty soon, though, she gets guidebooks and begins to explore the slower-paced, less flashy country she's in. She notices the windmills, the tulips, the Rembrandts. Her friends are busy, coming and going from Italy—bragging about their wonderful time there, and she listens longingly as they share experiences she will never have. Her pain at the loss of her dream never leaves, but she learns to enjoy the special, very lovely things Holland offers.

    That is exactly what it was like when my brother was born. Our family knew what it was like to have "normal" children, so having one with Down syndrome was different. It wasn't terrible, just different. We love him with all our hearts; he's adorable and loving and has a happiness and contentment that I envy. These past six years with my brother have taught me so much about not taking good health for granted, about what's really important in life, and about how much our perspective can change our attitudes.

5. **Lesson.** Our lives confront us with many happenings we don't want; often plans change because of some outside force we cannot control. Learning to roll with the punches you're thrown in life is a great quality. In the long run, God has everything under control, so if your plans don't work out, don't spend your life mourning your loss. "When one door of happiness closes, another opens; but often we look so long at the closed door that we do not see the one which has opened for us."

SPANKING? THERE'S GOTTA BE A BETTER WAY
by Gail Grobey

Gail gave this narrative speech in an argumentation class. Besides being a narrative speech, it's an example of invitational rhetoric (see Chapter 18); she invited her classmates, many of whom disagreed with her claim that spanking is wrong, to understand her perspective by telling this story.

My daughter Celeste [displaying the photograph] has always been a rather precocious child. She's picked up all kinds of concepts and language from listening to her future-English-teacher mom talk and has learned how to apply them. When given the opportunity, she'll wax lyrical in her piping four-year-old voice at some length about the Joker's role as antagonist in *Batman* and how Robin functions as a foil or why the conflict between the villain and the hero is necessary. She's constantly telling me when I'm stressed about school or work or the mess in the kitchen, "Mom, just breathe. Just find your center and relax in it."

Yes, she's a precocious child, but this time let me place the emphasis on child. Her temper is fierce and daunting, like her mother's! She can get very physical in her anger, striking out destructively at anything she can get her hands on. She can also be manipulative (which is really more like her father)!

At times, my patience is driven to the very end, and so I can understand why some parents turn to spanking. There are times when there seems to be no other alternative, when I can't think of any other way to get through to this completely irrational being. And there are a lot of things about me that would make me the ideal spanking parent: my temper, my impatience, my obsessive need to control. And after all, I was a spanked child. But when she was born, and I saw that tiny body and the light in her eyes, I made a conscious commitment never to strike my child.

As she's grown, that commitment has been challenged. About a year ago, she pranced into my room chanting in the universal language of preschoolers, "Look what I found! You can't have it." I looked down and in her hand was a large, inviting, bright red pill with irresistible yellow writing on it. I recognized it at once as one of my mother's blood pressure pills, and quite naturally, my first impulse was to snatch it.

I also recognized, however, that she was looking for just such a reaction from me. She had lately begun establishing clear patterns of button-pushing. I would say, "Give it to me." To which she would naturally reply, "No!"

And so it would begin. She was prepared to throw and fully enjoy the temper tantrum that would inevitably follow and tax me to the end of my patience. I repressed my impulse to aggressively take command and instead, bent down on one knee and asked her with casual awe, "Wow. Where'd you find it?"

She eyed me suspiciously, backing up. She said, "On the kitchen floor. It's mine. I'm keeping it."

All I could think of was how easy it would be to tip her over the edge into a major fight. (The big ones always begin over something small and silly—me attempting to exercise control over something and her asserting that this is not acceptable. We both get lost in our rage.) It would have been so easy to just grab the pill and move into fight mode. But I held firm to creativity over violence.

"Oh, Celeste," I said, "thank you so much. You are a real hero. You found that dangerous pill and picked it up before the dogs could eat it and make themselves sick. You saved them! What a hero!"

Gail puts a picture of Celeste on the table she's standing behind and introduces the characters, her daughter Celeste and herself, using vivid details. Listeners have mental images of the child and her relationship to her mother early in the speech.

Because she knows her audience pretty much disagrees with her position, she shows that she understands their frustration and their desire to deal with children who are angry and obnoxious.

Here is the point of climax, and Gail again clusters vivid details that enliven the scene. Her use of constructed dialogue, delivered with the vocal variations that would actually occur in the scene, keep the audience's attention.

Celeste "frames" the issue in terms of ownership and control, and Gail tries to see things from her child's perspective.

Here is an excellent example of re-sourcement (see Chapter 18) in which Gail reframes the discovery of the pill as a safety issue.

The change on her face was instant. She voluntarily and proudly relinquished the pill and dashed off to tell her grandma what a noble deed she'd just done. I remember saying out loud, "Whew. That was close!"

It seems like such a small thing, but I see it as representative of the greater whole. It's one of my proudest moments as a parent: Celeste and I both walked away with the feeling that we had accomplished something important. She experienced a boost in self-esteem, and I ended up holding firm to my commitment and reinforcing to myself my belief that there is always an alternative way to deal with children, no matter how small the situation or problem. One never needs to resort to violence.

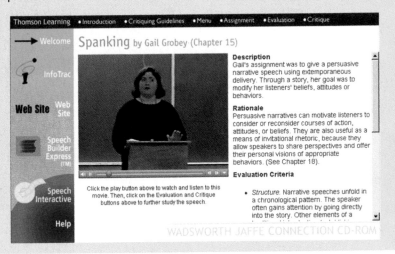

Gail's narrative provides an excellent example that others can use as a model for nonviolent childrearing. Choosing to tell a narrative, rather than building a case with examples, statistics, and other evidence, was probably more effective with her specific audience.

Informative Speaking

THIS CHAPTER WILL HELP YOU

■ Describe the global importance of information

■ Analyze an audience's knowledge of your subject

■ Create several types of informative speeches including demonstrations and instructions, descriptions, reports, and explanations

■ Use guidelines to make your informative speeches more effective

"Balance of Power" Mural ©1996 by Susan Kelk Cervantes, Juana Alicia, and Raul Martinez. (Mission Street Playground, Swimming Pool, Linda at 19th Street, SF, CA)

ALK INTO A THRIVING CORPORATION and you will see employees giving reports, providing instructions, demonstrating techniques and products, and updating their coworkers on the latest information related to their organization. Enter a school and you'll see students and teachers making announcements, discussing facts, defining terms, and explaining complex concepts. Now, take a moment and picture yourself fifteen years down the road. Where are you working? What instructions or directions are vital to your success? What information will you pass along to your coworkers or the public? What new information do you need to be healthier, more productive, or happier? Here are a few ways that people typically speak to inform:

- A member of the student government reports a committee's findings about the possibility of bringing a well-known entertainer to campus.
- A nurse demonstrates to first-time fathers how to wash a newborn.
- A teen explains to younger students some strategies for saying no to sex.
- Accountants present the annual audit to a client company's board of directors.

This chapter first examines the global importance of information. It then turns to audience analysis and distinguishes four levels of audience knowledge that should affect your informative strategies. Next, it describes demonstrations and instructions, descriptions, reports and explanations and includes skeletal outlines of speeches in these categories. General guidelines for informative speeches conclude the chapter.

Information Is Important Globally

Information Age
Thanks to technological innovations, more information is available today than in any other era.

Electronic Superhighways
Television, telephones, and computers linked up through networks.

Information Explosion
A metaphor comparing rapid information output to a bomb that scatters fragments of disconnected pieces in all directions.

Information Overload
A human response of being overwhelmed by the sheer amount of available data.

We are living in the **Information Age.** This means that a greater number of people, nationally and globally, have access to more information than any other humans throughout history have had. It also means that enormous industries exist to distribute this information through print and electronic channels with data bank storage and cable linkages that connect televisions, telephones, and computers into **electronic superhighways** (Elmer-Dewitt, 1993). You may experience this **information explosion** as a bombardment of fragments of disconnected, irrelevant facts, leaving you overwhelmed with **information overload.**

An example might clarify this concept. In one five-minute newscast, you learn that marchers gathered at the White House, a bridge collapsed in the Philippines, and a child was abducted in Virginia—but do any of these facts affect you personally? What's really important and what's trivial? What must you know to live better, and what's simply interesting?

Similarly, your listeners can feel overwhelmed with disparate facts and ideas unless you help them integrate new information with old. When you do this successfully, you not only help listeners make sense of their world but also provide them with basic information they can use to make wise decisions (Fancher, 1993). Let's say you gather and present data that clearly describe and explain various types of smoking-related illnesses. You've empowered audience members by furnishing information they can use to make wise lifestyle choices.

Having access to information is so important that world leaders consider the ability both to give and receive information to be a global human right that deserves to be protected by international law. Indeed, Article 19 of the Universal Declaration of Human Rights (1948) states:

Everyone has the right to freedom of opinion and expression; this right includes freedom to hold opinions without interference and to seek and impart information and ideas through any media and regardless of frontiers. (as quoted in Harms & Richstad, 1978)

Information Imbalance
Some people or groups have very little access to information in contrast to others that have it in abundance.

Article 19 recognizes the potential dangers of an **information imbalance,** which gives some people and groups lots of information, and others very little. Those kept in ignorance may lack fundamental understandings of the world. During the Cold War, for example, broadcasters created Radio Free Europe to provide listeners in Communist-controlled countries with information that their governments withheld. Today, there's concern about global Internet censorship by nondemocratic governments such as the People's Republic of China, Saudi Arabia, and Syria, which all restrict Internet access. North Korea is the most notorious; leader Kim John Il forbids all servers or Internet connections to the outside world ("Tear Down This Firewall," 2002). You can read Article 19 as well as the entire declaration of rights online at www.un.org/Overview/rights.html.

In summary, information is a valuable resource or commodity. U.S. culture has it in abundance; other nations have less. Some groups and social classes within the United States have access to information they need to be successful and healthy; others have limited access to the same knowledge. Finally, some individuals know how to take advantage of the information that is widely available; others do not (Maxwell & McCain, 1997).

Analyze Your Audience's Current Knowledge

When Dwight took public speaking, he saw an article in the *World Press Review* entitled "Longing for the Days of Harem." His curiosity was piqued; he knew little about harems, and he assumed his classmates were similarly unfamiliar with them. So he decided to give an informative speech on the topic. To increase his classmates' understandings, however, he first had to find out what they already knew and believed about harems. Then he adjusted his speech accordingly (Edwards & McDonald, 1993). Audiences can have no information, a minimum of information, forgotten or outdated information, or misinformation (see Figure 16.1), and each level of understanding calls for different strategies.

Presenting New Information

Some audiences are unfamiliar with your subject; they've never even heard of it, so the information you present will be novel. Your task, then, is to provide a basic overview of your

Figure 16.1 Early in your planning, assess your audience's current levels of knowledge about your topic and identify misconceptions or outdated information they may have. Doing so will help you devise strategies that will make your information more useful to your listeners.

topic. For instance, what do you know about DEET? Music thanatology? Emmaline Pankhurst? *Dundun* drums? I've heard speeches on each of these topics, and each speaker succeeded only because he or she followed these guidelines:

1. Provide basic, introductory facts—the "who," "what," "when," "where," and "how" type of information.
2. Define unfamiliar terminology and jargon clearly.
3. Give detailed, vivid explanations and descriptions.
4. Make as many links as you can to the audience's knowledge by using literal and figurative analogies—comparing and contrasting the concept with something that's already familiar to them.

Presenting Supplemental Information

The great inventor Thomas Edison once said, "We don't know a millionth of one percent about anything." This means that listeners may have vague or superficial knowledge about your subject but lack detailed, in-depth understandings. These listeners won't want you to rehash basic information; they'll want supplemental information. To illustrate, an audience somewhat familiar with Michael Jordan's life will be more impressed if you provide little-known information that gives additional insight into his character. Another example: most people learned in elementary school to select foods from several food groups, so a speech presenting the major groups is redundant. However, the same audience may lack information about specific elements of nutrition such as antioxidants—information that would help them choose foods more wisely. Here are two specific strategies to use with audiences whose information is limited:

1. Dig deeper into your research sources to discover additional, less familiar details and facts.
2. Go beyond the obvious and add in-depth descriptions and explanations to what is already familiar.

Narrow a broad topic and provide interesting and novel information about just one aspect of it. For example, explore only Michael Jordan's childhood or focus on his educational background instead of his sports career.

Presenting Review or Updated Information

This category of listeners once studied your subject, but they've forgotten some or most of what they learned, or they lack current, updated information. Your speech can function as a review that refreshes the audience's memories, reinforces their knowledge, and keeps their information current. This type of informative speech is typical in school or job settings. For instance, students may have studied the five canons of rhetoric, but they need to review them if they want to ace the test; workers may have read or heard about sexual harassment laws in company-wide seminars held two years ago, but a workshop on new regulations keeps them updated. With audiences in this category, you'll be more effective if you use these strategies:

1. When you review material, approach the subject from different angles—help listeners conceptualize it from different perspectives.
2. Be creative; use vivid supporting materials that capture and hold attention.
3. When appropriate, use humor, and strive to make the review interesting.
4. For both reviews and updates, present the most recent available information. Mills (1999) reports that our current proliferation of information results in 100 percent new knowledge every five years (at least in high-tech areas); consequently, what's learned earlier quickly becomes outdated. Overstated? Perhaps. But it's true that people who want to stay current must be lifelong learners.

Countering Misinformation

A final type of audience has misconceptions and misunderstandings about a subject that you can elucidate by clarifying definitions and facts and by countering misunderstandings. For instance, the saying, "A dog is a human's best friend," is well known and widely accepted in the United States. However, Stephen Budiansky (1999) presents scientific evidence suggesting that dogs don't really adore their owners; instead, they fake devotion to manipulate humans. If this is true, many or most people in your audience misunderstand dog behaviors! In other examples, Arab students sometimes speak to counter their classmates' misconceptions about Arab culture, and politicians clarify specific policy positions their opponents have distorted. When countering misunderstandings, you must present material that is inconsistent or contradictory to what they "know," and you will be wise to consider the following:

1. Prepare for emotional responses—often negative ones. (Think about it. Who wants to hear that her beloved Fido is really a con artist?) Consequently, present the most credible facts you can find and tone down the emotional aspect.
2. Look for information derived from scientific studies, especially quantification, when that type of support would be best.
3. Define terminology carefully; consider explaining the origin of specific words or ideas.
4. Counter the negative prejudices against and stereotypes related to a specific topic (such as Arab culture) by highlighting positive elements of the subject.

In summary, the amount of information your audience brings to your speech should make a difference in the strategies you select to present meaningful information. By assessing their knowledge about your subject in advance, you can more effectively craft a speech that meets their need to know.

STOP AND CHECK

ANALYZE YOUR AUDIENCE'S KNOWLEDGE

To determine your audience's prior knowledge—or lack thereof—regarding your topic, answer the following questions about your topic. (Refer to Chapter 5 if you need to construct a questionnaire to determine your audience's knowledge about your topic.)

You can answer these questions online under Stop and Check Activities for Chapter 16 at the Jaffe Connection Web site at http://communication.wadsworth.com/jaffe.

Web Site

Types of Informative Speeches

Informative speeches fall into several categories. Demonstrations and instructions, descriptions, reports, and explanations are some broad categories of informative speaking you may be called upon to give—both in college and in your eventual career. This section gives specific guidelines for these types of speeches.

Doing Demonstrations and Providing Instructions

Instructions provide answers to the question, "How do you do that?" On the day her company went public, Martha Stewart became a billionaire (although some of her later business dealings got her into trouble). What's her line of work? She gives demonstration speeches on television and creates instructional books and magazines. She's like thousands of teachers, coaches, and salespeople who both *show* and *tell* others how to do a procedure, how to use a specific object, or how to complete a task. Ms. Stewart, like other successful instructors, understands and implements a number of guidelines for giving demonstrations and instructions—guidelines that can help you succeed when you must give a "how-to" speech. (Unfortunately, no one can guarantee that you'll earn millions!)

Demonstrations
"How-to" speeches that both show and tell.

When you give **demonstrations,** you both show and explain how to do a process or how to use an item. The following tips will help you.

1. Your first step in preparation is to think through all the required stages or steps. As you proceed, ask yourself the following questions: What comes first? What's absolutely essential? Which step is easiest? Which is hardest? What does the audience already know how to do? Where will the audience most likely be confused? Which step takes the most time? Which take practically no time at all ("Demonstrative Speech," n.d.; Mannie, 1998)?

2. Next, work on the content of your speech. Organize the essential steps sequentially, and concentrate on clarifying and simplifying the ones that will probably cause difficulty or confusion. During this time, carefully preplan the environment to facilitate learning—this may mean your audience will have to move their chairs or stand up and spread out around the room. Or you may have to furnish supplies if you want them to do the project with you.

3. Plan your visual support. Ask yourself if actual objects are practical (see Chapter 12); if not, plan videotapes or other supplementary visuals. Then practice working with your props so you can use them and still maintain rapport with your audience (Flynn, n.d.).

The following outline shows the necessity of visual aids during some demonstrations. If this speaker had simply tried to describe how to create a cartoon face, he'd have surely failed! However, he drew cartoon features onto a transparency as shown in Figure 16.2, then he uncovered feature by feature as he progressed through his speech.

Specific Purpose: To inform my audience about simple features they can draw to create a cartoon character almost instantly.

Central Idea: By drawing simple shapes for eyes, noses, mouths, hair, and facial outlines, almost anyone can easily draw a cartoon.

I. First, select the eyes.
II. Then, draw a nose.
III. Choose a mouth.
IV. Add hair.
V. Outline your character's face.

Before he started, he had each classmate take out a pencil or pen and a blank sheet of paper. (He'd brought along several blank sheets of paper and several writing instruments, just in case.) Then, as he spoke, each student created her or his own cartoon.

Figure 16.2 For his speech on drawing cartoon faces, one speaker put a number of facial features on a transparency. He uncovered each row as he discussed the separate elements, and his listeners created personal cartoons, feature by feature, as he went along.

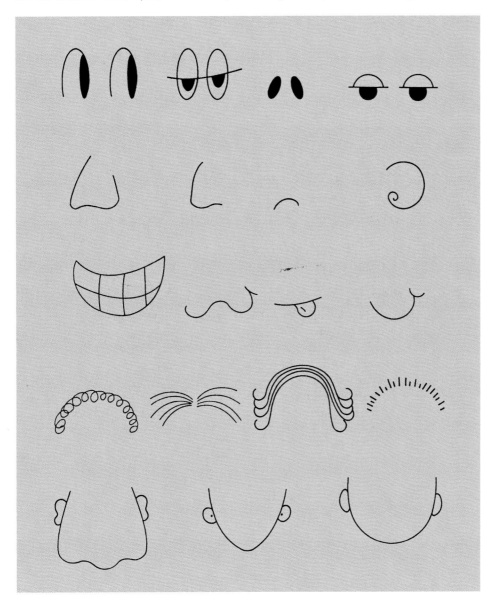

4. Make sure you time the entire process. If a task takes too long to accomplish in the time allotted for your speech, a better strategy is to demonstrate the process yourself and provide handouts with step-by-step instructions for listeners to use at home. One student failed to do this. She chose to have each listener complete a complicated origami project—folding a crane—in a seven-minute speech; twenty-two minutes later, her audience still had half-folded cranes when the class period ran out! Demonstrating the crane and providing each student with an instructional handout and a piece of origami paper would have been more successful.

Another strategy for a lengthy process is to prepare several versions of the item, stopping each at a different point of completion. Cooking and art demonstrations illustrate this well; a cooking instructor, for example, begins to prepare a complicated casserole. But rather than take twenty minutes on each step, he sets aside a partly-finished pan, reaches for a second pan which contains a more complete version of the casserole, then proceeds. Similarly, a sculptor does an essential step in creating a pot; then she leaves it to dry and takes up a pot she prepared in advance that's ready for the next step.

Not all "how-to" speeches require a demonstration. You can give people tips on how to resolve conflict or how to listen more effectively, on how to select a caterer for a major celebration or how to manage time effectively. In these cases, your focus is on providing instructions or pointers that will help audience members accomplish a specific goal.

Giving Descriptions

Descriptions answer the question, "What's it like?" Before you can describe an object, place, or event to someone else, you must first observe it carefully yourself. As you do, look for details, then select vivid imagery and sensory words that help people understand what your subject looks, smells, feels, or tastes like. A guide in an art museum, for example, walks her group from painting to painting, pointing out details of color, form, and texture within each painting that her audience would probably not see at first glance. Descriptions of places, objects, and events range from personal to global. Because listeners are generally more interested in topics that are close to their daily lives in location, time, and relevance, explicitly relate each topic to their perceived interests and needs.

Describing Places

People seek out useful information about places. A student visiting a campus, for example, needs to know how the place is laid out, so a college guide describes various parts of the campus as he shows the visitor around. Descriptions of different countries or sites such as national parks or tourist attractions similarly attract groups, and travel agents or park rangers are just two types of professionals who describe places.

When you describe a place, provide vivid details that help your listeners form precise images of the site. Take advantage of visual aids including maps, drawings, slides, brochures, or enlarged photographs, and consider a spatial or topical organizational pattern. By way of illustration, here are the main points of a speech about Thailand given by a Thai student:

Specific Purpose: To inform my audience about the beauty of Thailand and the many tourist attractions in it.
Central Idea: Thailand is a beautiful country with many scenic attractions that complement the human-made wonders to be found there.

  I. Geographic features

    A. Inland areas
    B. Famous beaches

 II. Tourist attractions

    A. Cities
    B. Temples and shrines

If you're searching for an international topic, places are good choices. Students have described Italian villas, African deserts, and the Taj Mahal, as well as local museums, Disney World, Carnegie Hall, the Mississippi River delta, and the Holocaust Museum in Washington, D.C.

Describing Objects

Descriptions of objects, including natural objects (stars, glaciers), human constructions (the Vietnam War Memorial), huge things (the planet Jupiter), or microscopic matter (microbes), are common. Students have described inanimate (computers) or animate (panda bears) objects by providing information about the origin of the object, how it's made, identifying characteristics, how it works, how it's used, and so on.

Topic choices range from personal to international. On the personal level, students have described body features such as skin or fingernails. They've talked about campus objects like a historical tree or a memorial plaque and explained cultural artifacts such as the Golden Gate Bridge, CD players, and guitars. International topics have included the Great Pyramids, the Great Wall of China, and African drums known as *dundun* drums. (Appendix C contains an outline of Josh Valentine's *dundun* drum speech.)

Describing Events

Consider discussing personal (birthday customs), community (local festivals or celebrations), national (elections), and international (the Russian launch of Sputnik or the bombing of Hiroshima) events or occurrences. Chronological, narrative, and topical organizational patterns are most common. The first two patterns work well for step-by-step events such as the launch of Sputnik or planning a wedding. The topical pattern is also useful for describing happenings that consist of several different components (birthday customs, for instance). Here is an example of a topical outline for a speech describing a sporting event.

Buildings such as the Yellow Crane Tower in Wuhan, China, are possible topics for informative speeches.

Specific Purpose: To inform my audience of the different events that occur in a rodeo.
Central Idea: Rodeos are athletic contests with people and animals competing in a variety of events.

I. Bull riding
II. Barrel racing
III. Bronco busting
IV. Calf roping

When you describe events or happenings in concrete detail and vivid language, your listeners can place themselves at the event. In other words, you speak so that they participate vicariously.

Presenting Reports

Think of a report as a way to answer the question, "What have we learned about this subject?" Giving reports is a global business that employs millions; around the clock, reporters collect and organize news and information about people and issues of public interest. For example, investigative reporters search for the answers to questions such as "What are scientists learning about the causes of attention deficit disorder?" And campus reporters pass along the information that university task forces have come up with. In classrooms and boardrooms, here and abroad, people give reports. This section discusses two common topic areas: people and issues.

Reporting About People

What individuals have shaped our world? What did they accomplish? How did they live? You can answer such questions by providing sketches of influential historical or contemporary characters. Biographical reports can be about philosophers (Kierkegaard), military men and women (Genghis Khan, the Amazons), artists (the Impressionists), writers (Toni Morrison), and so on. Don't overlook villains (Machiavelli) as well as heroes (Mother Teresa) for biographical subjects.

Generally, chronological, topical, or narrative organizational patterns best fit a biographical report. Fei Fei's outline is organized topically with two points: (1) Confucius's life and (2) his influence. She then uses chronological subpoints to develop her first point—Confucius's life.

Specific Purpose: To inform my audience of the life and ideas of the Chinese philosopher whose teachings influence more than a billion people globally.
Central Idea: Confucius, who lived in China about 2,500 years ago, developed a life-affirming philosophy that has influenced many Asian cultures.

I. Confucius's life

    A. Birth and youth
    B. Early career
    C. Period as a wandering scholar
    D. Later years

II. Confucius's influence

    A. His teaching method
    B. Concepts of *li* and *ren*
    C. Five relationships

In addition to individual subjects, consider speaking about groups of people such as skinheads, the Mafia, aborigines, or Motown musicians. Here is an outline of a student speech on the Amish that is organized topically:

Specific Purpose: To inform my audience about Amish people by describing their beliefs and explaining challenges facing their group.
Central Idea: The Amish are a religious group with written and unwritten rules for living that are being challenged by education and tourism.

I. The Amish people

    A. Number and location
    B. Historical information

II. Amish beliefs

    A. Written ordinances—Dortrecht Confession of Faith (1632)
    B. Unwritten rules of local congregations—Ordnung

III. Challenges to Amish culture

    A. Education and teacher certification
    B. Tourism attention

As you develop your major points, keep in mind your audience's questions: "Why should I listen to a speech about this person or group?" "What impact has this subject had on society?" "How does knowing about this individual or group tie into my concerns?" When you answer these questions, your listeners will better understand the relevance of the person or group. For links to biographical information on thousands of individuals, both contemporary and historical, visit the Internet site http://www.libraryspot.com/biographicalinfo.htm.

Reporting About Issues

Newspapers and magazines are good sources for a list of current issues that we discuss within our communities and our society as a whole. We debate welfare reform, immigration policies, legalization of marijuana, humanitarian aid to war-torn nations, plus local and campus problems—all complex and controversial. Generally, addressing issues allows us to create policies aimed at solving the problems and answering the question "What should we do about this problem?" Here are a few examples of controversial issues:

- What have we learned about the effects of marijuana on the body?
- What do we know about the effectiveness of various programs for rehabilitating juvenile offenders?
- What are the issues each side emphasizes in their support of or opposition to taxing the Internet?

Think of this speech as an investigative report, where you research the facts surrounding an issue and then present your findings. Your major purpose is to enlighten your listeners so that they have a factual foundation to use in formulating their own conclusions. Thus, reports are not intended to persuade or advocate one position or another. (However, you may follow up your report by giving a persuasive speech on the same topic.)

Informative speeches about current issues are common assignments in public speaking classrooms. Log on to InfoTrac College Edition to find up-to-date newsmagazines like *Time* and *Newsweek*, which provide answers to questions such as these: What exactly is the problem or issue? What are the current beliefs or theories commonly held about the issue? What is the extent of the problem (how many people does it affect)? How did this situation develop? What solutions are proposed? What are the arguments on both sides of the issue? Generally, pro–con, cause–effect, problem–solution(s), narrative, and topical patterns work well for investigative reports. Here is a pro–con outline for a speech on legalizing marijuana for medical use, with major points taken from articles found on InfoTrac College Edition.

You can present an investigative report on both sides of controversial issues such as the legalization of marijuana. What are the arguments for legalization for medical reasons? For religious reasons? For any reason?

Specific Purpose: To inform my audience about the supporters' and opponents' views about legalizing marijuana for medical use.

Central Idea: There are several arguments both for and against the legalization of up to three ounces of marijuana for private use and possession.

I. Many argue for the legalization of marijuana.

   A. Republican Governor Gary Johnson of New Mexico believes the war on drugs is ineffective, and legalization of marijuana would allow it to be a controlled substance that the government taxes and regulates.

   B. A lot of tax money is wasted funding arrests for minor possessions of the drug.

   C. The hemp plant is a good source of food, fuel, and fiber, according to Herer's book, *The Emperor Wears No Clothes*, which exposes the factual inaccuracies of those who oppose legalization.

   D. Some religious groups, like Rastafarians, use marijuana in their religious practices.

   E. The decriminalization of "soft" drugs like marijuana hasn't led to an increase in hard drug usage in the Netherlands.

II. A large group of people support current drug laws.

   A. Marijuana is a Schedule I drug, which has at least some negative physical effects on users including impaired memory, inability to perform complex tasks, and a depressed immune system.

   B. Eighty-five percent of people in the United States disapprove of legalizing drugs.

   C. There is a campaign of misinformation about legalizing drugs, financed by billionaire George Soros, including the "medical marijuana" hoax.

> D. Smoking marijuana for medical reasons is unnecessary because the active ingredient, TCH, has long been available under the name "marinol," which assures quality and dosage.
>
> E. Vermont State Senator Susan Streetser says legalizing marijuana would send the wrong message to children, and a major study shows that marijuana is a gateway drug for school-aged experimenters.

Issues for speech topics can be personal (eating disorders), campus (tuition hikes), local (potholes), national (teens and guns), and global (trade with nations that violate human rights). Many global decisions, such as what to do with nuclear waste, have long-lasting effects. Others, although less significant, are related to larger controversies. For example, the discussion of plastic surgery for Miss America contestants is associated with issues of women's rights and stereotypes of female beauty.

Explaining Concepts

Expository Speaking
The "speech to teach" that sets forth, discloses, unmasks, or explains an idea in detail so that listeners understand it.

Katherine Rowan (1995) of Purdue University focuses her research on explanatory or **expository speaking**—known more simply as the "speech to teach." Expository speakers set forth, disclose, unmask, or explain an idea in detail to increase listeners' understandings. Science and history teachers regularly define terms and explain concepts; parents answer the endless "whys" of four-year-olds with explanations. Effective expository speakers identify the hurdles listeners are likely to encounter in their attempt to comprehend the concept. They then plan ways to overcome the barriers and make meanings clear.

Defining Terms

Definitions answer the questions, "What is it?" or "What does it mean?" Definition speeches are common in educational institutions and workplaces—for example, a philosophy professor defines *justice*, a speech professor elucidates the concept of *confirmation* as it's used in the academic discipline, and an employer defines *sexual harassment* for new employees. Inspirational speakers also define words. Examples: a priest defines *peacemaking*; a commencement speaker defines *integrity*; a coach defines *commitment*. In short, although we see people act in ways we classify as just or as sexual harassment, we can neither see nor touch justice or harassment, and defining these terms helps us as a society discriminate between appropriate and inappropriate behaviors.

One effective organizational pattern for a speech of definition presents first the denotative then the connotative meaning of a word. (Chapter 13 discusses denotation and connotation in detail.)

> I. **Denotative Meaning:** Focus on the *denotation* of the term as found in reference books such as a thesaurus or etymological dictionary. The *Oxford English Dictionary* or another unabridged dictionary provides the most thorough definitions available. In addition, books in a specific academic discipline show how scholars in that field define the term; for example, the definition of *confirmation* you find in a dictionary will not be identical to the definition you'd find in a book on interpersonal communication. You can develop the denotative point of your speech by presenting the following:
>
> • Provide synonyms and antonyms that are familiar to your audience.
> • Explain the use or function of something you're defining.
> • Give the etymology of the word. What's its source historically? How has the concept developed over time?
> • Compare an unknown concept or item to one that your audience already knows. For example, "an Allen wrench" might be unfamiliar to some listeners, but "a wrench that looks like a hockey stick" or "an L-shaped wrench" helps them select the specific tool, given a line up of wrenches (Boerger & Henley, 1999).

II. **Connotative Meaning:** Focus on the *connotation* of the term by using realistic life experiences as creatively as you can. Here, draw from whatever you can think of that will elucidate or clarify the idea.

   1. Relate a personal experience that demonstrates the idea.
   2. Quote other people as to what the term means to them.
   3. Tell a narrative or give a series of short examples that illustrate the concept.
   4. Refer to an exemplar—a person or thing that exemplifies the term.
   5. Connect the term to a familiar political, social, or moral issue
      (von Till, 1998).

For example, in the denotative section of her student speech on *destiny*, Terez Czapp provided the dictionary definition then explained the etymology of the word like this:

> The Roman saying, *"Destinatum est mihi,"* meant, "I have made up my mind." In Rome, destiny meant a decision was fixed or determined. Later the word reappeared in both Old and Middle French in the feminine form *destiné*. Finally, from the Middle English word *destinee*, we get the modern form of the word.

Next she provided a transition to the connotative section—an extended example of a near-fatal car wreck that devastated her family—by saying, "However, it isn't the word's etymological history that is meaningful to me. You see, destiny is a depressing reminder of a car accident. . . ." Terez closed with a quotation by William Jennings Bryan, "Destiny is not a matter of chance, it is a matter of choice. It is not a thing to be waited for, it is a thing to be achieved." Including both denotative and connotative meanings provided a fuller picture of the concept of *destiny*.

Giving Explanations

Think of explanations as translation speeches in which you take a complex or information-dense concept and put it into common words and images that elucidate or clarify it. Explanations commonly answer questions about processes—"How does it work?"—or about concepts— "What's the theory behind that?" or "Why?"

How does a telephone work? How do Koreans greet one another? How is a levee constructed? To answer questions like these, you'll describe stages, ordered sequences, or procedures involved in processes—both natural and cultural. You can explain how something is done (bungee jumping, resolving conflict), how things work (elevators, cuckoo clocks, microwave ovens), or how they're made (mountain bikes, a pair of shoes). Not surprisingly, chronological patterns are common, as this outline demonstrates. Marietta was born in the Philippines and adopted by an American family when she was sixteen years old.

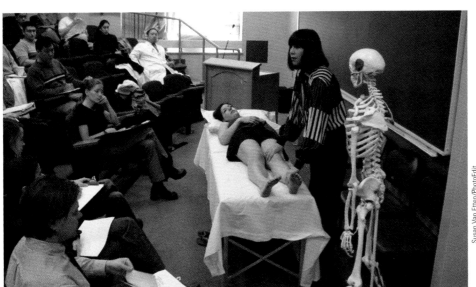

Every speaker who explains complex concepts or processes faces the challenge of making the subject understandable, relevant, and interesting.

Susan Van Etten/PhotoEdit

Specific Purpose: To inform my audience about the process of adopting a child from another country.

Central Idea: The four parts of the adoption process are application, selection, child arrival, and postplacement.

I. Application—the family and a social worker evaluate the adoptive home.
II. Selection—the agency provides pictures and histories of available children.
III. Child arrival—the child arrives with an "Orphan Visa."
IV. Postplacement—for up to a year, the family and a social worker evaluate the placement, after which time the adoption is finalized.

You can also explain concepts. What do we know about intelligence? What's in the mind of a serial killer? What is Johari's Window? These questions relate to concepts or abstractions—the principles, theories, and ideas we form mentally to explain both natural and social realities. For example, although we cannot know for certain what causes some people to kill repeatedly, we formulate theories or explanations for the unusual behaviors of serial killers.

Because concepts are sometimes difficult to define and explain, your major challenge is to make the complex ideas and theories understandable and relevant to the lives of your listeners. Here are some guidelines to follow for speeches about concepts:

● Simplify complex ideas by breaking them down into their component parts. For example, subdivide intelligence into categories that include social intelligence, spatial intelligence, and musical intelligence (Gardner, 1993).
● Carefully define your terminology, avoiding technical jargon. Exactly what falls into the category of spatial intelligence? Use examples that clarify this component of intelligence, or show the items from the tests that measure spatial intelligence.
● Clarify confusing details by using analogies, both figurative and literal, to compare the concept to something that listeners already understand. In this case, you might compare spatial intelligence to running a maze.
● Use detailed examples of concrete situations that illustrate the actions of people who test high in various kinds of intelligence.

The following example demonstrates a typical topical organizational pattern for an explanatory speech.

Specific Purpose: To inform my audience of core values of many groups in sub-Saharan Africa.

Central Idea: Four major value clusters are characteristic of many cultural groups in sub-Saharan Africa.

I. Spiritual force
II. Ancestralism and cyclism
III. Communalism
IV. Rationality

Here are a few concepts that students have defined or explained in their "speech to teach": types of relationships, autism, Afrocentrism, black holes, and False Memory Syndrome (thinking you remember something that happened—often as a result of psychotherapy—when the event did not occur).

We sometimes clash over theories, concepts, and ideas. For instance, exactly what does compassionate conservatism mean? People's ideas differ. What caused the dinosaurs to become extinct? Theories vary. What constitutes a date rape? Few people give the same answer. The purpose of explanatory speaking is not to argue for one definition or another but to clarify the concept, sometimes by comparing and contrasting differing definitions and theories regarding it.

INFORMATIVE SPEAKING IN AFRICA

Sean Sprague/PANOS Pictures

"Knowledge is power" could be the motto of these educators who provide health and child care information to mothers in Kenya.

THROUGHOUT PARTS OF AFRICA, public health educators give people data that may save their lives. For example, women in central Africa empower one another with facts they can use to protect themselves against sexually transmitted diseases. In remote areas of Kenya, a particular type of informative speaker is a person who travels, then brings back news of the world to tribal people where less than 10 percent can read and where televisions and radios are not accessible. Additionally, members of the community come together to give advice to newlyweds—they give the young couple practical "how-to" information they can use to build an effective marriage (Miller, 2002).

Guidelines for Informative Speaking

A common complaint about informational speaking is that it's not interesting (Goodall & Waaigen, 1986). To keep your audience's attention and to be both understandable and relevant, remember these guidelines for producing comprehensible messages (Rubin, 1993).

1. **Do an obstacle analysis of the audience.** Identify the parts of the message that are hard to understand, then work specifically on ways to make those sections clear. Next, identify internal barriers that might prevent your audience from learning your material. Choosing a scientific topic for an audience who thinks science is difficult and boring or challenging an audience's current misconceptions about a subject they hold dear are examples of topics that meet with psychological resistance. Plan strategies to deal with each obstacle (Rowan, 1995).

2. **Organize the material carefully.** Be kind to your listeners by stating your major points clearly and building in transition statements and signposts such as "next" and "in addition" that enable them to identify the flow of ideas. Use structures such as lists, comparisons–contrasts, or cause–effect patterns. Provide internal previews and summaries along with connectives that show how your material is linked—words and phrases such as *because* and *for example, therefore* and *as a result* (see Chapter 10). **Discourse consistency** also helps. This means you use a repetitive style such as beginning every section with a question or alliterating your main points throughout the entire speech (Rubin, 1993).

Discourse Consistency
Using a repetitive style such as alliteration of main points throughout the speech.

3. **Personalize your material for your audience.** Help listeners see the connection between your topic and their experiences, goals, beliefs, and actions. When they see the relevance of information to their personal lives, they're more likely to listen and learn effectively.

4. **Compare the known to the unknown.** Be audience centered and start with what's familiar to your listeners. Put simply, begin with their existing knowledge, then build on this foundation and show similarities and differences between what they already know and your topic.

5. **Choose your vocabulary carefully.** You may have heard lectures or reports that were full of technical information given in incomprehensible jargon; if so, you probably failed to understand the topic clearly. To clarify your ideas, define your terms and explain them in everyday, concrete images. Avoid trigger words—those with negative connotations—that might set off negative reactions in your audience.

6. **Build in repetition and redundancy. Repetition** means that you say the same thing more than once. **Redundancy** means that you repeat the same *idea* several times, but you develop it somewhat differently each time. Phrases such as *in other words* or *put simply* are ways to build in redundancy. Repeat and redefine the critical parts of the message to reinforce these crucial points in your listeners' minds (Thompson & Grandgenett, 1999).

7. **Strive to be interesting.** In your preparation, occasionally try to distance yourself from the speech and hear it as if it were being delivered by someone else. Do you find yourself drifting off? If so, where? Think of ways to enliven your factual material. Providing detailed descriptions, for example, engages your audience dialogically, because your listeners can use these descriptions to form mental images as you talk.

If you follow these guidelines, you will increase your listeners' motivation and interest in the topic. And your careful attention to details will help them understand the material more clearly.

Repetition
Saying the same thing more than once.

Redundancy
Repeating the same idea more than once, but developing it differently each time.

STOP AND CHECK

DO AN OBSTACLE ANALYSIS AND STRATEGIC PLAN

As you prepare your speech, ask yourself the following questions:

- What concepts or steps may be obstacles for this audience?
- What psychological barriers are likely?
- What is the best way to overcome these obstacles?
- Are the steps in order? Or are my main ideas clear?
- Where might I use alliteration, rhyming, or another form of discourse consistency?
- Where are my signposts and transitions? Should I use more?
- How, specifically, have I connected this material to the lives of my classmates?
- What do they already know that I'm building upon?
- Is my language clear?
- Where should I repeat an idea verbatim?
- Which ideas have I presented in a number of different ways?
- Would I be interested in listening to my speech if someone else were giving it? If not, how could I make it more interesting?

This form is also available online under Chapter 16 Forms at the Jaffe Connection Web site at **http://communication.wadsworth.com/jaffe**.

Web Site

Summary

We live in an Information Age where having the ability to give and receive information is empowering; those who lack information do not have the basic knowledge they need to perform competently in complex societies. Because of this, a variety of people in a variety of settings give informative speeches. Their goals are to present new information, to supplement what's already known, to review or update material, or to correct misinformation.

There are several categories for informative speaking that answer listeners' questions such as "How do you do that?" or "What's that mean?" These include demonstrations and instructions, descriptions, reports, and explanations.

Finally, remember the keys to informative speaking. Do an obstacle analysis that identifies elements within the topic or within the listeners that might prove to be barriers, then work to overcome those obstacles. Organize the speech and provide links that connect the material. Relate your topic to your listeners, and make vocabulary choices that clarify your ideas. Think of creative ways of presenting your information, and throughout your talk, tie abstract concepts to concrete experiences that are familiar to your listeners. Finally, include repetition and redundancy to reinforce the critical points of the message.

JAFFE ONLINE CONNECTION   JAFFE ONLINE CONNECTION

Use your CD-ROM and the Jaffe Connection Web site http://communication.wadsworth.com/jaffe to review the following concepts, answer the review questions, and complete the suggested activities.

KEY TERMS

Information Age (294)
electronic superhighways (294)
information explosion (294)
information overload (294)
information imbalance (294)

demonstrations (298)
expository speaking (304)
discourse consistency (307)
repetition (308)
redundancy (308)

APPLICATION AND CRITICAL THINKING EXERCISES

1. For your classroom speech consider a topic from the field of communication. For example, in interpersonal communication, topics such as how to work through conflict, how to become independent from parents, or how to successfully navigate the early stages of a romantic relationship are useful. From nonverbal communication come makeover speeches or speeches about time or touch. From mass communication, you could explain how camera angles communicate meaning or how emotions are expressed in email messages. Look for information that could help your classmates communicate better.

2. Within a small group in your classroom, discuss implications of the unequal distribution of information. Examples: What if only some societies know how to make sophisticated weaponry? What if some have information that benefits them economically and others do not? What if only some individuals or groups know their cultural history? What if only women were to have access to health information and men were excluded? What if only people under thirty-five years of age, with incomes over $80,000 a year, knew how to use computers to advantage?

3. Working with a small group, generate a list of speech topics in each of these four categories. For example, your audience

   • Is totally unfamiliar with these topics (medieval manuscripts, an unfamiliar composer)

- Has some knowledge of the topics, but not a lot (Singapore, the history of MTV)
- Has studied this topic, but needs a review (the five canons of rhetoric)
- Has outdated information (a new computer program)
- Has major misconceptions regarding the topics (tarantulas, gypsies)

Select a subject in two different categories and discuss how you would modify your speech strategies to accomplish your general purpose with each topic.

4. In a small group, think of creative ways to present an informative speech that reviews audience knowledge about one of these familiar topics:
   - Good nutrition
   - What to do in case of fire
   - How to read a textbook

5. Descriptions can be speeches in themselves, or good descriptions can be elements of larger speeches. To improve your descriptive skills, identify a place, an object, or an event, then make a list of vivid words that provide information about the look, the feel, the smell, the taste, or the sound of the item or place. Share your description with a small group of your classmates.

6. Log on to InfoTrac College Edition and do a PowerTrac search for the journal *Vital Speeches*. Skim the list of speeches and identify ten titles that appear more informative than persuasive. For example, "[Alzheimer's is] a Frustrating Disease" and "Marketing to Women 50+ on the Internet" seem more informative than "Dying Should Not Be an Event: Eliminating the Federal Estate and Inheritance Taxes" or "Violence Among Our Children: What Can Be Done?" which appear to take a specific position. Skim one of the speeches you've identified as informative and evaluate how well the speaker follows the guidelines found in this chapter.

7. Use www.alltheweb.com and search for the exact term *informative speaking*. Find a site from either a speech team (also called forensics team) or from a university professor that provides additional information about speaking to inform.

THE JAFFE CONNECTION WEB SITE

The Jaffe Connection Web site features review questions about the Web links and InfoTrac College Edition exercises referenced throughout the chapter. You can access this site via your CD-ROM or at http://communication.wadsworth.com/jaffe.

Web Links

16.1 Universal Declaration of Human Rights (page 295)
16.2 Biographical Links (page 302)
16.3 Informative Speaking (page 310)

Stop and Check Activities

16.1 Analyze Your Audience's Knowledge (page 297)
16.2 Do an Obstacle Analysis and Strategic Plan (page 308)

InfoTrac College Edition Exercises

16.1 Pro and Con Arguments for Legalizing Marijuana (page 303)
16.2 Evaluating Informative Speeches (page 310)

SPEECH INTERACTIVE ON THE JAFFE CONNECTION CD-ROM

Watch the following informative speech by Hillary Carter-Liggett and answer the questions for analysis under Speech Interactive on your Jaffe Connection CD-ROM.

STUDENT OUTLINE WITH COMMENTARY

SHAKESPEARE
by Hillary Carter-Liggett

General Purpose: To inform
Specific Purpose: To inform my audience about the Stratfordian and the Oxfordian theories regarding the author of Shakespeare's works.
Central Idea: Two men have been put forward as author of Shakespeare's works: Shakespeare, an actor from Stratford, and Edward deVere, the Earl of Oxford.

Introduction

I. Have you ever experienced writer's block—perhaps as you were preparing the speech you'll give today?

   A. If you were a respected author (or potentially one), you might pray for a muse, like the one young Will found in the noblewoman named Viola.
   B. This was the premise of the 1998 Academy Award winning Best Picture, *Shakespeare in Love.*

      1. Critics pointed out that the plot was ludicrous, fictionalized, and borderline sacrilegious—literature professors apparently want "only the truth" to be told.
      2. What would happen if the foundations of Shakespearean authorship were stripped away?
      3. Scholars reacted strongly when others suggested that the works of Shakespeare may have been written by someone else.

II. Why should we care when his words continue to move us to laughter and tears, hundreds of years after his death?

   A. According to the Internet Movie Database, in 1998 Americans spent more than $100 million to see *Shakespeare in Love.*
   B. The hundreds of millions spent on other versions of Shakespearean classics would be enough to sink the *Titanic.*
   C. His works are integral to education on almost every level, but what if the "triumph of truth" is merely cosmetic and our celebration of him merely supports deception?

III. To address these questions, we must look at the evidence about authorship: first, at the traditional Stratfordian school of thought; second, at the Oxfordian school of thought; third, at a comparison between the claims.

Body

I. Is it possible, as the Stratfordians suggest, that a man of humble origins could come into the world a pauper and leave it a literary prince?

   A. Josepb Sobran, author of *Alias: Shakespeare,* reminds us that a handful of wedding and birth announcements are all we have of the first half of his life.

      1. According to legal documents, shortly after he turned twenty-nine, he went to London to avoid prosecution for a deer-poaching incident.
      2. In London, he became an actor, and in 1594, became associated with the Chamberlain's Men.

Most people think Shakespeare wrote Shakespeare, but Hillary's speech shows that the prevailing theory has a credible challenger; her goal is to inform them of a theory that is unfamiliar to many in her audience.

To relate the topic to a college audience, she refers to a popular movie and to common educational experiences.

Her preview clearly provides a roadmap of her major points.

She starts with what's most familiar—the idea that William Shakespeare really wrote Shakespeare's works.

3. During this period, he supposedly turned out the bulk of his material.
4. In 1604, he went home to Stratford, and in 1616, he died.
5. In 1623, the first folio of Shakespeare's work was published.

B. With so little evidence about his life, is it any surprise that questions have been asked about the authenticity of his authorship?

1. Gail Kern Paster, editor of *The Shakespeare Quarterly*, writes in the April 1, 1999, *Harper's Magazine* that all his defenders have to prove is that he *could* have written the works, not that he *did* so.
2. Stratfordian scholars have some evidence that he did, indeed, write the works in question.

   a. The October 9, 1996, *Minneapolis Star Tribune* says that his name was on the plays when they were published.
   b. His contemporary, playwright Ben Jonson, both knew and worked with Shakespeare; he never even raised the question about authorship.

C. So why should we raise the question?

1. Irvin Matus, author of *Shakespeare, IN FACT*, believes intellectual snobbery and prejudice against the lower classes causes the questioning.
2. People are eager to deny that a man with a simple education could write masterpieces like *Macbeth* or *Othello*.

Providing source citations gives credibility to her information.

TRANSITION: Is the authorship question a case of class prejudice or the greatest case of mistaken identity in all literary history? Perhaps the answer lies in the Oxfordian school of thought—those who put forward Edward deVere, Earl of Oxford, as the author.

II. What evidence leads to deVere?

A. In the June 4, 1999, *Chronicle of Higher Education*, Roger A. Smitmatter looks to the Bible for proof of deVere's authorship.

1. In 1580, deVere purchased a Geneva Bible; 43 percent of Shakespeare's Biblical references are underlined or annotated in it.
2. The sonnets also seem to testify of deVere's authorship.

   a. Joseph Sobran writes, "Only in the sonnets does Shakespeare speak directly from his heart and in his own person."
   b. The subject of some of the sonnets was the young Earl of Southampton, Henry Wriothesley.
   c. In *Shakespeare, Who Was He?* Richard Whalen says deVere had a homosexual affair with the young earl, which would explain the love tributes in the sonnets.

B. It's logical that deVere would want to hide behind a pen name, because submitting one's work to the public was considered bad in his day.

1. The *Arte of English Poesie* (1589) says many noblemen wrote under pen names.
2. This book names deVere as the most accomplished of the lot.

Her transition statement summarizes the first point and introduces a second theory.

Hillary again cites sources to support the controversial theory.

(Note: she may not have come across other, contradictory sources that dispute this alleged affair.)

TRANSITION: There's something rotten in the state of Denmark, or at the very least, in the hallowed halls of academe, which is why we must look at what the evidence says about the lives of each candidate.

III. Like the three hags sought out by *Macbeth*, there are three areas to compare: their education, life experiences, and parallels between their lives and the literature.

A. In defense of Sweet William, his name is on the plays, and possession is nine-tenths of the law, but deVere's family crest is a lion shaking a spear.

The source from 1589 is much closer in time to the actual happenings and, thus, has a different kind of credibility than modern-day sources.

Her transition uses a literary allusion—"something rotten in the state of Denmark"—that comes from Hamlet. She also refers to the hags who are characters in Macbeth.

B. What of their education?

In this section she looks first, at one potential author's qualifications, then at the other's.

1. Shakespeare's education is defended in Irvin Matus's, *Shakespeare, IN FACT*, which reports he had the equivalent of a high school education at the Stratford Free School.
2. DeVere was enrolled in Cambridge at the age of nine, where he earned a bachelor's degree; he went on to earn a master's degree at Oxford and to study law (a common theme in the plays) at Grays Inn.

C. A man is not only that which he has read; his life experiences are also illuminating.

1. Shakespeare spent most of his life in Stratford and London; there's no evidence he traveled anywhere else.
2. DeVere spent much time abroad, specifically in Italy and France—common settings for the plays.
3. William was an actor and familiar with the theatre and, like many of his characters, must have been quite the rapscallion, as shown by his frequent legal bills like failure to pay debts and poaching of the royal deer.
4. DeVere was a member of the court and familiar with court procedures.

D. What about the evidence in the plays themselves?

Here she compares each potential author to the material in the plays themselves.

1. *Hamlet* is a good starting place.

   a. Shakespeare had a son named Ham<u>net</u>.
   b. DeVere, like Hamlet, was captured by pirates.

      1) His father-in-law, Lord Burghley, was arguably the model for Polonius.
      2) His mother, after her husband's death, married a man of much lower status—like Hamlet's mother.

2. *Othello* also has interesting parallels.

   a. Of Shakespeare's married life, we know little, but in his will, he left her his second-best bed.
   b. *Time Magazine* reports that deVere refused to see his royal wife for years after hearing rumors that she had been unfaithful.

3. *The Merchant of Venice* is a play about moneylending.

   a. Shakespeare was often in debt.
   b. Shylock lent Antonio 3,000 ducats to pay for three merchant ships that were lost at sea.

      1) DeVere provided 3,000 pounds for three merchant ships to look for gold ore; they came back empty and soon declared bankruptcy.
      2) Ironically, the ship's owner was named Locke.

         a) The prefix *shy* means shady or disreputable.
         b) Experts can find no precedent for the name *Shylock* anywhere in history.

Conclusion

Hillary ends with two allusions to material within Shakespeare's work. *All's Well That Ends Well* is the title of one play, and his phrase "a rose by any other name would smell as sweet" is well known.

   I. Obviously, we have just scratched the surface of the controversy.
  II. We've looked at the lives of each, and comparing them, we find there is a case to be made on each side.
 III. I leave it up to you to decide if all is truly well that ends well.
  IV. We are left to wonder if the plays, written by another author, still sound as sweet.

Persuasive Speaking

THIS CHAPTER WILL HELP YOU

■ Find a subject for a persuasive

speech

■ Decide on a claim of fact,

definition, value, or policy

■ Narrow the focus of your speech in

light of your listeners' beliefs,

attitudes, and actions

■ Identify organizational patterns for

your speeches including

problem–solution, direct method,

comparative advantages, criteria

satisfaction, negative method, and

Monroe's Motivated Sequence

Detail from "Desaparecidos Pero no Olvidados" Mural ©1999
by Carlos Madriz, Josh Short, and Mabel Negrette. (Balmy
Alley, Balmy at 24th Street, SF, CA)

F YOU WATCH *Court TV*, YOU'LL SEE DEFENSE and prosecution lawyers present conflicting interpretations of evidence, each hoping to persuade the jury to accept their version of what happened. C-SPAN provides coverage of the House of Representatives; it shows the "gentlewoman from Washington" and the "gentleman from Alabama" arguing against a proposed amendment that the "gentleman from Indiana" supports. Flip to a talk show and you'll hear representatives of various viewpoints argue for their beliefs and lifestyles. All these examples underscore the importance of persuasion in our society.

Persuasion is vital in a democracy where core values include citizen participation and freedom of speech. Centuries ago, Aristotle designated three arenas in which rhetoric, or the art of persuasion, functioned in a healthy democratic society: law courts, governing assemblies, and ceremonial and ritual occasions where the culture's core beliefs and values are reinforced. However, the role of persuasion varies across cultures, as the Diversity in Practice feature illustrates.

This chapter focuses specifically on the purposes and types of persuasive speaking. You will find information on selecting a topic, using what your listeners know and how they behave to narrow your speaking purpose, and strategies and organizational patterns that will be effective in conveying your ideas and supporting your positions.

DIVERSITY IN PRACTICE
PERSUASION IN OTHER CULTURES

NOT EVERY culture places the same value on persuasion as a means of publicly discussing issues and formulating reasoned conclusions, as these examples, from historical and contemporary societies, illustrate.

Rome

During Rome's long history as a republic, representatives of the people publicly debated issues that affected the entire community. However, by the first century A.D., emperors such as Nero and Caligula were dictators who made binding decisions and pronouncements, whether or not the senators approved; dissenters often met with torture or death. In one notorious incident, the emperor Caligula mocked the Senate's power by declaring his horse to be a senator!

The Soviet Union

When the Communists ruled the former Soviet Union, party leaders made decisions and spoke for the people. They strongly discouraged ordinary citizens from dissenting from the "party line," often through use of coercive force that could result in months or years in Siberian work camps.

Athabaskan Speakers

Speakers in this oral-based society of native Alaskans think it rude to explicitly state the conclusions they want listeners to draw. It is enough for them to simply present a set of facts and let audience members draw their own conclusions. This emphasis on information rather than persuasive strategies distinguishes their norms from those found in this text (Rubin, 1993).

International Negotiation

Many cultures are realizing the benefits of persuasive argumentation—at least in their dealings with representatives of the West. Because of trade negotiations, the existence of the United Nations, peace talks, and other international exchanges, many nations with different persuasive traditions are adopting strategies of Western rhetoric. Their leaders are often educated at U.S. universities, and they adapt their rhetorical strategies to communicate their nation's views to international audiences. One example is Takakazu Kuriyama, Japanese Ambassador to the United States from 1992 to 1995. He studied at Amherst College (Massachusetts) and Lawrence University (Wisconsin), and he intentionally adopted some U.S. rhetorical strategies when he dealt with members of Congress and representatives of the U.S. media (Ota, 1993).

Select Your Persuasive Topic

Choosing a persuasive topic for your classroom speech can be daunting. Even if you have some ideas for subjects, you may not know how to focus clearly on one specific purpose and one central idea. In this section, we will look at strategies you can use to find a subject. Then, we'll look at ways to select your claim and tentatively formulate your central idea.

Finding Your Subject

It is important to find a need that you can address by speaking out. Select a topic that matters to you. Especially in the area of persuasion, it's pretty hard to persuade others if you are neutral about the subject. So begin by considering your strong beliefs and feelings; then ask yourself what would improve society in general or people's lives in particular. Thinking about these ideas will lead you to a series of questions you can ask yourself as you search for an appropriate topic (Mullins, 1993).

- **My strong beliefs:** What ideas and issues would I argue for? What ideas and issues would I argue against?
- **My strong feelings:** What makes me angry? What are my pet peeves? What arouses my pity? What makes me sad? What do I fear?
- **My social ideals:** What changes would I like to see in society? What current problems or conditions could improve if we believed there is a problem, that there are solutions, and that we can be part of those solutions? Are there any causes for which I would sign a petition or join a protest?
- **My personal ideals:** What can make life more meaningful for others and for me? What activities will expand our horizons? What improves our health? What leads to more fulfilling personal relationships?

Here are some examples of classroom topics: censorship, high car insurance rates, downloading music from the Internet, affordable housing, international child sponsorship programs, the joys of skydiving, learning another language. You can see that they reflect strong beliefs and feelings and that the topics relate to social or personal needs.

Examine your strong beliefs and feelings, your social and personal ideals for topics. Loida believes international child sponsorship is a good thing. She uses her enthusiasm to convince her classmates that even college students can afford to participate in this charitable activity.

Michael Newman/PhotoEdit

STOP AND CHECK

SELECT YOUR TOPIC

Fold a piece of paper into fourths and label each quarter, using one of the following categories.

- My strong beliefs
- My strong feelings
- My social ideals
- My personal ideals

Next, make a list of possible topics within each section.

Now consider your classroom audience. Circle topics in each section that would be appropriate given this particular group.

Analyze the topics you've circled, and put an X by those you could discuss within the allotted time.

Finally, select the best topic, given your audience and the time constraints.

Access this Stop and Check Activity online under Chapter 17 at the Jaffe Connection Web site. Using the questions in this activity and InfoTrac College Edition, develop possible topics for your own speech assignments.

Web Site

Making Persuasive Claims

Selecting your subject is only the first step. After you know your topic area, ask yourself what claim you want to defend. A **claim** is an assertion that is disputable or open to challenge—a conclusion or generalization that some people won't accept, a statement that requires some sort of evidence or backing to be believed. We commonly make four types of claims: fact, definition, value, and policy.

Claim
An assertion that's disputable or open to challenge.

Factual Claims

Here you argue what exists or does not exist, what's led to a current situation, or what will or will not happen; you assess the validity of these claims using terms such as *true* or *false*, *correct* or *incorrect*, *yes* or *no*. These three types of **factual claims** are common:

Factual Claims
Arguments about existence, causation, or predictions.

1. *Debatable points* are things that either are or are not true, that did or did not happen (for example, there is life on other planets; Lee Harvey Oswald acted alone to assassinate President Kennedy; angels exist)
2. *Causal relationships* argue that a particular phenomenon is the result of something that preceded it and led to it (for example, secondhand smoke can kill your pet; television violence influences children to commit violent acts; aliens create crop circles)
3. *Predictions* contend that something will happen in the future (for example, a particular stock will gain in value; terrorists will succeed in launching another huge attack on the United States; the Mariners will win the World Series this year)

All these claims generate differences of opinion. Is there life on other planets? Science fiction writers seem to think so, but no one really knows for sure. If there are space aliens, did they create crop circles? Nobody can prove they did. What, if anything, links smoking to disease in pets? Or television violence to violent children? Studies often find correlations between two things, but a correlation is not the same as causation. That is, two things may appear together, but that does not mean one necessarily leads to the other.

Finally, claims about future happenings are open to debate. People lost huge sums of money in the stock market because their predictions proved wrong. The summer before September 11, 2001, a few FBI officials predicted attacks on the United States; unfortunately, no one paid much attention because such threats are common. Who could know that these threats were serious? And, of course, arguments about sports teams fuel many a conversation.

Definition or Classification Claims

One man shoots another. How should he be prosecuted? The answer depends on the category prosecutors decide fits the crime: was the killing *premeditated murder*? Was it unpremeditated *homicide*? Was it *self-defense*? Was he *insane*, incapable of making responsible decisions? The classification of the crime results in different charges and different sentencing possibilities.

Claims of definition or **classification** are needed when we must decide what kind of entity or phenomenon we have—when we categorize it. For example, people argue over the definition of *pornography*, of *anti-Semitic*, of *family*. They debate the meaning of *cruel and unusual punishment*. A group of young Palestinians strap bombs to their bodies and detonate them in crowded spots in Israel, killing themselves along with many Israelis. They are commonly called *suicide bombers* (a term that highlights their deaths); however, the Bush administration termed them *homicide bombers* (putting the emphasis on their victims). In their own country, many consider them *martyrs*.

Early in a discussion of issues, it's important to define terminology by setting the parameters of the category, then showing why the specific entity fits into that category. The abortion issue is contentious, partly because people classify or categorize the fetus differently. If you define someone as a *human person* from the point of conception, you will classify an eight-cell embryo differently than if you believe a *human person* exists only when brain waves are present (usually about twelve weeks into a pregnancy). The definitions you accept influence the kinds of decisions you consider proper regarding frozen embryos or late-term abortions—as well as capital punishment, censorship, family law, and diplomatic efforts in the Middle East.

> **Definition or Classification Claims** Determining which category an item belongs in.

Value Claims

When you judge or evaluate something using terms such as *right* or *wrong* (it's morally *wrong* to cut down the rain forest), *good* or *better* or *best* (that restaurant serves the city's *best* chili), *beautiful* or *ugly* (hybrid cars are *ugly*), you're making a **value claim.** Here is a value claim: "It's unfair for airlines to charge obese persons for two seats instead of one." Other examples include "It's better to have loved and lost than never to have loved at all" and "Environmental protection is more important than economic development." Value conflicts are hard to resolve when the people arguing disagree on **criteria,** or standards for deciding whether something is right or wrong, fair or unfair, humane or inhumane.

Consider a current movie that you loved and your friend hated. Why did you come to different conclusions about its merit? Because each of you had different criteria for deciding what makes a "good" or a "bad" movie. Let's say your criteria include romance, beginning-to-end action, and stunning visual effects—which this movie had. However, your friend likes movies only if the characters are realistic and the plot is unpredictable. Your movie fails to meet her criteria. You can argue for hours about the merits of the movie, but unless one (or both) of you adjusts your criteria, you'll never agree.

> **Value Claims** Arguments about right or wrong, moral or immoral, beautiful or ugly.
>
> **Criteria** The standards you use for making evaluations or judgments.

Policy Claims

These claims consider whether individuals or groups should act or not, and how they should proceed if they decide to do so. In short, **policy claims** often deal with problems and solutions, assessed by terms such as *should* and *would*. You'll commonly hear two major types of policy arguments:

1. **Arguments against the *status quo*** (a Latin phrase that means *the existing state of affairs*) are arguments for change, whether in policies or individual behaviors. (Congress should adopt a flat tax system; you should write your senator and urge a vote on the flat tax.)
2. **Arguments supporting the *status quo*** are arguments for the way things are—arguments against change. (The university should not raise tuition; the current sales tax rate is adequate.)

> **Policy Claims** Arguments about the need or the plan for taking action.
>
> **Status Quo** A Latin phrase that means the existing state of affairs.

For an example, look at the field of education. Many educational reformers believe teaching and learning within the United States needs improvement, and they argue against the status quo by first identifying educational problem areas, then proposing solutions that will truly improve schools and be workable. Various reformers argue for better teacher training, for smaller classes, or for vouchers as ways to solve some of the problems.

In short, within a single topic area, you can argue facts, show how an issue should be defined or classified, defend a value question, or formulate a policy to solve a problem related to the topic. Whatever you decide on as your major claim will be the tentative formulation of your central idea.

Let's say you decide to speak about ocean pollution—specifically, dumping garbage in the ocean. You have the option of focusing on facts, definitions, values, or policies surrounding the issue as the following illustrates.

Claim		Tentative Central Idea
Fact	Argue a debatable point.	Dumping garbage in our oceans is not excessive.
	Attempt to prove a cause–effect relationship.	Dumping waste products in the ocean poses health risks to seaboard residents.
	Make a prediction.	If we do not take seriously the issue of dumping garbage in the ocean, our beaches will become too contaminated to use.
Definition	Clarify denotative meaning or classification of a term.	Dumped garbage falls into the category of Non-Point Source (NPS) pollution or "people pollution."
Value	Argue something is right or wrong, good or bad, beautiful or ugly.	It is wrong to dump garbage in the ocean.
Policy	Propose a policy change.	We should stop dumping garbage in ocean waters.
	Propose a behavioral change.	Write your representative and voice your concerns about dumping garbage in the oceans.
	Argue against a policy change.	There is no good reason to stop disposing of garbage in oceans.

In summary, select the subject of your speech from topics and issues that concern you—from the personal level to the international level. Then, tentatively formulate your central idea by deciding if you want to argue a factual claim, a definition or classification claim, a value claim, or a policy claim.

Narrow Your Persuasive Purpose

Although the general purpose of your speech is to persuade, narrow your focus and specific purpose in light of what your listeners already know and do, how they feel, and what they consider important. Because all these factors are interrelated, keep in mind that one

STOP AND CHECK

MAKE FACT, DEFINITION, VALUE, AND POLICY CLAIMS

To better understand that discussions surrounding a controversial topic contain a mixture of factual, value, and policy claims, work alone or with a small group of classmates and choose a controversial topic such as euthanasia, gay marriage, affirmative action, environmental protection, or sex education. Then write out a factual claim, a value claim, and a policy claim relating to your topic. Afterward, share your claims with the class as a whole.

- Write a factual claim dealing with a debatable fact, causation, or a prediction.
- Define an essential term.
- Assess questions of good or bad, developing criteria for a decision.
- Decide whether or not the status quo needs to be changed, and frame your policy claim accordingly.

To understand how the same topic can be developed in different ways, compare the speech outline on sleep deprivation with the text of the speech on the same topic that appears in Appendix C.

speech may, in reality, have multiple purposes that exist on a number of levels. For instance, while you are trying to convince your listeners about hazards of dumping garbage in the ocean—focusing on their beliefs—you may also be reinforcing their health-related values and the negative attitudes they currently hold toward pollution in general.

This section will present specific strategies to use when you target your audience's beliefs and actions, their values, or their attitudes. (Chapter 18 provides detailed information on creating persuasive appeals.)

Focusing on Beliefs and Actions

What we believe to be true affects how we act. Our beliefs and actions, in turn, are influenced by our values and our attitudes. To illustrate, students who spend time studying outside of class believe their hard work actually benefits their learning and their grades; in addition, they feel it is good, even moral, to study hard, considering the amount of money they are spending on tuition. They also have positive attitudes toward education. This combination of beliefs, values, and attitudes leads them to act by scheduling time for reading their texts, working on class projects, and joining study groups. Figure 17.1 shows some possible combinations of belief and action that you should consider as you narrow the focus of your speaking intention.

Figure 17.1 Your audience members approach your topic with various combinations of beliefs and actions.

	Don't Believe	**Believe**
Don't Act	unconvinced	unmotivated, unfocused
Act	inconsistent	consistent

Unconvinced

Unconvinced audience members neither believe nor act. Take acupuncture as an example. Some listeners know nothing about this Chinese medical treatment; others know, but they don't believe it will help them. Still others have misconceptions about the practice. With all these listeners, you must produce enough evidence **to convince,** to persuade them to believe your factual claims before you call for action. The following general strategies are useful when your listeners are unconvinced:

To Convince
A persuasive purpose that targets audience beliefs.

- Begin with logical appeals. Build your factual case carefully, using only evidence that passes the test for credible supporting material.
- Prove your competence by being knowledgeable about the facts. Further, show that you have respect for your listeners' intelligence and for their divergent beliefs.
- Use comparatively fewer emotional appeals.

Unmotivated or Unfocused

Sometimes your audiences are already convinced, often because they know a lot about your subject. However, they don't act on their beliefs due to **apathy** or indifference (unmotivated listeners) or lack of specific know-how (unfocused listeners). Topics such as donating blood or getting a health checkup are in this category. Your purpose, then, is to actuate, or move them to behave in ways that are consistent with their beliefs, using two different persuasive strategies.

Apathy
Indifference due to lack of motivation.

- When your audience is unmotivated, give them good reasons to act. Use emotional appeals to show that behaving as you propose will fulfill their needs and satisfy them emotionally.
- When they lack focus, provide a detailed plan that spells out specific steps they can take to implement your proposals.

In both instances, show listeners that you have their best interests in mind as you appeal for action.

Inconsistency between belief and action is one of the best motivators for change. For example, these people may know that binge drinking is harmful, but they still go on binges. Highlighting this dissonance is a good way to persuade them to make some effort to moderate their alcohol consumption.

Inconsistent

When people act in ways that differ from their beliefs, they experience what various theorists call inconsistency, or **dissonance.** One influential theory of persuasion, called **dissonance theory** (Craig, 1998; Festinger, 1957), argues that humans, like other living organisms, seek balance or equilibrium. When challenged with inconsistency, they feel psychological discomfort, and they try to return to a place of psychological balance. Inconsistency between belief and action is one of the best motivators for change. (For additional information about this subject, use www.alltheweb.com to search for the exact phrase *cognitive dissonance*; use the Advanced Search feature to limit your hits to those with .edu in the URL. Then read one of the articles you find there.)

Sometimes people question or change their beliefs but continue to behave as if they were still convinced. For example, consumers lose faith in products that they continue to purchase; students continue to major in subjects that they know are not right for them; people persist in binge drinking, even though they think it's dangerous. With inconsistent audiences, either strengthen or reinforce wavering beliefs or persuade listeners to modify their actions to match their changed beliefs.

Here are a few specific strategies you can use when your listeners' actions are inconsistent with their beliefs.

- Support faltering beliefs by concentrating on logical appeals, using as much persuasive evidence as you can muster. Include emotional appeals as well, giving reasons for listeners to want to strengthen their wavering beliefs.
- When you want behaviors to change, appeal to emotions such as honesty and sincerity. Use narratives or testimonials that exemplify how you or someone else succeeded in a similar situation.

Consistent

When people act in ways that are consistent with their beliefs, they may need encouragement to "keep on keeping on." This type of audience is common in service clubs, religious organizations, and at political rallies. Here, your narrowed purpose is to reinforce both their beliefs and actions by following this set of guidelines.

- Help listeners maintain a positive attitude about their accomplishments. Use examples and testimony that illustrate how their efforts are making a difference in the world.
- Relate yourself personally to their fundamental beliefs and values.

Throughout this section, we have explored ways that audience beliefs and actions influence both your persuasive purposes and the methods you use to present your ideas. Although you continue to employ a variety of appeals in every speech, each type of audience requires somewhat different emphases and strategies.

Focusing on Values

As noted earlier, value claims argue that something should be judged or evaluated as moral or immoral, beautiful or ugly, right or wrong, important or insignificant, and so on. Here is a value claim: "Research on embryonic stem cells is wrong." To make an evaluation, you must first establish the criteria or standards on which to judge an economic policy by answering questions such as these:

- How do we make and apply moral judgments regarding bioethical issues?
- What criteria do we use?
- Where do these criteria come from?
- Why should we accept these sources?

Dissonance
Inconsistency or clash.

Dissonance Theory
Theory that humans seek stability or equilibrium; when faced with inconsistency they seek psychological balance that may motivate them to change in order to be consistent.

Within a single audience, listeners often vary widely in their views on issues such as embryonic stem cell research. Some know little about it. Others think it holds potential cures for dozens of diseases. Still others believe destroying embryonic life is immoral and unnecessary, and they offer adult stem cell research as an alternative.

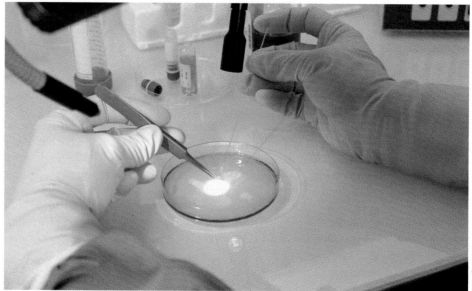

Index Stock Imagery

If your listeners agree with your criteria, it's easier for them to accept your evaluation. However, you can see that value questions are often conflict laden, for the standards used to make many value judgments are not universally accepted.

Because each individual's beliefs and experiences affect his or her value judgments, within a single audience they may vary so widely that some listeners view a topic as unethical whereas others view it as ethical. Furthermore, because values are assumptions about what is good, questions of value often generate strong emotional responses that are difficult to change. Remember the Ethical Quality Scale presented in Chapter 5? It is nearly impossible in one speech to move listeners from viewing a topic as highly unethical to the point where they evaluate it as highly ethical. Here are some tips for arguing a claim of value:

- Establish the criteria you have used to make your evaluation.
- Appeal to your audience's emotions. Use examples to help listeners identify with the issue. Appeal also to related values such as fairness, generosity, kindness, or freedom.
- As Chapter 8 pointed out, appeals to authority can be persuasive if the audience accepts the source as authoritative. Some audiences are moved by appeals to cultural traditions, words of philosophers, poets, scientists, or scriptures; others would discount those same authoritative sources.

Paul Southwick's speech, reprinted in Appendix C, argues that embryo adoption is an alternative to embryonic stem cell research. You can watch it under speeches for Chapter 4 on the CD that accompanies this text.

Focusing on Attitudes

As Chapter 5 pointed out, listeners can have positive, negative, or neutral attitudes about subjects, which we typically measure along a scale such as this:

Teenagers should be required to go through a series of graduated driver's licenses before they get an unrestricted license.

strongly agree	agree	mildly agree	neutral	mildly disagree	disagree	strongly disagree

Rebecca Ewing decided to argue for a graduated licensing process for teen drivers. If her audience shares her positive attitude toward changing the licensing process, she simply bolsters listeners' attitudes by emphasizing unpleasant or harmful aspects of the current system and highlighting the benefits of change.

However, when she faces a neutral audience, one that's neither positive nor negative, she must adjust her strategies. She first asks herself why they are neutral. Do they lack information? Or are they apathetic? Do they need to understand how the subject touches their lives directly? Her purpose with neutral listeners is to create or produce a desired attitude, in this case a positive attitude toward a graduated licensing system. She will first be sure her listeners understand the topic, then she will motivate them to care or to act.

When her listeners hold an opposite attitude—they are all negative toward a different licensing system because they feel the current system is just fine—her strategies again change. If they're mildly or moderately negative toward change, her overall strategy will be to lessen the negative and enable the audience to see positive aspects of the proposed system. If they're strongly against a graduated licensing system, she faces a hostile audience. Knowing this, Rebecca should set modest goals and aim for small attitudinal changes. (You can read her outline at the end of this chapter and view her speech on the CD that comes with the text.)

Perhaps the most distressing speaking situation arises when you face an audience that's hostile toward you personally. In these cases, it's important to emphasize common ground between yourself and your listeners. Barbara Bush (1990) faced this when she spoke at Wellesley College's graduation ceremonies. The class wanted a different speaker, and they expressed negative attitudes toward a woman whose fame resulted, not from her personal career but from her marriage. Humor was one way the First Lady turned a negative situation into a positive one. Her address is in Appendix C and on the CD that comes with this text under speeches for Chapter 18.

The following guidelines will help you plan effective speeches targeted toward attitudes:

- When listeners are positive, strengthen their emotional ties to the topic by using examples, connotative words, and appeals to needs and values that evoke emotional responses. Establish common ground throughout your speech (see Chapter 18).
- With uninformed audiences, present factual information early in the speech so they have a basis to form an evaluation. Then use emotional appeals to create either a positive or negative attitude toward the topic.

- With apathetic audiences, use emotional appeals. Link the topic to listeners in as many ways as you can. Appeal to values such as fairness and justice.
- When your audience is mildly negative, approach listeners directly. Make a clear case with objective data; present the positive facets of your subject, and link them to personal and community values your audience accepts. This way, even if they disagree with you, they will at least understand the rationale for your position.
- With negative audiences in general, approach your subject indirectly by establishing common ground on which you can all agree. For instance, begin with a statement with which everyone agrees and explain why there is agreement. Then make a statement that most would accept and explain why this is so. Move gradually to the point on which they think they disagree. By this time, they have already seen that they agree with you on many points, and as a result, they may be less negative toward your proposal (anonymous reviewer, 1993).

Generally, attitudes change incrementally. This means that listeners don't move rapidly from one extreme to another; rather, they change gradually over time. Each new encounter with the subject is only one small step that produces a slight attitude shift. Eventually, the small shifts add up to a measurable attitude change. Many people in the United States, for instance, once had a neutral or negative attitude toward schoolchildren with AIDS. However, over a period of months and years, after many speeches and much media coverage, many citizens began to fear them less and view them more positively.

Although we have discussed beliefs and actions, attitudes, and values as separate entities, the truth is that they're intertwined. Keep in mind the interrelated aspect of these cultural factors as you analyze your audience, select the specific purpose for your speech, and choose supporting material that will be persuasive.

STOP AND CHECK

ADAPT TO THE AUDIENCE'S ATTITUDE

Analyze the following public speaking situation: An anthropology major is going to present a speech on government funding for archaeological digs. Her claim is that the study of archaeology is important enough to receive government funding because knowing about other human cultures helps us to better understand our own.

Divide into three groups within the classroom. Each group will discuss how the speaker should prepare for one of the following audiences:

1. A group of anthropology majors who agree with her and are highly positive toward her topic.
2. An audience that knows nothing about anthropology but knows they are concerned about how their tax money is spent.
3. Listeners who feel that archaeology is a waste of time.

QUESTIONS

1. How will the speaker analyze the particular audience?
2. What purpose should she select for that group?
3. What specific strategies will she use to make her points?
4. What kinds of reasoning and evidence should she use?
5. What should she emphasize and why?

These questions are available online under Stop and Check Activities for Chapter 17 at the Jaffe Connection Web site. You can complete them there and, if requested, email **Web Site** your responses to your instructor.

Choose a Persuasive Pattern

After you have analyzed your audience by considering their positions regarding your issue, you then begin to look at the organizational pattern that will best communicate your ideas. In this section, we discuss common patterns used in persuasive public speaking.

Problem–Solution Pattern

The problem–solution pattern, described in Chapter 9, is commonly used in both informative and persuasive speaking. The goal of informative speaking is to increase your audience's understanding of the issue and the proposed solution or solutions. In persuasive speeches, however, your purpose is generally to convince or to advocate the implementation of a specific policy. When the intent is to convince listeners that there is indeed a problem, the outline looks like this:

Specific Purpose: To persuade my audience that there are too many air disasters but the problem can be solved by concentrating efforts in three areas.

Central Idea: Global air traffic has too many disasters and near disasters that could be minimized by working to eliminate the sources of the problems.

Stockphoto.com

In hundreds of persuasive speeches given after September 11, 2001, citizens and lawmakers alike discussed problems and proposed solutions that would prevent additional terrorist acts against the United States.

I. There are too many air disasters and near disasters around the globe.

   A. The problem involves near misses and crashes.

      1. The problem is extensive (statistics).
      2. This has negative implications for travelers.

   B. There are several causes of this problem.

      1. There are communication problems between crews and air traffic controllers.
      2. Weather is a consideration.
      3. Mechanical and maintenance failures cause disasters.

II. The problem can be minimized.

   A. Airplanes should be more carefully inspected and maintained.
   B. Both crew members and air traffic controllers should continue to receive on-the-job training both in communication and in understanding the effects of weather.
   C. Engineers and researchers should continue to develop state-of-the-art equipment to prevent some of these disasters.

When you aim less at convincing your audience of a problem, and instead argue for a particular solution, a good strategy is to present several possible solutions, then advocate or argue that one is best. This adds a third point to the outline.

I. Problem and need
II. Possible solutions
III. The one best solution

This is how a more complete outline looks:

Specific Purpose: To persuade my audience that incineration is the best solution to the problem of medical waste.

Central Idea: Of the three methods of medical waste disposal—steam sterilization, ocean dumping, and incineration—incineration is the best.

I. More and more medical waste is being generated, creating a need for a safe method of disposal.

   A. There are several waste products from medical procedures.

   B. The problem is extensive (statistics).

   C. Some of the waste products pose risks.

II. There are three ways to dispose of medical waste.

   A. One is the steam sterilization process.

   B. The second is ocean dumping.

   C. The third is incineration.

III. Incineration is the best solution.

   A. It completely destroys the product.

   B. Fire purifies.

Monroe's Motivated Sequence

Monroe's Motivated Sequence
A call to action in five steps: attention, need, satisfaction, visualization, and action.

Alan Monroe, a professor at Purdue University for many years, developed and refined a pattern that is commonly used in persuasive speaking, especially in speeches with the purpose of actuating behavior. **Monroe's Motivated Sequence** is a modified form of a problem–solution speech.

Before people act, they must be motivated to do what they know they should do. Because of this, it's important to provide emotional reasons as well as logical ones. Monroe's pattern includes the word *motivated*, because it has several built-in steps to increase motivational appeals. (Note that this pattern is not a formula in the sense that you have to include each element that Monroe describes. Rather Monroe suggests various ways you can develop each point in the speech.) Here are the five easily remembered steps in the sequence, as explained by Monroe himself (1962).

1. **Attention Step:** As with any other speech, you begin by gaining the audience's attention and drawing it to your topic.
2. **Need Step:** This step is similar to the problem part of a problem–solution speech. Monroe suggests four elements in establishing the need: (a) statement—tell the nature of the problem; (b) illustration—give a relevant detailed example or examples; (c) ramifications—provide additional support such as statistics or testimony that show the extent of the problem; and (d) pointing—show the direct relationship between the audience and the problem.
3. **Satisfaction Step:** After you've demonstrated the problem or need, shown its extent and its effects on the audience, you then satisfy the need by proposing a solution. This step can have as many as five parts: (a) statement—briefly state the attitude, belief, or action you want the audience to adopt; (b) explanation—make your proposal understandable (visual aids may help at this point); (c) theoretical demonstration—show the logical connection between the need and its satisfaction; (d) practicality—use facts, figures, and testimony to show that the proposal has worked effectively or that the belief has been proved correct; and (e) meeting objections—show that your proposal can overcome your listeners' potential objections.
4. **Visualization Step:** This step is unique from other patterns. In it, you ask the audience to imagine what will happen if they enact the proposal or if they fail to do so. (a) Positive—describe the future if your plan is put into action. Create a realistic positive scenario showing what your solution provides. Appeal to emotions—safety needs, pride, pleasure, and other emotions. (b) Negative—have listeners imagine themselves in an unpleasant situation because they did not put your solution into effect. (c) Contrast—compare the negative results of not enacting your plan with the positive results your plan will produce.

5. **Action:** In the final step, call for your listeners to act in a specific way: (a) call for a specific, overt action, attitude, or belief; (b) state your personal intention to act; and (c) end with impact.

As you might imagine, this pattern is good for a sales speech. It is also effective in policy speeches and other claims that include a "should" or an "ought." For example, after terrorists destroyed the World Trade Center, national leaders discussed homeland security—the need to be more vigilant, ways to solve the problem, scary scenarios if nothing is done, and calls for action to beef up security in the homeland.

STOP AND CHECK
USE MONROE'S MOTIVATED SEQUENCE

Working alone or with a small group, plan a short outline for a speech intended to motivate your audience to action. Choose one of these general topic categories:

- **Sales:** Convince your classmates to buy a specific product.
- **Public service:** Ask your listeners to donate time or money to a worthy cause.

Direct Method Pattern

In the **direct method,** sometimes called the **statement of reasons pattern,** you make a claim, then directly state your reasons to support it. Each point, thus, provides an additional rationale to agree with your views. It's a good pattern to use when listeners are apathetic or neutral, either mildly favoring or mildly opposing your claim. Consider it when your goal is to convince, although you can also use it to organize a speech **to actuate** (or motivate the audience to do something).

This outline for a speech on therapy dogs states four reasons these animals are helpful in health facilities, prisons, and shelter homes (Hunt, 2002).

> **Specific Purpose:** To persuade my listeners that therapy dogs provide psychological and physical benefits to people in distressing circumstances.
> **Central Idea:** Therapy dogs promote well-being, affection, communication, and movement.

I. They promote a general feeling of well-being (children, the elderly).
II. They provide unconditional affection to those who lack it (prisoners, people in shelters).
III. They interact with those who have trouble communicating (Alzheimer's patients, some psychiatric patients, stroke patients).
IV. They motivate simple activities (patting, brushing) for patients with physical limitations.

The intention of the following speech was to convince listeners that a particular policy should be enacted. The major points are factual claims of prediction that provide reasons to agree with the major claim.

> **Specific Purpose:** To persuade my listeners to believe that all primary and secondary students should wear uniforms to school.
> **Central Idea:** All students should wear school uniforms to eliminate social distinctions, save money, and prevent crime.

All pre-college students, even those in public schools, should wear uniforms.

Direct Method or Statement of Reasons Pattern
A method that makes a claim, then states reasons that provide a rationale for the ideas.

To Actuate
Motivate the audience to do something.

I. This will eliminate social distinctions between rich and poor.
II. It will save money.
III. It will prevent clothing-related crime.

As you can see, this pattern is a variant of the topical pattern. It's easy to use, both in speeches intended to convince and in those intended to actuate.

Comparative Advantages Pattern

Use a **comparative advantages pattern** for policy speeches arguing that one proposal is superior to competing proposals by comparing its advantages to those of the competition. Study the following outline from a speech to convince an audience of the superiority of osteopathic doctors:

Specific Purpose: To persuade my audience that a Doctor of Osteopathic Medicine (D.O.) is superior to a chiropractor for many reasons.
Central Idea: D.O.s are better than chiropractors because of their training and their ability to do surgery.

Doctors of Osteopathic Medicine (D.O.s) are superior to chiropractors.

I. They can do everything chiropractors do, and more.
II. Their training is superior because it includes courses comparable to those in medical schools.
III. Many D.O.s perform surgeries in hospitals with which they are affiliated.

You can also use the comparative advantages method when you want your listeners to act. For instance, in hopes of recruiting students, a representative of a small private college compares the advantages of her institution over larger state schools. Look for this pattern in advertisements, sales speeches, and campaign speeches, as this outline demonstrates:

Specific Purpose: To persuade my audience to purchase a specific brand of DVD player.
Central Idea: This brand of DVD player is superior to the competition in cost, features, and design.

Buy [a certain DVD player].

I. It costs less but provides the same features as the best-selling brand.
II. It is code free, meaning it's not limited to specific regions like the other brand is.
III. It has a cleaner, more usable front when compared to the more cluttered competitor.

It's easy to see that this pattern is related to reasoning by comparison and contrast, for you continually compare and contrast your proposal or product to other proposals and products the audience already knows.

Criteria Satisfaction Pattern

As defined earlier, criteria are standards that form a basis for judgments; the **criteria satisfaction pattern** first sets forth the standards to judge a proposal, then shows how the solution, candidate, or product meets or exceeds these standards. Because it describes the standards for evaluation at the outset, it is useful in speeches that argue value claims.

Let's examine the problem of hiring a new professor. The criteria section of an argument for a specific candidate answers the question, "What qualities does a good professor have?" The search committee might believe a professor should have good teaching skills, good interpersonal skills, and good research and writing skills. The second part of the speech—the satisfaction section—shows how the proposed candidate satisfies all the criteria. In this case, the candidate has a record of good teaching evaluations, she works well with people, and she has written two books and published several articles in academic journals.

The following outline demonstrates the criteria satisfaction pattern for the argument that using community service is a workable punishment for criminals.

Specific Purpose: To persuade my audience that community service meets all the criteria for a good punishment for nonviolent criminals.

Central Idea: Community service is a punishment that fits the crime, reduces recidivism, and is cost effective.

What does a good punishment for nonviolent felons look like?

I. The punishment fits the crime.
II. It reduces recidivism.
III. It is cost effective.

Community service is the best punishment for nonviolent crimes.

I. The punishment can be tailored to fit the crime.
II. It keeps felons out of prison where they can be influenced by career criminals.
III. It is far less costly to administer than incarceration.

You may find the criteria satisfaction pattern especially useful for controversial issues; this is so because at the outset you establish common ground with your listeners by setting up criteria on which you all agree. As in the direct methods pattern, consider building to a climax by developing the most persuasive criteria last.

Negative Method Pattern

When you use the **negative method pattern,** you concentrate on the shortcomings of every other proposal; then you show why your proposal is the one logical solution remaining. In other words, point out the negative aspects in competing proposals; then, after you've dismantled or undermined everyone else's plan, you propose your own. This pattern is often used to argue a policy claim that's one among many.

Negative Method Pattern
Point out shortcomings of other proposals, then demonstrate why your proposal is the one logical solution remaining.

Specific Purpose: To persuade my audience that global legalization of drugs is the only way to control the supply and demand of illicit drugs.

Central Idea: Because of the failures of drug enforcement agencies and education, we need to regulate drugs through legalization.

We need a solution to the problem of drugs around the world.

I. More drug enforcement agencies are not the answer.
II. Better education is not the answer.
III. Global legalization of drugs is the only way we will regulate supply and demand.

As you can see, you have many persuasive patterns from which to choose. As you plan your speech, use the pattern that is most appropriate to both your material and your audience. These patterns are not exhaustive, but they are among the most common you'll find in public speeches, advertisements, and other persuasive messages.

Summary

The best subjects for persuasive speeches come from the things that matter most to you personally. For this reason, ask yourself questions such as "What do I believe strongly?" "What arouses strong feelings within me?" "What would I like to see changed?" "What enriches my life?" Your answers will generally provide you with topics that you're willing to defend. Choosing your subject is only the first part of topic selection. You then decide whether you will argue a claim of fact, value, definition, or policy.

We consistently argue for our ideas in an attempt to influence one another's beliefs, actions, values, and attitudes, and we strategically organize our speeches and adapt our ideas to different types of audiences. However, assumptions and actions are always interwoven. The result is that while you are motivating listeners to act, you are also trying to reinforce their positive attitudes and beliefs. Throughout the entire time, you rely on underlying values to support your calls to action.

Choose from a number of common patterns to organize your major points. Consider the problem–solution pattern and its variant, Monroe's Motivated Sequence—both of which define a problem and identify a solution. The direct method, also called the statement of reasons pattern, directly lists arguments that support your claim. The criteria satisfaction pattern is good for value speeches because you first set up criteria or standards for judgment, then show how your proposal meets these standards. The comparative advantages method shows the advantage of your proposal over similar proposals; the negative method, in contrast, shows the disadvantages of every proposal but your own.

JAFFE ONLINE CONNECTION JAFFE ONLINE CONNECTION

Use your CD-ROM and the Jaffe Connection Web site http://communication.wadsworth.com/jaffe to review the following concepts, answer the review questions, and complete the suggested activities.

KEY TERMS

claim (318)
factual claims (318)
definition or classification claims (319)
value claims (319)
criteria (319)
policy claims (319)
status quo (319)
to convince (322)
apathy (322)

dissonance (323)
dissonance theory (323)
Monroe's Motivated Sequence (328)
direct method or statement of
    reasons pattern (329)
to actuate (329)
comparative advantages pattern (330)
criteria satisfaction pattern (330)
negative method pattern (331)

APPLICATION AND CRITICAL THINKING EXERCISES

1. Consider the relationship between beliefs and actions, and identify topics that might fall into each category. For instance, for the "unfocused" category: people often believe they should learn to study more effectively, but they don't know how to proceed. For the "unconvinced" category: people don't know enough about investing wisely, so they don't invest at all.

2. Listen to at least one persuasive speech on television, taking notes on the speaker's arguments. (C-SPAN is a good source for such speeches.) What kinds of claims does the speaker make? How does she or he support the claims? Who are the intended audiences? How effectively does the speaker adapt to audience beliefs, actions, attitudes, and values?

3. Use InfoTrac College Edition to do a PowerTrac search for the article titled "The Effectiveness of Humor in Persuasion," which describes a theory of persuasion called the elaboration likelihood model (ELM). Read the introduction and final paragraph of this article, and come to class prepared to discuss the ELM and the functions humor in persuasive messages.

4. To explore hostile speaking in greater depth, log on to the Internet and go to www.richspeaking.com/articles/Difficult_Audience.html. Compare the author's list of ten typical ways to respond to hostile audiences with his six positive alternative strategies.

5. With a small group in your classroom, identify areas in which national attitudes have changed—or areas in which your personal attitudes have changed. How did persuasive public speaking contribute to those changes?

THE JAFFE CONNECTION WEB SITE

The Jaffe Connection Web site features review questions about the Web links, Stop and Check activities, and InfoTrac College Edition exercises referenced throughout the chapter. You can access this site via your CD-ROM or at http://communication.wadsworth.com/jaffe.

Web Links

17.1 Cognitive Dissonance (page 323)
17.2 Speaking to a Hostile Audience (page 333)

Stop and Check Activities

17.1 Select Your Topic (page 318)
17.2 Make Fact, Definition, Value, and Policy Claims (page 321)
17.3 Adapt to the Audience's Attitude (page 326)
17.4 Use Monroe's Motivated Sequence (page 329)

InfoTrac College Edition Exercises

17.1 The Effectiveness of Using Humor to Persuade (page 333)

SPEECH INTERACTIVE ON THE JAFFE CONNECTION CD-ROM

Watch the following policy speech by Rebecca Ewing and answer the questions for analysis under Speech Interactive on your Jaffe Connection CD-ROM. In addition to Rebecca's speech, Speech Interactive features Paul Southwick's value speech (in Chapter 4 speeches) referred to on page 324 and printed in Appendix C.

STUDENT OUTLINE WITH COMMENTARY

THE CASE FOR GRADUATED LICENSING
by Rebecca Ewing

General Purpose: To persuade
Specific Purpose: To persuade (to convince) my audience that sixteen is too young for unsupervised driving and states should adopt a graduated licensing system.
Central Idea: Sixteen-year-olds are immature and lack drivers' training; to solve this problem, all states should adopt a graduated licensing system.

This speech was given in a state that had not yet changed the laws that license teenage drivers. Obviously, it would be unnecessary in a state with more restrictive laws.

Rebecca opens with an emotional, extended narrative.

Introduction

I. On a typical Friday night in a small Florida town, thirteen-year-old Margo and Crystal lost their lives when sixteen-year-old Nick drove foolishly, resulting in a deadly head-on collision.

   A. Nick crammed seven teens into the back seat of his Honda, where none wore seatbelts.
   B. He began driving too fast, and he speeded up and tailgated other cars when frightened passengers asked him to slow down.
   C. He lost control, jumped the median, and hit another car head on.
   D. Airbags saved the front seat passengers, but five backseat passengers were killed and two were injured.

II. Sixteen-year-olds face incredible responsibilities when they drive.

   A. Are they equipped to handle problems?
   B. Are they mature enough?
   C. Many teens have lost their lives because teen drivers lack proper training and have too much freedom at too young an age.

III. Sixteen is too young for teens to drive without adult supervision, and I think the evidence will show this.

IV. I will establish the dangers of giving licenses to sixteen-year-olds, then I will propose a solution that has proven effective in more than eighteen states.

V. Many of you disagree.

Here in the introduction she deals with her audience's attachment to the *status quo*.

   A. You probably think getting your license is a rite of passage; it's always been this way, why change now?
   B. I believe changing the law will save lives like Margo's and Crystal's—perhaps like yours and like mine.

Body

I. Statistics show that sixteen- and seventeen-year-olds are responsible for 11 percent of crashes, but they make up only 2 percent of the driving population.

By beginning her discussion with statistics, she shows the extent of the problem.

   A. Why are they responsible for so many crashes?

Quoting an authoritative source shows that she is not just giving her own opinion; more credible sources support her ideas.

      1. According to the University of North Carolina's Highway Safety Research Center, "A major reason that teens are involved in more driving accidents is that they are poorly trained by their parents and by drivers' attitudes."

         a. Parents need to take their children's passage into adulthood more seriously.
         b. They should take quality time to teach teens to drive defensively with good techniques.

      2. Another reason is teen attitudes.

         a. Teens see a license as a ticket to new freedoms.
         b. Caught up in the excitement of driving, they make mistakes.

Referring to her opening story creates continuity throughout the speech.

         c. If Nick had been more experienced and more mature, he probably would not have piled too many teens into his car, sped excessively, and tailgated at high speeds.

   B. *Readers' Digest* interviewed 400 teenagers, ages fifteen to nineteen, about their experiences with other teen drivers who had not been drinking and hadn't been using drugs—with shocking results.

TRANSITION: The problem is real. Teens don't have the maturity or judgment to handle the responsibility of driving without adult supervision, and we need to solve this problem.

II. Two major solutions have been proposed.

A. One approach is to raise the age that teens can get a license.

    1. *U.S. News & World Report* states that drivers over twenty-one have fewer accidents and other problems than other drivers; consequently, many countries don't even license drivers under age eighteen.

        a. But mass transportation is less available here.
        b. Teens drive to school and work, and parents don't want to chauffeur them around.

    2. Consequently, licensing only drivers over the age of eighteen is unlikely to pass here.

B. The National Highway Traffic Safety Administration urges states to adopt a graduated licensing program (a three-tiered system), which extends the time it takes to be qualified to drive.

    1. *Stage 1*: the teen obtains a learner's permit and drives with an adult.
        a. The teen becomes familiar with driving rules and regulations.
        b. Teens encounter problem situations with an adult beside them.
    2. *Stage 2*: after one year of good driving, the teen is issued a provisional license and drives without supervision during daylight hours, but with supervision at night.
    3. *Stage 3*: after six months with no accidents or tickets, the teen can get an unrestricted license.

III. There is evidence that the three-tiered system works.

A. California, Oregon, and Maryland report that accidents involving teen drivers dropped 5 to 16 percent.
B. This dramatic difference and the promise of lives changed impressed legislators in other states, where they are working to pass a similar system.
C. The more quickly this is adopted, the more lives will be saved.

Conclusion

I. I've shown you that sixteen is too young to drive independently and that a three-tiered system reduces the number of accidents involving teen drivers.
II. I urge you to contact your state's legislators and politicians and ask them to support the graduated licensing system, which might save the life of a sister, brother, friend, you, or me.
III. A graduated licensing system allows teens to accept responsibilities that go along with the privileges and to avoid Nick's mistakes; if he'd gone through a graduated licensing program, Crystal and Margo might be alive today.

Side notes:

She presents two approaches, but quickly shows that the first will probably not work. This leaves the second solution—the one that she proposes.

She describes her proposed solution is some detail.

Her conclusion presents a summary, a call to action, and a reference back to the emotional opening story.

Persuasive Reasoning Methods

THIS CHAPTER WILL HELP YOU

- Describe the elements of Toulmin's model of reasoning
- Define logos, or rational proofs
- Explain these types of reasoning and identify tests for each: analogy (metaphor and parallel case), inductive, deductive, and causal
- Recognize fallacious reasoning
- Define pathos, or emotional proofs
- Understand how appeals to emotions and needs are aspects of pathos
- Define ethos, or speaker credibility
- Identify ways ethos functions as a reason to believe
- Explain how reasoning strategies vary across cultural groups
- Identify elements of invitational rhetoric

"For the Roses/Para las Rosas" Mural ©1985 by Juana Alicia. (Treat Street at 21st Street, SF, CA)

FTER HOURS OF DELIBERATION, THE JURY was hopelessly deadlocked. The twelve jurors had been asked to decide if Kenneth Powell should be held responsible for the deaths of two men. One night, police officers stopped Powell's friend, Michael Fangle, who was driving while drunk. Police took him in, placed him in a drunk tank, and called Mr. Powell to come get him. Powell came, but instead of driving Fangle home, he returned the drunk man to his SUV, gave him the keys, and sent him out into the night. A few hours later, Michael Fangle—who apparently drank even more in the meantime—crashed into John Elliott's car. Both men died.

Prosecutors charged Kenneth Powell with manslaughter, aggravated assault, and vehicular homicide—death by car. All the jurors voted him "not guilty" on the manslaughter charge, but they disagreed on a verdict regarding aggravated assault and vehicular homicide. Some thought he was guilty as charged; others found the charges unreasonable. Throughout the trial, the jurors drew on their reasoning skills—skills described in this chapter—but they reasoned their way to different conclusions.

Every day you use your reasoning powers to make sense of your world and to make decisions that affect your life. Based on your observations, you've formed a number of conclusions that seem sensible to you. You may not think much about how you reason; you just "know" when something makes sense and when it does not. However, you may find that other people don't share your conclusions, and you may have felt compelled to explain them.

In the Western tradition, it's common to discuss three types of reasoning, which Aristotle explained in *Rhetoric* (1984):

> Of the modes of persuasion furnished by the spoken word there are three kinds. The first kind depends on the personal character of the speaker [ethos]; the second on putting the audience into a certain frame of mind [pathos]; the third on the proof, or apparent proof, provided by the words of the speech itself [logos]. (¶1356, 356, 20)

Ethos, pathos, and logos are not separate entities; they overlap to form a totality of "good reasons." In other words, emotion can be reasonable; reason can have emotional underpinnings; and it is both reasonable and emotionally satisfying to believe a credible speaker. In specific times, places, and situations, however, you may emphasize one reasoning type over the others. For instance, if you're explaining an economic recession, you'll use different kinds of reasoning or proofs than if you're explaining the accidental death of a young child to her kindergarten peers.

Using proofs from logos, pathos, and ethos effectively will empower you both as a speaker and as a critical listener within this culture. However, "winning" an argument is not always desirable or possible, and this chapter concludes with principles and forms of invitational rhetoric.

Use Toulmin's Reasoning Model

Watch a show like *Judging Amy*, and you'll see prosecutors charge defendants with crimes based on evidence that warrants their prosecutions. Every week, defense lawyers rebut these charges by attacking the claim, the evidence, the link to their client, and so on. Professor Stephen Toulmin (1958; Toulmin, Rieke, & Janik, 1984) diagrammed elements of an argument based on interchanges typically found in courtrooms. His linear model, shown in Figure 18.1, illustrates important aspects of reasoning and clarifies the relationships among claims, evidence or data, warrants, backing, qualifiers, and conditions for rebuttal that characterize traditional reasoning in U.S. culture. Learning to qualify your claim, justifying it with evidence, and planning ways to deal with counterarguments will make your speeches more persuasive.

Figure 18.1 Toulmin's model of argument.

SOURCE: ADAPTED FROM MACMILLAN PUBLISHING COMPANY, INC., FROM *AN INTRODUCTION TO REASONING*, SECOND EDITION, BY STEPHEN TOULMIN, RICHARD RIEKE, AND ALLAN JANIK. COPYRIGHT © BY MACMILLAN PUBLISHING COMPANY.

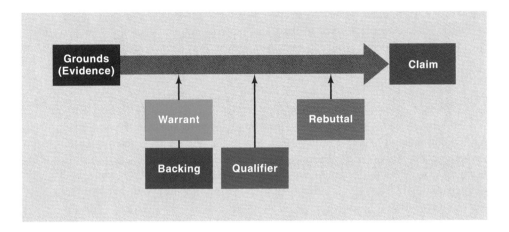

Claims

As Chapter 17 pointed out, claims are disputable assertions that require evidence or backing to be accepted. To review, factual claims argue about what exists, what causes something else, or what the future will bring. Definition or classification claims determine in which category a phenomenon belongs. Value claims deal with the rightness, the goodness, or the worth of a thing. Finally, policy claims argue over actions or proposals for change.

Grounds, Data, or Evidence

To support your claims, select facts, examples and narratives, quotations, statistics, and literal and figurative comparisons, as described in Chapter 8. Evidence is also called **data** or **grounds,** and providing your listeners with evidence enables them to weigh your argument and decide whether your conclusions make sense. Without sufficient and credible data, your claims will simply be unsupported **assertions.**

> **Data or Grounds**
> Evidence offered to support a claim.
>
> **Assertions**
> Claims put forth without any supporting evidence.

Warrants

The justification or reasoning that both you and your listeners use to connect your evidence with your claim is called a **warrant.** Switch your TV on to a police drama and watch the reasoning the officers use to justify an arrest. Officers must produce a warrant, which they can only get if they have sufficient data or grounds to make the arrest. Consider this scenario: The fingerprint on the gun (evidence) matches the suspect's print (additional evidence); the logical conclusion is that the suspect fired the gun (claim of fact), because each person has unique fingerprints (the warrant that connects or links the evidence to the claim).

> **Warrant**
> Justification or reasoning that connects the claim and the evidence.

Backing

When a warrant is not broadly understood or broadly accepted, you sometimes give reasons to support or defend it. These reasons are called **backing.** For example, *Court TV* broadcast a trial in which blood was found on a defendant's jacket (evidence). In case the jury didn't understand the link between the blood evidence and the perpetrator (warrant), the prosecution brought in several experts who explained the science of DNA (backing) and testified that the blood could only be the victim's (backing).

> **Backing**
> Reasons given to support the warrant.

Qualifiers

Qualifiers
Words and phrases that
limit or narrow the scope of
a claim.

Avoid words such as *always* or *never* when you make claims. Instead, use **qualifiers,** the words and phrases that limit or narrow the scope of your claim. Some common qualifiers are *in most cases, in males between the ages of seven and nine, among voters with a college degree,* and *usually.* For example, instead of asserting "one in eight women will get breast cancer," to have a more defensible claim add a qualifier such as "women *who live to the age of 110* have a one in eight chance of getting breast cancer."

Rebuttal

Rebuttal
Arguments that counter or
disagree with a claim.

Not all listeners will agree with your claims. As a "listening speaker," try to hear the arguments your audience members will raise in opposition, then prepare to counter their arguments directly. This is the **rebuttal** aspect of the model. It might help you to think of rebuttals as your listeners' arguments that begin with the phrase, "*But* what about . . . ?" Demonstrating that you've considered these counterarguments and that you still have good reasons for your claim enhances your persuasiveness.

In summary, if you learn to recognize the type of claim you are making, qualify it, provide evidence and backing to warrant it, then deal with potential audience rebuttals, you will be more effective in presenting your ideas to others and having them recognize your views as reasonable.

STOP AND CHECK

EVALUATING CLAIMS—A CASE STUDY

The relationship between Chinese women's strength and possible steroid use has been a question at several summer Olympic competitions.

AP/Wide World Photos

During summer Olympic competition, the question often surfaces: Are Chinese female athletes on steroids? Read the following elements of the argument, and then answer the question.

• Chinese female athletes have voices in the low range, compared to other women.
• They are comparatively large.
• They are heavily muscled.
• Their country has been advised by coaches from the former East Germany, which was found to provide steroids to its female swimmers for many years.
• George Steinbrenner of the Yankees baseball team said that it was impossible to build such a strong team in just two years without some explanation.

- Scientists admit that steroids can be administered in training so that they will leave no traces during the competition.
- The Chinese female swimmers used steroids in their training programs.

QUESTIONS

1. What is the claim?
2. Is the claim one of fact, value, or policy?
3. What is the warrant?
4. What possible rebuttal might an objector make? [*Hint:* But what about the population of China?]
5. Is there enough evidence, in your opinion, to warrant the claim?
6. What else might cause the swimmers' characteristics?

You can answer these questions online and, if requested by your instructor, submit them via email. Go to Stop and Check Activities for Chapter 18 on the Jaffe Connection Web site at http://communication.wadsworth.com/jaffe.

Web Site

Use Logos or Rational Proofs

Logos includes the verbal arguments you make relating to your subject. Also known as rational proofs, these arguments include analogy, inductive, deductive, and causal reasoning. As you might expect, these are not the only methods of sense making, as the Diversity in Practice feature on cultural reasoning explains.

Logos
Verbal arguments, arguments from the words of the speech itself.

DIVERSITY IN PRACTICE

THE INFLUENCE OF CULTURE ON REASONING

CULTURE INFLUENCES our reasoning strategies in a number of ways that can easily lead to misunderstandings between cultural groups (Hilliard, 1986).

- **Topics considered appropriate for discussion vary across cultures.** Some groups, for instance, would not debate such issues as gay rights, day care, or euthanasia. Openly speaking about sex is unthinkable to some cultural groups.
- **Cultural groups conceptualize issues differently.** Many people in the United States think of issues as problems and solutions that they can define, propose, test, and eliminate or enact; others see problems as the result of fate, evidence of a bad relationship with the deity or deities, or proof that people are out of harmony.
- **The norms for structuring and framing a discussion vary.** Rather than looking at causes and effects or pro and con arguments, then making claims and counterclaims, some cultural groups ground their discussions in the historical perspectives of the various participants. Still others rely on narrative structures to frame their speeches. In the United States, it's typical to frame debates as having a winner and a loser. But other cultures approach issues as an opportunity for a community of equals to cooperate in reaching consensus.
- **Levels of explicitness differ across cultures.** In the United States, many tend to state conclusions explicitly and concretely. In contrast, some cultures tolerate much more ambiguity in their conclusions; there, speakers exert influence through subtle metaphors and indirect suggestions.

● **Forms of proof are often dissimilar.** What's considered rational or irrational, what counts as evidence, and what constitutes a good reason varies across cultures. In contrast to reliance on facts, statistics, and studies by experts, some cultural groups find good reasons in narratives, analogies, traditional sayings, authoritative texts, and the words of wise, experienced elders.

● **The communication style varies.** The bias in mainstream U.S. culture is toward linear, analytical models of reasoning as depicted in the Toulmin model. Other cultural groups reason more holistically through drama, intuition, and emotional expressiveness.

To better understand the influence of diversity on reasoning, log on to www.yahoo.com. Under the general category Society and Culture, follow links to Cultures and Groups. There you'll find co-cultural groups including vegetarians, Goths, twenty-somethings, and people of color. Compare some topics the different groups discuss, or look at reasoning strategies a particular group uses to justify its positions.

Reasoning by Analogy: Figurative and Literal

Analogy
Comparison of one item that's less familiar or unknown to something concrete and familiar.

Chapter 8 described an **analogy** as a comparison between one item that is less familiar or unknown and something concrete that the audience already knows. In public speeches you can use both figurative (metaphor) and literal (parallel case) comparisons to draw conclusions. For example, we might ask, "What is the role of the United States in the world?" Common figurative analogies or metaphors compare our role to that of a police officer, kindly big brother, or a bystander or onlooker. Whichever metaphor is embraced can affect U.S. global policies. If we are "the police," our foreign policy will be different than if we are "bystanders." We also consider questions such as "What kind of health care system should we adopt?" If we use a literal analogy, we'll look around for a parallel case (a real country or state with a workable system) and decide whether or not that country or state is enough like ours to make their system work similarly well for us.

Figurative Analogies (Metaphors)

Reasoning by Metaphor
Comparing two things that are generally different but share a recognizable similarity.

When **reasoning by metaphor,** you figuratively compare two things that are generally different but share a recognizable similarity (Whaley, 1997). Metaphors are fundamentally dialogical, for they require your listeners to participate actively and make sensible connections between the two things you compare. For example, what images do these metaphors evoke in you?

● Good news is *music to our ears*; insecurity causes us to *play it by ear*; when we are getting along, we are *in harmony* or *in tune* with one another (McClain, 2001).

● The separation between Church and State is a *wall* or a *dance* or a *two-way street* (Voth, 1998).

● A teacher sees herself as a *police officer* or a *gardener* or a *ship's captain* in the classroom.

Metaphors can guide actions. For example, what if a teacher who keeps her classroom *shipshape* begins to think of herself as *sowing and nurturing seeds of learning* (Jaffe, 1998)? Metaphors can also arouse strong emotions, especially when they elicit positive images. For instance, Jesse Jackson uses images of a *patchwork quilt* or a *rainbow coalition* to evoke feelings of comfort, security, or beauty.

Use of analogy is a fundamental, universal form of reasoning. The scholar Brian Wicker (1975) explains that metaphor is an older, more poetic way of seeing the world, related to the modes of thinking of poets and storytellers—a continuation of our oral heritage. Aristotle associates metaphor with mental brilliance as seen in this quotation from *Poetics* (1984):

> . . . the greatest thing by far is to be a master of metaphor. It is the one thing that cannot be learnt from others, and it is also a sign of genius, since a good metaphor implies an intuitive perception of the similarity in dissimilars. (¶1459, 5)

In the following quotation, Asa Hilliard (1986) claims that metaphorical reasoning is typical of African and African American speakers.

> Early use was made of proverbs, song, and stories. Direct or symbolic lessons were taught through these. . . . Parenthetically, it is interesting that racist psychologists claim that Black people are not capable of "Level II Thinking," the kind of abstract thinking which is reflected in proverbs and analogies. To the contrary, this is our strong suit. . . . Psychologists . . . miss the extensive use of proverbs and analogies among us. (p. 287)

Literal Analogies (Parallel Cases)

Whereas metaphors highlight similarities between two *different* things, reasoning by **parallel case** or **literal analogy** points out likenesses between two *similar* things. We often use this type of reasoning to formulate policies by asking what another person or group decided to do when faced with a problem similar to our own. Here are some examples.

Parallel Case or Literal Analogy
Compares likenesses between two similar things; argues that what happened in a known case will likely happen in a similar case.

- How should your school solve parking problems on campus? Look at case studies of schools that solved similar parking problems, then infer that the other schools' experiences will be a good predictor of what might or might not work for yours.
- How should a local hospital keep health care costs under control? Look at cost-saving measures instituted by a hospital in a similar location.
- How should the state of South Carolina deal with welfare reform? Well, which states are most like South Carolina? What did they do? What positive or negative outcomes resulted from policies enacted in those states?

In summary, we commonly use actual cases based on real experiences to formulate policies and make predictions about the future. Then we predict that what happened in a known case will happen in a similar case that we project.

Testing Analogies

Reasoning by metaphor is not generally considered a "hard" proof, so you must make sure your listeners can sensibly connect your concept with whatever you use for comparison. Check to see that the comparison does, in fact, illuminate, clarify, and illustrate your idea. Parallel case reasoning is different; you can test it more directly by considering the following two questions.

1. Are the cases really alike? Or are you "comparing apples to oranges"?
2. Are they alike in essential details?

Reasoning Inductively

The **inductive reasoning** process involves using specific instances or examples and formulating a reasonable generalization or conclusion from them. Put another way, induction is reasoning from the particular to the general. Inductive reasoning is characteristic of many ethnic speakers who ground their knowing and reasoning in personal experiences that arise out of their relationship with others. Patricia Sullivan (1993), for instance, explains that African American leaders tie knowledge to human experiences, human actions, and the human life world.

Inductive Reasoning
Starts with specific instances or examples, then formulates a reasonable conclusion.

Knowledge does not exist for its own sake, or in the abstract, but exists as grounded in human experience. What is relevant is relevant because it makes a difference in people's lives.

Here is an example of induction from a *U.S. News and World Report* feature about inner-city debate teams (Morris, 2002):

- Darinka Maldonado got so involved in debate in her Bronx high school that she avoided negative peer pressure and earned a full scholarship to the University of Pittsburgh.
- Reena Rani, an immigrant from India who debates at her South Bronx high school, uses her debating skills to counter her father's and brother's arguments that she shouldn't aspire to a job because she's a female.
- Urban debaters, who are predominately minority, disadvantaged, and female, are excelling against opponents from wealthier schools with longer-established debate programs.
- LaTonya Starks, a former Chicago urban school debater and current Northwestern University student, says that being competitive as a debater improves the self-images of urban debaters.
- Angelo Brooks, coach of a Baltimore high school team, looks for students who are struggling academically, not overachievers. The tools of debate (research, listening, outlining arguments) have helped his debaters improve their grades an average of ten to fifteen points.

Generalization: Urban debate has had remarkable success in diverting at-risk kids from poverty, drugs, and violence.

Because you can only be sure of a conclusion when you're able to observe 100 percent of a population, it is ideal to look at every example before you form a conclusion. However, you can rarely observe every member of a specific group. (Imagine trying to survey every student who's participated in an urban debate league.) Instead, you select a representative sample, survey the characteristics of that sample, formulate conclusions, then generalize your findings to the larger population it represents. Take care here. If you only study inner-city debate programs in Atlanta or New York, don't assume that your conclusions apply to all urban debaters.

The three major tests for inductive reasoning are all linked to the tests you used to evaluate examples (see guidelines in Chapter 8 for evaluating examples).

1. Are enough cases represented to justify the conclusion? Or are you forming a conclusion based on only a few cases?
2. Are the cases typical? That is, do they represent the average members of the population to which the generalizations are applied? Or are they extreme cases that may show what could happen, but not what usually happens?
3. Are the examples from the time under discussion, or are they out of date?

Reasoning Deductively

Deductive Reasoning
Starts with a principle (the premise) and applies it to a specific case.

Inductive reasoning moves from specific examples or particulars to conclusions or generalizations, but **deductive reasoning** does the opposite. It begins with a generalization or principle, called the premise, and moves logically to an application in a specific case. (See Figure 18.2 for an example of the relationship between inductive and deductive reasoning.) In formal logic the deductive reasoning process is often shown in a syllogism such as this:

Major premise:	All Catholic bishops are unmarried.
Minor premise:	He is a Catholic bishop.
Conclusion:	Therefore, he is not married.

Figure 18.2 You observe a number of spaniels and inductively reason that they make good pets. Using that premise you deduce that Curly—the dog you want to buy—will be a good pet.

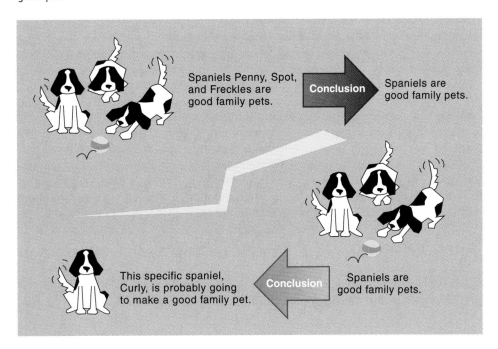

When you're sure of the major premise, you can state your conclusion with confidence. Because it is a rule or principle that members of the Catholic clergy cannot marry and remain in the priesthood, you can be sure that an individual who has risen to the level of bishop is unmarried. In contrast, many premises are less certain. Although some, such as "all men are mortal," are 100 percent true, others, such as "urban high school debaters get better grades," are not valid in all cases. For this reason, it's wise to qualify both your premises and your conclusions. Here is one example:

> Many students who participate in urban debate leagues get better grades.
> Yolanda Baylor is a debater at an inner-city high school in the South Bronx.
> She has a good chance of improving her grades.

When you reason deductively, you rarely provide the entire syllogism in your argument, leaving your listeners to fill in the unstated premises. Aristotle called this an **enthymeme.** For example, you might say, "Married? He's a Catholic bishop!" and let your audience make the necessary connections. Or (sitting with friends, discussing Marta's decision to participate in a study abroad program in Africa), "What a great opportunity! She'll never be the same again." Your friends use their generalizations about study abroad programs to make sense of what you've just said. The complete syllogism in this case runs something like this:

> Well-run study abroad programs in Africa broaden the participants' perspectives.
> Marta will participate in a study abroad program with a good reputation.
> Therefore, her view of the world will most likely be broadened.

Using enthymemes is inherently dialogical, for listeners must form conclusions based on their knowledge of what you don't say. However, if they know nothing about your subject—the rules regarding the Catholic clergy, for example—they'll miss your meaning.

There are two major tests for deductive reasoning:

1. For the conclusion to be valid, the premises must be true or highly probable.
2. To be reasonable, the conclusion must follow from the premise.

Enthymeme
Omitting part of the syllogism in an argument and letting listeners supply what's missing; inherently dialogical.

Reasoning Causally

Causal Reasoning
Links two factors in such as way that the first factor occurs before the second and leads to the second as a matter of rule.

One speaker made this assertion: "There were nine million immigrants last year, and there were nine million Americans out of work." Both of these facts can be verified by counting. However, if the speaker links the two, stating or implying that one results in or leads to the other, the speaker is using **causal reasoning,** and the statement sounds like this: "There were nine million Americans out of work *because* there were nine million immigrants." In the first statement, the two conditions exist together in time, perhaps by chance; in the second statement, the second condition *results from* the first and would cease to exist without it.

Because the belief in causation is a core Euro-American belief, this type of reasoning is common here. However, to be a cause, one factor must precede another and be linked in such a way *that the second factor follows as a matter of rule*. Thus, it is evident that the lack of oxygen to the brain (first factor) causes death (second factor)—this link is observed time after time. But other causal links are not as well proved, sometimes because many other factors may be linked to the effects. The causes of unemployment are much more complex than the flood of immigrants. The key to causal reasoning is to produce enough reasons to warrant the link or connection between the two factors.

Test causation by asking a series of questions to assess whether the reasoning is valid.

1. Is there a real connection? Does one follow as a result of the first, or do the two events simply exist together in time?
2. Is this the only cause? The most important cause? Or are there other factors?
3. Is the cause strong enough for the effect?

In summary, you use a variety of reasons to warrant your claims including figurative and literal analogies, inductive and deductive reasoning, and causal links. All of these types of reasoning fall under the category of logos, or rational proofs. (The Diversity in Practice feature provides additional information on men's and women's patterns in reasoning.)

DIVERSITY IN PRACTICE
REASONING AND THE SEXES

ALTHOUGH BOTH MEN and women reason inductively, a number of feminist philosophers argue that inductive reasoning is a *major* way that women draw conclusions. Women typically describe specific experiences of real people—the rape victim, the family without medical insurance, the student athlete whose sport was eliminated—then generalize from these examples. In short, women's reasoning is grounded in personal experiences that arise out of their interpersonal relationships (Griffiths, 1988; Jaggar, 1989; McMillan, 1982).

Women are commonly stereotyped as reasoning with their hearts rather than their heads—an overgeneralization that may have some basis in fact. Studies of women's patterns of thinking show the importance of emotion in their reasoning process. Alison Jaggar (1989), for example, believes emotions are essential to knowing. Although they are obviously different from what's termed "dispassionate investigation," emotions complement logic, and they are intertwined with rational proofs. Feelings, in this view, are not inferior to reason; furthermore, they are not something women must overcome in order to think clearly. Instead, emotions can be a source of knowledge in themselves, and "truth" or "knowledge" without them is distorted (Griffiths, 1988).

Not all scholars believe fundamental differences exist between men and women. Frank (1997) argues that evidence, linear thinking, and deductive logic are not inherently masculine; both men and women use them. Moreover, intuitive and emotional arguments are not inherently feminine; men often reason through experiences, emotions, and empathy.

The Laboratory for Complex Thinking and Scientific Reasoning, directed by Kevin Dunbar (2000) of McGill University, analyzed videotapes and audiotapes of women's and men's online thinking and reasoning during laboratory meetings by following a number of women scientists over extensive time periods. They found no major differences in inductive, deductive, or causal reasoning processes. However, they did find that, when given an unexpected finding, men scientists tend to assume they know the cause, whereas women track it down.

Whatever differences there may be, Asen (1999) argues that the "difference must be viewed as a *resource for*—not an *impediment to*—meaningful dialogue."

To learn more about gender and reasoning, log on to http://www.psych.mcgill.ca/perpg/fac/dunbar/women.html. Or read David Frank's 1997 article or related articles in the journal *Argumentation and Advocacy*, available on InfoTrac College Edition.

Recognizing Logical Fallacies

A **fallacy** is a failure in logical reasoning that leads to unsound or misleading arguments. As a speaker and as a critical listener, examine the arguments you hear to avoid being taken in by the following common fallacies:

Fallacy
Failure in logical reasoning that leads to unsound or misleading arguments.

Unsupported Assertion

In the **unsupported assertion** fallacy, the claim is offered without supporting evidence. Have you ever argued for a grade ("I deserve an A, so why did I get a B?")? If you really want to achieve a grade change, you'll have to produce some pretty convincing data to show that you deserve the A. Otherwise, your record will remain the same.

Unsupported Assertion
A claim presented without evidence.

Ad Populum or Bandwagon

The Latin phrase *ad populum* literally translates "to the people." This appeal to popular reason is another failure of evidence; rather than providing sound rational arguments, the speaker justifies a belief or action by phrases such as "Everyone's doing it" or "We all think this way." Think of how often the majority is wrong.

Ad Populum
An appeal to popular opinion.

Ad Hominem (Personal Attack)

Rather than evaluate the claim, the evidence, and the warrant or reasoning behind it, an *ad hominem* (literally, "against the person") attack discounts or demeans the messenger. For instance, one person presents good reasons against physician-assisted suicide. The listener says, "Of course, you believe that way; you're a fundamentalist Christian," ignoring the arguments and focusing, instead, on elements of the speaker's background. Again, a woman presents good reasons to report an incident of sexual harassment in the workplace. Her coworker just laughs and calls her a "frustrated feminist."

Ad Hominem
An attack on the messenger rather than the message.

False Analogy

The two things compared are not similar enough to warrant the conclusion in the fallacy of **false analogy.** For example, one Internet site, "Animal Auschwitz," compares the treatment of animals to the treatment of Jews, gays, and Jehovah's Witnesses during the Holocaust. Arguably, the treatment of animals is lamentable, but it is different in degree and kind from what happened in Nazi Germany.

False Analogy
Comparing two things too dissimilar to warrant the conclusion.

Post Hoc

The entire phrase describing this fallacy of causation is ***post hoc**, ergo propter hoc* (literally: "after this, therefore because of this"). It argues that because one event follows the other, the first must be the cause of the second. For instance, Maria's speech on lottery winners (see Chapter 9) told of Daisy, who was sued for half of her $2.8 million winnings by her son's teenaged friend. Before she bought her ticket, Daisy asked him to pray that she'd win;

Post Hoc
A fallacy of causation; a false cause.

afterward the teen felt that his prayer had caused her fortune. (The judge, however, ruled that there is no way to prove this.)

Overgeneralization

Overgeneralization
A fallacy of induction; generalizing too broadly, given the evidence.

This fallacy of inductive reasoning extends the conclusion further than the evidence warrants. For example, let's say you have a bad experience with a specific brand of computer, so you judge the whole line of computers (or worse, the entire company) as bad based on your one negative experience. People overgeneralize about blind dates, about partisanship of politicians, about student cheating, about members of ethnic groups, and so on. Jumping to a conclusion based on minimal evidence is **overgeneralization.**

Red Herring Argument

Red Herring
Introducing a side issue with the intent of drawing attention from the real issue.

The speaker dodges the real argument and intentionally digresses from the issue by introducing an unrelated side issue in an attempt to divert attention. The term derives from the days of fox hunting when a dead fish was dragged across the trail of a fox to set the dogs off in a different direction (Gass, 1999). Any time you think "That's beside the point" or "That's irrelevant," you're probably hearing a **red herring** argument.

False Dichotomy

False Dichotomy
An either-or fallacy that ignores other reasonable options.

The **false dichotomy** fallacy presents an either-or choice that overlooks other reasonable possibilities. As examples, you might hear "Either graduate from college or work in a low-paying job" or "Either athletes should be role models or we should ignore their private lives entirely." Such false choices overlook the range of possibilities between the two extremes.

In summary, an argument can be fallacious because it fails to produce evidence for the claim, or the support it presents is faulty. Fallacies also attack the messenger instead of the message. Furthermore, fallacies of analogy, of causation, and of induction are common. Learning to recognize irrelevant digressions and false choices will help you think more critically about the arguments you make and those you hear every day.

STOP AND CHECK

IDENTIFYING FALLACIES

Working alone or with a group of classmates, copy the list of common fallacies presented in this chapter and give an example of each. Use material from television shows (re-runs of *Seinfeld*, *Mad About You*, or *Home Improvement*, for example), personal experiences, letters to the editor, talk radio callers, and the like. Share your examples with other class members. You can complete this activity online and submit it to a classmate via email. Go to Activities for Chapter 18 at the Jaffe Connection Web site.

If you need more information or additional examples of fallacies, go to the Internet site http://commfaculty.fullerton.edu/rgass/fallacy31.htm, sponsored by Dr. Robert Gass, University of California, Fullerton. He provides definitions and humorous examples of these and other common fallacies as well as an assignment and links to other sites that explain fallacious reasoning.

Include Pathos or Emotional Proofs

Contrast the following situations:

● You're listening to a speaker who has all her facts and figures straight, and she provides evidence that passes all the tests: Her examples are representative, her statistics come from reputable sources, and she cites knowledgeable experts, but you still feel that there's no good reason for you to act. In other words, you're unmotivated—you are neither interested nor concerned.

● You're listening to a second speaker who similarly provides excellent evidence and sound reasoning. However, she links her topic to your core beliefs, values, personal goals, and emotions. You find yourself beginning to care about her subject, and you want to believe and act as she proposes.

The second speaker realizes what good speakers have always known—**motivation** is an internal, individualistic or subjective factor that results when listeners understand how topics affect their lives in a personal way. In short, we look for emotional and psychological reasons to believe and act. And in the end, our subjective reasons may be as powerful an influence as our logical ones; this demonstrates the power of emotions, which Aristotle called **pathos,** in reasoning.

Although you often respond subconsciously to emotional appeals, your responses can be conscious, and your thoughts may run something like this:

"She's right, that's *exactly how it feels* to go to bed hungry—and we shouldn't let it happen!"
"Writing my resume carefully *will help me* get a better job."
"I have to protest over *such a fundamental issue* as freedom of speech."
"I've experienced *frustration* just like that! I can relate!"

Pathos relies on two major, but intertwined, types of appeals: appeals to emotions and appeals to needs.

Appealing to Emotions

According to Aristotle, **emotions** are all the feelings that change people in ways that affect their judgment. Two general categories of emotions apply to speechmaking: Positive emotions are those we want to be part of our lives, and negative emotions are those we want to avoid or prevent. Political campaign ads provide an illustration of both kinds of emotions. Politicians try to engender hope if they're elected and fear of the consequences if they're not.

Positive Emotions

Psychologists say that we "approach" rather than "avoid" pleasurable emotions. Most people agree that love, peace, pride, approval, hope, generosity, courage, and loyalty are desirable. Additionally, we feel good about our core beliefs and values such as freedom and individualism. By appealing to positive feelings, you can often motivate your listeners to accept and act on your claims.

One of the best ways to appeal to emotions is to use narratives and examples, as this excerpt from a student speech demonstrates. Marieta, originally from the Philippines, was adopted into an American home when she was a teenager (Cribbins, 1990).

You might be thinking that adopting an international child is a lot of work. Well, it is, but I believe it is worth it. My parents say that bringing me into their family is one of the most gratifying things they have ever done. And their generosity has obviously benefited me. If it were not for my parents, I would not be able to continue my college education. I wouldn't have any parents or sisters to call my own. As far as I know, I would probably still be in an orphanage because I wouldn't have a place to go.

This personal story emphasizes generosity and hope as well as the underlying values of self-sacrifice for the good of others, education, family, and belonging. It provides a powerful argument for international adoption.

Negative Emotions

Some emotions are unpleasant, and we avoid negative feelings such as guilt or shame, hatred, fear, insecurity, anger, and anxiety. Appeals to negative emotions can be forceful—

Motivation
Internal, individualized factor that results when we understand how topics affect our lives in a personal way.

Pathos
Appeals or reasons directed toward audience emotions.

Emotions
Feelings that change people and affect their judgment; we tend to seek positive emotions and avoid negative ones.

and sometimes disastrous. Consider the rhetoric of hate groups who appeal to their audiences' weaknesses, rages, fears, and insecurities.

Don't reject the use of negative emotions entirely, however. Fear, anger, and guilt, for instance, can motivate us to avoid real dangers—a fact that the campaign against drunk driving uses effectively. Think of a story you've heard or a television ad you've seen that shows adorable children killed by drivers who "just this once" drove drunk. Don't they make you want to do something about the problem?

One way to arouse listener emotion is to use analogies. In this case Mike Suzuki uses anger to explore the use of Native American symbols as sports mascots. He wanted his fellow students (at a Catholic university that was undergoing a mascot change) to identify with the Native Americans' perspective, so he employed the following analogy:

> Opponents feel that non-Indian people do not have the right to use sacred Indian symbols. Phil St. John, a Sioux Indian and founder of the Concerned American Indian Parents group, said the behaviors of Indian mascots at sporting events were comparable to a Native American tearing apart a rosary in front of a Catholic church. Can you imagine someone dressing up as the Pope and swinging a cross wildly in the air at one of our football games? This is how some Native Americans feel when their sacred symbols are used in sports.

As you might imagine, it's easy to overdo negative appeals. For instance, excessive appeals to guilt or fear may turn the audience away from a speaker's beliefs. Here is how one listener reacted to a speech by a famous environmental activist (Roczak, 1992).

> [The activist's] presentation is meant to instill unease. In my case, she is succeeding, though not in the way she intends. She is making me worry . . . for the fate of this movement on which so much depends. As much as I want to endorse what I hear, [her] effort to shock and shame just isn't taking. . . . I find myself going numb.

He advises environmentalist speakers to evaluate the psychological impact of their appeals to fear and guilt and to consider presenting a "politics of vision" that connects environmental goals to positive emotions—to what is "generous, joyous, freely given, and noble" in people.

Appealing to Needs

One of the most widely cited systems of classifying needs follows the work of Abraham Maslow (1987). Maslow ranked needs into levels, each building on the others (see Figure 18.3). Everyone must satisfy basic needs in order to live. Although succeeding levels are important, they become less and less vital for survival. Briefly, Maslow's five levels and how they relate to public speaking are as follows:

1. **Basic needs:** It's been said that we can live forty days without food, four days without water, and four minutes without air. Thus, food, water, and air are basic survival needs. Shelter, sex, rest, and stress release are others.

   To appeal to this level in your speeches, show how your topic will help your listeners satisfy their basic survival needs.

2. **Security needs:** Once we have the basics, we need to feel secure and safe. The second level includes the need for self-preservation as well as secure employment as a means of obtaining the other needs. In addition, we need to feel we can take control of our circumstances.

   In your speeches, explain how to gain peace of mind, job security, safety and comfort, and better health.

Figure 18.3 Maslow's hierarchy of needs.

SOURCE: ADAPTED FROM *MOTIVATION AND PERSONALITY*, 3RD ED., BY ABRAHAM H. MASLOW. REVISED BY ROGER FRAGER, JAMES FADIMAN, CYNTHIA McREYNOLDS, AND RUTH COX. COPYRIGHT 1954, © 1987 BY ADDISON-WESLEY, LONGMAN, CO. COPYRIGHT © 1970 BY ABRAHAM MASLOW. REPRINTED BY PERMISSION OF PRENTICE-HALL, INC., UPPER SADDLE RIVER, NJ.

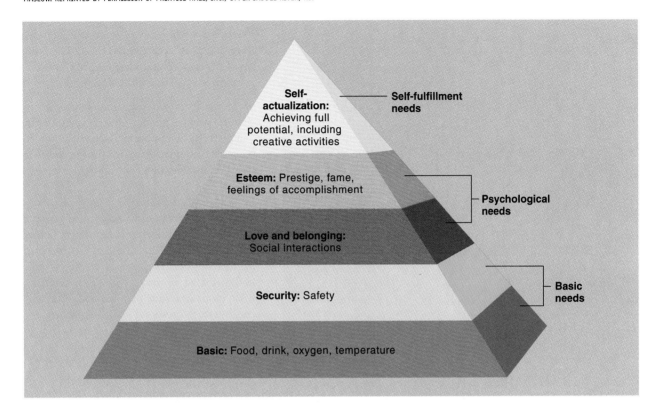

3. **Needs to love and belong:** Included here are our needs for love and affection, which can be met through meaningful, stable relationships with others, including friends, families, and social groups on whom we can depend.

   Address these needs in your speeches by showing how your topic helps your listeners be better friends, creates a stronger community, or builds ties between people.

4. **Esteem needs:** We need approval and recognition from others. We need to view ourselves as competent, respected individuals who can be proud of our accomplishments. This category includes self-respect and reputation.

   Demonstrate that you respect your listeners, and mention their accomplishments when appropriate. Find ways to make listeners feel competent to carry out your proposals. Let them know that their ideas, opinions, and concerns are significant.

5. **Self-actualization needs:** At the top level, we seek to reach our highest potential through personal growth, doing good deeds, creating unique works, and overcoming obstacles.

   Challenge your listeners to look beyond themselves and reach out to others. Encourage them to dream big dreams and accomplish unique things. The Army's slogan "Be all that you can be" is an example of an appeal to self-actualization.

   Return to the excerpt from Marieta's speech on international adoption and identify the different levels of Maslow's hierarchy of needs you find in her appeal. (To learn more about Maslow's work, use the Internet and search www.alltheweb.com for the exact term *Abraham Maslow*. Look for additional levels that other scholars have added to his hierarchy.)

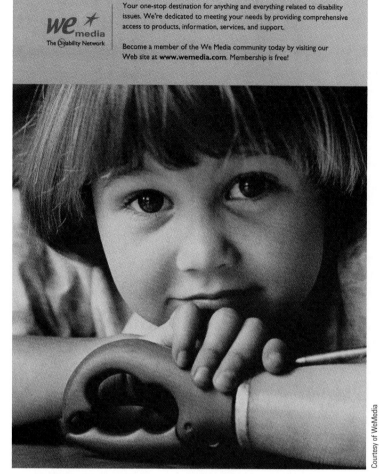

Your one-stop destination for anything and everything related to disability issues. We're dedicated to meeting your needs by providing comprehensive access to products, information, services, and support.

Become a member of the We Media community today by visiting our Web site at www.wemedia.com. Membership is free!

Courtesy of WeMedia

Examine this ad. What rational appeals are here? What emotional appeals? Are the appeals balanced? Why or why not?

Understanding Complex Motivations

As we've seen, using pathos is complex, because needs, wants, values, and emotions overlap. As you create emotional appeals, keep in mind four important factors that result in motivational variation from individual to individual (Griffiths, 1988).

1. *Sometimes you must choose between two desirable goals or feelings*—job security or the ability to reach your potential, for example. In contrast, you may have to choose between two undesirable things—"the lesser of two evils."

2. *Motives vary according to the circumstances of our lives.* Someone who's just broken up a significant relationship may worry more about belonging and self-esteem than a couple in a long-term relationship. You probably find that what motivates you is different from what motivates your parents, and your parents, in turn, respond to different appeals than do your grandparents.

3. *We sometimes respond out of mixed motives.* The alumna who donates out of loyalty to your school may also like the pride she feels when a building is named in her honor. Someone participating in an angry protest march may be acting out of underlying anxiety, fear, or frustration.

4. *Motivations are often group centered.* What we want for ourselves, we want for others—including our family, friends, members of our clubs, religious groups, schools, towns, states, society, and world. For this reason, speeches about child abuse in other countries motivate listeners who want security for themselves and their own families, as well as for strangers.

Testing Emotional Appeals

Emotions, although essential, are not always trustworthy, and it's appropriate to examine them to see if they make sense. Let's say you are using fear to motivate your audience. Ask yourself if the fear is justified or if you're making your listeners unduly fearful. Are you creating or playing on irrational fears? Although emotion is important in argument, excessive use of emotional appeals can cloud logical reasoning.

As a listener, ask questions such as these: "Why do I feel guilty?" "Is my guilt reasonable?" "Is this speaker using my feelings to manipulate me into action?" "Although the speaker is causing me to feel angry, is anger my primary emotion? Could it be that I am really fearful instead? That is, are her ideas challenging my cherished beliefs and creating anxiety that I am masking with anger toward her?" (anonymous reviewer, 1993).

Further, is emotion being used ethically? Generally, it is considered unethical to appeal to emotions in an attempt to bypass logical reasoning. For example, does an appeal to national pride create an argument for going to war in a way that clouds a more rational argument against military involvement? Does a speaker use fear to motivate listeners to act for his own profit rather than for the audience's good?

STOP AND CHECK

EVALUATING PATHOS IN CAMPAIGN ADS

A memorable political campaign ad was aired only once during the 1964 race between Democrat Lyndon Johnson and Republican Barry Goldwater. The Vietnam War was heating up, the Cold War was in full swing, and millions of Americans feared a final countdown that would unleash a nuclear attack. The Democrats took advantage of Goldwater's reputation as a military "hawk" in their ad, which showed a young girl pulling the petals off a daisy, while an off-screen narrator counts down— "10, 9, 8, 7, 6 . . ."

- What does the ad imply Goldwater would do as president?
- What emotion is stirred?
- If you were a college student dreading the draft, how might you respond?
- Is there enough information here for you to make a reasoned voting decision?

Other historical campaigns featured emotional appeals. President Ronald Reagan was famous for the ad "It's Morning in America," which showed scenes of happy families and beautiful homes. President Clinton's campaign featured his birthplace in Hope, Arkansas, and Clinton presented himself as "The Man from Hope."

- What emotions are aroused here?
- What values are represented?
- What do the ads imply that Reagan and Clinton will do as president?
- Is there enough information here for you to make a reasoned voting decision?

Develop Ethos or Speaker Credibility

A third type of **proof**—or reason to believe—comes from your personal qualities, as Chapter 5 pointed out. In fact, Aristotle (1984) believed that your character—a proof he called **ethos**—is the most effective means of persuasion you possess. Here is his explanation of speaker credibility.

> Persuasion is achieved by the speaker's personal character [ethos] when the speech is so spoken as to make us think him [or her] credible. We believe good [people] more fully and more readily than others: this is true generally whatever the question is, and absolutely true where exact certainty is impossible and opinions are divided. (¶1356, 4ff)

This simply means that people will place their confidence in you if they see you as personally believable, trustworthy, and of good character. Their inner dialogue—or reasoning—might look something like this:

> She really knows what she's talking about—she has obviously done her homework! In addition, she seems to have good intentions towards me; I trust her. Thus, I believe it when she tells me that . . .

In contrast, audiences frequently use a speaker's ethos as a reason not to believe what he or she is asserting to be true. Their reasoning may run something like this:

> He has no clue as to what he is talking about. I feel he isn't being entirely up front. He seems so arrogant—like he really doesn't care about us—he just wants us to sign up for his pet project. I don't trust him. Therefore, I don't really believe his information about . . .

We evaluate speakers in four areas: good sense, good character, goodwill, and dynamism. You can increase your ethos by demonstrating these characteristics.

Proof
A reason to believe.

Ethos
Personal credibility or character traits that make a speaker believable and worthy of the audience's confidence.

Demonstrating Good Sense

Good sense is a cluster of characteristics made up of several components.

- **Intelligence:** Show that you understand your subject and have up-to-date information about it. Discuss related historical developments, and link your topic to contemporary national and international issues. Listeners will recognize that you're not "bluffing your way" through your speech.
- **Sound reasoning:** Support your claims with trustworthy evidence and logical connections between ideas. Avoid fallacies and unwarranted or excessive appeals to emotions.
- **Composure:** Demonstrate composure by remaining calm rather than losing your poise in a stressful situation. For example, if you're agitated during a classroom presentation, your audience may wonder why you can't control yourself. However, if you are composed and controlled, they'll perceive you more favorably. However, note the differences in cultural expectations about composure described in the Diversity in Practice feature.

DIVERSITY IN PRACTICE
COMPOSURE IN OTHER CULTURES

CONCEPTS OF ETHOS depend on the cultural context. For example, credible speakers in the African American tradition are forceful and emotional rather than calm and composed (Kochman, 1990). Good speakers are genuinely intense in their expressions, and sometimes their emotions threaten to override the order and procedure common in the Euro-American style of public speaking. For this reason, listeners brought up in the Euro-American culture may consider these speakers loud.

Similarly, Janice Walker Anderson (1991) found that Arabs traditionally expect effective speakers to show their emotion and to heighten the audience's emotions through the rhythm and sounds of words. Overstating a case indicates the speaker's sincerity, not distortion; in contrast, a soft tone indicates the speaker is weak or dishonest.

Exhibiting Good Character

Character counts. Your listeners will believe you more readily if they trust you, so demonstrate honesty, integrity, and trustworthiness by documenting your sources and giving facts that square with what they know to be true. Choose topics that matter to you, and stick by your convictions, even when they are unpopular. Politicians get into trouble with constituents when they appear to be poll-driven and pander to the beliefs of a particular audience, waffling from one position to another according to what's popular instead of sticking by their core beliefs.

Expressing Goodwill

Identification or Co-orientation
Concerns shared among speakers and listeners that help overcome divisions and bring diverse people together.

Your listeners want to know you're concerned about them, that you can speak "their language." Kenneth Burke (1950), one of the twentieth-century's most respected rhetoricians, stressed the importance of "identification" with an audience. According to Burke, a variety of "divisions" separate us, but **identification,** sometimes called **co-orientation,** has the power to bring people with diverse beliefs and behaviors together.

Condoleeza Rice has credibility that is a combination of her experience as provost of Stanford University, her doctorate in economics, and her position as the first woman to be National Security Advisor.

But how do you identify with your audience? One way is to find areas of **common ground**—to emphasize ways you are similar to audience members. When your listeners share your beliefs, values, attitudes, and behaviors, it's easy to find areas of commonality to draw on. However, diversity issues make identification more difficult. When your listeners differ from you and from one another, apply this principle: Find areas of common ground and build on them. For instance, you share with every audience the needs for safety and self-esteem. Watch Barbara Bush's commencement address under Speech Interactive on your Jaffe Connection CD-ROM. Notice how she emphasizes shared values with her audience.

In the example that follows, Susan Au Allen (1993), president of the U.S. Pan Asian American Chamber of Commerce, emphasizes common ground with her largely African American audience.

> So I salute you, a cherished ally. . . . We are Japanese, Filipinos, Chinese, Asian Indians, Koreans, Vietnamese, Laos, Thais, Cambodians, Hmongs, Pakistanis, and Indonesians. Each has a distinct beautiful ethnic cultural heritage, but our goals are the same as yours. We want to remove racial barriers, we want equal opportunity for our members, and we want to create greater horizons for those who follow.

Although you'll usually rely on commonalities, in some cases your differences make you more credible, depending on the topic. For example, Gary suffered a stroke when he was seventeen years old; consequently, when he spoke about strokes and stroke victims, his words were much more persuasive because of his disability. Ariko spoke credibly about Japanese writing because she came from Japan.

Common Ground
Specific areas or concerns that both speakers and audiences consider important.

Showing Dynamism

Dynamism or forcefulness is a fourth trait that influences credibility. Chapter 14 pointed out that dynamism is linked to traits of extroversion, energy, and enthusiasm. This doesn't mean that you are not credible if you're not dynamic; however, your visible enjoyment of your topic, your enthusiasm, and your liveliness contribute to your ethos. Think of it this way: Wouldn't you be more likely to believe someone who states ideas forcefully rather than apologetically?

In conclusion, other cultures may not name these proofs in the way that Aristotle described them, but that does not mean these proofs do not exist in some form within the culture. Across the globe, public speakers appeal to their listeners' rationality, their emotional responses, and their assessment of speakers as trustworthy.

STOP AND CHECK

EVALUATING ETHOS

Log on to InfoTrac College Edition and do a PowerTrac search for the journal *Vital Speeches*. Read two speeches and identify ways the speaker demonstrates good sense, good character, and goodwill.

Incorporate Principles and Forms of Invitational Rhetoric

In many cases, marshaling your best arguments probably will not resolve disagreements, especially on issues like euthanasia and abortion. When others disagree heartily with your point of view, you may find it more satisfying to practice **invitational rhetoric,** a form of "sense making" identified by Sonia Foss and Cindy Griffin (1995). Rather than focusing on

Invitational Rhetoric
Inviting audiences to enter and understand the rhetor's world, then share their own perspectives; focuses on mutual understanding and mutual influence, not winning or change per se.

winning an argument, invitational rhetors invite their audiences to enter their world, understand it as they do, then present their own perspectives. Change may or may not result, but participants may understand one another better. Foss and Griffin identify three principles and two forms associated with invitational rhetoric.

Combining Three Principles

It's typical to think of traditional argument as verbal dueling in which one person wins the war of words; in contrast, invitational rhetoric focuses on mutual understanding and mutual influence based on the principles of equality, individual value, and self-determination.

1. **Equality:** Rather than trying to impose your "superior" views on others, as an invitational rhetor, you'll see your listeners as equals. You won't select strategies to overcome their resistance; however, you will identify possible barriers to understanding and try to minimize or neutralize them. In short, you'll be open to one another's viewpoints.

   For example, say it's an election year. Within your classroom are active supporters of three different candidates for an important office. You all have formulated what you think are good reasons for your choices. As an invitational rhetor, you share the path you've traveled in making your decision, and you invite your classmates to share theirs.

2. **Nonhierarchical value of all:** By approaching your audience as equals, you respectfully look for the value in their conclusions as well as your own. You won't attempt to demean their position and point out their deficiencies, and you'll try to maintain a positive relationship with those who differ from you.

   Back to the election. By not seeing yourself as intellectually or morally superior by virtue of your viewpoint, you respectfully accept the value of your classmates' conclusions, and you work hard to see the point of their reasoning. There's no yelling, no put-downs, no character assassination of the various candidates.

3. **Self-determination:** Invitational rhetoric may or may not result in change. If your listeners change their opinions or their behaviors, it won't be because you shamed or scared them into accepting your views. And you may modify your own positions as a result of their insights. In some instances, you and your listeners may agree to disagree while remaining respectful of one another.

   You and your classmates eventually split your votes, but regardless of who's elected, you have insights into the reasoning involved in each position, and you have learned more about working effectively in the political climate that will follow the election.

Including Two Forms

How does invitational rhetoric look in action? Two general forms are typical of this alternative way of approaching issues: offering perspectives and creating conditions that result in an atmosphere of respect and equality.

1. **Offering perspectives:** You explain what you currently understand or know, and you show a willingness to yield, examine, or revise your conclusions if someone offers a more satisfying perspective. When confronted with hostile or very divergent viewpoints, **re-sourcement** is one way to respond creatively by framing the issue in a different way.

Re-sourcement
Creatively framing a divisive issue or viewpoint in a different way that may be less threatening.

If this sounds complicated, read Gail Grobey's speech at the end of Chapter 15. By telling a narrative, Gail offers her perspective on not spanking children (to listeners who believed in spanking), and she reframes her daughter's discovery of a prescription pill. She calls it an act of heroism (saving the dog from danger) rather than accepting the ownership frame her daughter presents (it's mine, and you can't take it away).

2. **Creating conditions:** When you practice invitational rhetoric, you use two basic means to create conditions in which your audiences can feel safe, valued, and free to offer their own perspectives. First, you use **absolute listening,** or listening without interrupting or inserting yourself into the talk; this allows others to discover their own perspectives. You hear people out without criticism or counterarguments. Second, you use **reversibility of perspectives.** As others present their ideas, you attempt to think from their perspectives rather than seeing only your own. The Native American saying "Don't judge people until you've walked a mile in their moccasins" demonstrates this perspective taking.

Absolute Listening
Listening without interrupting or inserting oneself into the talk.

Reversibility of Perspectives
An attempt to think from the other's perspective as well as one's own.

Invitational rhetoric, a form of reasoning often associated with women, is a model of cooperative, dialogical communication in which you and your audiences generate ideas. Because it is rooted in affirmation and respect, it's arguably an ethical way of coming to conclusions. Further, because you're not intent on controlling the ideas of others, you can disagree without going to war.

Summary

You draw upon a variety of reasoning strategies to make simple daily decisions or to argue about complex national policy questions. Although it is often impossible to prove a claim beyond any doubt, you have several methods of reasoning to support your ideas.

Toulmin's linear model of reasoning shows that claims of fact, definition or classification, value, and policy are based on various kinds of evidence, with a connecting link or warrant and backing that justifies them. Listeners weigh the evidence, data, or grounds to see if it is sufficient and trustworthy enough to lead to the conclusion. To avoid overstating your claim, it is important to limit its scope by using qualifiers. Further, your arguments may be more persuasive if you rebut or counter the possible objections your listeners may have.

Aristotle presented three kinds of proofs thousands of years ago. The first, logos, or rational proof, comes from your words. Use analogies, both figurative and literal, to reason by comparison. You reason inductively by drawing generalizations or conclusions from a number of examples. Then, deductively apply these generalizations to particular cases. Finally, causal reasoning links things that exist in time in such a way that the second is a result of the first. All of these methods require the application of specific tests; otherwise, they may lead to fallacious or faulty conclusions.

Pathos, or emotional proofs, involves appeals to your listeners' positive and negative emotions as well as their needs. The chapter presented five basic needs: survival, security, belonging and love, esteem, and self-actualization. Emotions combine to form motivations that are both complex and mixed.

The third proof, ethos, comes from your personal credibility. To be believable, you should have good character, good sense, goodwill, and dynamism. Ethos varies across cultures.

Finally, an alternative way to make sense of complex issues is to practice invitational rhetoric based on equality, individual value, and self-determination rather than on control. You offer your perspectives and create conditions in which others are free to offer theirs. Use absolute listening and reversibility of perspectives as means of hearing and learning from the viewpoints of others. Change may or may not result.

JAFFE ONLINE CONNECTION JAFFE ONLINE CONNECTION

Use your CD-ROM and the Jaffe Connection Web site http://communication.wadsworth.com/jaffe to review the following concepts, answer the review questions, and complete the suggested activities.

KEY TERMS

data or grounds (339)
assertions (339)
warrant (339)
backing (339)
qualifiers (340)
rebuttal (340)
logos (341)
analogy (342)
reasoning by metaphor (342)
parallel case or literal analogy (343)
inductive reasoning (343)
deductive reasoning (344)
enthymeme (345)
causal reasoning (346)
fallacy (347)
unsupported assertion (347)
ad populum (347)

ad hominem (347)
false analogy (347)
post hoc (347)
overgeneralization (348)
red herring (348)
false dichotomy (348)
motivation (349)
pathos (349)
emotions (349)
proof (353)
ethos (353)
identification or co-orientation (354)
common ground (355)
invitational rhetoric (355)
re-sourcement (356)
absolute listening (356)
reversibility of perspectives (357)

APPLICATION AND CRITICAL THINKING EXERCISES

1. Find a letter to the editor in your local newspaper written by a citizen about a controversial topic. Identify the types of reasoning the author uses, then evaluate his or her arguments. Do they pass the tests for reasoning given in the text? Assess the effectiveness of the argument overall.

2. Find and discuss examples of reasoning that use emotional appeals—effectively and ineffectively. Look at letters to the editor (refer to Yan Hong Krompacky's letter in Chapter 14) or ads from current magazines. What appeals do you find to positive and negative emotions? To needs?

3. Watch a law and order movie or show on television and see if you can diagram the argument or case against the suspect using Toulmin's model. Who is arrested? For what (the claim)? On what evidence (the data or grounds)? What's the warrant (the link: think causal reasoning, inductive reasoning, deductive reasoning, parallel case reasoning, testimony by a credible source, emotional arguments)? Is there backing for the warrant? Is the claim or charge limited or qualified? How? What are the rebuttal arguments (the defense)?

4. Read the speech at the end of this chapter. Stop and answer the questions posed throughout.

5. With a small group within your classroom, make a list of possible speech topics that relate to each of the levels of need in Maslow's hierarchy.

6. With your classmates watch a movie like *Twelve Angry Men* or *The Castle* (a 1999 movie from Australia) and focus on the persuasiveness of the arguments stemming from logical and emotional appeals and from the credibility of each speaker.

7. Use InfoTrac College Edition's PowerTrac feature to search for the key term *fallacy*. Read a "facts and fallacies" article about a subject that interests you and identify the types of fallacies presented in it.

8. Visit the Internet site www.ncpa.org/debate2/debate01.htm. There you'll find a number of policy issues with links to further information on each topic. Using the Toulmin model as your framework, work with a partner to create a complete argument on a specific topic. Then refute the argument of another set of partners in a classroom discussion.

9. Stephen Toulmin is a major figure in argumentation. Go to a search engine such as www.alltheweb.com or www.google.com and search for the exact term *Stephen Toulmin*. Find out more about this important thinker whose work is studied by beginning speakers across the nation and the globe.

THE JAFFE CONNECTION WEB SITE

The Jaffe Connection Web site features review questions about the Web links, Stop and Check activities, and InfoTrac College Edition exercises referenced throughout the chapter. You can access this site via your CD-ROM or at http://communication.wadsworth.com/jaffe.

Web Links

18.1 Influence of Diversity on Reasoning (page 342)
18.2 Reasoning and the Sexes: Gender and Reasoning (page 347)
18.3 Fallacies (page 348)
18.4 Maslow's Hierarchy (page 351)
18.5 Debatable Topics (page 359)
18.6 Stephen Toulmin (page 359)

Stop and Check Activities

18.1 Evaluating Claims—A Case Study (page 340)
18.2 Identifying Fallacies (page 348)
18.3 Evaluating Pathos in Campaign Ads (page 353)
18.4 Evaluating Ethos (page 355)
18.5 Evaluate a Student Speech: The Benefits of Hunting (page 362)

InfoTrac College Edition Exercises

18.1 Reasoning and the Sexes: Gender and Reasoning (page 347)
18.2 Good Sense, Good Character, and Goodwill (page 355)
18.3 Identifying Fallacies (page 358)

SPEECH INTERACTIVE ON THE JAFFE CONNECTION CD-ROM

Speech Interactive features persuasive speeches by Paul Southwick, Hans Erian, Gail Grobey, and Rebecca Ewing.

STUDENT SPEECH
WITH QUESTIONS

THE BENEFITS OF HUNTING
Anonymous

This speech contains both sound and faulty reasoning. To guide your analysis, stop throughout your reading and answer the questions inserted between points in the text.

Animals, I'm sure, have a place in everyone's heart. No one would like to see animals live pitiful lives and die by the hundreds from overpopulation and starvation. Well, this has happened before, and it could very well happen again if hunting is once again abolished by people who are uneducated about its true benefits.

If the welfare of animals means anything to you, it is essential that you listen closely to the biological facts that support hunting as being beneficial to wildlife, for, in order to conserve wildlife, we must preserve hunting.

In the next few minutes, I will tell you about the damages resulting when people's right to hunt in certain areas is taken away. I will inform you of the uneducated ideas of animal activists and, finally, explain the differences between hunters and poachers.

a. What about the use of the phrases "I'm sure," "everyone," and "no one"? What effect does the use of the term "uneducated" have?

b. What claim is the speaker making?

So many people are unaware of the damage that occurs to the wildlife when hunting is taken away from a particular area. The best example of this happened in the state of Massachusetts. There, an animal rights group rallied and petitioned against deer hunting. Their efforts led to the banning of hunting in Massachusetts. During the period in which deer hunting was allowed, the deer population was around 100,000. Within the first year after the law was enacted, the population soared to 150,000.

Sounds good? Well, it wasn't! The overabundance of deer created a famine. Deer began to eat forest trees, gardens, and roots. They ate down to the foliage, leaving the plants unable to grow back the next year. Three years after the law went into effect, the deer population went from 150,000 to only 9,000. It took the state ten years to return the deer population to normal. Eventually, the hunting ban was reversed, and the deer population has remained at its carrying capacity. I think it is hunting that plays a major role in keeping species from overpopulation.

c. What kind of reasoning is the speaker using? Does it pass the tests? Do you think her conclusion is obvious? Why or why not?

d. She says in her introduction that she will present biological facts about hunting. Does she do so to your satisfaction?

People often argue that animals were fine before man invented guns. However, before the white men came over here with guns, there weren't sprawling cities like Los Angeles and Portland to take up most of the animals' habitat. In those days, there was far more land for the animals to live on. Today, modernization has pushed the animals into a smaller wildlife area, leaving them less food and less room for breeding. Therefore, it is easier for the animals to overpopulate. Hunting has played a major role in keeping the animal population at a normal number. If hunting is taken away, the animals are sure to overpopulate.

It has been proven that humankind, even in its earliest form, has always hunted animals. Here in North America, before white people and guns came over, Indians hunted animals on a consistent basis. They killed hundreds of buffalo by herding them over cliffs every year. They caught school after school of salmon that migrated up the rivers. These hunts have always played a major role in population management, whether or not you choose to label it as a law of nature.

e. What argument does the speaker attempt to rebut? Does she do so to your satisfaction?

However, people argue that Indians needed to hunt animals to live; whereas, today's North Americans don't need to kill animals to survive. So what if we can survive on fruit and vegetables? Humans are born omnivorous, meaning it is natural for us to eat both meat and plants. What is inhumane about eating an animal for food? Weren't we designed to do so?

f. Here is the second argument she attempts to counter or rebut. How well does she do it? Explain your answer.

People also argue that the laws of nature will take care of animals. Hunting has always been a major part of the laws of nature. Without mountain lions there to kill rabbits, the rabbit population would be a long-gone species because of overpopulation. Humans as well as mountain lions are animals. Our predation is as important to other animals, such as deer, as the mountain lion's predation is to rabbits.

g. *What is the third argument the speaker attempts to refute? What kind of reasoning does she use?*

h. *Which of the three arguments do you think she did the best job of refuting? Which argument did she refute the least adequately?*

Animal activists harass hunters all the time. These people have false perceptions of what hunting really is, and who hunters really are. At a rally against deer hunting a woman speaker argued that "Hunters are barbarians who are in it for the kill. Hunters would use machine guns if they could. Plus, the deer are so cute." I think that argument is pathetic and holds absolutely no validity.

Another instance of hunter harassment occurred at Yellowstone National Park. An animal activist was not satisfied with only verbal harassment, so he struck the hunter on the head twice. Are animal activists really the peaceful and humane people they claim to be? And they still believe that hunters are bloodthirsty, crazy, and inhumane!

i. *Do these two examples pass the tests for their use? Are they typical? How does the speaker generalize from them? How might she make her point instead?*

Many of these misperceptions about hunters come from the association of hunters with poachers. Hunters are not poachers!

Poachers are people who kill animals when they want, regardless of laws and regulations that were set to protect the animals. These are the kind of people who hunt elephants for their ivory tusks or kill crocodiles for their skins. Poachers kill deer in areas that are off-limits, during off-limited hunting seasons. These people are criminals who are extremely harmful to wildlife.

Hunters would turn in a poacher in an instant if they caught one. Poachers give hunting a bad image in the eyes of the public. It's too bad that the animal activists don't go after the poachers who are extremely harmful to animals, and stop pointing a finger at hunters who follow the laws and regulations.

j. *Why does the speaker contrast hunters to poachers? In what ways, if any, is this an effective argument?*

If hunting is banned, just imagine a drive through the mountains on a road covered with emaciated skeletons of cadaverous deer who died of starvation. No longer can you take a picture of Bambi, your favorite deer that you saw every year at Yellowstone National Park. For Bambi and his family were overpopulated, and they slowly wilted away until their final day. Too bad there weren't a few healthy bucks taken by hunting that year to keep Bambi and family at a cozy carrying capacity where there was plenty of delicious food for all of them.

k. *Here, the speaker uses a great deal of pathos. Identify emotional language and images. Is this effective? Why or why not?*

The argument that animal activists use against hunting is fabricated mainly from emotions. If they are personally against killing an animal, I can respect that. But they have no place trying to ban hunting. It is proven by biological facts that hunting is necessary for wildlife management. It provides millions of dollars that fund the construction of programs that help wildlife. It keeps species from overpopulating and starving to death. In order for wildlife to flourish at an optimum population number, hunting must continue to be a major part of wildlife management.

l. What does she put in her summary that does not appear anywhere else in her speech? If she had included it in the body of her speech and provided some evidence for that point, would her speech be stronger?

QUESTIONS

Now answer the following questions about the speech as a whole:

1. Overall, how would you grade the reasoning in this speech? Defend your grade.
2. How would you assess this speaker's credibility? How knowledgeable does she seem to be, and why? Does she show good sense throughout? Where (if at all) does she demonstrate goodwill toward listeners? Is there any way to assess her good character? Where (if at all) does she identify with her listeners?
3. How might you respond if you were an animal activist in her audience?
4. Where did you feel you would like to see sources cited?

You can answer these questions online and, if requested by your instructor, submit them via email. Go to Stop and Check Activities for Chapter 18 at the Jaffe Connection Web site at http://communication.wadsworth.com/jaffe.

Web Site

SOURCE: This speech was given at Oregon State University, Corvallis, on March 6, 1992.

Speaking in Small Groups

T HE ABILITY TO WORK WELL in small groups is essential because classrooms, businesses, and other organizations, here and abroad, regularly use cooperative work teams and groups to accomplish their work. In fact, in a recent survey conducted by Pennsylvania State University, 71.4 percent of corporate executives polled listed the ability to work in teams as a desirable quality in recent graduates (Galvin & Cooper, 2000). Task-oriented teams can produce excellent results, but they can also be dysfunctional and frustrating for participants, especially those who are unaware of the dynamics inherent in group work. This appendix first presents some advantages and disadvantages of group work. Next, it gives specific tips for working in two types of groups: investigative groups and problem-solving groups. A description of formats commonly used in public presentations of group findings concludes this appendix.

Advantages and Disadvantages of Group Work

You've probably heard the saying "Two heads are better than one." In fact, some people who work on difficult problems believe "The more heads the better." However, if you're trying to accomplish a task with a group plagued by scheduling conflicts, dominating members, or nonparticipants, you may be tempted to work alone. Truth be told, the many advantages of group work must be balanced against the disadvantages.

Advantages of Groups

Groups and teams have several advantages (Beebe & Masterson, 1990; Cooper, 1995):

- *Groups have access to more information and knowledge than do single individuals.* It stands to reason that the more people there are, the more experiences they've had and the more combined knowledge they have. For example, one person is an expert in one area, and another provides different expertise. Together, they pool their resources and generate more information than either one could produce individually.
- *The various viewpoints people bring to the group offer possibilities for more creative ideas to emerge.* By combining personalities and thinking and learning styles, the group as a whole can respond more creatively to an issue than if it relies on the ideas of one person. Diversity within a well-functioning group can also increase the members' understandings of various cultural perspectives.
- *Group work provides a deeper level of involvement and learning.* When all participants do research, discuss their findings with others, and listen to the information discovered by their teammates, they can do three to four times as much research in approximately the same time frame. In addition, during discussions they can ask and answer questions that clarify confusing ideas and sharpen their critical thinking skills. Consequently, many people learn better in small groups.
- *Many people enjoy working in small groups.* They are more motivated and have more positive attitudes when they don't have to deal with a subject or problem alone. In short, social interactions with others in the group can make teamwork satisfying; not only do participants learn about an issue, they learn about one another.
- *Working in small groups results in the co-creation of meaning.* Because of the nature of information sharing and decision making, small groups are inherently dialogical. Ideally, all members participate in discussing, refining, and evaluating ideas and solutions.

Disadvantages of Groups

Despite their many advantages, group work carries with it a number of disadvantages you should recognize and avoid whenever possible.

- *Working in groups takes more time.* Scheduling meetings and working around the schedules of other busy people takes time that often frustrates task-oriented group members.
- *Some members of the group do more work than others do.* It's true that some group members rely on others and do less work than they would if they were responsible for the entire project. The result is that hard workers often resent the slackers.
- *Some members of the group may monopolize the discussion and impose their ideas on others.* Dominators can take over a group for a number of reasons: One is linked to personality; some people are more extroverted and opinionated. Another is linked to sex; women often defer to men in mixed groups (Tannen, 1990).
- *There is a tendency toward groupthink* (Janik, 1971). Groupthink happens when the members pressure one another to conform to a decision (which may be unwise) to avoid conflict. A classic case occurred when President Kennedy and his advisers proceeded with the disastrous Bay of Pigs invasion of Cuba. Although an objective outsider might have predicted the unfortunate outcome, no one on the advisory team was willing to challenge the group's decision.

In summary, although group work offers many advantages, it also has disadvantages. However, these can be minimized by having group members be accountable to one another, by giving all members a chance to voice their opinion, and by avoiding agreement simply for the sake of peace.

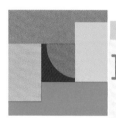

DIVERSITY IN PRACTICE

MALE AND FEMALE TENDENCIES IN GROUP INTERACTIONS

IN HER BOOK *You Just Don't Understand: Women and Men in Conversation,* Deborah Tannen (1990, 2000) identifies several differences in the conversational styles associated with males and females. John Cowan (2000) traces these differences to boys' and girls' playground experiences that he humorously suggests were "at least a light-year apart" (p. 307). However, male- and female-associated characteristics are tendencies, not absolutes, and researchers who take a "gender similarities" approach suggest that men and women, especially college students, may be more alike than different (Grob, Meyers, & Schuh, 1997). Nevertheless, Tannen's conclusions are widely discussed, and tendencies, like the following, have implications for communication in small group contexts.

- Men engage in "Report Talk." Their speaking is informative, and they rely more on facts, figures, and definitions and less on personalized information. In contrast, women tend to engage in "Rapport Talk" that stresses relationships. They personalize their information with examples and stories.
- Men interact with the goal of gaining power, status, and respect—whether or not they offend other group members. Women's goals, in contrast, are to help others and build relationships between people. They are less concerned about winning a persuasive argument.
- Men speak in a "dominant way," meaning that they interrupt and display their knowledge and expertise. They also control the topic and set the agenda. On the other hand, women express more agreement, making connections and smoothing relationships. Cowan (2000) says that men offer "assertion followed by counterassertion," whereas women offer "inquiry followed by counterinquiry" (p. 307). Although women suggest more topics than men, men choose which topic to discuss.

- Men explain more than women, and their explanations are lengthy. Women can and do explain, but they have fewer opportunities to do so in mixed gender groups.
- Men speak more. Conversational time is one-sided in their favor. Women listen more and speak less in mixed gender groups.

To learn more about Professor Tannen's work, go online and visit her Web page at http://www.georgetown.edu/tannen/, or go to www.alltheweb.com and search for the exact phrase *Deborah Tannen*. There you'll find interviews, excerpts from her books, and other interesting information about gender differences in communication that affect men's and women's talk in small groups.

Investigative Teams

Educators commonly ask students to team up to study a subject and present their findings to the entire class. For example, Eisen (1998) reported that biology students learned to do "science thinking" in small groups, and their classroom presentations honed organizational and speaking skills they'll use throughout their careers as scientists.

Investigative reporters (students and professionals alike) also team up to probe complex social issues. Because a seven-to-ten-minute report (described in Chapter 16) can only overview a controversy, many instructors ask students interested in a specific topic such as capital punishment or the abolishment of recess to study the issue in teams. Group members then present their findings in an extended period of time. In addition, reporters for a newsmagazine such as *Newsweek* or *Time* commonly work together on a major feature. One or two write the actual story, but you can find names of additional contributors at the end of the article. You'll also find sidebars and smaller, supplementary stories alongside the featured one, each written by a different member of the investigative team.

The advantages of teamwork, explained earlier in this chapter, converge in investigative teams. Obviously, a team can cover a national issue in a national magazine much better than a single reporter can. Similarly, students typically learn more and become more involved in a subject when they investigate it with others. Besides, the group shares the research burden, allowing a particular student to focus mainly on one area. Not only do team members learn more, others in the class benefit from the variety of perspectives they hear and the in-depth coverage they get when the group shares its findings publicly.

To research and report a topic effectively, the team should have several meetings that progress from initially getting acquainted with one another and the subject, moving through the research stage, and concluding with the final presentation.

First Meeting: Getting Acquainted

When you first gather, get to know one another and find out each person's interest in the topic. (This is a good time to exchange phone numbers or email addresses.) Then have each person share his or her knowledge about the subject. Leadership can develop informally, or you can designate someone to guide the meeting and keep people on task. One important role is that of a *gatekeeper*; this person makes sure that quiet people participate and that no one dominates the discussion. Another important role is that of a *recorder*, a person who takes notes (minutes) on what transpires during the meeting.

During this meeting, divide your subject into subtopics and have each member select specific aspects to research in depth. For instance, you might include a definition, the history, numbers and types of people affected, regions or areas affected, proposed solutions, or arguments for and against each solution. If the group is to be successful, it must hold members accountable. Consequently, before your meeting breaks up, ask all present to identify the areas and specify the methods (interviews, library research) they will use to investigate their subtopics. Then set a date, place, and time (beginning and ending times) for the next meeting.

Additional Meetings: Discussing the Subject

Begin each new meeting by approving the minutes of the previous meeting. Organize your group's work by writing out an explicit *agenda*, an ordered list of the items you'll discuss. Proceed by holding team members accountable for summarizing their work and answering questions the others ask. After everyone has contributed, discuss the following: What questions do we still have as a group? Are there gaps in our research? If so, where? What patterns or recurring themes are we finding? Are we beginning to detect a way to organize our final presentation?

Continue to use the gatekeeper role and have important discussion items recorded in the minutes. Focus on your final goal, which is to present your material publicly, in every meeting. To achieve this objective, work together to organize and outline your material into a coherent form. Review organizational patterns in Chapter 9, and think of creative ways to introduce and conclude your presentation (Chapter 10). Identify possible visual aids (assigning a person to create each one), and put someone in charge of requesting the equipment you will need for your presentation.

Before the group separates, have everyone state specifically what he or she will do during the period before the next meeting to forward the goals of the group. Always conclude by agreeing on a date, place, and time for your next meeting.

Final Meeting: Polishing the Presentation

In previous meetings you have researched various aspects of a complex topic. You've also used skills from the canon of arrangement or organization to shape your final product. Now, get together in one last meeting to make sure all the details are finalized. Give each group member a written outline or other record of what you've done. Rehearse the final presentation to make sure everyone knows her or his role and to iron out any glitches that arise. Check that visuals are made and equipment is ordered, then congratulate one another on a job well done.

Problem-Solving Teams

What is a problem? Professor Jack Henson (n.d.) defines a problem as *the difference between what is* (the present condition) and *what should be* (the goal). Put another way, a problem is the gap that exists between what we want and what we now have. Several years ago, Antioch College in Ohio confronted the issue of sexual offenses on campus by holding a two-year-long series of campuswide small group discussions. Leaders announced the resulting policy on sexual behaviors with a flurry of media attention. Both parties on a date must give verbal and willing consent at each increasing level of physical intimacy—they should ask first, even for a kiss. By following these rules, people aren't forced to participate in sexual activity against their will.

Although their solution is atypical, Antioch College's problem represents the type of issue we discuss in organizations on local, national, and global levels. Our challenges include child care on campus, wheelchair accessibility, global trade imbalances, elder abuse, safe water, and so on. When problems arise, we often form discussion groups, task forces, and committees in which we typically use a problem-solving method identified a hundred years ago by the educator John Dewey and modified several times since it was first explained.

The analytical, linear process of appraising problems and generating solutions presented here is typical of Euro-American culture, and it's used globally. For example, the Africa Region's Knowledge and Learning Center reported that women's groups in Senegal use a five-step process to solve community problems ("Senegalese Women," 1988). In many public contexts, following a structured, rather than a random, approach results in more effective group work. However, don't think of this process as strictly linear, proceeding from point to point in one direction only; your group may circle back to previous steps, and you may revise as you go along. What follows is a modification of John Dewey's original five steps.

Step One: Define the Problem

It's important at the outset to state the problem clearly. If you fail to do this, your work will be more difficult later, for it's hard to find a solution for something that is vague. Some problems are simple to define; for instance, "Whom shall we hire as the new basketball coach?" is easy to pinpoint when group members have in hand the previous coach's letter of resignation. However, many, even most, problems require narrowing the topic in ways similar to what you have done for your speeches throughout the term, following these three general suggestions:

- State the issue as a policy question, using the word *should*. For example, "Which athlete should we honor as outstanding gymnast? What should we do to prevent sexual offenses?
- Leave the question broad enough to allow for a variety of answers; put simply, use an open rather than a closed question. Thus, this yes or no closed question, "Should the student council repair acts of vandalism in the student union building?" is less effective for group discussion than the more open question "How should the student council ensure that campus buildings remain free from vandalism?"
- State the question as objectively as possible, avoiding emotionally charged language. "How can we get rid of this unfair grading system?" is less effective than "What changes, if any, should be made in the current methods of assigning grades?"

Step Two: Analyze the Problem

After you know the problem, begin collecting pertinent information using the guidelines described in Chapters 7 and 8. Look for the facts—including causes and effects—values, and policies that relate to your topic. Divide the relevant issues among group members and have them consult oral and print media and Internet sources for information by asking questions such as these:

- What are the factual issues involved? What's the history of the problem?
- What causes the problem? Which are primary causes? Which are secondary factors that contribute to it?
- What effects result from the problem?
- What values apply? Is it wrong or right? In what respects?
- Are any relevant policies involved? Any historical precedents?

So far, your group has defined the problem and analyzed related issues. You have also explored facts, possible causes, and resulting effects of the problem; finally, you have analyzed underlying values and related historical policies. Now you're ready as a group to explore possible solutions.

Step Three: Set Criteria for Deciding on a Solution

Because solutions must be realistic in terms of time, money, and ease of enactment, set up standards for determining an acceptable solution before you even begin to suggest possible solutions. As part of your consideration, Charles Kepner and Benjamin Tregoe (1965) suggest two vital factors: (1) What must we do? That is, what is *required*? (2) What do we want to do? In other words, what is *desired*? By way of illustration, we must solve the problem with less than $10,000; we want to solve it with less than $5,000. We must have the policy in effect by the beginning of the next school year; we want to have it implemented by the end of the spring term. As you might imagine, when you work within budget and time constraints, you'll automatically rule out some solutions as too costly or too time consuming.

Step Four: List Possible Solutions

During this period, your group's task is to generate as many ideas as possible. Because you're seeking possibilities, don't worry if all these suggestions aren't practical. Hold your judgment until later. One common way to generate ideas is through the process of *brainstorming*, in which group members offer a number of ideas for consideration. Don't overlook a mind map as described in Chapters 6 and 7 as a valuable way to record these ideas. Here are some tips for a successful brainstorming session:

- Have a recorder write down all the ideas presented, using a chalkboard, overhead transparency, or flip chart.
- Record all the ideas without judging any of them.
- Make sure each person in the group has an opportunity to contribute at least once.
- Piggyback off one another's ideas—that is, encourage group members to use one proposal as a jumping-off point for another.

After a successful brainstorming session, in which everyone generates ideas, begin to evaluate each idea against the criteria you set up earlier. Often your brainstorming session will lead you to rethink your criteria. Don't hesitate to circle back and make revisions at this time.

Step Five: Select the Best Solution

So far, your group has a good idea of the problem—its causes, effects, and history. You've decided on what is necessary for a good solution, and you've generated a number of ideas. It's now time to select the best solution, so you begin to evaluate the suggested solutions against the criteria you've set. You'll probably eliminate some ideas easily because they're too expensive, too time consuming, or don't fit your criteria for other obvious reasons. After you have pared down your options, analyze and weigh the merits of those that remain to find the one members of your group can agree on.

Presenting Your Group's Findings

Whether your group investigated a topic or solved a problem, prepare some way to report on your findings—both in writing and orally. First, summarize the work you completed. Then present the information you've discovered or the solution you've chosen, justifying your choice. For problem-solving groups, provide information on why you predict the solution will work, why it will be cost effective, and why it will be easy to implement. Then present your findings to the audience who will most likely be involved in its implementation. In general, there are three basic ways to present your conclusions.

A Final Report

When you choose this format, one member speaks for the entire group. A group giving an investigative report on a topic such as abolishing recess all gather data and work together to write up their findings, but only one member of the group actually speaks publicly.

A problem-solving team designates a presenter to define the problem and briefly explain background information related to it. Then, the presenter summarizes the decision-making process, identifies the criteria decided on for the solution, describes alternative solutions that were considered, and explains and justifies the group's final choice.

To illustrate, let's look at ways Antioch College might announce the new dating policy. To communicate with the college leadership as well as the public, the task committee writes a final report that details the procedures used and gives the underlying rationale for the decision. The committee chairperson then presents these to the board of trustees and to the student council for approval. A press release generated from the final report goes to newspapers in the area. Television stations pick up the story and send reporters to interview the committee spokesperson to gain additional information about the policy.

A Panel Discussion

In this format, all your group's members sit on a panel and discuss the issue in dialogical interactions. During your discussion, a leader or moderator asks a series of questions, and you take turns providing your insights on each one. In short, all members contribute from their store of information and opinions. Afterward, the moderator may open the discussion to the audience and encourage listeners to talk with panelists during a question-and-answer period. In this way, both your group and your audience cooperate in co-creating meaning.

Each member of a group that studied a current issue such as whether or not to abolish recess does research on the topic. They all locate pro and con arguments, find examples of schools that had abolished recess and those that decided to keep it, get quotations from experts on both sides of the issue, interview schoolchildren and teachers, and discuss among themselves their personal experiences with recess periods. In a group planning meeting, they share their findings and identify a series of questions to discuss; then on the day of their presentation, each member contributes to each question during their group's allotted half hour. Afterward, they invite audience questions.

The entire problem-solving group at Antioch College might appear in a town hall session at the college. There, in a free-flowing manner, each committee participant discusses the policy and the process the group went through to reach it; the committee chair acts as emcee. After the proposal is presented, audience members ask questions regarding implementation, consequences for breaking the rules, and so on.

A Symposium

In this format, each member of the group selects only one aspect of the problem and prepares and delivers a speech about it. After all the speakers have finished, the moderator usually opens up the floor for a question-and-answer period from the audience.

If a group investigating the topic of abolishing recess chooses a symposium format, their presentation would divide the topic into smaller topics, with each person discussing only one part. The first speaker leads off by telling the history of recess; the second overviews the controversy surrounding recess. The third presenter gives a case study of a school that decided to abolish recess, and a fourth relates a case study of a school that kept recess—after almost canceling it. The final speaker summarizes the issue. After they've all finished, a moderator opens up the floor for audience questions.

To inform parents of Antioch College's new policy, the committee might present a symposium during Parents' Weekend. Interested family members come to hear four task group members discuss the policy. The first discusses the history of the problem. The next speaker describes the campuswide discussions that took place over a two-year period. Another committee member details the specifics of the new dating code, and the final speaker tells why the committee believes this solution is workable. Parents are then encouraged to ask questions.

Speaking on Special Occasions

SPECIAL OCCASION SPEAKING OCCURS at celebrations, more solemn occasions, and occasions that reaffirm group values. These speeches share the general purposes common to all public speaking: to inform, to persuade, to entertain. But an important additional function, called the *integrative function*, helps bind members of the organization to one another and connects them firmly to their shared goals (Goodall & Phillips, 1984). This type of persuasive speaking reinforces and maintains the common belief-attitude-value cluster that influences the specific actions of group members.

This appendix provides guidelines for speeches of introduction, farewell, announcement, award presentation and acceptance, nomination, commemoration or goodwill, and eulogy. The Diversity in Practice feature describes some aspects of organizational culture that can affect your speech.

Introductions

Whenever people meet for the first time, they seek information about one another; introductions provide strangers with the knowledge they need to interact effectively. Introductions answer questions like these: "Who is this person?" "What might we have in common?" "What background experiences bring her here?" You may introduce a classmate, a newcomer to your workplace, or a speaker at a special event. Regardless of the type of introduction, keep your remarks brief. Chapter 2 provided guidelines for introducing a classmate. Here are some tips for introducing an unfamiliar person to your school or work environment.

- Provide the newcomer's name and job title.
- Give a few relevant details about the educational and occupational background as well as the personal characteristics the new person brings to the group or organization.
- Close by welcoming the newcomer to the group.

Here is a sample introduction of a student life employee, new to the campus. Notice that it briefly presents her qualifications and provides the students, to whom she's a stranger, with information about her background and some of her interests, which will help students relate to her.

> We are pleased to welcome a new Director of Student Life for the university: Janeen Bronstein. Janeen received both her bachelor's and master's degrees from Brandeis University. As an undergraduate, she decided upon a career in student life, so she worked as a resident adviser in her university's dormitories, and during two summers she administrated camping programs in upstate New York. She sought out activities that would give her a broad national and international perspective; for example, she spent a summer in Washington, D.C. where she was an intern in the Justice Department. That makes sense. One of her roles at the university will be to help us work out problems and disputes. Prior to coming here, she served as Director of Student Life at our sister campus in Japan. Fortunately for us, she decided to trade in Tokyo's subway crush for the complex freeway system of our metro area. Janeen comes with the highest recommendations from both the administrators and the students with whom she's worked.

Janeen, welcome. We know you will continue your tradition of interpersonal and administrative excellence and will be a wonderful addition to our student life staff.

To introduce a guest speaker, include some information about the occasion that precipitated the invitation as well as about the actual speaker. Here are some elements to include in such speeches:

- Greetings and/or a welcome to the group
- A statement about the occasion
- Announcement of the speaker's name and subject
- A brief account of the speaker's background, education, training, achievements, personality, or any other salient information that relates to the topic or the audience

Afterward, be prepared to make a few remarks that provide closure. Briefly thank the speaker, and make a simple, short remark relating to the central idea of the speech.

DIVERSITY IN PRACTICE
ORGANIZATIONAL CULTURE

IT'S COMMON NOWADAYS to think of organizations as small cultures within the dominant culture. An organization's culture is comprised of many elements that members of the culture know and newcomers must learn. For example, an organization's cultural environment includes these aspects (Pacanowsky & O'Donnell-Trujillo, 1983):

- **History**—the founders, the founding date, the founding mission
- **Political system**—the way power is distributed, who leads and who follows, and when
- **Distribution of wealth**—pay equity, merit pay, bonuses, stock options, and dues or collections
- **Art and music and dress**—group logos, songs, or uniforms
- **Language**—jargon or special in-group terminology
- **Rituals**—banquets, picnics, award ceremonies, installations, commencements
- **Folklore**—the narratives and myths, the heroes and villains, described in the stories passed from person to person within the organization (Bormann, 1985).

These last two aspects of culture are particularly relevant to public speaking. W. B. Ouchi (1998), author of *Theory Z: How American Business Can Meet the Japanese Challenge*, underlines the fact that an organization's symbols, ceremonies, and myths communicate the beliefs and values of the group. The organizational narratives—told and retold from generation to generation—explain what is valued, believed, and remembered. Knowing these symbols and stories is an important part of understanding the organization; using them in public speaking can act as a powerful form of proof to members of the organization.

Farewells

Saying good-bye is never easy; departures cause disruptions that affect those left behind, to a greater or lesser degree. This is true whether or not the person was well liked. For example, consider the varied emotions that arise when a popular professor leaves for a position in another university, a beloved rabbi retires, an unpopular manager is fired, the seniors on the football team graduate. All these departures signal changes in the social patterns of an organization. Because of this, farewell speeches function to ease the inevitable changes facing both the departing individual and the group.

People who leave bid the group or organization farewell; a representative of those who remain says good-bye on behalf of the group. Both speakers should express emotions—

especially appreciation, sadness, hope for the future, and affection for others in the group. Balance the sadness inherent in the occasion by remembrances of happy times; recounting humorous stories is one way to do this.

When you bid a group farewell because you are leaving, include some or all of these elements:

● Remind group members of what they've meant to you personally.
● List some lessons you learned from being with them.
● Tell humorous stories that you'll carry with you as happy memories.
● Express both your sadness at leaving and your hopes for the future.
● Invite people to write or visit you in your new location.

When you bid farewell to a departing member or members of an organization, you speak not only for yourself but also for the group. Remember these elements in your speech:

● Recognize the person's accomplishments that benefited the group.
● Recognize positive personal characteristics that you will remember.
● Use humorous anecdotes.
● Express your personal sadness and the group's sense of loss.
● Wish the person well in his or her new location.
● When appropriate, present a gift as a remembrance.

Announcements

Announcements are brief speeches that keep individuals and groups knowledgeable about the goings-on of organizations and groups to which they belong by providing facts about upcoming events or developments of interest to a specific audience. In clubs and organizations, businesses and faculty meetings, announcements are an agenda staple because they answer the questions "What's happening?" or "What's new?"

Essential to these short speeches are details regarding who, where, when, and how much it costs, as the following outline of essential points shows:

● First, draw your listeners' attention to the event.
● Provide such details as who, what, when, and where the event takes place.
● Give both the cost and the benefits of attending.
● End with a brief summary of important information.

Here's a sample announcement:

Remember when you were a little kid, and figures from the *Peanuts* cartoon strip were everywhere? I had a Snoopy tee shirt and couldn't wait for the annual "Great Pumpkin" show on TV. Well, you can return briefly to these beloved characters from childhood if you attend the campus production of *You're a Good Man, Charlie Brown*.

This play will be performed April 8 through 12 at Woodmar Auditorium here on campus. Evening performances begin at 8:00 P.M. In addition, there are 3:00 P.M. matinee performances on Saturday and Sunday afternoons. Tickets are $10.00— $5.00 with your student body card. You can purchase them in advance at the ticket window in Bauman Auditorium, or you can purchase them at the door at the time of the performance. This is a small price to pay for an evening with such memorable characters as Linus and Lucy.

Remember, *You're a Good Man, Charlie Brown* is playing April 8 to 12, with both evening and weekend matinee performances. You can get your tickets at the ticket office or at the door. It's worth it all just to see Snoopy dance!

Award Presentations

Award rituals express the common values of a group. Ordinarily, we recognize individuals for meritorious work or for character traits that embody our ideals. It's common to present recipients with a permanent memento of some sort. When you present an award, emphasize the group's shared beliefs, values, and commitments. In general, award presentations include similar elements:

- Name the award and describe its significance. What personal traits or accomplishments does it honor? In whose name is it made? Why is it given? How often is it awarded? How are the recipients selected?
- Summarize the selection criteria and reasons the recipient is receiving the award.
- Relate the appropriateness of the award to the traits of the recipient.
- Express good wishes to the recipient.

In some cultures, groups rarely single out one individual to praise over others. (New Zealanders, for instance, have the saying "The tall poppy gets mown down.") Consequently, the members of these groups tend to feel uncomfortable having their personal characteristics publicly acknowledged; when this is true, present the award or honor to the entire group rather than to an individual.

Acceptance Speeches

Accept an award with a brief speech in which you express gratitude to those who selected you, thank other people who helped you become eligible for such an honor, and reinforce the cultural values that the award demonstrates, as these guidelines and sample acceptance speech show.

- Thank those who honored you.
- Acknowledge others who helped you get it.
- Personalize what it means to you.
- Express appreciation for the honor.

> Thank you Professor Geffner for those kind words, and thank you, committee, for selecting me as the Outstanding Speech and Hearing Student this year. As you know, many other students are deserving of honor for their scholarship and their service to the clients in our speech clinic, and I know that each one deserves to receive recognition.
>
> Of course, no student can accomplish anything were it not for the support of a dedicated faculty—and the faculty we have here at St. John's University has been outstanding. I have been impressed, not only with their academic credentials, but also with the personal interest each one takes in the lives of each student who majors in speech pathology and audiology. Thanks also to my parents, who supported me both financially and emotionally through these past four years. I appreciate you all.
>
> Next year I will be attending graduate school at Northwestern University. I'm sure that when I'm homesick for New York I will remember this honor and be inspired by your confidence in me.
>
> Thank you once again.

Nominations

Think of a nomination as a short persuasive speech that does two things: It introduces your candidate to the group, and it presents brief arguments explaining why she or he should be elected. Be sure to include the following items:

- Name the office, and tell its importance to the organization as a whole.
- List the reasons the candidate is right for the office.

Because a nomination is a persuasive speech, two organizational patterns discussed in Chapter 17 work especially well: a direct method or statement of reasons pattern and a criteria satisfaction pattern, as these two brief outlines demonstrate:

Vote for Trung Vo-Vu for the office of treasurer.

I. He has been the treasurer of three organizations.
II. He is a business major.
III. He has worked part time in a bank, and he understands money management.

I. A president must have three important traits.

   A. She must have demonstrated leadership ability.
   B. She must be able to represent the organization to outside groups.
   C. She must have the ability to lead people to consensus when opinions differ.

II. Gisella Cassalino excels in all three areas.

   A. She has been vice-president of this organization and currently serves as president of the county's Partners with Disabilities organization.
   B. She is a communication major who gives public presentations with ease.
   C. She has served on a committee that mediates student grievances.

Commemorative Speeches

Commemorative speeches emphasize the common ideals, history, and memories the participants hold. Although the basic purpose of commemorative speeches is to inspire listeners by reinforcing their beliefs and values, they are often entertaining as well.

Frequently, guest speakers give commemorative speeches. In addition to reinforcing the ideals of the group to which they speak, they also aim to create or increase goodwill toward the organization they represent. A single large corporation may provide speakers for more than 1,000 events annually. You can hear goodwill speeches at breakfast, luncheon, and dinner meetings or at conventions and commencement ceremonies.

Although each speech is different, they all share some characteristics; speakers typically follow these guidelines:

- *Build the speech around a theme.* Find out in advance if one has been selected for the meeting; if so, prepare your remarks around it. If not, select your own inspiring theme. Farah Walters (1992), President and Chief Executive Officer, University Hospitals of Cleveland, explains her theme in this excerpt from a keynote address she gave before an organization called WomenSpace.

  Before preparing these remarks, I asked the leadership of WomenSpace if there was anything special that I should address. I was told that there might be some interest in learning a little more about who I am and how I got to be the head of one of America's largest academic medical centers; and I was asked if I would give my assessment of where women are today in the professional world, and where I think women will be in the years ahead. I will touch upon those topics, but in a particular context. And that context is in the title of my talk—"In Celebration of Options."

- *Inspire listeners.* Inspiration is often linked to positive emotions and values such as hope, courage, respect, perseverance, and generosity. See how many positive emotions and values you can identify in this excerpt from Barbara Bush's (1990) commencement address at Wellesley College.

Wellesley, you see, is not just a place, but an idea, an experiment in excellence in which diversity is not just tolerated, but is embraced. . . . Diversity, like anything worth having, requires effort. Effort to learn about and respect difference, to be compassionate with one another, to cherish our own identity, and to accept unconditionally the same in others. You should all be very proud that this is the Wellesley spirit.

- *Pay special attention to language.* To make your speech both inspiring and memorable, select words and phrases that are vivid, moving, and interesting. Begin by describing scenes in detail so that your hearers can form images in their minds; select words that are rich in connotative meanings. This excerpt from President John Kennedy's (1988) inaugural address shows the power of inspiring language.

  And so, my fellow Americans; ask not what your country can do for you—ask what you can do for your country.

  My fellow citizens of the world; ask not what America will do for you, but what together we can do for the freedom of man.

  Finally, whether you are citizens of America or citizens of the world, ask of us here the same high standards of strength and sacrifice which we ask of you. With a good conscience our only sure reward, with history the final judge of our deeds, let us go forth to lead the land we love, asking His blessing and His help, but knowing that here on earth God's work must truly be our own.

- *When it is appropriate, use humor.* For certain events, such as after-dinner speeches whose major purpose is to entertain, humor is almost essential. This example comes from the beginning of Donald Keough's (1993) commencement address at Emory University.

  President Laney and faculty and new graduates and nongraduates and those who would be graduates except you still have overdue library books and outstanding library fines; those who parked their cars three years ago and are still searching for them; family, friends, high school teachers who said you'd never amount to a thing— and you wish they were here so they could see you now in these black robes that make you look like Supreme Court justices; relatives who wish you well, parents and spouses who sold the family silver and took out second mortgages to get some of you here, I am honored and proud and delighted to be a part of Emory University's 148th commencement.

- *Be relatively brief.* These speaking occasions are generally not times to develop an extensive policy speech or to provide detailed information. Rather, they are times to reinforce important values and to state major themes.

Eulogies

Eulogies are perhaps the most difficult speeches you'll ever give, because the subject is a deceased person you probably knew fairly well. Don't worry about summarizing the person's entire life; instead, highlight things that celebrate the deceased's personality, and focus on sharing your feelings and your experiences to comfort other mourners. Here are some guidelines:

- If you're the only person giving a eulogy, consult family members and friends for insights and anecdotes that capture essential features of the deceased. This also gives you an opportunity to find out if there is information they'd prefer you *not* mention.
- Draw from your memories, and share appropriate feelings and experiences.
- Keep in mind your goal, which is to appropriately celebrate the deceased person's life by focusing on positive, memorable characteristics.
- Humor, used sensitively, can be appropriate and comforting.

- Consider using the wave pattern and organize your eulogy around a repeated theme like "Chet was creative . . ." or "John was a devoted friend . . ." or "Molly had enough energy for three people . . ."
- Sometimes lines from poetry or the deceased's favorite lyrics work well.
- Don't worry about delivery. You may break down and cry or otherwise show your emotions, but your audience will be sympathetic. If you think this will be a problem, consider writing out your eulogy and reading it in a conversational manner.
- Keep your eulogy short. Unless the family or director says otherwise, limit your remarks to five to ten minutes.

Famous eulogies include Queen Elizabeth's televised eulogy for Princess Diana and Senator Ted Kennedy's eulogy, delivered at John Kennedy Jr.'s funeral.

In summary, special occasion speeches function to integrate the members of the group to one another and with the community in which they exist. You'll hear these talks in a variety of organizations—from clubs and volunteer associations to business, educational, and religious institutions. You may have numerous opportunities to introduce newcomers, present awards, give announcements, and make other short speeches on special occasions. Three are available on the CD that comes with this text: Mark Anderson's wedding toast, an audio link to Dr. King's *I Have a Dream* speech, and a video clip of Barbara Bush's commencement address at Wellesley College.

APPENDIX C

Sample Speeches

A Self-Introduction
Outline of a Self-Introduction Speech (Chapter 2)

Jason Kelleghan

Jason's assignment was to introduce himself by telling a personal experience narrative that taught him a lesson. You can watch this speech on your Jaffe Connection CD-ROM.

Introduction

Since the beginning of time people have had the burning desire to explore unknown territory, seek out new lands, and go where no one has gone before. Men such as Lewis and Clark and Neil Armstrong have inspired us all to expand our boundaries. These men have risked injury, humiliation, even death. I have been one of those men, and this is my story.

Body

I. The summer before my senior year, I worked as a camp counselor in "Castle Rock," a park named after a gargantuan stone.

   A. Every Friday, my friend Keith drove down to visit, and we hiked the trails behind the park.
   B. Every time we passed Castle Rock, we admired it and fantasized about climbing it, but fear held us back until the fateful day we decided to climb it.

      1. Keith and I were inexperienced, and we lacked proper equipment.
      2. It was almost five stories high—mostly vertical, with a slight slope about three-quarters of the way up.

II. The morning of the climb, I packed food, water, and (for an unknown reason) an old rope I found in the garage.

   A. We began climbing, with me in the lead; it was so easy at first that we wondered why we had been so afraid.
   B. However, about three-quarters of the way up, I was stuck without handholds.

      1. Fortunately, there was a small ledge just above me; unfortunately, I had to let go of everything to leap up and grab it.

         a. I mustered my strength and successfully made the leap.
         b. Then I turned around to get Keith.

      2. Unfortunately, Keith is shorter than I, and he missed the ledge and began sliding down the rock, grabbing a handhold just before the falling-off point.
      3. I remembered the rope and threw it down to him, but it was too short; on the second throw, he caught it and I pulled him to safety.

   C. After what seemed like an hour of shaking, we realized that we had to continue; there was no way down.

      1. I had trouble finding a path.
      2. Keith somehow found the way to the top.

D. When we finally stood atop the rock, we felt that we had been where no one had gone before.

    1. But we soon spotted a trail on the other side; anyone could climb the rock—although a trail wouldn't be as much fun!
    2. Nevertheless, we took the trail down to safety.

E. On the way down we argued over who was the better climber.

    1. I said I'd saved his life, so I was.
    2. He said he was because he'd found the way to the top.
    3. I reminded him that he wouldn't have been on the ledge without me.

III. We climbed a canyon wall to settle our argument—first one up was best.

A. About ten feet up, I fell and sprained my ankle.
B. Keith kept climbing for a short time, but he soon slid clear to the ground.

    1. The canyon wall was soft dirt; the higher up, the softer the dirt.
    2. Keith had to rescue me.

C. We returned to the park before either of us could get another bright idea.

Conclusion

I have matured since that day. I don't climb rocks without equipment, nor do I chance death for fun. But I learned two important principles. First, life presents two types of rocks—one is tall and it appears scary and impossible to climb, but it is solid, and perseverance takes us to the top. The other is short and rough. It appears easy to climb, but we eventually realize it is not solid and it crumbles around us. We can choose which rock we'll climb. The second principle is this: No matter if you climb the solid or the soft rock, climb with a friend!

El Equipo Perfecto (The Perfect Team)
A Speech Delivered in Spanish and Interpreted in the Classroom (Chapters 13 and 15)

Uriel Plascencia; interpreter, Kelly Bilinski

Uriel's first language is Spanish, and he prepared a narrative speech (Chapter 15) in Spanish; then, in advance of the speech, he worked with a fellow student, going over his speech with her. On the day he spoke, she translated his words as he paused between ideas. One key to speaking through an interpreter is for Uriel to look directly at the audience at all times and to speak at his natural rate. Immediately, as Kelly finishes one phrase, he should go right into the next. He might want to use fairly long phrases in some places and short phrases in others, depending on the point he wants to make. Watch this speech on the CD that comes with your text. An interpreted speech sounds like this.

Cuando estaba en mi último año de Preparatoria, yo tuve buenos amigos. Nuestra amistad era muy fuerte que estábamos juntos mucho tiempo. (When I was a senior in high school, I had some very good friends. Our friendship was so strong that we spent a lot of time together.) *Nosotros éramos como un equipo en todos los aspectos porque estábamos en las mismas clases, hacíamos juntos nuestra tarea, practicábamos deportes y platicábamos mucho. Nosotros nunca tuvimos problemas serios.* (We were like a team in all aspects because we spent time in classes doing our homework, playing sports, and talking. We never seemed to have any serious problems.)

    En el principio del segundo semestre, se abrió un campeonato de vóleibol. (In the beginning of the second semester, there were openings for intramural volleyball.) *Yo no pensaba estar en estos juegos porque yo estaba muy ocupado con mis estudios.* (I didn't think about being in those games because I was very busy with my studies.) *Dos de mis amigos hicieron un equipo y me invitaron a formar parte del equipo, yo acepté estar en el equipo.* (Two of my friends made a team and they invited me to be a part of the team; I decided to play with them.) *Ellos me dijeron la hora y el día de nuestros partidos.* (They told me the time and the days that we were supposed to play.) *Un día, ellos me llamaron por teléfono para saber si yo iba a venir al partido y yo les dije que sí.* (One day, they called me to find out if I was coming to the game, and I said yes.) *Antes del partido, ellos me dijeron que yo iba a jugar el segundo juego.* (Before the game, they told me that I was going to play the second set.) *Cuando ellos terminaron de jugar el primer juego, yo fui a la cancha para hacer cambios y ellos no quisieron cambiarme.* (When they finished playing the first set, I came to the court to switch players, and they didn't want to switch the team.) *Ellos no quisieron que yo jugara con ellos.* (They didn't want me to play with them.) *Yo me sentí un poco mal y traté de entenderlos porque nosotros teníamos planes para el futuro.* (I felt a little bad, and I tried to understand because we had plans for the future.) *Ellos ganaron el juego y nos fuimos juntos de ahí. Ellos no se disculparon y no me dijeron nada acerca de esto.* (They won the game and we left from there together. They didn't apologize or even talk to me about it.)

Ellos me volvieron a llamar por teléfono para saber si yo iba a venir a los juegos finales y yo dije que sí. Yo fui muy emocionado a los juegos finales porque yo quería que fuéramos los campeones. (They called me again to find out if I was coming to the finals and I said yes again. I came to the game very excited because I wanted to win the finals.) *Antes del juego, ellos me dijeron qua yo iba a jugar el segundo juego. Ellos me volvieron hacer la misma cosa que última vez.* (Before the game, they told me that I was going to play the second set. They made me the same promise as the last time.) *Yo fui a la cancha para hacer cambios y ellos no quisieron cambiarme.* (I came to the court to switch with another player, but then they didn't want to switch.) *Ellos me rechazaron enfrente de muchas personas porque había mucha gente durante los juegos finales.* (They rejected me in front of many people because there were a lot of people during the finals.) *Ellos insinuaron que no me necesitaban.* (They meant they didn't need me.) *Yo estaba muy decepcionado y me sentí muy estúpido enfrente de ellos. Yo me fui de la cancha y no pude entender por qué ellos me hicieron esto.* (I was very disappointed and I felt so stupid in front of them. I left the court, and I couldn't understand why they made this promise to me.) *Nosotros no habíamos tenido problemas y no supe cuál era el problema.* (We hadn't had any problems, and I didn't know what was wrong.) *Yo me esperé para ver si ellos ganaban* (I waited there to see if they would win,) *pero no ganaron y me fui inmediatamente de ahí.* (but they didn't and I left immediately.)

Yo estaba pensando todo el día acerca de cuál fue el problema porque yo pensaba que nuestra amistad era más fuerte que un estúpido juego. (I thought the whole day about what was wrong because I believed our friendship was stronger than a stupid game.) *Ellos no podían decir que yo era un mal jugador porque yo era mejor que ellos.* (They couldn't say that I was a bad player, because I was actually a better player.) *Yo me sentí muy triste porque ellos no me habían hecho algo como esto antes.* (I felt very bad because they had made a promise like this before.) *Yo traté de entender la situación pero no pude.* (I was trying to understand the situation but I couldn't.)

Al siguiente día, (the next day) *uno de mis amigos me estaba buscando para disculparse. El sabía lo que hizo y trató de explicarme y disculparse.* (One of these friends was looking for me to apologize. He knew what he had done and he tried to explain to me and apologize.) *Yo lo perdoné.* (I forgave him.) *Cuando me amigo trató de disculparse, yo no lo estaba escuchando. Yo estaba escuchando mi corazón y a Dios.* (When my friend was trying to apologize, I didn't listen to him. I was listening to my heart and God.) *Yo aprendí de Dios a perdonar y esta es la razón por que yo lo perdoné.* (I learned from God to forgive, and this is the reason why I forgave him.) *Nosotros somos amigos otra vez.* (We are friends again.) *El aprendió una lección y estoy seguro que él no lo volverá a hacer a nadie.* (He learned a lesson, and I am sure that he won't do this again to anybody.)

An Indian's View of Indian Affairs
An Example of Narrative Reasoning (Chapter 15)

Chief Joseph

Chief Joseph of the Nez Percé Indian tribe told this story on January 14, 1879, before a large gathering of cabinet officers, congressional representatives, diplomats, and other officials. His speech shows that Congress has good reasons to act in behalf of his people.

My name is In-mut-too-yah-lat-lat (Thunder Traveling over the Mountains). I am chief of the Wal-lam-wat-kin band of Chute-pa-lu, or Nez Percé (nose-pierced Indians). I was born in eastern Oregon, thirty-eight winters ago. My father was chief before me. . . .

Our fathers gave us many laws, which they had learned from their fathers. These laws were good. They told us to treat all men as they treated us; that we should never be the first to break a bargain; that it was a disgrace to tell a lie; that we should speak only the truth; that it was a shame for one man to take from another his wife, or his property without paying for it. We were taught to believe that the Great Spirit sees and hears everything, and that he never forgets. . . .

We did not know there were other people besides the Indian until about one hundred winters ago, when some men with white faces came to our country. They brought many things with them to trade for furs and skins. They brought tobacco, which was new to us. They brought guns with flint stones on them, which frightened our women and children. Our people could not talk with these white-faced men, but they used signs, which all people understand. These men were Frenchmen, and they called our people "Nez Percé," because they wore rings in their noses for ornaments. Although very few of our people wear them now, we are still called by that name. . . . Our people were divided in opinion about these men. Some thought they taught more bad than good. An Indian respects a brave man, but he despises a coward. He loves a straight tongue, but he hates a forked tongue. The French trappers told us some truths and some lies.

The first white men of your people who came to our country were named Lewis and Clark. They also brought many things that our people had never seen. They talked straight, and our people gave them a great feast, as a proof that their hearts were friendly. These men were very kind. They made presents to our chiefs, and our people made presents to them. We had a great many horses, of which we gave them what they needed, and they gave us guns and tobacco in return. All the Nez Percé made friends with Lewis and Clark, and agreed to let them pass through their country, and never to make war on white men. This promise the Nez Percé have never broken. No white man can accuse them of bad faith, and speak with a straight tongue. It has always been the pride of the Nez Percé that they were the friends of the white men. When my father was a young man there came to our country a white man [Reverend Mr. Spaulding] who talked spirit law. He won the affections of our people because he spoke good things to them. At first he did not say anything about white men wanting to settle on our lands. Nothing was said about that until about twenty winters ago, when a number of white people came into our country and built houses and made farms. At first our people made no complaint. They thought there was room enough for all to live in peace, and they were learning many things from the white men that seemed to be good. But we soon found that the white men were growing rich very fast, and were greedy to possess everything the Indian had. My father . . . had suspicion of men who seemed anxious to make money. I was a boy then, but I remember well my father's caution.

Next there came a white officer [Governor Stevens], who invited all the Nez Percé to a treaty. . . . He said there were a great many white people in our country, and many more would come; that he wanted the land marked out so that the Indians and white men could be separated. If they were to live in peace it was necessary, he said, that the Indians should have a country set apart for them, and in that country they must stay. My father, who represented his band, refused to have anything to do with the council, because he wished to be a free man. He claimed that no man owned any part of the earth, and a man could not sell what he did not own.

Mr. Spaulding took hold of my father's arm and said, "Come and sign the treaty." My father pushed him away, and said, "Why do you ask me to sign away my country? It is your business to talk to us about spirit matters and not to talk to us about parting with our land." Governor Stevens urged my father to sign his treaty, but he refused. "I will not sign your paper," he said. "You go where you please, so do I; you are not a child, I am no child; I can think for myself. No man can think for me. I have no other home than this. I will not give it up to any man. My people would have no home. Take away your paper. I will not touch it with my hand. . . ."

Chief Joseph continues the speech, detailing years of treaty negotiations between the Nez Percé and the whites. His conclusion recognizes that the inevitable has happened; his people are powerless against the white settlers. But his final plea is for equal justice under law for the Indian as well as for whites.

SOURCE: From *Indian Oratory: Famous Speeches by Noted Indian Chieftains*, by W. C. Vanderwerth. Copyright © 1971 by the University of Oklahoma Press, pp. 259–284.

Dolphin Communication
Outline for an Informative Speech (Chapters 11 and 16)

Tanya Moser

Tanya's assignment was to prepare and deliver an informative speech with visual aids. Here's her content outline.

General Purpose: To inform
Specific Purpose: To inform my audience about studies being conducted in the area of human–dolphin communication.
Central Idea: Researchers have taught dolphins to communicate through a series of whistles and object association.

Introduction

I. "Hoop Right Frisbee In"; you may not understand this, but a dolphin trained to communicate with humans would know exactly what I meant.

II. Language forms a barrier that prevents us from communicating with life outside our "human" world, but studies involving the bottlenose dolphin show that we are not the only intelligent animals on earth, and communication with some animals is possible.

III. I first learned of the dolphin's ability to understand and communicate with humans when I read an article for a writing course; while researching the topic, I found several additional articles and books related to dolphin communication.

IV. I will explain the concept of dolphin intelligence, dolphin-to-dolphin communication, and dolphin communication with humans.

Body

I. Many scientists think that dolphins have a very high intelligence level and, in this area, they may be the animal closest to a human.

A. *Sea Frontiers Magazine* reports that dolphins have the highest ratio of brain-to-body size of any nonhuman animal; this ratio may indicate the ability to process large amounts of complex information.

B. However, intelligence is not entirely based on brain size.

1. It is also related to how information is processed and used.

   a. Quickness and efficiency are important.
   b. Flexibility, the ability to adapt to moment-by-moment happenings, is also important.

2. Dolphins have both quickness and flexibility.

C. Researchers have found that dolphins can mimic some human sounds.

   1. This indicates an ability to remember certain sounds.
   2. It also suggests they may be able to communicate in an artificial language.

II. Dolphins communicate among themselves.

A. According to *The Natural History of Whales and Dolphins*, they communicate through a system of whistles, clicks, rattles, and squeaks.

   1. Clicking sounds, which are used for navigation in deep waters, may also convey messages.

      a. Pulsed squeaks can indicate distress.
      b. Buzzing clicks may indicate aggression.

   2. Dolphins identify themselves through signature whistles.

      a. Each dolphin has a distinctive signature whistle it uses to identify itself to other dolphins.
      b. Mothers and calves find each other in large groups, even when other dolphins are also whistling.

   3. An article titled, "Those Dolphins Aren't Just Whistling in the Dark," suggests that dolphins may even pass down legends or stories.

      a. This idea seems a little far-fetched.
      b. However, animals seem to understand things in their own way.

III. Through training, captive dolphins have learned to associate sounds with objects and actions.

A. In one study, researchers used an underwater keyboard.

   [Display transparency showing the nine-key keyboard.]

   1. Symbols on each of nine keys represented a specific type of object.

      a. The symbol was not a picture of the object.
      b. The keys could be moved around on the board so that the dolphins could not memorize the location.

   [Display second transparency showing keys in a different position.]

   2. When dolphins pressed a key, a distinctive whistle was sounded, and they received the object associated with the symbol on the key.

      a. They soon learned to associate the symbol with the object.
      b. Dolphins would give the "ball" whistle before pressing the key.
      c. When they saw two items at once, such as a ring and a ball, they would make both whistles as they played with the objects.

   3. They remembered these sounds on a long-term basis.

      a. Researchers separated them from the keyboard for two years.
      b. When they saw it again, they happily began to whistle the various sounds.

B. Dolphins could understand "sentences" that combined various objects or actions they learned to associate with whistles.

1. Each sentence was two to five words long.
2. Sentences consisted of an indirect object, a direct object, and a term that connected them.

   a. For example, "HOOP RIGHT FRISBEE IN" meant, "Put the frisbee in the hoop on the right."
   b. Word order mattered; reversing the order in the sentence would result in a totally different response.

3. Dolphins could understand a variety of word combinations.

   a. Once an instructor said "WATER TOSS," thinking this was a nonsense sentence that would get no response.
   b. The dolphin quickly moved to the hose on the tank's railing and glided through it, sending out a spray of water.

Conclusion

I. In conclusion, we are not the only intelligent creatures on earth.
II. Dolphins are intelligent animals who communicate with one another and with humans through an invented "language" of whistles and clicks.
III. The next time you hear somebody talking to her dog as if it were a person, don't automatically assume that she is crazy; she may know something about communicating with animals that dolphin studies hint at.

References

Bower, B. (1984, December 1). Grammar-schooled dolphins. *Science News*, 346–348.
Curtis, P. (1987, January/February). Contact with dolphins. *Sea Frontiers*, 84–92.
Evans, P. G. H. (1987). *The natural history of whales and dolphins*. New York: Oxford.
Forcier-Beringer, A. C. (1986, March/April). Talking with dolphins. *Sea Frontiers*, 84–92.
Sayigh, L. S. & Pyack, P. L. (1989, Spring). Those dolphins aren't just whistling in the dark. *Oceanus*, 80–83.
Shane, S. H. (1991, March/April). The dolphin report. *Sea Frontiers*, 36–43.
Wintsch, S. (1990, Fall). You'd think you were thinking. *Mosaic*, 34–48.

The *Dundun* Drum
Outline of an Informative Speech (Chapter 16)

Joshua Valentine

Josh's assignment was to research, outline, and deliver an informative speech, using a visual aid. He created a multimedia presentation that showed pictures of the drum and played actual recordings, downloaded from the Internet.

General Purpose: To inform
Specific Purpose: To inform my audience about the *dundun* (which most will not have ever heard of), and to describe how and why it is used.
Central Idea: The *dundun* is an African drum with an interesting history that is used both musically and linguistically.

Introduction

I. Imagine that your friend asks you what you did over the weekend, but instead of using words, your friend simply beats a drum.

II. You will probably never have such an encounter, but in some cultures, music is used for purposes that are different from those we are accustomed to.

   A. *Webster's Dictionary* defines language as "any system of symbols, sounds, or gestures used for communication."
   B. Our culture does not have instrumental sounds that represent English words, but there are other cultures around the world where sounds have meaning.

III. I have been playing percussion since junior high, and I first learned about the *dundun* while attending a percussion workshop two years ago.

IV. Today, I will explain the history of the *dundun* as well as its linguistic use and its musical use.

Body

I. The Nigerian talking drum, *dundun* (pronounced *doon-doon*), actually does talk, in the Yoruba language.

   A. The *dundun* originated during the Oyo Empire of Yoruba-land in the fifteenth century A.D. for the purpose of worship.
   B. The Yoruba language is easily communicated on the *dundun*.

      1. This language is a tonal language.
      2. Yoruba speakers use three basic tones or pitches, with glides between them, as an essential part of how words are pronounced.

         a. Listen to this sound clip and try to identify the three main tones.

            [Play a sound clip, downloaded from the Internet.]

         b. If you have a sharp ear, you may also be able to pick out some slides essential to the Yoruba language.

      3. Melody is the basis for the Yoruba language since the same word pronounced with a different melody means something entirely different.

   C. The *dundun* functions by changing the tension of two skin heads using the leather straps that hold the heads in place.

II. The *dundun* was originally created to communicate.

   A. The Yoruba are a people of southwestern Nigeria who have used drums for spiritual communication throughout their history.

      1. The *dundun* was originally created as a tool for worship of the gods.
      2. Songs and hymns of praise were created entirely on *dundun* drums and are still recited today among the modern Yoruba people.
      3. Listen to the intensity of this spiritual worship song played on talking drums.

         [Play example, downloaded from the Internet.]

   B. The Yoruba also use their drums for social communication.

      1. The *dundun* has also been a part of day-to-day casual conversation.

         a. "A master drummer can maintain a regular monologue on a talking drum, saying 'hi' to different people, cracking jokes, and telling stories" (Plunkett).
         b. *Dundun* drummers are often heard speaking the names of friends and family on their drums as a greeting and sign of respect.

   C. The *dundun*'s secondary, yet most obvious, use is as a musical instrument.

      1. It became a musical instrument because of its use in worship.

    a. At first it was used mainly to communicate ideas, but since worship in the Yoruba culture is a corporate activity, people began coming together and music on the *dundun* was born.

    b. Religious songs are still recited today, although often only for their musical value, which is a complete switch from their origin.

2. Even everyday speech becomes song when the Yoruba use the *dundun*.

    a. The word *kabo*, which means *welcome*, is only a two-syllable word, so a more common phrase, "spoken" on a *dundun* is, "Welcome, we are happy that you arrived safely" (Drum Talk, Ltd).

    b. "Speech" on the *dundun* is always made rhythmic, even when it would not normally be rhythmic if spoken.

3. The *dundun*'s use as a musical instrument has spread far beyond Nigeria.

    a. Next to the *djembe*, the *dundun* is the most well-known and recognizable African drum used in America.

    b. "[It] fares well in jazz blues, R&B, rock and roll, reggae, classical music, even choral music" (Awe).

    c. This is a clip from a song by African American musician Francis Awe.

[Play clip downloaded from the Internet.]

Conclusion

I. Whether in language or in song, the *dundun*'s sound is always an unusually beautiful one.

II. Today, we have seen the origins of the Nigerian talking drum (*dundun*), its uses as a linguistic tool, and its uses as a musical instrument.

III. So next time you hear music as simple as a beating drum, you might remember that the drummer may be communicating much more than you think.

References

Awe, Francis. (1999). *Drum clinic by Francis Awe: Talking drum* [Online]. Available: http://www.after-science.com/awe/clinic.html

DeSilva, Tamara. (1997). *Lying at the crossroads of everything: Towards a social history of the African drum* [Online]. Available: http://www.artic.edu/saic/programs/depts/undergrad/Best_Thesis_Essay.pdf

Drum Talk Ltd. (2000). *Background information* [Online]. Available: http://www.drumtalk.co.uk/drum_background.html

Euba, Akin. (1991). *Yoruba drumming: The Dundun tradition by Akin Euba* [Online]. Available: http://www.music-research-inst.org/html/pubs/*dundun*.htm

How Bata drums talk and what they say [Online]. Available: http://www.batadrums.com/understanding_rhythms/talk.htm

Plunkett, Aaron. DU DUN [Online]. Available: http://www.world-beats.com/*dundun*.htm

Yoruba drums from Benin, West Africa the world's musical traditions 8 [Online]. Available: http://www.eyeneer.com/Labels/Smithsonian/yoruba.html

The Twenty-Fifth Amendment
An Informative Speech that Explains Presidential Succession (Chapter 16)

Loren Rozokas (American Legion Oratorical Contest Award Winner)
You can watch Loren's speech on Jaffe Speech Interactive on the Jaffe Connection CD-ROM.

Riding only two cars behind President John F. Kennedy through the streets of Dallas, Texas, on November 22, 1963, Vice President Lyndon B. Johnson could hear the shots that

killed his chief. Before the day was over, Johnson was sworn in as President of the United States and assumed command in the nation's capital.

The road to ratification of the 25th Amendment proved a long journey. The amendment, which addresses presidential chain of command, in case of death or resignation by a president, was noted in the original Constitution, but the wording was vague and led to confusion in its interpretation.

Perhaps the problem stemmed from the fact that the office of vice president was only important in the event of the death of the president.

From the very beginning, the founding fathers provided that executive power would rest in the hands of the president. They created the office of vice president, almost as an afterthought, in order to provide for a successor should the president die or resign. While they provided the vice president with an auspicious title, the power they provided was limited.

Some delegates at the convention, such as Massachusetts' Elbridge Gerry, felt the whole idea of a vice president was unnecessary. His opposition was so intense that he refused to sign the Constitution. Interestingly enough, he later served as vice president under James Madison.

Even the election of the vice president was dubious. In the beginning, the top two contenders ran against each other; one became president, while the runner up settled for a job with no power.

Because so many of the top office seekers did not get along, this caused great friction. Many vice presidents were virtually ignored by the chief executive in power.

As second in command, in 1880, Chester A. Arthur noted, "Being vice president isn't the most comfortable position to hold, you are a man waiting to fill another man's shoes." Within months of this statement, Chester Arthur got a chance to try those shoes on when his chief commander, James Garfield, died in September 1881.

Article 2, Section 6, of the Constitution was so obscure in its definition that when William Henry Harrison died in 1841, only a month after his inauguration, a problem immediately arose. John Tyler assumed the presidency. Congress believed Tyler was acting as the president, but, in fact, was not a true president. Tyler contended that, if he had the presidency, then he was indeed the president.

Research by constitutional historians, poring over the minutes and notes of the original drafters, determined that Tyler was wrong in his assumption. The early Constitution made no provision whatsoever that a vice president would become the top officer in the land upon the death, resignation, or removal of the president.

In short, Presidents Tyler, Fillmore, Johnson, Arthur, Roosevelt, Coolidge, Truman, and Johnson were not constitutionally certified presidents when they assumed the presidency as vice presidents. In fact, they were only acting presidents. Of all the presidents to succeed the office because of a vacancy, only Gerald Ford was bona fide president because of the ratification of the 25th Amendment.

This item of presidential succession took 127 years to clear up.

Employee Privacy and the Internet
Outline of a Persuasive Speech (Chapters 17 and 18)

Chris Farthing

Chris's assignment was to prepare and deliver a persuasive speech in the general topic area of electronic media.

Topic: Employee Privacy and the Internet
General Purpose: To persuade

Specific Purpose: To persuade my audience that companies deserve the right to monitor their employees' use of the Internet, email, and instant messenger services.

Central Idea: Companies own the equipment and they are paying for employees' time; therefore they have the right to monitor employees' time, but employees can protect themselves.

Introduction

I. Imagine Cheryl: she uses her coffee break to search the Internet for information about a cousin's health problems; her employee monitors this search and contacts the Human Resources Department, which records these visits in Cheryl's insurance files.

II. Any time you go to work, either now or in the future, your employer has the right to monitor your computer usage.

III. At a Web development company where I previously worked, two coworkers were reprimanded for misusing company time after they sent several inappropriate emails back and forth and surfed the Internet on company time.

IV. Today, I will summarize the history of Internet privacy issues, explain why employers should be allowed to monitor employees, describe what employers should do for employees, and finally tell what employees can do to protect themselves.

Body

I. Internet privacy and the workplace first became a major issue when the Internet became an increasingly popular way of communicating and doing business.

   A. Informationweek.com says, "When monitoring started to catch on a few years ago, it was in response to several high-profile sexual harassment cases. Now, employers are increasingly concerned about productivity and bandwidth."

      1. Employees download pornographic material from the Internet and cause a hostile environment for other employees who are subjected to unwanted images; they also send harassing messages to coworkers.

         a. SexTracker, a site that monitors pornography site usage, reports that 70 percent of porn traffic occurs during business hours (networkmagazine.com).

         b. The same source defines harassment as sexual, hateful, prejudicial, or inflammatory email.

      2. Networkmagazine.com also says, "Since the Industrial Revolution began and factories sprang up, productivity has become the god of industry. And if productivity is god, then the greatest sin one can commit is wasting time."

      3. As the Internet grew, employees began to download music, read news, and watch streaming videos, which greatly slowed down company networks, forcing them to pay for more bandwidth.

   B. Employers are legally allowed to monitor everything on company computers.

      1. CNN.com says, "U.S. law, which is backed by court rulings, makes clear that 'he who owns the computers gets to see what is going on with their computers,' he said."

      2. Instant messaging is currently the only safe haven for private communication, but soon even that will be open to scrutiny.

   C. Monitoring employees is a fast growing industry.

      1. Wired.com reports, "International Data Corporation (IDC) estimates that corporations worldwide spent $62 million on Internet filtering and monitoring software in 1999. An IDC study predicts that figure will rise to $561 million by 2005."

2. Msnbc.com says, "Interest in IM monitoring is soaring as companies not only look to record important communications but also control information leaks and discourage cyber slacking."

II. Companies own the employees' equipment and time; therefore, they should be able to monitor both as much or as little as they see fit.

A. Businesses want to know if people are doing anything illegal with company property.

1. Harassment—sexual or otherwise—is an example.
2. Illegally selling company secrets is another reason to monitor.
3. If I own something, I should be able to monitor my own property.

B. As long as employees are on a time clock, the company has the right to know what they are doing with their time.

1. Businesses want to know if people are using their time efficiently or slacking off.
2. Msnbc.com gives an illustration of wasted time, "If an employee surfs the Internet just 5 minutes of every hour at a pay of $15 per hour the loss to a business can be enormous. An eight-hour day has 40 minutes wasted, which becomes 200 minutes per week. At 48 weeks a year (4 allotted for vacation and sick time) that is 160 hours. This translates into $2400 on a single employee. For a business with only 500 personnel using computers that is $1,200,000."

III. Although they have the right to monitor employees, employers who want their employees' respect and loyalty should not abuse this tool.

A. Employers often expect more out of their employees, demanding long hours and stressful working conditions.
B. In order to allow employees to take care of personal needs, many businesses overlook limited personal emails and quick checks of personal information on the Internet.

1. Employees can go online during breaks and check personal stocks, read news, or even chat online for a short time.
2. Andrew Meyer of Websense, a company that makes Internet filtering software, explains, "If it's easier for me to do a five-minute, online banking transaction, it's a lot better than if I have to get in my car, go out to the bank, and spend 20 minutes in line" (networkmagazine.com).

C. Employers should also make plain their policy on use of company equipment and time so that employees know what is expected and can work accordingly.

IV. Employees can protect themselves from discipline by keeping their actions in line with their company's policy.

A. Make it a point to know your company's view toward using its time and network for your personal use.
B. If you are unsure of whether or not something is appropriate to do on a company computer, go and ask your supervisor.
C. If you don't think it's something you can discuss with your supervisor, you probably shouldn't do it at work.

Conclusion

I. Today we have discussed why businesses have the right to monitor their employees' actions on the Internet and on company computers.

II. We went over how Internet monitoring developed, why it is legal and appropriate, what businesses should do for their employees, and finally what you can do to protect yourself.

III. When you are using a work computer, hopefully you will stop to think that your company may be legally monitoring you, but as long as you are doing what you are supposed to do with company time and property, this should not cause pain or anxiety.

IV. But if Cheryl had thought through the implications of Internet monitoring, she might have done her research away from the workplace.

Embryo Adoption
A Persuasive Speech (Chapters 17 and 18)

Paul Southwick

Paul prepared this speech when he was a competitor on his speech team at Clackamas Community College. He delivered it at regional and national tournaments, and often took home a trophy. You can watch this speech under Speech Interactive for Chapter 4 on your Jaffe Connection CD-ROM.

There is something magical and beautiful that happens every winter, if we are lucky; snow. Thousands of snowflakes cover the ground and each snowflake is unique from the rest. Now, there is a new type of snowflake that science has led us to marvel at, the human embryo. Each little embryo is unique from the rest and is a mysterious new life beginning to grow. As *Citizen Magazine* reports in the October 2001 edition, Hannah Sterge, now a rambunctious two-year-old, was one of these snowflakes. The Nightlight Christian Adoption Agency in Fullerton California gave embryo adoptees this wintry name because the embryos are frozen and no two are alike.

However, a large amount of heat is threatening the existence of little snowflakes across the country. Many lobbyists are continuing to pressure the government for additional funding to obtain, destroy, and research on tiny, unsuspecting victims like Hannah Sterge. The United States government should discontinue its embryonic stem cell research and increase the funding for adult stem cell research.

Through the next few minutes we will examine the humanness of the embryo, then uncover the fallacies of embryonic stem cells, and finally slide into the benefits of adult stem cell research.

First, we will examine the humanness of the embryo. Many, including biologist Irv Weissman of Stanford University in a July 9th, 2001, *Newsweek* article, have treated the human embryo as merely a piece of tissue or lifeless substance. However, peering through medical history and concluding with medical expertise from our own time we will see that a human embryo is life in its most basic stage. Beginning with Dr. Bradley M. Patten's 1963 textbook, *Human Embryology*, we find that the culmination of the process of fertilization marks the initiation of the life of a new individual. Moving farther along in the timeline, in 1980 Dr. Jerome LeJeune, world renowned genetics professor, revealed that after fertilization has taken place a new human being has come into existence. Recent embryologists echo the words of Dr. Patten and Dr. LeJeune. Dr. C. Ward Kischer, professor at the University of Arizona college of Medicine, states in a July 16th, 2001, article that "The life of the new individual human being begins at fertilization. . . . Every human embryologist, world wide, know this . . . and it is so stated in virtually every textbook of human embryology."

At the June 2001 National Right to Life Convention in North Carolina, a lecture was given on human development. The lecture pertained to women who saw pictures of their unborn child at its earliest stage of development, mentioning that the child looked like a blob or a tadpole. The lecture affirmed the women; don't worry. That little blob in your tummy isn't going to be frog, a chicken, or a giraffe. It's a little human and its just going to get bigger. Since we know that the embryo is human, we should protect it.

After all, as Sen. Brownback of Kansas in the December 8th, 2001, issue of *World Magazine* points out regarding endangered-species laws, "You can't touch a bald eagle's eggs. You can't even mess with their habitat." As a society, we have recognized the importance of the beginnings of animal life, and it is time to recognize the importance of early human life as well.

Now that we have discovered the humanness of the embryo, wisdom's call beckons us to uncover the fallacies of embryonic stem cell research.

Many, including the National Institutes of Health and numerous mainstream media, are treating embryonic stem cells as a miraculous cure. Whether the cells are derived from unused embryos at in vitro fertilization clinics or as we have seen recently, through embryonic cloning, the hope of many science and research universities, like Johns Hopkins University, is that embryonic stem cells will one day be able to cure degenerative diseases like Alzheimer's and Parkinson's disease.

However, editorial page writer Richard Miniter, in the September 9th, 2001, edition of *Forbes Magazine*, reveals the reality of the situation, labeling embryonic stem cell research as "shaky" and "speculative." Mr. Miniter states bluntly and accurately that "[e]mbryonic stem cells have yet to save a single life." He credits researchers' demands for federal funding as stemming from the lack of private funding due to biotech companies viewing embryonic stem cell research as unprofitable.

Another complication with embryonic stem cell research is the high probability that transplanted embryonic cells will be rejected by the recipient. In July of 2001 Doctor Lauren Pecorino labeled immune rejection as a possible disadvantage to embryonic stem cells. Immune rejection is a large disadvantage because cells derived from an embryo may have a different immune profile than the person the cells would be transferred to, causing cell rejection.

Finally, we must uncover the fallacy that embryonic stem cell research does not destroy a human life. Though small, this human embryo will eventually grow into a fetus, then an infant, where the child will continue to grow and enter preschool like Hannah Sterge. Next, little Hannah will go through all the changes of puberty, go to college, possibly fall in love, get married, join the workforce, have kids, travel, and enjoy all that life has to offer. Unless, of course, life is cut off at its most basic stage and everything that follows is erased.

During the June 28th edition of *Fox News Sunday* one of embryonic stem cell research's proponents, Sen. Orrin Hatch from Utah, claimed that "an embryo in a petri dish is not a human life." Dr. Kischer profoundly asks the opposing question, is an embryo in a petri dish a human death? Of course not! "It is still a life process, but one that has been artificially suspended. This does not alter the integrity of the life process unless the manipulation is destructive."

Thankfully, there is a strong beacon of hope in the fact that adult stem cells are actively curing people and contain the promise of curing further degenerative diseases, without the destruction of a human life.

Adult stem cells are derived, without harm, from an individual and are naturally accepted and grown within that individual's system. In an October 2001 *Citizen Magazine* article, Michael Fumento, a science journalist and senior fellow at the Hudson Institute, states that there are many locations of adult stem cells, including bone marrow, newborns' umbilical cords, placentas, fat tissue, and virtually every part of the human body. Furthermore, a January 23rd, 2002, article in *New Scientist* reveals the eye-opening discovery of an adult stem cell that can turn into every single tissue in the body: muscle, cartilage, bone, liver, and different types of neurons. Additionally, the *Boston Globe* reported on January 24th, 2002, that some adult stem cell lines have grown in culture for two years and show no signs of aging. Though this discovery is very new and must still be confirmed by colleagues, Morphogen Pharmaceuticals Incorporated of San Diego has revealed similar results, and many more groups will likely follow suit.

Unlike embryonic stem cells, in recent months adult stem cells have cured a disease. On January 24th, 2002, *HealthScoutNews* reported that an early adult stem cell therapy cured "Bubble Boy" disease, a disorder that erases the immune system. Even more exciting is the scientific potential for adult stem cells to treat and cure heart disease, sickle cell anemia, radiation sickness, Parkinson's disease, and many others.

The greatest benefit of adult stem cell research and therapy is that human lives are not sacrificed. Contrary to popular belief, a large portion of people who could benefit from embryonic stem cell research are opposing the research on ethical grounds. An October 2001 *Citizen Magazine* article reveals two of these people as Andrew Sullivan and Mark Pickup. Andrew Sullivan is an HIV-infected journalist who contends, "If my life were extended one day at the expense of one other human's life, it would be an evil beyond measure." Another candidate for embryonic stem cell research, Mark Pickup, was tragically diagnosed with multiple sclerosis and is now confined to a wheelchair. Mark admits that sometimes it is tempting to wish that embryonic stem cell research could one day make him able to walk again, but he realizes something that many people have ignored. In Mark's own words, "To gain my freedom from disease, I would become more wretched by accepting the fruits of robbing another of life, existence and a place in the world. No! The cure would only increase the torment." Let us stand with Andrew Sullivan and Mark Pickup, rejecting life-destroying embryonic stem cell research while encouraging the development of life-giving adult stem cells, which every human being has been given.

Today, we have examined the humanness of the embryo, then uncovered the fallacies of embryonic stem cells, and finally slid into the benefits of adult stem cell research.

In order to take a step in the protection of human lives in the embryonic state, we can choose to accept the scientific and ethical support that human embryos are lives that deserve protection. Also, our government should encourage embryo adoption. This will ensure that every embryo has the chance to keep on living. Finally, our nation must take a larger stride in the exploration and development of adult stem cell research, which will keep little human embryos like Hannah Sterge alive, as well as finding very possible cures to degenerative diseases. When all is said and done on the embryonic stem cell research debate, we must look for wisdom from Dr. Suess who wrote, "A person's a person. No matter how small." In our case, even when they are the size of a snowflake.

The following speeches, both on the same subject, show how differently two people approach a topic depending on their purpose, their audience, and the context in which they speak. Angela prepared her speech for the classroom and delivered it extemporaneously on one occasion. Sonja prepared hers for competition in intercollegiate speech tournaments; she memorized it and gave it many times during the year.

Sleep Deprivation
A Persuasive Speech Outline (Chapters 17 and 18)

Angela Wilson

General Purpose: To persuade

Specific Purpose: To persuade (convince) my audience that sleep deprivation has three negative consequences.

Central Idea: When sleep is deprived, individuals suffer financially and relationally, and society as a whole suffers.

Introduction

I. We need food, water, shelter . . . and sleep to survive.
II. We are similar to rats in our need for sleep; without food, rats last sixteen days; without sleep they last only seventeen days.
III. As I began to study the effects of sleep deprivation on society, I found many interesting facts.
IV. Sleep deprivation affects society in three specific ways: our financial lives, our personal relationships, and our work environments all suffer.

Body

I. First of all, sleep deprivation affects us financially.

    A. Americans waste $70 billion a year in lost productivity, accidents, and medical bills.
    B. Americans fill over 14 million prescriptions a year to help them sleep; they also spend millions on OTC drugs, 33 million in grocery stores.
    C. In 1977 there were three sleep disorder clinics, now there are 377; we waste billions of dollars and hundreds of hours of labor building clinics because we aren't sleeping right.

II. Second, sleep deprivation affects our individual relationships.

    A. Because society is made up of interrelated individuals, when one person struggles, we all do.
    B. When sleep deprived, individuals have trouble controlling their emotions and behaviors.

        1. Small disagreements can become potentially explosive.
        2. Sleep deprivation leaves us feeling sluggish, tired, irritable, and depressed.
        3. Volunteers in an experiment, after going sleepless for some time, exhibited childish, masochistic, and paranoid behaviors; they also injured themselves.
        4. Sleep deprived individuals have increasingly aggressive behaviors.

III. And finally, sleep deprivation affects safety in our working environments.

    A. Volunteers, who were asked to refrain from sleeping for a certain amount of time, became listless, serious, and grim; they did poorly on tasks of vigilance, reaction time, and simple arithmetic.

        1. Imagine yourself as a truck driver, a fireman, or a schoolteacher.
        2. All of these jobs require vigilance, reaction time, and simple arithmetic skills.

    B. Examples of lives lost due to sleep deprivation are those of the *Challenger* space shuttle and Exxon *Valdez* oil spill.

Conclusion

I. In conclusion, I ask you to consider the facts and statistics I have presented.
II. Sleep deprivation really is a factor that affects our work, our personal relationships, and our lives.
III. Let those poor research rats be a warning to you, and go get some sleep!

Sleep Deprivation
A Persuasive Speech (Chapters 17 and 18)

Sonja Ralston

Since Congress has finally achieved a budget surplus, they've been able to devote their time to more important things, like declaring this week National Sleep Awareness Week. The

March 22, 1999, *USA Today* in part of a nineteen-article series on sleep deprivation warned that we are faced with a new national debt measured, not in dollars, but in lost hours of sleep.

William Dement, a sleep researcher at Stanford University, explains that a sleep debt accumulates night after night: if you skip one hour a night for eight nights, you'll owe your body as if you had stayed up all night long. And if you think only college students carry a sleep balance (akin to their credit card balance) somewhere deep in the red, keep in mind that James B. Mass, a sleep researcher at Cornell University, noted in the May 27, 1998, *Houston Chronicle*, "It's a national crisis." And it's affecting more than just our moods; every year the national sleep debt costs us $166 billion and 13,000 lives.

Before we can drift off for a good night's sleep we must first wake up to some of the alarming effects of sleep debts, then we can open our eyes to better understand their causes, and finally cozy up to some solutions at both the personal and the societal levels.

Unlike your loan shark, Big Tony, when you default on a debt to your body it can't exactly smash your kneecaps with a baseball bat. Instead it retaliates with the effects of sleep debts, which range from general fatigue to something as fatal as sleeping behind the wheel, and everything in between.

According to the December 12, 1998, edition of the *Tokyo Daily*, those most severely affected are "shift workers, parents of young children, and young adults, most notably students." However, it can affect anyone, especially those with high levels of stress in their lives, and according to a survey released last week by the National Sleep Foundation, 65 percent of adults are suffering from sleep deprivation, more than twice the number reported in 1991.

According to the *Orange County Register* of September 12, 1998, "an estimated 23 million Americans are afflicted with migraine headaches," the most common cause of which is a basic lack of sleep. And while these painful headaches can affect our moods and our productivity, they can also seriously affect our memories. Not getting enough sleep in and of itself can impair your memory, but that, in conjunction with frequent migraines, is enough to permanently damage your short-term memory retention. In the September 1998 edition of *American Health for Women*, Dr. Robin West, a psychologist at the University of Florida, Gainesville notes that being stressed strains the memory, but "add lack of sleep to the mix, and it's no wonder we're literally losing our minds." Being tired makes it hard to focus, which makes it difficult to get information into our short-term storage banks.

Also, our cumulative sleep debts have a serious impact on the monetary debt of American companies, who, according to the aforementioned *Houston Chronicle* article, lost $150 billion every year through the decreased productivity of their sleepy employees. People also spend money on sleep aids and caffeine pills.

Not surprisingly, people who carry high sleep debts are also more susceptible to disease and micro-sleep. Dr. Max Hirshkowitz, Director of Baylor, a sleep lab, explains in the May 27, 1998, *Sacramento Bee* that "micro-sleep" is the instantaneous dozing off which lasts less than a minute, but at 60 mph, five seconds is long enough. Micro-sleep is the attributed cause of such disasters as the Chernobyl explosion, the Exxon *Valdez* crash, and the twenty-five to fifty people killed every day in this country by those sleeping behind the wheel. That article goes on to exclaim, "that's like a 747 crashing every other week, with no survivors." Sadly, the National Highway Safety Administration reports that there will be a 20 percent increase in that number Sunday, the day we "spring ahead" into daylight savings time. So from headaches and memory loss to monetary costs and micro-sleep, sleep debts affect us all in some way.

Now that we understand why we need to be alarmed by letting our sleep balance plunge below zero, we can open our eyes to better examine the three causes of sleep debts. First, as Dr. Stanley Coren, a neuropsychologist at the University of British Columbia, explains in the August 2, 1998, edition of the *Boston Globe*, the "chronic lack of sleep experienced by the American population is a direct result of the industrial revolution." In the nineteenth century, the hours of the day were extended due to the widespread use of electric lights and the elimination of the midday nap. Experts at the National Sleep Foundation say we need between eight and nine hours of sleep a night to function at our peak, and most of us are only getting seven or less.

Having too much to do is another cause of sleep deprivation. Daily chores, TV, the Internet, caffeine, and simple insomnia, which affects over 35 million Americans, are all demands on our sleep time, and with 24-hour Wal-Marts, 120 channels on cable, and the world at the tips of our keyboards, there's always something to do, so sleep loses out.

And with all this, Dr. Judith Leech, head of the Ottawa Hospital sleep lab, presents the third cause in the April 19, 1998, edition of the *Ottawa Citizen*. She says that in addition to how much we sleep, "how well we sleep" is important. A fitful night of tossing and turning, although it may last ten hours, does us about as much good as six hours of deep, sound, relaxing sleep. So, the industrial revolution, too much to do, and poor sleep quality all influence our insufficient sleeping habits.

Now that we understand both the causes and the effects of sleep debts, we can cozy up to some solutions on both the societal and personal levels. Dr. Richard Costriotta, director of the University of Texas-Houston sleep lab, exclaims: "Welcome to the 90's" where more than half of us are sleep deprived and there's nothing we can do about it. Well, that's not quite true.

To completely eliminate this plague in our society, I propose that we undo the industrial revolution, destroy all the light bulbs, and revert to an agrarian society. Okay, so that's not really plausible, but there are steps we can take to eliminate our sleep deprivation without diminishing the last two centuries of progress.

First, we need to recognize the limitations of societal solutions. While some may say that big businesses will never be sensitive to the needs of their employees, an article in the March 28, 1999, *Times-Picayune* tells about several companies in the New Orleans area that have implemented nap time as part of the daily work routine. This drastically diminishes the sleep debts of their employees and increases productivity and benefits to the company.

If you're not lucky enough to work for one of these companies, don't worry, because most of the solutions lie on the personal level. In his 1999 book, *Power Sleep*, Dr. James Maas lists several tips for putting your sleep balance back in the black.

- First and foremost, make an appointment with sleep and don't be late.
- Secondly, turn the bedroom into a conducive sleeping environment; eliminate distractions such as the TV, computers, and work out equipment; make it quiet and dark, and lower the temperature so it's a few degrees cooler than the rest of the house.
- Next, establish a routine before bed; take a warm shower, eat a light snack with warm milk, unwind, and allow yourself twenty minutes to fall asleep.
- Finally, he advises to avoid evening exercise and caffeine and nicotine, if not altogether, at least within four hours of bedtime, because these activities lead to increased heart rate, which makes it difficult to relax.

By following these simple steps, we can eliminate our sleep debts and be happier, healthier, more productive individuals.

Today we've taken a look at our National Debt. Our national sleep debt, that is. First we woke up to some of its alarming effects, then we opened our eyes to better understand its causes, and finally we cozied up to some simple steps that both businesses and all of us can take.

Unlike so many other plagues that haunt our society today, we know both what causes and what cures sleep deprivation, so the real tragedy here is that two-thirds of us are still suffering unnecessarily.

So, before National Sleep Awareness Week and this tournament are over, take the time to pay off your sleep debt before your body declares biological bankruptcy. Sleep tight and don't let your sleep debt bite.

Mrs. Bush's Remarks at Wellesley College Commencement
A Commencement Address to a Hostile Audience (Chapters 17, 18, and Appendix B)

Barbara Bush

(You can watch this speech on your Jaffe Connection CD-ROM.) Administrators invited Mrs. Bush to speak at Wellesley College's commencement exercises, although students in the class wanted the novelist, Alice Walker. Facing a hostile audience, Mrs. Bush used humor to present her "goodwill" special occasion speech on Friday, June 1, 1990. After she thanked the president, recognized the platform party, the graduates, the parents, she said:

More than ten years ago when I was invited here to talk about our experiences in the People's Republic of China, I was struck by both the natural beauty of your campus . . . and the spirit of this place.

Wellesley, you see, is not just a place . . . but an idea . . . an experiment in excellence in which diversity is not just tolerated but is embraced.

The essence of this spirit was captured in a moving speech about tolerance given last year by the student body president of one of your sister colleges. She related the story by Robert Fulghum about a young pastor who, finding himself in charge of some very energetic children, hits upon a game called "Giants, Wizards, and Dwarfs." "You have to decide now," the pastor instructed the children, "which you are . . . a giant, a wizard, or a dwarf." At that, a small girl, tugging at his pant leg asked, "But where do the mermaids stand?"

The pastor told her there are *no* mermaids, and she says, "Oh, yes there are." She said, "I am a mermaid."

Now this little girl knew what she was, and she was not about to give up on either her identity or the game. She intended to take her place wherever mermaids fit into the scheme of things. Where do mermaids stand? . . . *All* those who are different, those who do not fit the boxes and pigeonholes. "Answer that question," wrote Fulghum, "and you can build a school, a nation, or a whole world."

As that very wise young woman said . . . "Diversity . . . like anything worth having . . . requires *effort*." Effort to learn about and respect difference, to be compassionate with one another, to cherish our own identity . . . and to accept unconditionally the same in others.

You should all be very proud that this is the Wellesley spirit. Now I know your first choice today was Alice Walker, known for *The Color Purple*. And guess how I know?

Instead you got me—known for—the color of my hair! Alice Walker's book has a special resonance here. At Wellesley, each class is known by a special color . . . for four years the Class of '90 has worn the color purple. Today you met on Severance Green to say good-bye to all of that . . . to begin a new and very personal journey . . . to search for your own true colors.

In the world that awaits you beyond the shores of Lake Waban, no one can say what your true colors will be. But this I do know: You have a first class education from a first class school. And so you need not, probably cannot, live a "paint-by-numbers" life. Decisions are not irrevocable. Choices do come back. As you set off from Wellesley, I hope that many of you will consider making three very special choices.

The first is to believe in something larger than yourself. . . . To get involved in some of the big ideas of your time. I chose literacy because I honestly believe that if more people could read, write, and comprehend, we would be that much closer to solving so many of the problems plaguing our society.

Early on I made another choice, which I hope you will make as well. Whether you are talking about education, career, or service, you are talking about life . . . and life must have joy. It's supposed to be fun!

One of the reasons I made the most important decision of my life . . . to marry George Bush . . . is because he made me laugh. It's true, sometimes we've laughed through our tears . . . but that shared laughter has been one of our strongest bonds. Find the joy in life, because as Ferris Bueller said on his day off . . . "Life moves pretty fast. Ya don't stop and look around once in a while, ya gonna miss it."

I won't tell George that you applauded Ferris more than you applauded him!

The third choice that must not be missed is to cherish your human connections; your relationships with friends and family. For several years, you've had impressed upon you the importance to your career of dedication and hard work. This is true, but as important as your obligations as a doctor, lawyer, or business leader will be, you are a human being first and those human connections—with spouses, with children, with friends—are the most important investments you will ever make.

At the end of your life you will never regret not having passed one more test, winning one more verdict, or not closing one more deal. You will regret time not spent with a husband, a child, a friend, or a parent.

We are in a transitional period right now . . . fascinating and exhilarating times . . . learning to adjust to the changes and the choices we . . . men and women . . . are facing.

As an example, I remember what a friend said, on hearing her husband complain to his buddies that he had to babysit. Quickly setting him straight . . . my friend told her husband that when it's your own kids . . . it's not called babysitting!

Maybe we should adjust faster, maybe slower, but whatever the era . . . whatever the times, one thing will never change. Fathers and mothers, if you have children . . . they must come first. You must read to your children, you must hug your children, you must love your children.

Your success as a family . . . our success as a society . . . depends *not* on what happens at the White House but on what happens inside your house.

For over fifty years, it was said that the winner of Wellesley's annual hoop race would be the first to get married. Now they say the winner will be the first to become a C.E.O. Both of those stereotypes show too little tolerance for those who want to know where the mermaids stand. So I want to offer you today a new legend: The winner of the hoop race will be the first to realize her dream . . . not society's dream . . . her own personal dream. Who knows? Somewhere out in this audience may even be someone who will follow in my footsteps and preside over the White House as the president's spouse. I wish him well.

The controversy ends here. But our conversation is only beginning. And a worthwhile conversation it has been. So as you leave Wellesley today, take with you deep thanks for the courtesy and the honor you have shared with Mrs. Gorbachev and me. Thank you. God bless you. And may your future be worthy of your dreams.

Bibliography

Allen, M., Berkowitz, S., Hunt, S., & Louden, A. (1999, January). A meta-analysis of the impact of forensics and communication education on critical thinking. *Communication Education, 48,* 18–30.

Allen, S. A. (1993, February 15). To be successful you have to deal with reality: An opportunity for minority business. *Vital Speeches, 59,* 271–273.

America 2000: A map of the mix. (2000, September 18). *Newsweek, 136*(12), 48.

American Heritage Dictionary of the English Language (4th ed.). (2002). Style [Online]. Available: http://www.bartleby.com

American Library Association. (1999, July 22) [Online]. Available: http://www.ala.org/org/html

Andersen, J. R., & Nussbaum, J. F. (1987). The public speaking course: A liberal arts perspective. *Communication Education, 35,* 174–182.

Anderson, J. W. (1991). A comparison of Arab and American conceptions of "effective persuasion." In L. A. Samovar & R. E. Porter (Eds.), *Intercultural communication: A reader* (5th ed., pp. 96–106). Belmont, CA: Wadsworth.

Annan, K. (2001, February 5). Idea of "dialogue among civilizations" rooted in fundamental UN values, says Secretary-General in Seton Hall address [Press release and text of address] [Online]. Seton Hall University, School of Diplomacy and International Relations, South Orange, NJ. Available: http://www.un.org/Dialogue/pr/sgsm7705.htm

Anokye, A. D. (1994, Fall). Oral connections to literacy: The narrative. *Journal of Basic Writing, 13,* 46–60.

Archambault, D. (1992, May 1). Columbus plus 500 years: Whither the American Indian? *Vital Speeches of the Day, 58,* 491–493.

Aristotle. (1984). *Poetics.* (I. Bywater, Trans.). New York: The Modern Library. (Original translation published 1954)

Aristotle. (1984). *The Rhetoric.* (W. R. Roberts, Trans.). New York: The Modern Library. (Original translation published 1954)

Arnett, R. C., & Arneson, P. (1999). *Dialogic civility in a cynical age: Community, hope, and interpersonal relationships.* Albany, NY: SUNY Press.

Arthur, A. (1997, July). Keeping up public appearances: Master the fine art of public-speaking and give a great presentation every time. *Black Enterprise, 27*(12), 54. [Available on InfoTrac College Edition]

Asen, R. (1999, Winter). Toward a normative conception of difference in public deliberation. *Argumentation and Advocacy, 35*(3), 115. [Available on InfoTrac College Edition]

A sweet deal? Schools across the country are making healthy profits from some not-so-healthy drinks. (1999, April 30). *Time for Kids, 4*(25), 4–5.

Augustine. (1958). *On Christian doctrine: Book IV* (D. W. Robertson Jr., Trans.). New York: Liberal Arts Press. (Original work published 416)

Ayres, J., & Hopf, T. S. (1989). Visualization: Is it more than extra-attention? *Communication Education, 38,* 1–5.

Ayres, J., Hopf, T., & Ayres, D. M. (1994). An examination of whether imaging ability enhances the effectiveness of an intervention designed to reduce speech anxiety. *Communication Education, 43,* 256.

Ayres, J., Hopf, T., & Edwards, P. A. (1999). Vividness and control: Factors in the effectiveness of performance visualization? *Communication Education, 48*(4), 287–293.

Barrett, H. (1991). *Rhetoric and civility: Human development, narcissism, and the good audience.* Albany, NY: SUNY Press.

Bartanen, M., & Frank, D. (1999, Summer). Reclaiming a heritage: A proposal for rhetorically grounded academic debate. *Parliamentary Debate: The Journal of the National Parliamentary Debate Association, 6*(1), 31–54.

Beatty, M., McCroskey, J. C., & Heisel, A. D. (1998, September). Communication apprehension as temperamental expression: A communibiological paradigm. *Communication Monographs, 65,* 197–219.

Becker, C. B. (1991). Reasons for the lack of argumentation and debate in the Far East. In L. A. Samovar & R. E. Porter (Eds.), *Intercultural communication: A reader* (6th ed., pp. 234–243). Belmont, CA: Wadsworth.

Becker, R. A., & Keller-McNulty, S. (1996). Presentation myths. *The American Statistician, 50*(2), 112–115. [Available on InfoTrac College Edition]

Beebe, S. A., & Masterson, J. T. (1990). *Communicating in small groups: Principles and practices* (3rd ed.). New York: HarperCollins.

Behnke, R. R., & Sawyer, C. R. (1999). Milestones of anticipatory public speaking anxiety. *Communication Education, 48,* 165–172.

Behnke, R. R., & Sawyer, C. R. (2001). Patterns of psychological state anxiety as a function of anxiety sensitivity. *Communication Quarterly, 49,* 84–95.

Bentley, S. C. (1998, February). Listening better: A guide to improving what may be the ultimate staff skill. *Nursing Homes, 47*(2), 56–58. [Available on InfoTrac College Edition]

Berger, P. (1969). *A rumor of angels: Modern society and the rediscovery of the supernatural.* Garden City, NY: Doubleday.

Bierhorst, J. (1985). *The mythology of North America.* New York: William Morrow.

Bippus, A. M., & Daly, J. A. (1999). What do people think causes stage fright? Naïve attributions about the reasons for public speaking anxiety. *Communication Education, 48,* 63–72.

Bitzer, L. F. (1999). The rhetorical situation. In J. L. Lucaites, C. M. Condit, & S. Caudill (Eds.), *Contemporary rhetorical theory: A reader* (pp. 217–225). New York: Guilford.

Blakeslee, S. (1992, March). Faulty math heightens fears of breast cancer. *New York Times,* Sec. 4, pp. 1, 2.

Bloch, M. (1975). *Political language and oratory in traditional society.* London: Academic Press.

Boerger, M. A., & Henley, T. B. (1999, Spring). The use of analogy in giving instructions. *Psychological Record, 49*(2), 193. [Available on InfoTrac College Edition]

Bormann, E. G. (1985). Symbolic convergence theory: A communication formulation. *Journal of Communication, 35,* 128–138.

Braithwaite, C. A. (1997). Sa'ah Naagháí Bak'eh Hòzhóón: An ethnography of Navajo educational communication practices. *Communication Education, 46,* 219–233.

Branham, R. J., & Pearce, W. B. (1996). The conversational frame in public address. *Communication Quarterly, 44*(4), 423–439. [Available on InfoTrac College Edition]

Brookhiser, R. (1999, November 22). Weird Al: A troubled and alarming vice president. *National Review, 60*(22), 32–34.

Brownell, W. W., & Katula, R. A. (1984). The communication anxiety graph: A classroom tool for managing speech anxiety. *Communication Quarterly, 32,* 243–249.

Budiansky, S. (1999, July). The truth about dogs. *Atlantic Monthly, 284*(1), 39+. [Available on InfoTrac College Edition]

Burgoon, J. K., Buller, D. B., & Woodall, W. G. (1989). *Nonverbal communication: The unspoken dialogue.* New York: Harper & Row.

Burke, K. (1950). *A rhetoric of motives.* Upper Saddle River, NJ: Prentice-Hall.

Burke, K. (1983, August 12). Dramatism and logology. *The Literary Supplement,* 859.

Burke, M. B. (1992). *Polar bears* [Student speech]. Jamaica, NY: St. John's University.

Bush, B. (1990, June 1). *Choice and change.* Address delivered at Wellesley College commencement, Wellesley, MA.

Bush, G. W. (2000, December 13). Text of George W. Bush's acceptance speech [Online]. Reprinted in the *New York Post.* Available: www.nypost.com

Bush, G. W. (2001, September 21). Address to the Nation. Delivered at a joint session of Congress [Transcribed by eMediaMillWorks Inc.]. *New York Times,* p. A17.

Bush, G. W. (2002). State of the Union Address [Online]. Available: http://www.whitehouse.gov/news/releases/2002/01/20020129-11.html

Bush, L. W. (2001, November 8). Address to the National Press Club. Washington, D.C.

Byrne, P. (2002, March 20–26). The rabbi who would save the world. *SF Weekly,* pp. 21–25.

Campbell, G. (1963). *The philosophy of rhetoric* (L. Bitzer, Ed.). Carbondale: Southern Illinois University Press. (Original work published 1776)

Carnahan, J. (1999, June 15). Born to make barrels: Women who put their stamp on history. Address given at the Trailblazer's Awards Ceremony, University of Missouri, St. Louis. *Vital Speeches of the Day, 65*(17), 529–531.

Carrell, L. J. (1997). Diversity in the communication curriculum: Impact on student empathy. *Communication Education, 46,* 234–244.

Cassady, M. (1994). *The art of storytelling: Creative ideas for preparation and performance.* Colorado Springs, CO: Meriweather.

Christensen, M. D. (1998, March). An idea is only the bait. *The Writer, 111*(3), 20–21.

Cicero, M. T. (1981). *Ad herennium: De ratione dicendi (Rhetorica ad herennium)* (H. Caplan, Trans.). The Loeb Classical Library. Cambridge, MA: Harvard University Press.

Clinton, W. J. (2000). State of the Union. Address delivered to a joint session of Congress, January.

Cloud, J. (1999, November 1). An end to the hatred. *Time Magazine, 154*(18), 62.

Collier, M. J. (1994). Cultural identity and intercultural communication. In L. A. Samovar & R. E. Porter (Eds.), *Intercultural communication: A reader* (7th ed., pp. 36–45). Belmont, CA: Wadsworth.

Columbia Encyclopedia. (1993). "Culture." [Available on InfoTrac College Edition]

Cooper, P. J. (1995). *Communication for the classroom teacher* (5th ed.). Scottsdale, AZ: Gorsuch Scarisbrick.

Cortese, A. (1990). *Ethnic ethics: The restructuring of moral theory.* Albany, NY: SUNY Press.

Coste, D. (1989). *Narrative as communication.* Minneapolis: University of Minnesota Press.

Cowan, J. (2000). Lessons from the playground. In K. M. Galvin & P. J. Cooper (Eds.), *Making connections: Readings in relational communication* (2nd ed.). Los Angeles: Roxbury.

Craig, B. (1998, April 15). Cognitive dissonance theory: Leon Festinger [Online]. COMM 3210 Online Syllabus. Available: http://spot.colorado.edu/~craigr/3210syll.htm#top

Crary, D. (2002, August 15). Going public with rape tough choice. AP. Available: http://www.washingtonpost.com

Cribbins, M. (1990). *International adoption* [Student speech]. Oregon State University, Corvallis.

Cuomo, M. (1999). New York Governor Mario Cuomo challenges President Reagan's portrayal of America as a "shining city on a hill." In R. Torricelli & A. Carroll (Eds.), *In our own words: Extraordinary speeches of the American century* (pp. 354–359). New York: Kodansha International.

Currey, J., & Mumford, K. (2002, September 18) Just talk: Guide to inclusive language [Online]. University of Tasmania. Available: http://student.admin.utas.edu.au/services/just_talk/Disability/disability.htm

Daniel, J. L., & Smitherman, G. (1990). How I got over: Communication dynamics in the black community. In D. Carbaugh (Ed.), *Cultural communication and intercultural contacts.* Hillsdale, NJ: Lawrence Erlbaum.

Davidson, J. (2001, November 15). Relaxing at high speed: You must take time. *Vital Speeches of the Day, 68*(3), 87–91. [Available on InfoTrac College Edition]

Davidson, W., & Kline, S. (1999, March). Ace your presentations. *Journal of Accountancy, 187*(3), 61. [Available on InfoTrac College Edition]

Delroy, K.-K. (1992). Ritual studies as a medium for communication. Paper presented at the Ethnography of Communication Conference, Portland, OR, August 13–15, p. 4.

Demonstrative speech (how-to). (n.d., accessed 2000, January) [Online]. Available: www.brazosport.cc.tx.us/~comm/demon.html

DePaulo, B. M., Blank, A. L., Swain, G. W., & Hairfield, J. G. (1992). Expressiveness and expressive control. *Personality and Social Psychology Bulletin, 18,* 276–285.

Detz, J. (1998, April–May). Delivery plus content equals successful presentations. *Communication World, 15*(5), 34–36. [Available on InfoTrac College Edition]

Dialects doing well. (1998, February 18). InSCIght on Apnet [Online]. Available: http://www.apnet.com/inscight/02181009/graphb.htm

DiMaggio, M. (1994). *You have my deepest sympathy: You just won the lottery* [Student Speech]. Jamaica, NY: St. John's University.

Dunbar, K. (2000). Gender, science & cognition [Online]. Available: http://www.psych.mcgill.ca/perpg/fac/dunbar/women.html

Dutton, B. (2001, December 20). Editorial one-sided [Letter to the editor]. *San Francisco Chronicle,* p. A22.

Dwyer, K. K. (1998, April). Communication apprehension and learning style preference: Correlation and implications for teaching. *Communication Education, 47,* 137–150.

Echo in introductions and conclusions. (n.d., accessed 1999, December 15). Instructional web page [Online]. Available: http://www.stlcc.cc.mo.us/fv/webcourses/eng020/testlocation/mensepage/Echo.html

Edwards, R., & McDonald, J. L. (1993). Schema theory and listening. In A. D. Wolvin & C. G. Coakley (Eds.), *Perspectives on listening* (pp. 60–77). Norwood, NJ: Ablex.

Eisen, A. (1998). Small group presentations in teaching "science thinking" and context in a large biology class. *Bioscience, 48*(1), 53–57.

Ekman, P., & Friesen, W. V. (1969). The repertoire of nonverbal behavior: Categories, origins, usage, and coding. *Semiotica, I,* 49–98.

Elmer-Dewitt, P. (1993, April 12). Electronic superhighways. *Time,* 50–55.

Emory University Department of Religion (2001, December 6). Statement on inclusive language [Online]. Available: www.emory.edu/COLLEGE/RELIGION/about/statement.html

Engnell, R. (1999). What is a central idea? Class handout for Introduction to Communication, George Fox University, Newberg, OR.

Fancher, M. R. (1993, August 8). Will journalism travel on the information highway? *Seattle Times,* p. A2.

Farmer, G. (1999, June 1). Cyberbabble and other facts: Life for the new millennium [Transcript]. *Vital Speeches of the Day, 65*(16), 509–511. [Available on InfoTrac College Edition]

Farthing, C. (2002, April 24). *Employee privacy and the Internet* [Student Speech]. George Fox University, Newberg, OR.

Festinger, L. (1957). *A theory of cognitive dissonance.* New York: Row, Peterson.

Fisher, W. R. (1984a). Narration as a human communication paradigm: The case of public moral argument. *Communication Monographs, 51,* 1–22.

Fisher, W. R. (1984b). The narrative paradigm: An elaboration. *Communication Monographs, 52,* 347–367.

Fisher, W. R. (1999). Narrative as human communication paradigm. In J. L. Lucaites, C. M. Condit, & S. Caudill (Eds.), *Contemporary rhetorical theory: A reader* (pp. 265–287). New York: Guilford.

Five keys to effective handouts. (1997, October 13). Buffalo Business First [Online]. Available: http://www.amcity.com/buffalo/stories/1997/10/13/smallb3.html

Flynn, L. R. (n.d., accessed 2000, January). Demonstration or "how-to" speech topics [Online]. Available: www.colin.cc.ms.us/flynn/Speech/DemoSpeech.htm

Font. (n.d., accessed 2000, January 3). Publications: Glossary of terms [Online]. Available: http://www.asme.org/pubs/glossary.html

Foss, S., & Griffin, C. (1995). Beyond persuasion: A proposal for an invitational rhetoric. *Communication Monographs, 62,* 2–18.

Frank, D. A. (1997). Diversity in the public space: A response to Stepp. *Argumentation and Advocacy, 33,* 195–197.

Freimuth, V. S., & Jamieson, K. (1979). *Communicating with the elderly: Shattering stereotypes.* Urbana, IL: ERIC Clearinghouse on Reading and Communication Skills.

Galvin, K. M., & Cooper, P. J. (2000). Perceptual filters: Culture, family, and gender. In K. M. Galvin & P. J. Cooper (Eds.), *Making connections: Readings in relational communication* (2nd ed., pp. 32–33). Los Angeles: Roxbury.

Gardner, H. (1993). *Multiple intelligences: The theory in practice.* New York: Basic Books.

Gass, R. (1999). Fallacy list: SpCom 335: Advanced argumentation [Online]. California State University, Fullerton. Available: http://commfaculty.fullerton.edu/rgass/fallacy31.htm

Gates, H. L. (1992). *Loose canons: Notes on the culture wars.* New York: Oxford University Press.

George Washington University Law School. (2000). Academic integrity: Citing responsibly; a guide to avoiding plagiarism [Online]. Available: www.law.gwu.edu/resources/citing.asp#what

Giller, E. (n.d., accessed 1999, December 28). Left brain/right brain religion [Online]. Available: http://www.sabbath.com/acfl.htm

Gingerich, J. (1999, February 24). *Peter Ilich Tchaikovsky* [Student speech]. Goshen College, Goshen, IN.

Goffman, E. (1959). *The presentation of self in everyday life.* Garden City, NY: Doubleday Anchor.

Goodall, H. L., & Phillips, G. M. (1984). *Making it in any organization.* Upper Saddle River, NJ: Prentice-Hall.

Goodall, H. L., & Waaigen, C. L. (1986). *The persuasive presentation: A practical guide to professional communication in organizations.* New York: Harper & Row.

Goodman, G., & Esterly, G. (1990). Questions—The most popular piece of language. In J. Stewart (Ed.), *Bridges not walls: A book about interpersonal communication* (4th ed., pp. 69–79). New York: McGraw-Hill.

Goody, J., & Watts, I. (1991). The consequences of literacy. In D. Crowley & P. Heyer (Eds.), *Communication in history: Technology, culture, society* (pp. 48–56). New York: Longman.

Gore, A. (2000, December 13). Text of Al Gore's concession speech [Online]. Reprinted in the *New York Post.* Available: www.nypost.com

Gozzi, R. (1990). *New words and a changing American culture.* Columbia: University of South Carolina Press.

Gray, G. W. (1946). The precepts of Kagemni and Ptah-hotep. *Quarterly Journal of Speech 31,* 446–454.

Gresh, S. (1998, December 1). Storytelling: The soul of an enterprise. Address given to the Rotary Club, Andover, MA, September 25, 1998. *Vital Speeches of the Day, 65*(4), 122–125. [Available on InfoTrac College Edition]

Griffin, C. W. (1998). Improving students' writing strategies; knowing versus doing. *College Teaching, 46*(2), 48–52. [Available on InfoTrac College Edition]

Griffiths, M. (1988). Feminism, feelings, and philosophy. In M. Griffiths & M. Whitford (Eds.), *Feminist perspectives in philosophy* (pp. 131–151). Bloomington: Indiana University Press.

Grob, L. M., Meyers, R. A., & Schuh, R. (1997). Powerful/powerless language use in group interactions: Sex differences or similarities? *Communication Quarterly, 45*(3), 282–303. [Available on InfoTrac College Edition]

Hacker, D. (1998). *A writer's reference* (4th ed.). New York: Bedford/St. Martin's.

Haiman, F. (2001, December 20).[Letter to the editor]. *San Francisco Chronicle,* p. A22.

Halstead, T. (1999, August). A politics for generation X. *Atlantic Monthly, 284*(2), 33ff. [Available on InfoTrac College Edition]

Harms, L. W., & Richstad, R. J. (1978). The right to communicate: Status of the concept. In F. L. Casmir (Ed.), *Intercultural and international communication.* Washington, DC: University Press of America.

Harnack, A., & Kleppinger, E. (1998). *Online!: A reference guide to using Internet sources, 1998 edition* [Online]. New York: St. Martin's Press. Available: http://www.smpcollege.com/online-4styles^help

Hart, R. P., & Burks, D. O. (1972). Rhetorical sensitivity and social interaction. *Speech Monographs, 39,* 90.

Harthorn, J. (1998, February 9). *Multiple sclerosis* [Student speech]. Newberg, OR: George Fox University.

Hawkes, L. (1999). *A guide to the World Wide Web.* Upper Saddle River, NJ: Prentice-Hall.

Healy, P. (2002, May 29). At Harvard, a word sparks a battle: Senior says his speech aims to redefine "jihad" [Online]. *Boston Globe*. Available: www.boston.com/globe

Heaphy, J. B. (2001). Commencement address [Online]. California State University, Sacramento. Available: http://www.commondreams.org/views01/1217-08.htm

Henson, J. (n.d., accessed 2000, February 1). Problem solving using group challenges [Online]. Available: http://www.bvte.ecu.edu/ACBMEC/p1998/henson.htm

Hilliard, A. (1986). Pedagogy in ancient Kemet. In M. Karenga & J. Carruthers (Eds.), *Kemet and the African world view* (p. 257). London: University of Sankore Press.

Hollingsworth, H. L. (1935). *The psychology of audiences*. New York: American Book Company.

Holzman, P. (1970). *The psychology of speakers and audiences*. Glenview, IL: Scott Foresman.

Howell, W. (1990). Coping with internal-monologue. In J. Stewart (Ed.), *Bridges not walls: A book about interpersonal communication* (5th ed., pp. 128–138). New York: McGraw-Hill.

How to become a good googler. (2002, August 27). CBSNEWS.com [Online]. Available: www.cbsnews.com/stories/2002/08/26/earlyshow/contributors/reginalewis/main519808.shtml

Humphrey, J. (1998, May 15). Executive eloquence: A seven-fold path to inspirational leadership. *Vital Speeches, 64*(15), 468–471. [Available on InfoTrac College Edition]

Hunt, C. (2002, February 4). Service and therapy dogs [Online]. Available: www.cofc.edu/~huntc/service.html#theralec

Hybels, S., & Weaver, R. L. (1992). *Communicating effectively* (3rd ed.). New York: McGraw-Hill.

Hypes, M. G., Turner, E. T., Norris, C. M., & Wolfferts, L. C. (1999, January). How to be a successful presenter. *Journal of Physical Education, Recreation & Dance, 70*(1), 50–53.

Internet Source Validation Project. (1999, July). [Online]. Available: http://www.stemnet.nf.ca/~dfurey/validate/termsi.html

Irvine, J. J., & York, D. E. (1995). *Learning styles and culturally diverse students: A literature review.* (ERIC Document Reproduction Service No. ED382 722 UDO3046). Available: http://ericae.net/faqs

Jaasma, M. A. (1997, summer). Classroom communication apprehension: Does being male or female make a difference? *Communication Reports, 10*, 218–228.

Jaffe, C. I. (1995). Chronemics: Communicating mainstream cycles to Russian Old Believer children. *World Communication, 15*(1), 1–20.

Jaffe, C. I. (1998, November). Metaphors about the classroom. A paper presented to the National Communication Association, New York City.

Jaggar, A. M. (1989). Love and knowledge: Emotion in feminist epistemology. In A. Garry & M. Pearsall (Eds.), *Women, knowledge, and reality: Explorations in feminist philosophy* (pp. 129–155). London: Unwin.

Jamieson, K. H. (1988). *Eloquence in an electronic age*. New York: Oxford University Press.

Janik, I. (1971, November). Groupthink. *Psychology Today*, 43–46.

Jenefsky, C. (1996, October). Public speaking as empowerment at Visionary University. *Communication Education, 45*, 343–355.

Jensen, J. V. (1997). *Ethical issues in the communication process*. Mahwah, NJ: Lawrence Erlbaum.

Jensen, K. K., & Harris, V. (1999). The public speaking portfolio. *Communication Education, 48*, 211–227.

Johannesen, R. L. (1996). *Ethics in human communication* (4th ed.). Prospect Heights, IL: Waveland Press.

Johnson, S. D., & Roellke, C. F. (1999). Secondary teachers' and undergraduate education faculty members' perceptions of teaching effectiveness criteria: A national survey. *Communication Education, 48*, 127–138.

Jordan, B. (1992, July 14). Excerpts from addresses by keynote speakers at the Democratic convention. *New York Times*, p. A12.

Jorgensen-Earp, C. (n.d.), "Making other arrangements": Alternative patterns of disposition [Unpublished course handout]. Lynchburg, VA: Lynchburg College.

Kao, E. M., Nagita, D. K., & Peterson, C. (1997). Explanatory style, family expressiveness, and self-esteem among Asian American and Euro-American college students. *Journal of Social Psychology, 137*, 435–444.

Karim, A. T. (2002, May 1). Terrorism: Addressing its root causes [Comments made in a question and answer forum] "Islam, 9/11, and U.S. National Security." American Council for Study of Islamic Societies, College of William and Mary, Washington, D.C., March 4, 2002. *Vital Speeches, 68*(14), 25–29.

Kennedy, J. F. (1988). Inaugural address. In J. Podell & S. Angovin (Eds.), *Speeches of the American presidents* (pp. 603–605). New York: H. W. Wilson.

Keough, D. R. (1993, May 10). The courage to dream: Seize the day. *Vital Speeches of the Day, 59*(15), 599–601.

Kepner, C. H., & Tregoe, B. B. (1965). *The rational manager: A systematic approach to problem solving and decision making*. New York: McGraw-Hill.

Khan, L. A. (2002, January 15). A century of great awakenings: "We have learned much about ourselves." *Vital Speeches of the Day, 68*(7), 222–224. [Available on InfoTrac College Edition]

Kiewitz, C., Weaver, J. B. III, Brosius, H-B., & Weimann, G. (1997). Cultural differences in listening style preferences: A comparison of young adults in Germany, Israel, and the United States. *International Journal of Public Opinion Research, 9*(3), 233–248. [Available on InfoTrac College Edition]

King, M. L. (1963, August 28). I have a dream. Address given at the March on Washington [Online]. Available: http://www.mecca.org/~crights/dream.htm

Kirkwood, W. G. (1992). Narrative and the rhetoric of possibility. *Communication Monographs, 59*, 30–47.

Kirshenberg, S. (1998, November). Info on the Internet: User beware! *Training & Development, 52*(11), 83–84. [Available on Infotrac College Edition]

Kochman, T. (1990). Cultural pluralism: Black and white styles. In D. Carbaugh (Ed.), *Cultural communication and intercultural contacts* (pp. 219–224). Hillsdale, NJ: Lawrence Erlbaum.

Krauss, B. (1993, March 28). Some secrets to a soulful, shining Sunday sermon. *The Honolulu Advertiser*, p. A3.

Learning styles, culture and hemispheric dominance. (n.d., accessed 1999, December 28) [Online]. Available: http://geocities.com/~mathskills/brain.htm

LeWare, M. R. (1998). Encountering visions of Aztlan: Arguments for ethnic pride, community activism and cultural revitalization in Chicano murals. *Argumentation and Advocacy, 34*(3), 140–153. [Available on InfoTrac College Edition]

Liebman, B. (1998, November). Sugar. (The sweetening of the American diet). *Nutrition Action Healthletter, 25*(9), p. 3. [Available on InfoTrac College Edition]

Lim, P. J. (2002, June 27). Credit squeeze: Card issuers raise the stakes with fees and penalties. *U. S. News & World Report, 132*(21), 38.

Luce, B. (2002). Top of their class [Online]. *Columns: The University of Washington Alumni Magazine.* Available: http://www.washington.edu/alumni/columns/june02/honors1.html

Lundsteen, S. W. (1993). Metacognitive listening. In A. D. Wolvin & C. G. Coakley (Eds.), *Perspectives on listening* (106–123). Norwood, NJ: Ablex.

Lustig, M. W., & Koester, J. (1993). *Intercultural competence: Interpersonal communication across cultures.* New York: HarperCollins.

Mabry, M. (1999, July 12). No money, no meds. *Newsweek, 84*(2), 32–35.

Machrone, B. (1993, Fall). Ziff-Davis/personal computing. Advertising supplement to the *New York Times.*

MacIntyre, A. (1981). *After virtue: A study in moral reasoning* (2nd ed.). South Bend, IN: University of Notre Dame Press.

MacIntyre, P. J., & MacDonald, J. R. (1998). Public speaking anxiety: Perceived competence and audience congeniality. *Communication Education, 47,* 359–365.

Maes, J. D., Weldy, T. B., & Icenogle, M. L. (1997, January). A managerial perspective: Oral communication competency is most important for business students in the workplace. *Journal of Business Communication, 34*(1), 6–14. [Available on InfoTrac College Edition]

Mannie, K. (1998, December). Coaching through demonstration: Focus only on the key points of the skill. *Coach and Athletic Director, 68*(5), 74–75. [Available on InfoTrac College Edition]

Marmor, J. (1996, December). Blurring the lines. *Columns, 16*(8), 22–27.

Marsella, A. J. (1993). Counseling and psychotherapy with Japanese Americans: Cross-cultural considerations. *American Journal of Orthopsychiatry, 63,* 200–208.

Martel, M. (1984.) *Before you say a word: The executive guide to effective communication.* Upper Saddle River, NJ: Prentice-Hall.

Martin, T. (2001, November 1). I am fearfully and wonderfully made: Living is an adventure. Address delivered at the Westover School, Middlebury, CT, October 11, 2001. *Vital Speeches of the Day, 68*(2), 61–63. [Available on InfoTrac College Edition]

Maslow, A. H. (1987). *Motivation and personality* (3rd ed.). San Francisco: Harper & Row.

Maxwell, L., & McCain, T. A. (1997, July). Gateway or gatekeeper: The implication of copyright and digitalization on education. *Communication Education, 46,* 141–157.

McClain, F. J. (2001, November 1). The music in your soul: A celebration of life. A speech delivered at fall convocation, Queens College, Charlotte, NC, September 18, 2001. *Vital Speeches of the Day, 68*(2), 59–61. [Available on InfoTrac College Edition]

McClearey, K. (1997). Text review. University of Southern Illinois, Edwardsville.

McCord, H., & McVeigh, G. (2002, June). Way beyond low fat! Brand-new "insider" tips for heart-healthy eating. (Nutrition News). *Prevention, 54*(6), 58–59. [Available on InfoTrac College Edition]

McCroskey, J. C. (1993). *An introduction to rhetorical communication* (6th ed.). Englewood Cliffs, NJ: Prentice-Hall.

McGuire, M., & Slembek, E. (1987). An emerging critical rhetoric: Hellmut Geissner's Sprechwissenschaft. *Quarterly Journal of Speech, 73,* 349–400.

McKeon, R. (1998). Creativity and the commonplace. In T. B. Farrell (Ed.), *Landmark essays on contemporary rhetoric* (pp. 33–41). Mahwah, NJ: Hermagoras Press.

McMillan, C. (1982). *Women, reason, and nature: Some philosophical problems with feminism.* Princeton, NJ: Princeton University Press.

McNally, J. R. (1969). Opening assignments: A symposium. *The Speech Teacher, 18,* 18–20.

Merriam-Webster online. (2002). [Online]. Available: http://www.m-w.com/home.htm

Messenger, J. (1960). Anang proverb riddles. *Journal of American Folklore, 73,* 235.

Miller, A. N. (2002). An exploration of Kenyan public speaking patterns with implications for the American introductory public speaking course. *Communication Education, 51*(2), 168–182.

Mills, D. W. (1999). Applying what we know: Student learning styles [Online]. Available: http://crsnet.org/crsnet/articles/student-learning-styles.html

Molloy, J. T. (1976). *Dress for success.* New York: Warner Books.

Monroe, A. H. (1962). *Principles and types of speech* (5th ed.). Chicago: Scott Foresman.

Morris, H. J. (2002, June 17). League of their own. *U.S. News & World Report, 132*(21), 50–51.

Morton, L. P. (1998). Segmenting publics: An introduction [Column]. *Public Relations Quarterly, 43*(13), 33–34. [Available on InfoTrac College Edition]

Muhovic, E. (2000). Visual aids for presentations [Online]. Center for Managerial Communications, Denver University. Available: www.du.edu/emuhovic/visualpresentations.html

Mullins, D. (1993). *Guest lecture.* St. John's University, Jamaica, NY.

Murray, D. M. (1998, May). Write what you don't know. *The Writer, 111*(5), 7–9.

Murray, I. (2002, February 13). Census nonsense. The American Enterprise [Online]. Available: http://www.theamericanenterprise.org/hotflash020213.htm

National Center for Victims of Crime. (2000). *Crime and victimization in America, statistical overview* [Online]. Available: www.ncvc.org

Nordlinger, J. (2001, December 17). The amazing George W. Bush, miracle in a men's room, Merry Christmas [Opinion commentary]. [Online]. *National Review.*

Novelli, W. D. (2001, November 15). Beyond fifty: America's future. Speech delivered to the Economic Club of Detroit, Detroit, MI, October 22, 2001. *Vital Speeches of the Day, 68*(3), 69–72.

O'Donovan, C. (1997, December). The X styles. *Communication World, 15*(1), 17–20. [Available on InfoTrac College Edition]

O'Neil, D. (1999, September 21). Ethnicity and race: An introduction to the nature of social group differentiation and inequality [Online]. Available: http://www.daphne.palomar.edu/ethnicity/default.htm

Ong, W. J. (1982). *Orality and literacy: The technologizing of the word.* New York: Methuen.

Online Writing Lab. (2002). Avoiding plagiarism [Online]. Purdue University Online Writing Lab. Available: http://owl.english.purdue.edu/handouts/research/r_plagiar.html

Osborn, M. (1967). Archetypal metaphor in rhetoric: The light-dark family. *Quarterly Journal of Speech, 53*, 115–126.

Osborn, M. (1977). The evolution of the archetypal sea in rhetoric and poetic. *Quarterly Journal of Speech, 63*, 347–363.

Osborn, M. (1997). The play of metaphors. *Education, 118*(1), 84–87. [Available on InfoTrac College Edition]

Ota, A. K. (1993, July 11). Japan's ambassador to U.S. sets welcome new tone. *Seattle Times*, p. A12.

Ouchi, W. B. (1998, Fall). The concept of organizational culture in a diverse society [Online]. SIETAR International. Available: http://208.215.167.139/sij-98-12/keynote03.htm

Outrage at Harvard over "jihad" speech: What's in a name? (2002, May 29). Reuters [Online]. Available: www.reuters.com

Pacanowsky, M. E., & O'Donnell-Trujillo, N. (1983). Organizational communication as cultural performance. *Communication Monographs, 50*, 126–147.

Pearce, W. B. (1989). *Communication and the human condition.* Carbondale: Southern Illinois University Press.

Pease, B. (1998, March 9). What's all this international business travel stuff, anyhow? (Preparations before going to business trips abroad, part 2). *Electronic Design, 46*(6), 146–149. [Available on InfoTrac College Edition]

Pennebaker, J. W., Rime, B., & Blankenship, V. E. (1996). Stereotypes of emotional expressiveness of northerners and southerners: A cross-cultural test of Montesquieu's Hypothesis. *Journal of Personality and Social Psychology, 70*, 372–380.

Peters, D. A. (1999, April 1). Boomers, bloomers, and zoomers. *Vital Speeches of the Day, 65*(12), 379–384.

Peters, D. (2000, May). Sweet seduction. *Chatelaine, 73*(5), 53. [Available on InfoTrac College Edition]

Peterson, M. S. (1997). Personnel interviewers' perceptions of the importance and adequacy of applicant's communication skills. *Communication Education, 46*, 287–291.

Pettit, R. (1990). *Who/what would you want in your band? Or why did I spend 25 years playing drums?* [Student speech]. Oregon State University.

plagiarism.org. (2002). The problem [Online]. Available: http://www.plagiarism.org/problem.html

Polkinghorne, D. E. (1988). *Narrative knowing and the human sciences.* Albany, NY: SUNY Press.

Porter, R. E., & Samovar, L. A. (1994). An introduction to intercultural communication. In L. A. Samovar & R. E. Porter (Eds.), *Intercultural communication: A reader* (7th ed., pp. 4–25). Belmont, CA: Wadsworth.

Prensky, M. (1998, October). Bankers trust: Training is all fun and games. *HR Focus, 75*(10), 11. [Available on InfoTrac College Edition]

Preparing the delivery outline. (1999, December 14). Speech assignments web page link: Riverdale School Speech Class, Upper Grades [Online]. Available: http://www.teleport.com/~beanman/english/delivout.html

Quintilian. (1920–1922). *The instituto oratoria of Quintilian* (4 vols.). (H. E. Butler, Trans.). The Loeb Classical Library. Cambridge, MA: Harvard University Press.

Radel, J. (1999, July). Effective presentations. Kansas University Medical Center on-line tutorial series [Online]. Available: http://KUMC.edu/SAH/OTEd/jradel/effective.html

Ray, G. B. (1986). Vocally cued personality prototypes: An implicit personality theory approach. *Communication Monographs, 53*, 266–276.

Ray, J., & Badle, C. (1993, February 3). Hosts of "Queer Talk" speaking on a talk radio call-in show. WABC, New York.

Readability. (n.d., accessed 2000, January 3). Planning, design, and production [Online]. Available: http://ibis.nott.ac.uk/guidelines/ch2/chap2-G-4.html

Reagan, R. (1986, January 31). Memorial service for the crew of the space shuttle *Challenger* [Online]. Houston. Available: www.eulogywriters.com/challenger.htm

Reynolds, J. (1995–1996). *The Dangers of DEET.* Forensics Competition. Spokane, WA: Whitworth College.

Reynolds, S. (1996, December). Selling to another language. *Communication World, 14*(1), 11. [Available on InfoTrac College Edition]

Richmond, V. P., & McCroskey, J. C. (1995). *Communication: Apprehension, avoidance, and effectiveness* (4th ed.). Scottsdale, AZ: Gorsuch Scarisbrick.

Richmond, V. P., & McCroskey, J. C. (2000). *Nonverbal behavior in interpersonal relations* (4th ed.). Boston: Allyn & Bacon.

Ridge, A. (1993). A perspective of listening skills. In A. Wolvin & C. Coakley (Eds.), *Perspectives on listening* (pp. 1–14). Norwood, NJ: Ablex.

Riding, R., & Cheema, I. (1991). Cognitive styles—an overview and integration. *Educational Psychology, 11*, 193–215. [Available on InfoTrac College Edition]

Roach, C. A., & Wyatt, N. J. (1995). Listening and the rhetorical process. In J. Stewart (Ed.), *Bridges not walls: A book about interpersonal communication* (5th ed., pp. 171–176). New York: McGraw-Hill.

Robinson, T. E. (1997, July). Communication apprehension and the basic public speaking course: A national survey of in-class treatment techniques. *Communication Education, 46*, 188–197.

Roczak. T. (1992, June 9). Green guilt and ecological overload. *New York Times*, p. A23.

Rodrigues, D., & Rodrigues, R. J. (2000). *The research paper and the World Wide Web* (2nd ed.). Upper Saddle River, NJ: Prentice-Hall.

Rokeach, M. (1972). *Beliefs, attitudes, and values.* San Francisco: Jossey-Bass.

Roper Starch. (1999). How Americans communicate. Poll commissioned by the National Communication Association. Available: http://www.natcom.org/research/Roper/howamericanscommunicate.htm

Rose, R. R. (1998, October 24). A definition [Online]. Filled Pause Research Center. Available: http://www.gm009a5328.pwp.blueyonder.co.uk/iidea/library/fp1.htm

Rosellini, L. (1999, November 1). An unlikely friendship, a historic meeting. *U.S. News & World Report, 127*(17), 68.

Ross, R. S. (1989). *Speech communication: The speechmaking system* (8th ed.). Upper Saddle River, NJ: Prentice-Hall.

Rothenberg, P. S. (Ed.). (1998). *Race, class, and gender in the United States.* New York: St. Martin's Press.

Rowan, K. E. (1995, July). A new pedagogy for explanatory public speaking: Why arrangement should not substitute for invention. *Communication Education, 44*, 235–250.

Rowland, R. C. (1990). On mythic criticism. *Communication Studies, 41*(2), 101–116.

Rubin, D. L. (1993). Listenability = oral-based discourse + considerateness. In A. D. Wolvin & C. G. Coakley (Eds.), *Perspectives on listening* (pp. 261–268). Norwood, NJ: Ablex.

Sawyer, C. R., & Behnke, R. R. (1999, Winter). State anxiety patterns for public speaking anxiety and the behavior inhibition system. *Communication Reports, 12*, 33–41.

Schrof, J. M., & Schultz, S. (1999, June 21). Social anxiety. *U.S. News & World Report, 126*(24), 53.

Schwandt, B., & Soraya, S. (1992, August 13–15). Ethnography of communication and "Sprechwissenschaft"—merging concepts. Paper presented at the Ethnography of Communication Conference, Portland, OR.

Scofield, S. (1999, August). An end to writer's block. *The Writer, 111*(8), 7–9.

Seattle. (1971). The Indian's night promises to be dark. From *Indian oratory: Famous speeches by noted Indian chieftains*, by W. C. Vanderwerth. Copyright 1971 by the University of Oklahoma Press, pp. 118–122. (Original work published 1853)

Seiter, J. S., Larsen, J., & Skinner, J. (1998). "Handicapped" or "handi-capable"? The effects of language about persons with disabilities on perceptions of source credibility and persuasiveness. *Communication Reports, 11*(1), 21–31.

Senegalese women remake their culture. (1988, December). *IK Notes World Bank, No. 3* [Online]. Available: http://www.africapolicy.org

Seymour, J. (1996, March 12). PC presentations: The schlepp factor. (Equipment for on-the-road presentations). *PC Magazine, 15*(5), 91–92. [Available on InfoTrac College Edition]

Shaw, B. (1993, February 1). An attitude about women: Democracy is not a smooth sauce. *Vital Speeches of the Day, 59*, 245–247.

Shipman, C. (2000, December/January). Searching for Al. *George Magazine, 102*(9).

Simon, R. (1999, November 29). The levels of his game. *U.S. News & World Report, 127*(21), 16–18.

Simons, G. F., Vazquez, C., & Harris, P. R. (1993). *Transcultural leadership: Empowering the diverse workforce*. Houston: Gulf.

Sitkaram, K. S., & Cogdell, R. T. (1976.) *Foundations of intercultural communication*. Columbus, OH: Charles E. Merrill.

Smith, A. L. (Molefi Asanti). (1970). Socio-historical perspectives of black oratory. *Quarterly Journal of Speech, 61*, 264–269.

Smith, D. (1996, February 7). Discussion leader: Globalization of the general education curriculum. George Fox University. Newberg, OR.

Sorokin, E. (2002, March 5). Berkeley conservatives tell of death threats for criticism [Online]. *Washington Times*. Available: www.washtimes.com

Spangler, D., & Thompson, W. I. (1992). *Reimagination of the world: A critique of the new age, science, and popular culture*. New York: Bear & Company.

Speech on jihad wins polite reception. (2002, June 7). *Las Vegas SUN* [Online]. Available: www.lasvegassun.com

Spitzberg, B. H. (1994). A model of intercultural communication competence. In L. A. Samovar & R. E. Porter (Eds.), *Intercultural communication: A reader* (7th ed., pp. 347–359). Belmont, CA: Wadsworth.

Staley, C. C., & Staley, R. S. (2000). Communicating in organizations. In K. M. Galvin & P. J. Cooper (Eds.), *Making connections: Readings in relational communication* (2nd ed., pp. 287–294). Los Angeles: Roxbury.

Statement on inclusive language. (2001, December 6). [Online]. Religion Department, Emory University. Available: www.emory.edu/COLLEGE/RELIGION/about/statement.html

Statham, S. (2001, July 1). Dead man watching. *Vital Speeches of the Day, 67*(18), 563. [Available on InfoTrac College Edition]

Sternberg, R. (1998). *Love is a story: A new theory of relationships*. New York: Oxford University Press.

Stewart, E. C., & Bennett, M. J. (1991). *American cultural patterns: A cross-cultural perspective* (rev. ed.). Yarmouth, ME: Intercultural Press.

Stone, G. (n.d.). Promotional Letter. New York: God's Love, We Deliver.

Stowers, R. H., & White, G. T. (1999, June). Connecting accounting and communication: A survey of public accounting firms. *Communication Quarterly, 62*, 23–31. [Available on InfoTrac College Edition]

Streicher, J. (1996, 1999, updated). *The five stages of culture shock* [Student speech]. George Fox University, Newberg, OR.

Sueda, K. (1995). Differences in the perception of face: Chinese *mien-tzu* and Japanese *mentsu*. *World Communication, 24*(1), 23–31.

Sullivan, P. A. (1993). Signification and African-American rhetoric: A case study of Jesse Jackson's "Common Ground and Common Sense" speech. *Communication Quarterly, 41*, 1–14.

Tannen, D. (1989). *Talking voices: Repetition, dialogue, and imagery in conversational discourse*. Cambridge: Cambridge University Press.

Tannen, D. (1990). *You just don't understand: Women and men in conversation*. New York: William Morrow.

Tannen, D. (2000, January 24). Guest appearance. *Hardball with Chris Matthews*. MSNBC.

"Tear down this firewall." (2002, August 19). *The Weekly Standard, 7*(46), 3.

Tembo, M. S. (1999, April). Your mother is still your mother. *World and I, 14*(4). [Available on Infotrac College Edition]

The Jefferson Muzzles. (2002). [Online]. The Thomas Jefferson Center for the Protection of Free Expression. Available: http://www.tjcenter.org/muzzles.html

Thiederman, S. (1991a). *Bridging cultural barriers for corporate success: How to manage the multicultural workforce*. New York: Lexington.

Thiederman, S. (1991b). *Profiting in American multicultural market places: How to do business across cultural lines*. New York: Lexington.

Thinking and learning skills. (1999, December 24). [Online]. University of Toronto. Available: http://snow.utoronto.ca/learn2/introll.html

Thompson, F. T., & Grandgenett, D. J. (1999, Fall). Helping disadvantaged learners build effective learning skills. *Education, 120*(1), 130–135.

Torrence, J. (1998). *Jackie tales: The magic of creating stories and the art of telling them*. New York: Avon Books.

Toulmin, S. (1958). *The uses of argument*. Cambridge, MA: Cambridge University Press.

Toulmin, S., Rieke, R., & Janik, A. (1984). *An introduction to reasoning* (2nd ed.). New York: Macmillan.

Truth, S. (1851, December). Ain't I a woman? In *Modern History Sourcebook* [Online]. Available: www.fordham.edu/halsall/mod/sojtruth-woman.html

Tuma, J. (2002, May). Falling off the high wire. *Diabetes Forecast,* *55*(5), 112. [Available on InfoTrac College Edition]

Ugwu-Oju, D. (1993, November 14). Pursuit of happiness. *New York Times Magazine.*

University of Minnesota, Duluth. (2002, February 20). Listening Skills. Student Handbook [Online]. Available: http://www.d.umn.edu/student/loon/acad/strat/ss_listening.html

Vanderwerth, W. C. (1971). *Indian oratory.* Norman, OK: University of Oklahoma Press.

Vatz, R. E. (1999). The myth of the rhetorical situation. In J. L. Lucaites, C. M. Condit, & S. Caudill (Eds.), *Contemporary rhetorical theory: A reader* (pp. 226–231). New York: Guilford.

Von Till, B. (1998). Definition speech. In C. Jaffe (Ed.), *Student resource workbook for public speaking: Concepts and skills for a diverse society* (2nd ed., p. 89). Belmont, CA: Wadsworth.

Voth, B. (1998, Winter). A case study in metaphor as argument: A longitudinal analysis of the wall separating church and state. *Argumentation and Advocacy, 34*(3), 127–139. [Available on InfoTrac College Edition]

Wallace, K. R. (1955). An ethical basis of communication. *The Speech Teacher, 4,* 1–9.

Walters, F. (1992, November 15). In celebration of options: Respect each other's differences. *Vital Speeches of the Day, 59*(22), 265–269.

Watson, B. (1997). "The storyteller is the soybean . . . the audience is the sun." *Smithsonian, 27*(12), 60–67.

Wehrly, B., Kenney, K. R., & Kenney, M. E. (1999). *Counseling multiracial families.* Thousand Oaks, CA: Sage.

Weider, D. L., & Pratt, S. (1990). On being a recognizable Indian. In D. Carbaugh (Ed.), *Intercultural communication and intercultural contacts* (pp. 45–64). Hillsdale, NJ: Lawrence Erlbaum.

Whaley, B. P. (1997, Spring). Perceptions of rebuttal analogy: Politeness and implications for persuasion. *Argumentation and Advocacy, 33*(4), 16–35.

Wicker, B. (1975). *The story-shaped world: Fiction and metaphysics, some variations on a theme.* Notre Dame, IN: University of Notre Dame Press.

Wierzbicka, A. (1991). *Cross-cultural pragmatics: The semantics of human interaction.* Berlin: Mouton de Gruyter.

Winans, J. A. (1938). *Speechmaking.* New York: Appleton-Century.

Wirth, D. (1999, October 29) *Arachnophobia: Overcoming your fear* [Student Speech]. Goshen, IN: Goshen College.

Wolvin, A. D., & Coakley, C. G. (Eds.). (1993). *Perspectives on listening.* Norwood, NJ: Ablex.

Yankelovich, D. (1999). *The magic of dialogue: Transforming conflict into cooperation.* New York: Simon & Schuster.

Zediker, K. (1993, February). Rediscovering the tradition: Women's history with a relational approach to the basic public speaking course. Panel presentation at the Western States Communication Association, Albuquerque, NM.

Zimmerman, T., & Goode, E. (1994, October 3). The mind of Aristide. *U.S. News & World Report,* p. 32.

Zuckerman, L. (1999, April 17). Words go right to the brain, but can they stir the heart? Some say popular software debases public speaking. *New York Times,* National Edition, pp. A17, 19.

Credits

This page constitutes an extension of the copyright page. We have made every effort to trace the ownership of all copyrighted material and to secure permission from copyright holders. In the event of any question arising as to the use of any material, we will be pleased to make the necessary corrections in future printings. Thanks are due to the following authors, publishers, and agents for permission to use the material indicated.

Text Credits

Chapter 1. 19: Wedding Toast, Reprinted with permission
Chapter 2. 30: Fig 2.1 From Brownell & Katula (1984). Reprinted by permission of The Eastern Communication Association **35:** Student speech with commentary: Self-introduction, by Mona Bradsher
Chapter 3. 44: NCA Excerpt, Endorsed by the National Communication Association, November 1999. Reprinted by permission of the National Communication Association.
Chapter 7. 127: Student outline with commentary: Medical misinformation on the Internet, by Quianna Clay
Chapter 8. 151: Student outline with commentary: Over-consumption of sugar, by Hans Erian
Chapter 9. 171: Student outline with commentary: You have my deepest sympathy: You just won the lottery, by Maria DiMaggio
Chapter 10. 191: Student outline with commentary: Peter Ilich Tchaikovsky, by Jennifer Gingerich
Chapter 11. 199: Student outline with commentary: The five stages of culture shock, by John Streicher
Chapter 12. 231: Student speech with visual aids with commentary: Terrestrial pulmonate gastropods, by Shaura Neil
Chapter 13. 253: "I Have a Dream." Reprinted by arrangement with the Estate of Martin Luther King, Jr., c/o Writer House as agent for the proprietor New York, NY. Copyright 1963 Dr. Martin Luther King, Jr., copyright renewed 1991 Coretta Scott King.
Chapter 14. 263: Immigrants, don't be in such a hurry to shed your accents, by YanHong Krompacky
Chapter 15. 289: Expemplum, by Jessica Howard **290:** Spanking? There's gotta be a better way, by Gail Grobey
Chapter 16. 311: Student outline with commentary: Shakespeare, by Hillary Carter-Liggett
Chapter 17. 333: Student outline with commentary: The case for graduated licensing, by Rebecca Ewing
Chapter 18. 351: Fig 18.3 Adapted from Motivation and Personality, 3rd ed., by Abraham H. Maslow. Revised by Roger Frager, James Fadiman, Cynthia McReynolds, and Ruth Cox. Copyright © 1954, © 1987 by Addison-Wesley Longman, Co. Copyright © 1970 by Abraham Maslow. Reprinted by permission of Prentice-Hall, Inc., Upper Saddle River, NJ. **359:** The Benefits of Hunting, by Anonymous
Appendix. 377: A Self-Introduction, by Jason Kelleghan **378:** The Perfect Team, by Uriel Plascencia; interpreter, Kelly Bilinski **380:** Excerpt from *Indian oratory: Famous speeches by noted Indian chieftans*, by W. C. Vanderwerth. Copyright © 1971 by the University of Oklahoma Press, p. 259-284. **381:** Dolphin Communication, by Tanya Moser **383:** The *Dundun Drum*, by Joshua Valentine **385:** The Twenty-Fifth Amendment, by Loren Rozokas **386:** Employee Privacy and the Internet, by Chris Farthing **389:** Embryo Adoption, by Paul Southwick **391:** Sleep Deprivation, by Angela Wilson **392:** Sleep Deprivation, by Sonja Ralston

Photo Credits

Chapter-Opening Murals photographed by Jonathan Fisher
Chapter 1. 6: © David Young-Wolff/PhotoEdit **13:** AP/Wide World Photos
Chapter 2. 23: Michael Newman/PhotoEdit **26:** Wadsworth-Thomson Learning **32:** Todd Eckelman
Chapter 3. 40: AP/Wide World Photos **42:** Courtesy of Seeds of Peace Organization, www.seedsofpeace.org
Chapter 4. 58: Jacques Chenet/Woodfin Camp & Associates **64:** © Matthew McVay/Stock, Boston Inc./PictureQuest
Chapter 5. 72: Dick Blume/The Image Works **79:** Jack Jaffe **82:** Wadsworth-Thomson Learning **83:** AP/Wide World Photos
Chapter 6. 93: Hans-Erik Lundin/www.ocf.org **97:** © Pictor International/Pictor International, Ltd./PictureQuest
Chapter 7. 104: Wadsworth-Thomson Learning **107:** Fox News Network, L.L.C. **111:** Wadsworth-Thomson Learning **112:** Infotrac College Edition © Gale Group **113:** Courtesy Bob Drudge. Copyright © 2003 Refdesk.com, www.refdesk.com **116:** Copyright © 2002 Yahoo! Inc. All Rights Reserved. **117:** Copyright © 2003 Fast Search & Transfer ASA **118 (left):** Courtesy Raven Sky Sports, www.hanggliding.com **(right):** Courtesy United States Hang Gliding Association, Inc., www.ushga.org
Chapter 8. 133: © Ed Kashi/CORBIS **136:** Charles Gupton/corbisstockmarket.com **138:** Josh Nauman **141:** David Schull/*New York Times* **143:** Powerpoint slide created by Spencer MacRae **147:** George Tarbay, NIU Media Services
Chapter 9. 158: © Edward R. Degginger/Bruce Coleman, Inc./PictureQuest **162:** AP/Wide World Photos
Chapter 10. 179: Josh Nauman **182:** AP/Wide World Photos **186:** © Bettmann/CORBIS
Chapter 11. 197: © Peter Chapman Photography **202:** Mark C. Burnett/Stock, Boston
Chapter 12. 214: Jose Pelaez/corbisstockmarket.com **218:** ©Jeff Greenberg/PhotoEdit
Chapter 13. 239: © John Davis/Pictor International, Ltd./PictureQuest **241:** Joel Simon **245:** Wadsworth-Thomson Learning **248:** © Kyle Krause/Index Stock Imagery/PictureQuest **250:** Josh Nauman
Chapter 14. 259: AP/Wide World Photos **261 (left and right):** Wadsworth-Thomson Learning **264:** AP/Wide World Photos **270:** AP/Wide World Photos
Chapter 15. 277: Franz Lanting/Minden Pictures **280:** Photo (c) Kenji Kawano **283:** Printed with permission of Houghton Mifflin Publishing Company. All Rights Reserved. **284:** CNN
Chapter 16. 301: © Keren Su/Index Stock Imagery/PictureQuest **303:** © BSIP Agency/Index Stock Imagery/PictureQuest **305:** © Susan Van Etten/PhotoEdit **307:** Sean Sprague/PANOS Pictures
Chapter 17. 317: © Michael Newman/PhotoEdit **322:** © Creasource/Series/PictureQuest **324:** Index Stock Imagery **327:** Stockphoto.com
Chapter 18. 340: AP/Wide World Photos **352:** Courtesy of WeMedia **354:** AP/Wide World Photos

Artists' Credits for Mural Art

Cover: "Culture of the Crossroads" Mural © 1998 by Precita Eyes Muralists. Directed by Susan Kelk Cervantes. (McDonald's Building, 24th Street at Mission, SF, CA) www.Precitaeyes.org

Chapter 1, pp. 2-3: "Culture of the Crossroads" Mural © 1998 by Precita Eyes Muralists. Directed by Susan Kelk Cervantes. (McDonald's Building, 24th Street at Mission, SF, CA)

Chapter 2, pp. 20-21: Detail from "Family Life and Spirit of Mankind" Mural © 1977 by Susan Kelk Cervantes and Judith Knepher Jamerson. (Leonard R. Flynn School, East Wall, Army Street at Harrison, SF, CA)

Chapter 3, pp. 36-37: Detail from "Family Life and Spirit of Mankind" Mural © 1977 by Susan Kelk Cervantes and Judith Knepher Jamerson. (Leonard R. Flynn School, East Wall, Army Street at Harrison, SF, CA)

Chapter 4, pp. 54-55: "Learning Wall" Mural © 1989 by Keith Sklar. (SFSUD Headquarters, Franklin at Hayes, SF, CA)

Chapter 5, pp. 70-71: "Educate to Liberate" Mural © 1988 by Miranda Bergman, Jane Norling, Maria Ramos, Vicky Hamlin, Arch Williams. (Hayes Street and Masonic, SF, CA)

Chapter 6, pp. 88-89: Detail from "Family Life and Spirit of Mankind" Mural © 1977 by Susan Kelk Cervantes and Judith Knepher Jamerson. (Leonard R. Flynn School, East Wall, Army Street at Harrison, SF, CA)

Chapter 7, pp. 102-103: "Time After Time" Mural © 1995 by Betsie Miller-Kusz. (Collingwood Street near 19th Street, SF, CA)

Chapter 8, pp. 130-131: Detail from "Carnaval" Mural © 1995 by Joshua Sarantitis, Emmanuel Montoya, and Precita Eyes Muralists. (PG&E Yard Wall, 18th Street and Harrison, SF, CA)

Chapter 9, pp. 154-155: "Desaparecidos Pero no Olvidados" Mural (c) 1999 by Carlos Madriz, Josh Short, and Mabel Negrette. (Balmy Alley, Balmy and 24th Street, SF, CA)

Chapter 10, pp. 174-175: "The Chant of the Earth, The Voice of the Land" Mural © 1991 by Betsie Miller-Kusz. (Market Street and 19th Street, SF, CA)

Chapter 11, pp. 194-195: "Family Life and Spirit of Mankind" Mural © 1977 by Susan Kelk Cervantes and Judith Knepher Jamerson. (Leonard R. Flynn School, East Wall, Army Street at Harrison, SF, CA)

Chapter 12, pp. 210-211: "Immigrant Pride Day Community Mural" Mural © 1998 by Precita Eyes Muralists. (Mission District, SF, CA)

Chapter 13, pp. 234-235: "Life" Mural © 1997 by Gretchen Rosenblatt. (16th Street and Market, SF, CA)

Chapter 14, pp. 256-257: "Carnaval" Mural © 1995 by Joshua Sarantitis, Emmanuel Montoya, and Precita Eyes Muralists. (PG&E Yard Wall, 18th and Harrison, SF, CA)

Chapter 15, pp. 274-275: Detail from "Culture of the Crossroads" Mural © 1998 by Precita Eyes Muralists. Directed by Susan Kelk Cervantes. (McDonald's Building, 24th Street at Mission, SF, CA)

Chapter 16, pp. 292-293: "Balance of Power" Mural © 1996 by Susan Kelk Cervantes, Juana Alicia, and Raul Martinez. (Mission Street Playground, Swimming Pool, Linda at 19th Street, SF, CA)

Chapter 17, pp. 314-315: Detail from "Desaparecidos Pero no Olvidados" Mural © 1999 by Carlos Madriz, Josh Short, and Mabel Negrette. (Balmy Alley, Balmy at 24th Street, SF, CA)

Chapter 18, pp. 336-337: "For the Roses/Para las Rosas" Mural © 1985 by Juana Alicia. (Treat Street at 21st Street, SF, CA)

CD-ROM: "Culture of the Crossroads" Mural © 1998 by Precita Eyes Muralists. Directed by Susan Kelk Cervantes. (McDonald's Building, 24th Street at Mission, SF, CA)

Index